Starve and Immolate

New Directions in Critical Theory

NEW DIRECTIONS IN CRITICAL THEORY
Amy Allen, General Editor

New Directions in Critical Theory presents outstanding classic and contemporary texts in the tradition of critical social theory, broadly construed. The series aims to renew and advance the program of critical social theory, with a particular focus on theorizing contemporary struggles around gender, race, sexuality, class, and globalization and their complex interconnections.

STARVE

The Politics of

AND

Human Weapons

IMMOLATE

Banu Bargu

Columbia University Press
New York

COLUMBIA UNIVERSITY PRESS

Publishers Since 1893

New York   Chichester, West Sussex

cup.columbia.edu

LIBRARY OF CONGRESS CATALOGING-IN-PUBLICATION DATA

Bargu, Banu.
  Starve and immolate : the politics of human weapons / Banu Bargu.
    pages cm. — (New directions in critical theory)
  Includes bibliographical references and index.
  ISBN 978-0-231-16340-8 (cloth : alk. paper)—ISBN 978-0-231-16341-5 (pbk. : alk. paper)—
ISBN 978-0-231-53811-4 (e-book)
  1. Hunger strikes—Turkey—History—21st century.   2. Protest movements—Turkey—
History—21st century.   3. Prisoners—Civil rights—Turkey.   4. Political prisoners—Turkey. 5.
Human body—Political aspects—Turkey.   6. Government, Resistance to—Turkey.
7. Turkey—Politics and government—1980- I. Title.

  HN656.5.Z9H844 2014
  303.48'409561—dc23   2014001323

COVER & INTERIOR DESIGN BY **MARTIN N. HINZE**

COVER PHOTO BY **GENÇER YURTTAŞ**

For my parents,
Gülçin and Simav Bargu

Contents

Acknowledgments

The research for this book began, informally, on a late summer night in 2001, when I encountered the funeral march of a death faster in a shantytown of Istanbul, a death faster who had passed away only a few hours earlier and whose news had reached me through a strange series of inexplicable contingencies; a chance encounter, a spontaneous get-together, a birthday celebration, a phone call received by one of the people at that celebration from the acquaintance of an acquaintance, an announcement of the situation, a brief pause, an impulsive decision, a fast drive, and there I was, in the neighborhood where a growing crowd of people came together in front of the dimly lit patio of a shabby, unpainted house from which the lifeless body of a young woman would shortly be taken.

The silent grief of the crowd gathering before the "resistance house," as its occupants named it, was interrupted by the greetings of newcomers, whispers among those organizing the funeral march, and the opening and closing of the front door, in the two small and simple rooms behind which several others on the fast unto death were awaiting their turns to die. The crowd got bigger as journalists, artists, writers, and university students trickled into the neighborhood. It was not long after my arrival that a few people brought out long sticks with edges wrapped in rags and turned them into torches with slowly growing flames. Their light soon fell upon the dead body of a woman held on a stretcher and carried on the shoulders of the crowd. She looked young, beautiful, and pale, emaciated and frail, as she lay amidst a sea of red carnations, with a red headband around her forehead. The crowd, with anger, hope, and sorrow almost tangible, held up a banner that celebrated her immortality and declared her a "revolutionary martyr."

The sight of this march meandering in the neighborhood, the torches that broke apart the dark night sky, the slogans and hymns of the crowd, and the dead body of the death faster irretrievably etched that night in my memory and interpellated me to the work that today culminates in this book. Throughout that summer, I regularly visited the "resistance houses" in various shantytown neighborhoods, the few and fast disappearing enclaves of the extraparliamentary left in the city, in order to get to know these individuals and to understand why they were participants of a fast unto death. These early encounters left me thoroughly perplexed by what I observed and learned: how these individuals, with shrunken bodies and sullen faces, managed their own self-starvation, how they arrived at the edge of death and looked at it squarely, how they remained hopeful and resolute, unwavering in their commitment and certain of the imminent victory of their cause. With pronounced cheekbones and shiny eyes, they nurtured their convictions while they starved their bodies in a world that was oblivious to their story. I was fascinated and repelled at the same time, and felt both with such intensity that I could not but pursue this inquiry.

Most of those individuals I met that summer are long dead. They have become "martyrs" of the revolutionary community, immortalized by their sacrificial acts, especially for those who revere their memory and seek to follow in their footsteps. Many others that I met over the course of my official research period three years later, individuals who were participants in the death fast struggle but had quit or had been made to quit the fast, survive as veterans. Some of these individuals have suffered severe corporeal and emotional damages from long durations of starvation and, at times, its improper, nonconsensual, and highly controversial, medically administered termination. Others—fewer to be sure—remain committed to the revolutionary cause despite the damages, losses, and defeats they have individually and collectively suffered. Regardless of how one may evaluate their actions, their political cause and convictions, their tactics and strategies, the corporeal and self-destructive techniques of their struggle, all of which present immense theoretical and political problems that this book sets itself the goal to tackle, one cannot but be silenced and humbled before the depth of their dedication, their determination, strength, and courage as individuals. This book takes its inspiration from their commitment to live and their readiness to die for their convictions.

In a political present dominated by values of self-interest, instrumental calculation, well-being, and security, a present in which absolute dedication, heroism, and self-sacrifice have little currency, these individuals appear curiously archaic or dangerously prefigurative of a different politics. But the book's purpose is neither to condemn nor to condone these individuals. The purpose of the book, rather, is to theorize their agency, its aspirations, contradictions, and implications by engaging with them critically. The book therefore takes inspiration from their example not necessarily as a model to be emulated or vilified but, rather, as suggestive of a possibility, an opening, an alternative path of envisioning politics beyond its present form, a politics animated by the desire for justice and insistent in its urgent call to bring it into being. The book is motivated to understand what is gripping in this form of radical politics, what are the subversive and emancipatory potentialities entailed by it, and what are its shortcomings, reversals, and failings.

This is why the greater part of the analysis in the book is based on ethnographic and archival research carried out in Turkey. The research brings together multiple accounts of the same series of events in the form of narrations and practices, explanations and justifications from a variety of actors involved in the death fast struggle in different capacities: former participants of the hunger strike and fast unto death, their families and relatives, human rights defenders, intellectuals, artists, doctors, lawyers, state officials, prominent politicians, and members of parliament. The contextual immersion, observation, and first-hand interactions with the participants of the death fast struggle grant us access to highly personal, differentiated, involved narratives, which complicate the conventional approach to human weapons that simply folds them into a fear-mongering discourse of national security and terrorism. Working through the voices of these actors and their supporters conveys the rich and paradoxical complexities of their situation and traces the trajectory of the death fast in a way that appreciates the internally fraught, multilayered, vivid, and distinctive features of the movement. But the voices of those at or near the helm of the state also show how the participants of the death fast struggle and their actions were perceived. Their presence in this book offers us access to the reception of the struggle from within dominant narratives of power, documenting how it was politically discussed and judged and how its goals, arguments, demands, and practices were interpreted as security threats and emplaced within a discourse on terror, bringing into light the articulation of the historical, structural, ideological, and pragmatic reasons for the choice of strategies that were deployed by the state to address the struggle. In short, the juxtaposition of these perspectives enables us to comprehend the complexities and stakes of the death fast struggle from opposing viewpoints. The resulting analysis troubles an easy judgment, I think, and thereby aspires to keep open a space in which critical theory can operate.

Approximately one hundred in-depth interviews constitute the main body of documentation from whose transcription and translation most of the direct quotations in this book are derived. These interviews were conducted in full confidentiality during June 2004–August 2005 in Istanbul and Ankara, Turkey. I have purposefully abstained from conducting interviews in prison or while an interviewee was on hunger strike. I have adopted the method of coding the interviews by the dates on which they were carried out in order to protect the identity of my interlocutors. For the same reason, I have not indicated their organizational or institutional affiliations or sympathies. Throughout this endeavor, I have attempted to reflect the voices of the participants of the death fast struggle and their supporters as well as their opponents and critics as truthfully as possible. Any factual errors, oversights, or gaps that may have been further exacerbated by the difficulty of accessing individuals and archives, inadvertent mistakes in transcription, and problems of translation, of course, remain mine alone.

This project was long in the making and it would not have possible to bring it to fruition if it were not for the generous support of several institutions. At its inception at Cornell University, the project received institutional and financial support that enabled the conducting of extended fieldwork and provided time for composition. The ethnographic component of this project was carried out with the support of the Luigi Einaudi Fellowship awarded by the Institute for European Studies at Cornell University. The Committee of Muslim Societies and the Graduate School at Cornell University provided travel funding which enabled further trips to the field and the presentation of the work to diverse audiences. The Mellon Fellowship allowed the writing up of the early incarnation of this project as a doctoral dissertation. The second home for this project was the New School. The project benefited from annual research funds that made possible recurrent trips to the field for follow-up interviews and further research. The research leave supported by the New School gave the necessary time to revise the manuscript for publication. Finally, Kadir Has University in Istanbul, Turkey provided collegial conditions of study that facilitated the final revisions.

My project benefited immeasurably from the support of outstanding teachers and mentors. Susan Buck-Morss and Nancy Fraser were the two exceptional women without whose inspiration, critique, guidance, and encouragement the project would have long been abandoned. Richard J. Bernstein and Richard F. Bensel were terrific mentors. Wendy Lochner benevolently took on the project as editor. Amy R. Allen graciously lent her support to the project at a very critical juncture. To all of them I am deeply indebted.

Every project has its own difficulties, but the amount of death and destruction that infused every detail of this one became a heavy burden for me to bear, emotionally and intellectually. Without the support and encouragement of teachers, colleagues, students, and friends, I would have not been able to carry this project through. At Cornell I was fortunate to learn from the scholarship of Isaac Kramnick, Jason Frank, Geoffrey C. W. Waite, Peter U. Hohendahl, Anna Marie Smith, Diane Rubenstein, Natalie Melas, Mary Katzenstein, and Barry Maxwell. I am also deeply grateful to the camaraderie and intellectual fellowship of Ute Tellmann, Leila M. Ibrahim, Katherine Gordy, Shannon Marriotti, Megan Thomas, and Israel Waismel-Manor, all of whom contributed to the early stages of this project. At Boğaziçi University I was fortunate to have been the student of Yeşim Arat and Taha Parla, who became crucial interlocutors for this project while I was conducting my fieldwork. At the New School I benefited from having brilliant interlocutors who were also my most challenging critics: Andreas Kalyvas, Victoria Hattam, Andrew Arato, Eli Zaretsky, Ross Poole, Dmitri Nikulin, Oz Frankel, Jeremy Varon, Orit Halpern, Cinzia Arruzza, Miriam Ticktin, Rafi Youatt, Paul Kottman, and Inessa Medzhibovskaya. I thank them all. My graduate students at the New School were crucial for the development of this project to its current form. I am grateful for their critical engagement, inspiration, and provocations. It is my pleasure to thank Pavlina Majorosova, Peter Galambos, Scott Ritner, and especially Jordanco Jovanovski for research assistance related to this project. My book greatly benefited from the discerning eye of Susan Pensak at Columbia University Press. I doubt that this project could have been completed if it were not for the friendship of Merve Mısırlı, Michael F. Gasper, Yektan Türkyılmaz, Meltem Sancar, Jonathan Phillips, and Seda Altuğ.

This work would not have been possible without the humbling generosity of all the research participants whose names I cannot recite for reasons of confidentiality. My debt to those remarkable individuals, who have opened their homes and hearts to me, shown me enormous hospitality, and entrusted me their memories, experiences, ideas, views, emotions, and dreams, is immense. During my fieldwork I benefited from the help of individuals and institutions, which offered documents, access to archives, contacts, and ideas. Special thanks to Oral Çalışlar and Yücel Sayman for granting me access to their private collections. I would like to mention the collaborative efforts of the following institutions: the Human Rights Foundation of Turkey, Human Rights Association, Istanbul Bar Association, Contemporary Lawyers' Association, and the Architects' and Engineers' Chambers Association of Turkey. Many other organizations, ranging from prisoner rights associations to independent law bureaus, from newspapers and journals to cultural centers, helped me locate materials difficult to find, individuals difficult to reach, stories difficult to forget. To all I extend my sincere thanks.

It is to my loved ones that I owe the most. They have supported me, unconditionally and in so many ways, throughout the vicissitudes of this project, as well as before and beyond. This book could not have been written without Mediha Sangar, who passed away in 1993, having taught me, long before I encountered Plato, that only an examined life is worth living and that death is not an end. It is my hope that my work lives up to her memory. Massimiliano Tomba brightened even my darkest days with his love. Without my siblings, Berna Bargu and Arda Dermanlı, my life would have been impoverished of joy. I dedicate this book, with love and respect, to my parents, Gülçin and Simav Bargu. I am forever grateful to them for all they have given me and for being my source of inspiration in the quest for dignity, equality, and justice.

Abbreviations

Legal Political Parties

AKP
Adalet ve Kalkınma Partisi
Justice and Development Party

ANAP
Anavatan Partisi
Motherland Party

CHP
Cumhuriyet Halk Partisi
Republican People's Party

DP
Demokrat Parti
Democrat Party

DSP
Demokratik Sol Parti
Democratic Left Party

DYP
Doğru Yol Partisi
True Path Party

EMEP
Emeğin Partisi
Labor Party

FP
Fazilet Partisi
Virtue Party

HADEP
Halkın Demokrasi Partisi
People's Democracy Party

İP
İşçi Partisi
Workers' Party

MHP
Milliyetçi Hareket Partisi
Nationalist Action Party

ÖDP
Özgürlük ve Dayanışma Partisi
Liberty and Solidarity Party

RP
Refah Partisi
Welfare Party

SİP
Sosyalist İktidar Partisi
Socialist Government Party

TİP
Türkiye İşçi Partisi
Workers' Party of Turkey

TSİP
Türkiye Sosyalist İşçi Partisi
Socialist Workers' Party of Turkey

Extraparliamentary and/or Illegal Organizations on the Radical Left

Dev-Genç
Türkiye Devrimci Gençlik
Federasyonu
Revolutionary Youth Federation
of Turkey

Dev-Yol (DY)
Devrimci Yol
Revolutionary Path

Dev-Sol (DS)
Devrimci Sol
Revolutionary Left

DH
Direniş Hareketi
Resistance Movement

DHKP-C
Devrimci Halk Kurtuluş Partisi-
Cephesi
Revolutionary People's Liberation
Party-Front

KPİÖ
Komünist Parti İnşa Örgütü
Communist Party Building
Organization

MKP
Maoist Komünist Parti
Maoist Communist Party

MLKP
Marksist Leninist Komünist Parti
Marxist Leninist Communist Party

PKK
Partiya Karkerên Kurdistan
Workers' Party of Kurdistan

PKK-DÇS
Partiya Karkerên Kurdistan–
Devrimci Çizgi Savaşçıları
Workers' Party of Kurdistan–
Revolutionary Line Warriors

TDP
Türkiye Devrim Partisi
Revolution Party of Turkey

THKO
Türkiye Halk Kurtuluş Ordusu
People's Liberation Army of Turkey

THKP-C
Türkiye Halk Kurtuluş Partisi-
Cephesi
People's Liberation Party-Front of
Turkey

THKP-C/MLSPB
Türkiye Halk Kurtuluş Partisi-
Cephesi/Marksist Leninist Silahlı
Propaganda Birliği
People's Liberation Party-Front of
Turkey/Marxist Leninist Armed
Propaganda Unit

TİİKP
Türkiye İhtilalci İşçi Köylü Partisi
Revolutionary Workers' Peasants'
Party of Turkey

TİKB
Türkiye İhtilalci Komünistler Birliği
Revolutionary Communists' Union
of Turkey

TİKB(B)
Türkiye İhtilalci Komünistler
Birliği (Bolşevik)
Revolutionary Communists' Union
of Turkey (Bolshevik)

TİKP

Türkiye İşçi Köylü Partisi

Workers' Peasants' Party of Turkey

TKEP/L

Türkiye Komünist Emek Partisi/
Leninist

Communist Labor Party of Turkey/
Leninist

TKİP

Türkiye Komünist İşçi Partisi

Communist Workers' Party of
Turkey

TKP(ML)–TİKKO

Türkiye Komünist Partisi (Marksist
Leninist)–Türkiye İşçi Köylü
Kurtuluş Ordusu

Communist Party of Turkey
(Marxist Leninist)–Workers'
Peasants' Liberation Army of Turkey

TKP/K

Türkiye Komünist Partisi/Kıvılcım

Communist Party of Turkey/Spark

TKP/ML

Türkiye Komünist Partisi/
Marxist Leninist

Communist Party of Turkey/
Marksist Leninist

**Other Organizations and
Institutions in Turkey**

ÇHD

Çağdaş Hukukçular
Derneği

Contemporary Lawyers'
Association

DETAK

Devrimci Tutsak Aileleri Komitesi

Committee for the Families of
Revolutionary Captives

DETUDAK

Devrimci Tutsaklarla Dayanışma
Komitesi

Solidarity Committee for
Revolutionary Captives

DGM

Devlet Güvenlik Mahkemesi

State Security Court

DİSK

Devrimci İşçi Sendikaları
Konfederasyonu

Confederation of Revolutionary
Workers' Trade Unions

EGM

Emniyet Genel Müdürlüğü

General Directorate of Turkish
National Police

HAK-İŞ

HAK İşçi Sendikaları
Konfederasyonu

HAK Trade Unions' Confederation

HYD

Helskinki Yurttaşlar Derneği

Helsinki Citizens Assembly

İHD

İnsan Hakları Derneği

Human Rights Association

İHH

İnsan Hak ve Hürriyetleri İnsani
Yardım Vakfı

Human Rights and Liberties
Humanitarian Aid Foundation

KESK
Kamu Emekçileri Sendikaları
Konfederasyonu
Confederation of Public Laborers'
Trade Unions

MAZLUMDER
İnsan Hakları ve
Mazlumlar için Dayanışma
Derneği
Solidarity Association for Human
Rights and the Oppressed

MGK
Milli Güvenlik Kurulu
National Security Council

MİT
Milli İstihbarat Teşkilatı
National Intelligence Agency

ÖZGÜR-DER
Özgür Düşünce ve Eğitim
Hakları Derneği
Association for Free Thought
and Educational Rights

RTÜK
Radyo ve Televizyon Üst Kurulu
Higher Board of Radio and
Television

TAYAD
Tutuklu Aileleri ve Yakınları
Dayanışma Derneği
Solidarity Association for the
Families and Relatives of the
Arrested

TBB
Türkiye Barolar Birliği
Union of Bar Associations of
Turkey

TBMM
Türkiye Büyük Millet Meclisi
Grand National Assembly of
Turkey

TİHV
Türkiye İnsan Hakları
Vakfı
Human Rights Foundation of
Turkey

TMMOB
Türkiye Mimar ve Mühendis
Odaları Birliği
Architects' and Engineers'
Chambers Association of Turkey

TTB
Türk Tabipleri Birliği
Turkish Medical Association

TUYAB
Tutuklu Yakınları Birliği
Union for the Relatives of the
Arrested

Tüm Yargı-Sen
Tüm Yargı ve İnfaz Kurumları
Çalışanları Sendikası
All Judicial and Penal Institutions
Employees' Union

Türk-İş
Türkiye İşçi Sendikaları
Konfederasyonu
Confederation of Turkish Trade
Unions

YÖK
Yüksek Öğretim Kurulu
Council of Higher Education

Starve and Immolate

Introduction
The Death Fast Struggle and the Weaponization of Life

Prison is the only place where power is manifested in its naked state, in its most excessive form, and where it is justified as moral force.

—Michel Foucault, "Intellectuals and Power"

In October 2000, hundreds of political prisoners in Turkey went on hunger strike. They announced that their main goal was to halt the introduction of high security prisons and to prevent cellular imprisonment. A month later, and in the absence of any response from the government, they declared the transformation of their hunger strike into a fast unto death and began to launch teams of death fasters, selected from those already on hunger strike, and concatenated according to expected dates of death, on the path to self-destruction. Individual death fasters, donned with a red headband to mark their advancement toward martyrdom, saw their struggle as advancing the cause of revolution. Their experience in hitherto existing prisons, architecturally set up in the form of large wards where prisoners lived a collective life and established self-governing "communes," formed the basis of their solidarity and political will; these wards also became the foundations of their claim to an alternative sovereignty. In defense of the communist revolution, which these prisoners saw as emanating from prison wards as the new front of struggle, they launched a movement by forging their lives into weapons. They starved and burned themselves to death. They meticulously managed their self-starvation, with precise intakes of sugar, salt, and water, and at times, vitamin supplements, in order to prolong or hasten their labor of dying. They coordinated this labor with others, across ideological differences, organizational affiliations, prison wards, and prison walls. This book tells their story.

As the silent army of death fasters scattered all over the country's prisons marched toward death, negotiations with the government came to an impasse. The popular mobilizations, petitions, sit-ins, demonstrations outside the prisons did little to alter this stalemate. In December 19–22, 2000, most of these prisoners were forcibly transferred to the high security prisons they were struggling against by an unprecedented "security operation" in which, not unlike the Attica recapture but on a much greater scope and scale, the Turkish state dispatched thousands of heavily armed personnel against the political prisoners on hunger strike, simultaneously attacking and invading some twenty prisons under its own control. This security operation, named "Operation Return to Life," declared the intention of rescuing the prisoners from their path to self-destruction; ironically, however, it alone resulted in the death of thirty prisoners and two security personnel (some of them burning to death, others shot or poisoned by gas), the severe wounding of hundreds of prisoners, and many instances of maltreatment, torture, and rape, complaints regarding which were filed with human rights organizations.

At the time of the operation, the construction of F-type prisons (as high security prisons have come to be known in Turkey) was incomplete; some buildings were barely finished, others had no running water or proper heating. But the government's hasty decision to open these prisons was, according to members of parliament across the political spectrum, symbolically and strategically long overdue. Not only were the overcrowded, unhygienic, and disease-infested communal wards of existing prisons extremely obsolete, but they were also the source of radical politics incommensurable with the sovereignty of the state. The high security prisons, originally stipulated as part of the 1991 Law for the Struggle Against Terrorism (but not yet put into practice by 2000), were not only the architectural underpinnings of a new penal regime that became the basis of a vigilant security apparatus, but they would also constitute the building blocks of a transfigured and strengthened sovereignty, a sovereignty that was now wounded by those who threatened to die rather than submit themselves to the state.

While the repeated broadcasts of the violent security operation were largely successful in intimidating the public into silence, they were less effective in putting an end to the movement. Defying the state's expectations, the violence that the security operation unleashed upon prisoners increased the number of participants in the hunger strike and led more prisoners to escalate their protest, by either transforming their hunger strike into a fast unto death or resorting to acts of self-immolation. While prisoners affiliated with three outlawed leftist organizations initially spearheaded the struggle, the number of organizations that participated in the death fast movement increased to a dozen after the state's security operation. At its peak, the number of prisoners who participated in the movement reached some fifteen hundred individuals—encompassing nearly the entire population of prisoners affiliated with the extraparliamentary and outlawed left. This participation was complemented by solidarity hunger strikes, self-immolations, urban guerrilla attacks, and suicide attacks outside the prisons in an escalating spiral of violence that only alienated the movement further from mass support and had no positive political effect on the government's unyielding stance in support of high security prisons. If anything, it lent further support for official arguments that these prisons were absolutely crucial in the vigorous "struggle against terrorism."

For several months after the security operation, the militancy of the movement crested both in terms of the radicalism of its discourse, asserting a "right to die," and in terms of its casualties due to self-inflicted violence. In response to the increasing death toll and the prospect of even higher casualties, given the number of prisoners on the brink of death by self-starvation in prison cells, the state resorted first to artificial feeding and, when that did not create the intended deterrence on prisoners, to discharging prisoners on the death fast almost en masse, by the provisional suspension of their sentences or by presidential pardon, on grounds of their deteriorating health. Beginning in May 2001 the discharge of prisoners constituted the turning point in the trajectory of the movement.

Once these prisoners were released from prison by state authorization to the care of their families, many of them quit the death fast. They dispersed to their hometowns across the country or went to Europe, seeking political asylum or looking for refuge in self-imposed exile. Some remained in Turkey's largest urban centers like Istanbul and Ankara and continued to organize around the associations for prisoners' families; others quit politics altogether; and still others faced a new struggle against Wernicke-Korsakoff, a debilitating disorder of the central nervous system common to hunger strikers due to prolonged durations of starvation and vitamin deprivation. Meanwhile, a handful of ex-prisoners continued to fast in their private beds, carrying out the labor of dying now in the "resistance houses" that welcomed them in the urban shantytowns that have traditionally been enclaves for the radical left. In these neighborhoods, now transformed into small pockets of insurgent activity, relatives, neighbors, and comrades surrounded those still on the death fast and continued to pressure the government for concessions to relax solitary confinement in the F-type prisons, which had already become functional fixtures on the Turkish penal landscape.

When ongoing attempts of civil society organizations to reach a compromise, led by several bar associations and supported by trade unions, occupational chambers, and human rights organizations, were officially rejected by the government after the first anniversary of Operation Return to Life, the already precarious public support waned even further. In 2002 most of the leftist organizations called off their participation in the movement, without, however, conceding that the movement had come to an end. In spite of the steadfast adherence to the death fast by only two of the dozen leftist organizations that had once been part of the movement, the general mood on the left was one of retreat.

In the following years the movement continued to have an even more marginal presence, making not the headlines but small corners of newspapers whenever another death transpired as the result of the fast unto death, self-immolation, or occasional suicide attack. When mainstream media found the casualties of the death fast struggle worth reporting, rather than human tragedies that should scandalize the public they became numbers indicating the already meaningless death toll in the protracted, low-intensity "war against terrorism." In the meantime, the trauma of witnessing the self-induced deaths of a generation of dedicated leftist militants deepened the political paralysis for many of the interested and committed public intellectuals, artists, and human rights defenders in Turkey. While they had mobilized in favor of the prisoners in the early days of the hunger strike, pulling together their resources and connections, signing petitions, organizing press conferences, sit-ins, and events, translating books on prison struggles from around the world, writing letters, articles, and columns, their efforts vanished into thin air. The government proved highly adept at diffusing whatever pressure these intellectuals generated, and the publicity never turned into a significant mass support.

Soon the sympathetic parties in civil society were reduced to passive spectators, having to watch, on one side, prisoners march to their self-inflicted deaths and, on the other, the state's high security prison project put into practice, without being able to put a stop to either process. Their difficulty was also encumbered by their position vis-à-vis violence: defending the right to resist the violence of the state, on the one hand, and taking distance from the violence of the outlawed leftist organizations carrying out the struggle, on the other hand. Their sense of ethical responsibility and humanitarian commitment to the "right to life," to making sure that militants did not die, stood in tension with their political support for the struggle against high security prisons, whose predominant technique was self-destruction and most prominent claim the "right to die." These positions squeezed the most outspoken members of the intelligentsia, human rights defenders, and trade unionists into a difficult middle ground, as a result of which their efforts were not appreciated either by the state or by the militants. Their efforts did not translate into building nonviolent popular resistance against the high security prisons, nor could they help arriving at an amicable agreement between the state and the militants. In the face of the personal tragedies they witnessed as well as the general public's growing acceptance of and indifference to these tragedies, their involvement soon decelerated and came to a standstill.

According to the participants of the death fast struggle, civil society had, once again, failed the left. It was not until 2006, over five years into the struggle, when a prominent lawyer and human rights defender launched a fast unto death, in connection with the floundering movement, that shook off some of the inertia in the public sphere. In question, however, was no longer the very existence of high security prisons but only the regime of cellular isolation that came to define the conditions of imprisonment in these new penal institutions. With the new moral, humanitarian call, which framed cellular isolation as a form of torture, the mostly subsided struggle found renewed public support and gained the necessary momentum that culminated in a gesture from the government, which relaxed conditions of solitary confinement in high security prisons.

When it was formally called off on January 22, 2007, the death fast had lasted a little over six years—a total of 2, 286 consecutive days of sustained, relayed self-starvation that had involved several thousands of people. The movement claimed 122 martyrs, most of whom had died self-inflicted deaths. The end of the death fast struggle was announced in radical newspapers to the shrinking audience of the extraparliamentary left of Turkey as a great victory. However, the concession of the government, which allowed up to ten prisoners to come together for social activities (for no longer than ten hours per week) in the F-type prisons, now without the controversial requirement of "successful" participation in prison "treatment and rehabilitation programs," was so minimal, particularly in comparison with the initial demands and militancy of the movement, that this was hardly an occasion for celebration. The anticlimactic ending, rather, came as a relief from the vicious cycle of self-destructive practices that dominated the politics of the radical left in the last decade and shackled resistance to a stalemate between a small group of defiant insurgents and a recalcitrant, increasingly securitized government.

WHY THE DEATH FAST STRUGGLE?

While this book tells the story of the death fast struggle, this is not its only purpose. The second aim of the book is to interrogate the death fast struggle around the question of its dominant form of political action: self-destruction. It asks: Why did modalities of self-destruction such as hunger striking, death fasting, self-immolation, and suicide attack become the prevailing tactics in this movement of political prisoners? The technique of self-destruction as the basis of political action is radical and enigmatic in general: it is self-inflicted, painful, potentially irreversible, and final, therefore existential and embroiled within a logic of sacrifice that is opposed to our conventional notions of instrumental action because it renders difficult, if not altogether impossible, the achievement of political ends through means lesser than death. But given the nature of the declared aims of the political prisoners who participated in the struggle and the reactions of the state, that such an irreversible and final technique should be the predominant form of political action appeared only to augment this enigma.

The ostensible aim of political prisoners was to halt the introduction of high security prisons, the F-types. Surely, this was a goal that had a significant self-interested component that followed, rather transparently, from an intimate knowledge of Turkish penal practices and an accurate prediction regarding how conditions of imprisonment would change as a result of the move away from prisons based on communal wards to prisons with cells. In addition to struggling for better conditions, the prisoners' movement also served a symbolic purpose, drawing attention to how the Turkish state governed its prisons, its human rights record, and the numerous problems associated with different elements of the criminal justice system, including the conditions of detainees in relation to convicts, the precarious status of prisoner rights, ongoing human rights violations, the unavailability of mechanisms for addressing grievances, and the lack of public scrutiny over the management of prisons. The struggle cast light on the state of Turkish democracy; it brought into the spotlight the high numbers of political prisoners in Turkey's prisons, especially vis-à-vis the country's European counterparts, and their problematic legal status, which is stipulated as a function of laws that regulate the "struggle against terrorism." Moreover, the struggle was important for its capacity to problematize cellular imprisonment at a time when high security prisons have become widely accepted and have proliferated around the world.

However, despite the hard facts of prison conditions and the very real problems emanating from every aspect of the penal system in Turkey, which the struggle threw into sharp relief, there was something elusive and puzzling about the radical nature of the struggle that emerged from Turkey's prisons. The opposition to F-type prisons, venerable as it was as the movement's expressed goal, was never a fully satisfactory explanation, given the high levels of participation, the zeal and dedication of its participants, and, most importantly, the technique of struggle that became the central feature of the movement.How was it that this relatively limited political goal of protesting conditions of imprisonment could warrant such an existential, total response? The ends simply did not seem to measure up to the means: either the arduous labor of dying, enduring months of prolonged self-starvation and suffering the slow decomposition of the body, or the brutal agony of consuming one's flesh in flames. The finality and pain that such violent political practice entailed appeared to far exceed the potential, plausible gains that might have been achieved through a collective struggle that resorted to other, perhaps more ordinary, practical, and customary tactics. Since all the participants of this struggle happened to be openly declared Marxists of different ideological stripes, whose "repertoire" of political action did not include or lend justification to such corporeal tactics (especially until the late 1970s), the choice of these self-destructive practices appeared all the more counterintuitive.[1] Even the common argument that these practices were rendered necessary due to the specific conditions of the prison where there was a dearth of possible forms of political action did not seem to ring completely true, since similar tactics were utilized outside the prisons where other methods of struggle were surely available.

If understanding the choice of the corporeal and destructive technique of political action in its various modalities, deployed by the movement as its central tactic, thus appeared as the key to unlock the enigma of the struggle from the point of view of its participants, it also seemed quite central to understanding the Turkish state's otherwise inexplicably heated reaction to this struggle. The coordinated security operation targeting the already frail political prisoners on a fast unto death appeared so out of measure, even given the state's own roots in an authoritarian tradition of statecraft and its history of repressive practices toward political dissent, that it could be read as the symptom of a deeper problem.

From the beginning of the struggle, the state's perspective was shaped by the perception of a grave threat posed by political prisoners, a perception that was nurtured, of course, by the Kemalist state tradition whose primary reflex toward the political left, and especially its radical variants, has always been one of criminalization and punishment. This reflex had long transformed prisons into sites of confrontation, a tendency that intensified with the 1980 coup d'état. Therefore, this was not the first time there was unrest in prisons, nor were the numbers of prisoners participating in the struggle a great fraction of the total prison population (even though they corresponded to a significant fraction of the political prisoner population). Furthermore, to a state whose policy had been oriented toward the fervent elimination of the currents it considered to be on the "extreme" left in connection with its "struggle against terrorism," should the political prisoners' self-destructive practices not have seemed as an apposite occurrence?

Nevertheless, the official perspective on the death fast struggle as a "crisis" and the ensuing measures set into motion to deal with this crisis gave away an evaluation of the resistance of political prisoners not simply as a struggle against prison conditions but, rather, as a formidable challenge directed at the state itself. The prisoners' tactics were simply intolerable to the state, and the state went to extremes in order to put an end to this movement. From the disproportionality of force deployed in Operation Return to Life to the controversial "amnesty" legislation passed in order to dampen down the overcrowding in prisons, from the endorsement of artificial feeding, in order to resuscitate those on the brink of death, if only to continue to imprison these individuals in high security prison cells, to the collective pardons issued to discharge dying prisoners on the death fast, the state's response was comprehensive and total. As was the case for the political prisoners, but from the opposing viewpoint, the necessity of implementing F-type prisons was never a fully satisfactory explanation, given the vocalized and fast-forming unity across the political spectrum at the level of official politics, the zeal of government officials and bureaucrats in trying to suppress the movement, the belligerent discourses that were marshaled for justification, and the complex array of tactics that were deployed in response to the prisoners. Once again, there was something peculiar about the form of the prisoners' struggle and its implications that proved fertile for the attribution of such significance by the state to an otherwise marginal movement.

This book therefore explores the death fast struggle by placing self-destructive techniques of political action at the center of its inquiry in order to theorize this highly particular form of struggle in which life is forged into a weapon. Since the sustained duration of the movement and the high numbers of its participants, its elevation of the fast unto death to centrality, its complementing of the death fast with self-immolations and suicide attacks have rendered it uniquely resourceful to explore this counterintuitive form of political action, this book utilizes the in-depth study of the death fast struggle in order to contribute to the understanding of human weapons. What are the reasons for choosing such tactics? What are the justifications provided for this choice? What are their ethical and political implications? Through this inquiry, the book attempts to interpret the growing centrality of a novel set of practices of resistance that have entered the political scene in Turkey and to scrutinize their meaning, function, and effects, without whose analysis both the opposition of political prisoners and the reaction of the Turkish state are bound to remain opaque.

THE LOCAL AND THE GLOBAL

The book's focus on the self-destructive techniques of this movement illuminates the specificities of the political context in Turkey, but it also has political and theoretical repercussions that exceed the boundaries of Turkish politics.

While the death fast struggle, with its goals and demands, practice and discourse, was specific to the Turkish scene in many ways, it also had an important kinship with other instances of political struggle around the globe.

The death fast struggle in Turkey spanned the same decade as a large number of mass hunger strikes of varying durations that sprang up in different places. Scores of hunger strikes have been performed by immigrants, refugees, and asylum seekers (sometimes involving hundreds of individuals) in detention centers across Australia, Greece, Italy, Bulgaria, France, Spain, Finland, the United Kingdom, the United States, Canada, Japan, Malaysia, Indonesia, Trinidad and Tobago, Mexico, Bahrain, among others.[2] These hunger strikes were often complemented by other acts of self-harm (such as self-infection, self-mutilation, sewing of lips and eyelids) and, at times, different forms of self-killing. Our knowledge of these hunger strikes and other self-destructive practices is still very limited, not only contingent upon what gets officially reported by local authorities, what portion of these instances makes the global news, and how much coverage they are given, undocumented and unnamed as their performers already are, but also because of the relative paucity of studies focusing on such actions as forms of resistance. Nonetheless, the increasing number of organizations that monitor the status of immigration detention centers, the growing body of news reports, documentation, and scholarship on immigration and population movements all point us to the fact that self-destructive forms of resistance are fast becoming a common feature of detention centers around the globe.[3]

Among prisoners, widespread instances of hunger striking have also been noted around the globe, including locations as diverse as South Africa, Australia, Israel/Palestine, and China, among others.[4] Of these protests, those carried out by the prisoners under "indefinite detention" in Guantánamo Bay Prison, and their subsequent nonconsensual artificial feeding by the prison authorities, have received the most public attention, happening as they have been in the wartime detention center, already controversial due to its offshore location, unclear status vis-à-vis international rules of war, and denial of fundamental rights, such as habeas corpus, to the detainees under its supervision. The occurrence of hunger strikes in Guantánamo under the auspices of a country that deems itself the beacon of democracy has been particularly scandalous as it has exposed the human rights practices of the United States to widespread criticism.[5] Since the actions of Guantánamo prisoners deeply resonate with those of the political prisoners in Turkey, it is worthwhile to examine them in further detail.

The several waves of hunger strikes that have taken place in Guantánamo since 2002 were carried out in protest of the prisoners' detention without trial and their ongoing experience of different forms of inhumane treatment, including physical, psychological, and religious abuses, degrading conditions of shelter, as well as not having access to proper food and clean drinking water.[6] While the mass hunger strikes in 2002 were relatively short in duration and conducted in the form of relays, without serious harm to the individuals involved, the protests of several individuals who did continue to fast for over sixty days and approached death were terminated by nonconsensual artificial feeding.[7]

A second wave of hunger strikes in mid-2005, which started out as the refusal of one meal per day, was soon converted into a fast unto death, in a form of escalation highly resonant with the trajectory of the death fast struggle in Turkey. The death fast in Guantánamo involved around two hundred prisoners (corresponding, approximately, to one-third of the total prisoner population) who, in addition to fasting, also refused showers, clothes, and recreation time, not unlike the dirty protest of the Provisional IRA prisoners in Maze Prison three decades ago.[8] The Guantánamo prisoners demanded fair trials, the amelioration of their conditions (such as access to clean water, edible food, sunlight, medical treatment, letters from their families), equal treatment of prisoners across the different divisions of the prison, and respect for their religious beliefs and practices.[9] Even though the prisoners called off the strike upon the establishment of a prisoners' grievance committee and promises that conditions at Guantánamo would be made to comply with the Geneva Conventions, they recommenced the hunger strike in August 2005 in the absence of any concrete measures by the prison administration and carried on, with decreasing participation, until 2006.[10] The procedure of nonconsensual artificial feeding by military medical staff also continued, despite widespread criticism from the broader medical community.[11]

Acknowledging the administration of "involuntary" feedings upon prisoners on hunger strike, Department of Defense officials emphasized the humane and professional conduct of the medical staff and the necessity to carry out these interventions to secure the health of the prisoners. According to the words of Joint Task Force Guantánamo Deputy Commander Brig. Gen. John Gong, "We have an ultimate responsibility that every detainee on our watch is taken care of."[12] Officials also argued that most instances of artificial feeding were consensual, despite counterallegations. Secretary of Defense Donald Rumsfeld argued that it was the decision of the commanders and medical experts to intervene when they saw fit.[13] In 2006 the instructions for the treatment of detainees issued by the Department of Defense gave further official affirmation to the procedure of "involuntary" feeding on hunger strikers in critical condition as a necessary measure to "prevent death or serious harm."[14]

Despite the difficulties of accessing accurate information regarding what happens at Guantánamo, we know that the Guantánamo prisoners have repeatedly resorted to individual and coordinated acts of self-killing in addition to multiple hunger strikes. In August 2003, 23 prisoners attempted (unsuccessfully) to hang themselves in their cells. Of these, 10 attempts were reported to be simultaneous.[15] These incidents were only a fraction of the 120 "hanging gestures," as the U.S. government called them, that came out of a pool of 350 instances of reported "self-harm," for 2003 alone. According to government officials, who subsequently referred to these acts of self-harm as "manipulative self-injurious behavior,"[16] the purpose of these actions was "a coordinated effort to disrupt camp operations."[17]

In 2006 three prisoners (who had been participants of previous hunger strikes) were found dead on the same morning, having hanged themselves in their cells using bedsheets. While officials, including Defense Secretary Rumsfeld, had explained away the earlier hunger strikes as the prisoners' way of attracting press attention,[18] the official evaluation of these new self-killings was different. In a press conference Navy Rear Adm. Harry B. Harris, commander of Joint Task Force Guantánamo, argued: "I believe this was not an act of desperation, but an act of asymmetric warfare aimed at us here at Guantánamo."[19] Emphasizing that this was not a simple suicide but a political act, Harris continued: "We have men here who are committed jihadists. They are dangerous men and they will do anything they can to advance their cause."[20]

The recognition by officials of the *political* nature of the Guantánamo prisoners' practices of self-destruction, whether the ultimate goal attributed to them is one of attracting publicity, disrupting the operations of the prison, or advancing their cause as part of asymmetric warfare, is important as a public acknowledgment of these acts as different from personal acts of suicide. Perhaps this merely registers what is all too well known to the prisoners themselves, but it is still significant, especially in light of how frequently these acts tend to be conflated, at times purposefully, with suicides in order to conceal the occurrences of resistance or to neutralize their reverberations, not only in Guantánamo but across detention centers and prisons around the globe. The recognition granted to these acts by United States officials has served to underscore the fact that these acts do not often arise from personal despair or psychological pathologies but are conscious, voluntary, politically motivated, and orchestrated, thereby directly contributing to their political and subversive qualities as acts of protest. As the officials well understood, these acts were calculated responses, arising out of the problems of their immediate material conditions, but they were not necessarily limited in their political purpose to those conditions. Rather, they were acts of corporeal, existential, and total resistance and refusals to participate in one's own dehumanization.[21] In short, they were occasions in which actors forged their lives into weapons of political struggle and which became performances that incited further state violence through repeated medical interventions in the form of artificial feeding.

Like their more mediatized counterparts in Guantánamo, detainees in tens of detention facilities around the world and the prisoners in Turkey have also been resorting to self-destructive acts as a form of political resistance. In fact, the very synchronicity of these multiple struggles and their wide-ranging geographical distribution suggest that we are faced with a global political phenomenon. This does not mean that these struggles are organically connected, nor that the individuals who resort to these tactics fight for the same cause. Regardless of whether those prisoners at Guantánamo were "committed jihadists," as Commander Harris called them, it is certain that the prisoners in Turkey, or detainees and asylum seekers around the globe, subscribe to a wide array of beliefs and political views that cannot be reduced to or subsumed under jihadism. The differences across them, in terms of their ideological viewpoints, sociological characteristics, the internal organization of their respective movements (if they are connected with one) and the relation of these movements to the contexts out of which they emerge, are not negligible, nor should we ignore these differences.

Each struggle has its own specificity, complex set of determinations, particular trajectory, distinct discourses, and, of course, divergent effects and reverberations. It is nonetheless noteworthy that, precisely despite their very important differences, political actors around the globe in comparable situations increasingly resort to a repertoire of self-destructive techniques that they share in common. Scholars suggest that military and civilian prisons, especially supermaximum security facilities, detention centers, and refugee camps, are fast converging in terms of their structural features, as well as the practices that govern them, troubling an easy separation of Guantánamo as the "exception" from the otherwise legally, politically, socially acceptable norms reigning everywhere else.[22] The globally homogenizing spaces of confinement, with cellular isolation and panoptic surveillance, are increasingly germane to similar modalities of protest. It is in this light that one may agree with Harris's characterization of Guantánamo prisoners, "dangerous men [who] will do anything they can to advance their cause," as an illuminating remark for all those individuals, men, women, and even children who, treated as a "danger" to society, go to extreme lengths to assert their political voice and forge their lives into weapons around the world.

A NOTE ON CONCEPTUALIZATION

The convergence of disparate, unrelated struggles around the globe toward a common repertoire of self-destructive techniques is of central interest to this book. In fact, if one can speak of a global conjuncture in which radical movements operate and resistances, individual or collective, are staged, our conjuncture is marked by the increasing prevalence of the *weaponization of life*. In this conjuncture the Turkish case constitutes an important, though by no means singular, example. This characterization does not imply that the technique of self-destruction is completely unprecedented or novel. In fact, hunger striking, for example, has entered the modern political scene with the actions of British suffragettes in the early twentieth century and became well-known through Gandhi's repeated hunger strikes, which were formative for the constitution of modern India.[23] What I want to underscore, rather, is an intensification: both an ever more frequent resort to this form of political action as well as a growing tendency to orchestrate this technique with the coordination of a multiplicity of individuals, ranging from several to hundreds at a time. This intensification renders the weaponization of life an emergent repertoire rather than an isolated, random tactic, an individual act.

By the *weaponization of life,* I refer to the tactic of resorting to corporeal and existential practices of struggle, based on the technique of self-destruction, in order to make a political statement or advance political goals. I coin the term *human weapons* to designate the actors who forge their lives into weapons of political struggle by a resort to self-destructive techniques. As a tactic, the weaponization of life encompasses a series of practices that range from varieties of nonlethal self-mutilation (which include forms of amputation, maiming, infection with disease, sewing of eyes and mouth, temporary starvation, all inflicted by and upon oneself) to the more fatal actions of self-immolation (understood as setting oneself on fire), temporally indefinite hunger strikes, fasts unto death, self-killing (through a variety of methods including hanging, drinking pesticide, slitting wrists, overdosing on medication, and swallowing cyanide capsules), and forms of suicide attack (involving, again, different forms of actions such as the detonation of bombs strapped upon the body, driving a loaded vehicle into a target to induce explosion, participation in military assaults with no chance of survival, and so on).[24]

Overall, the various modalities of the weaponization of life have different temporalities and degrees of certainty in their fatality. Some extend the period of fatality over a long period of suffering whereas others are more instantaneous. Those modalities, such as indefinite and nonrelayed hunger strikes or fasts unto death, which prolong the labor of dying, are also more prone to interruption and termination, though generally not without reversible health effects. In contrast, self-immolations and suicide attacks bring about much more immediate deaths. Self-destructive acts also span a continuum with respect to the reach of violence they perform. Echoing Oliver Grojean, it is important to stress that "the common perception of the hunger strike as a type of non-violent action here seems misleading."[25] While all of the modalities involve violence to the actor performing these acts, they fall into a spectrum with respect to violence on others: on one end are acts that are entirely self-directed (such as death fasts and self-immolations), which I will refer to as *defensive* forms of weaponization of life, and on the other are acts that are simultaneously other-directed (such as suicide attacks), which I will refer to as *offensive* forms of weaponization of life.[26] Most of the organizations that resort to the weaponization of life (such as PKK, Hamas, Islamic Jihad, Tamil Tigers, and al-Aqsa Martyrs Brigade) have utilized both defensive and offensive forms, sometimes within the same campaign, along with other, more common violent tactics, such as guerrilla warfare.[27] As a result, a categorical separation between these forms, in which defensive forms are construed as nonviolent as opposed to offensive forms that are recognized as violent, does not seem to be accurate, especially from the perspective of those who resort to them.[28]

I therefore suggest viewing these different modalities of the weaponization of life as a continuum.[29] Situating these acts on a continuum does not intend to obliterate the political and ethical differences between the defensive and offensive forms of self-destruction, only to underscore the affinities in their technique. Overall, I use the weaponization of life as an overarching umbrella concept that involves these different modalities of action whose core commonality is that the performance of self-destruction is integral to the actor's political intervention.

The weaponization of life is a tactic in which the body is utilized as the conduit of a political intervention. However, it is important to emphasize that even though this intervention is made through the body, it is irreducible to the corporeality of the body. There are two main reasons for this. First, the corporeality of these performances presents a paradoxical combination of instrumentality and the abolition of instrumentality. On the one hand, the body is an intermediary, a means of staging a protest that advances certain specific demands as the political ends of that protest. On the other hand, the body is not an empty, mediate vessel to achieve political ends precisely because its deployment only by way of its destruction defies the distinction between means and ends and obliterates instrumental rationality. Second, the intervention often has a metaphysical element attached to it, an element regarding the meaning of existence.[30] The self-destructive act makes a commentary on the meaning of life by conveying the prioritization of the life of a political cause over the biological existence of its proponents. These acts say, in a sense, it is not worth living life if you cannot live it according to your own political convictions; it is not worth living life if you are forced to live a mere existence that is predicated on renouncing or not living up to your political cause. Without this metaphysical component, it would be difficult to understand the specificity of self-destructive practices vis-à-vis other practices of resistance, their extremity, existential and total nature, and, further, to separate these acts from suicides.

For these reasons, I find it more apt to refer to this tactic as the weaponization of *life* and not the weaponization of the body. I use this characterization also in order to highlight the violence that inheres in the weaponization of life less as a political instrument than as a form of political *expression*. Among theories of violence, Frantz Fanon's argument that, under circumstances of colonial rule, violence is entwined with the political expression of the oppressed has an important place, emphasizing the transformative function of violence beyond an instrumental relation to the political end of fighting colonial domination. According to Fanon, violence is not viewed simply as a means to an end, justified by the legitimacy or desirability of the end, but becomes formative and redemptive of the colonized subject, if not even therapeutic: violence is the process of the constitution of the colonized into a human being.[31] His view that violence becomes a sign and means of the political subjectification of the colonized, particularly in the absence of other opportunities to individuation, has suggestively been applied to human weapons.[32]

While I am skeptical of this romanticization and justification of violence as a means of subject formation, a view that is authorized or at least rendered plausible by Fanon himself, I think he is nevertheless correct to problematize the reduction of violence to a simple means.[33] In the transformation of human life into a weapon, there is both the desire to pursue particular political goals and an assertion of subjectivity (that may or may not have been denied previously) in which one's humanity is constitutively entwined with a *politicized* interpretation of life itself. In other words, what is asserted is less an abstract political subjectivity or a universal notion of humanity than a situated and radicalized understanding of what it means to be human as synonymous with a political existence in conformity with the specific cause that subjectivity is marshaled to express. The body becomes the "organ" of representation that articulates this coterminous assertion of the frustrated existence of an individual, class, or community and the political desire for nondomination and emancipation.

But the weaponization of life, understood as a form of expression, also invites us to complicate our understanding of violence by restoring an independent role to *form* as having distinctive qualities, certain political and ethical effects of its own. I find Walter Benjamin's interpretation of violence illuminating in order to conceive of the weaponization of life as a particular form of violence whose technique of self-destruction renders it not only expressive of a content but also with specific implications of its own. Benjamin draws attention to instrumental modalities of violence that instantiate the sovereign power to make or preserve the law, but he also distinguishes a different kind that is not a means to an end (nonmediate violence). Benjamin gives the example of a sudden angry outburst as the example of the kind of violence that is "not a means but a manifestation."[34] He then identifies a certain variety of expressive violence, which he qualifies as "pure" and "divine," aporetically intimating its relation to transcendent, messianic justice. Following his thought, we may think of the weaponization of life not only as the political expression of passions (such as rage) but also as articulating, in its very form, a similar aporia: the desire and call for justice and, at the same time, the recognition of the impossibility of its realization under the political conditions in which these violent performances take place. Thus self-destruction as *form* is intimately, if aporetically, connected with a transcendent justice, which in its turn gives meaning to life and death and animates this violence.[35] This complex determination of form, consequently, creates highly specific effects, such as the cultivation of a theologized discourse of martyrdom that permeates the content being expressed in these violent political practices.

By conceptualizing self-destructive practices as the weaponization of life, with particular emphasis on their expressiveness, therefore, this book takes critical distance from approaches that conflate these actions with *suicides*, on the one hand, and that subsume them into *terrorism*, on the other. The first move, in part a result of Émile Durkheim's influential categorization of voluntary deaths under the rubric of suicide, works in the present to neutralize the political and often collective quality of these actions. Durkheim's original classification is problematic not only because its criteria for distinguishing between different categories of suicide is primarily based on individual moral dispositions of egoism versus altruism but also because it groups together self-induced deaths pursued in fulfillment of social obligations, religious ideals, and political motivations in the same subcategory of "altruistic suicide," losing the specificity of self-destructive acts carried out as a political intervention.[36]

At the same time, in politics, calling these acts *suicides* has the rhetorical function of assigning responsibility solely to the actor who performs the act of self-killing, thereby individualizing the action, obfuscating its political message, and even working against the very purpose of action. In most contexts these rhetorical effects are compounded by the evocation of the religious prohibition on suicide. As an exemplary instance of this move, one may recall that, in the context of prison struggles in 1981, the British government insisted on calling Bobby Sands's death on the hunger strike a suicide, presenting him "as having the initiative and thus deciding his fate."[37] In contrast, his supporters viewed his death as martyrdom, emphasizing the self-sacrificial nature of his course of action and attributing the responsibility of his death to the government's policies in response to which he starved himself to death. Either way, the choice of vocabulary defining the act clearly shows that the nominal operation is cryptonormative, incorporating a judgment of the cause for which the self-destructive act is performed.

On the other hand, the second move of folding self-destructive practices within a discourse of terrorism is also problematic for two reasons. First, the definition of *terrorism* is not free of ambiguity and contestation. In the context of its evolution, the term has experienced a semantic reversal: having originated from the practices of Jacobin government, it has come to denote the oppositional practices directed at established political rule that threaten to challenge the status quo through the deployment or threat of violence. More important, however, is that the proliferation of the semantic possibilities of the term has rendered it difficult to distinguish terrorism from other forms of violence. At times the distinction rests on the status of the perpetrators of violence as nonstate actors, at other times it is based on the noncombatant status of the targets of violence. Moreover, each definition is quickly complicated by counterinstances: the arbitrary, illegitimate use of violence by state agents against the civilian population has been labeled state terrorism,[38] acts directed at combatants (such as those in military bases or on patrol), particularly within the context of invasion and warfare, are frequently called terrorist attacks, even violence directed at property and cybernetic information systems have been included within the definition of terrorism (for example, ecoterrorism and cyberterrorism). As a result of its malleability and multivalence, the term has become a loose cannon that has lost whatever analytical precision and effectiveness it may have originally commanded.

Second, as a result of the definitional ambiguities and the political stakes of these ambiguities, the public and scholarly discourse on terrorism has become an ideological battlefield in which even the deployment or avoidance of the term itself has been transformed into a signifier of a normative and political position. It is not only that states confer illegitimacy upon their political contestants when they label their acts "terrorist" but also scholars who reproduce the same charges of illegitimacy at the discursive level while also revealing their own political sympathies in relation to these acts. Once again, as in the application of the category "suicide," the labeling of these acts as "terrorist" does the cryptonormative work that incorporates a judgment of the cause for which the self-destructive act is performed.

While some instances of political, self-destructive violence may have their roots in personal motivations akin to those that lead to suicide, and while more assertive and offensive modalities of self-destruction, such as suicide attacks by nonstate parties directed against civilians, may fit a rigorous definition of terrorism, I think it is analytically and politically worthwhile to dissociate the weaponization of life from these conceptual apparatuses. This move enables us to analyze the meaning and functions as well as the reasons and justifications for self-destructive tactics in connection with political struggle and to situate these forms of action within a theoretical discussion of power and resistance rather than immediately be implicated in their condemnation or espousal. This approach does not imply that we should not ultimately judge these acts, only that political and normative judgment should come ultimately.

Following this path, this study is interested in inquiring what material, political, and social conditions produce self-inflicted death as a form of resistance and the predominant alternative to existing hierarchies of power, what mechanisms make the self-infliction of death appear as the only agency possible, rather than ask, for example, whether self-immolation is suicide, whether it is morally acceptable or justifiable, whether it is terroristic, and so on. Instead of imposing moral judgment through the characterization of these acts as suicidal or terrorist, this study is concerned with understanding their relation to the conditions out of which they emerge as well as also how they come to be shaped by the perception and experience of those conditions and how they in turn express those perceptions and experiences. Finally, suspending preemptive judgment also allows us to be attentive to the multifarious ideological, political, and cultural effects the deployment of the weaponization of life may have upon the world of those who plan, coordinate, perform, and support these acts, highlighting the specific consequences that flow from the very form of struggle.

AIMS OF THE BOOK AND ITS FRAMING

There are thus two interrelated aims of this book. The first is to tell the story of the death fast struggle in Turkey. The second is to interrogate this story from the angle of self-destructive practices in order to deploy its findings toward the theorization of this emergent repertoire of action that increasingly stamps the radical struggles of our present.

There is a burgeoning literature that addresses the rise of self-destructive forms of political struggle, particularly in the last three decades, marshaling various explanations and interpretations in order to illuminate this complex and elusive phenomenon. One of the most common explanations is to place these actions within a framework of fanaticism, mostly driven by religious beliefs.[39] The weaponization of life, particularly in its more aggressive, offensive modalities, it is argued, is motivated by Islamism in its fundamentalist version that condones violence against its infidel enemies and seeks political supremacy through the waging of holy war in which individual self-sacrifice in the name of God is sought in order to achieve the status of martyrdom and a rewarded afterlife.[40] Following this line, the more defensive modalities of self-destructive practices, such as self-immolation, have been associated with Buddhism and Christianity.[41] A corollary of the religious fundamentalism argument points to the existence of "cultures of violence"[42] or "cultures of death" in which martyrdom is exalted, even if this exaltation may not be solely due to religious convictions.[43] Scholars have argued that self-destructive practices can arise from a nonreligious construction of victimhood and the view that the political body is an "afflicted body" that needs to be reversed by radical action.[44] It is a logical consequence, the argument goes, that struggles will be directed toward the attainment of martyrdom in geographies where the constant presence of violence, exacerbated by religiosity, has shaped popular culture and mechanisms of subjectivation to foster a widespread acceptance of self-destructive acts and even grant them legitimacy.[45]

The emphasis on religion has led to the construction of lineages for these contemporary practices through historical narratives of religious martyrdom. Of central interest to the Islamism thesis is the genealogy that emphasizes the Karbala event of 680 CE (where the prophet's grandson Husayn was killed with his seventy-two men in the fight over the succession of the caliphate after Mohammed's death), which has generated the Shia interpretation of Husayn's death as a willful act of martyrdom that was intended to inspire others to fight against injustice. The anniversary of Husayn's death is commemorated through a series of rituals that enact the suffering of Husayn on the battlefield: self-flagellation, self-mutilation, and other forms of self-harm are regular components of the Ashura, pointing to a continuing tradition in which martyrdom commands great value. On the more aggressive end, the seditious sect of Ishma'ili "assassins," also known as the Hashishiyun, led by Hassan Sabbah in the late eleventh and early twelfth centuries, has been recognized as a medieval precursor of today's suicide attackers, based on their practice of carrying out suicidal missions in order to kill those in power, particularly prominent members of the Sunni ruling elite.[46] On the other hand, others have pointed to the early Christian martyrs as generative of a discourse of martyrdom in the face of persecution.[47] The traditions of apocalyptic prophecy and eschatology connected with Judeo-Christian thought that have given rise to the heretical millenarian movements in early modern Europe have also been considered as potential sources of the proliferation of martyrdom today.[48] Historical precedents of self-immolation have also been traced back to early Buddhist practices dating from circa fifth century.[49] Overall, while such lineages tend to associate martyrdom with particular religions, they rather suggest that a common heritage of martyrdom lies at the source of all modern religions.

Despite the powerful evocation of traditions of martyrdom as antecedents of contemporary political practices of human weapons, recent scholarship has shown that religion, while an important source of motivation for some of these actions, is by no means the sole or even the main determinant.[50] While religious beliefs may have some role in inspiring the actions of these agents, these constitute *one* among many motivations that instigate self-destructive practices.[51] Religion sometimes simply serves as a justification, "rationalizing narrative" or consolation rather than a direct motivation.[52] In fact, studies have suggested the relevance of highly this-worldly rationales, such as the desire to combat imperialist domination and foreign occupation and the quest for national independence, as more prominent motives in the name of which self-destructive techniques are widely used.[53] As Diego Gambetta notes, counter to their common public perception, "more than half of total world missions, even if one excludes the anarchists and the Kamikaze and counts only from 1981 to September 2003, were carried out by *secular* groups."[54]

Another common strand of explanation resorts to individual psychology, attempting to pin the reasons for performing such acts to trauma and post-traumatic disorders, depression, and, at times, personal pathologies.[55] In these approaches the self-destructive act becomes a function of the personal life story of the actor and the experiences (such as the loss of a loved one, poverty, unemployment, humiliation, and so on) that result in social exclusion, grief, desperation, and hopelessness about the future, which then propel individuals to self-destructive actions. For many strands of liberal thought, whose political analyses are based on the model of the rational, self-interested individual, for whom self-preservation should be a priority, the explanation of individual trauma or psychopathology is expedient in order to account for the reasons why individuals would choose to give up their lives, consciously and willingly.

The problem with this group of explanations is that, in addition to the tendency to construe these individuals as irrational, disturbed, brainwashed, or suicidal, it tends to lose sight of the political context in which these actions take place, the conditions that give rise to them, and the ideological dispositions, motivations, and demands of the political groups and organizations that coordinate them.[56] While individual reasons for participation in such actions are doubtless important, scholars have suggested a wide array motivations that may or may not be political: protecting family and country; expressing solidarity with members of a group; avoiding the guilt of nonparticipation; taking revenge; acquiring prestige and glory; and acting on beliefs and emotions, such as devotion, disappointment, desire for the afterlife, fury, and hatred against the enemy, among others.[57] However, particularly when these actions are not spontaneous but rather part of organized movements or campaigns, the directly political, organizational motivations stand in tension with narratives that privilege personal motivations that are often deemed nonpolitical. Organizational motivations include weakening and demoralizing the enemy, escalating the conflict, drawing publicity for the cause, retaliating, improving political reputation before the opposed forces or vis-à-vis rival organizations, and increasing the morale of one's political constituency.[58] Given this diversity and the complex interaction between the individual and organizational motivations, interpretations that focus mainly on personal experiences of trauma appear reductionist, lopsided, and incomplete at best.

A different thread of explanations focuses on the balance of power between conflicting parties in which self-destructive techniques are commonly used, often by the weaker party against the strong.[59] Situating these practices within the context of the changing nature of warfare and increasing asymmetries, scholars argue that the resort to "suicide missions" becomes a strategic choice that violent organizations make.[60] This choice is contingent upon the objective constraints of these organizations, constraints such as the degree of asymmetry vis-à-vis the enemy, technological resources, the availability of volunteers, and level of popular support, as well as their ideological orientation.[61] Particularly where weapons and resources are scarce, the argument goes, groups or organizations resort to "human capital" to make up for what they lack in terms of technology or money.[62] By deploying militants in sensational acts of violence, they achieve a greater impact than what they can otherwise achieve. As these methods command a much amplified media presence, they become effective and efficient ways of furthering the struggle and drawing attention to their cause. Moreover, the success of these operations motivates other organizations to emulate and adopt similar tactics, creating a "social learning" or contagion effect.[63] At the same time, competition among various organizations for the loyalty and support of their constituencies tends to create "outbidding" and increase the propensity of suicide operations, particularly if the popular reception of these acts is positive.[64] In light of this strategic, calculative framework, political actors embedded in asymmetric conflict situations become the favored precursors of contemporary self-destructive actions rather than prior instances of religious martyrdom. Here we can find references to the Russian anarchists in the nineteenth century who resorted to suicidal missions to assassinate political figures, as well as to the Japanese kamikaze fighters. Such an approach also fosters the possibility of sustained comparisons with radical organizations in asymmetric situations that do not carry out self-destructive missions, such as Baader-Meinhoff, Red Brigades, ETA, and the IRA.[65]

The greatest merit of this approach is to counter the demonization of self-destructive acts and to present an analysis of these actions as conscious, calculated choices given the structural constraints of conflict situations, such as the absence of effective access to conventional means of political struggle or equivalent technological and financial resources among conflicting parties. However, one of the drawbacks of this approach is that that it focuses exclusively on the analysis of the given situation without problematizing the broader structures and relations of power that go into the making of the given situation. Another problem is that while the perspective of asymmetric warfare gives a strong account of the causes of the resort to self-destructive violence, it fails to conceptualize the specificity of this form of violence vis-à-vis other forms of resistance, except as a cheap, short-circuiting alternative to the methods of struggle that require greater resources and broader popular support.

While generally utilizing the insights of this body of scholarship regarding how power differentials in situations of asymmetric conflict tend to shape choices of political action, I take a different theoretical track—one that problematizes the power relations that produce asymmetric conditions and operate through them, shaping not only the strategic choices of political actors but also the political subjectivities of those who make those choices of political action. In order to explore the specifically self-destructive form of the weaponization of life, I think we need a more comprehensive account of the nature of power relations that agents resorting to oppositional practices are situated in and conditioned by, concurrent with an analysis of asymmetry and its implications. If we are to restore a rigorous specificity and independent role to *form*, it is necessary to analyze the kind of power relations that are being confronted, relations which inform the expressive capacity of the oppositional action and condition the flow of the content of resistance into the specific variant of struggle, involving a complex negotiation of the meaning of life and death in relation to power and justice. This is why contemporary strands of biopolitical theorization that tackle the intimate and intricate relationship between life and power in modern societies are of immense relevance for human weapons. Since self-destructive practices work by forging life into a weapon of struggle, they necessitate a deeper understanding of the nature of power relations in which life becomes an object, a target, an objective in response to which death, and especially self-inflicted death, becomes constituted into a distinct site and form of resistance.

My reading builds upon a Foucauldian perspective on power relations and takes as its point of departure Michel Foucault's dual thesis on how life becomes an object of regulation and how death falls from the purview of the political in light of the emergence of biopolitics as a new modality of power with modernity. As the seminal theorist of the biopolitical problematic, Foucault makes a strong case for transformation in the nature of power regimes toward the regulation of the well-being of individuals and populations and away from rule based on corporeal loyalty and the extraction of death. He thereby draws up a stark contrast between sovereignty based on the power *of* life (and death) and governmentality based on the power *over* life.[66] This account has the great merit of depicting the entry of life into the political sphere, both at the level of the individual body through disciplinary power and at the social level in the form of population management through biopower. Foucault's reflections on the prison have become a natural starting point for analyzing modern practices of punishment, with great relevance to the high security prison whose architectural design furthers panoptic surveillance, individualized and docile subjectification, and normalization in a power regime based on disciplinary domination rather than corporeal punishment.[67] Foucault's analysis of the prison also draws attention to a politics of space, through its enclosure, organization, and utilization, which provides the necessary foundation upon which to build a micropolitical analysis of asymmetric conflict situations within institutional structures. At the same time, his work on the development of governmental techniques that manage the life processes and well-being of populations through the regulation of flows and contingencies has become an indispensable reference point to understand the political tactics deployed under the expansive category of "security."[68] Overall, Foucault has taught us to pay attention to the conjoined workings of disciplinary and biopolitical discourses and practices in order to advance the analysis of power in the present.[69]

However, the two theses of the Foucauldian account, if taken to their logical conclusions, tend to produce two consequences that present theoretical difficulties in light of contemporary politics, constituting important shortcomings
to the otherwise potent insights of this account. First is that the general tenor
of the argument regarding the transformation from sovereignty to biopolitics
gives the impression that sovereignty is in the process of disappearance, dissolution, and replacement by the techniques of government that focus on the
administration of life processes and well-being. Second, the narrative of the
progressive totalization of biopolitical government tends to foreclose possibilities of resistance or at best tether resistance to forms that mimic the biopolitical
logic of affirming life and making claims for greater rights and well-being.

Through a close engagement with theorists of biopolitics, especially Foucault and Agamben, this book argues against both of these tendencies.[70] On
the one hand, the book makes a case, theoretically and empirically, for *biosovereignty*, which indicates the contradictory amalgamation of sovereignty
and biopolitics as the distinguishing feature of contemporary power regimes.
In response to the argument that sovereignty, in the traditional sense of the
power to command life and death, is fast becoming an artifact of the past, this
book maintains, on the contrary, not only that sovereignty continues to be
prominent, but also that it refounds and installs itself in new, albeit contingent, configurations based on the fertilization and mutual interpenetration
of sovereign tactics with biopolitical tools of government. Rather than disappearing or enfeebling, the sovereignty with which we are faced is recalcitrant,
seasoned, and self-invigorating; it grows and augments itself by increased
control and governance over life. Sovereignity and biopolitics come together
in the form of a *biosovereign assemblage*, which the book traces in the specific
example of the Turkish state.

On the other hand, by critically reconstructing and extrapolating from the
otherwise limited and pessimistic account of resistance provided by theorists
of biopolitics, according to whom power penetrates every facet of life and
shapes subjectivities in ways that preclude or greatly limit the potentials of resistance, the book argues that biosovereignty continues to produce new forms
of resistance. Since biopolitics functions by extending control over life itself,
the argument goes, then resistance to it must accordingly occur as a response
to this control and at this level. When theorists of biopolitics do in fact carve
a role for resistance, however, this resistance is based on turning the logic of
biopolitics against itself through struggles that demand better conditions of

life and greater well-being. However, this book contends that there is also a negative form of biopolitical struggles, based not on the affirmation of life but on its willful destruction.

I theorize the self-destructive practices that forge life into a weapon as a specific modality of resistance, which I will call *necroresistance*. I argue that the reasons for the growing prevalence of human weapons should be sought in the new and contextually specific constellations of the increased biopoliticization of sovereign power; indeed, precisely as a response to this development. The contours of this kind of resistance are shaped not only by the biopolitical valorization of life but also by the ongoing, modulated, and fortified presence of the sovereign power of life and death. I interpret necroresistance as a form of *refusal* against simultaneously individualizing and totalizing domination that acts by wrenching the power of life and death away from the apparatuses of the modern state in which this power is conventionally vested. In this effort I argue not only with and against Foucault but also through Agamben and other scholars who have developed Agamben's provocative thesis on "bare life" in new directions.

The overarching theoretical goal of this book, then, is to show the link between specifically self-destructive violence and the power of the state, or how fatal corporeal acts of insurgence reveal, communicate with, and perform a response to the continuing presence of sovereign power, but in specific forms whose corporeality and relation to death are conditioned by biopolitics. The book relies on the in-depth study of the death fast struggle as a suggestive example to unpack the characteristics of this novel form of insurgent politics in relation to transformations in the nature of power relations. Through this situated analysis, the book seeks to offer new ways of thinking about human agency and the possibilities and limitations of radical political resistance in the present.

METHODOLOGY

This book casts the death fast struggle as an instance that crystallizes a conjuncture in which the process of the *biopoliticization of sovereignty* meets the *necropoliticization of resistance*. In order to reveal the internal dynamics, lived experience, and ideological understanding of the actors that are situated amidst these interrelated tendencies, I study the death fast struggle as an exemplary but not exceptional instantiation of the conscious, voluntary, protracted, and strategic deployment of self-destructive practices as part of a political struggle in a context that is characterized by overt efforts at transforming and revamping the sovereign power of the Turkish state.

In this study I proceed by weaving together political theory and political ethnography. I draw upon detailed fieldwork, combining contextual immersion, personal observation, and in-depth interviews. I bring this research together with an array of resources: parliamentary proceedings, prisoner letters, press releases by various civil society organizations and minimally circulated reports prepared by human rights agencies, excerpts from leftist journals, pamphlets, and daily newspapers. These primary sources nourish us with a thorough and vivid sense of the movement and the context, allowing us to trace the trajectory of the death fast in a way that appreciates and conveys the rich details and paradoxical complexities of the situation.

The ethnographic component of this work is particularly important in order to access the world of the death fast struggle as a movement that emerged from and occupied margins otherwise difficult to penetrate, a movement that, in fact, stood at the intersection of multiple margins, objective and subjective. The death fast struggle was at the margins geographically: it occurred in a country that borders Europe and the Middle East, being part of both and neither fully. It was at the margins spatially: the movement was initiated in prison wards, continued in prison cells, and disseminated into the shantytowns in big cities, whose inhabitants were increasingly constructed as "others" of mainstream urban life.[71] It was at the margins legally: the participants of the struggle were not only prisoners affiliated with extraparliamentary leftist organizations and parties, outlawed by the Turkish state, but they were also carrying out and supporting acts of self-destruction whose legal status was ambiguous. The movement was at the margins ideologically: the organizations orchestrating the struggle constituted the "radical" end of the political left, arguing for the overthrow of the constitutional order with violence, if necessary. The movement was also at the margins epistemically: the participants of the struggle lacked the privilege that would qualify their experiences as a source of knowledge, their utterances as political voice, their desires as legitimate interests.[72] Finally, the movement was at the margins politically: it was composed of individuals and organizations that, far from participating in mainstream politics, were rather included in it only as a threat to be overcome or eliminated. If these distinct margins came to intersect, under the increasingly unsparing and intensifying domination of the Turkish state over its insurgents, in the position inhabited by leftist political prisoners in Turkey, it was not long before the same intersection was appropriated and transformed into a "space of death."[73] As a result, the literal margins of the political overlapped with its metaphorical margins: death relegated to the borders of biopolitics was concretized in these overlapping sites of marginality and transformed into the venue of radical politics.

Without an ethnographic account, it would be difficult to capture the fleeting spaces and temporalities of these intersecting margins that were briefly opened up to visibility as actors located in those sites staged fatal political interventions and which were subsequently closed to public scrutiny as the state attempted to push them further into the margins, if not erase them altogether. In that brief aperture created by the movement's coming into existence and subsequent passing, therefore, the ethnographic work attempts to grasp in situ what happened in these margins, how they were shaped, perceived, and dealt with by the center, as well as the relationality of the center to its margins, and to catapult the way in which this relationality was experienced by a multiplicity of actors into the field of theory. As such, the empirical research is not a mere complement, but an indispensable part of the effort of political theorization pursued in this book.

The narrative's focus on the weaponization of life as it becomes the interface of confrontation between the insurgency and the state allows us entry into two spheres at once: the sphere of resistance and the sphere of power. On the one hand, it provides important clues regarding the objects, objectives, desires, strengths, weaknesses, and contradictions of resistance; in short, it opens a path to its theorization and critique. At the same time, it enables us to gauge the approach of power—its fear and hostility, decisiveness and commitment, reactions, calculations, discourses, justifications, and stratagems— toward the weaponization of life, allowing us access to its objectives, desires, strengths, weaknesses, and contradictions; in short, the internal configuration of the power regime, the differential modalities of power that operate in tandem and their interrelations. In other words, the ethnographic account of the margins gives an account both of the margins and the center, or more accurately, of their dynamic relationality.

The work as a whole learns from the "anthropology of the margins" as an integral part of the work of political theorization.[74] According to Veena Das and Deborah Poole, "anthropology of the margins offers a unique perspective to the understanding of the state, not because it captures exotic practices, but because it suggests that such margins are a necessary entailment of the state, much as the exception is a necessary component of rule."[75] In keeping with the emphasis on the margins, a crucial antecedent of this work is Allen Feldman's account of the dirty protest and the hunger strike of Irish political prisoners in the cells of Maze Prison.[76] Feldman's narrative combines great ethnographic acumen with profound theoretical sophistication while relaying the violent struggles in Northern Ireland, both outside and inside prison. This study takes inspiration from his work, which highlights the body as both an extension of the state apparatus and a counterinstrument of protest. Like Feldman's masterful work, this book attempts to bring the lived experience of corporeal violence to bear on its theorization, albeit with different theoretical preoccupations that center on biosovereignty and necroresistance.

As a work in political theory, this book insists on the centrality of ethnographic research as an indispensable resource, which allows us to hear the marginal voices that make up the death fast struggle, but it also cautions us against taking them at their word. The reading I give the death fast struggle builds on narratives by the participants of the movement, but ultimately diverges not only from the ways in which they individually perceive and present themselves as participants but also from the collective statements and evaluations issued by the radical organizations with which they affiliate their politics. The book attempts to analyze the resistance beyond how that resistance understands and presents itself to itself, to its supporters and opponents, and to the public at large. At the same time, my reading builds on the accounts of state officials, public authorities, and prison administrators, but takes distance from the way in which they portray the struggle as well as the practices of the state addressing that struggle. The book therefore attempts to analyze power beyond its self-representation, by making the case that the transformation in the central categories of our political world must be studied and understood from the perspective of their most subversive opponents that find themselves in the margins, their demands, views, reactions, and ultimately, transformations. Without attention to the stories that become subjugated by the dominant narratives of power, we are left to take power at its word. It is not possible to have a truthful grasp of the political relations and arrangements that define our world, let alone begin to think beyond them, without attending to the resistances they provoke and coming to terms with how these resistances interpret them.

Consequently, my practice is to read the varied interpretations of multiple actors gathered through ethnographic research in relation to one another. At the same time, I treat these narratives as living texts of political theory that facilitate our entry into the margins and the center alike. As raw and unmediated convictions, statements and interpretations, these narratives, especially the voices of those who inhabit the margins of the political, constitute subjugated knowledges, according to Foucault, "knowledges that have been disqualified as nonconceptual knowledges, as insufficiently elaborated knowledges: naïve knowledges, hierarchically inferior knowledges, knowledges that are below the required level of erudition and scientificity."[77] Bringing these knowledges to bear on questions of political theory, such as power, resistance, sovereignty, and agency, entails a practice of political theory that aggressively questions any strict separation between the histories of political thought and the diverse ways in which ideas are put into practice. It interrogates the moments in which political theory becomes lived experience and traces the theoretical contradictions and practical dilemmas of political agents that become accentuated and acute as they are violently acted out. It puts these live texts in conversation with the great thinkers of politics.

Overall, this method signifies my understanding of the enterprise of critical theory today: as thinking in the conjuncture, through the case at hand, from the event, in its concreteness, immediacy, and often daunting complexity about a political problem that is of universal significance.[78] At the same time, treating subjugated, disqualified knowledges at the same level with prominent theorists of politics is my way of writing a more egalitarian "history of the present" in order to assess the ambiguous, dangerous, multifaceted, obscure, and intriguing legacy of human weapons.

ORGANIZATION OF THE BOOK

The main thesis of the book, namely, the stark contrast between the *biopoliticization of sovereignty* and the *necropoliticization of resistance* as the dual political logic of the present, is mirrored in its organization. The architecture of the book replicates this contrast by developing the narrative of the death fast struggle around the central antagonism between the state and the insurgents. It begins from a description of the death fast struggle as an event. It then unpacks this event, first by venturing in the realm of the state and second by moving to the realm of the insurgents. Meanwhile, it portrays the opposition between the state's goal of introducing a penal regime that controls life and the prisoners' goal of protesting this control by a resort to death. It juxtaposes the discursive and practical techniques deployed in the service of these goals by the state and the insurgents respectively. In other words, it tells the same story twice, from opposing perspectives, the contrast between and the combination of which tells another story that is irreducible to each story alone. The main intention of the book's architecture, therefore, is to cast power and resistance not only in a binary opposition but also as two faces of the same coin. At the same time, the architecture aspires to enact a displacement from the conventional sites of political action to enclaves of insurgency by shifting our political gaze from the center of the political stage to its margins. We therefore move from the domain of power to the domain of resistance, from the center to the margin, from life to death.

The analysis opens by the depiction of the death-event of a hunger striker in the death fast struggle. Focusing on the relationship between the state and the insurgent's body as key to the significance of that scene, chapter 1 takes up this relation as a symptom of the nature of the dominant power regime. It develops the conceptual apparatus of the book by charting the changing nature of sovereignty and resistance within a biopolitical problematic. Through a close engagement with Foucault's work, and a discussion of Agamben and others who have utilized the biopolitical paradigm, I introduce and develop the concepts of *biosovereignty* and *necroresistance*. Having presented the theoretical problematic of the book, its conceptual tools, and main arguments, I turn to the specific study of the death fast struggle in Turkey in order to illustrate, complicate, further explore, and elaborate this apparatus.

Chapters 2 and 3 explore biosovereignty in the context of its development. Chapter 2 provides the historical background on Turkey, its traditions of statecraft and treatment of radical currents on the left as its "internal enemies," which frame the way in which the state perceived the challenge of the death fast struggle as a "crisis" of sovereignty. The prison becomes an emblematic site for securitization and the stage for a highly politicized confrontation between the state and the insurgents. In this light, I interpret the introduction of a new, selectively engineered, and isolationist penal regime as a crucial moment in the transformation of sovereign power in line with the state's security considerations. I analyze the state's rationales for reforming its penal apparatus couched within a discourse of a "war against terrorism" and the reestablishment of the state's sovereign authority over insurgents. I discuss how the spatial rearrangement of the penal landscape through the introduction of high security prisons modeled after the super-max becomes symptomatic of the development of the biopoliticization of sovereign power.

Chapter 3 continues the investigation of biosovereignty by looking at the tactics of its implementation. It challenges the conventional understanding of governmentality in which traditional techniques of power based on the ex-traction of the corporeal loyalty of citizens are left behind in favor of new ones based on the administration of their lives and well-being. In contrast, I show how this "transition" to the governmental technologies of life builds upon a substrate of old techniques and instruments of sovereign power that, far from disappearing, are thereby reformed and refurbished. I argue that the Turkish state introduced a new penal regime by making law, implemented that regime by making war, and, finally, secured that regime by making peace, including the issuing of amnesties and artificial feeding of hunger strikers at the brink of death. These stratagems were used to implement a new rationality of politi-cal rule. In fact, the transition toward a more efficient, effective, customized, and calculated penal government of "internal enemies" was continuously but-tressed, pushed forth, and implemented by traditional instruments of sover-eignty. The chapter thereby depicts the amalgamation of sovereign power with disciplinary and biopolitical logics of political rule in an emergent biosover-eign assemblage.

Chapters 4, 5, and 6 turn to necroresistance. Chapter 4 shifts the gaze from the center to the margins. Moving away from the mainstream of the political sphere dominated by the state, the political parties in the parliament, and pub-lic institutions, it turns to document the emergence of islands of alternative power at the margins—the prison wards that were transformed into semiau-tonomous spaces where prisoners lived a communism-in-practice. It depicts these spaces as sites in which actors brought their insurgent political ideals into life. I argue that these spaces became pivotal for the formation of a strong collective will and a shared political identity that facilitated these actors' en-try into a struggle with the state, contesting its sovereignty and defending a rival form of power based on their claim upon the right of life and death, and that decided on necropolitical resistance as the method of expressing politi-cal voice from the margins. The chapter then chronicles the emergence of the death fast struggle, its demands, the main incidents that shaped the prisoners' course of action, and the debates that surrounded their choices, especially how the weaponization of life became the favored tactic of the movement. It analyzes the paradoxical "right to die" that was asserted by these prisoners against the state, especially its policy of nonconsensual artificial feeding. The chapter concludes by providing an account of how the protracted struggle was brought to an end by the movement's tactical instrumentalization of a human rights discourse in a final attempt to gain mass support in place of the radical, albeit failed, politics of human weapons. Overall, I put forth a reading of the trajectory of the movement through the contradictory development of voice and will, undergirded by a politics of space.

Chapter 5 continues the exploration of necroresistance by delving further into the discourses and practices of human weapons, their cultural world, rituals, values, and myths. It presents the political cosmology that envelops the experience of self-destructive practices and the rites that develop around it as specific effects that follow from this particular *form* of political action. Drawing upon the diverse meanings, interpretations, and formulations with which the participants of the death fast struggle understood and constructed their actions, goals, and desires, I present the peculiar qualities of their militancy and their relation to death, their ideas about martyrdom, and, finally, the contradictory interpretations of their agency as different cultural and metaphysical coordinates of the weaponization of life. I draw attention to how self-destruction works to generate a new constellation of practices, meanings, and values that sustain the radical political community that endorses this form of political action. The chapter proceeds by tracing a dialectic between the living and the dead in which human weapons are embedded and through which their subjectivity is shaped. Based on an analysis of the preparatory, funeral, and commemorative rituals that surround the weaponization of life, I call attention to three moments of this dialectic: namely, the transition of the militant to martyrdom even before the performance of the self-destructive act, the fusion of the militant and the martyr in the dead body, and, finally, the movement of the martyr into a new stage of militancy through its appropriation by the living and incorporation into practices of everyday life. Through this analysis, I show how the theologization of leftist politics at the margins occurs through the movement of the category of martyrdom to prominence.

Chapter 6 highlights the multiple meanings of the weaponization of life as a political tactic. Through an analysis of the self-interpretations of participants of the death fast, especially with respect to the role of the body, violence, death, and the meaning of sacrifice, I identify three distinct readings that present themselves as different ways of conceptualizing the weaponization of life. As an act of *resistance*, I argue, the movement sought to defend human dignity against the cell as a form of torture and to articulate itself with the broader societal struggle for the deepening of democracy. As an act of *class war*, the movement saw itself as part of the struggle against capitalism, demonizing the state as the representative of the class enemy. As an act of *refusal*, the movement launched an ideological offensive against the state's sovereign power whose legitimation is based on the sanctity of human life, asserting a "right to die" in the name of an alternative order. As a result of these multiple threads, I show how the death fast struggle also constituted a contradictory assemblage (like the power regime it was opposing), which advanced biopolitical claims regarding prison conditions, on the one hand, while it constituted a necropolitical refusal of the existing order, on the other hand. Finally, the book closes by discussing the implications of human weapons for a theory of biosovereignty and necroresistance.

Chapter 1
Biosovereignty and Necroresistance

The room where Mehmet stayed was barely furnished—one bed, one nightstand, one chair—and full of the acrid, acetonic smell of death.[1] His hiccups and occasional moans, uneasily blending with the singing of the birds in front of the window of the shanty house in Küçükarmutlu, Istanbul, interrupted the heavy silence. Mehmet's body was small, shrunken and emaciated from months of deliberate, disciplined, and meticulously managed self-starvation. From under the many layers of sheets and blankets that covered him, despite the blazing heat of the Istanbul summer, his bones protruded like sharp knives pointing to the walls around him. On those walls were pictures of deceased militants that permeated the whole house with their ghostly presence and a placard that read: "Long Live Our Death Fast Resistance!"

In this shantytown neighborhood upon a hill overlooking the Bosphorus, the many one-story houses—some partially constructed, some left without the final coating—were of the familiar kind in Istanbul built under the radar of municipal officials by the influx of immigrants who came to the city from rural Anatolia in search of a better life. Built with cheap construction materials, reflecting the poverty of their inhabitants and the precariousness of their status, and without official construction permits, these houses were of the kind that sprang up overnight, became part of the ever expanding contours of the city, and yet faced continuous danger of demolition by authorities. Separated from one of the most expensive and chic districts of Istanbul by the highway that led up to the Fatih Sultan Mehmet Bridge, connecting Europe to Asia, the neighborhood had unpaved, dusty roads, intermittent bus service, plumbing and electricity legally provided after long struggles and populist land grants from incumbent governments, and a population that served as the informal and flexible labor force of the growing metropolis. This new working class was essential in the economies and functioning of the largest cities and yet unable to earn their deserved share in them. At the same time, this neighborhood was one of several shantytowns, which had their own traditions of organized resistance that developed through the mobilization of their inhabitants for access to urban services and violent struggles between radical leftist and ultranationalist militants who parceled different neighborhoods in the ideological battles of the 1970s.[2] Like their Islamist counterparts in the late 1980s and 1990s, though less successfully than they, leftist militants had been organizing in these shantytowns since the late 1960s, offering their inhabitants informal networks of relief, economic solidarity, and even physical protection.[3]

In one of these shanty houses, the hunger striker lay in bed, reduced to a skeleton wrapped in a thin, almost transparent layer of skin, with the greenish gray hue of death, in marked contrast with the bright red headband tied around his forehead, a headband he was ceremoniously given to wear when he embarked on the hunger strike unto death. Mehmet had been brought here when he was discharged from prison on account of his deteriorating health and pending death, after having starved himself for several months in a prison ward, which he used to share with other political prisoners, and, after December 2000, in a high security prison cell under solitary confinement. Having been discharged from prison in the early summer of 2001, but not having quit his fast unto death, he continued his struggle in bed, though now he was surrounded by comrades and supporters in the neighborhood that welcomed him. There were others, too, individuals like Mehmet, in different houses of the same neighborhood and in other shantytowns, similarly progressing toward their deaths as part of the same struggle.[4]

The struggle had begun many months ago as a hunger strike, but was soon converted to a fast unto death. At that time the cravings for food had already largely disappeared and Mehmet was still in relatively good health. For many weeks he had experienced the slow decomposition of his body with an alertness of the mind. He spent his days assiduously reading the daily papers, writing letters, signing petitions, conversing with comrades, and analyzing the political situation.[5] In fact, the whole ordeal had been more tolerable precisely because he was conscious of the significance of his action and the prospect that he may not survive it.

Since then, however, his body had slowly wasted away. First it became more difficult to get up and walk because of the constant fatigue; then came the aches and the cramps; soon after, the objects and faces around him became indistinct, and vertigo and nausea set in as he slowly lost his sight. Voices grew distant, and they blurred into that constant ringing and humming in his ears.[6] Sores appeared in his mouth; the sugary water became increasingly difficult to swallow; and whenever he managed to take small sips, which required an exaggerated self-assertion, he had to begin another struggle against the urge to vomit.[7] Finally, wounds around his body from lying down for so long made it difficult to move even in bed.

Nevertheless, the long labor of dying, prolonged even further by the use of vitamin B1 in the initial phases of the struggle, continued without wavering commitment. Despite the excruciating pain of fasting for hundreds of days and the convulsions of a decomposing body, Mehmet remained firmly convinced of the righteousness of his cause and the inevitability of the struggle's imminent victory. In fact, he and the others around him were so convinced of the correctness of the struggle that they deemed those who quit not simply weak or cowardly but outright "traitors" to the revolution.[8] Mehmet was no traitor, a fact that he would prove by taking the struggle to its very end, unless a victorious ending would enable him to end his fast before he passed away. Until that victory came along, Mehmet continued to fast. Even as his consciousness became intermittent, he carried on, responding to visitors by little more than squeezing back the hands that held his own. In his lucid moments, he made his left hand into a fist and raised it up high from where he lay, now and again whispering the movement's slogans with barely discernable words: "Long Live Our Death Fast Resistance!" and "We Are Right, We Will Win!"

When Mehmet passed away after a long and painful struggle with death, leaving behind a corpse that was the grotesque imitation of the man he had once been, his death was commemorated by his comrades carrying, along with red banners that declared his immortality, his photos from a time when he was still young and vibrant. As everyone who came together in the little neighborhood square before the shanty house knew, he did not simply die but "fell martyr."[9] His death was thereby transformed; no longer was it merely an ending but rather a beginning—a second life, similarly political, though now eternal. As martyr, he would be remembered as the man he had once been and would forever remain, as a fighter who had not waivered in his commitment and had given up his life for his cause. As the slogan went, "The Martyrs of the Revolution are Immortal!"

TWO DEATH-EVENTS

The account of Mehmet, the hunger striker from Turkey, and his corporeal struggle resonates, in an uncanny way, with the detailed description of the gruesome torture and execution of Damiens the regicide with which Foucault's great book *Discipline and Punish* begins. In that vignette Foucault quotes historical accounts that describe in excruciating detail how the regicide is punished on a public stage on behalf of the king whose life he attempted to take. The executioner subjects Damiens to a terrible session of corporeal pain in which his flesh is cut off and burnt with a boiling mixture of metal, oil, and wax, and his body torn into pieces. Damiens is physically tormented until he is granted a final relief in death. Indeed, it is against the background of Foucault's memorable aperture into the nature of power via Damiens's torture that I would like to pose the death of Mehmet the hunger striker.

After being taken on a cart "wearing nothing but a shirt, holding a torch of burning wax weighing two pounds" to the scaffold in Place de Grève, Damiens would be subjected to the following tortures: "the flesh will be torn from his breasts, arms, thighs and claves with red-hot pincers, his right hand, holding the knife with which he committed the said parricide, burnt with sulfur, and, on those places where the flesh will be torn away, poured molten lead, boiling oil, burning resin, wax and sulfur melted together and then his body drawn and quartered by four horses and his limbs and body consumed by fire, reduced to ashes and his ashes thrown to the winds."[10]

Witness testimonies that Foucault quotes repeat the operation in detail, but also mention that it did not proceed smoothly, because the sulfur used to burn Damiens's skin was poorly heated, the steel pincers that tore his limbs had to be used more than once in each area and were left twisted, and the horses proved to be inexperienced in quartering a body. In fact, Foucault continues to quote, upon several unsuccessful quartering attempts of the horses, "the executioner Samson and he who had used the pincers each drew out a knife from his pocket and cut the body at the thighs instead of severing the legs at the joints; the four horses gave a tug and carried off the two thighs after them, namely, that of the right side first, the other following; then the same was done to the arms, the shoulders, the arm-pits and the four limbs; the flesh had to be cut almost to the bone, the horses pulling hard carried off the right arm first and the other afterwards."[11] According to these reports, Damiens was still alive even after the quartering was successful. Finally, the trunk of Damiens's body along with his severed limbs were burned in a fire, which lasted for four hours, until everything was "reduced to ashes."[12]

Here we have two death-events: two individuals, two corpses. One in mid-eighteenth-century France, the other at the turn of twenty-first-century Turkey. One upon the public scaffold in the town square of Paris, the other in a bed of an Istanbul shanty house. One as the unruly subject of a king, the other the unruly citizen of a democratic republic. One tortured and dismembered, the other starved and decomposed. In Damiens's situation, it is the king's executioner who inflicts a painful death; in Mehmet's situation, death is self-inflicted, and the hunger striker is his own executioner. In the former, the type of violence at work is brutal, bloody, vengeful, and slaughtering, whereas in the latter, it is bloodless, slowly decomposing, and self-destroying. In the former, pain is extreme and sudden; in the latter, subtler and more sustained. Damiens's executioner represents the king and, through the king, the body politic of the French people; Mehmet represents an alternative body politic, a revolutionary collective struggling for communism for the peoples of Turkey. Damiens's death is a public display to the people, precisely so that it constitutes an example to others to dissuade them from repeating the regicide; Mehmet's death aspires to be public(ized) and no less exemplary, but this time to persuade others to emulate the act and mobilize in its wake. Damiens is alone, but Mehmet is part of a movement composed of a coalition of outlawed organizations.

However, separated as they are by several centuries, different political regimes and cultures, the two scenes are marked by significant similarities. Both Damiens and Mehmet have committed *political* crimes: Damiens has attempted to take the life of the king, while Mehmet has been a committed communist militant. Both have been condemned to punishment: one by corporeal pain, the other by imprisonment. Both have resisted: Damiens by the refusal of a confession despite the possibility of a less painful death, Mehmet by the refusal to submit to solitary confinement in prison despite the possibility of acquiescently doing his time and thus surviving his sentence. Finally, both individuals take part in spectacles, performances of power upon the body. In the first situation, it is the king's executioner who transforms Damiens's death into a spectacular ordeal; in the second, the self-inflicted death of the hunger striker is also spectacular. Both performances attempt to call upon, enlist, and incite their audiences to hear and comply with their core message.

Most important, there is a certain equivalence between these two death-events, a common core, a constitutive relationship between the state and the body established through the performance of violence. This core relation is what we call *sovereignty* or the power of life and death. Both spectacles perform and produce this relation, a direct and transparent tie between the individual and the state: in the one between the monarch and the disobedient and unruly subject, in the other between the disobedient and unruly citizen and the modern state. In the first case, violence is deployed by the state; in the second, against it. The difference in the directionality of violence, of course, transforms the two death-events into opposites: in the former, violence functions to restore, affirm, and display the power of the state, whereas in the latter, violence functions to contest and challenge it. The death of Damiens serves the rule of the French king, the death of Mehmet serves the insurgency against the Turkish state. Both death-events delineate the body as the site of the exercise of power. What is at stake in both is who will have the final word on what Foucault calls the "body of the condemned," but what I will call, in the spirit of shifting our perspective to resistance, the "insurgent's body."

If we consider these scenes as stylized, ideal types, they can be taken as equivalent in the core relation that is performed through corporeal violence with two opposing vectors: political power and its counterpower, sovereignty and resistance. Both vectors are at work in both scenes, but to different degrees. Sovereignty is more pronounced in the scene of Damiens's punishment, whereas resistance is more pronounced in Mehmet's death. However, resistance is also in play in Damiens's scene, and sovereignty in Mehmet's. We can view the opposing vectors of this relation as presenting two intertwined questions that separate the relation between the individual and the state into its constitutive components: What do the differences between the two death-events tell us regarding sovereign power, on the one hand, and resistance, on the other? This chapter intends to chart the changing nature of sovereignty and resistance theoretically by working with, through, and beyond Foucault in the exploration of the biopolitical problematic.

FROM SOVEREIGNTY TO BIOSOVEREIGNTY

Sovereignty and violence are intimately linked. As Max Weber defines it, the modern state has the "monopoly of the legitimate use of physical force within a given territory."[13] The modern state is vested with sovereignty, the supreme power of the political entity, by which it legitimately claims to hold at its disposal the life and death of the inhabitants of that territory within which it commands the monopoly of physical force. However widely accepted, this definition is lacking in that it does not specify the kind of force the state lays claim to, just that it has monopoly over its use and that this monopoly is legitimate. However, the kind of force a sovereign entity controls, monopolizes, and exercises is just as important in order to define sovereignty. In fact, a key to understanding the nature of power is the specific technologies deployed for its exercise, especially the technologies of violence. Hence, the distance between the brutal and vengeful violence performed in the execution of Damiens the regicide and the silent and structural violence performed by solitary confinement in a high security prison cell gives us an insightful indication regarding not only the transformation in punitive practices but also the transformation in the nature of sovereignty. Foucault is the theorist who has done most to draw our attention to how these techniques of power and the kind of violence that inheres in them are strongly correlated with the dominant characteristics of a power regime.

It is well known that one of the most important contributions of Foucault's analysis of power is his displacement of sovereignty from the center stage of political theorization. Foucault's famous argument is that there exists a historic transformation of power from sovereignty to governmentality, or from the vocabulary and practices of the power *of* life (and death) toward the power *over* life, marking the advent of modernity.[14] This is a radical claim, if only because, for the tradition of modern political theory, sovereignty is the central concept.

Foucault defines sovereignty as the "right to take life or let live"; it is a power that is ultimately based on the "right to kill."[15] The power of life and death, and all the derivative powers that follow from this ultimate source, find expression in the law articulating the rights of the sovereign and its subjects. Foucault's reference to sovereignty as a juridical and prohibitive power reflects a lineage of theorization that stems from early modern and modern thinkers such as Jean Bodin, Thomas Hobbes, and Jean-Jacques Rousseau. Sovereignty, in this conception, corresponds to command.[16] It is repressive, and it functions on the basis of the extraction of corporeal loyalty. From the supreme, commandeering force that decides on the life and death of the subjects of a political entity, there issues a discursive and practical system of juridical-political rule, which is used first to describe, justify, strengthen, and later to challenge and delimit the modern, centralized state. This development also echoes the historical evolution of sovereignty in Western societies in terms of both the operation of power relations and their articulation in political discourses that revolve around a system of rights.

Foucault follows the development of sovereignty from the absolutist state of monarchic dynasties to the modern liberal-democratic state of parliamentary regimes, but he significantly complicates this progressive narrative in which the royalist roots of sovereignty have given way to more enlightened constitutional forms that bring significant limitations to the absolute and arbitrary nature, indivisibility, prerogatives, and other defining features of the supreme power of the political community. Foucault acknowledges that, with modern revolutions, sovereign power has shifted from the monarch to the people, and the juridical structure of sovereign power has become solidified in a system of rights. But, emphasizing the discontinuities in the development of sovereignty, he points to the emergence and growth of different forms of power relations, which must be taken into consideration in relation to sovereignty in order to understand how power operates in modern societies.

Foucault's argument is that our preoccupation with law as the main language of sovereign power has occluded our understanding of the workings of power.[17] Viewing the political sphere from the framework of law, particularly in its democratic version of rights and liberties, tends to conceal the workings of a multiplicity of techniques in the service of social control in the substratum of society, undergirding the juridical formation of power. Foucault's approach, therefore, asserts that sovereignty is only one of the poles of power in contemporary societies. The successive moments of the trajectory of sovereign power that Foucault zooms in on coincide, historically, with the emergence of new modalities of power whose skillful depiction by Foucault puts pressure on our conceptualization of the core political relation between the state and the individual and enables us to theorize the changing nature of sovereignty and resistance alike.

Of the three moments in the evolution of sovereign power that I would like to distill from Foucault's account, the first is its monarchical form where the definition of sovereignty as the power of life and death has an immediate and concrete referent in the monarch's person and the might of his sword.[18] The violence emanating from the command of the monarch is deployed over a territory in order to extract political, economic, legal, and corporeal obedience from the people.[19] The breach of the sovereign's law or interference with the extraction of obedience meets punishment that is similarly corporeal, vengeful, and spectacular, as every crime is, at the same time, a personal assault on the sovereign. The excessiveness of punishment is necessary for the restitution of sovereignty because any breach of the sovereign's law is synonymous with a "revolt, or insurrection against the sovereign"; hence punishment is the "sovereign's personal vendetta."[20] This is the moment of ritualized raw violence, as concretized in the torture of Damiens, when sovereign power most approximates its *absolute* form. It conforms to Bodin's sixteenth-century definition of sovereignty as "the absolute and perpetual power of a commonwealth,"[21] even though, as Bodin was quick to acknowledge, its actual exercise was limited by customary restrictions as well as divine and natural law.

The second moment in the trajectory of sovereign power corresponds at once to its democratization and its displacement from centrality. With the age of revolutions, monarchs are replaced by the "people" as the new sovereign. Power is depersonalized by the rise to prominence of democratically made or legitimated law. Sovereignty is still repressive, but it follows a juridical rationality and enters a process of formalization. Despite its democratic extension (or perhaps because of it) to encompass citizen participation, sovereignty also begins to lose its hold over society. Foucault shows that this Rousseauean moment of sovereignty is its highest point before its decline due to the competition posed by the emergence of a new form of power now striving for ascendance. Disciplinary power pervades the social sphere, emerging out of and penetrating the domains where the sovereignty of the democratic state is unable to reach. This is the *panoptic* moment.[22]

In contrast to sovereign power as extraction in its absolutist moment and juridical regulation in its popular, democratic moment, discipline is marked by surveillance and normalization through relays of power concretized in institutions, such as the prison, clinic, army, school, and new fields of knowledge, such as penality, medicine, psychiatry, and education. A different corporeality is at work here. Rather than the object of raw extraction, the individual body becomes both the bearer and vehicle of power relations and their object of inquiry, intervention, and point of application. Disciplinary power operates through a different technology of the body based on its mastery, domination, and artful utilization. The body is explored and learned; different fields of knowledge study the individual's qualities and capacities; they observe, measure, rank, compare, and differentiate bodies. With the deployment of these knowledges, the body is also dominated: hierarchized, economized, distributed within enclosed spaces, surveilled, rewarded and punished, controlled, compelled to conform to norms, and, ultimately, pushed to interiorize its own subjection.[23]

Disciplinary power is not prohibitive, it is prescriptive; it does not only delimit a field of action but constructs the very agent who will act; it is not concerned with the power to kill but with the power to make the body work and conform through enclosure and panoptic supervision.[24] Sovereignty is territorial, while discipline is individual and individualizing.[25] Foucault depicts disciplinary power as the opposite of sovereign power: "the exact, point-for-point opposite of the mechanics of power that the theory of sovereignty described."[26] It is nonjuridical, social, minute, multiple, invisible, everyday, supervising, productive, and generative.[27] And yet disciplinary power whose spread is facilitated by capitalism is largely complementary to the power of the state all the while it is rendered invisible by the egalitarian formalism of popular sovereignty.[28]

The third moment in the trajectory of sovereignty that we can glean from Foucault's work refers to the transformation enacted by its relation to biopower. Biopower, or what Foucault has later tended to study as the apparatus of security and "art of government,"[29] is the power *over* life; it is the administration of the well-being of a population. This new modality of power, counterposed to individualizing disciplines and considered to be operative at the aggregate social level, is now "precisely the opposite right" of sovereignty because it is the power "to 'make' live and 'let' die" instead of the sovereign power to "take life."[30] Instead of ruling over a territory, it is focused on ruling over the population that inhabits the territory. Instead of ruling through law, it transforms the law into its own tactic of management. Instead of prohibiting or prescribing, it is interested in regulating circuits and flows and managing resources and contingencies.[31] Instead of panoptic supervision, it is concerned with efficient regulation and the optimization of circulation. In short, instead of ruling, it is *governing*. Through the regulation of the population's life processes (health, nutrition, fertility, sexuality, and mortality) and conditions of well-being (hygiene, sanitation, immunization, work, urbanization, and environment), it creates new areas of knowledge and puts different knowledges to work. Biopower opens up and accesses new domains of life for political intervention. This is the moment not of brutal violence, nor of panoptic surveillance, but of *policing*; namely, the regulation of contingency (crime, for example), according to the probability of its occurrence, its distribution, and cost efficiency, and the optimization of its treatment.

The biopolitical processes, identifiable particularly since the nineteenth century, transform the object and objective of power relations. From a preoccupation with death, there is a shift toward life and well-being, from "taking life or letting live" to "making live or letting die." Death, the insignia of sovereignty, fades away; it begins to lose its political purchase, its public significance and relevance.[32] In the displacement of death from being the privileged stake of politics, Foucault famously argues, "the ancient right to take life or let live was replaced by a power to foster life or disallow it to the point of death. . . . Now it is over life, throughout its unfolding, that power establishes its dominion; death is power's limit, the moment that escapes it; death becomes the most secret aspect of existence, the most 'private.'"[33] Suicide, Foucault contends, once unacceptable to the sovereign with the monopoly over the right to take life, is silently granted as an "individual and private right to die, at the borders and in the interstices of power that was exercised over life."[34] The rational, efficient, and productive management of individuals and things begins to take over the logic of sovereignty.[35] The stark difference in the field of punishment, a symptomatic arena of the state's operation from which the nature of sovereign power can be read and analyzed, is the most vivid evidence of this transformation. Death, which is absolutely central to sovereignty, "now becomes the moment when the individual escapes all power, falls back on himself and retreats, so to speak, into his own privacy. Power no longer recognizes death. Power literally ignores death."[36]

For Foucault, then, the emergence of both disciplinary power and bio-power has profoundly modified the ways in which society operates, situating us in a *biopolitical* problematic. The acuity of this insight has dramatically, definitively, and perhaps irreversibly altered our understanding of modern societies. However, while this account makes a case for the evolving nature of power, what is less clear is how we may theorize the modulation in sovereignty itself, given the scale and scope of this transformation. What happens to sovereignty within the biopolitical problematic? Does it tend to weaken and regress or to grow stronger and more total? On this score Foucault provides a more mixed record. Foucault often underscores how new modalities of power have decentered sovereignty. However, he describes this transformation in contradictory and inconsistent, often asymptotic, ways. He points to the withdrawal and supersession of sovereignty while, at the same time, he postulates its continuing relevance and even its resurgence.

On the one hand, he puts forth that the sovereign right to kill has been "replaced" or "supplanted."[37] This does not mean that sovereignty completely disappears, but that it loses its centrality. He argues, for example, that there has been a reversal in the right to kill.[38] He claims that "traditional, ritual, costly, violent forms of power . . . soon fell into disuse and were superseded by a subtle, calculated technology of subjection."[39] He asserts, "the old power of death that symbolized sovereign power was now carefully supplanted by the administration of bodies and the calculated management of life."[40] As modern power becomes interested in the management of life rather than the exaction of death, death is relegated to the literal and figurative margins of power.

On the other hand, Foucault also makes the opposite argument, not only maintaining that sovereign power continues to animate the state but also underscoring its transmutation within the biopolitical problematic due to its interaction with new modalities of power. In this line of reasoning he posits: "there is not the legal age, the disciplinary age, and then the age of security. Mechanisms of security do not replace disciplinary mechanisms, which would have replaced juridico-legal mechanisms."[41] What changes is the "dominant characteristic" of the power regime.[42]

At times Foucault suggests that different modalities of power function independently, yet in ways mutually supportive and reinforcing. Popular sovereignty enables the development and functioning of discipline, as its "other, dark side," concealing from view the domination inherent in its norms.[43] Meanwhile, discipline ensures the submission of subjects as the condition and support of juridical rights and liberties, while it opens new domains for the effective intervention of state institutions.[44] In a parallel fashion, biopower and disciplinary power also coexist and operate in tandem, both establishing power over life, but at different scales (one at the level of the population, the other at that of the individual) and with distinct techniques.[45]

At other times Foucault avers that different modalities of power imbricate each other, modulating each other through their intertwining, accentuating certain features and attenuating others.[46] Foucault intimates, for example, that while initially disciplinary communities (especially religious communities like the mendicant monks and Brethren of the Common Life as well as freemasons) constitute an oppositional force to sovereignty,[47] discipline manages to colonize society as a whole and is incorporated into sovereignty, particularly through the vehicle of the family, which mediates both apparatuses of power.[48] Disciplinary power colonizes the law, resulting, most significantly, in the generalization of imprisonment as punishment.[49] Torture, insofar as it remains as the trace of archaic, absolutist sovereignty, is nonetheless "enveloped, increasingly, by the non-corporeal nature of the penal system."[50] Surveillance, normalizing judgment, and examination as disciplinary techniques become part and parcel of state apparatuses. In fact, indicating the synergy between discipline and sovereignty, Foucault even calls the panoptic formation "the oldest dream of the oldest sovereign."[51] The Napoleonic attempt to enhance the state's panoptic abilities while preserving the spectacular, ritual aspect of sovereignty is the historical example of the integration of these powers.[52] At the same time, the growing prominence of the police is an example of how sovereign power is modified by biopower utilized in the service of the state.[53] This imbrication is not only instrumental for the perpetuation of biopolitics, it is also beneficial, and indeed, necessary for the perpetuation of sovereignty: "the governmentalization of the state has nonetheless been what has allowed the state to survive."[54]

Finally, Foucault also conceptualizes the conjunction of different modalities of power in a contradictory unity, held together through a novel technology adopted by the state—racism. This technology, based on setting apart "what must live and what must die," allows the coexistence of the power *of* life with the power *over* life, both individually and collectively.[55] Racism enables the exercise of sovereignty to protect the "pure race" against threats, biopolitically defined, while it enables the exercise of disciplinary and biopolitical techniques of government to intervene in the well-being of racialized populations in selective, differentiated ways. Racism, as the "basic mechanism of power, as it is exercised in modern States," sutures sovereignty, discipline, and security together, allowing them to become "absolutely coextensive" with one another.[56] The exceptional experience of the world wars, Foucault maintains, point to this specific conjunction of powers that combine the extreme focus on the administration of life with the extreme extraction of death. Racism institutionalized in the Nazi and Soviet states constitutes the exemplary link between two conceptions of power, bringing them together in a deadly combination. But while the Nazi and Soviet states are exemplary, Foucault insists, all modern states are "demonic combinations" of these modalities of power.[57] In this conception, sovereignty becomes "thanatopolitics," the reverse of biopolitics. Ultimately, contends Foucault, this contradictory combination of biopolitics and its reverse remains a paradox. It is the coexistence of the machinery of death and the political concern for life, which Foucault calls "one of the central antinomies of our political reason" that becomes the dominant characteristic of the late modern age.[58]

To theorize the transmutation of sovereignty within the biopolitical problematic, then, is to follow Foucault down the theoretical path that opens up when he suggests that this process is not the replacement of sovereignty or its sequential regression and disappearance in the face of the new, but, rather, a significant and specific transfiguration through the interrelation of different modalities of power. In the transformation "from a regime dominated by structures of sovereignty to a regime dominated by techniques of government," the new techniques of biopolitics do not replace those of sovereignty but rather bring about the latter's sharpening into a politics of death that starkly contrasts with the politics over life.[59] In the biopolitical problematic, "the problem of sovereignty is not eliminated; on the contrary, it is made more acute than ever."[60] The paradox, then, of the relations of power in contemporary formations is the existence of this contradictory conjunction of sovereignty, discipline, and government, of a politics *of* life (and death) and a politics *over* life itself. I will call this paradoxical coexistence, the object of this book's investigation, *biosovereignty*.

Biosovereignty names an incipient regime of power, one that takes as its starting point Foucault's remarks on the paradoxical coexistence of thanato-politics and biopolitics. It builds on Foucault's observations on the conjunction of different modalities of power, but sharpens what remains latent, contradictory, and often confused in his attempts at theorizing this conjunction. Biosovereignty builds on the argument that neither sovereignty, nor discipline, nor security singly defines the dominant characteristic of the contemporary power regime. It denotes a power regime whose dominant characteristic is precisely this new conjunction, which denies one or the other, conceived in their analytically distinct and ideal-typical forms, the role of being the privileged marker of the power formations in the present. Rather, it poses their *articulation* as the "dominant characteristic" of the present.

Since biosovereignty marks the theoretical imbrication and operational mingling of different modalities of power, it implies that none remains in its analytically pure and distinct form, as separately and independently constituted and operative in this conjunction. Sovereignty persists, but it is permeated and transformed, not only with the invasive diffusion but with the conscious, voluntary, and rational adoption and incorporation of disciplinary and governmental techniques. Meanwhile, disciplinary and governmental techniques are also transformed as they are fused with the traditional and recalcitrant prerogatives of sovereign power. On the one hand, we have the conjoined deployment of techniques based on corporeal violence along with those that convey an invisible, individualizing, and internalized violence folded within the management and optimization of the living. On the other hand, the discourses and practices that privilege the sanctity of life and the improvement of well-being rise to prominence as the justification and selective deployment of the power to kill. Different technologies of violence, brutal and corporeal, individualizing and surveilling, regulating and policing, are put to use in mutually reinforcing and interpenetrating ways in the service of power. Consequently, biosovereignty names the emergent regime of power in which techniques targeting the administration of life are brought within the fold of sovereign decisions, while the power of life and death is marshaled in support of life and well-being. Neither sovereignty nor biopolitics can be reduced to opposing poles; their mutual interpenetration also designates the end of a strong conceptual contrast between them. Biosovereignty is therefore the expression of an unstable, contingent, and changing intersection between sovereignty, discipline, and security.

While I am suggesting biosovereignty to name an incipient power regime theoretically, I would also underscore that, in reality, this amalgamation is not an already finished product but an ongoing process in formation. As a becoming, *biosovereignization* is not unidirectional; it involves twists and turns, progressions and reversals, differentiated speeds and intensities, completely predictable determinations as well as contingencies, trials, and errors. In calling this formation biosovereignty, I want to draw attention to the *emergent* structure of articulation of different modalities of power, keeping the structure of articulation, which is always bound to contingency, context, and historicity, as well as the forces of contestation, as an open question. This structure cannot be imputed an essential, unchanging nature but must be analyzed anew, according to the specific histories, spaces, practices, discourses, forces, and counterforces that determine the characteristics of each power formation. The structure of articulation of biosovereignty as a highly complex and overdetermined artifact in formation, flux, and modulation needs to be studied, analyzed, and interpreted in its concreteness in order to understand how power operates in a given context.

The concept of assemblage (*agencement*), which Gilles Deleuze and Félix Guattari develop based on Foucault's work, is particularly helpful to conceptualize the structure-in-formation of biosovereignty.[61] Deleuze and Guattari deploy this term to denote complex formations that arise at the intersection of discrete multiplicities. An *assemblage* is a formation that is characterized by novel qualities that cannot be attributed to the individual multiplicities prior to their intersection.[62] The idea of an assemblage combines an event, a formation, produced by an intersection that cannot be reduced to its components and its process of becoming. The example provided by John Phillips is vivid and revealing: "The *wound* as an event which brings the knife and the flesh together can be reduced to neither knife nor flesh."[63] Each assemblage can be analyzed according to its content and expression. Its content is comprised of the actions, practices, techniques that make up its machinic element. Its expression consists of signs that make up its enunciative element. Composed of practice and discourse, the machinic and the semiotic dimensions, an assemblage provides a shifting matrix of meaning and action out of which stable and consistent apparatuses may eventually emerge.

The concept of assemblage is more useful than the Foucauldian counterpart of apparatus (*dispositif*) to conceptualize the structure of articulation
of biosovereignty because it is able to denote processes of modulation and
transformation within the becoming of a structure rather than a structure that
is already constituted and stable.[64] An assemblage, according to Deleuze and
Guattari, has "lines of articulation or segmentarity, strata and territories; but
also lines of flight, movements of deterritorialization and destratification."[65] It
designates the stratification, territorialization, and organization of phenomena into a structure as well as their continuous rupture and flight away from
that structure. Assemblage, therefore, allows us to consider the determinacy
of structure and the indeterminacy of change within the same concept. As
Nicholas Tampio argues, "the brilliance of the concept of assemblages is that it
describes an entity that has both consistency and fuzzy borders."[66] Pointing to
the merits of the concept of assemblage, Couze Venn maintains that "it focuses on process and on the dynamic character of the inter-relationships between
the heterogeneous elements of the phenomenon. It recognizes both structur-
izing and indeterminate effects: that is, both flow and turbulence, produced in
the interaction of open systems. It points to complex becoming and multiple
determinations. It is sensitive to time and temporality in the emergence and
mutation of the phenomenon; it thus directs attention to the *longue durée*."[67]

The *biosovereign assemblage*, then, refers, on the one hand, to the discourses and practices, signs and actions that define the power regime that currently
emerges at the intersection of different modalities of power, and, on the other
hand, to the processes of localization and condensation of forces in apparatuses along with concurrent processes of deterritorialization and dispersal
that deform and deflect these forces away from those apparatuses.[68] As every
form of power involves a counterpower, the biosovereign assemblage, too, creates its own forms of resistance. New relations of power and counterpower
come into being from the contingent, heterogeneous, multiple, and highly
differentiated discourses, practices, and techniques that are in the process of
territorialization, deterritorialization, and reterritorialization within each biosovereign assemblage.[69]

As Aihwa Ong contends, "assemblages are thus experimental systems, that
is, open-ended and responsive to unfolding elements and events, so that solutions to particular challenges are not given in advance."[70] The biosovereign
assemblage, with its contradictory constitution that brings together the extraction of bodies with their management, the power to kill with the power

to regulate life, is the process of creating solutions to problems of rule and government of biopoliticized individuals and populations as well as the process by which these solutions are unhinged and upended through forces of resistance and refusal. Since biosovereignty is distinguished by its paradoxical combination of the power *of* life with the power *over* life, this emergent conjunction also produces lines of flight that respond to its paradoxes. *Life* as a field of knowledge, political intervention, violent extraction, surveillance, and optimizing regulation is the object of the biosovereign assemblage. *Death*, as we shall see, becomes its new line of flight.

RESISTANCE TO POWER

Just as sovereignty is intimately linked with particular technologies of violence, so is resistance. Since subjects are shaped in and through power relations, their practices, including their practices of resistance, carry the stamp of the power regime that molds their subjectivities. As a counterpower, resistance is shaped by and responds to the dominant characteristics of the prevailing power regime and the technologies of violence it deploys upon its objects. It is the link between sovereignty and resistance as power and counterpower that enables us to read the kind of violence deployed not only as a symptom of the nature of sovereignty but also, in reverse, of the nature of resistance, even if resistance may be formally nonviolent itself.

Power, in Foucault's conception, is a relation that requires freedom and agency. Therefore, it always calls for and incites a response in the form of a reaction, transgression, reversal, or counterforce. Power breeds resistance.[71] Freedom is the "permanent provocation" of both power and resistance; it is inherent to agency.[72] Foucault argues that resistance is copresent with power, almost like a shadow: "Where there is power, there is resistance, and yet, or rather consequently, this resistance is never in a position of exteriority in relation to power. . . . These points of resistance are present everywhere in the power network . . . by definition, they can only exist in the strategic field of power relations."[73] Foucault's statement displays his understanding of power as a relation that immanently gives birth to its own counterpower, which contests and reacts to power. That resistance immanently responds to power means that it is also shaped by the nature of relations it contests. Power and resistance mutually implicate one another. They are intrinsic to each other's presence and form. Therefore it is not possible to discuss the nature of power relations without reference to the multiple struggles and resistances that accompany, imply, shape, deflect, and respond to those power relations. In Foucault's words: "there is no relationship of power without the means of escape or possible flight. Every power relationship implies, at least in potentia, a strategy of struggle."[74]

Such a conceptualization, which allows tackling resistance mainly as the immanent counterforce, or reaction to power, has deeply divided interpreters on the role of resistance for Foucault. Some, following Jon Simons, have argued that Foucault posits "an ethic of permanent resistance."[75] Others have been troubled by the ubiquitous role of power and the absence of any space for agency to emerge from "inside" power relations: if subjectivities are constituted within power relations, how then are they capable of resistance, how would they engage in resistance, and for what reasons?[76] If the subject is an "effect of power," how and why does it resist power?[77] Still other commentators have questioned the normative and justificatory grounding of Foucault's espousal of resistance, particularly when his theory seems to view norms and truths as a function of power relations.[78] The same ambiguity that plagues the justifications for Foucault's own political commitments is also valid for the subjects he theorizes. According to Richard Bernstein, "what is never quite clear in Foucault is why anyone should favor certain local forms of resistance over others. Nor is it clear why one would choose 'one' side or the other in a localized resistance or revolt."[79] In short, we lack a convincing Foucauldian theory of resistance.

Nonetheless, it is Foucault's strength to couple power and resistance, or at least the possibility of resistance, which prevents him from falling into a completely dystopic view of society and keeps open the possibility of change. While Foucault has been rather evasive about analyzing resistance, there are recurrent affirmations of resistance in his work, coupled even with a romanticization of revolution (as in the Iranian case). Furthermore, we know that Foucault was actively involved in resistance, especially around prison struggles, and there is much evidence to suggest that he thought of his intellectual work as a contribution to political struggle.[80] As a whole, resistance remains a continuous point of reference for Foucault's work, both a "tactical reversal" of power and an "aesthetics of existence," in which new forms of life and subjectivity are formed through practices of the self.[81] However, while resistance constitutes an irreplaceable element in his thought, it is left largely undertheorized.

But the intimate connection between power and resistance, or the possibility of imagining these two vectors of politics as if they were two sides of the same coin, also enables us to extrapolate from and build on Foucault. In proceeding, we would not only have to piece together the scattered comments in Foucault's oeuvre on resistance but, more important, to read Foucault's observations on power in reverse. Following this path will lead us to trace a historical trajectory for resistance analogous to the one for power relations. Just as we can identify different moments in the development of power relations in Foucault's thought, we can also identify different moments in the trajectory of resistance, moments that roughly correspond to those of power relations. In the three power regimes discussed by Foucault, whose dominant characteristics are defined by sovereignty, discipline, and security, respectively, we can point to distinct forms of resistance that correspond to and react against these power regimes, replicating and deflecting their dominant features at the same time.

In the power regime characterized by absolute sovereignty, the exploration of resistance takes us back to the example of Damiens. According to Foucault, Damiens the regicide is the "absolute criminal," the condemned. In fact, he is much more than that. Damiens is the political insurgent par excellence because while he has targeted the physical body of the sovereign, he has also breached his imaginary body, the *body politic*.[82] In attacking the king, therefore, Damiens has attempted not only to take the life of the king, but attacked the kingdom as a whole. Damiens's crime is thus no simple transgression of the law, but a direct act of rebellion.

In detailing his execution, however, Foucault portrays him as the exemplary victim of the archaic modality of sovereign power. His flesh and limbs are torn apart, his body is cut into pieces; in short, Damiens is subjected to the worst of agonies and humiliations in the public square. What tends to drop out of this account is this: while this ritual of vengeful punishment goes on, his confessors are unable to extract a confession out of Damiens. Quoting the depictions of Damiens's execution, Foucault notes: "It is said that, though he was always a great swearer, no blasphemy escaped his lips; but the excessive pain made him utter horrible cries, and he often repeated: 'My God, have pity on me! Jesus, help me!'"[83] A different source confirms this observation: "Monsieur Le Breton, the clerk of the court, went up to the patient several times and asked him if he had anything to say. He said he had not; at each torment, he cried out, as the damned in hell are supposed to cry out, 'Pardon, my God!

Pardon, my Lord.'"[84] Despite repeated attempts at extracting a confession, Damiens retains his silence. "Monsieur le [sic] Breton went up to him again and asked him if he had anything to say; he said no. Several confessors went up to him and spoke to him at length; he willingly kissed the crucifix that was held out to him; he opened his lips and repeated: 'Pardon, Lord.'"[85]

The confession is important, Foucault notes, not only during the judicial process to establish the "truth" of the crime but also at the site of the public execution because it constitutes an acceptance and affirmation by the condemned of the charges and the punishment falling to his lot.[86] In other words, it is a sign of ultimate submission to the sovereign power that has judged and decided the fate of the criminal selected for brutal execution. The confession redeems the violence of the sovereign and affirms its justice by the person who has unsuccessfully threatened it and is destined to be crushed under its weight as punishment. The confession recuperates the sovereign whose bodily vulnerability has been exposed by the regicide attempt; it restores his might and authority by the exercise of force over the vulnerable "body of the condemned." The great act of disobedience displayed by Damiens the regicide is not only that he attempts to assassinate the king but that he refuses to admit guilt and ask for clemency from the sovereign despite the torture he is subjected to. It is a sign that he continues his disobedience until his painful end. Damiens asks for mercy from God, but that is another story.

Damiens's resistance on the scaffold is perhaps meager, particularly in comparison to the disorder and unrest that spectacles of corporeal punishment occasionally inspire in the people standing by, an aspect of the scene that is of great interest to Foucault. Especially when the condemnation is found unfair, excessive, or wrong, the solidarity between the people and the criminal is strengthened to the detriment of the sovereign's authority. As Foucault recognizes, the criminal's attitude of nonrepentance intensifies his greatness in the popular mind, encouraging further protests around the scaffold against the executioner and other officials that represent sovereign power.[87] The popular support for the unyielding criminal has significant repercussions for the sovereign's authority and status before the people, the erosion of which contributes to the slow displacement of punishment out of public view. It is from this perspective that Foucault views the scaffold: as a confrontation between the "vengeance of the prince and the contained anger of the people, through the mediation of the victim and the executioner,"[88] whose unintended effects eventually catalyze the transformation of punishment toward the modern prison system. However, the "condemned" in this account becomes just the vehicle of confrontation between the sovereign and the people, a voiceless victim and a passive screen upon which a power struggle is projected. But Damiens is not (simply) a victim, and his resistance to utter a confession is the greatest testimony to his disobedient and unrelenting agency on the scaffold—refusing to submit to the earthly sovereign, seeking clemency only from the divine.

The concealment of punishment from public view, through the substitution of torture by imprisonment, and the accompanying decorporealization of violence mark an important shift in resistance. With the concurrent democratization of sovereignty and rise of capitalism, accompanied by the rise of popular and class struggles (which Foucault largely omits), we arrive at the second moment in the development of power relations where the disciplinary characteristics of the new power regime take precedence over those of sovereignty. Punishment now works by situating the subject in a system of deprivations rather than by inflicting pain. While imprisonment still operates through the body, it is less direct, less immediate, and less bloody. It aims for submission without corporeal violence. Violence does not disappear but changes form: constant surveillance, measurement, study, control, prescription, and normalization constitute an invisible structural violence that shapes subjects situated in panoptic institutions. Through this invisible and continuous violence, discipline seeks to mold the soul: by choosing to suspend liberty, it attempts to dominate and transform the subject into an obedient and "docile" member of society.[89] The disciplinary mechanism necessitates an "enclosed, segmented space, observed at every point, in which the individuals are inserted in a fixed place, in which the slightest movements are supervised, in which all events are recorded."[90] It individualizes and isolates: "solitude," argues Foucault, "is the primary condition of total submission."[91] The subjection of individuals to atomizing and subjugating disciplinary mechanisms significantly limits the possibility of resistance, especially collective resistance.[92] In fact, popular revolt now gets inscribed within a discourse of monstrosity that feeds into the construction of the criminal.[93]

While Foucault tends to personify disciplinary power as a force with a tight clasp on subjects who are slowly transformed into passive and obedient bodies, more like objects, subjectified only by their subjugation, he also mentions that the system of social control is not without contestation, that the tactics of domination "have always met with resistance; they have given rise to struggles and provoked reaction."[94] He particularly notes the emergence of struggles in prison.[95] As for the individual prison revolts themselves, we do not learn what motivates them, which prisoners participate in them, how they are organized and conducted, their modes of operation, and finally what they achieve. Even though we know that Foucault's own activism came at a time when political prisoners in French prisons (especially imprisoned Maoist militants) staged hunger strikes and joined other prisoners in multiple acts of resistance in the early 1970s, Foucault does not reveal to us whether the prisoners who occasion his work are motivated by specifically political crimes and carry out resistance for political causes or whether they are political by virtue of their reaction to the machinery of power functioning through the limitation of transgressive social action.[96] As such, these acts of resistance are not analyzed to draw out an autonomous logic of their own, but appear as a function of the power/knowledge structures and technologies of domination that individuals are resisting and are thereby making visible.[97] The problem with this conceptualization of resistance is its secondary or derivative nature, despite its role in informing Foucault's normative stance against domination.[98]

According to Allen Feldman, Foucault "abandon[s] the body to the monopoly of the state apparatus."[99] He analyzes how force is applied to the body, how the body is both presupposed and constituted by power, and how, finally, discipline is interiorized by the body and administered toward its self-subjugation. However, Foucault does not pay sufficient attention to how the body, objectified by the operations of power, can also be countermobilized and transformed into an instrument that can be used against the state. He tends to construe the body as a "passive site" that is enfolded into power relations. However, building on his analysis of the prison struggles in Northern Ireland, Feldman argues, the body can also become an agency by which the violence of the state is inverted: "The body as the terminal locus of power also defines the place for the redirection and reversal of power."[100] Through a series of mimetic reversals, displacements, and substitutions, "agency, as a self-reflexive framing of force, subjectivates exteriority and refolds the body."[101] Discipline divides the prisoner into a body and a self; the self becomes a part of the panoptic machine that applies discipline to its own body. However, Feldman demonstrates, the "self-bifurcation of the prisoner" also provides the conditions of possibility for the objectification of the body into an instrument against the panoptic machine.[102] The possibility of this transformation, through the mimetic reversal of the use of force on the body, according to Feldman, constitutes the basis of prison resistance, resistance that Foucault celebrates but does not theoretically account for. Whereas Foucault might account for prison resistance by reference to the incompleteness of the subjugation of the prisoner to disciplinary power, leaving open the possibility of agency to push back against power, Feldman turns to the divisive function of disciplinary power that turns the body into an independent force, even where power's reach might appear complete. The body, then, becomes crucial for understanding resistance especially in asymmetric contexts like the prison, detention center or refugee camp.[103]

In Foucault, there is a certain functionalism that renders the presence of prison struggles, like struggles in other disciplinary institutions, a response to domination and subjugation that is important insofar as they thwart the full reign of social control. Prison struggles, for example, become a conclusive demonstration that the prison system has failed in providing the necessary corrective to criminality and its ultimate rehabilitation. They also stand as proof against the flawed circular logic of offering prison reform as a solution to the ills and insufficiencies of the prison. Alternatively, they demonstrate that the prison has been successful insofar as its intent was never to eliminate criminality and achieve rehabilitation, but rather the regulation and control of criminality.[104] Consequently, there is an implicit acknowledgment that these struggles do not add up to a substantial challenge.[105] Like the capillary, dispersed, local, and diffuse modality of power they respond to, resistances to discipline generally remain local, dispersed, and without totalizing aspirations. Foucault argues: "there is no single locus of great Refusal, no soul of revolt, source of all rebellions, or pure law of the revolutionary. Instead there is a plurality of resistances, each of them a special case."[106] The prison remains firmly entrenched precisely because its failures are compensated by its successes as an instrument of social control. The continual production of delinquency through the prison system serves as a mechanism that infiltrates, polices, and divides social struggles, instills fear, supervises the limits of illegalities, and hence functions to dominate the lower classes and, through them, the rest of society. Although resistance to discipline exists (even though Foucault leaves us in the dark regarding how it exists), it remains overshadowed by the functional efficiency and effectiveness of disciplinary institutions for social control. Ultimately, we are left with a rather pessimistic stance on the possibility of change despite the recognition that multifarious acts of resistance are everywhere present.

When we turn to the third moment in the trajectory of power relations marked by the emergence of biopower, Foucault is more illuminating regarding the changing nature of resistance. There are two elements that internally deter-mine the ends of biopolitics, both in the sense of purpose and limits: power's invasion of the social body through the administration of life, on the one hand, and its disqualification of death from the political sphere, on the other hand. The first points to the permeation of relations of power into every facet of life and the increasing totality of domination. The second element, the designation of death as the outer limit of politics, implies that life is the supreme value of the new regime of power, based on survival and well-being. As the object of power becomes life itself, the object of resistance, too, is determined.

Like power, resistance, too, becomes preoccupied with life, with de-mands focused on prosperity and well-being. With biopoliticization, Fou-cault asserts, "life as a political object was in a sense taken at face value and turned back against the system that was bent on controlling it . . . what was demanded and what served as an objective was life, understood as the basic needs, man's concrete essence, the realization of his potential, a plenitude of the possible."[107] The quality of life and fostering its potential thereby become the center of oppositional demands, the main source of rights: "The 'right' to life, to one's body, to health, to happiness, to the satisfaction of needs, and beyond all the oppressions or 'alienations,' the 'right' to rediscover what one is and all that one can be, this 'right'—which the classical juridical system was utterly incapable of comprehending—was the political response to all these new procedures of power which did not derive, either, from the traditional right of sovereignty."[108]

Similar to antidisciplinary struggles, biopolitical struggles also reflect and repeat the dominant characteristics of the power regime in which they are embedded by mobilizing around the politicization of life, its regulation, and securitization, but on a grander scale. With modern biopolitics, life is not only the new object of politics, the domain of investigation, intervention, and regu-lation, but it is also appropriated as the object of counterpolitics. We therefore encounter a multitude of resistances in a variety of areas of social life subjected to biopolitical regulation, resistances that focus on demanding better condi-tions, the fulfillment of needs, the provision of services that address wealth, welfare, education, health, and the environment. These struggles strive for redistribution, for the rectification of socioeconomic injustices, and recogni-tion, for the rectification of cultural and symbolic injustices.[109] However, in this picture, the refusal to submit to power, the act of absolute confrontation, begins to appear curiously archaic, almost as a luxury enjoyed by early modern subjects faced with absolute sovereignty operating corporeally and brutal-ly.[110] It is as if the muted, diffused, and elusive operations of disciplinary power and biopower, functioning through the very subjects they shape, deploying upon them surveillance and policing as more invisible though no less effec-tive techniques of violence, tend to preclude wholesale disobedience from the repertoire of oppositional practices. As sovereignty recedes, so does rebellion.

While our perusal of Foucault's writings helps us identify different forms of resistance that roughly correspond to different modalities of power, it falls short of being commensurate with the complexity of the late modern power regime I am calling *biosovereignty*. If the biosovereign assemblage de-notes an incipient regime that is different from each of its components singly and involves, instead, their conjunction as a becoming, resistance cannot be limited to biopolitical forms but must also involve other incipient forms of action that correspond to the continuing presence and modulations of sov-ereignty and echo its complex structure of articulation with other modalities of power. What practices and discourses of resistance does the biosovereign assemblage generate as it takes shape? What forms of resistance respond to it, functioning in turn to undermine its formation, as lines of flight that deter-ritorialize its operations?

Foucault's analysis does not provide immediate answers to these ques-tions, but his reflections on the politicization of life as the object of politics in the biosovereign assemblage lay the groundwork for further theorization. It is especially significant that the resistances Foucault's analyses on biopower are able to shed light upon are limited to those struggles that take life as their object in a positive way, to demand greater rights, security, and well-being, resources and recognition, rather than those struggles that politicize life in a purely negating way, by rebelling against the life constructed and offered with-in the biosovereign power regime. Having focused on the biopolitical aspect of the new power regime, Foucault views only the affirmative pole of social and political struggles. Just as he tends to neglect the sovereign element of contemporary power formations, he also fails to address the forms of resis-tance that strive to perform disobedience and disrupt the political rationality of securitization, those struggles that confront and negate the complex struc-ture of articulation of the emergent power regime—struggles that proceed not by the *politicization of life* but the *politicization of death*.

Forms of struggle in which life is transformed into a weapon, not in or-der to affirm greater rights and privileges, better conditions and standards of well-being, but as a rejection of domination, constitute the kinds of resistance that disappear from the lens of Foucauldian biopolitics due to its preoccupation with the valorization of life. Compounded by the overall neglect of resistance in Foucault's work, it is understandable to arrive at a lacuna, or at best a skewed appreciation of affirmative forms of biopolitical resistance. However, Foucault's groundbreaking reflections on biopolitics should be brought to bear on contemporary forms of resistance based on self-destructive practices, or what I will call forms of *necroresistance*. This is because the very antinomy of modern political reason that Foucault identifies as the paradoxical coexistence of the politics *of* life and politics *over* life, or the reversal of biopolitics into thanatopolitics, is what we now come to observe in the field of resistance. As biosovereignty brings together the differential logics of biopower and sovereign power in a contradictory combination, so does resistance bring together the differential logics in incipient forms of action. We should, therefore, learn from Foucault that it is always in relation to the dominant characteristics of the power regime that we must interrogate practices of resistance, but also pressure Foucault's reflections on power toward current forms of resistance that seem to belie his expectations.

SACRIFICE AS COUNTERCONDUCT

In the genealogy Foucault presents for biopolitical government, pastoral power occupies an important place. Focusing on the relationship between the ruler and his subjects as that between a shepherd and his flock, Foucault analyzes the beneficent qualities of this form of power, its emphasis on care and protection, especially the sacrificial devotion of the shepherd to his flock.[111] Since pastoral power comes to define how the Christian Church governs the "souls" of the faithful, Foucault is keen to mark its distinction from "political power."[112] However, the distinction does not reside in the separation of the secular and the sacred domains of authority. Rather, it arises from the type of power at work: political power *rules*, whereas pastoral power *governs*. Through the management of the lives and conduct of the faithful, both individually and as a community, the pastorate exemplifies power as "conducting."[113]

One of Foucault's most sustained discussions of resistance concerns precisely those that oppose pastoral power or power as conducting.[114] Examples of counterconduct involve a range of radical groups (Anabaptists, Waldensians,

Hussites, Beghards, Beguines, and so on) and a range of practices (ascetism, refusal of baptism, mysticism, eschatological beliefs) and, finally, their utmost radical form, the Protestant Reformation. What Foucault calls "revolts of conduct" or forms of "counter-conduct" are important for three reasons.[115] First, even if they do not immediately involve politics, these revolts, which are generally religious in form, provide antecedents to resistances to modern forms of governmental power, for which pastoral power constitutes a central historical source (along with traditions of raison d'état and the police).[116] Foucault hints that these practices inform the religious revolutionaries of the English revolution, the clubs of the French revolution, and even the workers' councils of the Soviet revolution.[117] He argues that this development is also facilitated by the appropriation of pastoral functions by the political government, as a result of which these resistances also assume a more political character. Other examples from the eighteenth century onward include the refusal of soldiering and medicine as well as the formation of secret societies like freemasonry.[118]

Second, these resistances are not responses to pastoral power only, but, rather, to the imbrication of pastoral power with civil government, through the introduction of the judicial and penal function into the Church (via techniques such as the obligatory confession, religious court, Purgatory, indulgences, etc.). On the one hand, this means that, despite the separate genealogy of governmental power Foucault draws up, he is attentive to the penetration of pastoral power by elements of sovereignty and in fact characterizes revolts in response to this amalgamation: "So, from the twelfth century, the Church was penetrated by a judicial model that was a major reason for anti-pastoral struggles."[119] This is important for us, as it lends support to the argument that radical resistance as the refusal to submit to power has a special relation to sovereignty, even though this point tends to drop out of the Foucauldian account of resistance in general. Just as radical counterconduct finds "major reason" to operate in the penetration of the judicial model into pastoral power, we can extrapolate, contemporary "revolts of conduct" find their rationale in the ongoing sovereign presence in the biopolitical problematic.

Third, these revolts are important because they entail a questioning of how one should conduct oneself and, as a result, they involve the potential transformation of subjectivity. The predominantly religious forms of counter-conduct achieve self-transformation through practices that require self-mastery, the cultivation of alternative modes of sociality and faith, and the distancing from the conduct required, affirmed, and promoted by the Church.[120]

These forms of conduct are oppositional, but they operate on the terrain of conduct that was itself brought into being by the operation of pastoral power. In other words, they are enabled by the development of government, but they utilize the tools of government against government, by deploying those same tools simultaneously toward self-transformation and toward the conduct prescribed by the pastorate. Extending his conceptualization of counterconduct to the operation of governmentality in its modern form, Foucault argues, these resistances were aimed at the "rejection of *raison d'État* and its fundamental requirements" by the mobilization of elements that were in themselves enabled by the development of governmentality.[121] As a result, counterconduct in modern regimes of power involves pitting society against the state in a revolutionary way, with the eschatological hope of a "final time, of a suspension or completion of historical and political time, when . . . the indefinite governmentality of the state will be brought to an end and halted" through the emancipation of civil society from the state.[122] Again, the specificity of this revolutionary form is, first, that it mobilizes on the terrain that is itself brought into being by governmentality, and, second, that it depends on the revolutionizing of conduct at the level of individuals as well as at the social level by the development of alternative practices of subjectivity that refuse obedience and assert their own truth against that of the governmental apparatuses of the state.

Having delineated resistance as counterconduct, Foucault increasingly takes the direction of an exploration of ethics and the practices of the self that constitute and affirm the possibilities of cultivating individual subjectivities as forms of resistance to processes of normalization and control.[123] I will not pursue this direction, which, while interesting as an exercise in understanding Foucault's work, wends us away from the analysis of incipient forms of more *collective* and overtly *political* resistance based on the weaponization of life. However, I would like to make a brief detour through Foucault's reflections on the protests in Tunisia and Iran because they resonate with his conceptualization of collective resistance as counterconduct and therefore provide further grounds to develop a nuanced understanding of resistance in contemporary power regimes.[124]

Remarking on the protests of Tunisian students in 1968, Foucault notes: "During those upheavals I was profoundly struck and amazed by those young men and women who exposed themselves to serious risks for the simple fact of having written or distributed a leaflet, or for having incited others to go on strike. Such actions were enough to place at risk one's life, one's freedom, and one's body. And this made a very strong impression on me: for me it was a true political experience."[125] Finding in the commitment of Tunisian students to Marxism something at once existential and passionate, especially vis-à-vis their European counterparts, Foucault diagnoses that this was less about the scientificity and accuracy of Marxism, its internal debates and splits, than about its ability to ignite the struggle, constitute a "moral force, an existential act that left one stupefied."[126] Impressed and inspired by the "direct, existential... [and] physical commitment" of Tunisian students and their radicalism, which involved heavy personal costs, Foucault asks: "what on earth is it that can set off in an individual the desire, the capacity, and the possibility of an *absolute sacrifice* without our being able to recognize or suspect the slightest ambition or desire for power and profit?"[127]

It is clear that the sacrificial dimension of the Tunisian scene grips Foucault. It becomes a counterpoint that casts the contemporaneous European struggles in a weaker light by its very intensity. The "total experience" of the Tunisian protests is something Foucault attempts to replicate in his own political involvement with prison struggles in France, political activity with a "personal, physical commitment that was real and that posed problems in concrete, precise, definite terms, within a determinate situation."[128]

Foucault's exaltation of the existential commitment, passionate sacrifice, and intense desire that characterize the Tunisian struggle is echoed in his observations on the Iranian revolution a decade later. In Iran Foucault was fascinated with the "political spirituality" of those in revolt, particularly their deployment of Shia narratives and rituals, among which martyrdom figures prominently.[129] He was interested in how the centrality of martyrdom in Shia Islam involved a commitment to continue the struggle for justice by remembering those who had fallen and "to defend the community of believers against the evil power."[130] Because of the exaltation of martyrdom, particularly in the month preceding the celebration of Imam Husayn's death, Foucault noted that "the crowds [were] ready to advance toward death in the intoxication of sacrifice."[131]

The religious form of the Iranian revolt, the radicalized Shia interpretation of Islam, was important because it gave its participants an alternative framework of conduct that enabled them to question and transform their own conduct and refuse obedience to the state. Religion thus provided the "political spirituality" that guided the individuals and masses into action against the state.[132] The religious form also resonated with the "revolts of conduct" against pastoral power in early modern Europe that based their counterconduct on radicalized interpretations of Christianity against the established Church. In fact, Foucault saw deep parallels between the oppositional function of Shi'ism and the Anabaptists in Münster, for example.[133] Religion, according to Foucault, was not the "opium of the people" in Iran,[134] neither was it an "ideological cloak,"[135] but the very spiritual resource by which Iranians not only made a revolution but also revolutionized their own subjectivity as the precondition of a "true revolution."[136] If Foucault's eager espousal of religious discourse as the dominant form of counterconduct is highly problematic because it ignores the class-based mobilizations in Iran, it also betrays his inclination to fold the specificities of the Iranian struggle into a genealogy inspired by early modern European history. However, it is still noteworthy that he did not adopt the progressivist view of history, in which religion is either premodern or anti-modern, but rather saw it as the familiar, accepted, and customary form of expression of the "discontent, hatred, misery, and despairs" of the common people, one that transformed these experiences into a political force.[137] Foucault was also keen to separate political spirituality from religious rule: "The spirituality of those who were going to their deaths has no similarity whatsoever with the bloody government of a fundamentalist clergy."[138]

As a radical form of counterconduct, the revolt in Iran was revolutionary not only because it was based on the transformation of subjectivity through the reorientation of conduct but also because it provided the possibility of a collective opposition that could nevertheless take on the state in a highly asymmetric condition. Foucault recorded, for example, how Iran's "immense movement from below" changed the parameters of conventional politics. He was impressed by how "this movement ha[d] just thrown half a million men into the streets of Tehran, *up against machine guns and tanks*"; how they were "under the threat of bullets," "perhaps at the risk of a bloodbath," "at the cost of their own lives," putting strong and repeated emphasis on the risks taken by individuals who participated in the struggle.[139] The Iranian people opposed a highly armed regime "with bare hands," but armed with "determination" and "courage," which in turn disarmed the repressive forces of the regime.[140] They took to the streets to "face the machine-guns bare-chested."[141] They demonstrated an "intensity of courage,"[142] and each one "staked his life and his death" in the confrontation with the regime.[143]

This highly asymmetric confrontation was motivated, at least in part, by martyrdom, which constituted an important element of the "political spirituality" of the Iranian masses. Martyrdom valorized and popularized political action oriented toward sacrifice, which corresponded in Foucault's view to the more authentic and "true" form of politics with which he was fascinated. It may be that this fascination was simply a function of Foucault's personal relation to "limit-experiences" and his interest in self-sacrificial practices.[144] It may also be that he saw in these political experiences a counterpoint to Western modernity, which he was intent to criticize; domination and docility contrasted with revolt and authenticity, schematically put, as a dichotomy between the West and the non-West.[145] While Foucault's tendency to blend a romantic orientalism (or, perhaps more positively, a counteroccidentalism) with a nostalgia for authentic politics undoubtedly colored his reflections on Iran, these aspects do not cancel out the importance of his appreciation for this struggle as a radical refusal of obedience, which is of greater relevance for our purposes. In this light it is important that he saw in the revolutionary movement of an unarmed people against an armed regime a form of radical resistance, a collective counterconduct, that is itself enabled by the practices of government, but uses those practices against the state and against being governed. Although Foucault did not theoretically articulate the correspondences between his reflections on counterconduct against modern forms of governmentality and what he saw in Iran, it would not be inaccurate to view them as strongly related. His attentiveness to the indigenous forms of political spiritualism that enable the sacrificial dimension of the acts of resistance in Iran also remains of great relevance to the theorization of necroresistance, as it points to the discursive and practical conditions of possibility of staging acts of absolute refusal under asymmetry produced by the current organization and nature of power relations. Foucault saw the uprising in Iran as a "radical rejection," expressed by real collective will, "of everything that had constituted, for years, for centuries, its political destiny."[146] That is why he viewed the protests in Iran as "the first great insurrection against global systems, the form of revolt that is the most modern and the most insane."[147]

While Foucault's romanticization of revolution and willingness to lend public support to Islamist radicalism, especially without an erudite familiarity with its ideological and political implications, stand in tension with some of his most prominent contributions to the critique of power relations, these elements also point to an alternative strand in his thought that allows us to think resistance as counterconduct. The problem is that this strand in Foucault's thought is not organically connected with his reflections on modern governmentality. If we take up Foucault's observations on Tunisia and Iran in connection with his remarks on the modern power regime, conceived as an amalgamation of sovereignty, discipline, and biopower, we can draw several important conclusions that would have otherwise remained less evident.

First is that these struggles respond to the expanding government of conduct, which reaches such an extent that the relations of power appear as a form of "political destiny," as Foucault put it in relation to Iran.[48] In other words, insofar as modern power functions biopolitically by extending control over life itself, it appears immutable and eternal, unquestionable as if it were a destiny. In response, resistance to it also germinates in increasingly existential, total forms of counterconduct. Second, these struggles are themselves enabled by the terrain paved by government. They operate by turning the elements of the same terrain against the state. In so doing they direct their opposition to the sovereign element that is still present within the biopolitical problematic, with which they enter into direct communication as they struggle over the power of life and death that is vested in the modern state. Third, and following from the second conclusion, insofar as the antistatist forms of resistance advance a refusal of obedience to the state (a form of resistance that had hitherto appeared as reserved to a long-superseded form of absolute sovereignty and not to a biopoliticized form of power), they also differ from those struggles that demand better conditions of life and greater well-being as forms of resistance that turn biopolitics against itself. In this sense they tend to defy the kind of resistance that was theorized by Foucault as prevailingly life-affirming struggles that tend to arise in response to the emergence of biopower. Fourth, such resistance that negates life, which in Iran draws its spiritual resources of self-denial, asceticism, and martyrdom from a radicalized Shia Islam, tends to create its own forms of spirituality. These forms of spirituality are absolutely necessary for the self-transformation of political actors in revolt and the will to perform actions of great risk to their lives and bodies, enabling them to assert a "refusal to obey" at the cost of their own death. It is in the willful transformation of subjectivity that the sources of such radical resistance can be found. These conclusions, insofar as they indicate not only the ways in which life and power are implicated but also the forms in which death and resistance can be entangled, therefore, constitute the groundwork upon which we will further develop the analysis of human weapons.

LIFE AS THE SUBJECT-OBJECT OF HISTORY

Since Foucault, many scholars have taken up the project of thinking the relation between life and power in modern power regimes. In this endeavor they have generally drawn upon the productive ambiguity in Foucault's thought regarding the relationship between sovereignty and biopower and their co-functioning.[149] One of the most important and influential contributions to this nexus has been that of Giorgio Agamben, who has proposed the thesis that, *pace* Foucault, the implication of life in sovereignty is not a new phenomenon characterizing modernity but rather inscribed in the very structure of sovereignty since its inception in the ancient world. The upshot of Agamben's sophisticated analysis is that life is produced by sovereignty as its vulnerable other, not merely neutralized (i.e., *depoliticized*) but forcibly stripped of its political qualities (i.e., *dispoliticized*).[150] Since Agamben's category of "bare life" has had significant consequences for the theorization of power and resistance in the last decade, it is worthwhile to work through his contribution, as his conclusions directly pertain to the theorization of necroresistance.

The ambiguous link in Foucault between the juridico-institutional and biopolitical models of power, between the technologies of the state and the technologies of the self, between the dimensions of totalization and individualization, a link Foucault never quite clarifies, lies in the relationship between sovereignty and life, according to Agamben. Since Agamben defines his project as one that sets out to "complete," if not to "correct," Foucault's thesis on the relationship between life and power, his critique of Foucault provides the most lucid entry point into his theoretical contribution.

Agamben criticizes Foucault on several fronts. First, he argues, Foucault completely misses the structure of the "exception," or what Agamben calls the "ban," as the originary political relation that is "consubstantial with Western politics."[151] This relation indicates the way in which sovereignty and life are inextricably and structurally connected. Following Carl Schmitt, Agamben contends that it is the power to name the exception and to suspend the law that gives sovereignty its essential character and structure of operation.[152] Furthermore, the production of life as "bare" or sacred is the result of the exceptional structure of sovereignty.

Accordingly, sovereign power operates by producing a distinction between natural life shared by all living beings (*zoē*) and politically qualified life exclusive to human communities (*bios*).[153] This philological distinction is then used to justify the outcasting of biological life as not properly belonging to the political. Natural life is banned or suspended from being the proper object of politics through an "inclusive exclusion (an *exceptio*)."[154] Just as the sovereign is both inside and outside the juridical order, by virtue of his ability to decide on the exception, so is life both inside and outside in relation to law. It is included by way of its abandonment by the political.[155] The metaphysical concept of life that is so produced by the sovereign operation is what Agamben calls "bare life" (*la nuda vita*).[156]

Neither natural nor political, *bare life* is the politicization of natural life as excluded from political life, constituting a life that is thereby dispoliticized, dispensable, and exposed to violence. Bare life is symbolized by the figure of the *homo sacer*, an elusive figure that Agamben revives from Roman law, from sources such as Festus and Macrobius.[157] Both "august and accursed,"[158] the figure of the homo sacer is the embodiment of a life that has been stripped of its political qualities and pushed out of the juridical domain. Having been condemned for a crime (thus in a similar position to Damiens), this life is punished by being put into a position from whence it can be killed "*without committing homicide and without celebrating a sacrifice.*"[159] The position of being excluded from the traditional forms of capital punishment (and therefore from the domain of human law) and from the religious domain of sacrificial rites (and therefore from the domain of divine law) provides, according to Agamben, a symptomatic limit position that sheds light on the constitution of the political as such.

Agamben claims that the production of bare life is the founding on which every sovereign order rests: Bare life is the "original—if concealed—nucleus of sovereign power."[160] Produced by its exceptional structure, bare life is diametrically opposed to the sovereign; it is nonsovereign.[161] Sovereign power can kill; bare life, as its inverse mirror image, is what can be killed.[162] Sovereignty, therefore, is the capacity to make life bare, to dispoliticize life and reduce it to vulnerability.[163] Bare life is also the point of intersection and entwinement between sovereignty and biopower. Scholars have called the Agambenian amalgamation of sovereignty and biopolitics, ontologically linked through the structure of exception, "bio-sovereignty." It is important to note here that the Agamben-inspired iteration of "bio-sovereignty" is different, for reasons that will become clear in the following discussion, from the concept of *biosovereignty* proposed in this book.[164]

This brings us to Agamben's second critique of Foucault. Having injected a Schmittian structure into Foucault's theorization of the articulation of sovereignty and biopower and posited an originary articulation between them, Agamben criticizes Foucault for mistaking what is a constitutive relation with a historical conjunction that Foucault locates only within modernity. What Foucault theorizes as a modality of power emerging with modernity is, according to Agamben, a power that modernity simply brings into the spotlight. Agamben's argument is that life has always been the object of politics, in fact produced by politics, as the "hidden nucleus" of sovereignty. With modernity, contends Agamben, this nucleus only becomes visible.

Unlike Foucault, Agamben contends that what characterizes modernity is not so much the implication of life in politics but rather the increased indistinguishability between natural life and political life, or the *politicization of bare life*, which thereby obscures the relation of the ban.[165] This is corollary to the generalization of the "state of exception" into the norm such that the initial function of sovereign power to manufacture the distinction between natural life and political life begins to disappear, and it is no longer clear what is to be kept outside the order, by what abandonment or inclusive exclusion the political should be constituted. Just as Roman sovereignty manufactures bare life in the figure of the homo sacer and keeps it in a relation of ban vis-à-vis the political sphere, modern sovereignty manufactures bare life in its citizen-subjects as always vulnerable to its violence and keeps them all potentially in a relation of ban vis-à-vis the political community. The *Muselmann* in the concentration camp, an abject being who has become devoid of his political rights as well as his humanity, the limit figure between life and death, is homo sacer's paradigmatic expression in modernity.[166] Democracy only generalizes the figure of the homo sacer, inscribing the exceptional structure of sovereignty in the sacred body of each individual, who thereby embodies both the norm and the exception, being both the bearer of rights and the figure of subjection. "Modern democracy does not abolish sacred life but rather shatters it and disseminates it into every individual body, making it into what is at stake in political conflict," argues Agamben.

Third, Agamben criticizes Foucault for not connecting his analysis of biopolitics with totalitarianism and for neglecting to extend his analysis into what Agamben perceives to be the primary spaces of biopower, the camps, where power confronts its victims without any mediation and with the greatest intensity.[167] Fundamentally different from those spaces of confinement, such as the prison and the asylum, to which Foucault attends, the camps are marked by the operation of the state of exception.[168] More important, Agamben contends, Foucault's neglect of the camp also prevents him from reckoning with the close proximity between democracy and fascism. According to Agamben, the camp is the "hidden matrix and nomos of the political space in which we are still living."[169] Modern democracy, uncannily resembling fascism, is essentially another version of the sovereign exception, which functions by producing sacred life in every one of its members.[170] Thus

> modern democracy presents itself from the beginning as a vindication and liberation of zoē, and that it is constantly trying to transform its own bare life into a way of life and to find, so to speak, the *bios* of zoē. Hence, too, modern democracy's specific aporia: it wants to put the freedom and happiness of men into play in the very place—"bare life"—that marked their subjection. Behind the long, strife-ridden process that leads to the recognition of rights and formal liberties stands once again the body of the sacred man with his double sovereign, his life that cannot be sacrificed yet may, nevertheless, be killed.[171]

The more life is politicized as the source of rights, the more it comes to be caught in the sovereign exception; the politicization of bare life ends up with its sacralization and further permeation by sovereignty. Agamben's "biosovereignty" has the power to decide on when and which life is valuable and politically relevant.[172] The decision on what life is to survive is Agamben's version of what Foucault calls racism: "a third formula can be said to insinuate itself between the other two, a formula that defines the most specific trait of twentieth-century biopolitics: no longer either to make die or to make live, but to make survive. The decisive activity of biopower in our time consists in the production not of life or death, but rather of a mutable and virtually infinite survival."[173] In contrast to Foucault, Agamben injects the sovereign with the power of decision, not only over life, as a distinction between "what must live and what must die," but also over what constitutes life as such, life worthy to be kept alive, defined in a metaphysical way.

Three theoretical consequences stand out among the conclusions we can draw from Agamben's criticisms of Foucault vis-à-vis the relation of power and life. First is that, by such a temporal and spatial extension of the biopolitical paradigm, Agamben eliminates the very ambiguity Foucault sustained in the articulation of sovereignty with new modalities of power. This ambiguity involved an unresolved paradox for Foucault: the reversal of biopolitics into thanatopolitics or the coexistence of the power to kill with the power to make live. In Agamben, sovereignty is both biopolitical and thanatopolitical from its inception in the ancient Greek polis.[174] As such, Agamben brings "bio-sovereignty" to a theoretical standstill. Eliminating Foucault's historicization of power regimes, Agamben's "bio-sovereignty" reveals little about the historical transformations, shifts, and discontinuities of sovereignty, if such transformations are possible at all. Rendering "bio-sovereignty" abstract, metaphysical, transhistorical, and teleological, Agamben's analysis lacks historical specificity and diachronic change. In this light, Ernesto Laclau argues, that wavering between a genealogical and a structural argument, Agamben leaves the impression that the "*origin* [of a concept] has a secret determining priority over what follows from it."[175] At the same time, Agamben's concept of biopolitics is excessively juridical and is "blind to all the mechanisms operating beneath or beyond the law."[176] Agamben's work is therefore anti-Foucauldian in method and spirit (though Agamben asserts that he follows Foucault in the paradigmatic method).[177] In Agamben, the politics that is intimately bound up with life seems to elude the very potentiality of life in changing or creating possibilities for change.

Second, in Agamben's reading, life becomes a metaphysical concept and, further, one that is not simply the object of power relations but its subject as well. But this is a peculiar subject, one that lacks any agency except being a function of sovereignty, on the one hand, and any specificity, on the other. In Agambenian "bio-sovereignty," not simply the individual or the population but *life* "now itself becomes the place of a sovereign decision."[178] Once life is fixed as the sacred *subject* of sovereignty by being the bearer of rights, on the one hand, and the *object* of the exercise of power trapped in the structure of the exception, on the other, the sacred source of rights is constantly undermined by the capacity of subjects to be killed in the name of life. It is no longer the individual of liberalism or the public of republicanism that is deemed the subject of political action and intervention but *Life* as the metaphysical product of sovereignty, which animates a singular direction of history inevitably leading toward totalitarianism. Sovereignty and biopolitics are entangled in producing the Life of the homo sacer as the subject-object of politics, albeit one with little potential for political action.

Thirdly, Agamben's theory of "bio-sovereignty" leaves us in the dark regarding the possible or actual resistance of Life as the subject-object of power. Since sovereignty involves not only the manufacture of naked life but also its submission to power for its constitution, Life appears as completely captured by the apparatus of the exception. Indeed, Agamben seems to be pessimistic about the possibilities of resistance: "The 'body' is always already a biopolitical body and bare life, and nothing in it . . . seems to allow us to find solid ground on which to oppose the demands of sovereign power."[179] Whatever resistance might occur, its only result can be to entwine us further into the law, into the exceptional structure of biopolitical sovereignty, thereby hastening our entrapment in the camp. In the absence of any room for contingency, we can only become more vulnerable. Didier Bigo argues: "by exaggerating the capacity of the actors speaking in the name of the sovereign and by essentializing sovereignty though a conception that plays against (yet with) the rule of law . . . Agamben ignores the resistance of the weak and their capacities to continue to be humane and to subvert the illusory dream of total control."[180]

Even if one were to accept a limited agency for the modern homo sacer, Agamben's theory still falls short of providing a differentiated analysis for subjects who are racialized, gendered, and classed in divergent ways.[181] Agamben never clarifies how the wide-ranging examples of bare life he provides (the comatose, the asylum seeker, the guinea pig, Jews in the concentration camps, modern-day refugees) are connected and fated in the same way and to the same violence. Take the case of the comatose patient and the refugee. Rendering them equivalent blinds us to the enormous gap in their availability for and vulnerability to the death operation of sovereignty. In other words, what Hugo Reinert has called their "necroavailability" is far from being the same.[182] Thomas Lemke's criticism of Agamben is pertinent here: "Even if all subjects are homines sacri, they are so in very different ways."[183] Since the camp is a threshold beyond which only bare life exists, Agamben "cannot analyze how inside 'bare life' hierarchizations and evaluations become possible, how life can be classified and qualified as higher or lower, as descending or ascending."[184] We are therefore never informed about the "actual transgressions of these banished individuals." [185] They are of little relevance to our sealed destiny as *homines sacri*.

For Agamben, those who are openly homines sacri only reveal the ontological fate of modern citizens, just as the exception reveals the rule. As Peter Fitzpatrick aptly notes, homo sacer wavers between referencing ordinary citizens in contemporary liberal democratic states, on the one hand, and all those groups (refugees, detainees) who are trapped in the camp, on the other hand.[186] Such oscillation makes the situation of those groups reflect what awaits ordinary citizens. In other words, insofar as life is sacralized and structurally caught in the ban, it is always threatened with being deemed of no value and exposed to violence. According to Jef Huysmans, making bare life the ontological "specter" of politics "does not simply depoliticize histories of sociopolitical struggles and the locales of these struggles. The metaphysics of pure life seeks to ontologically erase them. The result is an apocalyptic political vision in which not fear of the enemy but the collapse of order into anomic, self-referential life is the defining principle of politics."[187]

In Agamben's work there is a constant yearning for a nonsovereign politics, a politics without the ban, but since bare life is already limited in its capacity for action, it is unclear how this could be achieved.[188] Agamben also calls for a transformation of bare life into a *form-of-life*, a "life for which living itself would be at stake in its own living,"[189][190] or a "*bios* that is only its *zoē*."[190] The primary division between bare life and form-of-life, a division that has replaced the one between man and citizen, constantly subverts the possibility of the cohesion of form and content into an empowered life in which happiness is possible. An organic, singular life that is immediately political because it carries within it a potential of happiness, a life that unites *bios* and *zoē*, Agamben contends, is the sine qua non of a nonsovereign politics: "A political life, that is a life directed toward the idea of happiness and cohesive with a form-of-life, is thinkable only starting with the emancipation from such a division, with the irrevocable exodus from any sovereignty."[191]

Agamben postulates an exodus through passive refusal whose exemplar is Herman Melville's Bartleby, the scrivener who, "with his 'I would prefer not to,' resists every possibility of deciding."[192] This scrivener, by passively refusing to scribe while holding the possibility of scribing as a potential, annuls the hold of sovereign power over him; he withdraws, so to speak, from sovereignty.[193] While the "pure, absolute potentiality"[194] of Bartleby's refusal may obstruct the operation of "bio-sovereignty," as a form of resistance it remains purely individual (and individualizing) and ethical.[195] It is unclear how his re-fusal to decide would eventually render him immune to his becoming a homo sacer (which he always already is). As such, resistance in Agamben's work is transformed into passive contemplation, a stubborn yet inactive refusal rather than any active resistance or revolutionary, transformative politics.

Overall, Agamben's call for an ethical and singular conception of Being that can free life from the dominion of "bio-sovereignty" provides an ontolog-ical answer to a political problem. A far cry from resistance, only aporetically intimating the possibility of the "politics to come" through a messianic prom-ise, Agamben's theory takes away the counterpower that Foucault grants to every subject.[196] The homo sacer may want to resist sovereignty, but, it seems, the Life inhering in him, as the subject-object of history, is destined to remain bound to its creator—sovereignty.[197]

NECRORESISTANCE AND BARE LIFE

In spite of its problems, the figure of the homo sacer has been found by recent scholarship to resonate with a wide array of populations that are marginal-ized and vulnerable: refugees, immigration detainees, unlawful combatants, ethnic minorities, aboriginal populations, those demanding death with dig-nity, women subject to honor killings, even the third world poor: in short, all those who are excluded from legal protection and thus vulnerable to absolute violence (with impunity).[198] However provocative, the association of bare life with these populations obscures the real differences in the status and vulner-ability of these populations, on the one hand, while it erases the active and ongoing resistances that these groups perform, on the other.

Drawing upon Foucault and Agamben, Achille Mbembe has maintained that it is in *necropolitical spaces* that lives are rendered disposable and reduced to "death-in-life," where bare life can be found.[199] Necropolitical spaces are those sites of exception, such as the slave plantation, the colony, and territories under occupation, where populations are not killed but "subjected to condi-tions of life conferring upon them the status of *living dead*."[200] Mbembe has called the combined power of sovereignty, disciplinary power, and biopower that operates in these spaces of exception *necropower* and defined it as a "terror formation."[201] Populations that are forced to live in these exceptional spaces are reduced to bare life by necropower, whose logic of maximum destruction evades the explanatory force of biopower or sovereignty alone.

While ostensibly following the dystopic view of Agamben regarding resistance, Mbembe's definition of *necropolitics* as the "subjugation of life to the power of death"[202] also opens to a second interpretation, one that draws attention to how death itself can be a form of resistance.[203] This latter form of necropolitics, a necropolitics from below, as it were, is one in which "resistance and self-destruction are synonymous."[204] Mbembe alludes to how in spaces of exception death can become the mediator of freedom, the idiom of agency, inscribed in the "logic of martyrdom" through the figure of the suicide bomber. This interpretation is important because, even though it accepts the production of bare life in spaces of exception, it engages self-destructive practices as practices of resistance. It thereby opens the stage of politics, once again, to the phenomenon of resistance. It raises the question of how to theorize the relationship between bare life and self-destructive resistance, which pursues a different theoretical route to account for what we identified earlier as a strand in Foucault's thought that intimated self-destructive resistance by way of characterizing existential, sacrificial practices of resistance as counterconduct.

How, then, does the thesis of bare life pertain to forms of resistance based on the technique of self-destruction, or what I call *necroresistance*? Scholarship suggests two opposing answers to this question. One, building on Agamben's arguments, is the claim that necroresistance is the politicization of bare life. Analyzing practices of refugees who resort to self-destructive acts, such as sewing their lips and eyelids, and going on hunger strikes in protest of their detention, Jenny Edkins and Véronique Pin-Fat, for example, have argued that the resistance of individuals who are reduced to bare life in refugee camps (which are contemporary expressions of the camp) arises from the "*assumption of bare life*, that is, the taking on of the very form of life that sovereign power seeks to impose."[205] Identifying such practices as the *embrace* of the life constituted by the sovereign exception, they contend that refugees thereby contest sovereignty. The refugees' demand for recognition as "nothing but life," "viscerally reveals and draws attention to the refugees' own person as the bare life produced by sovereign power: it is a re-enactment of sovereign power's production of bare life on the body of the refugee."[206] This reenactment mobilizes bare life against sovereignty as the only form of resistance possible in order to reveal sovereignty for what it really is—a relation of violence rather than a relation of power.

In a parallel fashion, Ewa Płonowska Ziarek ventures that the British suffragettes' hunger strikes in the early twentieth century are exemplary of how
bare life can be mobilized for resistance.[207] Ziarek contends that hunger strikers mimicked the hidden irrational violence of the sovereign state against their
own bodies in their self-destructive practices, on the one hand, and, by so doing, they also usurped the state's power over bare life, on the other. These suffragettes thereby became the embodiments of both bare life and sovereignty
at once. Forging a "new type of link between bare life and political form that
would be generated from below, as it were, rather than imposed by a sovereign
decision," the suffragettes have shown how bare life is not simply caught up in
the ban but rather embedded within a terrain of relations in which contestation is possible. Such contestation, enacted by the *mobilization* of bare life,
according to Ziarek, creates a new weapon for oppositional movements, one
in which life produced by sovereignty as damaged and degraded can be turned
against itself to call for the transformation of law.

Such celebratory accounts of bare life, however, are problematic for several reasons. First, in Agamben's construction, homo sacer represents abjection. The *Muselmann* in the concentration camp and the comatose patient, as
products of the sovereign decision, both reside on the border of life and death;
they are at the threshold of humanity itself, unable, therefore, to engage in
any political action except survival. However, the situation of the agents who
actively contest their conditions and put up a resistance cannot be considered
to be in the same category of abjection with these figures. Despite a certain
structural homology in the vulnerable, dispoliticized, and abandoned position to which they are pushed by the operation of sovereignty, others such as
refugees, detainees, prisoners, citizens all have agency and exercise it in different ways. Even when sovereignty does its utmost to reduce individuals to bare
life, it cannot succeed in eradicating their agency.[208] The mere fact of resistance
itself indicates that the sovereign attempt at dispoliticization remains only a
fantasy, that it has not neutralized and cannot eliminate the oppositional politics of those subjected to its violent operation.

Second, the utilization of bare life implicates populations in the definitional categories and distinctions produced by sovereignty itself by way of defining
them in terms of how they are rendered vulnerable by the sovereign exception.
In other words, it accepts the sovereign operation that is based on the denial
and forcible removal of political status to the actions of these individuals as
the determining quality of their subjectivity; it assumes their dispoliticization.

The valorization of bare life as the new subject-object of politics implicitly accepts (and therefore reproduces) the sovereign operation, which functions by separating biological from political existence in order to render life bare.

Third, the accounts that celebrate bare life focus on the fact that resistance is corporeal, that it is carried out by the mobilization of the body as the conduit of resistance, rather than on its self-destructive quality. Self-destruction in this perspective is no different from other forms of violence; it is the mimicry of state violence, directed upon the body, as if the body were already and completely integrated into the apparatus of state sovereignty. Self-destructive resistance is therefore also rendered a function of sovereignty, just like bare life itself, emanating from the state rather than from the agency of those who oppose the state. What is not problematized here is that it is precisely the violence in survival as produced by sovereignty that self-destructive practices of resistance contend with and stake in order to make a political intervention. From the point of view delineated by Agamben, which entails starting out from the premise that subjects are always already constituted as bare life, the source and desire of their action and what they intend to express remain rather unclear or already subsumed in the operation of sovereignty. In contrast to these interpretations, it might be helpful to recall Feldman's argument, working on a Foucauldian register but critiquing and going beyond Foucault, that the mimicry of violence on the body can be the source of transforming the body from the object of the state to an instrument against it, but that this transformation itself is based on the interiority of agents, their bifurcation. Self-destructive violence, from his perspective, rather shows the shortcoming of power to manufacture its subjects in its own image and to overcome their alterity because it cannot prevent mimetic reversals in which the body is turned against the state.[209]

In this vein, Diane Enns holds a nuanced position when she interprets self-destructive acts not simply as the acts of bare life, but as a course of action resulting from the reduction of the individual to bare life through the victimization of a colonizing state. Enns marks the ceasura between Agamben's abject figure of the camp, the *Muselmann*, who has lost all hope and therefore does not resist but only strives to survive, and the Palestinian suicide bomber who might be desperate enough to forgo his own life but who also resorts to sacrificial violence in order to generate hope for others.[210] Nonetheless, she still interprets the suicide bomber as a figure of bare life, one whose status reflects "abject vulnerability, reduction to a life devoid of any political meaning except that by which he is excluded, and by the fact that his or her life would be extinguished with impunity if the act did not already accomplish death."[211] Stripped of human rights, dignity, and access to politics, she argues, despairing individuals resort to violent sacrifice as a way to reclaim meaning, if not for themselves then at least for their people.[212] However, Enns argues, such sacrifice cannot be considered a strategy of resistance, but rather "a desperate refusal of bare life to the condition of being occupied, as well as one of the most horrific and counter-productive examples of violent retribution."[213] As a result, necroresistance appears both as the effect of being reduced to bare life and a desperate, almost nonpolitical reaction to it.

This brings us to the second answer given to the question regarding the relationship between necroresistance and bare life. This is the position that necroresistance is carried out not to embrace bare life, even if to upend it, but as a struggle not to be reduced to bare life. This answer conceptualizes necroresistance as the preference and assertion of death over and against a life that is stripped of political meaning and whose terms are dictated by the sovereign exception. From this perspective, necroresistance is not the resistance *of* bare life but resistance *to* bare life.

In this vein, critiquing Edkins and Pin-Fat's interpretation that resistance is an appropriation of bare life, Patricia Owens argues, "the politics emerging out of these actions is based on the transcendence of bare life, not its celebration."[214] Similarly, Sigrid Weigel's argument that the suicide bomber is not homo sacer, but the "counter-image" of homo sacer echoes this position: "For while [homo sacer] represents bare life that may be killed but not sacrificed, the [suicide bomber] embodies a life that sacrifices itself in order to kill. Through this act, the life defines itself as more and other than bare life, since it posits itself as consecrated or sanctified, and is mediated by images that draw on the traditional iconography of passion and martyrdom."[215]

Accordingly, if necroresistance is the *refusal* of bare life rather than its politicization, this refusal is both normative and empirical: it opposes that the position of bare life ought to define a human being and that it does. In protesting the severing of the political meaning of life from its biological existence, necroresistance, according to this view, opposes the valorization of survival over political existence, thereby defying the logic of the production of life by sovereignty. This approach criticizes the politics of survival associated with bare life while it also contests the equation of vulnerability with powerlessness. It puts forth the argument that, in contrast to embracing pure existence and its vulnerability and activating it, these agents actively seek to avoid and refuse it by sacrificing their biological existence in the name of their political existence. It sheds light on the self-destructive technique of these practices not as the mimicry of sovereign violence through the politicization of life but as the politicization of death. This move separates these self-induced deaths from ordinary acts of violence and attributes to them political and spiritual meaning. *Pace* Enns, this would not be a meaning intended only for the people who are left behind but also a meaning for the actors themselves, one that complements in death the political lens through which these actors view their own existence in life.

In his work with Australian immigration detainees, Richard Bailey takes issue with the tendency in the scholarly literature to depict detainees as victims only.[216] Critiquing Agamben for his failure to see the presence of collective resistances in the camp, Bailey finds the camp to be a site where individuals refuse to abandon their politics in order to reject their reduction to bare life. He contends that as they struggle for their rights the detainees themselves make a distinction between biological existence and political life, a distinction that is unavailable to bare life: "For bare life the only politics is physical survival, whereas these detainees were determined to survive *and* to assert their politics."[217] Where Bailey finds bare life in these immigration centers is not in resistance but in the situation that some individuals decline toward due to severe mental illness or when the hunger-striking detainees are fed intravenously in order to make them survive against their will.[218] Accordingly, it is in situations where the human being is robbed of agency altogether that the category of bare life makes most sense.

DEATH AGAINST LIFE

Bailey's contribution is important not only because it evaluates necroresistance as a refusal of bare life but also because it does so on the basis of ethnographic material that brings the voices of detainees into the realm of theory and attempts to understand how they view their own actions, lives, and position vis-à-vis bare life. In fact, his work shows how there is much to gain by engaging with the perspective of resistance itself. However, such an endeavor requires venturing into the world of the agents who resist and understanding their interpretations of their own actions, their justifications for the use of violence, the relation they establish to their own bodies, their lives, and actions, their status in the existing political order, with all the problems, excesses, shortcomings, and contradictions in their discourses. By venturing into the world of resistance, we do not confine ourselves to the limits and limitations imposed by power relations, which not only shape the dominant characteristics of resistance but, more important, constrict our political vision in recognizing what is and is not admissible to count as a form of resistance.

In fact, insofar as the current power regime, which I have called the *biosovereign assemblage*, is not a transhistorical and teleological formation, as Agamben claims, but, rather, an incipient formation that combines different modalities of power and whose articulation is dependent upon context and history, in a process of becoming, it is necessary to study it in its specificity and contingency. Positing the biosovereign assemblage as a counterpoint to Agambenian "bio-sovereignty" entails a study of the practices and discourses of power and resistance, both the strategies and techniques of violence utilized to consolidate the biosovereign formation as well as those used to contest it, by attending to the actual agents producing and performing them. This requires an engagement with the perspectives of those who are in positions of authority, with the official capacity to wield power, as well as the perspectives of those in resistance, in order to arrive at a holistic understanding of the power regime in which sovereignty, biopolitics, and resistance are constitutively and irreducibly entangled with one another.

With this purpose, we will now turn to the analysis of biosovereignty and necroresistance in Turkey as a particular instance of the relationship whose theoretical derivations discussed so far will be juxtaposed against its empirical determinations. The guiding threads of the analysis will be the evolution of sovereignty into biosovereignty along with the ascendance of disciplinary power and biopower, on the one hand, and the emergence of necroresistance as a novel form of political opposition, on the other.

Before proceeding, however, several points that will propel the inquiry further must be recapitulated from the discussion in this chapter. I have argued that *biosovereignty* is the novel amalgamation of sovereign power with the forces of discipline and security—a conjunction that marks the dominant characteristic of the contemporary power regime. Biosovereignty combines the power *of* life with the power *over* life, including the power over the definition of life, in an assemblage whose structure of articulation is to be discerned from the specific context in which it is found and the cultural and political traditions, economic conditions, social and political forces through whose interaction it takes shape. However, it is important to underscore that what defines this assemblage is neither sovereignty nor biopower singly but rather the form of their conjunction, which gives our power regime its unique character.

In this assemblage, the politicization of life, both at the individual and the aggregate levels, is both the modus operandi and the boundary that marks the limits of its operation. In biosovereignty, life is the object and objective of power; it is the supreme value of the system, even though the control and government of life is undergirded and maintained by sovereign power of life, exercised in the form of the power to kill. The biosovereign assemblage governs individuals, populations, goods, services, territories, relations, and movements within its purview by relegating death to its margins. The logic of the exception, neglected by Foucault but proposed by Agamben, is one of the central mechanisms by which the power regime justifies bringing death back in, despite its contradictory relationship to life as the supreme value. This regime's political object of investigation, intervention, and control is therefore not simply life as such, but rather life and death in their aporetic combination. As such, biosovereignty revolves around and legitimates itself through a highly complex discourse on life and death; its sanctity, inviolability, sacredness, security, purity, health, and quality, on the one hand, and its dispensability, violability, impurity, and dangerousness, on the other.

The paradox of the present that Foucault identifies as the reversal of biopolitics into thanatopolitics, or their uneasy coexistence through the persistent mediation of other modalities of power by sovereignty in the biopolitical problematic, also takes place in the field of resistance. Against the increasing grip of domination upon every facet of life, we find the development of novel forms of resistance that challenge it through a mobilization from the symbolic margins of power. Resistances based on demands for greater rights and privileges, better conditions and standards of well-being, coexist with their inverse, with resistances that disrupt biosovereignty by rejecting its domination and refusing obedience. While both kinds of resistance are conditioned by the dominant power regime and operate by turning life as the object of power back against the state, they differ with respect to how they relate to the different components of the amalgam that characterizes the biosovereign assemblage. In contrast to life-affirming struggles, which demand new rights, redistribution, or recognition, in the way Foucault originally describes resistance to biopower, necroresistance negates life and turns death against the power regime, engaging in an ultimate refusal of biosovereign domination. However, it directs its opposition primarily to the sovereign element that is part of the biosovereign assemblage. By wrenching the power of life and death from the modern state into the hands of those who resist, necroresistance directly communicates with and responds to sovereignty. Nonetheless, it does so in ways enabled by the terrain of biopolitics itself.

As we have seen, contemporary forms of necroresistance based on the weaponization of life resonate more with the forms of existential, sacrificial, and total protest Foucault found in Tunisia and Iran, rather than the conventional forms of protest that surrounded him in Western Europe. Like the Tunisian and Iranian protests, necroresistance is existential and requires total commitment, but its differentiating quality, brought forth by biopolitics, is its corporeality and self-destructive technique. With biopolitics, the body (whether individual or social) is reconfigured as the intermediary through which life can be accessed and regulated. Necropolitical resistance transforms the body from a site of subjection to a site of insurgency, which by self-destruction presents death as a counterconduct to the administration of life. Practices of necroresistance are thus both creative and destructive lines of flight that constantly escape being co-opted into the biosovereign assemblage and destabilize the assemblage itself.

In this connection, the important theoretical reflection concerning whether the insurgent's body is produced as bare life, and, if so, whether its dispoliticization is appropriated or reversed through the course of struggle, remains inconclusive. Even though Agamben's account of the relation between power and life does not provide satisfactory answers to the ambiguities and problems of the analysis of biosovereignty that I have delineated, it is necessary to keep the relationship of necroresistance to bare life as an open question that can only be answered by the examination of the accounts of actual agents who engage in resistance. How do agents in resistance perceive their lives and their relation to the state? How do they view their political existence vis-à-vis survival? Is necroresistance only a tactic that politicizes death in conditions of asymmetry under biosovereignty or does it also challenge the exaltation of life as a supreme value, thereby critiquing the "hegemony of biopolitical reason"?[219] The relation between necroresistance and bare life can only be settled by the meanings attributed to struggle by agents who take into their hands the power of and over death to contest the power of and over life.

Chapter 2
Crisis of Sovereignty

P risons may be the emblematic structures of disciplinary power, as Foucault has taught us, but they are also spaces that belong to the state. As part of the penal apparatus of the state, they reveal how the state performs and reproduces itself through the exercise of the sovereign right to punish. The notoriety of Turkish prisons is therefore a transparent reflection of the authoritarian and repressive nature of Turkey's state tradition. Kemalism, named after the founder of the republic, Mustafa Kemal Atatürk, as the official republican ideology of the regime, plays an indispensable role in determining the contours of the dominant tradition of statecraft. The constitutive features of Kemalism are important as they make up the parameters by which the state defines itself, perceives its unity, and asserts itself as an actor on the political stage.

In the Turkish tradition of statecraft, constantly worried about its hard-won sovereignty and unity, the identification of internal threats to security, real or perceived, have always occupied a privileged place. Intolerant toward dissent, the state has more or less continuously pursued a proactive and vigilant policy of criminalizing and punishing its radical challengers. Hence, even though their numbers have ebbed and flowed, *political* prisoners have always had a continuous and unique presence in Turkish politics as a direct outcome of the security interests of the state. The situation of political prisoners can therefore be considered to be the barometer of Turkish democracy.

Identification of the extraparliamentary left, or what official discourse often refers to as the "extreme left," as a critical security threat as well as criminalization of leftist dissent have been crucial for the establishment of prisons as an ongoing site of contestation, particularly since the advent of the cold war. This situation has been compounded by Turkey's own checkered history, with periods of democratic politics and consecutive reversals in the form of coups d'état. As a result, since the 1970s, prisons have been catapulted to the symbolic forefront of political confrontation. At the end of the twentieth century, when the Turkish state was undergoing a transition from an authoritarian and tutelary to a more liberal-democratic regime, the situation of the country's prisons came under increased scrutiny. Complemented by the high numbers of political prisoners and a consistently worrisome human rights record, the conditions of prisons were considered to be a direct reflection of the regime's democratization. However, the ways in which the prisons were perceived and debated in the sphere of official politics revealed that more was at stake than merely the transition from authoritarian to democratic politics: prisons were symptomatic of a deeper issue regarding how the Turkish state imagined its sovereignty.

In this context the mass hunger strike conducted by political prisoners presented an acute and urgent political problem. To address this problem, the Turkish parliament convened for a special session to discuss the state of the country's prisons. The debates that took place in parliament starkly portray how the elected representatives of the people across the political spectrum concurred in the view that prisons were in dire need of reform. Moreover, they reveal how the mass hunger strike in the prisons was perceived as a real political crisis that precipitated the need to reconsider the nature of the state's sovereignty. This chapter presents the authoritarian state tradition in Turkey and its relationship to internal security threats, chronicles the emergence of prisons as site of political struggle with the state, and discusses how the "prisons problem," increasingly a euphemism for the hunger strike, was interpreted as a "crisis of sovereignty" from the point of view of the agents at the helm of the state.

THE KEMALIST STATE TRADITION AND BIOPOLITICS

The state tradition in Turkey is marked by its strong capacity to shape and influence politics, both independently from forces in civil society and from governments, whether appointed or elected.[1] This tradition, inherited from its imperial past, characterized by a high centralization of absolute power and the relative absence of civil society, has been critical in rendering the state a unique presence in the political sphere, if not *the* primary actor in politics.[2]

However, the authoritarian state tradition in Turkey is not only the legacy of its imperial past but also a rigorously reinvented practice of rule based on an assertive program of nation building and modernization in the early republican period. Having achieved national liberation in the aftermath of the First World War and abolished the monarchy, the republican forces in Ankara established their worldview and program of action as the ideological framework that would guide the bureaucratic and military elite who took charge of the state under the new regime. Since its adoption by the Republican People's Party (Cumhuriyet Halk Fırkası) in 1931 as the official program of the single-party regime and incorporation into the Constitution six years later, Kemalism has largely defined the parameters of Turkish political culture, demarcated the field of political contestation, and constituted the central anchor of the regime up to this day.

As a positivist, modernizing ideology, Kemalism was the cement of the incipient nation-state. Through Kemalism, a new framework of legitimacy was constructed for the republic in which religious allegiance was replaced by national identity. Embodied in the figure of the charismatic leader-founder, Kemalism became the signifier of popular sovereignty and progress. It was characterized by an unrelenting project of national development, which found its most cogent expression in the goal of "attaining the level of contemporary civilizations."[3] The project of modernization, synonymous with Westernization, since "contemporary civilizations" were always the euphemism for Western powers, entailed the far-reaching transformation of society from above, through a combination of radical cultural reforms, social engineering, and economic development. Kemalism was an elitist republicanism combined with authoritarian pragmatism. These qualities, embedded within each principle of Kemalism, contributed to the construction of the hegemonic identity of the state, enabling its constitution as a unitary actor, relatively independent from society, and the construction of challenges to the state as internal security threats and therefore the objects of repression.

Kemalism was symbolized by the Six Arrows, each corresponding to a constituent principle: republicanism, nationalism, populism, étatism, secularism, and revolutionism/reformism. The principle of *republicanism* asserted that the idea of popular sovereignty is best embodied in the "republican" form of state. The republic was positioned against monarchy, substituting the National Assembly as the highest organ of legislation and administration in place of the sultanate, on the one hand, and against theocracy, substituting national identity in place of the religious ties of a community of believers (*umma*) as the basis of its legitimacy, on the other.[4] *Republicanism*, at times used synonymously with democracy, depended not on the direct participation of the people in the government,[5] but on the representation of the national will initially by the parliament, later by the single party and its leading cadres, and, finally, by Mustafa Kemal himself, as the founder and leader of the party and the state.[6] The position of Mustafa Kemal as the "founding father" of the republic became entrenched in the paternalistic attitude of the republic toward the people who needed to become "mature" enough for self-government.[7] The elitist and "tutelary" form of republicanism became solidified in the motto "for the people, despite the people," while the substantiation of republicanism with democratic pluralism awaited the people's political "maturation."[8] Meanwhile, until after World War II, the Republican People's Party actively monopolized the political sphere: parliamentary opponents were eliminated, democratic experiments were short-lived, and popular insurrections were forcefully suppressed by the party-state.

The second of the Six Arrows, the *nationalism* principle, entailed a non-ethnic and territorial definition of membership to the nation, based on the commonality of "language, culture, and ideal." At the same time, it sought to promote peaceful international relations while preserving the unique character of Turkish society. Thus, as a principle, it was based upon a nonirredentist and psychocultural view of national identity as a substitute for religious ties in the establishment of unity within the territorial borders of the newly founded state. However, the increasingly abstract and homogeneous conceptualization of the unity of the nation and the active process of assimilation of various ethnic but Muslim minorities under the unifying identity of Turkishness paved the way for an ethnicist interpretation of nationality.[9] That the idea of homogeneity in unity—an indivisible nation, an indivisible state, and, more significantly, an indivisible people—prevailed within Kemalist ideology is evinced by how allusions to "peoples of Turkey" were gradually replaced by those to the "Turkish people."[10]

Populism, the third of the Six Arrows, claimed the absolute equality of the people in legal terms. But it also described the people of Turkey as a harmonious mass composed of different occupations rather than social classes.[11] Thus, whereas the principle of *populism* endeavored to eliminate distinctions and privileges, on the one hand, it denied the existence of social classes, on the other.[12] It reflected the ideal of a classless, organic society divided only along corporatist lines, one that functioned without conflict. By abolishing political inequalities, the state rendered class distinctions and social privileges nonpolitical, but it also preemptively foreclosed their repoliticization by asserting their nonexistence and, therefore, nonlegitimacy. The rejection of class-based politics lent justification for economic reforms that focused on rapid capitalization and the creation of a national bourgeoisie rather than on redistributive policies throughout the process of modernization and development.[13]

The fourth arrow, *étatism*, aimed to foster economic development as the prerequisite of national independence. While private enterprise was assigned the central role in the economy, *étatism* entailed large-scale state intervention; for example, setting up public economic enterprises, encouraging, protecting, and, if necessary, regulating private entrepreneurship, and establishing an amicable relation between capital and labor.[14] While the ensuing mixed economy, accompanied by central planning, was largely a practical response to the urgency of development in the absence of initial capital accumulation, as well as to the post-1929 crisis context, it also strove to foster the development of a national capitalism.[15] Kemalist *étatism* was ideologically positioned against both liberalism and socialism, with the contention of being a "Third Way" peculiar to Turkey.[16] If the belief in the priority of rapid industrialization justified a top-down engineering of the economy in the eyes of the Kemalist elite, it also provided the state bureaucracy with more power, thereby reinforcing its authoritarian tendencies and autonomy vis-à-vis the rest of the social body.[17]

The fifth arrow, *secularism*, was one of the fundamental pillars of Kemalist ideology. Politically, the abolition of the caliphate in 1924 paved the way for the separation of affairs of the state from religion. Radical reforms such as the removal of Islam as state religion from the Constitution, the abolition of courts based on religious law (*Sharia*), the outlawing of religious orders, convents and schools, as well as Muslim dress and headgear, and the adoption of the Latin alphabet in place of Arabic script confirmed that secular reforms were not limited to politics but cast a wide social and cultural net. Identifying religion to be a matter of conscience and adopting modern science as the guiding principle of action, Kemalism asserted secularization as the indispensable precondition of progress and modernization.[18] While the principle of *secularism* guarded the new government against unwelcome opposition from traditional centers of religious power, fortifying the national basis of its legitimacy, it also contributed to the making of the "new citizen," one whose culture was devoid of religious obscurantism and rationally constituted according to principles of positivist thinking.[19] Identity construction and social engineering went hand in hand: the invention of a glorious national history reaching back to pre-Islamic societies, such as the Hittites and the Sumerians, was coupled with the translation of the call to prayer (*ezan*) into Turkish, and the creation of a Directorate of Religious Affairs, under the office of the Prime Ministry, responsible for tasks from appointing religious personnel to overseeing the content of religious education. Such attempts revealed that secularism was intended to create a nationalized religion.[20] Turkish secularization was primarily concerned with the decentering of popular religion and its substitution by a "civilized" and rationalized version of Sunni Islam under state control.[21] It facilitated the promotion of a "renovated and turkified Islam that could help the state propagate new values."[22]

The last arrow of Kemalist ideology, which can be translated both as *revolutionism* and as *reformism*, installed the principle of change within the heart of the ideology while it paradoxically formulated change as the protection of Kemalist achievements. The semantic ambivalence in the principle regarding radical change might have stemmed from the officially promoted efforts of language "purification," by way of eliminating Arabic and Persian words from the language and substituting Turkish neologisms in their place,[23] but the duality also reflected a deeper ambivalence regarding how Kemalists situated themselves and their actions with respect to the Ottoman past. Wanting to emphasize their revolutionary character, the Kemalist elite celebrated the radicalism of the new regime and its transformations while, at the same time, they were careful not to reject the past tout court but rather to maintain a tight control over the direction and substance of social change. Change was not foreclosed completely, in tandem with the goal of modernization, but was limited to progress within the framework of the new order, making sure that the new reforms themselves would not be subject to upending.[24]

Overall, the Six Arrows of Kemalism constituted a coherent worldview and a program of action whose goal was to transform the remains of the Ottoman Empire into a modern, independent nation-state. Because of its role as a *constituent* ideology, animating the self-understanding of the founding cadres and the retrospective narration of the struggle for the founding,[25] Kemalism drew its strength from its ability to create a new state that would endure. This achievement became, in turn, the evidence of the validity and legitimacy of Kemalism as its founding ideology. The ability of the ruling elite of the republic to utilize Kemalism as a political resource, combining the coercive authority derived from their position of power with the persuasive force of the constituent ideology, to garner the consent of different sectors of society and provide them with a national-popular program, and political, moral, and ideological leadership, transformed Kemalism into the hegemonic ideology of Turkey.[26]

The hegemony of Kemalism, which buttressed the strong state tradition in the new republic and affirmed its relative autonomy vis-à-vis the social sphere, also endowed it with a unique opportunity not only to modify, shape, and control society, according to the outlines of the republican program, but also to improve its well-being, foster its growth and strengthening, and increase its productive forces and quality of life, according to the program of modernization. The social engineering responsible for in the making of the "new citizen" involved, alongside the social and cultural reforms that put into effect the directives of the Six Arrows, the deployment of a whole range of *biopolitical* techniques by which a healthy, productive, and docile population was to be produced out of the ruins of a collapsed empire whose diverse peoples had been devastated, dislocated, and decimated by incessant warfare, heavy taxation, poverty, disease, and malnourishment. Kemalist cadres predicated the health of the new *body politic* upon the health of the citizen's body and vice versa. To this effect, they resorted to techniques of population management that had been introduced in the late Ottoman period, especially in the second half of the nineteenth century, but deployed them with greater rigor and intensity.[27]

In order to achieve the desired improvement of the population as part of the modernization program, the Kemalist state intervened, with varying degrees of success, in the spheres of individual and public health, tackling a range of issues such as high rates of child mortality, high rates of morbidity due to preventable diseases and epidemics, widespread alcohol use and venereal disease, and low rates of reproduction, among others. Through a series of measures, not all of which were systematic, via the formal education system as well as semi-independent institutions (such as hospitals and clinics, voluntary sports organizations, local party branches, and newspapers), the state attempted to educate citizens on how to achieve personal hygiene, conducted large scale vaccinations, instituted preventive health care, encouraged reproductive health and higher birth rates, fought prostitution and alcohol, and paid special attention to the development of physical education and sports.[28]

While this modernist deployment of biopolitics upon the social sphere was largely contemporaneous with similar techniques utilized in the West (and especially took inspiration from Soviet Russia and Nazi Germany's achievements in educating and improving the well-being of their people under similarly dire circumstances of postwar reconstruction), it was comparatively mild in its racism. Scholarship shows that a racialized discourse did become an important component of the biopolitics of the Turkish party-state, especially in the 1930s, in an effort to prove to the West that the Turks were "white" and not of an inferior race, and that they, too, had an "innate ability to modernize."[29] This period also corresponds to a more ethnic definition of Turkishness and the racialized overtones in the identity construction of the Kurds and the non-Muslim populations within Turkey. Although there was a lively discussion regarding the benefits of eugenics in the early republican period, the actual policies of the state remained at the level of positive encouragement of reproduction rather than forced sterilization (however, the prohibition of marriage for the disabled in the early republican period should also be noted).[30]

Nonetheless, it would be inaccurate to assert that racism became the primary mechanism for combining the sovereignty of the Turkish state with the development of biopolitics during this period. Biopolitics in the early republic remained largely instrumental for the state and relatively extraneous to it; it was deployed, but without a real internalization of its techniques as state logic. These techniques were part of a "civilizing" mission in which the creation of a strong nation was understood to depend on the fostering of a healthy population that would constitute a productive workforce, with a greater readiness for national defense and dynamic growth potential. The identification of the healthy body politic with national unity, however, did lead to the construction of dissent as a "foreign" and "subversive" element that endangered the republic. In the realm of official ideology, radical political opposition to Kemalist principles was interpreted as a dangerous force that weakened the nation and should be expunged, like a healthy body expunges disease.

While the presence of an official ideology is always in contradiction with democracy, the situation in Turkey was complicated by the fact that it was within the framework of official ideology that democracy was eventually introduced. This development further contributed to the strong presence of the state as a political actor, despite the eventual enlargement of the democratic field of contestation.[31] In fact, it set strong limitations on what could count as legitimate political contestation and created an enduring bifurcation between the state and politics, the former not only as an active agent in the latter but also as the underpinning guarantor that continuously inspects it, controls its development, and keeps it within assigned limits defined by Kemalism.

In this context, the Democrat Party (Demokrat Parti), against which the Republican People's Party (CHP) experienced a dismal defeat in Turkey's first free elections in 1950, did not significantly diverge from Kemalism. Rather, DP accepted, utilized, and further reproduced Kemalism, albeit with a more liberal economic interpretation of the *étatism* principle, relaxing some of the controversial reforms of *secularism* (reverting to the recitation of the *ezan* in Arabic, for example), and adopting a more pro-Western stance in international politics. In distinction from the early republican period's biopolitics directed at the health, education, and fertility of the population, the interventions of the state on the social body during the democratic period, beginning in the 1950s, took on the additional dimension of targeting social welfare and aid, particularly in order to alleviate the growing disparities of income and assuage social conflict.[32] Despite broad continuities with the ideological orientation of the single-party period, DP's increasing authoritarianism and aggressive pursuit of economic and social aggrandizement for its populist base through a dense network of patronage relations paved the way for its ousting from power by the 1960 coup d'état.[33]

Given the strong state tradition and its relation to the field of politics, it is not surprising to find that the 1960 coup, as well as the subsequent military reversals in 1971, 1980, and 1997, have all been carried out as interventions into politics so that in these "states of exception" deviations from original Kemalist principles at the hands of political parties could be corrected and the country put back on the "right course."[34] Acting as a bulwark against the "deformation" of the constituent principles of the regime, the military thereby strengthened the unitary agency of the central state apparatus vis-à-vis successive governments, which were tolerated only insofar as they were able to include, appropriate, and internalize Kemalist principles, and, once again, enshrined Kemalism's position as the "only" official ideology of the republic in the 1982 Constitution.

The hegemonic status of Kemalism, its propagation through the state apparatuses, both repressive and ideological, and its recurrent reinforcement by the military, has had important consequences for Turkish politics. Not only has it granted a privileged role to actors who are part of the state bureaucracy, by virtue of a relative autonomy from political and social forces and a strong and unified capacity to influence the direction of politics, but it has also enabled the state to carry out the Kemalist program of top-down modernization, relying on disciplinary and biopolitical techniques. Elected governments have largely accepted and reproduced this autonomy and have been deeply invested in guarding the state's hard-won sovereignty and unitary identity, as well as its achievements in social, economic, and cultural transformation. As a result, rival ideologies and their proponents have been constructed as "enemies" and "foreign bodies" that threatened the health of the body politic.[35] This orientation has led to the privileging of raison d'état over political contestation, while it has also facilitated the entrenchment of an authoritarian attitude toward dissent, one that has remained operative even during periods of democratic government. As a result, the state has treated the politicization of differences of ethnicity, class, religion, and language with great suspicion. With little room for opposition, especially in radical form, the constricted political space in the republic has largely been occupied by the state as one of the main political actors of Turkish politics.

THE CRIMINALIZATION OF THE LEFT

Nevertheless, the foundational principles of Kemalism have met radical opposition from different quarters: Islamists, Kurdish nationalists, and leftists have each presented different challenges to the principles of secularism, nationalism, and populism, as well as to the homogeneous unity of the nation-state envisioned by the ruling elite. Oppositional currents emerging from these quarters have almost always been regarded as "divisive currents," with their roots outside the country as an indication of their "foreignness" and subversiveness to the project of national unity and sovereignty entailed by Kemalism. As such, they have been considered instruments of foreign powers that plant and nurture the seeds of domestic contention to weaken, destabilize, and ultimately divide the country in their own interests.[36] Classifying these oppositional currents as "internal threats," the state has viewed them with suspicion and hostility, pointing to their invisible or potential ties to external enemies and regarding them as insidious, debilitating, dangerous, and perhaps even more recalcitrant against attempts at elimination than their external counterparts. As a result, the state has put much effort in devising strategies to confront and neutralize these threats to its security, with serious legal repercussions for their proponents.[37]

The political left has particularly borne the brunt of Kemalist authoritarianism from the very inception of the republican regime. Although the nationalist cadres of the nascent Turkish state were able to establish amicable and beneficial relations with the young Soviet Union while navigating the tensions between the powers occupying the remains of the Ottoman state, these ties slowly withered away after Turkey's declaration of independence. Communist forces active in the country were suppressed and eliminated by nationalist cadres during the years of the War of Independence (1919–22) and the early republic.[38]

Despite this rocky beginning, the leftist opposition in Turkey followed the Communist International in its support of the Kemalist struggle for national independence as a progressive element in the international fight against imperialism and an example to other oppressed nations in the East during the initial period of the republic. At the same time, the Kemalist reforms against theocracy and monarchy, on one hand, and strides against semi-feudal structures, on the other, were welcomed as the "bourgeois democratic revolution" that would facilitate the development of the working class and set the stage for a future proletarian revolution. However, because of their "bourgeois" character, the leftists expected that there would be objective limits to how far Kemalist reforms could extend. Land reform, for example, stood at the boundary of how radically Kemalists would be willing to transform social relations, in their view. Those on the left were quick to predict that Kemalists would not risk distributing land to poor peasantry since it would undermine their alliance with the landowners. And they were accurate in their prediction.

As a result, the left occupied an awkward position from which it had to build a precarious combination of support and opposition to the Kemalist regime.[39] Especially during the Second World War, after the decentralization decision taken by the Communist International in 1939, leftist opposition was largely settled on the strategy of advancing the "national front" against fascism and imperialism in compliance with the urgency of the international situation and promoting a noncapitalist path of development where possible.[40] This meant that the left accepted an increasingly muted role with respect to Kemalist cadres politically and allied itself with Kemalism ideologically, except for launching criticism against wartime policies that encouraged profiteering and calling for democratic elections.[41] The interpretation of the Kemalist revolution as the first bourgeois democratic step in liberation within a linear and stagist construction of history strengthened this alliance, as it was expected that this crucial phase would enable the development of a national capitalism and a national proletariat, which could then be organized for the next socialist stage. The Kemalists and the leftists therefore shared the desire to attain full national independence and commonly emphasized developmentalism. The low profile of the left was also a consequence of difficulties organizing, as the communists were often the first to be adversely affected by the repressive practices of the center.

After the transition to democracy in 1946, leftist opposition had a brief period of legal freedom, both under the auspices of the Democrat Party and as small but short-lived independent parties. However, the optimism generated by the sweeping victory of DP, which broke the political monopoly of the Republican People's Party and dislodged it from power, did not last long. Leftist opposition was soon disillusioned with the DP government in the face of its similarly authoritarian tendencies, visibly pro-Western posture, populist concessions in religion, networks of patronage, rapid program of industrialization without concern for growing disparities, and its welcoming of the support of foreign capital.[42] The left largely interpreted the changes brought about by the Democrats as a retreat from the progressive aspects of the Kemalist regime, such as nationalism, étatism, and secularism. The McCarthy-like anticommunist attitude of the new government, soon actively closing down leftist parties and instigating waves of persecution directed at intellectuals and militants, added material force to this disillusionment.

In this light, the leftists welcomed the military coup of 1960 as a restoration of the Kemalist order against the excesses of democracy through the intervention of the progressive forces of the state.[43] Carried out by colonels instead of the High Command, the coup of May 27, 1960, enlisted the support of CHP and based its legitimacy on a coalition of republican politicians, bureaucrats, civil servants, students, and leftist intellectuals, all of whom came together around the goal of completing the unfinished Kemalist revolution. The new regime indicted the Democrat Party government for having created a "tyranny of the majority" and put its leading political figures on trial. Prime Minister Adnan Menderes and two ministers of his cabinet were convicted of treason and hanged.

After the adoption of the more libertarian and democratic 1961 Constitution, the Turkish political scene witnessed an unprecedented spread of communist, socialist, and social-democratic ideas and the formation of several dozens of groups and organizations that together constituted an extraparliamentary leftist opposition. This growth was soon translated into parliamentary representation. In 1965 the Workers' Party of Turkey (TİP) won fifteen seats.[44] In the meantime, the growing popularity of the left drifted the Republican People's Party, the heir of the single-party state, leftward. The new leadership of Bülent Ecevit signified the left-of-center stance.

In stark contrast to the elitist "monoparty" period,[45] the rising demands for social justice and welfare on the streets evidenced a dramatic change in the dynamics of Turkish politics, forged through political pluralization, economic development, industrialization, urbanization, and rising social inequalities. The general strike of June 15–16, 1970, demonstrated the mounting strength of the left, despite persistent attempts at repression.[46] A strong indication of the increased politicization of the masses and the expanding influence of leftist ideas was the establishment of the Confederation of Revolutionary Trade Unions (DİSK), with which trade union membership rose from 250 thousand to around 2 million. However, the emergence of the trade union movement, activism among university students, labor strikes, and other social struggles also accentuated the hostility of the state toward the left.

The March 12, 1971 intervention of the High Command was effected through a memorandum, which installed a group of technocrats in power without suspending the parliament. The new cabinet under Nihat Erim was accompanied by constitutional amendments restricting rights and liberties (of the 157 articles of the 1960 Constitution, 57 were amended). The hanging of three popular leftist student leaders—Deniz Gezmiş, Yusuf Aslan, and Hüseyin İnan—in 1972 exemplified the politics of the 1971 coup, especially in contrast to the 1960 coup in which the three political figures who were hanged were the top three officials of the DP government. If the state's earlier corrective was against authoritarian populism, this time it was against left-wing politics from below. This intervention also signaled the intensification of the left's further criminalization.

The 1970s were a period of growing political polarization between the left and the right that was quickly translated into extremely sectarian politics and escalating violence, which rendered civil war a plausible threat. The parliament was at a political stalemate due to unstable coalition governments and feuding between the two major parties: the left-of-center Republican People's Party under Bülent Ecevit's leadership and the right-of-center Justice Party (Adalet Partisi) under Süleyman Demirel's leadership, which continued the line of the Democrat Party suppressed by the 1960 coup d'état. The oil crises and the embargo following the Cyprus invasion of 1974 hampered the economy and isolated Turkey in the international sphere. The two Nationalist Front (Milliyetçi Cephe) coalitions and the following minority cabinet of the Justice Party allowed right-wing parties, the Nationalist Action Party (Milliyetçi Hareket Partisi) led by Alparslan Türkeş and the National Salvation Party (Milli Selamet Partisi) led by Necmettin Erbakan, to play a disproportionately powerful role in relation to the number of seats they commanded in parliament. While the incorporation of ultranationalist and Islamist currents into government further polarized the political sphere, the internal politicking between coalition members brought the parliament to an impasse.

The ineffectiveness of the parliament to address the country's deepening economic crisis and social problems pushed politics to the streets in a rising tide of violence that claimed many lives. Right before the 1980 coup, an average of fifteen to twenty individuals were killed on a daily basis in street vendettas between right-wing "commandos" unofficially linked to the National Action Party and left-wing "revolutionaries" linked to numerous splinter organizations and factions on the extraparliamentary left, a number of which had grown out of the youth organizations of the Workers' Party (TIP) and taken increasingly radical, vanguardist directions. These forces divided urban neighborhoods according to opposing ideological orientations and spheres of influence. At the same time, leftist factions were highly conflicted among themselves and capable neither of unified action nor of decisive social mobilization.[47] During the same period, the general militarization of daily life was compounded by numerous assassinations of intellectuals, journalists, and politicians, whose perpetrators remained largely unknown. Bloody May Day in 1977 left 36 dead (5 of whom were shot by unknown snipers, the rest crushed in the stampede) and 130 wounded. Increasing extremist violence in the streets went hand in hand with rising sectarian tensions between Sunnis and Alevis.[48] The ongoing organized assaults on Alevi communities, in the form of raids on coffeehouses, homes, and shops, reached a peak with the massacre in the southeastern province of Kahramanmaraş in December 1978. This attack alone took the lives of more than 100 people.

One of the most important aims declared for the military coup d'état of 1980 was, in the words of the High Command, to put an end to the "terror" and "anarchy" caused by the threat of communism on the streets and to bring order to a country that not only lacked proper government by the civilian parliament but also had become unruly and "ungovernable." The state was, once again, intervening in politics to curb the contestation and violence among extremes, impose constraints upon political actors and civil society, end radical social mobilization, and correct the deviation of the country from Kemalist principles. The project of eliminating internal threats to security was soon transformed into political engineering and refounding when the military not only declared a "state of exception," in which all political opposition was brutally suppressed, but also dissolved the 1960 Constitution (already constricted by the amendments of 1971) and set up a new constitutional order.

As soon as the military took over, it shut down the parliament and banned all political parties, expropriating their assets and prohibiting party leaders from political activity. The military also embarked on a campaign against civil society, disbanding all associations and trade unions, including DİSK, still the largest workers' organization at the time.[49] According to the statistics compiled by human rights organizations, a total of 23,677 organizations were banned by military rule. Major newspapers and journals were banned, some of them permanently, along with hundreds of films. The Kurdish language was made illegal. Classes on religion became a compulsory part of primary and secondary education. A Council of Higher Education (Yüksek Öğretim Kurulu) was set up in Ankara, putting an end to university autonomy. During the coup, some 30,000 people were fired, forced to resign, asked to retire from their jobs, or exiled to remote posts in the rural provinces. Those who were forced to resign include 3,854 teachers and 120 university professors. Another 30,000 people sought political asylum in European countries; 14,000 individuals lost their citizenship; 388,000 individuals could no longer hold a passport and were, in effect, imprisoned within the country. Over 300 people simply disappeared; another 300 died in prisons.[50]

The criminalization of dissent reached unprecedented numbers in the history of the republic. In three years 650,000 people were arrested, 230,000 were prosecuted, and some 65,000 were convicted. The number of arrests comprised about 2.6 percent of the adult population, although unofficial estimates are twice this figure.[51] Nearly of half of those who were prosecuted (98,404 individuals) were charged with membership in illegal organizations. A third of those who were prosecuted (71,000 individuals) were charged with crimes defined by three infamous articles of the Penal Code: 141, 142, and 163. These articles stipulated significant limitations on the right to organize (141) and freedom of expression (142 and 163), rendering even nonviolent propaganda punishable. A symbolic climax was the prosecution of approximately 7,000 individuals with the death penalty, even though capital punishment had not been carried out in Turkey since 1973. Of the 517 individuals eventually condemned to death, 50 were executed.[52] The first two of these executions occurred only a month after the military assumed power. One from the "extreme" right and another from the "extreme" left, these executions were singled out to represent the alleged "even-handedness" of the new regime against both radical ends of the political spectrum.

Despite its rhetorical neutrality and ostensible equidistance to both extremes of the political spectrum, the conservative sympathies of the military inevitably colored the legal, political, and economic order that the military sought to put into place. On the economic front, the military installed the IMF-prescribed economic stabilization program introduced in January 1980 (which included a devaluation of the currency by one-third of its value) and facilitated the emergence of an open and competitive market economy oriented toward growth by exports and flexible currency exchange rates, moving away from the previously heavily state-regulated economy based on import substitution and fixed exchange rates.[53] Politically, it put into place new limits on contestation. The new electoral law introduced a 10 percent national threshold, which intended to preclude small or regional parties from gaining representation in parliament and leverage beyond their actual popular support, while it also encouraged a two-party system gravitating around centrist parties. The Constitutional Court was assigned the responsibility and power to close down political parties considered to represent ideological extremes, whether from an ethnic, a religious, or a class perspective.[54] Legally, the 1982

Constitution, adopted by a national referendum under military rule,[55] introduced many loopholes through which fundamental rights and liberties (especially the right to strike and the right to free assembly) could be restricted.[56]
Meanwhile, the new Constitution guaranteed a prominent role for the National Security Council, composed in part of ministers of the government and
in part of the High Command, as an advisory board to the government. If
the decision on the "exception" reveals the real locus of sovereignty, the 1980
coup, through which the military usurped this power permanently, not only
confirmed the military's constituent role but also integrated it into the civilian
order as a limiting force upon elected governments through the stipulations of
the 1982 Constitution.[57]

The first elections took place in November 1983 under the auspices of
military rule in order to transfer government to civilian hands. However, the
return to normalcy from the military coup came gradually, in subsequent
waves of democratization.[58] Martial law was fully in effect until March 1984
and was only gradually phased out in July 1987. In its place, a regional "state
of emergency" was put into effect (in the eastern and southeastern provinces
where the Kurdish population is concentrated), with extraordinary provisions for the governing officials to override constitutional rights and liberties
if and when necessary. The state of emergency was also gradually phased out
throughout the 1990s and lifted completely only at the end of 2002, upon two
decades of low-intensity warfare with the Partiya Karkerên Kurdistan (PKK)
that undergirded the long transition to civilian rule.[59]

During the protracted process of civilianization, oppositional political
currents, which were deemed to be targeting the "constitutional order of the
state, the indivisible unity of the country, and the welfare of the nation,"[60] continued to be considered pernicious, centrifugal forces whose suppression by
legal and illegal means was considered legitimate. Torture, despite the process
of democratization and the ratification of the European Convention for the
Prevention of Torture and the United Nations Convention Against Torture
in 1988, remained rampant, especially under police custody, and, according to
the United Nations Committee Against Torture, "systematic."[61] Even though
the armed struggle of the Kurdish separatists led by PKK soon surpassed leftists as the highest priority on the list of strategic security concerns defined by
the National Security Council, the extraparliamentary left continued to retain
its role as an "internal threat" to security and order, especially as it became
more militant and violent in the early 1990s. Despite the collapse of the Soviet

Union that led to the waning of radical-revolutionary leftist politics around
the world, the extraparliamentary left in Turkey gained a new momentum
with the armed struggle of the Kurdish nationalist movement, rapid social and
economic transformation, and the culture of collective resistance in prisons.
Meanwhile, the large flows of migration from the countryside into the cities
nourished all radical movements – leftist, Islamist, and ethno-nationalist,
which competed for this constituency.[62]

In response, the hostile relationship of the Turkish state with its radical
challengers took an important turn with the promulgation of the Law for the
Struggle Against Terror in 1991.[63] The antiterror law not only folded the state's
"internal threats" into the category of "terror," adopting discourses and practices of securitization and preempting the global turn to antiterrorism legislation
by a decade, but it also dictated policies and procedures that would ensure the
distinctive treatment of "terrorists" vis-à-vis other populations who infringed
the laws. This law donned the state with the ability to pursue its vigilant persecution of dissidents and oppositional forces with impunity and with remarkable continuity, now through democratic rule under successive governments,
despite their ostensible ideological differences. The antiterror law also marks
an important turning point in the history of biopolitics in Turkey, precisely
because it signals that the hitherto predominantly extraneous and instrumental deployment of governmental techniques by the state in order to foster the
health and well-being of the population in line with the program of modernization is now being supplanted by a rethinking and reorganization of the state
apparatuses and their practices around questions of *security*—the redefinition,
classification, regulation, and management of threats as an integral part of the
health and well-being of the population. From now on, biopolitical techniques
are no longer simple tools to be imposed upon the social sphere, but become
part and parcel of the construction of sovereign power itself, manifest most
clearly in the exercise of its right to maintain public order and to punish those
who attempt to subvert it, selectively and with respect to security objectives,
biopolitically defined. Here, we have an infusion of biopolitics into the very
tissue of sovereign power. The process of securitization precipitated by the
antiterror law in the spheres of policing and imprisonment technologies refers
to an integration of sovereignty and biopolitics and their mutual penetration
at an unprecedented level.

The antiterror law thereby provided the conditions of possibility for
the intensification of the state's pursuit and containment of its challengers:

Kurdish separatists, radical leftists, and political Islamists. Torture remained a widespread and systematic practice.[64] The hawkish approach to the Kurdish question, exacerbated by armed conflict with PKK in the southeast, was complemented by extensive profiling, wiretapping, and other means of covert domestic surveillance as well as by security operations in urban centers against Kurdish and leftist opposition and the forcible suppression of erratic insurrections in the shantytown neighborhoods and other spontaneous riots. However, the vigilance displayed by civilian governments did not prevent the military intervention of February 28, 1997, fourth of its kind in the republic's history. This "soft" or "postmodern" coup,[65] as observers have called it, came at a juncture of intensified social conflict and the growing rise of political Islam.[66] It did not suspend civilian rule, but only reprimanded the government with a harsh statement warning against religious extremism. The coalition government of Tansu Çiller's True Path Party (Doğru Yol Partisi) and Necmettin Erbakan's Welfare Party (Refah Partisi) was eventually pressed to resign, reaffirming the military's role as the "guardian" of national sovereignty and its core republican principles. The hegemony of Kemalism was thereby reasserted, without significant discontinuity in the repressive attitude of the state toward its challengers. It was only as the military gained control over the Kurdish insurgents, under the added pressure of a long-desired European Union membership, that successive constitutional reform and democratization packages were allowed to pass in parliament, now dominated by the Justice and Development Party (Adalet ve Kalkınma Partisi) under the leadership of Recep Tayyip Erdoğan. AKP's strong popular support enabled the government to facilitate the process of democratic reform in order to consolidate the precarious transition from the bureaucratic-authoritarian and tutelary regime to civilian democracy, a process that, despite its contradictions, continues to this day.[67]

PRISONS AS SITES OF CONFRONTATION AND THE ANTITERROR LAW

In the post-1980 context, the measures that sought to eliminate internal threats to security, whether by military intervention and the forceful repression of radical opposition or the criminalization of opposition through the punitive policies of successive democratic governments, produced momentous consequences for the country's prisons. Two of these consequences stand out among others: first, the informal but consistent partition of prisons, with corresponding rules and regulations, according to prisoner status and, second, the entrenchment of prisons as a symbolic site. By the mid-1990s, prisons in Turkey, especially the wards in which political prisoners were confined, had become sites of a highly politicized confrontation between the state and the insurgents. Prisons were transformed into a direct and transparent interface between the state and its unruly "crowd."[68]

In the first half of the 1980s the military regime's punitive practices were exceptionally harsh, in keeping with its ideological commitment to eliminate political extremes. As a result, those who were affiliated with radical politics, left and right, were subjected to the grinding mill of the military prison. Moreover, those detained for "political" reasons were treated very differently from prisoners held for "ordinary" crimes, although this distinction in status was not yet codified into the law. In fact, one of the first moves of the military was to impose upon political prisoners the status of "arrested personnel," a status beneath the lowest private in the chain of command, according to the military's criminal procedural code of regulations called 13/1. The task of the prison commanders was to make the "arrested personnel" accept and respect the military chain of command and discipline, through a variety of measures, including making prisoners salute all military personnel (including privates) as "commander," coercing them to walk and talk like soldiers, sing military marches, repeat the national anthem and Atatürk's famous "Speech to the Youth" by heart, recite prayers at meals, and wear prison uniforms. In cases of disobedience to the inculcation of a militarized dispoliticization and Turkification, violence was rampantly applied.

The internal partitioning of prisons between those held for "political" crimes and "ordinary" crimes was therefore largely an effect of the differential treatment of prisoners by the military administration on a day-to-day basis, ranging from simple disciplinary measures to physical violence used to make them submit. It was not that violence was lacking in the interactions of the military command with "ordinary" prisoners. Violence was widespread. However, the violence directed at "political" prisoners was of a different caliber, both in its arbitrariness and brutality and in its specific design to eliminate dissident identities and political affiliations.

The fierce experience of the military prison led to the emergence of individual and collective resistances in prisons, initially against the ongoing practices of torture and degrading treatment and, in successive stages, over access to health care, lawyers, visitors, and the regulation of daily life in prison. Although the brutality of prison life somewhat subsided with the transition to civilian rule in 1983, prison struggles increased in rigor. As we will see in detail in the next chapter, a whole range of issues revolving around life in prison soon became politicized, ranging from what prisoners could read, eat, wear, and keep as personal belongings, to how often they could receive family visits, legal consultation, and medical care. Tactics of prison struggles varied: sometimes prisoners only shouted slogans, banged on bars, resisted body counts and ward searches, boycotted court hearings and visits; other times they organized uprisings, carried out violent occupations (of wards, yards, and main hallways), and took prison guards hostage; occasionally, they also resorted to hunger strikes of various durations, acts of self-immolation, protest self-hangings, and death fasts. These acts of resistance achieved mixed results, but collectively they functioned to reinforce the internal partitioning of the prisons among "ordinary" and "political" prisoners. In the 1990s, especially in the aftermath of the promulgation of the antiterror law, the crackdown on the radical left in urban centers and the intensification of low-intensity warfare against Kurdish separatism in the east continued to fill prisons with younger generations of militants. As political prisoners increased in numbers, prison struggles became more confrontational. The prison assumed the status of an independent site of hostile political engagement between the state and those it considered to be "internal threats."

By the late 1990s the ongoing struggles of political prisoners in many prisons across the country had produced a complex and internally differentiated penal sphere based on a myriad of arrangements, partitions, and selective practices, formal and informal, regular and ad hoc, that regulated prison life in a way that acknowledged, at least de facto, differential rights and privileges accorded to political prisoners in comparison to other prisoners held for "ordinary" crimes. The legal ambiguities and discontinuities created by different and, at times, inconsistent executive decrees issued by various governments to govern the prisons and address their problems, coupled with practical measures taken by prison administrations and their concessions to the political prisoners in their attempt to assuage the ongoing unrest, led to the emergence of a certain autonomy of the wards of political prisoners from the administrative procedures and practices that regulated the lives of the rest of the prison population. Accordingly, even though political prisoners had to answer to body counts and were subjected to random searches and seizures conducted by the prison administrations, even though they nominally had to follow the general rules of conduct applicable to conditions of imprisonment, they were otherwise permitted to organize their daily lives themselves, without much interference from the prison administrations. Over time, the wards of political prisoners were transformed into self-governing enclaves, whose existence eased the burden of prison administrators in regulating daily life in the prison and ensured the maintenance of order and peace within large groups of politicized individuals, on the one hand, while, at the same time, it increased the frequency of collective mobilization and unrest, and, as a result, the anxiety and troubles of prison administrators and state officials, on the other hand. The experience of collective life in the prison wards reinforced the prisons as sites of confrontation with the state while, at the same time, they became a venue of generating political leadership for the radical left, both inside and outside prisons.

If the rapid growth in the numbers of political prisoners was one factor contributing to the radicalization of prison struggles and the strengthened autonomy of prison wards, the other factor was undoubtedly the impact of the antiterror law. The stipulations of the antiterror law affirmed the distinct status of political prisoners vis-à-vis other prisoners, even if it did so at the expense of bringing political prisoners within the fold of an expansive discourse of terrorism and its attendant practices of securitization. The antiterror law contained a stipulation for the conditional release of prisoners for crimes committed until 1991 (Provisional Article 1), by which those who had been given the death penalty would be released after ten years, life imprisonment would be commuted to eight years, and all other sentences would be commuted to one-fifth of their term. With this article, most prisoners incarcerated since the 1980 military coup would be released. The antiterror law therefore established a break between the preceding military coup and the democratic regime, instituting new forms of criminalization instead.

Several controversial aspects of the antiterror law are worth highlighting because they have had important repercussions for delineating the vicissitudes of oppositional forces in their interaction with the state and their specific form of criminalization in the 1990s under the aegis of a democratic regime. The most prominent characteristic of the law was its scope, determined by the rather loose and broad definition of *terrorism*. According to Article 1 of this law, terrorism was defined as

> any kind of act done by one or more persons belonging to an orga-
> nization with the aim of changing the characteristics of the Republic
> as specified in the Constitution, its political, legal, social, secular and
> economic system, damaging the indivisible unity of the State with its
> territory and nation, endangering the existence of the Turkish State
> and Republic, weakening or destroying or seizing the authority of
> the State, eliminating fundamental rights and freedoms, or damaging
> the internal and external security of the State, public order or general
> health by means of pressure, force and violence, terror, intimidation,
> oppression or threat.[69]

Written in such a way as to encompass opposition to the state from a wide spectrum of positions (whether based on ethnicity, religious affiliation, or class politics), the law included not only "force and violence" but also manifold forms of "pressure," "intimidation," and "threat" to the unity of the state, its constitution, internal and external security, public order, and health within the scope of terrorism. Article 2 further broadened the universe of "terror" crimes by defining not only those who committed crimes to attain the goals stated in Article 1, but also those who were *members* of organizations aspiring after these goals (regardless of whether they had committed such crimes themselves) as "terrorist" offenders. Meanwhile, the criteria for establishing membership in "terrorist" organizations were left largely ambiguous. The law's infamous Article 8 prohibited not only demonstrations and marches but also written or oral propaganda, "regardless of the methods, intentions, and ideas behind such activities," thereby greatly restricting the freedom of expression.[70] In the name of the "struggle against terror," the law extended protection to antiterrorism police, shielding them from prosecution with the protective provisions specified for civil servants and, in case of prosecution, waiving remand and assuring financial support for their legal expenses out of resources allocated to the Ministry of Justice. The law therefore not only left room for torture and maltreatment of detainees but also sanctioned state-sponsored violence by lending protections to the perpetrators of such violence.

Because the antiterror law created a two-tier criminal justice system, one for "ordinary" offenses and the other for "terror" crimes, it wedged the respective prisoner populations further apart, situating them in considerably different conditions at four separate stages in the system: (1) detainment and arrest, (2) trial (with or without remand), (3) sentencing, and (4) execution of sentence. As such, even though the state did not officially recognize a separate class of prisoners with political status, it indirectly fixed their status (and hence, treatment) as different from ordinary offenders once they were captured by the state apparatus.

Accordingly, those detained as suspects for "terror" offenses would be subject to exemptions from the stipulations of the Criminal Procedural Code (Law No. 3842) otherwise instated to protect the rights of detainees and organize legal procedures for detention and trial. While detainees suspected of "ordinary" crimes could benefit from legal counsel immediately, those detained as suspects for "terror" crimes did not have to be reminded of their rights as part of due process.[71] Furthermore, they could be held in incommunicado detention for forty-eight hours and, if the crime was collectively committed, up to fifteen days (this amount went up to thirty days if the crime was committed in a region where the "state of emergency" was still in effect).[72] Such practices legalized a whole set of infractions upon fundamental rights, while they created a significant time frame for arbitrary detention. They put the suspects of "terror" crimes at the mercy of security forces and provided ample opportunities, if not incentives, for the use of torture under detention.

The situation was no better at the stage of trial. The antiterror law assigned jurisdiction over "terror" cases to the State Security Courts (DGM), special courts of law equipped with increased discretionary powers. For "terror" crimes, trials would generally proceed with remand, jump-starting imprisonment much before the trial's end was in sight (and, most frequently, trials went on for several years before they could be concluded). At the sentencing stage, Article 5 of the antiterror law allowed the discretionary increase of the sentences of crimes committed with a "terrorist intent" by half and prevented their commutation into lesser forms of punishment (such as fines). The conditional release of "terrorist" offenders was also tied to more stringent criteria: the earliest that those convicted of "terror" crimes could be discharged was upon the completion of three-fourths of their sentences, while this period was set at two-fifths of sentences for "ordinary" crimes.

While these stipulations of the antiterror law already determined two very distinct paths in the criminal justice system, another provision (Article 16) was that the sentences for "terror" crimes should be executed in "special" penal institutions in which convicts and detainees would be barred from having open visitation or communicating with other prisoners. This article thereby introduced the model of the high security prison as the proper site of punishment for "terrorists." Although there had been several attempts by various governments throughout the 1990s to open high security prisons in accordance with the antiterror law, these efforts had been suspended, having encountered serious prisoner resistance and public controversy. The threat of the full implementation of Article 16 by way of introducing cellular confinement either in new penal institutions or by the piecemeal renovation of existing prisons loomed large in the second half of the 1990s. This threat led to the escalation of organized resistance on part of political prisoners, who were the first constituency destined for cellular confinement. While the mass hunger strike in 1996 (which ended with 12 casualties) led to the temporary abandonment of the high security prison thanks to the reconciliatory moves of the government, the mass hunger strike launched in October 2000, this time with greater participation, precipitated a full-blown crisis for those at the helm of the state. The death fast struggle catapulted the prisons not only to public view but also to top priority on the government's agenda.

THE OFFICIAL DIAGNOSIS OF THE PRISONS PROBLEM

In the eyes of state officials, prisons were a continually bleeding, nonhealing sore. They were dysfunctional, ineffective, and embarrassing. Instead of being sites of discipline and order under the tight control of the state, they had become places of disobedience and disorder. Instead of venues for punishment, they had turned into the breeding ground of crime. Instead of rehabilitating criminals and transforming them into law-abiding citizens, they tended to produce more experienced and audacious criminals. Instead of curbing terrorism, they had become "command centers" for further terrorist activity.[73] They were, in short, institutions in dire need of reform. Mainstream newspapers covering the "prisons problem" had already carried the state's perspective to their headlines, which proclaimed: the "Confession of the State: Terrorists in Charge of Prisons."[74] Newspapers referred to prisons as "factories of crime."[75] Beyond this sensationalism, however, stood a real problem, acknowledged not only by the state but also by forces in civil society. At this point, institutions such as the Union of Bar Associations (Türkiye Barolar Birliği) and the Istanbul Bar had already been solemnly convening working groups, organizing conferences, and writing reports in order to delineate the problems in the criminal justice system, discuss possible solutions, and inform the public.[76]

For the state, prisons were simply disastrous for public relations. On the one hand, there was the notorious reputation of prisons inherited from the legacy of the military coup d'état, a reputation that reinforced Turkey's compromised human rights record and put the Turkish state in a difficult position vis-à-vis the West, especially the European Union. On the other hand, and what prevented Turkey from writing off this reputation as an artifact of the authoritarian past, was the recurrence of violent incidents behind prison walls, which frequently made the national news. Uprisings of political prisoners, internal settling of accounts by the mafia, and the security operations of the gendarmerie often resulted in high numbers of prisoner casualties and the scandalous discovery of vast amounts of weaponry, cell phones, and illicit drugs smuggled inside prisons. The incidents that leaked to the media raised many questions and occasioned much public criticism (both national and international) concerning the state's human rights abuses, lack of security in its prisons, and the disproportionate use of force by the security forces to impose order. These incidents put democratically elected governments into a much more difficult position than the military. They troubled national claims of having achieved civilianization and democratization in the postcoup era to the outside world, while, internally, they weakened popular faith in the state's ability to protect the lives entrusted to its control and increased government officials' own worries vis-à-vis their electoral constituencies about their ability to solve the thorny issues enveloping the criminal justice system.

These concerns were no doubt aggravated by the mass hunger strike of political prisoners launched in October 2000. The sheer numbers of prisoners who participated in the strike, coordinated across the country in forty prisons, and the militancy with which the prisoners were struggling constituted living proof of the severity and seriousness of the situation in the country's prisons. For the government in need of formulating an urgent response to the hunger strike, the current unrest in prisons was an alarming symptom of deeper problems that needed large-scale reform, reform that could not be carried out without a parliamentary discussion that generated a broad coalition of support across the political spectrum. Under these conditions, the Turkish Grand National Assembly gathered for a special session devoted to discussing the "prisons problem" on November 21, 2000. The debate in parliament revealed, however, that more than prison reform was at stake. The parliamentarians were quick to diagnose the current situation not simply as a crisis of prisons but rather as a "crisis of sovereignty." This was because the political prisoners' resistance was perceived as an outrageous challenge to the state from within those sites allegedly under its most intimate control.

At the special session of the parliament, Minister of Justice Hikmet Sami Türk presented the situation of prisons in austere terms, representing the general sentiment of the coalition government of three parties led by Prime Minister Bülent Ecevit: the social-democratic Democratic Left Party (Demokratik Sol Parti), center-right Motherland Party (Anavatan Partisi), and ultranationalist Nationalist Action Party. Minister Türk admitted that there were serious problems at every level of the penal system, even though a "concentrated effort was being made in order to create an environment that was respectful of human rights, befitting of modern states, [and] to establish order, discipline and security fully in prisons and detention houses."[77]

According to Minister Türk, the prison population was now higher than ever before in the history of the republic (see figure 2.1). At the time of his speech, there were 73,748 individuals in prison, exceeding the total capacity of prisons in use (designated for 72,575 individuals).

Overcrowding, Türk opined, resulted from the fact that the pace with which new prisons were being built was not keeping up with the growing numbers of prisoners: every month an additional 372 people were admitted to facilities that were already filled to capacity. Existing prisons were simply inadequate to house the growing prisoner population. Türk did not probe deeper into the reasons why the prisoner population might be growing at such a fast pace. Whether the higher prison population was a consequence of overall population growth, increasing crime rate, widening definitions of crime, more vigilant policing and law enforcement that brought greater numbers of offenders into the criminal justice system, increased numbers of trials with remand, or a host of possible other factors, was irrelevant for the government whose main concern was to frame the "prisons problem" as a technical problem (overcrowding) with a technical solution (new prisons) rather than a political problem (justice) that required social, economic, and cultural reform.

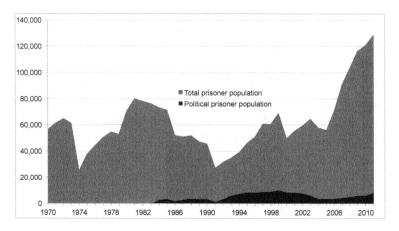

Figure 2.1   PRISONER POPULATION OVER TIME
Compiled from statistical data published by the Ministry of Justice. ABCTGM, "Statistics," http://www.cte.adalet.gov.tr/ (Last accessed December 1, 2012.)

But the swelled prison population was only the surface of the problem. The composition of the prison population was a complicating factor. The political prisoner population of Turkey corresponded to approximately 15 percent or one-seventh of the total prison population (see figure 2.2).[78] Around 70 percent of the political prisoner population comprised prisoners associated with the Kurdish struggle (numbering around sixty-five hundred to seven thousand), another 20 percent comprised prisoners with extraparliamentary leftist affiliations (numbering around fifteen hundred to two thousand), while the rest were imprisoned for cases related to radical Islamist organizations and other "terror" crimes.[79] The political prisoner population had quadrupled since the early 1990s, and this steady increase corresponded to the promulgation of the antiterror law (see figure 2.3).

The third crucial issue was critical security failures. Originally built outside cities, most prisons had been encircled by residential neighborhoods as urban settlements spread outward. These locations facilitated the escape of prisoners as well as the smuggling of illegal substances and weapons into the prisons. Security failures were also connected to the high rate of prisoners imprisoned for "terror" crimes and the increased activities of criminal gangs, leading to escapes and casualties due to violence among prisoners or violence by state

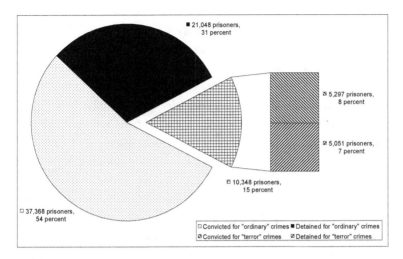

Figure 2.2   INTERNAL DISTRIBUTION OF THE PRISON POPULATION (AS OF 1999)
Compiled from statistical data published by the Ministry of Justice. ABCTGM, "Statistics," http://www.cte.adalet.gov.tr/ (Last accessed December 1, 2012.)

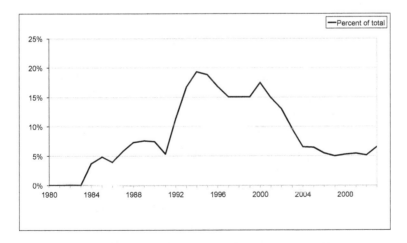

Figure 2.3   PRISONER POPULATION HELD FOR "TERROR" CRIMES OVER TIME (AS PERCENT
OF TOTAL PRISON POPULATION)
Compiled from statistical data published by the Ministry of Justice. See ABCTGM,
"Statistics," http://www.cte.adalet.gov.tr/ (Last accessed December 1, 2012.)

personnel. Only a year earlier in 1999, ten prisoners had died in the security operation conducted at Ulucanlar Prison, Ankara. Even the parliament's own Human Rights Investigation Commission voiced serious concerns that security forces might have used disproportionate force and resorted to torture during their intervention.[80] On the other hand, in the recent riot at Uşak Prison, instigated by the mafia leader Nuri Ergin and his followers (also known as the Nuriş gang), 6 prisoners were killed and thrown out the window, making national headlines. According to the figures provided by the General Directorate of Prisons and Detention Houses, another 16 prisoners had died because they were executed by fellow political prisoners after being tried in the mock tribunals operated by terrorist organizations themselves. In addition to these casualties, in the ten riots that occurred in 1995–2000, nearly 400 prisoners were seriously injured. In these violent incidents, 205 of the prison personnel were also injured and 9 were killed.[81]

Overall, in the last seven years, 51 prisoners had escaped, 27 prisoners had died in the security operations of the gendarmerie (see table 2.1), 26 prisoners had died because of internal clashes and conflicts, and 12 prisoners had died in the 1996 death fast, adding up to some 116 prisoner casualties. Adding the numbers of prisoners who were involved in conflicts, uprisings, escape attempts, and other infractions, and factoring in the general destitution of living conditions in the prisons, the country's prisons appeared to be forlorn institutions.

Having sketched out different facets of the "prisons problem," Minister Türk placed the blame on a combination of factors: deficient physical infrastructure, insufficient financial resources, inadequate and lenient legislation, and understaffing. The inadequacy of existing prisons was obvious enough. But the limited budget allotted to the Ministry of Justice slowed down the construction of new prisons, created delays in the transportation of prisoners to court hearings, and impaired the provision of adequate heating and food for prisoners.[82] The legislation concerning the administration of penal institutions was outdated and haphazardly supplemented by decrees and statutes adopted at different times based on conjunctural needs.[83] Penal institutions were administered according to the Law on the Administration of Prisons and Detention Houses (Law No. 1721), dating from 1930, and the Law on the Execution of Punishments (Law No. 647), dating from 1965, and various other bylaws, statutes, and executive decrees (such as the Bylaw on the Administration of Penal Institutions and Detention Houses and the Execution of Punishments).[84] Recent legislation enabled prisoners to be conditionally released after completing two-fifths of their sentences, and the ceilings imposed on prison terms, Türk argued, made punishment too lenient and annulled any deterrence function. Furthermore, prison staff was largely uneducated and severely underpaid. Prisons were also understaffed in that only 25,122 of the 31,194 positions were filled (while 43,345 positions would have been necessary to administer existing prisons at full capacity). In other words, the prisons were run by only 60 percent of the personnel originally stipulated as required for their proper administration.

However, the root cause of the "prisons problem," according to the minister, was the *spatial* organization of the prisons. Prisons were laid out in dormitory-style wards. The size and capacity of wards varied, but they usually housed around thirty to one hundred individuals each. These crowded wards compromised security and order because they made it possible for some prisoners to control and dominate others. Türk argued that wards also allowed prisoners "to act collectively, to create damage in the buildings, to render those in charge ineffective, to succeed in actions such as having the doors left open, taking hostages, extracting tribute, preventing searches, digging tunnels and escaping, and instigating uprisings."[85] The minister claimed that terrorist organizations and gangs used wards to maintain "their group discipline in prisons and detention houses, and furthermore, [to sustain] their relations with the outside [world]," making prisons "ideological training grounds."[86] Prisons had thus been transformed into educational and organizational "headquarters" in which terrorist identities were reinforced, subversive ideologies were disseminated, and new plans to undermine the state were concocted.

Member of Parliament Beyhan Aslan, speaking on behalf of the Motherland Party in the coalition government, described the situation in even more apocalyptic terms:

> *Today, unfortunately, the prisons in which there are terrorists, mafia and gang members, are not under the sovereignty of the State of the Republic of Turkey....* Prisons are training camps that educate militants for the organization of terrorist offenders, [they are] the command headquarters for gang members and the mafia. There are kings in prisons. Aghas have sprung up in prisons. When the sovereignty of the state was compromised, terrorist offenders, mafia and gang members have

Table 2.1 MAJOR SECURITY OPERATIONS IN PRISONS (1995–2000)

DATE OF OPERATION	PRISON	CASUALTIES	NAME OF DECEASED PRISONERS
September 21, 1995	Buca, Izmir	3 prisoners dead, 40–56 wounded	Uğur Sarıaslan Yusuf Bağ Turan Kılınç
December 13–15, 1995	Ümraniye, Istanbul	36 prisoners wounded	
January 4, 1996	Ümraniye, Istanbul	4 prisoners dead, 36 prisoners wounded	Abdülmecit Seçkin Orhan Özen Rıza Boybaş Gültekin Beyhan
September 24, 1996	Diyarbakır	10 prisoners dead, 46 wounded	Erkan Hakan Perişan Hakkı Tekin Cemal Çam Ahmet Çelik Mehmet Namık Çakmak Rıdvan Bulut

Date	Location	Casualties	Names
September 26, 1999	Ulucanlar, Ankara	10 prisoners dead, 28 prisoners wounded	Edip Direkçi, Mehmet Kadri Gümüş, Mehmet Aslan, Kadri Demir, Halil Türker, Abuzer Çat, Nevzat Çiftçi, İsmet Kavaklıoğlu, Aziz Dönmez, Önder Gençaslan, Ümit Altıntaş, Zafer Kırbıyık, Mahir Emsalsiz, Habib Gül
January 25, 2000	Metris, Istanbul	13 prisoners wounded	
July 5, 2000	Burdur	61–70 prisoners wounded	

Compiled with data from TİHV, *İşkence Dosyası*; İHD, *Sessiz Çığlık*; and Demirci and Üçpınar, *İzmir Barosu İnsan Hakları Hukuku*.

become sovereign over prisons with violence, by intimidating the administration with threats, and sometimes, with bribes. The administration cannot carry out body counts, cannot enter wards; the administration is overawed and ousted. The detainees and convicts entrusted to the state are deprived of completing their sentences in peace. . . . We are openly and clearly pronouncing this: *the ward system has become bankrupt.*[87]

Even though the parties in the parliament pointed fingers at each other, especially at those who had previously been in power, for pursuing policies that had brought the country's prisons to the brink of ruin and not addressing the problems in a timely and effective manner, a surprising consensus in the way parliamentarians across party affiliations perceived the "prisons problem" soon emerged. What initially began as a general diagnosis of the situation in prisons and its causes quickly turned into a diagnosis of the lack of state sovereignty over prisons. From the perspective of those in parliament, the unruly "crowd" in the prisons threatened the *sovereignty* of the state and threatened it all the more dramatically the more crowded prisons got. The threat was such that those state officials at the point of contact with prisoners were simply "overawed and ousted" by the prisoners.[88]

As Member of Parliament Hayri Kozakçıoğlu, speaking in the name of the center-right True Path Party (DYP) in opposition (alongside the Islamist Virtue Party [Fazilet Partisi]), argued:

In Turkey, the person in prison has no security of life; the person in prison does not have the most important right, the right to live. We have not been able to provide this, the security of life. The person who enters the prison entrusts himself to the state. The person who enters the prison leaves his security to the state. Yes, but what happens when he leaves it to the state?! The authority of the government has negated the gravitas of the state. Now, can you imagine, what great anguish, what great pain must those individuals, whose relatives were killed in prison, have gone through, and they are still enduring this pain. Yes, how is Mr. Minister of Justice going to give an account of that person who has been killed inside [the prison] to the spouse, children, mother, father; what will he say? The person you entrusted to me, you entrusted to the state and to the government, I could not protect;

they were taken hostages, I could not go and save [them]; I could not even conduct a [security] operation; and what is more, I could not even approach those prisons where these incidents were taking place; is he going to say this?! If this is said, will this be an attitude that befits the state?! And how will the children of those who are deliberately tortured and killed in prison ever again trust the state, how will they view the state from now on, how will they trust the services of justice? Hence, in my opinion, this is the greatest negligence that has been committed. *The repute of the state has disappeared. The trust in the state has disappeared. The government has completely lost its authority and surrendered the prisons to these groups.*[89]

Lamenting the loss of state authority, Kozakçıoğlu's criticism of the government's failure to control prisons not only affirmed the definition of the "prisons problem" as a lack of sovereignty but also provided indications regarding the new directions the restoration of sovereignty should take. Important in the rhetorically powerful statement drawing attention to the horror with which these terrorist groups, which have "stopped state authority from entering prisons," must have come to be perceived by the Turkish public were two elements: the necessity of reinforcing the strong state tradition vis-à-vis its challengers while, at the same time, holding the state democratically accountable to its citizens. How was the state going to protect its people if it could not protect its prisoners from one another? How could it be sovereign over its territory if it could not exert sovereignty over its own prisons? How could it pretend to be democratic, if the people could no longer entrust their lives to the state?

If at the source of the strong state lay its ability to punish, at the source of democratic accountability lay its ability to secure the "right to live." When the two elements became contradictory goals, with attendant practices that came into conflict with one another, those at the helm of the state found themselves at a crossroads. Should the state rule by force, prioritizing its ability to control, dominate, extract, or should it govern gently, by protecting lives and caring for the welfare, rights, liberties of its citizens? Put differently, those electorally given the power to decide the future of the Turkish state found themselves at a crossroads between the assertion of authoritarian sovereignty and the implementation of liberal-democratic governmentality. It was obvious that the old techniques of naked domination, while utilized rampantly during the military "state of exception," were no longer legitimate in tandem with the fruition of the process of civilianization of the post-1980 regime and had, moreover, become more of a liability. On the other hand, the conditions of "gentle" government, respectful of fundamental rights, responsive to citizen demands, and yet with the necessary strength to ensure safety and order, inside the prisons as well as outside, were hardly in place when the state's very sovereignty over its prisons was at stake.

The parliamentary debate identified the spatial organization of prisons as the main culprit that exacerbated the negative effects of crowding, especially on the political prisoner population. The "prisons problem" therefore sprang from the explosive combination of the unruly activities of terrorist organizations, the mafia, and the gangs, which capitalized on the opportunities afforded by the spatial organization of the ward-based prisons and was exponentially compounded by the woefully neglected budgetary, educational, and infrastructural restraints and deficiencies. However, it was the ongoing hunger strike that vastly complicated the problem and transformed it into a *crisis* of state sovereignty, which necessitated not only prison reform but, through it, the restoration and refurbishment of sovereign power itself through its biopoliticization.

The hunger strike precipitated a crisis at several different registers. First, the hunger strike brought the conditions of prisons under the spotlight. It stirred public discussion and brought on criticism of the state, both for its inability to secure the lives of prisoners placed under its control and for the violations of human rights in prisons. The "crowd" congregating in places that should be under the state's tightest and most complete control attacked the very legitimacy of the state predicated not only on providing protection, security, and peaceful conditions for its citizens, inside and outside prisons, but also on caring for the well-being of its citizens, defined in terms of fundamental rights such as the right to life and bodily integrity and the right to be protected from arbitrary violence coming from other citizens as well as the security apparatus of the state. It proved that the state could not guarantee the safety and well-being of prisoners allegedly under its own control and ensconced within its own institutions. It therefore presented an important threat to the strong state tradition and the Turkish state's self-representation as the "benevolent father" of its citizens that, paternally responsible for their safety and care, would ensure their unity, independence, and security, both as a nation and individually.

Second, the hunger strike demonstrated that the sovereignty of the state in prisons had been lost over to radical organizations affiliated with terrorism and criminal gangs. Not only did the state fail to provide security by preventing criminal activity outside the prisons, it also failed to curb criminal activity inside the prisons. Having practically taken over the administration of prisons, political prisoners and their mafia counterparts had literally evicted the state from the wards and declared their own sovereignty in those spaces. Illegal organizations had become influential over the broader prisoner population and, in case of political prisoners, achieved a level of coordinated action that enabled them to launch hundreds of individuals on hunger strike across the country. In the eyes of those in charge of the state, the scale and synchronization of the protests only served to confirm that these organizations simply flourished in the current prison conditions. The "internal" threats of the regime had literally become internal, emerging, as they were, from the most intimate spaces of state control.

But this was not all. What really transformed the challenge of the hunger strike into a crisis of sovereignty was the ideological threat presented by the unruly "crowd" in the prisons. It would be wrong to attribute the ideological threat simply to "terrorism," generally, or even to the radical leftism and revolutionary aspirations of these political prisoners, more specifically. The prisoners were certainly ready to defend their political convictions and even prepared to engage in acts of violence that challenged the "monopoly of the legitimate use of physical force within a given territory" vested in the state, according to Weber's famous definition.[90] By participating in acts of violence, prisoners had already challenged the state's role of being the exclusive agent that can use force with the legitimacy of law. However, by engaging in self-destructive violence, practically usurping the power of life and death normally reserved for the state, the prisoners were no longer simply opposing the state's monopoly over violence. Unlike conventional acts of violent resistance (such as clashes with the security forces, occupations, even hostage scenarios), the *necropolitical* nature of the current resistance challenged, along with the *monopoly* of violence, what I will call the state's *monopsony* of sacrifice.

Monopsony, derived from Ancient Greek *monos* (single) and *opsonia* (purchase), refers to a situation that is the inverse of a monopoly, derived from *monos* (single) and *polein* (to sell). Whereas monopoly refers to a situation where there is one supplier or provider of a product or a service that has no substitute, monopsony refers to the opposite situation in which there is only one buyer or receiver.[91] Building on Weber, we can say that the modern state is not only the sole provider of legitimate force; it is also the sole receiver of political self-sacrifice. However, necropolitical resistance denies the state's status as the sole, legitimate locus for the political demand for life and as its exclusive recipient. In the mass hunger strike of political prisoners, the prisoners were prepared, committed, and determined to sacrifice their lives in their struggle against the state, in the name of a nascent "revolutionary community," represented immediately by their respective (outlawed) political parties and, more symbolically, by the "peoples of Turkey" in whose name they were struggling. As we shall see in the following chapters, these prisoners also utilized a discourse of self-sacrifice and a political spiritualism that befitted and nourished their necropolitical resistance. The alternative order in whose name these prisoners were ready to give up their lives constituted an indictment of the Turkish state as illegitimate, while it also enabled the "terrorist" organizations able to command such politically motivated self-sacrifice to emerge as claimants of an alternative sovereignty. The attack on the state's monopsony of sacrifice was also an ideological threat to the foundations of its authority.

The "prisons problem," which quickly became a euphemism for the weaponization of life, therefore reflected a deep anxiety on part of the government and parliamentary opposition alike. The officials believed that the state was not *sovereign* in its own prisons. They were concerned that the loss of state power translated into the defilement of the legitimate foundations of state authority by the very internal enemies identified by the Kemalist regime as threats to its unity. The hunger strike emerging from the belly of the state had turned into a caustic crisis of sovereignty, which necessitated measures that would not simply restore sovereignty in its old form but, rather, reconfigure it in the way most appropriate to the "level of contemporary civilizations" the country had aspired to achieve since its republican founding. The latter goal required a new way of governing commensurate with the country's process of democratization while not compromising the power to rule. The modernization of prisons would be, at one and the same time, the modernization of the state's sovereign power.

Chapter 3
The Biosovereign Assemblage and Its Tactics

Once the "prisons problem" was formulated as a crisis of state sovereignty, the solution dictated itself. The crisis could only be resolved if the visibly tarnished sovereignty of the state could be reestablished. However, it was also clear that the reconstitution of the state's supreme power over prisons could not simply reinstate traditional methods and practices, since they were what precipitated the current crisis in the first place. The state should gain back its control over the prisons, but, meanwhile, the prisons should be reconfigured to enable the reconfiguration of sovereignty itself. As prisons became a synecdoche for the state, their transformation would also become a synecdoche for the transformation of sovereign power.

The special parliamentary session on the nature and gravity of the "prisons problem," which became a euphemism for the threat posed by the hunger strike, did not only transpose it to a general register by claiming it to be a problem of sovereignty. It also pinpointed its root cause in technical, and therefore practically alterable, terms concerning the spatial organization of prisons. Since the ward system had rendered prisons ungovernable, it was argued, the reestablishment of control over the unruly "crowd" in prisons must have as its core strategy the changing of their spatial order, which amplified the negative effects of crowding and turned prisons into sites of political rebellion. The expedient and necessary solution, then, was the substitution of wards by cells, thereby replacing collective confinement by solitary confinement. This simple spatial, technical modification at the ground level would then enable the state to build its wounded sovereignty bottom-up in a new configuration.

If high security prisons, based on cellular confinement, thus appeared as a concrete and tangible cure for the crisis of sovereignty, this was because, as "special" penal institutions, they would not only guard against security failures but also provide effective punishment, not only achieve intimate, individualized control over prisoners but also enable the state to attend to their well-being and rehabilitation. Through high security prisons, the state would thereby both renew the conditions of political rule and secure the conditions of gentle, effective, and efficient government. The ability of the state to punish effectively and protect the "right to live" could thus intersect in the new penal regime and constitute the basis for governing society at large.

Once a general consensus was established in parliament on the necessity of implementing a disciplinary penal regime, the impending question became one of tactics. What were the best methods by which the implementation of high security prisons could be made to serve the following strategic objectives? (1) The restoration of sovereignty over the prisons and the neutralization of radical opposition; (2) the reparation of the authority of the state harmed by the ideological challenge of necropolitical resistance; and (3) the establishment of popular confidence in the state's commitment to the struggle against terrorism without disrespecting democratic sensibilities, which entailed the expectation that the state should respect fundamental rights, protect the lives entrusted to its institutions, provide for their well-being, physical and mental health, and treat them humanely. In sum, the question now was how to implement biopolitical government and strengthen sovereignty while winning over the bodies and minds of its citizens, insurgent or not. However, despite the fact that initially there were two tendencies in policy circles regarding what tactics to use, one dovish and the other hawkish, the oscillation between them was soon resolved in favor of the latter.

In keeping with its strategic goals, the state deployed a three-pronged approach: making law, making war, and making peace. It made *law*, selectively aiming at a particular group of offenders considered to be its "internal enemies," those who threatened the state's security interests, and singled them out as the objects of the new penal regime. It made *war*, invading its own prisons, capturing its own prisoners, and transferring them to the new, high security prisons where a disciplinary penal regime would be materially solidified. It continued its warfare, in individualized form, by "saving" the lives of hunger strikers, resuscitating them by nonconsensual medical interventions. And finally, it made *peace*, giving prisoners a second lease on life through the granting of selective pardons.

Paradoxically, it was the traditional markers of sovereign power that were deployed in putting into place a disciplinary penal regime that would become the building block of biopolitical government. However, in the process, these classical instruments of sovereign power were also reconfigured in keeping with the transitional aspirations of the Turkish state toward a more rational, efficient, effective, modern, and "civilized" mode of government, concerned with the well-being of its population, individually and at large. The sovereign instruments actively deployed were penetrated by different bodies of specialized knowledge, customized management, and administrative mechanisms that were geared toward the promotion of security, health, and productivity. Meanwhile, new nodes of expertise that concerned itself with studying and administering different aspects of the prison population—prosecutors, psychiatrists, physicians, and prison staff—as instruments of biopolitical government became vested with the exercise of sovereign power at the local level, deciding on the lives of political prisoners. The result was the emergence of a *biosovereign assemblage*, which combined, in a novel way, the power *of* life and death with an expanding power *over* life. This chapter examines how the F-type prisons as the new model of securitized government came to be the solution to the crisis of sovereignty and analyzes the discursive and practical tactics through which they were justified and put into place.

HIGH SECURITY PRISONS

According to state officials and parliamentarians, the ward system had rendered prisons entirely dysfunctional. It enabled the continuation of criminal activity within prisons, subjected individual prisoners to psychological and social pressures, thereby perpetuating the survival of illegal organizations, and occasioned collective struggles through which prisoners defied the state's power and authority. What prisoners, especially political prisoners, exalted as their communal life in prisons, was, to state officials, evidence that illegal organizations prevented individuals from exercising their free will and thwarted the state's efforts of rehabilitation.

In order to overcome the threat to sovereignty posed from within prison wards, it was imperative to get rid of prison wards. This meant transforming the spatial ordering of prisons. The solution to the "prisons problem," according to officials, depended on the replacement of the prevalent method of *collective confinement* in large wards by *solitary confinement* in cells. Fortunately, the Turkish state did not have to reinvent the wheel. In installing what Foucault famously described as a *disciplinary* penal regime, those at the helm of the state could look to the West. They could draw inspiration from supermax prisons in the United States and their European equivalents. Despite the various controversies surrounding these institutions, their prevalence in Western countries reinforced their status as models that could be emulated.[1] In the view of state officials, exemplary prisons such as the H-blocks in Northern Ireland, the Stammheim in Germany, Marion (Illinois), Pelican Bay (California), Red Onion State Prison (Virginia), and Florence ADX (Colorado) in the United States combined the highest levels of security with "humane" conditions of imprisonment that complied with human rights. The institutional design and internal administration of these prisons appeared to provide the perfect conditions for controlling, disciplining, training, educating, and resocializing prisoners, thereby fulfilling the rehabilitative function of imprisonment as well as its punitive function. Moreover, these institutions presented the possibility of exerting individualized control over prisoners. Prisoners could be divided and grouped according to criteria provided by modern behavioral and medical sciences, each group of prisoners could then be targeted with specific "treatments" customized according to their personalities, criminal tendencies, prior offenses, socio-economic background, and behavior in prison. Through the lure of rewards and incentives (such as early discharge and quotidian privileges) and fear of additional punishment (such as deprivation of customary rights while in prison), individuals could be conditioned to change their ways and thereby remolded into law-abiding citizens.

The F-type prison project, which sought to implement the supermaximum security prisons of the United States and Western Europe in the Turkish context, entailed the construction of high security prisons based on cells (for up to three prisoners) and the remodeling of wards in existing medium security prisons known as E-type and special type prisons into similar units by installing internal divider walls (bringing each ward to a size that would only house six to ten prisoners). In addition to the partitioning of space in order to achieve individualized or small group confinement, the F-type prisons were designed to increase maximum visibility. Fully equipped with camera surveillance in each unit, these prisons were *panoptic* in structural design and operational technologies. F-type prisons contained two kinds of units: cells for three prisoners and solitary cells.[2] The former units had two floors, each of which was twenty-five square meters. The lower level had a shower, toilet, sink, and table, and the upper level was designated as the sleeping area with beds and lockers. Each unit had access to an enclosed yard area of fifty square meters. Single-prisoner units, on the other hand, were ten square meters with similar furnishing. Two or three of the single-prisoner units had access to the same yard area, but doors could only be opened from the outside such that the prisoners could be let out to the yard area without contact with others in adjacent cells.[3] The yard area was sealed with walls five meters tall. These prisons were designed to include vocational workshops, an infirmary, laundry, library, kitchen, visitation rooms, and gym facilities.

The implementation of high security prisons was a project in planning over the last decade. Its legal basis had been prepared through the antiterror law of 1991, with Article 16. Although this article had not yet been fully implemented, various governments had made agreements with contracting firms for the construction of high security prisons and for the internal restructuring of existing ones. Accordingly, the internal restructuring of 97 E-type and special type prisons had already begun in 1996, but only four of them (Bingöl E-type, Isparta E-type, Eskişehir Special Type, and Kartal Special Type) were fully completed and 53 others were under construction by November 2000.[4] An additional eleven F-type and two other "room-type" prisons were contracted in 1999 in Ankara, Izmir, Edirne, Bolu, Kocaeli, Tekirdağ, and Adana. Each prison was designed with 103 three-prisoner units and 59 one-prisoner units, housing up to 368 prisoners. In November 2000, six of these prisons were near completion. Two D-type prisons (a slightly different and larger version of the "room-type" prison) in Denizli and Diyarbakır were also on their way, with a capacity to house 688 and 744 prisoners respectively.

The General Directorate of Prisons and Detention Houses praised the F-type prisons, emphasizing their stark contrast to traditional ones. In a document published on the directorate's official Web site to introduce these prisons and present justifications as to why they were deemed necessary, it was maintained that the F-type prisons would

> establish order, discipline, and security in penal institutions, to ensure that the convicted and detained inmates get the maximum benefit from modern treatment methods, to minimize the failures of discipline and order created by the crowded ward system, to prevent the feelings of hostility and negative psychological effects of crowded life on convicts and detainees, to prevent the spread of contagious diseases or to correct the negative conditions of hygiene that might result from crowding, to prevent security weaknesses, to provide the convicts and detainees with opportunities of social, cultural, and sports activities and more private living spaces.[5]

It was understandable that the directorate would repeatedly emphasize how these prisons would aid the establishment of order and discipline and serve the state's security concerns. What was more interesting was the directorate's argument that the high security prisons were also in the interests of prisoners. These prisons would not only guarantee their security but also provide them with better, healthier conditions, both physically and psychologically, as well as greater opportunities for self-betterment. These were "civilized" spaces of confinement that met modern standards of hygiene, comfort, and privacy and that facilitated rehabilitation through modern "treatment methods." The new prisons would eliminate the negative effects of the "crowd," in terms of both its unruliness and the pressures it put on each individual's living conditions, psychology, and behavior. Each prisoner would have a private "room" that would liberate him/her from those communal pressures that had previously encouraged crime and inhibited rehabilitation. Officials insistently rejected any implication that these "rooms" were "cells," associated with solitary confinement and arbitrary violence in the public imagination.[6] The privacy of personal "rooms" would not only ensure a cleaner, healthier environment but also allay the "hostility" toward the state fostered by collective life in prison. Individuals could complete their sentences in peace while, at the same time, developing their vocational skills, working in ateliers, and enjoying cultural and sports activities.

The directorate also recurrently iterated that the F-types were in complete conformity with, if not surpassing, the prison standards recommended by the United Nations and the European Council. They specially cited and emphasized the F-types' convergence with the recommendations of the European Council's Committee for the Prevention of Torture and Inhuman or Degrading Treatment or Punishment (CPT).[7] In fact, as Penny Green has persuasively argued, the evolution of high security prisons was also driven by pressure from Europe, in line with the recommendations of the CPT to move toward "smaller living units," on grounds that ward-based prisons involved a "lack of privacy," the "risk of intimidation and violence," as well as the "maintainance of the cohesion of criminal organizations," echoing almost verbatim the justifications provided by the directorate in support of high security prisons.[8] The new prisons, officials assured, were not violating human rights; they were protecting them. They were in line with the international human rights regime and thus approved by the "modern" Western world. The F-type prison project, the directorate argued, would be beneficial to all parties involved: to the state, in terms of security and international recognition; to the prisoners, in terms of well-being and rehabilitative treatment; to the public, in terms of good conscience.

The discourse of the directorate, reflecting the official view on high security prisons, was symptomatic of the objectives intended with the new penal regime. If the most immediate purpose was to reassert state control over prisons, based on disbanding the collective life and putting an end to the subversive actions of political prisoners in the wards, its longer-term goal of producing proper citizens, by means of education, training, and rehabilitation, was also consistent with the authoritarian reformism and modernist social engineering of the Kemalist state tradition. Kemalism had been used both to eliminate "internal threats" by criminalization and punishment and to modernize, to bring a strong and unified Turkey to the "level of contemporary civilizations." These aims were closely connected: the unity of the nation-state hinged on the struggle against divisive social forces in order to make way for modernization. The difference of the current interest in the new penal regime from the customary reflexes of the Kemalist state tradition was simply that the control of dissent should no longer be achieved via a traditional, predominantly violent, and arbitrary exercise of supreme power in punishment, but rather a more "modern," disciplinary, rehabilitative, hygienic, technologized, and streamlined mode of individualized imprisonment, with the ability of productively shaping individual offenders into remorseful, docile, and tame citizens. This meant less a regime more tolerant of radical dissent than a regime whose statecraft adapted to present-day requirements and sensibilities and whose governmental technologies were in compliance with both democratic accountability and international standards of human rights. The F-type prisons should therefore make the country's penal apparatus worthy of Turkey's place among Western, civilized countries of the world. After all, high security prisons were a product of Western civilization.

DEMOCRACY AGAINST TERRORISM

When the parliament convened for a special session on the "prisons problem," political prisoners had been on hunger strike for a month. The hunger strike carried a particular urgency. Every day brought the hunger strikers closer to death, so a timely and effective response was necessary.

While a general consensus was reached in parliament on the diagnosis of the "prisons problem" as a crisis of sovereignty, whose solution would be the implementation of high security prisons, there was no clear agreement on the tactical choices that should be pursued in the short term. In fact, there were two main tendencies, corresponding to different courses of action.[9] Schematically put, one tendency was dovish, the other was hawkish. According to the former tendency, the government should treat political prisoners as no different from other prisoners—as "ordinary" criminals. Viewing them as convicts and detainees, with grievances arising from prison conditions, the government should, directly or via intermediaries, negotiate with them and try to resolve the situation before anyone died. This course of action meant folding prisoner demands within a framework of democratic contestation, rather than viewing their opposition as a threat to state sovereignty. Following this route certainly did not imply that the government should meet all the demands of the prisoners, but it did implicate the government in being responsive to them, respecting their rights as citizens and demands as legitimate grievances.

While this accommodating perspective would allow the government more space to maneuver politically, it also limited the tactics it could use against the prisoners with impunity.

According to the hawkish tendency, the government should not negotiate with "terrorists." These prisoners were critical threats to national security and their demands were nothing resembling grievances over prison conditions (as we shall see in detail in the next chapter, the demands of the prisoners included the closing down of the F-type prisons, abolition of state security courts and the antiterror law, among other things). By displaying their willingness and determination to sacrifice their lives in allegiance to the directives of illegal terrorist organizations, these prisoners showed themselves to be "enemies of the state" who, therefore, had to be carefully isolated from one another and the rest of the prisoner population and irreversibly crushed. Such disciplined and dedicated mass participation in the hunger strike demonstrated what a formidable, organized force these terrorist organizations had become (thanks to the ward system). Capable of ordering individuals to embrace a painful, prolonged, and self-induced death, the illegal parties behind these prisoners seemed to command greater loyalty, obedience, and commitment than the state had ever enjoyed over its own soldiers. One of the top decision makers in government argued: *"While the state could command armies to fight and die in the name of the nation, it certainly could not order them to starve themselves to death."*[10]

In this light, the utilization of a language of democracy and human rights by these prisoners should be understood as a manipulative tactic that sought to confuse the public as to their real intentions: to disrupt, violently, the constitutional order, and to establish their own sovereignty under the guise of a class dictatorship. In parliament the representatives of the nation already admitted that the state had lost its sovereignty over prisons to these groups. In this light, negotiating with these prisoners would not merely be construed as a democratic concession but would further risk granting them recognition as a competing locus of power, a claimant for the support, loyalty, and sacrifice of the Turkish people with equivalent legitimacy. The proponents of this tendency argued for the necessity to display a vigilant attitude toward these prisoners, refrain from any negotiations, and demonstrate the might of the state in an exemplary fashion. The state should not give in to their blackmail.

The coalition government reflected both tendencies and initially oscillated between them. In a press statement, Prime Minister Ecevit reiterated the parliamentary consensus on the necessity of high security prisons. Wards transformed prisons into *"centers of action of terrorists and the mafia,"* maintained Ecevit, "similarly, in most of the prisons, there is neither *security of life,* nor *State authority* any longer."[11] In contrast, the high security prisons were hygienic and modern; they contained "rooms," not cells; and they enabled a "healthy" life: "convicts will be able to stay in one-two-three-[person] *rooms* [that are] healthy in every way. They will be able to come together in activities such as sports and library [*sic*]. The structuring and arrangements of the most civilized and democratic countries will be valid in our country, too."[12]

In contrast to the "civilized" and, doubtless, *civilizing* project of the high security prisons, emulated from the arrangements of the "most civilized and democratic countries," stood the "inhumane" leaders of the hunger strikers: "some *terrorists* in prisons are trying to prevent the transition to the F-type, by dragging the *youth* that they have taken under their influence into a death fast," Ecevit contended. "For that reason, almost 250 young individuals have come to the brink of death. This *inhuman action* must be put to an end."[13] Referring to prisoners as citizens "gone astray" and "terrorists," on the one hand, and as "youth" who have been "dragged" into the death fast under the influence of "terrorist" leaders, on the other, Ecevit encapsulated the government's wavering attitude toward those on the hunger strike in one breath. This discourse imputed a certain naïveté to the rank-and-file militants in the hunger strike, whose youthful militancy gravitated against their better sense, allowing them to be pressured ("dragged") into this (obviously) irrational path of self-destruction, whereas it recognized in their leaders the real "terrorist" threat. At once criminalizing and patronizing, demonizing and ready to forgive (if selectively), the state emphasized its role as the protector of life and embodiment of humanity against the "inhumane" protest of the prisoners, a role that would become central in the reconfiguration of its sovereignty.

At the same time, the oscillation could be observed further in that even while expressing the state's determination to put an end to the traditional ward system, Ecevit accepted an offer by an informal committee, comprised mainly of renowned public intellectuals, writers, and journalists, volunteering to act as an intermediary between the government and the prisoners.[14] The members of this committee, dubbed the committee of intellectuals, offered to talk to the prisoners in Sağmalcılar Prison (Bayrampaşa, Istanbul), where the selected representatives of political prisoners were located.[15] Prime Minister Ecevit referred to the task undertaken by this commission as a "mission of humanity" against the hunger strike as an "inhumane" method of political action.[16] The meetings held by the parliament's official Human Rights Commission at the same prison complemented the efforts of the informal committee of intellectuals at arbitration.[17]

At the talks in Sağmalcılar Prison, the committee of intellectuals agreed with prisoner concerns regarding how the ongoing arbitrary violence in prisons might be aggravated if prisoners would be locked into solitary cells. The committee concurred with the prisoners' assessment that the move toward cellular confinement was irreversible. The negotiations were thus steered in the direction of finding an intermediate solution between the traditional wards and the solitary cells of the high security prisons, even though the prime minister, who was not completely unfamiliar with the reality of Turkish prisons (having been imprisoned himself in the 1980 military coup), insisted that the new prisons were not based on cells but "rooms." The discussions with the committee focused on how the units in newly built F-type prisons could be redesigned to house a larger number of prisoners in each unit through minor architectural adjustments (e.g., the walls and doors in between adjacent three-person cells could be taken down to create larger units). The situation and content of these negotiations were regularly reported to the minister of justice and thus conducted within his knowledge. The talks reached an optimistic peak when, also due to increased public pressure by street demonstrations and the vocal opposition by human rights organizations, trade union confederations, and prominent occupational organizations, such as the Turkish Medical Association (TTB), Architects' and Engineers' Chambers Assocation of Turkey (TMMOB), and bar associations, the minister of justice announced a reprieve: the F-type prisons would not be put into use until a "public consensus" around them was created, involving the approval of civil society associations and the public at large.

However, despite growing prisoner expectations regarding a settlement, the government alluded to the possibility of some architectural and legal adjustments, but eschewed commitment to an agreement on remodeling high security prisons and specifying how many prisoners would be allowed to congregate in their new form. In vague pronouncements the prime minister indicated the desirability of a "public consensus" generated in an "environment of dialogue"[18] and repeated that architectural adjustments in the high security prisons would be "considered" based on the recommendations of civil society organizations. However, he also referred to public debate as if it were simply a means of generating consent to the government's original plan of introducing the F-types: debate would mainly be a means of persuading the broader public to the government's position (so that "preparations could be made" and "the realities [regarding the F-type prisons] can be better understood").[19] While the gesture of reprieve sounded like an agreement was on the horizon, nothing specific was put on the table. In response to the mixed messages coming from the government, a double-talk that the prisoners interpreted as insincere and manipulative, the prisoners told the committee that they would not quit the strike.

Meanwhile, events taking place outside the prisons caused the situation to escalate even further. On November 22, a militant was killed while conducting an armed attack upon a police station in Dudullu, Istanbul.[20] On December 9, a militant on hunger strike in front of the Municipal Palace of Rotterdam, along with twelve others in a Netherlands solidarity action with the prisoners in Turkey, was stabbed to death.[21] That same day several militants putting up flyers on the walls in support of the death fast were gunned down by the police in Istanbul, leaving one dead and two wounded.[22] The dose of violence in the interventions of the riot police was also visibly increasing, with more protestors wounded and detained in demonstrations outside the prison walls. On December 10, eight other outlawed leftist parties, which had withheld participation in the death fast struggle until then, announced that they also began a hunger strike of indefinite duration.[23] The escalation crested when, on December 11, an armed attack was conducted upon a police bus in Gaziosmanpaşa, Istanbul, resulting in the death of two policemen (Ali Acur and Tahir Toka) and the wounding of thirteen others. The responsibility for this attack was assumed by TKP(ML)–TİKKO, one of the three organizations that had initiated the death fast.[24] In the message TKP(ML) issued, the attack was cited as proof of the determination of the death fast struggle and justified as retribution for the deaths of Cafer Dereli and Özkan Tekin, the two militants who had been killed by then.

In the next two days the police force took to the streets.[25] In an illegal demonstration, unprecedented in the history of the republic, over two thousand members of the riot police (Çevik Kuvvet) marched in protest against poor weapons, low pay, and the restrictive laws on the use of weaponry that allegedly tied their hands against "terrorist attacks."[26] The December 12 demonstration in Istanbul spread to other big urban centers, including Izmir, Adana, Mersin, Gaziantep, and Antalya.

In a press conference on December 11, 2000, Prime Minister Ecevit warned that the hunger strike had gone over fifty days. Approaching the threshold of sustainability, he resorted to a discourse of life against the deadly actions of the prisoners, emphasizing the sanctity of human life: "This is a very upsetting event. *The human is a being whose life is very valuable. People have the right to take the life neither of others, nor of their own.*"[27] Ecevit pleaded with the families to convince the prisoners to quit the hunger strike: "I call out primarily to the mothers and fathers of these youth: Please do not give an opportunity to your children to relinquish themselves. This death fast should come to an end at once. I await the necessary contributions by the families regarding this."[28] Repeating the minister of justice's declaration that transfers to F-type prisons would be indefinitely postponed, he also warned that the state would not accept extortion by the prisoners: "Those who prepare and orchestrate these actions would like to make certain demands upon the state. It is not possible to accept this."[29] What was at stake was not simply territorial control over prisons but control over the "value" and use of human life: it was the illegal organizations who were squandering the lives of individuals whereas the state wanted to protect them; the prisoners were "relinquishing" their lives in their "inhumane" action—lives that belonged to the state. The state could not accept alternative claimants to its sovereignty, nor could it tolerate a challenge to its *monopsony* of sacrifice.

It is impossible to know exactly what happened behind closed doors between the dovish and hawkish factions in the government and the state bureaucracy during those few days. It is also difficult to ascertain whether the government had genuinely intended to come to an agreement with the prisoners on hunger strike or whether the talks had been a way of keeping up the appearances of democratic accountability while carrying out extensive preparations for the repressive security operation that would shortly follow. However, it is possible to pinpoint, with relative certainty, that Prime Minister Ecevit's speeches to the press beginning on December 11 signaled the end of the government's oscillation between the conciliatory and noncompromising tendencies and its resolution in favor of the latter. Within a few days of the negotiations, the government had already lost patience with the prisoners, increasingly gravitating toward treating them as "terrorists" and "enemies of the state."

Meanwhile, the negotiations between the intellectuals' committee and prisoner representatives had culminated in a possible agreement around the number of eighteen to twenty prisoners per unit (in place of the one to three prisoners per unit originally stipulated in the F-type prison project and the thirty to one hundred prisoners per ward currently held in the existing prisons).[30] In place of three-person cells, the two plausible formulae agreeable to the prisoners were nine plus nine and twelve plus six, implying that smaller wards would be created in F-type prisons by connecting six, nine, or twelve different cells.[31] In a press statement on behalf of the negotiation committee, Member of Parliament Mehmet Bekaroğlu expressed his expectation that the matter would be resolved shortly, claiming that a concrete solution was in the making.[32]

However, on December 14, the minister of justice rejected this agreement, maintaining that the prisoners' proposal for units that would house eighteen to twenty prisoners was "no different from the continuation of the ward system" and, hence, unacceptable. He also foreclosed the possibility of further negotiations.[33] The committee members announced that the talks had come to a halt.[34] On the same day, Prime Minister Ecevit indicated, even more forcefully, the shift of mood against the prisoners:

> Our Government has done everything possible to end the death
> fasts in prison without any casualties. Members of parliament, civil
> society organizations, writers, and artists have also made great efforts
> on this issue. All kinds of worries about F type prisons have been
> overcome. In spite of this, those who organize and uphold the death
> fast are continuing to insist on demands that no state could accept. In
> this situation, if there are some deaths, the responsibility will lie with
> those who have pushed them to death.[35]

Criticizing the public for paying too much attention to what was going on in the prisons, Ecevit blamed the media for deepening the crisis by providing undue visibility and publicity to the cause of the prisoners. This declaration foreshadowed the censorship that was imposed later the same day when a ruling of the state security court set a precedent for charging and imprisoning reporters, who continued their favorable coverage of the hunger strike, for "aiding and abetting terrorism."[36] News related to prisons would henceforth be monitored by the Higher Board of Radio and Television (RTÜK). The prime minister's gesture signaled the end of public debate (days after highlighting its necessity and desirability). Soon after, the committee of intellectuals resigned from its "mission of humanity," declaring that there was nothing left for it to do.

In this brief aperture of a few weeks, the government was straddled between a reconciling tendency that exemplified a desire to solve the crisis within democracy, through the use of the negotiation committee, the reprieve gesture, and calling upon a wider public discussion of F-type prisons, however limited, and a hawkish tendency that insisted upon a hard line on the high security prisons and refused committing to any concrete concessions, forcefully suppressing street protests, calling for censorship, and viewing prisoner demands as "extortions." The oscillation was so evident that the prime minister could, in one and the same speech, express both tendencies. Discursively, this oscillation was manifest in referring to individuals on hunger strike as "youth," as "children" who had been led astray, on the one hand, and to those who "prepare and orchestrate," "organize and uphold" the hunger strike as leaders of "terrorist organizations" who "pushed [the youth] to death," on the other. Compassion and tolerance were possible toward the former (and only then as a "mission of humanity"), but vigilance and rejection were due the latter. It is important to note, however, that despite this wavering between the democratic tactics of negotiation, reconciliation, public discussion, and consensus building, and the authoritarian tactics of the struggle against terrorism, the diagnosis of the crisis and the overarching strategy to solve it had already been set up on the register of sovereignty under the leadership of the same government. In this sense the oscillation and disagreements within the official sphere should be interpreted against the background of a fundamental consensus, not as irreconcilable tendencies that endangered the unity of state policy, but, rather, as competing alternatives whose differences would soon become redundant.

THE BIOSOVEREIGN ASSEMBLAGE

At this critical juncture the escalation of conflict on the streets gave ammunition to the interpretation of the perpetrators of the death fast as "enemies of the state" and the hawkish tendency found greater resonance in policy circles. In keeping with the consensus in the parliament regarding the "prisons problem" as a crisis of sovereignty, the government's interpretation of the recent events as further threats to the sovereignty of the state by illegal organizations, now resorting to violence on the streets and attacking the security forces, propelled the state further on the path of a comprehensive and aggressive set of practices to solve the crisis once and for all. In order to implement high security prisons while reestablishing its sovereignty, the state deployed traditional instruments of sovereign power. In a three-pronged program it made law, war, and peace so as to put into operation innovative techniques of biopolitical government.

However, in resorting to classical tactics of sovereign power, the state fertilized them with disciplinary and biopolitical tactics as well. Neither the law, nor the war, nor the peace was exactly conventional. While pursuing these tactics, the state systematically relied on the biopolitical alterization of populations, their partitioning and hierarchization, their selective targeting and specialized management, as well as the deployment of psychiatric, criminal, and, most important, medical knowledge in order to control the life and death of bodies that were the conduits of lives forged into weapons against the state itself. At the same time, the state enveloped its use of traditionally sovereign instruments in a biopolitical discourse based on the value of human rights, the sanctity of human life, and the necessity of guaranteeing its security. While the state employed both real and symbolic violence in the name of protecting its sovereignty and security interests, these tactics were justified as protective measures for the betterment of human rights, the sacredness of human life, and the well-being of all. The "humanitarian" nature of these tactics was also contrasted with the "inhumane" nature of necropolitical resistance. The state utilized juridical means in tandem with violent, disciplinary, and ideological mechanisms, buttressing each one further to its advantage with the help of the others. Meanwhile, sovereign tactics also modified the exercise of disciplinary power and biopower. A host of new professionals who administered the penal apparatus of the state as prosecutors, psychiatrists, physicians, and prison staff in direct contact with prisoners appropriated the power to decide on their lives, making decisions ranging from whether or not they deserved to congregate with other prisoners to whether they should be "saved" by artificial feeding. As a result, the Turkish state entered into a process of *biosovereignization*.

Making Law

The first step in the implementation of high security prisons was juridical. Law was instrumentalized in order to address one of the most pressing obstacles to penal reform—overcrowding. The pressure of the growing prison population could only partially be alleviated with the construction of additional prisons. Given the rate of increase in the prison population, only if a new prison (F-type or not) were to be built every month would the state be able to keep up with the increased need for space. Since this approach was not economically sustainable and temporally feasible, it was considered necessary to decrease the existing number of prisoners and distribute a lesser number into the newly built units. The spatial restructuring of existing wards into smaller units, which was slowed down because they were still in use, also made their evacuation a practical necessity.

In order to decrease the prison population, the government passed a highly controversial "amnesty" bill. The Law for Conditional Release and Postponement of Court Cases and Punishments for Crimes Committed until April 23, 1999, was so stipulated that it would dramatically reduce the country's prison population almost by half in one stroke.[37] As important as the numbers of prisoners who would be discharged from prison, however, was the issue of which groups of prisoners would be discharged. The law was highly selective. It grouped prisoners according to crimes they had committed or were being tried for, it hierarchized certain crime groups vis-à-vis others and attached different degrees of leniency to them, and, finally, it indirectly isolated political prisoners, as those folded within the antiterror law, as the real constituency of the new penal regime.

The conditional release bill was proposed to parliament on December 8, 2000, within three weeks of the special session on the "prisons problem" and in the midst of the turmoil surrounding the death fast. But the bill had its own checkered history. A prior version of the bill had been offered by Rahşan Ecevit, vice president of the Democratic Left Party and the spouse of the Prime Minister Bülent Ecevit, two years ago, on the occasion of the seventy-fifth anniversary of the foundation of the republic, as the state's paternalistic gesture toward its prisoners. The proposal, in original form, entailed a limited amnesty for those prisoners Mrs. Ecevit referred to as the "victims of fate." The proposal excluded crimes committed against the state (in line with constitutional restrictions) along with others deemed hurtful to "public conscience" (ranging from forgery and bribery to torture crimes). It suggested commuting death penalties to thirty years of imprisonment, life sentences into twenty-four years, and subtracting twelve years from all other sentences. The parliament had passed the bill in August 1998 after broadening its scope, but President Süleyman Demirel had vetoed it. Since no further agreement had been reached between the coalition partners at the time, the bill was shelved (and not sent to the presidency again, which is necessary for its rectification as law).

Now, given the consensus around the necessity to solve the "prisons problem," the bill was revived and brought to parliament once again by the government. However, the conditional release bill led to fierce parliamentary debates. The opposition parties fervently argued against the bill, criticizing it on different grounds. These grounds included: (1) the absence of conditions necessitating the issuing of an amnesty, such as war, revolution, or other major social transformation; (2) the ambiguity concerning the nature of the bill as either a limited amnesty or a conditional release, which would have different implications for the penal regime and the prison population; (3) the arbitrary scope of the bill and inconsistencies in its formulation; and, finally, (4) the contradiction between the bill and the equality clause in the Constitution (Article 10). These criticisms are important because they depict both the interplay between the different tendencies in the parliamentary sphere, one that sought to make use of the law as an expedient tool of sovereign power, and the other that cautioned against the abrogation of legality and the assertion of state impunity.

The first criticism concerned the issue of whether utilizing lawmaking in the service of expediency would enhance or detract from the state's authority, already tarnished by the ongoing hunger strike. The opposition parties raised doubts about whether the issuing of an amnesty in the absence of a radically transformative event comparable to revolution was warranted. While the amnesty would reinforce the paternalistic attitude of the Kemalist republic vis-à-vis its citizens, as one that cares for its citizens, educates them, forgives them, and gives them second chances even if they have made mistakes, it would also compromise justice, especially for those citizens who had been affected by the actions of those in prison. Further losing trust in the state, what, then, could prevent those citizens from striving after securing their own justice? Member of Parliament Ahmet İyimaya from the True Path Party voiced the opposition's concerns when he argued, "an amnesty is the parliament's temporary abrogation of its own law, of the law it legislates, of the decisions of the judiciary, of their execution. If its conditions are lacking, this amnesty only feeds crime; if the conditions are lacking, this amnesty only leads to the alienation of the nation from its state."[38] Positioning the amnesty as another form of the "state of exception" in which the sovereign suspends its own laws, the opposition thus argued against measures that reflected traditional repertoires of supreme rule, especially in the absence of conditions necessitating the "exception." Similarly, Member of Parliament Salih Çelen criticized the current amnesty by drawing a parallel with its precedent also issued by Ecevit's government in 1974: "Mr. Prime Minister has transformed the streets into open prisons, the country into a bloodbath with the amnesty he issued in 1974."[39]

The second line of criticism was directed at the ambiguous legal nature of the bill. While the bill had been popularized in the press as an "amnesty," its legal status was, in fact, a "conditional release" based on legislative prerogative. According to the conventional judicial procedure for conditional release, the criterion of "good conduct" would be key in deciding whether or not a prisoner could benefit from the law. In contrast, the legislative prerogative effectively eliminated this criterion, substituting in its place new criteria based on the nature and classification of crimes, grouped together and ranked by those who stipulated the law. In this sense the bill was akin to an amnesty issued for certain crimes. Thus, while the legal nature of the bill was analogous to a conditional release, its qualifications and restrictions effectively rendered it an amnesty, about the issuance of which the opposition was particularly averse under the current political conjuncture.

A third consideration was the scope of the bill. Members of the opposition argued that the arbitrary boundaries of the bill led to many inconsistencies. While some crimes (e.g., threats and torture) were excluded from the scope of the law, other more severe crimes (e.g., murder and murder by torture and/or rape) were included. How could the government justify an outcome in which those convicted of rape were released, for example, while others convicted of extortion were kept in prison? Not surprisingly, the bill also excluded "terror" offenses. How could the government justify forgiving crimes committed against individuals while excluding crimes committed against the state from its own forgiveness? According to Member of Parliament Mehmet Ali Şahin, speaking on behalf of the Virtue Party:

> The government . . . has turned to the nation, has turned to the people, and is saying: One of your relatives may have been killed, you may have been harmed by a crime, my people, forget these, forgive them because I am forgiving them in your name, my people, please, sacrifice. Dear Friends, should those who demand sacrifice from others not first make sacrifices themselves? Those who ask from their citizens to forgive those crimes committed against themselves or

their relatives, that is, the government and state power, should first
portray this sacrifice for the crimes committed against themselves.[40]

A final criticism of the bill concerned equity. The bill determined which prisoners were eligible for conditional release according to the nature of the crime
committed rather than the sentence received. But, the opposition argued, all
convicts should have equivalent status based on their sentences, regardless of
the crime committed.[41] Member of Parliament Mustafa Kamalak, speaking on
behalf of the Virtue Party, claimed, "the state is obligated to treat all convicts
of the same status equally."[42] It was not equitable to release one convict sen-
tenced to seven years, for example, while keeping another with the same sentence, simply because the crimes they had committed were different.

Despite the plausible objections and reservations voiced in parliament,
the government single-handedly rejected all motions to amend the bill.[43]
Responding to criticisms, Minister of Justice Türk insisted that the bill was,
simply, necessary. Its mixed legal nature had a precedent in the antiterror law,
which contained a conditional release clause.[44] Minister Türk maintained that
the bill was not an amnesty but a conditional release, even though the two
could often approximate one another. There were two important elements that
distinguished this bill from being a kind of amnesty: (1) prisoners discharged
according to this law would go back to prison if they breached the conditions
of their release, and (2) detainees could also benefit from this law. Rebutting
the argument that the state should treat all convicts equally, he claimed that
equality was not a criterion applicable for the execution of sentences since
penal laws could and often did stipulate differential penal regimes (e.g., according to whether the convict is juvenile or female or according to whether
the crime is terrorism and organized illegal activity). Citing the 1982 Constitution, which imposed limits upon the scope of *any* amnesty that could be
issued by the parliament (permitting amnesty for crimes committed against
the people, but not for crimes against the state), Minister Türk contended that
the Constitution itself discriminated between crimes (by altogether excluding
some crimes from amnesty).[45] He purported that in this bill "it is not possible to find any situation that is against the Constitution when the legislator
discriminates, in an amnesty law or in a conditional release or reprieve law,
according to the qualities of crimes, the dangers they carry for society, or their
moral evilness."[46] Hence he defended the legality and, indeed, the necessity to
stipulate differential penal regimes for convicts in different categories.

Without a doubt, the primary rationale for pushing this bill was one of necessity and expediency, predicated upon the bill's promise to solve the "prisons problem." This expediency was expressed in the most explicit and starkest terms by Member of Parliament Ahmet İyimaya, spokesperson for the True Path Party: "Today, prisons have transmuted into internal headquarters where criminal plans are made [and] orders are issued. *In the prisons, there is no state sovereignty but the sovereignty of gangs.* One of the main reasons behind the insistence for the amnesty is the understanding that we can only temporarily solve this problem . . . by way of emptying out the convicts and detainees."[47] Insinuating that opposition to F-type prisons was the equivalent of treason, Member of Parliament Beyhan Aslan, from the coalition partner Motherland Party, argued as follows:

> Our prisons are extremely full. You are certainly aware that our prisons are insufficient in terms of physical circumstances. . . . Let alone enabling rehabilitation, the prison has almost become a mechanism that produces crime. Especially, the prisons and wards in which the political detainees and convicts are held have assumed the quality of [illegal] organization camps. In these places, unfortunately, there is a vacuum of authority; the last prison rebellions have also shown this. . . . Those who oppose the F-type prison, those who protest the meals, those who go on hunger strike are those who want prisons to be [illegal] organization camps again, those who would like to bring in weapons, to bring in drugs, to bring in heroin there; they are the traitor forces that would like to drag Turkey into chaos.[48]

The bill would solve the "prisons problem" by reducing the size of the prison population itself, which would enable the state to deal with more manageable numbers of prisoners in prisons that would thus more easily be architecturally transformed into securitized spaces based on cellular confinement.

However, the more important immediate impact of the bill would be the dispersion of the unruly "crowd" in the prisons. In this light, the bill was deemed expedient because it could create a rift in prisoners, subjecting them to differential regimes of punishment and thereby impeding their unified militancy. By creating the expectation of early discharge for different groups of prisoners, the bill would exacerbate existing divisions among them and create a concrete incentive to stop them from joining or supporting the hunger strike.

Thus a sizable group of political prisoners imprisoned for "aiding and abetting terrorism" in relation to charges associated with PKK was included among the potential beneficiaries of the Law for Conditional Release. This selective inclusion, it was expected, would create a serious division among the political prisoner population, preventing the participation of Kurdish political prisoners in the death fast (which, if they did participate, might bring the numbers of protestors up to ten thousand). Similar differentiations among prisoners would deepen the de facto gulf between "political" prisoners and "ordinary" prisoners, particularly weakening the latter group's attempts to stage hunger strikes and other protest actions in solidarity with "political" prisoners. At the same time, the law was also useful because it diverted the public's attention away from the hunger strike and to the controversial content of the bill.

Finally, through the making of this bill, we can observe that insofar as law was utilized as an instrument of the legislative prerogative of sovereign power, it was infiltrated by biopolitical considerations that took as its object the prison "population" and sought to mold that population, by dividing it into subgroups, ranking and hierarchizing them, and subjecting them to differentiated penal regimes in which they would receive customized treatment. The divisions among the prisoners stipulated by the bill via the classification of crimes and their corresponding degrees of mercy were concerned with the efficient distribution of prisoners' bodies across penal space, their allocation and management, and the destabilization of the potential unity of the prison "crowds." Meanwhile, the law also reasserted a fundamental distinction between "terrorist" and "ordinary" criminal profiles, performing leniency much more liberally in the case of the latter and reinforcing the differentiated ways of punishing these crimes. Through this bill the state would thus decide who warranted early discharge and who must be kept inside the prisons, but the decision itself was conditioned by the numbers and unruly practices of the bodies in prison and the problem of their government. Therefore the most important effect of the bill would be the singling out of certain prisoner constituencies as targets of the new penal regime: prisoners held for terrorism, organized crime, and criminal gangs, as well as prisoners who participated in prison struggles.[49] As a result, these subpopulations would be stigmatized vis-à-vis their pardoned counterparts, while also being physically and symbolically isolated from the rest of the prison population.

The bill was passed in parliament on the same day. In a revealing statement on December 9, 2000, the day after the parliament passed the Law for Conditional Release, Prime Minister Ecevit reiterated the necessity of the spatial reconfiguration of existing prisons and the introduction of high security prisons. "The Conditional Release approved by TBMM (Grand National Assembly of Turkey)," Ecevit insisted, "is in fact not an amnesty, but [it is] to give a chance to those who have gone astray. If those taking advantage of this opportunity commit crimes again, they will heavily pay for the consequences. One benefit of the law that was passed in the parliament last night is the decrease of the *crowding* in prisons approximately *by half*. Thereby, the prospect of making a healthy arrangement of prisons will be gained."[50] Breaking the good news of the prospect of discharge to the prisoners, Ecevit confirmed the status of the Law for Conditional Release as an effective and expedient tool for reducing the prison population in line with the project of the securitization of prisons.

But the vicissitudes of the law did not end here. President Ahmet Necdet Sezer vetoed it on December 14, 2000. In his veto decision the president provided a detailed jurisprudential critique, drawing attention to the law's internal inconsistencies and the clauses that violated constitutional equality. Rejecting differentiation between convicts due to the nature of the crimes committed (such that even if two convicts had received similar sentences, only one could be conditionally released, because of different crimes committed), the president argued for *equal* treatment of convicts with *equal* sentences. In his veto decision the president argued that the absence of consistent criteria determining the exclusions also rendered the law problematic. While recognizing the legislative prerogative to decide which crimes could be included in the scope of the law, the president expressed concerns about how the scope would nonetheless effect the "tranquility of society," "understanding of justice," the characteristics of "rule of law," "equality" before the law, and nondiscrimination. More important, the president criticized the grounding of the law in considerations of *expediency*: "The use of the right of amnesty with thoughts that lack legal value, such as the decrease of the population in prisons, diminishes the trust in society toward justice and the laws. The announcement of such a law will destroy the belief that 'The foundation of the State is justice,' will disrupt societal order and will injure the citizens' trust in justice."[51] Such (mis)use of the legislative prerogative, he feared, would further damage the authority of the state.

Despite the president's veto, the government decided to keep the law "as is" and asked the parliament for another vote. The law was passed (282 to 85) and sent back to the president. Because no changes were made in parliament, the president had to sign the law, but applied to the Constitutional Court for its cancellation. The Constitutional Court decided on the constitutionality of the law on July 18, 2001, partially enlarging its scope in light of the equality clause but not rejecting it tout court. The Constitutional Court maintained that the parliament had the discretion to decide which crimes should be included in the scope of this legislation. The crimes excluded from the law were justifiable because they constituted "crimes against society," because of their severity, and because their exclusion entailed a legal advantage (i.e., the protection of internal and external security). Thus the sovereign expediency of utilizing legislation to solve the "prisons problem" received the highest possible constitutional confirmation.

By August 23, 2001, 33,109 people had taken advantage of this legal opportunity: 23,350 were discharged from prison, an additional 2,527 received reductions in their sentences but could not be released, and 7,332 others avoided going to prison altogether. As a result, the Turkish state effectively reduced its prison population by enacting its prerogative of making law, exerting, in the meantime, a highly specialized management of its prison population, dividing and hierarchizing prisoners, distinguishing "political" prisoners vis-à-vis "ordinary" prisoners, selectively targeting the former for customized and disciplinary treatment under the new penal regime. In attempting to restore the state's sovereignty over prisons, law became the instrument with which the prison "crowd" could be dispersed, divided, and selectively marginalized. Carried out in the name of the people, the well-being of the prison populations, and public security, the new penal regime was also thereby clothed with the legitimacy of the law. The law was not only instrumental in implementing high security prisons; in the meantime, it was also infiltrated by the logic of securitization.

Making War

As those on hunger strike approached death and the negotiations of the committee of intellectuals came to a halt after the refusal by the Ministry of Justice to entertain its halfway solution of eighteen to twenty-prisoner wards, Minister of Justice Türk declared that the hunger strikes were no longer considered to be incidents limited to the prisons but had become "actions targeting the disruption of the order."[52] Minister of Interior Affairs Sadettin Tantan declared: "The real purpose of death fasts and similar actions is to provide advertising oxygen for terror. It is imperative to know that for the state accepting to give concessions in the face of these actions will have no other result than the encouragement of terror."⁵³ These declarations of the exhaustion of diplomacy between the state and the prisoners were a definitive signal regarding the radicalization of the conflict and the switch to the second step of the state's three-pronged approach. Retrospectively, it is possible to interpret these statements as a declaration of war on the part of the Turkish state upon those it considered to be the belligerent competitors for sovereignty, competitors scandalously arising out of its own prisons and holding the state hostage by their self-destructive actions. Meanwhile, citing discussions in the European Parliament, mainstream newspapers already declared that, in the confrontation between the state and the prisoners, the West was on the side of the state.⁵⁴

On December 19 the Turkish state launched a coordinated attack on twenty prisons around the country, unleashing over eight thousand security personnel equipped with heavy artillery, gas bombs, and bulldozers.⁵⁵ The security operation was carried out under the auspices of a "general search."⁵⁶ Otherwise aiming to find forbidden items in prison, the general search this time also aimed to find hunger strikers and, once found, to transfer them immediately to various F-type prisons, some of which were still partially under construction. It was later revealed to the public that a secret meeting was held on December 15, 2000, with the participation of representatives from the Ministries of Interior, Justice, and Health, the National Intelligence Agency (MİT), the High Command of the Gendarmarie, and the General Director of the Turkish National Police (EGM). The final decision for the security operation was allegedly made in this meeting.⁵⁷ Minister of Interior Affairs Sadettin Tantan later admitted, "We prepared the operation in one year, we finished it in one week."⁵⁸

"Operation Return to Life" was the name given to the state's invasion of its own prisons, reflecting its ostensible purpose of saving the prisoners on the brink of death from their own self-destruction. The date of the security operation was carefully chosen in light of the mission to "save lives." December 19, 2000, corresponded to the sixty-first day of the fast until death. In the previous death fasts of 1984 and 1996, the first deaths had occurred on the sixty-third day. Thus the state's military intervention came at a time when it was thought that prisoner deaths were imminent. Minister of Justice Türk explained: "It is unthinkable that the state will be a spectator to people being steered toward death. The purpose of this intervention is to save the lives of people. At the same time, the state's authority shaken since 1991 in various prisons will be properly constituted."⁵⁹ One of the highest elected officials of the cabinet argued: "There can be no such thing as a human right to annihilate human life."[60] Those at the helm of the state consistently remarked: "We are defending the right to live."[61] Now the state's strategic objective of restoring sovereignty by way of implementing securitized prisons was increasingly conjoined with the protection of life.

Second, the "rescue" mission also reflected the government's belief that the "youth on hunger strike had no individual will of their own."[62] We have seen Ecevit's paternalistic remarks referring to these prisoners as "youth" indoctrinated and "led astray" by "terrorist leaders." Under the name of political education, or by psychological, social, and political pressure, these prisoners had been brainwashed in the prison wards and thus "lost" over to these illegal organizations. The fear of being cast out and deemed "traitors" by their fellow prisoners had clouded their better judgment.[63] Once they were separated from each other and put into the new "rooms" of the high security prisons, officials calculated, prisoners would voluntarily abandon the hunger strike. The operation would "liberate these youth and give them their freedom"—the freedom not to participate in the hunger strike.[64] According to one of the top officials at the General Directorate of Prisons, the operation sought to rescue those individuals that terrorist organizations "sacrificed" for their own calculations: "These are deceived youths."[65] Each person transferred to the new prisons, out of the reach of terrorist organizations, would be a life "saved."

In his press conference on the same day the armed operation into prisons began, Prime Minister Ecevit remarked: "We had been showing great patience in the last weeks in order not to be forced into an armed struggle like this. Not only we as government but many civil society institutions, journalists, writers, artists, prosecutors, doctors, all have tried to bring these terrorists back into a normal path by way of reason and without necessitating such an intervention, but no results were attained. *This struggle is the enterprise of protecting and saving terrorists from their own terror.*"[66]

In "saving terrorists from their own terror," the state's security forces had to fight their way into the prisons.[67] In this operation prison walls were bulldozed, holes were drilled into rooftops, and wards were set on fire as swat teams entered the buildings with machine guns amidst dense clouds of gas. Finding themselves in conditions of asymmetric warfare, prisoners responded by piling up their beds, chairs, lockers, personal belongings, and the LPG tanks used for cooking in the communal kitchens as barricades to block the entry of soldiers into their wards. They manufactured gas masks from plastic water bottles, fought back with weapons of their own making from pieces of furniture, and set their bodies on fire. The utilization of self-immolation, alongside the fast unto death, as a different modality of self-destruction began in the confrontation between the security forces and the prisoners during this operation. The resistance of the prisoners led to the prolongation of the security operation to up to three days in several prisons.[68] As part of the conclusion of the security operation, most political prisoners on hunger strike were relocated to three of the newly built F-type prisons, female political prisoners were transferred to the Women's and Children's Prison and another special security prison in Istanbul, and several hundreds were taken to hospitals for the treatment of severe wounds.[69] Overall, around thirteen hundred prisoners were relocated. Those who did not participate in the hunger strike (mainly PKK-related prisoners) were not moved. Most of them did not participate in the resistance and suffered no injuries: "not even a nose bleed," according to the minister of justice.[70]

Ostensibly intended to "save" lives, this operation resulted in the deaths of two soldiers and thirty prisoners, dangerously wounding hundreds of others.[71] During the transfers, the prisoners reported that they were severely beaten, tortured, and, at times, raped. According to the report prepared by Contemporary Lawyers' Association (ÇHD), based on the initial observations of lawyers and families, some prisoners had simply become unrecognizable due to beatings.[72] The lawyers and families of the prisoners transferred into the F-type prisons also reported many other abuses to human rights organizations. The reports included instances of beatings with truncheons and sticks, kicking, slapping, punching, cursing, stripping naked and conducting cavity searches, spraying with cold water, shaving of beards and hair, sexual harassment, rape with truncheons, forced singing of the national anthem and kissing the boots of the gendarmes, and urination on the head.[73] That prisoners were suffering from wounds, broken arms and ribs, and other health problems was also observed and reported by Member of Parliament Mehmet Bekaroğlu, who visited Sincan F-type Prison in Ankara as the representative of the parliament's own Human Rights Commission on December 31, 2000.[74]

In this short but violent episode of warfare, the state's security personnel had wrecked vengeance upon the "enemies of the state." And yet Prime Minister Ecevit evaluated the operation as a major victory:

It has been a very successful operation, I congratulate all our security forces; all have worked in complete harmony. In fact, the preparations for this harmonious effort have been under way for weeks. In this way, a terrorist nest is thus now *extinguished*; after this all the developments the state requires will take place in a healthy manner. These prisons will be saved from being terrorist nests. May the result be beneficial to our nation. *We have two martyrs*; I wish them God's mercy. I hope that the injured will get well soon. May this result be beneficial for our nation.[75]

Adopting a highly belligerent and hawkish tone, Ecevit intimated that the security operation had been in planning for weeks, putting into doubt the authenticity of previous efforts at negotiation with the prisoners via the committee of intellectuals. He celebrated the security operation as an effective and successful effort in clearing the way for the implementation of high security prisons. When asked why prisoners were forcibly relocated to the new high security prisons on whose use the government had previously declared a reprieve, the minister replied that the military operations had rendered most of the currently occupied prisons unusable.[76] Against reproaches that the state had not kept its word, the prime minister replied, "You should look at the result we have achieved. . . . Prisons are no longer the headquarters of terrorist organizations."[77] Symptomatic of the attendant dehumanization of "terrorists" at work in the deadly outcome of the operation conducted to "save lives," Ecevit mentioned only the two soldiers among the thirty-two individuals who had lost their lives. The soldiers were the "martyrs" of the nation, while the rest were simply "extinguished" in the "war against terrorism."[78]

In order to demonstrate that it was regaining control over prisons, the state had staged a public spectacle.[79] The mainstream newspapers announced the operation with sensationalist headlines, largely complicit with the government's discourse against the prisoners.[80] *Milliyet*, based on the press statements of the minister of interior about the good health of the hunger strikers taken to hospital, declared the whole death fast to be a lie: "Fake Fast, Bloody Meal."[81] *Hürriyet* announced the operation upon prisons with sexualized language: "The State Went In."[82] Many columnists praised the state for the operation, affirming that it was intended to "save lives."[83] These newspapers claimed that the leaders of terrorist organizations had ordered prisoners to burn themselves to death, declaring that these terrorist organizations were worse than the religious fundamentalist Hizbullah.[84]

The spectacle of power performed by the security forces and overseen by the government was televised live and then repeatedly broadcast over many television channels for days. Like the public spectacle of Damiens's torture and execution that Foucault conveys, the public spectacle of the invasion of prisons, where the bodies of the "internal enemies" of the state were being kept, was a ceremony that displayed the restoration of a wounded sovereignty. It showed dissymmetry and excess; it sought to affirm the state's superiority over its contestants and to eliminate its adversaries, all the while affirming the autonomy of the state vis-à-vis civil society whose criticisms of F-type prisons had had no bearing on the state's policy.[85] The violence employed by the state security personnel was disproportionate and brutal, discriminating and vengeful. It terrorized its audience and successfully silenced public criticism for many months to come. The security operation in the prisons was complemented with increasing repression on the streets. Over two thousand demonstrators were detained, during which many reports of torture, degrading treatment, and abuse were filed with human rights organizations. The reruns of the operation footage on television were supplemented with stylized displays of weapons and cell phones that had allegedly been captured from prisoners. Along with this visual material were circulated voice recordings of conversations, which the government had tapped into and then used as part of allegations that prisoners had been receiving their orders to carry out "acts of terrorism" (especially orders to immolate themselves) via direct phone calls from their fugitive leader hiding in Brussels.[86] Thus the state was also utilizing a common trope in the Kemalist tradition wherein internal opposition was always considered to be organically linked to and complicit with outside forces that endangered the hard-won sovereignty and precarious unity of the nation. Since the "internal enemy" was being directed by outside forces to weaken the nation, the hunger strike and the supporting demonstrations on the streets were the equivalent of treason.

Unlike the traditional spectacles of violence performed by absolute sovereignty, however, the modern spectacle of the Turkish state was steeped in biopolitics. It was wrapped in the power to "make live" against those who forged their lives into weapons; it was a rescue operation to "save terrorists from their own terror."[87] The violent spectacle was justified by a discourse on the sanctity of life, in protection of which the state could kill, torture, and violate the insurgent's body. Paradoxically, the invisible panopticon of the high security prisons was put into effect by a contrastingly visible and public manifestation of power, staged as an invasion of prisons, which intended to display the state's vitality in all its vigor and supremacy. But the attendant and implicit violation of the insurgent's body was carefully hidden away from sight, as it was taking place during and after the conquest of prisons, in the nontelevised encounters between the security forces and the prisoners behind the walls. The effects of this violence could only be read off the burned corpses that were silently carried away into the morgues from the prisons and the wounds of the prisoners observed and reported by their lawyers only when they were allowed to see them. The state was proud of its violence and embarrassed about its actual effects, registering in its own way the paradoxical combination of its power to kill (*sovereignty*) and its power to make live (*biopolitics*). Operation Return to Life symbolized the intermingling of different modalities of power into a singular combination, a *biosovereign assemblage,* in which life permeated the mechanisms of death and the age-old violent "sword" of the state were exercised and justified in the name of the protection of life.

After the transfer of prisoners into the high security prisons, and to the dismay of state officials, scores of new prisoners joined the hunger strike while others converted their ongoing hunger strike to a fast unto death.[88] Meanwhile, the supporters of prisoners began resorting to armed attacks, including one suicide attack, outside prisons.[89] The prisoners stubbornly continued to fight a protracted war from inside the cells of the F-type prisons and the hospital rooms where they were taken to get medical care for the wounds incurred during the security operation. The war between the prisoners and the state soon entered a new phase with the onslaught of artificial feeding.[90]

The application of artificial feeding, or nonconsensual medical intervention, to resuscitate hunger strikers who lost consciousness was the continuation of warfare in corporeal form. It epitomized the contradictory combination of life and death in the biosovereign assemblage that was emerging through this violent chapter in Turkish history. On the one hand, the insurgent body was worthless, a body that, as Ecevit remarked, was not even killed but "extinguished" insofar as it was part of a "terrorist nest."[91] This was a body that could be beaten, kicked around, stripped naked, harassed, and raped, behind closed doors, especially as it resisted and refused compliance with orders. On the other hand, the insurgent body was absolutely precious and endowed with inestimable value as a symbolic conquest and the bearer of a life that must, under any condition, be made to live. Artificial feeding reinforced the violability of the insurgent's body and the absolute necessity to save it from its own terrorism.

The forces deployed in this battle were no longer the security personnel of the state but its medical professionals. The state instrumentalized medical knowledge in order to take control over the lives that were forged into weapons against the state itself.[92] By sanctioning artificial feeding, often without the informed consent of the prisoners on the fast unto death, the state put the physicians on the frontline in the highly personalized and ongoing struggle fought on hospital and infirmary beds, with no other weapons than plastic feeding tubes, intravenous solutions, and syringes. Intensive care units became intensive zones of conflict.

This controversial phase of highly irregular biopolitical warfare was divisive in the medical community. Most physicians publicly argued against medical intervention on ethical and political grounds, claiming that its nonconsensual nature violated the basic and universally accepted value of patient autonomy.[93] They cited the documents issued by the World Medical Association, partially in reaction to governmental pressures on medical staff around the globe to feed fasting prisoners nonconsensually, even forcibly, in order to prevent their deaths. According to the Declaration of Tokyo, issued in 1975, prisoners on hunger strike would not be artificially fed, if the physicians confirmed them as "capable of forming an unimpaired and rational judgment concerning the consequences of such a voluntary refusal of nourishment."[94] According to the Declaration on Hunger Strikers, also known as the Malta Declaration of 1991, which provides the framework of basic human and patient rights as it relates to health care professionals, the physician caring for the hunger striker should not forcibly feed the patient without the patient's consent. When the patient loses consciousness, the physician must take into consideration the patient's prior declarations of informed refusal of food. If there is an informed and voluntary refusal, the declaration posits that forced feeding is unjustifiable. In the absence of the possibility of ascertaining consent, the Malta Declaration relegates the decision to intervene to the individual physician. The options available to physicians in this situation are either to decline treatment (in line with the declared will of the hunger striker) or to go ahead with treatment (despite the patient's prior instructions to the contrary, especially if the physician considers that the patient's refusal of treatment is a result of peer pressure). It is also possible for the physician to resign from his/her role in order to avoid making this decision. In any case, physicians should have the freedom to decide without pressure from nonmedical authorities. If the hunger striker repeats the refusal of treatment after resuscitation, the physicians should respect this decision and not impose further nonconsensual treatment.[95]

In addition, the physicians in Turkey also referred to the 1998 European Union Member States Ministry Committee's Recommendation Decision R(98)7, which affirmed the primacy of patient privacy and consent in order to protect the rights of prisoners. In this light a large group of the medical community argued that the informed consent of the patient was necessary for them to conduct artificial feeding. In the absence of informed consent, the physicians held that the decision to resuscitate a hunger striker must be left to the individual physician who should not be pressured by either the Ministry of Health or the Turkish Medical Association. As an ethical matter, the physicians contended that this decision must be independent of political considerations and calculations.

Despite the objections of physicians, the Ministry of Health decreed that public hospitals should feed the hunger strikers and embraced resuscitation as a way to give the prisoners a second lease on life. In support of this decision, state officials cited letters and petitions from the families of the hunger strikers urging and "authorizing" medical intervention. Moreover, the same decree insinuated that those physicians who refused to conduct artificial feeding would face judicial consequences.[96] The members of the Turkish Medical Association had to navigate a complex terrain woven together by the dictates of their own conscience, the standards of medical practice, the expectations of the public, the declarations of refusal by the prisoners, the state's decree in favor of artificial feeding, and the struggle around the high security prisons.[97] Dr. Metin Bakkalcı of the Turkish Medical Association maintained that it was impossible for them as doctors to condone an action such as hunger striking that threatened human life. On the other hand, it was also impossible for them to obey the government's command to intervene without the consent of the patient: "What they wanted from us was in fact this: forced feeding. This is not a medical procedure; it has no place in medical training, it has not had one, it cannot have one."[98] While physicians could not bring themselves to support self-destructive protest, neither did they want to become the apparatchiks of the state.[99] As a result, the Turkish Medical Association officially refused the state's attempt at instrumentalizing medicine to "make live."[100]

Nonetheless, some physicians argued that the official refusal of the Turkish Medical Association concerning artificial feeding also infringed on their professional decision making, as much as the state's pressure in favor of feeding did, contending that thereby *both sides* politicized bedside clinical judgment."[101] During the first months of 2001, many instances of state-sanctioned artificial feeding allegedly took place, which resuscitated hunger strikers on the verge of death, often multiple times, despite repeated declarations of refusal by prisoners. The Human Rights Association (İHD) of Turkey reported that forty-six individuals had been subject to "forced intervention" until the summer of 2001.[102] The physicians who conformed to the state's decree authorizing medical intervention in the form of artificial feeding thereby appropriated the power of life and death, acting at the extremities of the state, at its point of contact with the bodies of the insurgents. Willingly arrogating to themselves the power to decide who should be made to live and who should be allowed to die, they became active vehicles of the biosovereign assemblage. In contrast, the physicians who refused to intervene and who openly spoke out against artificial feeding were prosecuted for supporting "terrorism."[103]

Meanwhile, individual hunger strikers fought corporeal battles on hospital beds, pulling out the IV needle when they gained consciousness only to find it put back in after they had passed out the next time they woke up. Prisoner rights organizations and the supporters of the hunger strikers conducted campaigns to publicize these medical interventions as "forced feeding" and drew attention to the disabilities and complications caused by the improper (and nonconsensual) termination of hunger strikes. Around this time, a guerrilla attack on a patrolling police car in Bahçelievler, Istanbul, on April 2, 2001, resulted in the deaths of two policemen. Conducted by the Fırat Tavuk Death Fast Brigade (named after a prisoner who had immolated himself in prison during Operation Return to Life), the attack was publicly assumed by DH-KP-C, one of the main organizations of the death fast, and announced with a declaration that called for an end to forced feeding, which accused the state for all those participants of the death fast left with disabilities because of the improper procedures used in these nonconsensual medical interventions. The declaration asserted: "Against the state which creates violence and oppression, there must be the people's justice. No people can remain without justice."[104]

Making Peace

No state can afford to wage an endless war, especially against its own people. The security apparatus of the state had won control over the prison wards and dispersed the unruly "crowd," but it was unable to bring their unruliness to an end. The bodies of the insurgents continued to host a protracted conflict. The continuation and expansion of the hunger strike belied official expectations that prisoners would quit once they were placed into individual cells. The persistence of the death fast mocked the rhetoric about "saving lives" especially because now the absence of ward conditions neutralized the state's claims about how prisoners were forced to participate in the hunger strike due to peer pressure and rendered participation purely voluntary. The *willing* weaponization of life undermined the legitimacy of the state as much as the actual deaths of prisoners. Meanwhile, the first death due to self-starvation occurred on March 21, 2001, with Cengiz Soydaş in Sincan F-type Prison.[105] Many others soon followed, some of them taking place outside of prisons.[106] These successive deaths, now and again supplemented with urban guerrilla warfare tactics outside of prisons, demonstrated that the "prisons problem" had not been fully solved, but was rather transformed into a prolonged, low-intensity conflict. The state might have won the physical struggle for sovereignty, yet how could it restore its legitimacy in the face of this continued challenge?

In response to the rising number of deaths, the state resorted to another traditional instrument of sovereign power: making peace (and making it on its own terms). As the final step of its three-pronged approach, the state resorted to several measures of peacemaking. In order to consolidate the new penal regime, spectacularly catapulted into operation, the parliament passed an amendment to Article 16 of the antiterror law in order to relax the stipulation of absolute solitary confinement, introduced mechanisms of surveillance over high security prisons, and most importantly, issued pardons to discharge prisoners at the brink of death. These measures were justified on the basis of the state's obligation to secure the "right to live," and they enabled the state to prevent the occurrence of new deaths in prisons while further legalizing the securitized penal regime.

As originally written, Article 16 endorsed absolute solitary isolation and blocked any kind of sociality within the prison, even precluding participation in state-sponsored "rehabilitation programs" in the event that these programs involved the concurrent participation of more than one prisoner. In order to lessen the highly impractical conditions of cellular confinement in F-type prisons, to dispel public doubts about their administration, and to permit the use of common areas for education, sports, counseling, and occupational activities built into them, the government passed an amendment in May 2001. The amendment allowed access to social spaces within these prisons, but made it contingent upon "treatment" or "correction,"[107] i.e., "successful" participation in prison "rehabilitation programs." Vague criteria such as responsiveness to rehabilitation and adaptive prisoner behavior were to define successful participation, giving leverage to a host of experts, prison administrators, counselors, psychologists, and other personnel to exercise professional judgment in determining whether or not prisoners should remain in isolation. With great room for arbitrary practices, medical and psychological knowledges would henceforth be deployed as instruments of control while socialization with other prisoners became the reward for rehabilitation.[108] Meanwhile, the new experts assumed the right of decision, if not on the life and death of prisons, then at least on the quality of life determined by access to human contact.

In addition, new legislation was passed in parliament, specifying the establishment of special courts to oversee matters pertaining to the execution of judicial sentences (*infaz hakimlikleri*), and prison monitoring boards (*cezaevi izleme kurulları*) to scrutinize human rights violations in the prisons.[109] While the former legislation extended the sphere of legal control over prison practices to address prisoner grievances, the latter sought to make prisons more transparent to the public. However, in contrast to the prisoners' proposal of establishing inspection boards comprised of representatives from civil society associations, the new law stipulated that the members of the monitoring boards would be assigned by the Judicial Courts Justice Commission (*adli yargı adalet komisyonu*). The inspection of the state's prisons by individuals appointed by the state raised questions about how independently they could function vis-à-vis official policies and expectations.[110] Human rights organizations were quick to criticize the inadequacy of these reforms and to claim that they functioned to legitimize the status quo.[111]

The most significant peace gesture was yet to come, however. At the end of May 2001, the Ministry of Justice began the discharge of prisoners who were still on a fast unto death. Authorization for this new policy was found under Article 399/2 in the Criminal Procedural Code, according to which prisoners, the execution of whose sentences created risk to their lives, could have their sentences postponed for up to six months. The degree of lethal risk involved in continued imprisonment was to be determined for each prisoner on hunger strike by a commission of physicians at the Council of Forensic Medicine (Adli Tıp Kurumu). If the prisoner's condition was critical, his/her sentence would be postponed and the prisoner would be released. The prisoner would need to check in every six months for a medical examination by the forensics council's physicians to ascertain that his/her condition was still inappropriate for further imprisonment. Unless the prisoners recovered, this reprieve could be renewed indefinitely. This policy was supplemented by the president's discretionary ability to grant individual pardons under Article 104 of the 1982 Constitution. In contrast to Article 399 of the Criminal Procedural Code, which only postponed punishment, the presidential pardon permanently released a prisoner.

Under both these policies, convicted prisoners were discharged en masse over the next two years. Detainees also benefited from the state's turn to forgiveness: either Article 399 was applied to them or, where this was not possible, the courts overseeing their cases set them free.[112] By January 2002, 182 convicted prisoners had benefited from the postponement of their sentences and were released from prison according to Article 399. Another 71 prisoners under remand were discharged from prison by court decisions. Moreover, the president pardoned 25 prisoners based on Article 104 of the Constitution. By October 2004, the number of prisoners discharged went up to 660, out of which 189 were pardoned by the president, 391 received reprieves of their sentences, and 80 were released by court decisions.

After violently and vengefully suppressing the opposition, the state thus turned to forgiveness. The state's newfound leniency and peacefulness were obviously motivated by calculations; they helped prevent additional deaths in the prisons, transfer the costly and difficult care for prisoners in critical condition to their families, generate new divisions among the prisoners with prospects of pardon, and neutralize the prisoners' struggle by further dispersing the unruly "crowd." The state's turn to peace can also be understood as the prevalence of the more conciliatory tendency over the hawkish one, whose military success in clearing the way for the high security prisons was overshadowed by the use of disproportionate force and high number of casualties in the prison operation, the injuries and abuses suffered by the prisoners, and the onset of repression on the streets, all of which caused the government to become an object of criticism and reprobation, both nationally and internationally.

However, the state's turn to peace may also be interpreted in keeping with its process of *biosovereignization*. The aim of such peacemaking, which relied

on the instrumentalized extension of legal control over prisons, the co-optation of the medical apparatus in resuscitations, the deployment of medical,
psychiatric, and rehabilitation experts in prisons, and the selective release of
prisoners through individualized amnesties, was to normalize the exceptional
situation created by the crisis of sovereignty, consolidate the achievements of
the security operation and the securitized prison, and build a reconfigured
sovereignty that would repair the state's tarnished authority by reaffirming its
grounding on the "right to live." The state's forgiveness would demonstrate
that its beneficence was greater than its punitiveness, that it could forgo its
right to punish to ensure the prisoners' "right to live" and even enhance their
well-being. Having eliminated the overwhelming security threat in the prisons, the state could now reinvent itself in the role of the benevolent protector
and paternalistic caretaker of the people. At the same time, this turn revealed
that the reconfiguration of its supreme powers would now prioritize its ability
for "gentle" government, one that would be respectful of fundamental rights
and responsive to democratic sensibilities, rather than its former tradition
comprising exceptional, authoritarian, and violent practices.

The biosovereign assemblage now sought to make these prisoners live,
not necessarily because their lives were valuable in themselves, but because
the state was invested for reserving for itself the *monopoly* over life and death
and reinstating its *monopsony* of sacrifice while, at the same time, moving further along the path of biopoliticization. If the prisoners released from prison
were to continue their self-destructive protest outside, their deaths would
have nothing to do with the state; such deaths could thus become private affairs, pushed out of the domain of biosovereignty. The prisoners' lawyers (or,
at times, family members), who applied for these legal opportunities to get
their clients (or relatives) out of the F-type prisons, were, in fact, unwitting
aides of the state's campaign to constitute the hitherto defiant prisoners as
new subjects accepting pardon, hence recognizing the state's sovereign authority, and submitting to its benevolence. As a result of these measures, the
state's commitment to the "sanctity of human life" was ensconced in peace.
The state could now rebuild its authority through the silent, pervasive, and
intensive management of life, modeled after the high security prison, but
certainly not limited to it. Meanwhile, the contradictory combination of the
power to kill and the power to make live was consolidated in the emergent
biosovereign assemblage.

Chapter 4
Prisoners in Revolt

While the Turkish state was debating, diagnosing, and devising solutions for the "prisons problem," political prisoners argued that the real problem was the state itself. As if it were not enough that they were subject to repression on the streets, curtailed in their political activities, classified and treated as "terrorists," subjected to torture and manifold forms of inhumane treatment, and tucked away behind bars for years at a time, the Turkish state now wanted to annihilate them completely, not by killing them but by rendering them politically dead.[1] In their opinion, solitary confinement was the desire of the state to achieve total control, to break prisoners' solidarity, to isolate and atomize them, to destroy their political identity and convictions—in short, to purge political opposition. And the desire of total control was hardly limited to the prisons.

According to political prisoners, the high security prison was emblematic of a much larger project to transform Turkish society. In this project, which they referred to as "cellularization" (*hücreleştirme*), the "cell" would be the new model of social organization, just as it would be the basic unit of the new penal space. This was a project of atomization, intended to break all networks and social ties of solidarity, to disband all attempts at collective organization geared toward the securing of greater rights and liberties from the state. Cellularization was the fantasy of neutralizing dissent in order to transform citizens into consumers, solidarity into competition, and sociality into individualism. Cellularization was the marriage of neoliberal capitalism and the authoritarian state. With political prisoners treated as "internal enemies" of the state and subjected to the grinding structural violence of cellular confinement, there would be no one to struggle for the people, to defend their rights, to act in the name of marginalized and deprived populations, to be a "barricade against the assaults."[2] Hence, the prisoners cautioned, if it were to succeed, the high security prison project would soon transform the entire country into an unbounded prison, a prison without walls and yet a prison from which there was no escape. As a result, the F-type prisons appeared as the spatial symbols of the injustice of the existing order and portents of its disastrous future. The F-type prisons constituted an existential threat to the peoples of Turkey.

But the high security prisons were also an immediately and transparently existential threat to the political prisoners themselves. This is because they had predicated their survival upon the collective forms of life they had developed in the wards of existing prisons. As a result of countless struggles over decades, they had appropriated those spaces that belonged to the state, shaped them according to their own will and political ideals, and transformed them into islands of communism. As spaces that had become more or less autonomous from prison authorities, the wards were sites in which political prisoners practiced what they preached. They organized and managed their daily lives, provided for their needs, advanced their education, and engaged in politics according to the very principles for which they landed in prison.

The experience of a communism-in-practice at the margins of the political sphere turned prison wards into enclaves of insurgency. The appropriation of these spaces by their inhabitants and the alternative experience of everyday life this appropriation made possible rendered wards crucial for the formation of a collective will and a shared political identity that reinforced the solidarity of political prisoners and facilitated their entry into a common life-and-death struggle with the state. Prison wards thereby became the material congeal-ment of the political prisoners' competing claim to power from the margins. Political prisoners believed that the wards, signifying the power of society against the state, of communism against capitalism, of dissent against authori-tarianism, should be protected at any cost.

If the very marginality of the wards, reflecting the asymmetry between the movement comprised by political prisoners and the might of the state, set lim-its to the forms their struggle could take, their venerable tradition of resistance also privileged certain repertoires of political action. At the same time, their view of the F-type prison project not only as an oppressive penal regime that must be *resisted* but also as a holistic strategy of state power that must be *chal-lenged* by a counterpower, epitomized by its ability to command life and death, strengthened their inclination to choose a radical confrontation with the state as the appropriate strategy of struggle. Especially in light of the absence of conventional means and mechanisms of political voice that could enable the articulation of their desires and demands in public and publicly recognized forms, and the military assault of the state on the prisons, violence quickly became the dominant medium of this confrontation and self-destructive prac-tices the principal kind of violence performed by the prisoners. Against the state's goal of introducing a regime that controls life, the political prisoners set themselves the goal of struggling against it by resorting to death. The *weapon-ization of life*, as the predominant tactic of the ensuing struggle, became the venue of these agents' refusal, characterizing the specificity of the death fast movement.

This chapter narrates the story of Turkey's prisons once again, but from the opposing point of view. We therefore shift our gaze from the center to the margins, from the domain of the wielders of power to the domain of resistance, from the control over life to its contestation by the politicization of death. The chapter proceeds by depicting prison wards and how they came into being. It recounts the emergence of the death fast struggle, the main incidents that shaped the prisoners' course of action, and the debates that surrounded their choices. It analyzes the internal structure of the prisoners' coalition and zooms in on fissures and conflicts among the organizations that eventually tore their coalition apart. It scrutinizes their demands, especially the paradoxical "right to die" that came to characterize necroresistance, and traces how the instru-mentalization of human rights allowed the movement to bring itself to an end. Overall, this chapter discusses how the movement's practical and discursive trajectory, a dialectics of voice and will undergirded by a politics of space, was shaped in response to the *biosovereignization* of the state.

WARD COMMUNES AND FREE CAPTIVES

One of the most appealing images of communism in the history of radical political thought is, without a doubt, Karl Marx and Friedrich Engels's depiction of an arrangement that would let one "hunt in the morning, fish in the afternoon, rear cattle in the evening, criticize after dinner . . . without ever becoming hunter, fisherman, shepherd or critic."[3] For the leftist militants of Turkey, like their counterparts around the globe, this vision was a continuous source of inspiration. It expressed the desire to transcend the fixed and restricted roles assigned to individuals by a specialized and sophisticated division of labor dictated by capitalist relations of production, roles that denied personal autonomy and command over how to live one's life. In Marx and Engels's vision, the narrow, repetitive, and monotonous labor that transformed producers into appendages of machines and reduced them to levels of bare subsistence was akin to a prison of necessity. The only way to experience freedom beyond necessity was to break out of the prison that confronted individuals not as their own creation but as something foreign and restricting. The communal organization enabling such freedom would eliminate inequality and privilege, put an end to exploitation, and ensure the relation of each individual to the social whole in an unmediated transparency. This, Marx and Engels believed, would be the only way in which each individual could actually flourish as an individual and live a dignified life. In this alternative order, the political sovereignty of the state, defined primarily by class domination, would be eliminated and replaced with the collective determination of human destiny by society itself. The Paris Commune, if short-lived, was the first historical attempt at realizing this vision that established the *commune* as the form of life appropriate to a communist politics.

For the leftist militants of Turkey, whose convictions aligned with this vision, it was ironically in prison wards where they set up and experienced the revolutionary commune. Individuals who got involved in radical politics, took active roles as part of the extraparliamentary leftist opposition, and subscribed to the ideas propagated by outlawed leftist parties eventually landed in prison. Once in prison, the majority of these individuals would be assigned to prisons that had an already existing political prisoner population, often to wards with other political prisoners. The "political" wards, as they became known, were often strictly separated from the wards of "ordinary" prisoners and divided according to political affiliation: there were wards that belonged to prisoners of the Kurdish cause and wards that belonged to the organizations of the radical left. If the numbers of political prisoners were sufficiently high, the wards could even be separated according to ideological orientation and organizational affiliation within the left. In contrast, in smaller prisons where political prisoners were not sufficiently concentrated to make up a ward of their own, they stayed with "ordinary" prisoners but tried to maintain their distinct identity by acting as a group.

What was distinctive about "political" wards was the way most of them were quickly organized into what prisoners called *ward communes*. Ward communes comprised of various committees with the responsibility of organizing and managing different facets of prison life for the prisoners of the same ward, which could involve between thirty to one hundred individuals (or more, depending on the degree of "overcrowding" in the prison). Prisoners assumed membership on these committees by election or by rotation, depending on existing numbers. The ward commune oversaw a range of functions, including planning, coordinating, distributing, and managing daily tasks and activities, providing for basic needs, and handling relations with the outside world.[4]

For example, the money, clothes, food, and medicine brought to prisoners by their families were handed over to the commune, which distributed them back to prisoners according to need. The commune thus made sure that those prisoners without means would be fed, dressed, and taken care of as much as their more privileged comrades. Even though the prison administration supplied food, most prisoners found it unpalatable and insufficient and therefore recooked it, adding ingredients that would make it taste better, and supplemented it with other dishes. The ward commune made sure that acceptable meals were prepared for the whole ward and that food was distributed equitably.[5] Since the political prisoners rejected prison uniforms, the commune also had the responsibility of providing clothes. It made sure that all members were adequately dressed, with clean underwear and socks, sweaters, pants, and shoes that would keep them warm in the harsh winters. The wards were almost never properly heated, and showers grossly inadequate, with limited hot water under the arbitrary control of the administration. Because of the difficult conditions, most prisoners got sick frequently. When prisoners fell ill, the commune supplied the basic over-the-counter medication and arranged for prisoners to be sent to the infirmary inside the prison (which often required lengthy negotiations with the staff) or to outside hospitals if the severity of their condition warranted (which required even lengthier negotiations).[6] The ward commune also identified the necessities that were not provided by the prison or the prisoner families and tried to procure them using the ward's common resources.

One of the most important functions of the ward commune was the planning and organization of daily activities. The day was divided into different slots. Every hour of the day was structured.[7] On a typical day, prisoners in the ward would wake up at the same time and then line up in the yard for physical exercise. The morning exercise was the first collective activity. Calisthenics would be followed by breakfast and cleaning up. The day would continue with educational sessions in which prisoners would work on joint projects, including the preparation of skits, publications, and posters, and participation in reading groups. Reading materials ranged from daily newspapers and current books to Marxist-Leninist classics and leftist periodicals. After lunch there would be a break for individual recreation and reading. This time was often devoted to reading literature, writing personal letters, keeping journals, and engaging in hobbies and handicrafts, such as knitting, lacing, and woodwork. In the late afternoon, there was time for team sports in the yard, political discussions, and leisure. Volleyball and soccer were the most favored sports, and teams of different wards competed in tournaments. Conducting group conversations and doing the paced walk in the yard (*volta*) were important parts of recreation. Different committees appointed by the commune organized cooking, cleaning, laundry, and various other household tasks, convening at specific times during the day. Dinner was eaten collectively, and clean up would be followed by a slot for watching a television program selected by prisoners' representatives or by general vote.[8] Special occasions (associated with the history of an organization, past struggles, or the death of comrades) would be celebrated or commemorated together. Everybody would be in bed around the same time. Sleeping during the day, unless due to illness, was most often prohibited. Through everyday practices, the ward commune enabled prisoners to make the prison their own.[9]

The commune also took on other functions. It helped its members obtain an education, to do time in self-discipline, and to keep intact their sense of identity, community, and solidarity with comrades. It established a sense of ideological and cultural continuity on the radical left by constructing a bridge between different generations of prisoners and enabling the transfer of the practical knowledge of survival in prison and the training of further militancy. At the same time, the commune often served as a shield of protection against arbitrary intrusions and rights violations by the prison administration and security forces by coordinating collective resistance or making sure that prisoners looked out for each other. The commune acted as an umpire in solving conflicts between prisoners without the intervention of the prison administration. Its decisions ranged from the channeling of social pressure and reprobation of prisoners found at fault to passing "sentences" with more serious ramifications.[10] Especially if the breach concerned an issue with ideological and political import (which could also involve issues carrying over from the past or acts outside the prison) rather than a quotidian matter, the commune could punish individuals after trying them in mock trials. According to the alleged severity of the crime, the punishment could range from the temporary exclusion of individuals in the ward to their permanent ostracization. They could be given the "dirty work," punished with "silent treatment," and, in some severe cases, even face capital punishment.[11]

Thus the ward commune enabled prisoners to live according to the dictates of their politics. With such meticulous planning and rigorous discipline, prisoners might not be able to do whatever they desired, but they could surely participate in all aspects of daily life and take turns in assuming responsibility. As a model of communism-in-practice, life in the wards allowed prisoners to transcend the position of captivity that was imposed upon them and have a say over the organization of their own lives. The wards permitted prisoners to experience freedom in prison, breaking the cage of imprisonment in the very spaces otherwise under the control of their arch-enemy, the state. As a result of their experience, the prisoners often called themselves "free captives."[12]

As Henri Lefebvre famously argues, space is a social construct. It is the everyday experiences, meanings, and values that *produce* space and condition the practices and perspectives of those who occupy that space.[13] In the case of prison wards, the objective marginality of these sites, combined with their isolation from the outside world, provided the conditions of possibility of their transformation.[14] However, it was the collective life of political prisoners, their subjective experiences of deprivation, arbitrary violence, intrusion, on the one hand, and autonomy, solidarity, and equality through communism, on the other hand, that allowed the *production* of the prison wards into spaces of freedom within captivity.

Like the Paris Commune, the ward commune was also the product of a besieged community. If behind the organization of the Paris Commune stood not only class identities but also, and perhaps with greater significance, neighborhood solidarity, the organization of the ward commune was also a product of the place-bound solidarity of the prison ward.[15] Similar to the Paris Commune, the ward commune also contained in embryonic form the ideological and practical claim of a different form of community upheld as a positive horizon of emancipation. At the same time, this claim acted as an alternative to the sovereignty of the Turkish state, more threatening precisely because it was emerging out of the spaces that should be under its firmest control. These wards became spaces in which a *constituent* power was assembled; they were transformed into the breeding grounds of an insurgent politics. As marginal sites in which a revolutionary collective was brought into life through everyday practices, they were *constituent spaces.*[16]

The intensity and significance of the lived experience of the ward commune, which fortified already existing ideological commitments, in turn contributed to the emergence of a distinct, radical, and unified collective will among prisoners of different affiliations and sectarian differences. It reinforced the political prisoners' desire to create an alternative order outside of the prison and their determination to fight the state, which they recognized as the common enemy, in defense of their own spaces in prison. The death fast did not simply take place in prison wards; prison wards were the spatial determinants of this movement, producing it, as it were, through the social construction of the ward commune, with a distinct spatiality.[17] As that spatiality was transformed, so was the movement.

RESISTANCE IN TURKISH PRISONS

The wards that eventually became islands of lived communism were not created overnight. They were the result of many difficult, unrelenting, and heroic struggles of generations of political prisoners, individual and collective. These struggles have become increasingly more collective and more corporeal, with hunger strikes rising to prominence in the last few decades.

Earliest references to hunger strikes in the prisons of the republic go back
to the 1930s. In 1932, individuals associated with the Communist Party staged
a hunger strike in Istanbul Prison first to protest the long detention period
before their appearance in court, and later, upon the conclusion of the trial, to
protest their sentences.[18] One of the most well known instances of resistance
emerging from Turkish prisons is the hunger strike of the famous communist poet Nazım Hikmet, who was condemned to fifteen years, on grounds
of "inciting cadets to rebellion" when his poems were found in the lockers
of students at military school, and another twenty years in a military trial for
"inciting the army to rebellion."[19] In 1946, eight years into his combined sentence of twenty-eight years, Nazım Hikmet appealed to the parliament to have
his unjust punishment rescinded. Unfortunately, his appeal did not generate
any response. Another appeal by his lawyer in 1950 for a special amnesty was
subsumed within the bill for general amnesty proposed by the Republican
People's Party. However, this bill did not carry the vote in parliament. Nazım
Hikmet began a hunger strike on April 8, 1950, which immediately created a
national and international uproar, in light of his worldwide fame, his ill health,
and the circumstances of his sentence.[20] In a letter to his family announcing
his hunger strike, the poet emphasized that his decision was not indicative
of his despair or cowardice, but, rather, a "consciously, hopefully utilized last
opportunity" to attain "justice and the truth," for which the poet declared his
readiness to die.[21]

Having been convinced by the government that officials were attending
to his case, the poet stopped the hunger strike the next day. When nothing
happened, he resumed his hunger strike on May 1. His mother's hunger strike
in solidarity to publicize the poet's cause was perhaps the first time a hunger
strike was being used outside the prison in Turkey. Nazım Hikmet called off
his hunger strike after eighteen days, upon the landslide election victory of
the Democrat Party, when he was convinced by public pressure to stop his
strike until the new government was set up.[22] The new government's general
amnesty did not include political prisoners, but Nazım Hikmet was finally
released in July 15, 1950, after a reduction of his sentence by two-thirds. The
effectiveness of the poet's hunger strike set a strong precedent that would be
emulated by generations of political prisoners, especially as political repression and brutal prison conditions colluded.

Without a doubt, the darkest times in Turkish prisons coincided with military takeovers. The next well-known hunger strike episode coincides with the

1971 military intervention. This hunger strike of twelve days was conducted by the three leftist student leaders (Deniz Gezmiş, Yusuf Aslan, Hüseyin İnan) in Mamak Military Prison. Commencing their action on April 18, 1972, they stated that their hunger strike was in protest of the increased poverty of the working class, the curbing of rights and democratic liberties, military tribunals, political assassinations, torture, and the censorship of the press. The hunger strike was the "last protest action we could carry out for the working class of Turkey and our people," they maintained, as narrated by their lawyers.[23] They called off their hunger strike upon the persuasion of their lawyers a few days before their execution so that they would not stagger while walking to the gallows, which could be used as negative propaganda against them.[24] All three were hanged on May 6, 1972.

The most violent prison conditions in Turkey were experienced during the 1980 coup d'état. It is now well documented that political prisoners were systematically subjected to torture and inhumane treatment, including daily beatings, electric shocks, solitary isolation, rape, and various other forms of physical and psychological torture and humiliation under military rule.[25] Diyarbakır Military Prison was perhaps the most notorious prison in the country, with mostly Kurdish political prisoners, subjected not only to brutal forms of torture but also a process of forced Turkification.[26] Metris Military Prison in Istanbul was also exemplary for its brutality.[27] Overall, prisons became the main pillar of the military regime, with greater longevity than the coup d'état itself.[28]

Against the rampant violence in the military prisons, prisoners spearheaded the opposition to military rule, making prisons into one of the most important sites of political resistance in Turkey. Even though the streets grew silent after the military takeover, prisons did not. Prisoners resisted their dehumanization and tried to stage acts of collective protest in order to push back against the violence that was unleashed upon them. In the overall "state of exception" created by the 1980 military intervention, wards were transformed into spaces of normality carved and sustained by prisoner solidarity, necessary for survival.[29] Families of prisoners, when they were allowed to visit, constituted the single most important venue for the transmission of news from inside the prisons to the general public, and, even then, only intermittently. The most significant evidence of prison violence in the hands of prisoner relatives was the laundry of prisoners, heavily stained with blood, handed over during visitation days to their families.[30] When the news of prisoner resistance leaked outside, it helped undermine the legitimacy of the military regime.

As the military administration of prisons gave a free rein to a regime of terror from which there seemed to be no way out, it was only by the most fatal actions of individual prisoners that resistance could come forward. The first protest actions came in the form of several noncoordinated self-killings in Davutpaşa and Mamak Military Prisons (see table 4.1).[31] A hunger strike attempt in Diyarbakır Military Prison in January 1981 was brutally repressed. Two months later, in March 1981, prisoners affiliated with the Kurdish movement managed to conduct the first death fast, which was called off after forty-three days and one casualty (see table 4.2). The conditions got worse. The next protest to occur in Diyarbakır Military Prison was the self-destruction of Mazlum Doğan, who hanged himself in his prison cell on the night of Newroz (March 21, 1982), the festival celebrated for the coming of spring by the Kurds with symbolic connotations of redemption from tyranny. This was followed by the simultaneous self-immolation of four prisoners on May 17, 1982. This paved the way to the second fast unto death initiated in Diyarbakır Military Prison on July 14, 1982. After the death of four prisoners and the promise of the administration to end torture, the death fast was called off in September.[32] Another death fast in September 1983 was called off after twenty-six days without casualties. A fourth death fast, which began in response to the murder of one prisoner by torture and two subsequent self-killings in protest, on January 14, 1984, lasted fifty-four days and incurred two casualties. These death fasts were largely successful in bringing the worst period of Diyarbakır Military Prison to an end during which at least eighteen individuals lost their lives as a result of torture. Protest hangings by individual prisoners continued for several more years against the policies of violence, intimidation, and the extraction of forced confessions.

Meanwhile, several hunger strikes were taking place in Istanbul prisons. A seventeen-day hunger strike in April 1981 and a twenty-eight-day hunger strike in April 1982 in Metris Military Prison, and a twenty-seven-day hunger strike in July 1983 in Metris and Sağmalcılar Prisons were carried out, alongside several self-killings, with varying degrees of success, in protest of torture and repression in prisons. A short-lived hunger strike in Ankara's Mamak Military Prison in 1982 was soon aborted when most prisoners quit under repression from the administration, leading to scorn from other prisoners.[33] Even though a fifty-day hunger strike in the same prison in 1984 succeeded in pushing back

Table 4.1   SELF-KILLINGS IN TURKISH PRISONS (1980–2000)

YEAR	NAME OF PRISONER	PRISON	DATE OF DEATH	METHOD
1980	İrfan Çelik	Davutpaşa Military Prison, Istanbul	September 14	Self-hanging
	Bekir Bağ	Mamak Military Prison, Ankara	November 12	Self-hanging
1982	Ahmet Erdoğdu	Mamak Military Prison, Ankara	February 10	N/A
	Mazlum Doğan	Diyarbakır Military Prison	March 21	Self-hanging
	Kenan Çiftçi	Diyarbakır Military Prison	April 21	Self-poisoning
	Necmi Öner	Diyarbakır Military Prison	May 17	Self-immolation
	Eşref Anyık	Diyarbakır Military Prison	May 17	Self-immolation
	Ferhat Kutay	Diyarbakır Military Prison	May 17	Self-immolation
	Mahmut Zengin	Diyarbakır Military Prison	May 17	Self-immolation
	Hakkı Hocaoğlu	Metris Prison, Istanbul	November	Self-hanging
1984	Yılmaz Demir	Diyarbakır Military Prison	January 8	Self-hanging
	Remzi Aytürk	Diyarbakır Military Prison	January 28	Self-hanging
	Selahattin Kurutuz	Diyarbakır Military Prison	May-June	Self-hanging

	Hüseyin Yüce	Diyarbakır Military Prison	May 23	Self-hanging
1986	Suphi Çevirici	Diyarbakır Military Prison	May-June	Self-hanging
1996	Selami Zoro	Erzurum E-Type Prison	October	Self-immolation
	Süheyla Alagöz	Sivas E-Type Prison	October	Self-immolation
	Hamdullah Şengüler	Sağmalcılar Prison, Istanbul	November	Self-immolation
	Vedat Aydemir	Sağmalcılar Prison, Istanbul	November	Self-immolation
1998	Sema Yüce	Çanakkale E-Type Prison	March 21 (died in June)	Self-immolation
	Fikri Baygeldi	Çanakkale E-Type Prison	March 26	Self-immolation
	Vedat Azat Emirhanoğlu	Burdur E-Type Prison	April 4	Self-immolation
	Adem İnce	Çankırı E-Type Prison	April 27	Self-hanging
	Ayhan Yılmaz	Bingöl Special Type Prison	September 1	N/A
	Mehmet Halit Oral	Kahramanmaraş E-Type Prison	October 9	Self-immolation
	Mehmet Gül	Amasya Special Type Prison	October 19	Self-immolation
	Ali Aydın	Bartın Special Type Prison	October 20	Self-immolation
	Bülent Bayram	Adıyaman E-Type Prison	October 21	Self-immolation

	Selamet Menteş	Midyat Special Type Prison	October 23	Self-immolation
	Aynur Artan	Midyat Special Type Prison	October 22-23	Self-immolation
	Mirza Sevimli	Erzurum Special Type Prison	October 26	Self-immolation
	Mehmet Aydın	Çanakkale E-Type Prison	November 13	Self-immolation
	Erdal Çeken	Mardin E-Type Prison	November 13	Self-immolation
	Kadri İlhan	Siirt E-Type Prison	November 16	Self-immolation
	Cemil Özalp	Diyarbakır E-Type Prison	November 27	Self-immolation
1999	Serpil Polat	Sakarya E-Type Prison	February	Self-immolation
	Yavuz Güzel	Bartın Special Type Prison	November 30	Self-immolation
	Takibe Gültekin	Sivas E-Type Prison	December 12	Self-immolation
2000	Çiğdem Burgan	Ümraniye E-Type Prison, Istanbul	September	Self-hanging

This table is limited to the self-killings of "political" prisoners. Compiled from journal archives and checked against the following sources: Mavioğlu, *Asılmayıp da Beslenenler*, 373–91; Mazlumder, *1998 Yılı Cezaevleri Raporu*; "Diyarbakır Zindanı"; "'Güneşimizi Karartamazsınız!'"78.

Table 4.2 HUNGER STRIKES AND DEATH FASTS IN TURKISH PRISONS WITH CASUALTIES (1980–2000)

	START DATE	PRISON	DURATION	ORGANIZATIONAL AFFILIATION	NAME OF DECEASED PRISONER AND LOCATION OF DEATH	DATE OF DEATH
1	March 4, 1981	Diyarbakır Mil-tary Prison	43 days	PKK	Ali Erek	April 20, 1981
2	July 14, 1982	Diyarbakır Mil tary Prison		PKK	Kemal Pir	September 7, 1982
				PKK	M. Hayri Durmuş	September 12, 1982
				PKK	Akif Yılmaz	September 15, 1982
				PKK	Ali Çiçek	September 17, 1982
3	January 14, 1984	Diyarbakır Military Prison	54 days	PKK	Cemal Arat	March 2, 1984
				PKK	Orhan Keskin	March 3, 1984
4	April 11, 1984	Sağmalcılar Prison, Istanbul, and Metris Prison, Istanbul	72 days	Dev-Sol	Abdullah Meral (Sağmalcılar Prison)	June 15, 1984

#	Date	Prison	Duration	Organization	Name	Date
				TİKB	M. Fatih Öktülmüş (Sağmalcılar Prison)	June 17, 1984
				Dev-Sol	Haydar Başbağ (Sağmalcılar Prison)	June 17, 1984
				Dev-Sol	Hasan Telci (Sağmalcılar Prison)	June 26, 1984
5	January 11, 1988	Diyarbakır Military Prison	38 days	PKK	Mehmet Emin Yavuz	February 18, 1988
6	July 1989	Eskişehir Special Type Prison & Aydın E-Type Prison	35 days	PKK	Hüseyin Hüsnü Eroğlu	August 2, 1988
				PKK	Mehmet Yalçınkaya	August 2, 1988
7	March 1993	Muş E-Type Prison		PKK	Abdullah Fidan	April 9, 1993
8	July 14, 1995	20 Prisons	36 days	PKK	Fesih Beyazçiçek (Yozgat E-Type Prison)	July 23, 1995
				PKK	Remzi Altıntaş (Amasya E-Type Prison)	August 11, 1995

9	May 20, 1996	43 Prisons, 8 organizations	69 days	TKP(ML)	Aygün Uğur (Ümraniye Prison, Istanbul)	July 21, 1996
				DHKP-C	Altan Berdan Kerimgiller (Sağmalcılar Prison)	July 23, 1996
				DHKP-C	İlginç Özkeskin (Sağmalcılar Prison)	July 24, 1996
				TKP(ML)	Ali Ayata (Bursa Special Type Prison)	July 25, 1996
				MLKP	Hüseyin Demircioğlu (Ankara Central Closed Prison)	July 25, 1996
				DHKP-C	Müjdat Yanat (Aydın E-Type Prison)	July 25, 1996
				DHKP-C	Ayçe İdil Erkmen (Çanakkale E-Type Prison)	July 26, 1996

			July 26, 1996
	Tahsin Yılmaz (Sağmalcılar Prison)	TİKB	
	Ulaş Hicabi Küçük (Bursa Special Type Prison)	TİKB	July 27, 1996
	Yemliha Kaya (Sağmalcılar Prison)	DHKP-C	July 27, 1996
	Osman Akgün (Sağmalcılar Prison)	TİKB	July 27, 1996
	Hayati Can (Sağmalcılar Prison)	TKP(ML)	July 28, 1996
	Mirza Çubukçu (Batman E-Type Prison)	PKK	November 27, 1998
10	November 14, 1998	20 prisons, 16 organizations	

Compiled from the following sources: Mavioğlu, *Asılmayıp da Beslenenler*, 373–91; Okuyucu, *'96 Ölüm Orucu*; Mazlumder, *1998 Yılı Cezaevleri Raporu*.

against the arbitrary violence in the prison, not resisting in prison and reformist politics are still dubbed in leftist jargon as "Mamakification."[34]

In November 1983 the military regime officially ended with the holding
of elections. However, in contrast to expectations, civilian prison administrations across the country upheld the military's efforts to impose discipline in
the prisons by enforcing compulsory prison uniforms in January 1984. Protests soon followed. The next major death fast in the country occurred in Metris and Sağmalcılar Prisons largely in response to the imposition of prison
uniforms. This death fast, which started on April 11, 1984, and lasted seventy-
two days, was also the first one conducted by prisoners of the Turkish left.
Prisoners affiliated with two organizations (Dev-Sol and TİKB) began a hunger strike, which was converted into a fast unto death on the forty-fifth day.
The main demands of the prisoners were the end of torture and repression in
the prisons, freedom to exercise the right of defense, the abolition of prison
uniforms, better living conditions, and the recognition of "political" status.
The death fast was called off when it succeeded in gaining some concessions
from the prison administration upon the death of four prisoners.[35]

In July 1987 a fifty-day hunger strike against prison uniforms in Istanbul's
Sağmalcılar Prison quickly spread to other prisons around the country. In
February 1988 a thirty-eight-day hunger strike against prison uniforms, which
began in the same prison and spread to others, finally succeeded, with one
casualty in Diyarbakır Military Prison, whose control was passed over to the
Ministry of Justice only in May 1988. Prison uniforms were abolished. However, in August of the same year, Minister of Justice Mehmet Topaç issued a
circular, reinstituting prison uniforms.[36] In response, over two thousand prisoners across twelve prisons went on hunger strike in October 1988. After one
month, prisoner resistance annulled the circular.

The next hunger strike with casualties occurred in 1989 in protest of prisoner relocations from Eskişehir to Aydın Prisons.[37] Eskişehir Prison was vacated and closed on June 22, 1989, after two big tunnels were discovered. However, prisoners on hunger strike experienced severe beatings and maltreatment
during the relocation, which resulted in the death of two prisoners on August
2, 1989. The strike was called off on August 19 without any further casualties.[38]

Until the end of the 1980s, protests were generally concerned with stopping torture, arbitrary violence, and fundamental rights violations in prisons.
It is important to note that these protests continued even after the transition
to civilian rule, which did not immediately alter prison conditions but rather

presented significant continuities with the preceding military rule. The promulgation of the antiterror law in 1991 can be said to mark an end to the first wave of prisoner protests after the military coup d'état. The antiterror law, while conditionally releasing many of the political prisoners of the 1980s, also created an "exceptional" regime within democracy whereby torture, maltreatment, and degrading treatment could be perpetuated with impunity, in the name of security and the success of the "fight against terrorism." While torture became extremely prevalent during the 1990s as a result, its main location shifted to pretrial detention and police custody instead of the prison. Decried and condemned as it was by the public, torture of leftist and Kurdish militants had become so prevalent in Turkey that militants joked about the experience as a means of socialization. On the one hand, this relocation enabled the new wave of prison struggles to focus on the betterment of prison conditions and prisoner rights rather than fighting torture in prison. On the other hand, while the aim of torture might have been to produce broken and docile subjects, its usual consequence for those who continued to be part of the struggle was the creation of an even more determined militant, equipped with a profound hostility to the state that would enable even more dramatic acts of violence, inside and outside prison. As a result, the confrontation between prisoners and the state continued in this decade with great rigor.

In the second wave of prison protests that began in 1991, the pronounced aims were focused on securing common living areas, gaining rights to communal cultural, social, and sports activities, ensuring the circulation of publications inside the prison, stopping the arbitrary confiscation of letters and publications, and guaranteeing rights to open visitation, private consultation with lawyers, and access to health care. At the same time, because the antiterror law also prepared the legal framework for the introduction of high security prisons, opposition to successive government attempts to introduce high security prisons also became an important feature of prisoner protests during the 1990s. Protests in this decade were more collective and often conducted simultaneously across different prisons. Finally, this decade was also one in which the struggles of Kurdish prisoners and those on the Turkish left became largely autonomous from one another (solidarity actions notwithstanding) and assumed broader political goals than merely the struggle for better conditions of imprisonment.

For Kurdish prisoners affiliated with PKK or other, smaller ethno-nationalist radical organizations, these goals involved the democratic resolution of the Kurdish question, the recognition of cultural rights, and the cessation of military conflict. While prisoners affiliated with PKK conducted mass hunger strikes, they advanced demands regarding the recognition of their status as "prisoners of war" and the peaceful resolution of the ethnic conflict ravaging the country through guerrilla warfare and counterinsurgency.[39] For example, the mass hunger strike organized by Kurdish political prisoners in July 1995 was carried out in over twenty prisons with the participation of five thousand prisoners and ended with the deaths of two prisoners. [40] A similar hunger strike was initiated in Diyarbakır Prison on March 27, 1996. On April 25, eighteen prisoners announced that they would conduct a hunger strike of indefinite duration, eliminating the relays among prisoners. Their demand was the acceptance of their status as "prisoners of war," the response of the government to the unilateral cease-fire declared by PKK, the end to military operations, and permission for independent, international observers to inspect war crimes in accordance with the Geneva Convention. PKK called off the hunger strike at the end of May 1996 without any deaths. Furthermore, self-immolations in prisons became a frequent tactic of PKK-affiliated prisoners in the 1990s. Several individually driven self-immolations in 1996 in protest of forced confessions and the harsh security operation into Diyarbakır Prison with ten casualties were followed by an exponential rise in self-immolations in 1998 (see table 4.1). In response to the imprisonment of PKK leader Abdullah Öcalan, around seventy prisoners attempted self-immolation. These self-destructive practices resulted in sixteen casualties. A two-week collective hunger strike, launched on November 14, 1998, in twenty prisons, was also supported by the Turkish left and ended with one casualty.

For those on the extraparliamentary left, the goals of prison struggles in the same period involved advancing prisoner rights, on the one hand, and opposing attempts at introducing high security prisons, on the other. The latter goal began taking precedence as the "political" wards, which by then had begun to achieve a certain autonomy from prison administrations, became stronger. While the methods of protest varied, individual and relay hunger strikes became the most frequent tactics of struggle in prison. There were also several riots in which prison wards were occupied by prisoners and wardens were taken hostage.

The first mass hunger strike of the 1990s conducted by those on the radical Turkish left occurred when, in November 1991, the government introduced the renovated version of Eskişehir Prison, which had been restructured according to the cell system, with 432 single-prisoner cells, and 206 political prisoners from various prisons around the country were transferred to Eskişehir Special Type Prison. After reporting severe beatings and torture as they were transferred to the prison, prisoners went on hunger strike, demanding that this prison be closed. A committee of physicians from the Turkish Medical Association (TTB) was sent to check on these allegations and confirmed that 119 out of the 198 prisoners showed signs of torture. Other prisoners in Sağmalcılar (Istanbul), Buca (Izmir), and Ceyhan Special Type Prisons launched solidarity hunger strikes when the news reached them. Upon the inspection of the prison by Minister of Justice Seyfi Oktay and Minister of State Mehmet Kahraman, with other members of parliament and representatives of human rights organizations, the government decided to close down the prison. The prison was vacated by November 28, 1991.[41]

The next few years witnessed political prisoners' growing power in prisons, parallel to their growing numbers, with largely autonomous ward practices. However, prisoners soon met an increased intensity of violence in security operations conducted by the gendarmerie, under the auspices of searches, often leading to clashes, beatings, and other violations, at times with several casualties. For example, the security operation in Buca Prison on September 21, 1995, resulted in three deaths and forty-seven prisoners severely wounded, whereas the one in Ümraniye Special Type Prison led to the death of four prisoners by severe beatings. In response to this escalation of violence in prisons, death fasts and self-immolations soon reemerged.

The first death fast of the 1990s carried out by the Turkish left took place in the summer of 1996 by over fifteen hundred prisoners with a host of different political affiliations. Launched on May 20, 1996, as a mass hunger strike of indefinite duration, the action was transformed into a fast unto death on July 3, 1996. This death fast came as an effort to prevent the government's second attempt to revive the Eskişehir Special Type Prison. Meanwhile, Mehmet Ağar (the former police chief responsible for counterterrorism programs) became the minister of justice of the coalition government made up of Motherland Party (ANAP) and True Path Party (DYP). Minister Ağar issued three executive decrees on May 6, 8, and 10, 1996, dubbed as the "May Decrees," ordering the transfer of eighty prisoners back into the Eskişehir Prison.[42] The prisoners went on hunger strike, demanding the cancellation of these decrees, the cessation of violence against the families and relatives of prisoners, the end to arbitrary violations of the right to legal counsel and health care, the end to arbitrary transfers of prisoners across prisons (especially to prisons far from the places where their trials were taking place), and, most important, the closing down of the Eskişehir Prison, which they referred to as the "coffin." The prisoners also included a general call for an end to disappearances, extrajudicial killings, torture, and state terror directed at the Kurdish people and the laboring masses of Turkey in their list of demands. In the meantime, elections were held and the government changed.

When the first prisoner death due to self-starvation occurred on July 22, PKK launched a hunger strike in solidarity, putting additional pressure on the newly elected coalition government, composed of the Welfare Party (RP) and the True Path Party (DYP). An informal agreement was reached between the government and the prisoners on July 28, following the deaths of eleven prisoners. Minister of Justice Şevket Kazan announced that Eskişehir Prison would be closed to political prisoners and canceled the decrees in return for the ending of the death fast. The collective, coordinated action of prisoners had thus given the prisoner representatives enough leverage to halt the transfer of political prisoners to the Eskişehir Special Type Prison, which had been the major aim of the fast. The death fast was called off with success, but another prisoner died on the way to the hospital, bringing the total number of casualties to twelve (see table 4.2). Meanwhile, the European Commission's Committee for the Prevention of Torture delegation visited the Eskişehir Prison, upon the invitation of the Turkish government, and colluded with the Turkish state's position, claiming that the prisoners' allegations regarding the "coffin cells" in the prison were "unjustified."[43]

The mass hunger strike of 1996 marked a qualitative difference from its precursors in two significant ways. First, it was much broader in its scale and scope. Not only did it result in the participation of larger numbers of prisoners, it was also conducted through the coordination of multiple organizations. In earlier hunger strikes, decision making had been much more decentralized, divided by prison and, within prisons, by political affiliation. In 1996 the illegal organizations that participated in this action included seven different groups: DHKP-C, TKP(ML), TKP/ML, MLKP, TKEP-L, TDP, and DH. An eighth organization, TİKB, supported the action as a hunger strike of indefinite duration, refusing to call it a death fast.[44] The greatest numerical support came from the political prisoners imprisoned in relation to the Kurdish struggle (i.e., mainly those charged for PKK-related cases), albeit well into the hunger strike, as an act of solidarity. Overall, the strike had the involvement or support of almost all political prisoners affiliated with over a dozen different organizations in prisons scattered across the country.

Second, the death fast of 1996 was marked by the creation of a body of political representatives by the prisoners to streamline their coordination. The Central Coordination of Prisons (Cezaevleri Merkezi Koordinasyonu), the informal board organization composed of prisoner representatives of the major political parties of the radical left, was established in Sağmalcılar Prison in Istanbul, where there were a high number of political prisoners and leadership cadres. The CCP comprised the following eight organizations: DHKP-C, TKP(ML), TKP/ML, TİKB, MLKP, DH, TKİP, and TKEP/L. Those organizations not on the board but with a prison constituency (though in smaller numbers) were THKP-C/MLSPB, TDP, Dev-Yol, TKP/K, and TİKB(B).

Before the establishment of CCP, collective resistance had been more or less spontaneous and reactive, spreading across the country as news were haphazardly relayed from one prison to the other. Creation of the board allowed political prisoners to plan and act in concert, bringing together different prisons and a motley of organizations in those prisons. The main principle of the CCP was to generate a mechanism of centralized decision making to coordinate prisoner resistance and develop collective responses when there was an attack on one prison. According to the CCP, prisoners should not begin a protest that would involve other prisons without the permission from the board, except in self-defense. When a security operation took place in a provincial prison, for example, the news should be directly and immediately relayed to Sağmalcılar Prison, where the course of action would be decided. All other prisons would then follow the response strategy decided by the board.[45] This central direction, it was expected, would effectively demonstrate the organized power of political prisoners and give them greater leverage in their negotiations with state officials.[46]

Unfortunately, the gains of the 1996 death fast proved to be temporary and superficial. Only a year later a new decree was issued under the new Minister of Justice Oltan Sungurlu, authorizing units for four to six prisoners for the following groups: homosexuals, bisexuals, those in peril in prison (generally referring to prisoners convicted for sexual offenses), the mentally ill, those with contagious diseases, those who want to be alone, those who are not wanted in the wards, ward aghas, mafia leaders, and assassins. The ministry now referred to these units as "small wards" instead of cells. While this development did not immediately impact political prisoners, it did signal to them that the state had not given up on its plans to securitize its prisons.

Meanwhile, there was an escalation of violence in prisons, as searches and security operations became more frequent and utilized new kinds of heavy weaponry and gases. Between 1996 and 2000 the severity and brutality of the prison operations carried out by security forces in Diyarbakır, Ulucanlar, and Burdur Prisons sparked prisoner unrest and led to many casualties (see table 2.1).[47] The operation in Ulucanlar Prison, Ankara, by the gendarmerie on September 26, 1999, was particularly brutal, as the excessive use of violence even came into question by the parliament's own Human Rights Investigation Commission.[48] When the news of the operation in Ulucanlar Prison reached Istanbul, the CCP coordinated prison riots across the country within hours. Prisoners stormed the administration of the Çanakkale Prison, took prison staff hostage, and occupied it for over twenty-four hours. The protests were ended only upon an informal agreement with the Ministry of Justice that the security operations would be called off.[49] After this incident, prisoners began to expect retribution from the state. The covert and protracted struggle in the prisons had not ceased; on the contrary, it was soon to break out into an open confrontation.

THE EMERGENCE OF THE DEATH FAST STRUGGLE

In the early months of 2000, the stalemate between the prisoners and the state presented a bleak picture for the future. The prisoner representatives at Sağmalcılar Prison concurred that all of the security operations in prisons were "rehearsals" for the transition to F-type prisons and that a further escalation of violence would soon follow. They were also of the same opinion with respect to the nature of F-type prisons: unlike previous assaults upon prisoners, the "cellularization" entailed by high security prisons was an attack of a different caliber, a strategic maneuver to liquidate not only political prisoners but also any form of radical opposition with subversive potential. In light of these views, prisoners with different affiliations began extended rounds of discussions to find the most effective way to proceed. However, despite its ability to create and manage coordinated action, the CCP was not free of disagreements.

While all groups and factions agreed that collective resistance was imperative, there was no agreement on either the choice of tactic or the timing. Two
tendencies quickly became apparent. The first tendency argued for the staging of a preemptive hunger strike that would be converted into a death fast
before a bloody security operation took place. Representatives of prisoners
affiliated with the Revolutionary People's Liberation Party-Front (DHKP-
C) and Communist Party of Turkey (Marxist Leninist)–Workers' Peasants'
Liberation Army of Turkey (TKP(ML)–TİKKO), whose total prison membership far outweighed all the other parties put together on the Turkish left,
subscribed to this position, which had several different rationales.[50]

First, the correct choice of tactic, these groups contended, would be crucial in portraying the militancy of prisoners. The death fast was the most effective tactic in their opinion because it would demonstrate the determination
and commitment of the militants to the broader public. The prisoners cast the
contestation between the state and revolutionary organizations as a battle of
wills. Especially in prison, where there were limited means of struggle, they
argued, "the communist and revolutionary will of prisoners [was] the only
materiale of war."[51] Against the state's will of imposing F-type prisons, which
meant death to political prisoners, the prisoners' could assert their own will
by resisting these prisons to the death. Displaying their willingness to die rather than accept the terms dictated by the state, prisoners could counteract the
pervasive and totalizing domination the state intended to install in the society
at large through the F-type prisons. The fast unto death would thus constitute
a frontal assault against the state, proving to the world that "Revolutionary
Captives Cannot Be Taken Over!"[52]

Second, these groups maintained that the death fast commanded a certain
gravity and moral weight by putting the lives of prisoners at stake. The seriousness of the situation, they argued, would trigger greater mobilization outside
the prisons, without which it would not be possible to win. At the same time,
because the temporal horizon of the death fast spreading the confrontation
over two months, there would be more time to organize outside mobilizations. In contrast, other forms of struggle, such as taking prison staff hostage,
constructing blockades in prison wards, occupying sections of the prison, and
other similar actions, these organizations argued, would lack the legitimacy
that a death fast would have for the masses outside. These other tactics might
appear too belligerent and even cause supporters on the outside to be more
reluctant to take action.

Third, while these prisoners saw that in order to be effective, prison struggles had to have the support of the masses, they also thought that since the
attack targeted the prisons, the most militant response should come from the
prisoners themselves.[53] They considered that the mobilization outside, weak as
it already was, would be doomed to fail in the absence of a strong stance from
the inside. Any weakness or failings of the prisoners would be exponentially
compounded on the outside.[54] This position was also in keeping with the vanguardist orientation of these organizations (see chapter 5). They contended
that the F-type prison sought to crush the political identity of revolutionaries
in prison, which they equated with the future of the masses, and to humiliate
the leaders of popular struggle. Even though they agreed that the real target
of the high security prison was the masses, they did not expect the masses
to put up a firm resistance in the absence of a tough stance from prisoners.[55]
As a result, vanguardist, preemptive action from the prisons would show the
people that their trust in revolutionary organizations was not misplaced, while
also convincing them to join the struggle against the state. Finally, their interpretation of the 1996 death fast as a success in securing concessions from
the state strengthened their case that the death fast was the best resistance
against high security prisons.[56] Some factions within these organizations also
saw the death fast as a way to secure a victory against the state without incurring a heavy death toll.[57] In sum, these organizations claimed that only a
fast unto death could give the prisoners the necessary power to negotiate with
state officials and that, even if this power might not be sufficient to prevent
the opening of the F-type prisons, then it would at least secure them the least
disadvantageous transition. In this light, they further argued that the hunger
strike should be launched as soon as possible in order to prevent or delay the
opening of F-type prisons.

By contrast, a second tendency among prisoners, affiliated with several
different organizations like the Revolutionary Communists' Union of Turkey
(TİKB) and the Marxist Leninist Communist Party (MLKP), maintained
that it was too early to begin a fast unto death. They concurred with the hardliners that the high security prison was a "strategic assault" targeting the working class by way of attacking its vanguard organizations; they had shared this
diagnosis with the groups arguing for the immediate commencement of a
death fast for several years now.[58] They, too, considered the cells of F-type prisons to be "death cells."[59] However, they strongly argued for privileging other,
more "active" kinds of resistance and leaving the death fast as a last resort.

This faction argued that the struggle with the state on F-type prisons would not be limited to a single confrontation, such as a death fast, but would rather necessitate a multipronged, long-term strategy.[60] Even if the death fast might eventually be conducted, the argument went, the inauguration of the hunger strike should be held off until more publicity had been generated and greater popular mobilization against the F-type prisons, with the widest possible social coalition, had been set into motion.[61] This group contended that the activation of social forces outside prisons was particularly important because the anticipated assault of the state could only be stopped by large-scale social mobilization. "We were aware that the forces that could repel this attack were outside," one of these ex-prisoners argued, "[it was] the struggle of the forces outside."[62] Another former death faster convincingly summarized their position at the time as follows: "You can never win only with the prisons. Unless there is a mobilization outside that supports it, the inside is always bound to lose. Social pressure is imperative."[63]

While pressing for the activation of social opposition, the proponents of this position also believed that the death fast should be a response to the impending security operation and not a preemptive move. Only when the struggle outside had failed to stop the opening of the F-type prisons would the timing be right, in their opinion, to launch a death fast. In the words of a former participant of the death fast, "We wanted to do all we could in order to establish an inside-outside relation which would trigger the public outside into action because we believed that life outside was also being cellularized. And that's why we emphasized the need for people to better own up to this [struggle]. We tried to organize this and, as a last resort, when there was nothing left to do, we maintained it was necessary to begin the death fast."[64]

Meanwhile, the security operation at Burdur Prison on July 5, 2000, was interpreted as another signal of the escalation of violence.[65] Although there were no casualties, the operation drew wide media coverage because a bulldozer destroying the prison wall had cut off the arm of a prisoner, which was later found by dogs in the municipal garbage. Furthermore, there were seriously wounded prisoners, allegations of rape, and many other abuses reported by prisoners after the operation. The Burdur operation provoked intense debates among prisoners, whose representatives reached the conclusion that a death fast would constitute the most effective response, that it was "necessary" and "inevitable," but that it must be planned with caution and that no other method of protest could be ruled out. After this agreement in mid-August

2000, the former faction began pressing to initiate the hunger strike at once. The fear was that if prisoners did not commence the hunger strike immediately, the government might pass an amendment on Article 16 of the antiterror law when the parliament went into session in September. With this cosmetic amendment lifting absolute isolation in high security prisons, the public opposition against these prisons could be diffused and further legitimacy generated for the transfer of political prisoners into the F-types.[66] This group of prisoners also considered that the government would probably issue an amnesty that would further harm the prison movement, sowing divisions among them with the expectation of early release for some prisoners, and lead to the diversion of the political agenda in general.

Despite the arguments of the hardliners, the prisoners subscribing to the latter tendency insisted on the inaccuracy of this timing, pushed to wait until a broader coalition was generated between organizations inside prisons and the social forces outside, and claimed that the establishment of unity among oppositional forces was more important than the timing of the struggle. They also did not credit the speculations regarding the impending amnesty.[67] As a result, the groups arguing for immediate action decided to launch the hunger strike without the support of the groups in the second faction. In preparation for launching the hunger strike, two organizations, DHKP-C and TKP(ML), issued a joint statement condemning the preparations for a military intervention in prisons and called for public support on October 10, 2000:

> We have nothing to lose but our bodies. We have a great world to win. We are revolutionaries, we are right, and we will eventually win. We state that no massacre, attack, maneuver, or psychological warfare can stop us from being the conductors of our rightful struggle. We call upon all the oppressed, all those progressive, democratic, revolutionary persons and institutions to be attentive to the preparations for attacks and massacres directed to prisons and to take a concrete stand against the attack.[68]

With this declaration, contentions among prisoners were not resolved but shelved. The death fast struggle would be launched by the two outlawed leftist parties (soon to be joined by a third), but the full coalition involving a dozen affiliations would not coalesce together for another three months. In one of the few scholarly analyses of the Turkish hunger strike, Patrick Anderson persuasively argues that the prominent feature of the struggle was the absence of a "single figurehead" like Bobby Sands or Gandhi and that the "coalition" was, instead, the "primary unit of action and signification."[69] We are now in a position to observe that this statement is only partly accurate. While it is correct to note the collective nature of the movement, defined by high numbers of participants and different political affiliations, which prevented any one individual from becoming the figurehead of the struggle, this coalition was far from monolithic, constructed with difficulty, and certainly fragile. The initial disagreements that divided the political prisoners never disappeared, even at the highest point of participation. These debates would resurface in the later stages of the movement when the expected results were not forthcoming. The alternative claim to power asserted through necropolitical resistance was marred by internal strife from its inception.

Demands of the Prisoners

The mass hunger strike was launched on October 20, 2000, by prisoners affiliated with DHKP-C, TKP(ML), and TKİP in Ümraniye, Bursa, Çankırı, and Aydın Prisons.[70] It spread to Çanakkale, Bartın, Gebze, and Malatya Prisons on October 23. This was followed by Bayrampaşa, Buca, Uşak, Ceyhan, and Ulucanlar Prisons on October 26. Prisoners publicized their hunger strike by issuing a communiqué.[71] This declaration summarized the different forms of social opposition against high security prisons and the state's repression of these forces until that date. In light of the state's decisive stance in putting into effect the cellular prisons, the prisoners stated: "It is now the prisoners' turn, our turn to talk."[72] The prisoners argued that the "state's assault can only be pushed back by a line of struggle, a resistance that is ready to pay a price," since "this has been the only language that governments understand."[73] They cited previous victories against the state, the retreat of repression in military prisons during the coup d'état, the abolition of prison uniforms, and the closing of Eskişehir Prison in 1991 and 1996 as successful precedents of this struggle. The prisoners declared that in light of past victories and martyrs they would "once again make the enemies of the people kneel before them."[74] The prisoners adopted a decidedly noncompromising tone: "We will not enter those cells. They may massacre all of us, we may fall martyr in death fasts, only one comrade may be left in prison. But even in that situation, they will not be able to put that captive alive in the cells. We will wreck the cells upon the heads of those who had them built."[75]

The bold communiqué also contained a list of demands. These demands were not limited to the abolition of high security prisons but asked for democratization of the legal and penal apparatus of the state tout court. They involved significant legal, executive, and institutional changes; they pertained to the laws, the courts, the security personnel, *and* the prisons. The chief demand of the death fast, of course, was the closing down of F-type prisons. But this was one demand among nine. The prisoners asked for the abrogation of the antiterror law with all its legal consequences. Most of the prisoners participating in the hunger strike were directly affected by the stipulations of the antiterror law and hence wanted it changed. But they were also critical of this law because of its implications for Turkish democracy at large, which they saw as being undermined by the security interests of the state. Connected to this demand was the abolition of state security courts (DGM), under whose jurisdiction fell cases connected to the antiterror law. In operation since 1984, these tribunals had greater discretionary powers and handled offenses against the "indivisible unity of the State with its territory and nation," the constitutional order, and national security.[76]

Another demand was the cancellation of the working agreement put into effect on January 17, 2000, between the Ministries of Justice, Internal Affairs, and Health, dubbed the Tripartite Protocol.[77] This agreement curbed prisoner rights by executive decree, restricting their access to legal counsel, medical care, and family visitations. The protocol also impaired lawyers' access to their clients by subjecting them to physical searches and otherwise violating lawyer-client confidentiality by inspecting documents after consultations (Articles 6 and 11). It sanctioned medical intervention, i.e., artificial feeding, on prisoners on hunger strike (Article 19). It ordered that medical examinations of prisoners subject to the antiterror law (and the Law for the Struggle Against Interest Based Criminal Organizations) be conducted in the presence of the gendarme, obliterating doctor-patient confidentiality (Article 66). In sum, the protocol took away most of the de facto prisoner rights that had been gained through prison struggles over the past three decades.

Next on the list of prisoner demands was that prisons be periodically and publicly inspected and that these inspections have legal standing and protection. The prisoners did not want state-appointed committees to carry out these inspections for fear that they would do little more than give a rubber stamp of approval to ongoing human rights abuses in prisons. Instead, they proposed that these inspections be conducted by nongovernmental committees constituted by lawyers selected by the Union of Bar Associations of Turkey (TBB), doctors chosen by the Turkish Medical Association (TTB), the families of prisoners, and representatives of human rights organizations, prisoner rights organizations, and the All Judicial and Penal Institutions Employees' Union (Tüm Yargı-Sen)—the trade union for state employees working in the field of criminal justice.[78] In other words, they wanted inspections to be public and independent.

The next three demands were concerned with reparations for previous abuses and injustices. The prisoners wanted those responsible for previous security operations in prisons to be publicly prosecuted for the violence committed against prisoners. These operations in the last five years had caused the deaths of twenty-seven prisoners and the serious wounding of many others in the Buca (Izmir), Ümraniye (Istanbul), Diyarbakır, Ulucanlar (Ankara), and Burdur Prisons (see table 2.1). Another demand was the release of prisoners whose health was failing due to severe illnesses, participation in the death fast of 1996, or exposure to violence during past prison operations, along with those whose situation had gotten worse because they were denied access to proper medical care. In addition, prisoners also asked for the trial and punishment of those security officers responsible for torture in pretrial detention. They complained that even though they had repeatedly filed grievances with public prosecutors and the human rights commissions of the parliament, those responsible for torture were still immune to prosecution. Their immunity arose, the prisoners argued, either via the refusal of courts to try their cases or, in the event that their cases were tried, through the courts' dismissal of charges based on lack of evidence or due to statutory limitations.

The final and most sweeping demand on the list was a call that expressed the desire for nonoppression. The prisoners asked for the abolition of all antidemocratic laws that restricted the struggle for democracy and liberty. This demand incorporated a call to end the oppression of the Kurds and other ethnic minorities within Turkey. Given the status of the 1982 Constitution, made and ratified under the aegis of the military, this demand entailed the implicit call for a new, civilian, and democratic constitution. It involved a plea for the redefinition of citizenship, away from the privileging of the Turkish population and based on the equal incorporation of other ethnic groups, both in law and in practice. It also sought to garner the support of Kurdish political prisoners for the death fast.[79]

While the signatories of this communiqué claimed that they would continue to fast until all their demands were met, the most obvious stake of contestation and the focal point that condensed all the other demands in the declaration was the abolition of F-type prisons.[80] This appeared first in the list of
demands and would later form the crux of the negotiations with the intermediaries (like the committee of intellectuals) who went into prison to carry out
talks regarding the hunger strike. In practice the acceptance of this demand
alone would be a significant achievement; it could bring solitary confinement
to an end, address the various conditions of imprisonment that had been the
terrain of continuous struggles between prisoners and officials since the 1980
coup d'état, and secure in the form of legal rights what generations of prisoners had been fighting for. Such a victory would also serve as a tacit recognition
of the power of political prisoners.

The all-encompassing nature of the list of demands, hardly attainable solely by means of prison struggle, was both strategically and ideologically motivated. Strategically, the prisoners viewed these demands as cohering together
into a minimalist package of democratization, a baseline agenda to be pushed
forth by forces of social opposition. By bringing together the concrete problem posed by the F-type prisons with other, more inclusive demands relating
to the penal, legal, and political system, the prisoners sought to merge their
own immediate struggle with the broader political struggle for democracy,
involving the support of the masses and civil society organizations outside
the prisons. The prisoners wanted to build a coalition among all the social
forces fighting for the deepening of Turkish democracy, a coalition that would
take the high security prisons to be the material symbol and focal point of
the broader transformation that the progressive Turkish and Kurdish forces
desired to achieve.

Ideologically, however, the reason for having a wide range of demands was
to expose the real "truth" of the Turkish state to the masses. The undemo-
cratic, oppressive, "oligarchic" and "fascist" nature of the Turkish state, they
contended, could not be thoroughly understood by the masses unless it was
shown to them by their vanguards.[81] The prisoners, as the vanguards of the
progressive social forces in Turkey, were directly confronting the state and
could therefore penetrate the veneer of ideological manipulation from their
standpoint in the line of fire. Exposing the "truth" of the state to the masses
by their inclusive demands and staking their lives to assert these demands, the

prisoners believed, would shake and awaken the masses, educate them about political realities, and demonstrate that the state was not invincible. Seeing that oppression was shared and change was possible—change brought about by the heroic struggles of the vanguard forces—would propel the masses to action. In this sense the expository function of the death fast resonated with the vanguardist orientation of the large portion of the Turkish left while it also resembled the anarchist "propaganda of the deed" in spirit (see chapter 5).

Finally, on a more tactical level, the prisoners thought that, even though it might not be possible to achieve all of these goals, the inclusion of more general demands would give them maneuvering space in their negotiations with state officials. For example, if the state made certain concessions on the F-type prisons, they could envision themselves making concessions from the more general demands, such as the closing down of state security courts. They therefore considered it necessary to have a broad range of demands that would not only help define the nature of their struggle as democratic and secure the support of broader oppositional forces but also strengthen their possibility of gaining concrete results through negotiations.

Escalation

Although some eight hundred prisoners began to refuse food under the banner raised by these nine demands, the mobilization it provoked within society at large remained limited. Mobilization had already begun over the summer of 2000 in Istanbul and Ankara. Every Saturday at noon, a group of prisoner families, especially mothers, met at the crowded public square in front of the Lycée de Galatasaray in Beyoğlu, Istanbul. In preceding years, this site had been used and popularized by the demonstrations of the "mothers of the disappeared."[82] In Ankara the corresponding site was on Yüksel Street, a crowded intersection and popular spot. Once the hunger strike was launched, these demonstrations became a regular fixture of the urban landscape. As it progressed, the riot police grew fiercer and more violent in suppressing them.

Other mobilizations took place as well. For example, trade union representatives, human rights organizations, lawyers, and organizations of prisoner families carried out a campaign called "No to the Cell-Type Prison" and conducted marches, sit-ins, and other actions to create awareness. The Intelligentsia and Artist Initiative Against the F-Type Prison (F-Tipi Cezaevine Karşı Aydın ve Sanatçı Girişimi) issued a declaration against these prisons on October 28, a week after the hunger strike's launch. This declaration, intended to create greater public awareness around the prisons and to put pressure on the state, was signed by prominent figures in Turkey's public life.[83] The same initiative called for a mass demonstration supported by trade unions, legal socialist parties, prisoner organizations, human rights organizations, and other civil society organizations. Various journalists repeatedly discussed the situation of prisons in their columns. A conference on prison conditions, organized by TAYAD (Solidarity Association for the Families and Relatives of the Arrested), was held in Istanbul on November 10–12, 2000, with the participation of academics, doctors, lawyers, and journalists.[84] Petitions were signed, tables were set up, pamphlets were distributed.

On November 14, four TAYAD members (Şükran Ağdaş, Şenay Hanoğlu, Gülsüman Dönmez, and Fatma Şener) began a hunger strike of indefinite duration to be converted into a fast unto death outside prison walls. A week later, they were joined by four others (Özlem Kahraman, Asibe Yılmaz, Halise Ateş, and Zehra Kulaksız). In late November, families connected to TAYAD also went on hunger strikes and death fasts in other cities, such as Bursa, Adana, Ankara, Ordu, Izmir, Kırşehir, and Trabzon.[85] The demonstration in Ankara against F-type prisons on November 25, 2000, was the highest point of mass mobilization, but it remained limited to seven thousand people.

These limited social pressures mobilizing around the hunger strike of political prisoners failed to provoke an immediate response from the government. In return, the prisoners converted the hunger strike into a fast unto death on November 19, 2000. This conversion meant a more restricted intake, limiting the prisoners' diet to sweetened water and a few pinches of salt a day. The transformation of the hunger strike into a death fast was announced with a new declaration from prisoners in Ümraniye, Bursa, Çankırı, and Aydın Prisons, again associated with the three organizations that launched the hunger strike. A comparison between the two declarations reveals only two minor changes in the list of demands. First, the demand about the closing down of state security courts along with all their legal implications (involving the sentences these courts have issued) was trimmed down. Now the demand made no reference to legal implications but encompassed only the closing down of the courts. Second, the explicit reference to "Kurds and other minorities" in the last demand was removed. In the new version, the last demand read as a call for an end to all antidemocratic laws and the abolition of oppression. It is possible to speculate that this change was a tactical maneuver in order to make the demands appear more realistic, on the one hand, and more appealing to a general audience, on the other. At the same time, the removal of the Kurdish reference is most likely a function of the understanding that PKK would not be participating or supporting this movement (as it had done in 1996). Overall, the declaration announced the prisoners' determination to continue the fast until death or until these demands were met.[86]

Beginning on November 19, 2000, teams of death fasters were serially launched, initially with ten days between each team, and later at greater intervals (see table 4.3). Usually comprising three to fifteen militants, these teams were formed through complex selection procedures and considerations. The actual inauguration of fasting was also accompanied by elaborate ceremonies in which militants would swear an oath to uphold the struggle at any cost and tie a red headband, the symbol of the death fast, around their foreheads. These ceremonies marked the ritual initiation of militants into the new phase of the struggle (see chapter 5).

The conversion of the hunger strike into a fast unto death spurred greater mobilization outside prison walls. Those on the death fast called on the other organizations represented in prisons to join in, but a broader coalition could not be established at the time. Instead, seven other organizations (TİKB, TKP/ML, MLKP, TDP, DH, THKP-C/MLSPB, DY) launched a five-day solidarity hunger strike on November 14–19, 2000.[87] Of the organizations still arguing that the time was not ripe for a death fast, TİKB responded to the hardliners by suggesting that the ongoing death fast should be temporarily suspended or else called off on grounds that the effectiveness of the struggle was being compromised. Their argument was that proposals advanced by prisoners on the death fast and their supporters in the form of smaller wards (possibly composed of twelve prisoners each) in place of cellular confinement in F-type prisons were giving mixed signals to the state in terms of the radicalism of the death fast.[88] Meanwhile, the death fast gained the support of some nonpolitical prisoners in Turkey. For example, thirteen of the prisoners held for "ordinary" crimes in Çankırı E-type Prison went on a two-day hunger strike and another twenty-three went on hunger strike indefinitely on December 4, 2000.[89] Fellow prisoners in European prisons (eleven prisoners in the Netherlands, one in France, and ten prisoners in Germany) went on solidarity hunger strikes of varying durations beginning in late November.[90] Different members of the Intelligentsia and Artist Initiative Against the F-type Prison went on hunger strike on December 7. As a result of growing pressures, the government initiated talks with prisoners through the committee of intellectuals on December 9.

Once the negotiations were initiated, nine other organizations that had initially abstained from participating in the movement joined in on December 10 with a ten-day solidarity hunger strike. When Minister of Justice Türk announced a reprieve in the opening of the F-type prisons on December 11, until a broader public consensus could be achieved, it seemed as if the end of the death fast was in sight. Different civil society organizations, bar associations, trade unions, occupational chambers, and human rights organizations announced that they would be monitoring the government's promise to postpone the opening of F-type prisons. Legal socialist parties EMEP, HADEP,

Table 4.3   TEAMS OF DEATH FASTERS AND THEIR LAUNCH DATES

DEATH FASTER TEAM	LAUNCH DATE
1	November 19, 2000 (with relays on November 22 and 25)
2	November 29, 2000 (with relays on December 2 and 5)
3	December 14, 2000 (with relays on December 15-25)
4	May 11, 2001 (with relay on May 20)
5	June 3, 2001
6	July 28, 2001
7	September 26, 2001
8	May 1, 2002
9 Zehra Kulaksız Team	November 30, 2002
10 Gültekin Koç Team	October 20, 2003
11 Sevgi Erdoğan Team	July 25, 2004
12 Fidan Kalşen Team	May 9, 2005
13 Cengiz Soydaş Team	May 1, 2006

ÖDP, SİP, and TSİP issued a joint press statement, venturing their support for the "public inspection role" assumed by civil society organizations in the growing public debate on prisons.[91] The prisoners already on the death fast interpreted the government's message of reprieve as a positive but unsatisfactory sign, refusing to quit the death fast upon this announcement. Negotiations of prisoner representatives with the committee of intellectuals in Sağmalcılar Prison proceeded until December 14 when the concrete counteroffer to keep prisoners in eighteen-to-twenty-person wards instead of one-to-three-person cells was rejected by the government. The armed attack on a police bus in Istanbul, conducted by militants of TKP(ML)–TİKKO, one of the three organizations that initiated the death fast struggle, did not serve the purpose of adding further pressure on the government. On the contrary, it spurred the riot police to take to the streets and added to the government's frustration with the prisoners.[92]

Days later, a fierce security operation was unleashed upon the prisons participating in the hunger strike. According to the prisoners and their supporters, the Operation Return to Life conducted during December 19–22, 2000, simultaneously upon twenty prisons around the country, was both violent and cynical, though not completely unexpected. The cynicism, according to the prisoners, was due not simply to the state's deployment of thousands of security personnel to attack the prisons allegedly under its own control. Rather, the cynicism lay in the purported rationale of the security operation, i.e., saving and bringing back to life the prisoners on the brink of self-starvation, "saving terrorists from their own terror," as Prime Minister Ecevit remarked. The death toll of the security operation and the number of those who incurred severe wounds revealed a grave discrepancy between the name and conduct of the operation. While the human cost of the operation may in part be a result of the active resistance the prisoners put up to defend their wards, the disproportionality of the force and the weaponry employed in the operation were astonishing in themselves.[93] Whatever one may say regarding the irony of the state having to invade its own prisons, the clash between the armed forces and the starving prisoners presented a memorable and disturbing contrast.

Operation Return to Life marked a new stage in the escalation of the struggle, not only due to the state's resort to violence but also because the participants of the movement began resorting to acts of self-immolation. The first ten instances of self-burning occurred during this security operation. These prisoners (all of whom except for one were prisoners affiliated with DHKP-C) set themselves on fire in order to thwart the attack, to gain time for the relocation of hunger strikers within the prison to areas unaffected by the fires and gas clouds, and to protest the operation itself.

Despite prisoners' attempts to defend their wards, it was not long before the state's security forces cut through the barricades of the prisoners: 942 prisoners were taken to three F-type prisons put into immediate use despite their contested status in public opinion and the minister's preceding reprieve declaration; 308 prisoners were taken to Sincan F-type Prison in Ankara, 317 prisoners were taken to Edirne F-type Prison, and 317 prisoners were taken to Kocaeli F-type Prison. Another 95 female prisoners were taken to Bakırköy Women and Children's Prison and Kartal Special Type Prison. 237 severely wounded prisoners were taken to hospitals.[94] In addition, prisoners were transferred to provincial E-type medium-security prisons, such as those in Izmir, Manisa, and Kütahya.

The continuous reruns of operation footage broadcast on television, especially of the state bulldozing its way into prisons, were very effective in silencing the general public. According to participants of the death fast struggle, under siege and invasion in the televised spectacle of sovereign power were no longer only prisons but the dissent of an entire country, silenced and overawed into submission. Accompanied by displays of rows of weapons and cell phones allegedly captured from within the prisons, the news presented many allegations that prisoners had been receiving phone calls from their fugitive leaders in Europe ordering them to burn themselves to death and to carry out acts of "terrorism." State officials claimed that the causes of casualties in the prisons operation were not the disproportionate use of force by security personnel but the use of weapons secretly stockpiled by the prisoners and their self-destructive acts. The acts of self immolation were enthusiastically used by the state as propaganda against the prisoners, presenting them both as brainwashed "youth" and fanatical "terrorists" while justifying the operation that "saved" their lives.

It is impossible to say with certainty what happened in the prisons during those three days and in the immediate aftermath of Operation Return to Life that led to the deaths of thirty prisoners and two security personnel. The public trial continues to this day. However, it would not be a mistake to claim, based on the autopsy reports released to the press, that the real cause of death for most prisoners was neither self-starvation nor self-immolation but the wounds incurred by weapons used by security forces, in addition to suffocation and burning by the gas bombs that were thrown into the prisons.[95] Similarly, these reports cast doubt on the allegations that the two security personnel were killed by prisoners but suggested instead that they were killed by friendly fire.

As a result of the discrepancy between their experience of the security operation and its presentation to the public, the prisoners soon added a new demand to their original list of demands, asking for full disclosure of what really happened during the security operation and the public trial of all of those who were involved in its planning and execution. Meanwhile, DHKP-C militant Gültekin Koç entered police headquarters in Şişli, Istanbul and detonated the bomb on his body on January 3, 2001, killing one policeman and doing significant damage to the building. In the public announcement issued by DHKP-C claiming responsibility for the attack, the action was explained as an "act of justice" in response to the security operation of December 19–22, 2000.[96]

In the aftermath of the military operation in prisons around the country, the state's security forces continued a vigilant operation against civil society. Human rights defenders also bore the brunt of state repression. The police raided ten branches of the Human Rights Association (İHD), detained its staff, and confiscated archival material. Some six branches were temporarily sealed and shut down. Similarly, community and cultural centers where panels and meetings on the F-type prisons were held were subjected to searches, with thirty people detained.[97] Other planned gatherings were not permitted. The leaders of Tüm Yargı-Sen, the trade union of workers in the judiciary and penal institutions, were detained upon issuing press statements critical of the prison operation. On February 6, 2001, members of the central board and the Ankara branch of the trade union were detained for trial at the state security court of Ankara by Public Prosecutor Nuh Mete Yüksel for "aiding and abetting terrorist organizations."[98] Overall, in the next two months following the operation, 2,800 people were detained in protests against the F-types, of which 190 were eventually arrested.

Legal socialist parties, such as ÖDP, SİP, and EMEP, quickly distanced themselves from the radical supporters of the death fast. Even before Operation Return to Life, the socialist ÖDP issued a circular prohibiting its members from participating in demonstrations related to prisons and its branches from allowing prisoner relatives to use their space to stage solidarity hunger strikes.[99] SİP leader Aydemir Güler announced the liquidation of the radical left. He argued that "revolutionary democracy had been upholding its political existence through the prisons agenda for a long time and had fallen off the politics of the country . . . It is unnecessary to say that revolutionary democracy has fallen outside of politics. This current is experiencing a large liquidation in this period. Activity could be sustained on the prisons agenda but political enlivening could not have been achieved . . . The prison operation is surely a bloody liquidation, but of course, at the same time, it is the elimination of the lack of a political line."[100] The leftist newspaper *Evrensel*, close to EMEP, published a piece condemning the participants of the death fast struggle with "irresponsible petit bourgeois leftism."[101]

Birikim, the influential journal of socialist theory and culture in Turkey, published pieces on the hunger strike, which, while critical of Operation Return to Life, emphasized the sociological and ideological distance of supporters of the "extreme" left from "moderate/democratic" groups on the left, at times in language that could hardly hide the class contempt felt by the democratic socialists for the participants and supporters of the death fast. Accordingly, the constituency of the "extreme" left, who participated in and supported the death fast struggle, could "find a place for themselves among the masses who came not even from the lowest ranks of societal hierarchy but who could be considered 'outside of society,' from those who were unemployed, those pushed to temporary, undocumented, fugitive, 'illegal' or dubiously legal means of subsistence, those who could not establish themselves or who refused to do so, and were nourished by the pessimistic reaction and rage that arose from the condition of actual exclusion or subjective feeling of exclusion."[102] The illegal organizations that capitalized on this constituency considered victory not as effecting social transformation but in expressing a "hopeless rebellion," which consisted of resisting through armed struggle, or rather, being able to die in the struggle.[103] Those in prison were no longer "one of us," but the ones who "flowed from the shanty towns, like a muddy torrent, young people without a future and without hope. People who are darkened by the consciousness that they can never be a real part of this society."[104] The same author continued, "even though our name is subsumed under the same heading with these people . . . it is difficult to say that we share the same street, same neighborhood, even the same restaurant, let alone the same political goal."[105]

But while the wave of repression on social opposition attending Operation Return to Life managed to intimidate many individuals and marginalize the death fast struggle, even on the left, it was unable to put an end to the struggle itself.[106] To the contrary, the organizations now participating in the struggle went from three to eleven. The prisoners affiliated with the organizations that had launched a solidarity hunger strike before the prison operation continued to uphold the hunger strike after being placed in F-type prisons along with the prisoners affiliated with the first group.[107] The peak of the death fast struggle in terms of participation, therefore, came after Operation Return to Life, when some 1,500–2,000 prisoners were involved (corresponding to an overwhelming majority of the leftist prisoner population). Of these prisoners, those on the death fast went up to 395, while the number of prisoners on hunger strike of indefinite duration increased to 1,118, bringing the total of those prisoners engaged in self-starvation to 1,513.[108] Only a few days later, on December 26, 2000, the number of prisoners on hunger strike was reported to be 1,596, with 432 on a fast unto death.[109] In a rare display of solidarity, most leftist factions, groups, and organizations acted together, including the organizations that were reticent before the launch of the struggle, doubling the number of prisoners engaged in some form of self-starvation. With a joint declaration on February 3, 2001, the remaining nine organizations announced their formal participation in the death fast. Through this declaration, and one issued on February 10, the coalition of a dozen organizations announced their determination to continue the struggle together. The various streams of resistance had now converged into a coordinated, collective fast unto death, commanding the political prisoner population on the Turkish left almost en masse.[110] This is the point when the "coalition" as the predominant form of organization reached its fruition.[111] Now carried out with even greater determination, the death fast became the means by which political prisoners claimed a voice from the depths of the cells in the new high security prisons.

Right to Die

By March 2001, with the full participation of outlawed leftist organizations with constituencies in prison, the number of death fasters had increased to around 500 prisoners and the rest of the political prisoner population was on indefinite hunger strike.[112] The prisoners on the death fast had also quit taking vitamin B1, which helped prolong the process of self-starvation and was important for the recovery of the body with less damage in case the fast was terminated. The first death due to starvation occurred in an F-type prison cell, 153 days after the initiation of the strike. Following the death of Cengiz Soydaş on March 21, 2001, the supporters of the hunger strikers carried out an armed attack against a patrolling police car on April 2, 2001, in Bahçelievler, Istanbul, resulting in the deaths of two policemen. Responsibility for this attack was claimed by the Fırat Tavuk Death Fast Brigade, an armed faction of DHKP-C. The armed unit was named after a militant who died after setting himself on fire during the prisons operation of December 19–22, 2000.

The deaths of another nineteen people from self-starvation (five of whom carried out the hunger strike in solidarity outside prison) and the self-immolation of a militant in Germany in support of the hunger strike marked the month of April. However, despite the increasing death toll, there was no compromise from the state. Instead, rumors regarding artificial feeding circulated among prisoners.

Referring to this medical practice as "forced intervention" (*zorla müdahale*) to emphasize its nonconsensuality, the prisoners argued that ever since they had been evacuated from the wards and taken to hospitals they had been subjected to intense pressures to quit the hunger strike and were even fed intravenously against their will. Some hunger strikers described the ongoing struggle they had to wage from their hospital bed: they would fall unconscious, the medical staff would give them the IV, they would wake up and take it out, continue the fast, loose consciousness again, only to find the IV back in their arm when they woke up.[113] Prisoners contended that resuscitation through intravenous feeding should be considered a form of torture and that their "right to die" should be respected. They also declared that the negligent or intentionally malignant administration of artificial feeding (by the exclusion of a much needed vitamin B in the liquid mixture given intravenously) had caused serious disabilities in many prisoners. One of the most prevalent effects of such artificial feeding was the increase in those diagnosed with the Wernicke-Korsakoff syndrome—a thiamin (vitamin B1) deficiency, due to starvation, sometimes aggravated by the improper termination of a hunger strike.[114] In severe cases, individuals with Wernicke-Korsakoff syndrome would practically regress into a state of mental infancy, become for the most part immobilized and sometimes even delusional, and thus require continuous health care.[115] Medical interventions personalized the war between the state and revolutionaries by localizing this war in each militant's own body, marking a new, intensified phase of the struggle. Death became the prisoners' weapon to fight the forced administration of life upon their bodies.

However, as the death toll increased and public support waned, the differences in the fragile coalition of leftist parties began to resurface. The latecomers, the group of organizations that joined in the struggle after Operation

Return to Life, argued that, in light of the "narrowing down" of the support for the struggle, the focus of the movement should be turned to the problem of isolation in F-type prisons rather than the closing of the prisons themselves. The closure of high security prisons now appeared too unrealistic and noncompromising, and they thought that upholding this demand would impede the possibility of further negotiations with the government. This faction maintained that the movement should fight for the creation of common living areas for fifteen to twenty-five individuals in F-type prisons (this could be achieved, they argued, by leaving the doors of adjacent cells sharing the same hallway unlocked during the day) and the abolition of the requirement for participation in "treatment," i.e. the prison-run "rehabilitation programs," as a precondition of utilizing common areas in these prisons.[116] In contrast to the revolutionary rhetoric and the noncompromising stance of the first group of organizations, the second group favored the adoption of the language of human rights and the involvement of transnational and supranational organizations (such as Amnesty International and the European Parliament) that could pressure the government, to create greater publicity for the movement.[117] The meeting the supporters of this group arranged with the minister of justice, head of the General Directorate of Prisons and Detention Houses, and a member of parliament (also member of the parliament's Human Rights Commission) on April 12, 2001, however, did not achieve any results.[118] Nor did the meeting with members of the European Parliament, including Daniel Cohn-Bendit, who suspected double-talk on the part of the prisoners oscillating between defining the struggle as an opposition to isolation, on the one hand, and a struggle against imperialism and the IMF, on the other.[119] While these initiatives did not lead the state to compromise, they did manage to shake the prisoners' already fragile coalition.

In May 2001 the death fasters issued a new declaration, announcing an abridged list of demands.[120] The first demand was no longer the abolition of F-type prisons, but the *end to isolation*. However, the abolition of the disciplinary penal regime imposed via cellular confinement could only be achieved, the prisoners argued, by actually modifying the spatial layout of the high security prisons. They proposed that the state combine adjacent cells, by removing the separating walls to enable more prisoners to stay together, and lift the preconditions regarding prisoner conduct to access areas designated for common use in the F-type prisons. Second on the list was a call for the abolition of all the prohibitions and disciplinary practices that sought to destroy their identity as "political" prisoners. The third item was an assertion that their demands were "legitimate and democratic." Finally, the prisoners wanted the state to give up the policy of artificial feeding upon loss of consciousness. The prisoners claimed that there were at least thirty people who had experienced nonconsensual medical intervention and were suffering from a resultant disability such as memory loss.[121]

This new set of demands was not the same as those proposed by the second group (whose proposal was the creation of common spaces by unlocking adjacent cells), as it still pushed for architectural changes in the F-type prisons, but it was indicative of a compromise between the two factions. It also signaled retreat from the original objectives of the movement. In the meantime, the state's olive branch, consisting of several new laws and amendments, appeared wholly unsatisfactory to the prisoners. The amendment of Article 16 of the antiterror law appeared to create the opportunity for socialization in the F-type prisons, but it gave legal backing to "rehabilitation programs" administered by prison authorities in which prisoners had to participate in order to gain access to common spaces.[122] Because political prisoners rejected these programs in principle, this amendment, in effect, enhanced the legality of ongoing practices of cellular confinement in the F-type prisons. The law establishing special courts to oversee infractions in prisons and prison monitoring boards represented improvements that were negligible insofar as they made the state in charge of its own inspection. If the prisoners did not trust the state, why should they trust the officials appointed by the state to monitor the state?[123]

Three other prisoners died of self-starvation during May. At the end of May 2001, the Ministry of Justice began to release the participants of the death fast from prison, with a view of preventing the growing number of deaths inside prison walls. The prisoners' release, chosen in place of resuming negotiations, was carried out by the provisional suspension and reprieve of their sentences or by permanent presidential pardon. These pardons, whether temporary or permanent, were justified on the grounds that the prisoners' deteriorating health was not compatible with life in prison and that their sentence (or detention) could not be executed as long as it presented a serious risk to the prisoner's life.[124] Some prisoners, especially those affiliated with the hardliners, considered this move to be another one of the state's tactics to divide and weaken the struggle and argued that the death fast should be continued outside of prisons, while others considered it a concession of the state to the struggle and an opportunity to get out of prison. Most prisoners did not shy away from using the state's turn to compassion and applied to be considered for the amnesty (though some were released without having had to apply). Physicians from the Council of Forensic Medicine were asked to determine who was eligible for parole based on physical examinations. Fasting militants on the verge of death were released into the world, either singly or a few at a time, beginning on May 31, 2001.

As the participants of the death fast were ejected from prison, new challenges awaited the movement. One of the biggest challenges was to sustain the hunger strike outside the prisons. Already in prison some participants had stopped fasting after being subject to artificial feeding, losing the will or the well-being to fight for the "right to die." In the absence of the shared spatial experience of the prison, it proved extremely difficult to maintain the collective will of self-starvation, with the exception of some extraordinarily committed individuals. Many participants quit fasting when they were released from prison; others were pressured to quit by their families; still others were made to quit by their organizations. As more people quit the fast, they were ostracized and accused of "treason" by the supporters of those who continued.[125] These tensions created hostilities within the movement. Second, it became difficult to justify the reason why the death fast should still be the dominant tactic of the struggle. Many participants argued that there were many different ways of struggling against F-type prisons, especially now that they were outside, so self-destructive practices began to lose their appeal. Third, it became increasingly difficult to sustain the unity of the movement, again in part due to the loss of the shared spatial experience of the prison, which had been critical in fortifying a unified front among the prisoners and enabling them to transcend their sectarian differences and divergent political views.

Nonetheless, some of the prisoners discharged from prison announced that they would continue to fast outside in order to ensure the survival of the death fast struggle. They argued that quitting now meant playing into the hands of the state, whose tactical maneuver of releasing prisoners was carried out, in their view, precisely to break the movement. Since F-type prisons were firmly in place, the reasons for the struggle were still intact. The struggle must therefore continue until demands were met. These prisoners were affiliated with the hardliners, especially two of the three organizations that initiated the struggle. In contrast, prisoners affiliated with the organizations in the second group (except MLKP) refused to continue the death fast outside the prison (while still actively participating in prison). This difference regarding whether or not to uphold death fasting outside of prisons furthered already-existing tensions in the coalition of parties that comprised the movement.

The ex-prisoners who declared their will to continue fasting were placed in houses among family, friends, and supporters in shantytown neighborhoods, such as Küçükarmutlu and Alibeyköy, where their organizations drew the bulk of their supporters. These houses, referred to as "resistance houses," were often visited by journalists, human rights defenders, intellectuals, and artists as an expression of solidarity. On June 4, 2001, a new team of death fasters launched by the prisoner rights organization TAYAD, comprising of three women, joined the ex-prisoners in Küçükarmutlu's resistance houses.

Each month over the summer brought the death of several new militants. In the fall the death toll increased again. Another eighteen militants were dead between September and December 2001: one from suicide attack (killing two policemen and a civilian, wounding twenty-one others), four from hunger strike and self-immolation combined, nine from self-starvation. Four individuals were killed in police raids of the "resistance houses" in the shantytowns.[126] Table 4.4 shows a breakdown of casualties according to causes of death.

Yet the public grew accustomed, if not numb, to the news of death. Each death barely found a small corner in the newspapers, which reported the death fast struggle with lesser frequency, if they mentioned the struggle at all. In

Table 4.4   CAUSE OF DEATH IN THE DEATH FAST STRUGGLE

CAUSE OF DEATH	CASUALTIES
Self-starvation due to death fast	67
Self-Immolation	24
Self-immolation while on death fast	22
Suicide Attack	5
Killed	24
Killed while on hunger strike or death fast	9
Died of medical neglect or health complications	2
Total	122

place of the disruptive impact it initially generated, the *weaponization of life* became the tactic of an isolated politics, isolated from the support of the masses and their daily struggles. It kept failing to unite, lead, and inspire; failing, in other words, to generate popular support for the prisoners' alternative claim to power, to bring the experience of a different form of life in prison wards into mainstream politics, to carry the reality of the margins to the center. The movement had reached an impasse.

Around the time of the first anniversary of the Operation Return to Life, an important initiative to disrupt the stalemate emerged under the leadership of lawyers. This was the proposal called "Three Doors, Three Locks" put forth by the Istanbul, Izmir, Ankara, and Antalya Bar Associations.[127] According to this proposal, the doors of three cells, each containing three prisoners and opening to the same corridor in the F-type prisons, could be left open during daytime so that nine prisoners could interact freely. Neither a return to the ward system, nor the continuation of isolation, this proposal sought a middle-ground solution to the "prisons problem," one that would bring the fast unto death to an end while also softening cellular confinement. By the time the proposal was articulated in the public sphere, 36 individuals had died on the death fast, bringing the death toll to 87 individuals. Over 300 had become disabled due to artificial feeding. Around 150 individuals were still fasting.[128]

Despite the broad support rallied behind the proposal from trade unions, occupational chambers, prisoners' rights associations, and human rights organizations, it was rejected by the Ministry of Justice.[129] In order to justify this position, the ministry marshaled a number of arguments: (1) such a proposal was legally unacceptable because it conflicted with Article 16 of the antiterror law (which allowed access to common areas only on the basis of participation in "rehabilitation and educational programs"); (2) discipline and security would be damaged because (a) the corridors would be unusable for services, such as distributing letters and meals, conducting counts and searches, and controlling the internal traffic of prisoners; and (b) the prisoners could destroy the cameras watching the corridors, communicate with other prisoners in corridors nearby, break the iron doors in between corridors, begin rioting, and finally occupy the prison; (3) a riot in the prison would destroy the electronic system, whose replacement would bring a great financial burden upon the state; and (4) the prison personnel would lose confidence and motivation.[130] In the event that the proposal was accepted, the ministry argued, penal reform would have failed and prisons would revert back to their state of "anarchy" prior to December 19, 2000, emboldening those on the death fast. On these grounds the ministry announced that it would not accept this proposal. Minister Türk discredited the proposal by arguing that it encouraged those on the death fast, who, he declared, were of the "same mentality as Muhammed Atta," thereby insinuating that these prisoners were as dangerous as those "terrorists" who carried out the suicide attacks of September 11.[131] In place of Three Doors, Three Locks, the ministry pointed to the legal reforms underway (such as the amendment of Article 16 of the antiterror law and the establishment of prison monitoring boards and special courts overseeing prisons) and issued an alternative executive decree. According to this decree, prisoners selected by a commission appointed by the prison administration could get together in groups of ten or less in the common spaces of the prison for five hours a week on the condition that they quit fasting and agreed to participate in at least one of the activities of the "rehabilitation program." Needless to say, the prisoners uniformly rejected this decree.

Upon the failure of the Three Doors, Three Locks initiative, the illegal organizations supporting the death fast struggle began to withdraw their militants from the ongoing hunger strike. Ex-prisoners in "resistance houses" in Alibeyköy and Gaziosmanpaşa announced that they would no longer continue the fast outside.[132] Eight organizations issued a statement announcing that they had called off the death fast for their own prisoners and supporters in May 2002. These were TKP(ML), TKP/ML, MLKP, TİKB, TDP, DH, THKP-C/MLSPB, and TKP/K. Announcing the ethical and moral victory of the movement, they jointly argued that the resistance movement had "disrupted the plans of fascism" and played its "revolutionary role," having proven the "superiority of the revolutionary will."[133] They asserted that a new stage had arrived in the "great resistance" and that the struggle would be continued by other means until the "terror of the cell and isolation" were fully trampled.

The atmosphere of defeat, marked by dwindling public interest, ninety-two militants already dead, and no more than a superficial change in the state's disciplinary penal regime now in place, that occasioned this decision stood in stark contrast with the victorious proclamations of these parties. With this decision, the organizations in the second group in the coalition, advocating the postponement of the death fast in the initial discussions, were withdrawing from the struggle, tagging along TKP(ML) as one of the hardliners with them. Another hardliner, TKİP, had quit the struggle without an announcement. These organizations (and others without official participation) claimed a death toll of nineteen individuals (see table 4.5).

At this stage, only two organizations out of the multiparty coalition continued to uphold the fast unto death. DHKP-C, as one of the three organizations that had initiated the struggle, had deployed the greatest variety of tactics and incurred most of the death toll (see table 4.5). It was now joined by TKEP/L (initially from the second group) in continuing the death fast, which they claimed was the (only) correct line of action, regardless of changing circumstances.[34] They held that the death fast should go on as a matter of principle, even if this meant having only a few prisoners on the fast unto death. The slogan "Till the End, Till Eternity, Till the Last One of Us" ("Sona, Sonsuza, Sonuncumuza") was coined to express their determination.

Two years into the struggle, therefore, the death fast was already much abated in its level of participation, public support, and vigor. However, its continuation even by a few militants and political defense by the supporters of the remaining two organizations had symbolic value. It attested to the fact that neither had prison conditions been ameliorated nor had any of the prisoner

Table 4.5 DISTRIBUTION OF CASUALTIES ACCORDING TO POLITICAL AFFILIATION AND CAUSE OF DEATH

POLITICAL AFFILIA-TION	SELF STAR-VATION	SELF-IMMOLATION	SUICIDE ATTACK	KILLED	OTHER	TOTAL
DHKP-C	42	23	5	17	2	89
KPİO	1					1
MLKP	2					2
PKK-DÇS				2		2
TAYAD	7			4		11
TİKB	4					4
TKEP/L	2			1		3
TKİP	1					1
TKP(ML)	6	1				7
TKP/ML	2					2
TOTAL	67	24	5	24	2	122

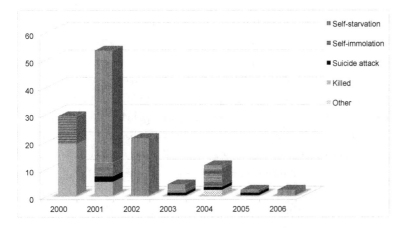

Figure 4.1   DISTRIBUTION OF DEATHS OVER TIME

demands been met. For the next few years, deaths would continue to occur, though with less frequency, as a result of self-starvation, self-immolations, and occasional suicide attacks (see figure 4.1).

END TO ISOLATION

"End Isolation, Stop the Deaths!" This was the only slogan around which different social forces mobilized in the last couple months of 2006 in order to bring the long durée of the death fast struggle to a close by pressuring the Ministry of Justice, now run by the AKP government, to take action.[135] This mobilization emerged, after a long period of inactivity, around the increasingly critical situation of Behiç Aşçı (pronounced Ash-chu), the prominent lawyer and human rights defender, who began a fast unto death at his own home on April 5, 2006.[136] Aşçı had chosen this date, recognized around the world as Lawyers' Day, to draw attention to his choice of fasting as an extension of his advocacy for many former participants of the death fast struggle and other leftist militants still imprisoned in F-type prisons.

The extension of legal advocacy into political activism, Aşçı argued, was both in line with his self-perception as a "revolutionary democratic lawyer"[137] and rendered inevitable, given his loss of faith in the possibility of law to deliver justice.[138] During the press conference announcing his decision, Aşçı began his speech by stating, "I am on the death fast because I am a revolutionary lawyer."[139] For Aşçı, his political identity as a "revolutionary lawyer" meant that his legal practice was inseparable from his own position as an activist in the struggle for rights and liberties. As he spoke, a placard on the wall behind him announced: "Resistance is a right where there is no justice."[140] Declaring that he had observed and experienced too many wrongs to keep on believing that law could dispense justice, Aşçı announced that he had decided to continue his legal practice by other means. If war, according to Carl von Clausewitz, was the extension of politics by other means, Aşçı's death fast would be the extension of his legal practice by the only means he had left at his disposal: his life. Where *representing* his clients was ineffective, he would *present* their case with his life, making it his own.

The participation of such a person of recognized stature and public repute in the death fast struggle did not go unnoticed.[141] Aşçı's participation not only reinvigorated the debates around high security prisons in the public sphere after a hiatus of almost five years, but it also (even if slowly) mobilized other sectors of civil society, especially representatives of democratic mass organizations. Among these were the Turkish Medical Association (TTB), Union of Bar Associations of Turkey (TBB), Architects' and Engineers' Chambers Association of Turkey (TMMOB), Confederation of Revolutionary Trade Unions (DİSK), Confederation of Public Laborers' Trade Unions (KESK), HAK Trade Unions' Confederation, Human Rights Association (İHD), Solidarity Association for Human Rights and the Oppressed (MAZLUMDER), International Amnesty Organization Turkey Branch, Human Rights Foundation of Turkey (TİHV), Helsinki Citizens' Assembly (HYD), Human Rights and Liberties Humanitarian Aid Foundation (İHH), and Association for Free Thought and Educational Rights (Özgür-Der).

This was an important development especially because many trade unions, intellectuals, activists, human rights workers, legal socialist parties, and even the illegal organizations that had formerly participated in the prisons struggle had distanced themselves from the death fast in the intervening years. They had been debilitated by the impasse the movement had reached and claimed that the hardliners had not caved in at crucial moments when an agreement with the state could have been reached, therefore missing important opportunities for ending the struggle with relative success. They had also been alienated by the revolutionary rhetoric of the movement and the high stakes of participation.¹⁴² They had become disillusioned with hunger striking as the primary tactic of struggle and its supplementation with self-immolations and suicide attacks. They criticized these militants' insistence on the weaponization of life, arguing that the means of the struggle had become its end. They even considered the technique of struggle to be the "fetishiza-tion" of death.¹⁴³ Moreover, they interpreted this insistence on upholding the death fast, now that the struggle was largely monopolized by the sympathizers of DHKP-C, as a self-righteous display of obstinacy against the state and a form of self-aggrandizement, as opposed to a strategic deployment of the radi-cal left's increasingly scarce human resources.¹⁴⁴ Consequently, the movement, already marginal in its inception, had been further marginalized, having lost its supporters even on the left. The hardliners that led the struggle had been abandoned by their own allies.

In such a conjuncture, the lawyer Aşçı's statements to the press represented a new turning point in the discursive world of the movement. Aşçı drew atten-tion to the meaning of being locked up in a cell and the deleterious impact it had on prisoners' mental and physical integrity.¹⁴⁵ He focused on the problem of *isolation* and its impact on the well-being of prisoners. Cellular confinement meant isolation; isolation meant sensory deprivation, lack of human contact, and physical vulnerability; therefore, cellular confinement meant torture. The unacceptability of torture rendered it necessary to oppose and fight isolation.

The only demand the lawyer put forth in his fast unto death was a *concrete* concession on the part of the state to end the absolute regime of isolation in prisons. Meeting this demand did not necessitate closing down F-type prisons but merely entailed improvements within them, improvements that would permit prisoners greater opportunities for socialization. "We are not demand-ing the demolition of prisons," he declared. "Confinement is already a punish-ment, we are only against adding on top of this a second, a third punishment. This is torture."¹⁴⁶ Speaking on behalf of all political prisoners, Aşçı argued:

> What we want is the abolition of architectural isolation or a concrete step toward its abolition. We are not articulating a formula on this issue. We want the ministry to articulate it. That is, whether it will be three doors, three locks, whether the single-person beds will be changed with bunk beds and the three-person cells will be converted into six-person ones, let the ministry say. There are hundreds of

formulae the ministry can suggest. We are dependent on the ministry, that is. If the ministry takes a step, we will quit the death fast. We particularly emphasize that abolition of isolation is a matter of a longer duration. The struggle against isolation will not end even when the ministry takes a step and we quit the death fast. The struggle against isolation will continue, but the death fast will end. Because isolation will continue with its different dimensions. The death fast is only a means that aims [to achieve] a retreat in the abolition of isolation [*sic*]. Other means are other methods of struggle that will be conducted in the prison itself.¹⁴⁷

Aşçı's plea represented a significant retreat from the ambitious demands of the death fast struggle, encompassing as they had been a holistic transformation of the legal and political system. Not only were the broader demands for democratization dropped, but even the demand for the abolition of F-type prisons was now significantly watered down to the relaxation of isolation in high security prisons. A struggle for democracy was thereby being substituted by a democratic struggle against isolation. Isolation was now presented within a human rights discourse as a penal practice that denied human dignity rather than within the discourse of revolutionary struggle. Reformulated as such, the question of isolation was no longer about the sovereign imposition of a biopolitical spatial logic to achieve totalizing disciplinary control and surveillance, but, a form of punishment that was not "humane."

The reformulation of the death fast struggle as a movement against isolation disentangled the opposition to F-type prisons from the communist experience of the prison wards, an experience whose spatial grounding had enabled the critique of "cellularization" in the first place. It openly portrayed that the prisoners could no longer make an alternative claim to sovereign power as the revolutionary vanguard of the people. The movement had failed in its ability to put forth a hegemonic project that would provide a coherent and convincing alternative to the sovereignty of the Turkish state outside of prisons. With the state's strategic negligence, the movement's marginality had been accentuated while its unifying and mobilizing power had been attenuated. The inability of the movement to create a "hegemonic sovereignty" was decisive for the shift toward humanitarian empathy.¹⁴⁸ The communism at the margins that had transformed prison wards into *constituent spaces* was therefore submerged in a despatialized call for humanity across prison walls, neighborhoods, and borders. The uncompromising stance emanating from the experience of *ward communes* was thus deflected into an abstract, universal call for human rights, which could not contest the state's rebuilding and reconfiguration of its sovereignty bottom up, but instead submitted to it, confining itself to demanding more "humane" conditions of confinement.

In a press release Aşçı declared: "I have no personal demands. My only demand is the abolition of isolation in prisons. . . . I don't view my act as an act of suicide. Of course, I, too, love to live and want to live. But I don't want to live watching my clients being kept under conditions of isolation. I don't want to live watching them consume and destroy themselves every day. I owe them a *debt of conscience* and I must pay this."[149] From his perspective, Aşçı's death fast was only the assumption of the moral obligation he felt toward those who had lost their lives in the struggle and those who continued to struggle.[150] This was a *moral* call that intended to appeal to the "conscience" of the people and their humanitarianism. The call asserted that it was enough to be human to support the demands of the prisoners. The people might have little in common with those from the margins, but should nonetheless meet them on the basis of a humanitarianism whose *ultima ratio* was that no one should have to seek death in order to make oneself heard. The lawyer demanded the people apply to the prisoners the dictates of a universal morality in which different values could coexist and not pass judgment on the specific implications of their radical political identities. Radical politics was thereby displaced to the domain of morality.

In the absence of the death fast struggle's effective hegemonic appeal to the masses, this moral call was set to work (or set to do the political work). The movement had hitherto called for a militancy that made moral concerns subsidiary to the political, advocating the transformation of lives into weapons and asserting the primacy of the "right to die." The very radicalism of the movement was predicated on the fact that the prisoners had wrenched away the power of life and death from the state into their own hands. Their militancy and alternative claim to power was supported by their ability to command the power of life and death, impinging not only on the state's *monopoly* of violence but also on its *monopsony* of sacrifice. Advocacy against state-sponsored artificial feeding had been built around the very notion that prisoners were ready to die in the name of their political identity and convictions rather than live a life that was imposed on them by the state.

In contrast, the moral call voiced by the lawyer sought to advance claims against isolation on the grounds of the basic and universal "right to live," substituting it in place of the "right to die." The deliberate effort to distinguish the fast unto death from a nihilistic or suicidal act that did not value life in itself (Aşçı had argued, "Of course, I, too, love to live and want to live") ultimately hoped to persuade the audience that this struggle was life-affirming more than it was life-negating.[151] The hunger strike was not suicidal; it intended to advance a political cause that involved a more humane and dignified life. The prisoners now sought to meet the audience through the moral affirmation of life itself, to which politics would henceforth become subordinate.

The most outstanding quality of this moral appeal was its instrumental role in establishing a new bridge of solidarity between the progressive social forces in civil society and the radical and radically marginalized participants of the death fast struggle. The call would succeed insofar as it was able to muster the contradiction between political voice and collective will. Initially the prisoners had a strong collective will arising out of the shared experience of prison wards, but no political voice. Their discourse remained marginal to the political sphere, just as they remained in the margins. The profound discrepancy between their earnest, strong, and unified will and the lack of voice was translated into a readiness to weaponize their lives in the name of contesting the state while publicizing and popularizing their cause. On the other hand, the progressive forces in civil society commanded political voice but lacked (or soon lost) the collective will and determination to speak and act. These denizens of the public sphere had been reduced to the role of spectators, passive witnesses to the opposing spectacles of violence performed by the state and the insurgents. This renewed moral call sought to resolve the contradiction by uniting those who had political voice and yet little or no collective will with those who had collective will and yet little or no political voice—an alliance between the privileged and the dispossessed. The person of the lawyer was a bridge between the two, reminding the people of their moral responsibility to intervene on the basis of a shared humanity and translate the violence of the weaponization of life into the language of rights.

As a moral call, the struggle against isolation capitalized on guilt and shame. The hunger strikers called upon those who possessed symbolic privilege and retorted that they ought to assume responsibility for their inaction. They sought to mobilize the people by imparting shame upon their passive spectatorship or insufficient involvement: if those with political voice did not ally with those without voice, they would be just as responsible for the subsequent deaths as was the state. Inactivity implied tacit consent. Aşçı's decision to fast was intended to reveal to the audience the burden of shame they all carried because, unlike them, he had refused complicity. The movement also strove to make the audience aware of the debt they had (unwittingly or not) incurred to those who had no voice. The militants had been the ones who struggled for emancipation; they had been the ones who performed the *labor of dying* in order to claim a just life for all. Their work had defended the rights of all because their deaths claimed voice not only for those who lacked it but also for those who failed to exercise it. If it were not for them, who knows what incursions upon democracy and human rights might have been weathered at the hands of a state apparatus determined to impose its cellular vision on society, its project of biosovereignty? For the audience, becoming aware of their indebtedness to those who had no voice meant interrupting their labor of dying; hence, if this moral command were to successfully mobilize the audience, it would already imply that those who lacked voice were no longer without it.

At the same time, the shift in the movement's discourse implied repositioning the death fast as a method of protest, one among many, instead of the only possible and plausible tactic of struggle both inside and outside the prison. While Aşçı's reframing sought to confer on the fast unto death its lost legitimacy as an effective political tactic within the repertoire of oppositional social forces, it also softened the uncompromising message hitherto conveyed by the weaponization of life as a *refusal* to submit to biosovereign domination.

While this reconceptualization of the struggle was important in its own right, it also expressed the desire to bring the fast until death to a close, but in a way that would not permit the impression that those who had already lost their lives had died in vain.[152] It was not possible to terminate the death fast without a compelling justification or, better still, some concession from the state (even if that concession was only symbolic). A tangible gain would enable the movement to claim that their victory vindicated their militancy, whereas the unilateral abandonment of the fast at this stage would inevitably entail a disastrous defeat.

The desire for a victorious ending to the death fast struggle, in the form of a concrete concession weakening the regime of isolation, was an ironic moment, as the desire to end the death fast was incorporated into the political ends pursued through the death fast. As a "sacrifice to end all sacrifice," the death fast was now paradoxically being carried out at least in part to bring the death fast struggle itself to a close. The very self-referentiality assumed by the struggle attested to how the militants were ensnared by the circle of violence they had woven through acts of *necroresistance*, a vicious circle in which voice could be achieved, if it was achievable at all, through the anticipated impact of death upon an audience increasingly acclimated to death. In this vicious circle, the ultimate victory kept being deferred into the future because of the growing futility of each new death. Aşçı could help the movement exit the circle of violence if his labor of dying could be interrupted before it culminated in death.

Tied to the expectation of a concrete gain that had been out of reach for ordinary militants was the prominent role accorded to Aşçı. As the lawyer of many leftist prisoners, he was a well-respected figure with social stature, which provided him with the capability of participating in public discourse. As a human rights defender, he was a figure around which different social forces could rally. Even participants in the movement now seemed to believe that it would not be the "ordinary" death faster performing self-destruction to achieve voice, but, rather, someone with stature who could secure the success the movement would like to claim credit for achieving.[153] Because Aşçı had social standing and commanded public respect, his death fast could express the collective will of the movement more effectively than the death fast of "ordinary" militants. The instrumentalization of human rights discourse went hand in hand with the strategic deployment of privilege.

Not surprisingly, public intellectuals, human rights defenders, prominent writers, artists, and journalists, as well as the leaders of democratic mass organizations did rally around Aşçı, publicizing his case and paying him visits at his home to show their support. In a public declaration of solidarity called "Isolation Is Torture!" with almost three hundred well-known signatories, these leaders of public opinion called for an end to cellular confinement. At the time, there were two other female militants on the fast until death: Sevgi Saymaz inside Uşak Prison, and Gülcan Görüroğlu, a former prisoner, a death faster whose fast had been terminated by "forced feeding," and a mother of two, in her home in the province of Adana. None of these women drew the kind of publicity that surrounded Aşçı's fast. The only hunger striker whose name appeared in the declaration "Isolation Is Torture!" was Aşçı. He was accorded indisputable centrality, even though all of those still on the death fast were collectively (though anonymously) acknowledged.[154]

While gender bias might also underlie the disproportionate recognition accorded to Aşçı's fast compared to that of the "ordinary" female militants, the more important reason (in many ways not unrelated to gender) was that the other militants lacked the social standing Aşçı enjoyed. This gap between Aşçı and the other militants in stature, amplified in time by the differential publicity and recognition, in fact relegated rank-and-file militants to an even more profound invisibility, only partially compensated by their sporadic association with Aşçı and the mediation of his image. "The state got used to the deaths," Aşçı argued, "that is why someone who had status, who was powerful, a lawyer, should lie down to death. There are untouchables of this system, an appreciation of status. That is why when I started the death fast, it became news much more [often]."[155] Aşçı conceded that his participation was a strategic deployment of his privilege in order to draw publicity.

This fragile and belated alliance between the dispossessed and the privileged, through the participation in the death fast of the reputable figure of Aşçı, set the two poles of the contradiction into dialectical motion to achieve the concrete goals that could not be achieved by the recurrent performances of necroresistance. It finally conferred a will upon those with political voice and a voice upon those who had the will. Thus, ironically, it was the repetition of the sacrificial gesture by a recognized lawyer and the instrumentalization of a discourse on human rights that eventually translated the collective will of the margins into audible political expression, by rallying oppositional forces that pressured the state to respond to the movement and thereby enabling the interruption of the lawyer's "sacrifice to end all sacrifice" before a new death occurred.

Eventually, the Ministry of Justice issued a statement on January 22, 2007, in which prisoners were granted ten hours of social time per week in high security prisons.[156] This statement thereby doubled the time allowed for socialization while it also relaxed the conditions of access to socialization, namely, the requirement of participation in prison "rehabilitation programs" (until this time, the prisoners who refused to participate in these programs had been denied even the five hours of social time). The popular pressure and the significant decline of Aşçı's health worked in harmony. It is also highly likely that the assassination of the Armenian journalist Hrant Dink on January 19, 2007, and the popular outrage it generated motivated the government to act in order to prevent the death of another prominent figure. Whatever the exact determinants of this concession, it was successful in bringing the death fast struggle to a definitive end. Upon the issuing of the statement, Aşçı, Saymaz, and Görüroğlu as the last three of the long chain of death fasters, announced that they were terminating their fasts, declaring their determination to continue the struggle against isolation by other means. The death fast had indeed been a "sacrifice to end all sacrifice," but only because the labor of dying was now successfully terminated. The failed politics of the weaponization of life achieved this ending by its instrumentalization of a universal morality that transcended marginality, but without overcoming it. When the death fast struggle was reframed on the "right to live," it unwittingly affirmed the "sanctity of human life," a claim that had ironically stood at the core of the state's justification to use violence in order to reestablish its control over prisons and its authority over the prisoners. When the death fast was called off, it was the ideological hegemony of the Turkish state that was further consolidated. Despite the government's concession and the movement's declaration of its ideological victory, the outcome was hardly a success. The movement had incurred 122 deaths (see table 6.1). The despatialized claim to a shared humanity based on the "right to live" was substituted for the counterhegemonic and partisan claim to the "right to die," a claim that dissipated along with the constituent spaces at the margins. Through a humanist discourse that affirmed the sacredness of life, what had been a destructive line of flight from the biosovereign assemblage was now ensnared and incorporated within it.

Chapter 5
Marxism, Martyrdom, Memory

For the extraparliamentary, illegal leftist opposition in Turkey, the adoption of the weaponization of life as the predominant tactic of struggle entailed an existential and passionate commitment to Marxism. The radical organizations that participated in the death fast struggle subscribed to different currents of Marxism, which provided diverse readings of world politics and Turkey's role within it, the history of the country, the level of its socioeconomic development and nature of its production relations, and the character of the state, prescribing in turn the different revolutionary strategies to be followed and the forms of organization best suited for their favored strategy. While these differences, further complicated by local debates, historical events, social networks, and particular experiences, soon hardened into distinct group identities and endowed the left with a highly sectarian culture, the commitment to Marxism nonetheless constituted a common moral compass, which guided generations of militants against the injustice of the capitalist economy and the oppression of the state. As a moral compass, Marxism drew the dividing line between right and wrong, between the just and the unjust. It was therefore thanks to their existential commitment that militants of different organizational affiliations and ideological convictions could see themselves as standing together on the same side of that line, transcending the differences among them.

In prison this existential commitment found its expression as the willingness to sacrifice one's life for the revolutionary cause. It developed out of and in turn further developed a cultural repertoire of conduct that was deeply oppositional to the forms of conduct required, encouraged, and affirmed as appropriate for prisoners by the state, laws and regulations, governmental decrees and circulars, and the orders of prison administrators. Collective life in ward communes as alternative modes of sociality already prescribed in detailed manner how each prisoner should conduct oneself in prison. Moreover, the intense periods of collective resistance against the arbitrary and violent intrusions of the state, built upon the spatial experience of the prison wards, further delineated a clear framework of *counterconduct* based on corporeal practices that required self-discipline, solidarity, dedication, and conviction. This repertoire of conduct helped transform prisoners on an individual level and gave them the power, determination, and courage to refuse obedience to the state. It enabled them to carry out acts of self-destruction and assert their political agency as a group from a position of intense marginality.

However, the growing centrality of necroresistance as a form of collective counterconduct also enacted a profound transformation in the politics of Marxist organizations and their supporters. The novel orientation toward death in the discursive and practical world of the radical left led to the development of what Foucault has called a "political spirituality."[1] This political spirituality not only altered the ideological views of these organizations and those of their militants but also produced elaborate rituals that have come to assume a vital function for the way in which ideology is lived and reproduced. Martyrdom became the main element of this spirituality and the resource with which collective and existential opposition could be justified and sustained in a highly asymmetric situation. *Marxist martyrdom*, as a secular theology, turned into the paradoxical vehicle of a sacrificial, vanguardist militancy. It brought into being the *militant-martyr* as the new revolutionary subjectivity of necroresistance conceptualized as collective counterconduct. This chapter explores the ideological leanings of the extraparliamentary left in Turkey and the *theologization* of their politics through necroresistance. It analyzes the rituals, metaphors, and symbolisms that mark, politicize, resignify, and commemorate death. It thus gives a portrait of the rituals by which the Turkish left has produced a movement that has grounded its very existence, meaning, and legitimacy on the sacrifice of life for the attainment of political ends, without, however, openly relying on an organized religion for support.

THE MULTIPLE MARXISMS OF THE DEATH FAST STRUGGLE

Mapping the extraparliamentary left in Turkey is a difficult task. The tapestry of radical organizations, having largely been woven in the aftermath of the 1960 coup d'état, includes many shades of red.[2] This is because the spread of social-democratic, socialist, and communist ideas in the 1960s and the 1970s produced, through the contentious splintering and radical sectarianism of different factions, over forty groups, circles, and organizations, which carved themselves unique places on the left.[3] However, the suppression of civilian politics, the repression of dissent, the imprisonment of leadership cadres, and the dissolution of organizational ties rendered most of these groups defunct by the end of the 1980 coup d'état.

On the other hand, struggles in prisons and the Kurdish armed struggle have been the practical transmission belts of radical traditions across the decades interrupted by military takeovers. At the same time, growing disparities of wealth and increased inequalities arising from rapid socioeconomic transformations caused by the neoliberalization program of the 1980s have contributed to their survival. During the 1980s, internal migration from rural areas to urban centers facilitated the substitution of the traditional working class with a less qualified, flexible, and precarious labor force, lacking in customary rights and welfare provisions. At the same time, economic development achieved by export-oriented growth strategies, integration with the world market, privatization of state economic enterprises, and shrinkage of the welfare state as part of the complex process of globalization endowed the left with a new constituency and renewed militancy despite the worldwide collapse of the socialist bloc. As a result, a handful of extraparliamentary groups were able not only to survive the destruction of the left the 1980 coup put into motion, but also to thrive further.

The illegal organizations that participated in the death fast struggle represent a rich array of Marxist thought as interpreted in the vernaculars of local class struggle and traditions of resistance. These groups are inheritors of various distinct syntheses of Marxism with Leninism, Stalinism, Maoism, Hoxhaism, Castroism, on the one hand, and with currents such as focoism (focalism), workerism, and syndicalism, on the other. In addition to the general ideological differences between these currents and the world-historical events that have triggered their divisions, the specific history of the Turkish debate on the left has created many splits and separations that have, through intense rivalries across factions, solidified into different group identities. These identities have in turn shaped a highly sectarian culture that has generally foreclosed cooperation and collective action. That the death fast struggle became the coordinated effort of a dozen different organizations (despite the presence of internal disagreements) is all the more remarkable given this history.

In spite of the organizational multiplicity and ideological heterogeneity of the organizations that make up the radical Turkish left, certain common threads can be identified as providing the conditions of possibility of the joint effort of the death fast struggle and thus making up the ideological core of their coalition. First, these organizations share a highly secular, materialist worldview, with a firm commitment to establishing justice in *this* world. Marxism is first and foremost a secular morality for those on the Turkish left, one that frames the world in dichotomous, partisan terms as a contestation between justice and injustice, right and wrong, friend and enemy. Second, the Marxist militants of Turkey diagnose the injustice of the current order and contend that the exploitative and oppressive capitalist relations of production must be abolished. They see the antagonism between classes as the main political divide and all agree in principle that the struggle of the working class is the means through which existing power relations can be overturned. However, depending on how they read Turkey, namely, its political history, path of development, imperial heritage, position in the global economy, presence of feudal remains in its economic and social structure, class composition, and the belated and warped process of industrialization, they espouse different revolutionary strategies.

Third, the organizations that make up the death fast struggle all share the contention that the existing order cannot be changed solely by democratic, legal means and that therefore its revolutionary overthrow is necessary. Moreover, they agree that revolution cannot be achieved without violence. While some of these organizations privilege urban guerrilla warfare and argue that the revolution should first be carried out in cities and then spread out into the countryside, others argue that rural guerrilla warfare should take the lead, spreading the revolution from the countryside into the urban centers. Some defend the thesis of general strike while others argue for the necessity of a people's war. In general, all these organizations advance a combination of legal and outlawed struggle and argue for the coordination of organized resistance among students, laborers, intellectuals, and across institutions of civil society, with violent forms of struggle undertaken by specifically trained and selected cadres.

Fourth, especially in light of the relative weakness of the industrial labor force in Turkey, these organizations place great emphasis on the vanguard role of the party as the political organization of the working masses and the representative of their authentic interests. The party is in charge of delineating the strategy of revolution and developing tactics suitable for the concrete situation. Among its objectives is the training of cadres, the dissemination of propaganda, and the education, organization, and mobilization of the working class. The revolution should be the work of the people, but the vanguard organization is responsible for directing, motivating, channeling, and leading the people toward victory. Interpretations of vanguardism differ across organizations, but the common denominator is the expectation that the party will exercise political, cultural, moral, and ideological leadership to guide the masses toward the appropriate analysis of the existing order and prescribe the right course of action.

Finally, a fifth commonality is the historically intimate relationship of these groups with Kemalism, a relationship which has become radically severed after the 1980 coup d'état. We have already seen how leftist opposition in the early republican period, after consecutive attempts of elimination by the nationalist forces, trod a fine line between support for the transformative elements in Kemalist reforms and opposition to their bourgeois limitations. An important claim that resulted from the experience of this period was that the Kemalist revolution was left incomplete by the founding cadres or, worse, was purposefully betrayed by subsequent governments.[4] One of the central goals of the Turkish left has therefore entailed continuing or deepening the Kemalist revolution in a more socialist direction.[5] With the attainment of full national independence and socioeconomic development as the central concern of progressive forces, the various factions on the left have shown remarkable consistency in their allegiance to the Kemalist revolution as a historical and foundational source of legitimacy.[6] The purpose of deepening the Kemalist revolution has revealed a stagist philosophy of history, in which Kemalism was seen as the necessary precondition for progress in a more socialist direction.

Economically, the left has enthusiastically defended the Kemalist revolution as a break from the feudal, imperial past, which, by setting up a national capitalism (or preferably, a non-capitalist "Third Way" of development) would prepare the grounds for a socialist economy. However, the left has been more hesitant about the political achievements of Kemalism, especially its relationship to democracy. On the one hand, the left has argued for greater rights and liberties against the authoritarian tendencies of Kemalism; on the other hand, the left has been lukewarm about "bourgeois" democracy and inclined to a Jacobinist, top-down approach to social change, an inclination it shared with the Kemalists. On this note, it is significant that the left, despite initially welcoming the transition to democracy in the 1950s, was quickly disillusioned with Democrat Party's authoritarianism, interpreted it as a counterrevolutionary step away from Kemalism, and welcomed the military intervention of 1960 as the restoration of a radical republicanism. According to Ahmet Samim, "by its failure to accurately understand the meaning of the 1950 and 1960 events, the Turkish left was theoretically and politically shackled to an obsolete and romanticised vision of an alliance between the working masses and a 'progressive' state bureaucracy."[7] This halfhearted loyalty to democracy and the attempts to synthesize Kemalism and socialism in a specifically "Turkish way," has largely set the tone for the debate of the 1960s and limited the ideological spectrum of the left to a left-wing Kemalism.[8]

However, in the second half of the 1970s, and especially after the coup d'état of 1980, the left's relationship to Kemalism changed dramatically. Since then the radical left has approached the Turkish state with caution, if not enmity, diagnosing it to be a "fascist," "oligarchic" dictatorship and the organized power of the "class enemy." The disillusionment with whatever progressive elements the left once saw in the Kemalist civilian and military bureaucracy has further radicalized the left, but it has not dissuaded these organizations from the desire to capture state power to utilize it according to their own transformative agenda. As a result, this distancing from Kemalism and the state has stopped short of a critique of sovereignty, with the implication that anarchism has never found a significant following in the radical left of Turkey.

In order to make sense of the ideological positions of the array of organizations that partook in the death fast struggle and to map their interpretations of Marxism beyond the commonalities identified so far, it is necessary to take into account how the intellectual-political debate has unfolded in the local vernacular. Two moments of this debate, which combined Marxist currents from around the world with the particular history of Turkey, have been seminal for many of the subsequent divisions and independent formations on the left. First is the split that materialized at the end of the 1960s between the proponents of the national democratic revolution (NDR) thesis and the socialist revolution (SR) thesis. Second is the splintering of groups following the NDR line into three main currents: Maoists, vanguardists, and workerists.

The first split between NDR and SR depended primarily on a diagnostic disagreement as to what the Kemalist revolution had accomplished and a prescriptive disagreement as to how the "correct" revolutionary strategy must be formulated. The thesis of socialist revolution, advocated by the Workers' Party of Turkey (TİP) in the legal sphere and the Communist Party of Turkey (TKP) in the illegal sphere, entailed the claim that the bourgeois revolution in Turkey was more or less completed and that therefore the next step should be the establishment of a noncapitalist path of development.[9] For the Workers' Party of Turkey, the contradiction between capitalism and feudalism in Turkey had been solved in favor of capitalism because of the development of market relations since the late Ottoman era.[10] Similarly, Kemalist reforms and the transition to multiparty democracy had led to the withering away of feudal ties and the influence of religion in society, strengthening the working class.[11] Because the bourgeois revolution had been achieved, the democratic struggle against feudal remnants could not constitute a separate stage of struggle by itself.

However, the party also concluded that it was impossible for Turkey to develop further on a capitalist path, as European countries had done in the past, because the conditions of development had changed with the entry of Western capitalism into the phase of imperialism. In order both to prosper and to advance according to the schema of societal evolution, Turkey had to free herself from the web of dependency created by the imperialist countries and attain real political independence. Because the collaboration of past governments with the world bourgeoisie foreclosed this option, independence could only be regained through socialism. Accordingly, the anti-imperialist and antifeudal struggles should be subsumed under a socialist struggle.

The proponents of SR advanced a blend of parliamentarism, trade unionism, youth organizations, and illegal activity. The Workers' Party pursued parliamentary means (and attained an electoral victory in 1965 by gaining parliamentary seats), but the Communist Party supplemented the legal struggle with an underground organization. Treading a pro-Soviet line, offshoots of the advocates of SR gained strength in the second half of the 1970s with such parties as the Socialist Workers' Party of Turkey (TSİP).[12] Two of the dozen organizations that participated in the death fast struggle, namely Communist Party of Turkey/Spark and Revolution Party of Turkey (TKP/K and TDP, respectively), came out of variants of the Communist Party tradition. While the latter group advocated the SR thesis, to direct forces of struggle under the leadership of the party toward a popular socialist revolution carried out by mass mobilization and armed struggle, TKP/K, following the unique Dr. Hikmet Kıvılcımlı, stood closer to the NDR thesis with its advocacy of democratic revolution.[13]

Despite its short-lived success, the Workers' Party of Turkey is often venerated as a school for the Turkish left. As an important center for the dissemination of Marxist thought, the party became the wellspring for later radical politics in Turkey. The socialist revolution thesis advocated by the Workers' Party, however, was rapidly challenged by the thesis of national democratic revolution, which advocated the establishment of complete independence and democracy as the first revolutionary stage ahead.[14] In contrast to the SR position of the indivisibility of the bourgeois and socialist revolutionary stages, the proponents of NDR argued that the main task of socialists should be to struggle for a "real" bourgeois democratic revolution to be carried out against feudalism and imperialism, exemplified by the collaborationist bourgeoisie and the landed oligarchy.[15] According to Mihri Belli, the main theorist of NDR, Turkey was a semifeudal, semicolonial, and dependent capitalist country. The interests of the dominant classes were tied to the persistence of dependency relations with imperialist centers. The purpose of NDR should be to attain "complete independence" and institute democracy, signifying the completion of the Kemalist revolution that had been abandoned halfway through.[16] The revolution would then create a favorable environment for the development of productive and democratic forces. Afterward, the ripening socioeconomic conditions would require a second stage of socialist revolution. In a third-worldist perspective, the idea of national liberation, now interpreted to encompass the liberation from relations of economic dependency, took center stage.[17] Anti-imperialist rhetoric replaced anticapitalism as the rallying point of leftist opposition.

The followers of the NDR thesis built their revolutionary rhetoric on the idea of a national front, based on an alliance of the proletariat, the petty and national bourgeoisie, the army, the bureaucracy, students, and intellectuals. This grand alliance would fight against imperialism under the ideological leadership of the proletariat. But much of the real expectation was placed on the progressive sections in the army.[18] The early proponents of NDR hoped for a pro-socialist military junta that would enable the swift conquest of state power, the enactment of democratic reforms, grand-scale nationalization of industries, and top-down social transformation. In order to install democracy, Belli argued, it was possible, if not necessary, to go beyond the limits of democratic contestation. NDR's opposition to the legalist line of the Workers' Party of Turkey soon paved the way for alternative struggle methods beyond the framework of legality.[19] The youth organizations that subscribed to this line such as the Revolutionary Youth Federation of Turkey (Dev-Genç) soon advocated the use of violence, supporting a possible progressive coup d'état and, when it was seen that the 1971 intervention proved conservative, gliding toward guerrilla warfare. Ironically, despite the rhetoric of establishing the broadest possible national coalition against imperialism, the most vanguardist groups came out of the splits among the proponents of NDR.

Without going into the intricate details of internal debates that produced a great many divisions, we can sketch out the genealogy of groups within the NDR sphere in three major branches. The Maoist branch developed against the proponents of a progressive junta, advocated by Belli, and argued instead for the broadest possible national coalition. This coalition should also include the peasantry and organize a people's war from the countryside under the leadership of the proletariat. Advocated by the pro–Chinese Revolutionary Workers' Peasants' Party of Turkey (TIİKP), Maoism accused the Soviet Union (and its followers in Turkey) of social imperialism, identified the contradiction between the two great powers of the cold war and Turkey as the determining element of the struggle, and supported national liberation movements in other parts of the world.[20] Claiming the revolutionary heritage of Mustafa Kemal, TIİKP (and its successor TİKP) became an ardent defender of the ideological underpinnings of the Kemalist regime and treated them as goals to be taken to their natural conclusions. The distinction that was drawn by TİKP in its early years, between the heritage of the national liberation movement and Mustafa Kemal as the national hero, on the one hand, and Kemalist ideology as the ideology of the bourgeoisie, on the other, was lost in time, as the party line drew closer to nationalism.[21]

Even though the two sister Maoist organizations that participated in the death fast struggle had roots in the circles that splintered from the NDR line, they are the inheritors of groups that broke from TİİKP, soon after it was formed, espousing a more critical line vis-à-vis Kemalism and advocating revolutionary violence.[22] The groups in this branch, led by İbrahim Kaypakkaya, evaluated the Kemalist revolution as the movement of the comprador bourgeoisie and landed oligarchy and moved toward a categorical rejection of Kemalist ideology.[23] The collaboration of the Kemalist republican elite with imperialism, argued Kaypakkaya, prevented it from transforming the semifeudal and semicolonial structure of the country into national capitalism. He underscored the dubious relationship of Kemalism with democracy and maintained that in reality it was a "military-fascist dictatorship" that oppressed other ethnicities.[24] His views on the oppression of the Kurds as a people were also markedly different from the largely nationalist orientation of other factions.[25] The followers of Kaypakkaya argued for a "democratic people's dictatorship" based on a worker-peasant alliance that would replace the Kemalist government, which they condemned for its promotion of a national bourgeoisie, exploitation of the people, and making the country part of the international imperialist front. In the struggle against the regime, the three weapons of the people were the party, the militia, and the united popular front, all to be built within armed struggle.[26] Following this branch, we can locate several organizations within the death fast struggle: the Communist Party of Turkey (Marxist Leninist)–Workers' Peasants' Liberation Army of Turkey [TKP(ML)–TİKKO], which later renamed itself the Maoist Communist Party (MKP), and the Communist Party of Turkey/Marxist-Leninist (TKP/ML) are direct descendants of this Maoist line.

The second branch of the NDR thesis consists of groups and organizations that have grown out of the People's Liberation Army of Turkey (THKO). This line followed the NDR thesis in maintaining that Turkey was a semidependent, semicolonial, and backward capitalist country. With the aim of establishing a "completely independent" Turkey, THKO identified the fight against American imperialism as the precondition for liberation. As such, the impending war would take place between the revolutionary front of compatriots (formed by national classes, with an emphasis on the rural poor) and the reactionary front of imperialists and their local allies, i.e., the non-national strata.[27] This group strove to complete the Kemalist revolution by overthrowing the order that had displaced the achievements of Mustafa Kemal. Highly influenced by the Cuban, Algerian, and Vietnamese revolutions, and the writings of Carlos Marighella and Che Guevara, the group adopted the strategy of guerrilla warfare, based on small groups of militants, to incite the rural proletariat to a popular war.[28] After the leaders of this organization were hanged by the 1971 military intervention, the movement distanced itself from Kemalism, continued illegality, and guerrilla warfare, and developed relations with the Palestinian and Kurdish struggles. Some factions moved toward a Maoist line, others adopted an Albanian line, still others criticized the focoist past as "adventurism" and sought to establish connections with the traditional working class. These factions moved further toward anticapitalist struggle, combining the organization of poor peasants through rural cooperatives with the militant organization of the working class, directing acts of violence against the military and bureaucratic apparatuses of the Turkish state. The groups that started out as Guevarist and evolved into different forms of Leninist workerism led to many splinter groups. Three of the organizations that participated in the death fast struggle, the Communist Labor Party of Turkey/Leninist, Communist Workers' Party of Turkey, and Revolutionary Communists' Union of Turkey (TKEP/L, TKİP, TİKB) come out of this lineage, emphasizing the necessity of the revolution to be built on the support and active participation of the traditional working class.

The third main branch of the NDR thesis is the group advocating "vanguardist warfare," represented in the 1970s by the People's Liberation Party-Front of Turkey (THKP C). This organization, led by the charismatic Mahir Çayan, espoused the idea of a "continuous revolution" between the democratic and socialist stages and defended the ideological vanguardism of the proletariat in the democratic revolution over the primary force of the peasantry.[29] The distinguishing feature of this line was the adoption of what Çayan called a "politicized military war strategy" in which all democratic and economic struggles would be subjected to armed struggle.[30] It diagnosed the historical moment as the "covert occupation" of the country by a neoimperialist, globalizing capitalism, leading to relative economic prosperity.[31] This prosperity kept the oppressed masses pacified by the neocolonial "oligarchic" dictatorship (of

the comprador bourgeoisie and feudal remnants) through an "artificial balance."[32] The People's Liberation Party-Front of Turkey insisted that this artificial balance could only be destroyed by means of "armed propaganda" or sensational acts of violence carried out by vanguardist military forces comprising
urban guerrillas, against the agents of imperialism and finance capitalism, on
the one hand, and state officials, torturers, and the "enemies of the people,"
on the other. The impact of these sensational actions, it was argued, would
be to display the vulnerability of the existing order and expose the political
"truths" that are concealed from the masses by the "artificial balance"; hence
these actions would shake up the masses, raise their consciousness, and trigger mass mobilizations that would lead to anti-imperialist and anti-oligarchic
revolution.[33] The "vanguardist warfare" strategy espoused by THKP-C came
very close to the anarchist "propaganda of the deed."

After the death of Çayan and the leadership cadres of the organization, different factions emerged. Among the offshoots of this branch, some circles distanced themselves from armed struggle and moved toward a pro-Soviet line,
such as the Liberation Group (Kurtuluş), others placed a greater emphasis on
popular organization, such as the Revolutionary Path (Dev-Yol), and still others became more ardent defenders of vanguardism, such as the Revolutionary
Left (Dev-Sol). Several organizations that stem from the further splits within
this current participated in the death fast struggle. These include the Revolutionary People's Liberation Party-Front (DHKP-C), Resistance Movement
(DH), People's Liberation Party-Front of Turkey/Marxist Leninist Armed Propaganda Unit (THKP-C/MLSPB), and Revolutionary Path (DY). Finally, the
Marxist Leninist Communist Party (MLKP) was formed by groups that broke
away from the main descendants of each of the three branches of the NDR,
promoting its unique blend of Maoist, workerist, and vanguardist warfare.

As this brief portrait of the complex mosaic of leftist organizations and
their evolution suffices to show, the organizations that made up the radical left
in Turkey represented a wide array of political positions. Each organization
waged an endless, hairsplitting ideological battle in its publications against the
rival organizations it considered to reflect reformist or revisionist deviations
from the "correct" revolutionary position, represented, of course, by their
own. The distances between these positions, even when they were not theoretically insurmountable, were compounded by practical differences: distinct
histories and localities of struggle, leaders and social networks, organizational
cultures, favored markers of identity, all worked to distinguish groups from

one another and to exaggerate differences even further. The sectarian culture and intergroup conflict on the radical left produced a rich spectrum of radicalism while also preventing coordinated action.

On the other hand, more important than the scientificity, accuracy, persuasiveness, and even popularity of the specific theoretical diagnoses and strategic prescriptions espoused by each organization was perhaps their proponents' naive but genuine and passionate commitment to the struggle for justice under the banner of Marxism. This struggle took on convoluted theoretical forms and obscure vocabularies hard to master even by those who defended them, presented the world in binary terms that oversimplified conflicts and reduced everything to opposites, was highly patronizing, absolutized differences, and took pride in not compromising; however, its role as a moral compass was not obliterated by these shortcomings. Militants of different stripes were dedicated to uphold this secular morality that distinguished between the oppressors and the oppressed and were willing to sacrifice their lives in its defense. Without this commitment, it is difficult to explain the fervor with which ideological battles were waged, names were called, relations were broken, and violent conflicts broke out. It is also impossible to understand that what so vehemently separated these organizations from one another was also what put them on the same side and eventually brought them together in the same struggle.

Given the highly divided nature of the Turkish left and the militant defense of ideological differences, we may wonder how the death fast struggle was indeed conducted as a coalition of a dozen organizations. In fact, the collective experience of the prison, with its isolation from the world, propensity to expose prisoners to violence, precarity of rights, as well as its alternative forms of sociality and experiments in self-government through ward communes, was crucial in creating a common ground among individuals with different affiliations and the collective will to struggle together. The experiences of collective prison resistance since the 1980s also enabled the convergence of these otherwise different organizations on a common set of demands. As we have already seen, the coalition was never free of tensions and disagreements, but coordinated action was nonetheless possible. As prisoners forged their lives into weapons, their existential investment in the struggle against high security prisons was less about advancing the particular current of Marxism they subscribed to than about preserving their common political identity and "way of life" as defined by Marxism in general. However, the widespread adoption of necroresistance transformed its practitioners in unexpected ways, producing considerable ideological effects. The most significant ideological effect was the emergence of a *sacrificial Marxism* through the theologization of their politics.

SACRIFICIAL MARXISM

In his much acclaimed study, Benedict Anderson views the cenotaphs and tombs of Unknown Soldiers as the most important symbolic expressions of the culture of nationalism: "Void as these tombs are of identifiable mortal remains or immortal souls, they are nonetheless saturated with ghostly *national* imaginings."[34] The ability of nationalism to inspire people to die and kill has always been a perplexing feat. For Anderson, these emblems of nationalist imaginaries point to the intimate relationship of nationalism with death and, ultimately, with religious thought. In search of an explanation for their power, Anderson turns to the cultural roots of nationalism.[35] He argues, "the cultural significance of such monuments becomes even clearer if one tries to imagine, say, a Tomb of the Unknown Marxist or a cenotaph for fallen Liberals. Is a sense of absurdity avoidable? The reason is that neither Marxism nor Liberalism are much concerned with death and immortality."[36]

Notwithstanding the irony of an embalmed Lenin, the Tomb of the Unknown Marxist will perhaps never be erected. However, the growing centrality of necroresistance on the left has rendered such a tomb less of an absurdity. The death fast struggle raises the question of how the development of such a direct and metaphysical relation with death within Marxism (or different currents of Marxism) has been possible.

As one of the early critics of the worldliness of Marxism, Ernst Bloch has argued that there is an inherent lack in the materialist and atheistic "fixation" of Marxism, preventing it from adequately responding to the problems of the soul, community, and hope.[37] According to Bloch, "throughout all the movements and goals of worldly transformation, this [utopian tendency] has been a desire to make room for life, for the attainment of a divine essence, for men to integrate themselves at last, in a millennium, with human kindness, freedom, and the light of the *telos*."[38] Hence, Bloch argues, while the problem of sustenance and well-being might be solved by Marxist reason, Marxism fails to address the experience and desire for transcendence. "Dialectics has voided the economy, but the soul and the faith it was to make room for are missing," contends Bloch. He holds that the only way to realize the "freely self-chosen community above society . . . and above a social economy thoroughly organized along communist lines, in a classless, and therefore non-violent, order" is to follow a metaphysical guide that complements communism to answer the "socially irremovable problematics of the soul."[39] Hence Marxism does not do away with the human need for mysticism.

Yet, unlike movements that are motivated by religion, the participants of the death fast struggle avowed their atheism. Unlike varieties of liberation theology or Judeo-Christian socialism, the death fast struggle did not weave together Marxism with Islam. Nor was this a form of Alevi leftism.[40] While it is true that part of the constituency of the radical left came from an Alevi background, it would be simplistic to reduce the ideology of the death fast struggle to the sociological profile of its participants, who nonetheless professed atheism. While it could be argued that the movement appropriated some aspects of Alevi cultural symbolism (such as the red headband and references to a Shia and specifically Alevi history of oppression and sacrifice), the identification of the death fast with Alevism is misleading because of the overall absence of religious belief and Islamist politics in the movement. It would be more accurate, instead, to observe that the death fast struggle reconfigured Marxism into a political mysticism, a secularized political theology. As Bloch suggests, the necessity of giving meaning to life and death especially in relation to acts of self-destruction paved the way for a theologization that created its own solutions to the problem of *faith* in the absence of commensurate spiritual resources that could be tapped from within Marxism: the political cause and its victory was transformed into a new form of faith, and rituals that reproduced and disseminated the convictions of its participants were invented.[41]

In the death fast struggle the theologization that accompanied the adoption of the weaponization of life occurred through a *displacement* of two major theoretical components central to the indigenous interpretations of Marxism.[42] First was the transmutation of the stagist view of revolution. We have already seen that the schism between the socialist revolution and national democratic revolution theses was one of the major fissures on the Turkish left. With the adoption of necroresistance, this fissure, which had already lost its significance in the aftermath of the 1980 coup, was replaced with the understanding of a continuous and unified stage of revolutionary action, but one whose main line of contention was now constituted by the role envisioned for *sacrifice*. The new alignments on the left were no longer really driven by the diagnosis of the country's economic and political status, based on modes of production, class composition, and integration into the world economy (and their corresponding strategies of democratic and socialist revolution), but by the prominence accorded to self-destructive forms of struggle in advancing the revolutionary endeavor. The new alignments were based on the centrality of sacrificial action. It was not that any group categorically rejected the resort to necroresistance, but there emerged a significant difference between those who deemed it secondary versus those who considered it central. Either way, what was displaced from centrality was class struggle as the motor force of history. In the emergent vision the revolutionary process now stretched from oppression to final and absolute victory as a unified chain of struggles that would be driven forward by self-sacrificial acts, if not as the sole tactic then at least as one prominent as any other.

The second displacement concerns the reinterpretation of vanguardism. Despite their multiple differences, organizations on the radical left largely concurred on the necessary role of the vanguard party in the revolutionary endeavor. With the adoption of necroresistance, the party's ideological, political, and cultural leadership of the masses was redefined to constitute the conduct of exemplary and heroic deeds based on the performance of acts of sacrifice on behalf of the working and oppressed classes. The vanguardist expression of class struggle would henceforth be played out in the persons of communist militants and their confrontation with the state. This reinterpretation, particularly prevalent in the factions coming out of the "vanguardist warfare" branch of the NDR thesis, involved the transformation of the "politicized military war strategy," which advocated carrying out sensational acts of violence against official and economic targets of strategic value in order to expose political "truths." Now the conduct of heroic acts of self-sacrifice became the novel form of propaganda aiming to disrupt the "artificial balance" of the existing order and to expose the "truth" of the state. Sacrificial propaganda could be armed or unarmed, depending on whether the chosen form of weaponization of life was offensive or defensive. On the other hand, for factions that came out of the Maoist or workerist traditions, which placed greater emphasis on popular participation in the struggle, this displacement also grew to be apparent in the reconsideration of the vanguard role of the party, but in a different way. Accordingly, the party was no longer simply the political representative of the interests of the masses; it became their allegorical embodiment. If the person of the communist militant now stood for the people, the sacrificial acts conducted in struggle could be understood as standing in for popular warfare. As a result, martyrdom became a new form of vanguardist militancy for large sections of the Turkish left despite their ideological differences.

Indeed, the central vehicle for this double displacement has been *martyrdom*, ensconced in ritual practices that have become crucial for the reproduction of the cause.[43] For a long time the word for martyr in Turkish, i.e., *şehit* (derived from the *shahid* in Arabic) has been commonly used in mainstream discourse for the soldier who has lost his life in combat or on duty.[44] The same word is now frequently used in the lexicon of the Marxist left for anyone who has died in the name of the cause, whether this death has been intentional or unexpected. This usage has short-circuited debates in Islam regarding whether self-destruction is admissible by applying the expression "to fall martyr" to those killed in armed conflict as well as those who lost their lives as a result of self-starvation, self-immolation, or suicide attack. However, while disengagement with such controversy has helped in circumventing the negative connotations that the religious prohibition on suicide might have for self-destructive actions, it has not been able to resolve the tension between the left's lack of belief in the afterlife and investment in the attainment of immortality. This tension has become even more pronounced with the intriguing slogan of the death fast struggle: "Martyrs of the Revolution Are Immortal!"

From a materialist point of view, the prominence that martyrdom has attained on the left is a paradox.[45] This is not intended to imply that either sacrifice or martyrdom has hitherto been completely foreign to revolutionary struggles. The communist movement has incurred many losses, renowned or anonymous. What is paradoxical is the celebration of death as sacrifice, the growing quest for heroism and immortality, and the yearning for martyrdom. What I would like to draw attention to is the qualitative difference between what could be termed *Marxist sacrifice* and a *sacrificial Marxism*. The latter, exemplified by the death fast struggle, concerns the systematic appropriation of martyrdom as a central ethico-political value and its transformation into a vehicle for the ideological and cultural propagation of the revolutionary struggle and the dissemination of its heritage.

The most telling symptom of sacrificial Marxism in the context of the death fast struggle is the shift from the *hunger strike* of unlimited duration to the *fast unto death*. We have already seen how this shift, announced one month after the initiation of the hunger strike, was part of the escalation of the struggle. Its declared purpose was to stress the determination of the militants to continue their hunger strike until death if their demands were not met. The practical expression of this determination was the adoption of a harsher nutritional regiment, limited to the intake of sugary water and salt only, aimed at accelerating the process of dying. Discursively, however, while the idea animating the hunger strike is a combination of the perennial Marxist concern with *hunger* and the common political strategy of the *labor strike*, the death fast shifts the focus from life to death, with unmistakably theological, particularly Islamic, connotations associated with fasting.[46] This is the case even though the politics of self-starvation has nothing to do with religion.

We could interpret this change in vocabulary as a strategic move that aims to up the ante for the struggle. We could interpret it simply as a tactical utilization of popular culture in a country whose population is predominantly Muslim and for whom fasting has immediate relevance. However, it is also possible to read this transformation as symptomatic of the theologization of Marxist politics related to the *politicization of death* in the context of resistance. Just as the religious fast expresses the unquestionable conviction in God, the death fast expresses a similar conviction, this time in the righteousness of the revolutionary cause. Just as the religious fast is motivated by the idea of self-discipline in the attainment of the purity of faith and submission to God, the death fast utilizes self-discipline in the attainment of the purity of militancy and submission to the revolutionary cause. The willingness to sacrifice is elevated into the marker of conviction for both.

This theologization is both a result of the adoption of necroresistance and its precondition. On the one hand, it is understandable that the ability to continue fighting for the communist cause in the growing absence of a popular following, combined with the general passivity and disinterestedness of the masses, necessitated a strong, unqualified, and unconditional conviction, especially in the face of the difficult nature of the corporeal struggle ahead. On the other hand, the repetition and elevation of sacrifice perpetuate this unconditional conviction, suffusing the gaps and silences of the otherwise secular worldview of these militants and transmuting Marxism into a new faith. Consequently, the theologization of the fundamental ideological views of these organizations has culminated in a *sacrificial Marxism*, which has in turn proven to be fertile ground for the reproduction and dissemination of these convictions through the exaltation of martyrdom.

An important implication of sacrificial Marxism is the transformation of the communist militant into the *militant-martyr*. In this transformation there is a double theoretical movement as well: on the one hand, there is the profanation of self-sacrifice, which is rationalized and secularized as an ideological weapon of revolutionary struggle rather than a component of religion and faith-based struggles, while, on the other hand, this comes with the attendant sacralization of the communist ideal, which becomes a new transcendence. As the communist ideal is sacralized and relegated to an imaginary and mythical future, through a continuous deferral of victory, the chain of revolutionary martyrs stretches endlessly from the depths of history to an imagined end point of final victory, an end uncharted and unconfined by geographical, cultural, or historical boundaries. Built painstakingly by each death, communism becomes the ultimate reward not in the afterlife but for those who will live afterward: it is posterity who will benefit from the actions of those who sacrifice themselves and who will commemorate the martyrs as immortal.

The theologized politics of the weaponization of life operates as a *dialectic* between the militant and the martyr, the human and the weapon, the living and the dead, steered by the "consciousness of sacrifice," which now replaces "class consciousness" in more conventional Marxisms. In the first moment of this dialectic, the performer of the self-destructive act moves from militancy into martyrdom, even prior to her departure from the world of the living. The second moment is the unique fusion of the militant and the martyr in the dead body, the only tangible material artifact of the spectacle of death. The final moment is the movement of the martyr into a new (perhaps higher) stage of militancy. The dead are appropriated by the communities who espouse self-destructive practices; their memories are incorporated into practices of everyday life and cultural and ethical codes; the images, utterances, and recollections of their sacrificial acts reenter circulation in the political imaginary. In the presence that the militants establish through their absence, they are endowed with a new agency that contributes to the organization of the past, present, and future experience of the living and becomes an ongoing wellspring of legitimacy for the perpetuation of a radical politics built on necroresistance. Their absence gives meaning and legitimacy to the continuation of the struggle through the repetition of the sacrificial act itself. Each death begins a new dialectic as others, motivated by the memory, legacy, and example of the martyrs, conduct new acts of sacrifice in their honor.

In what follows we will look at the preparatory, funerary, and commemoratory rituals enveloping this dialectic. These rituals are important because they express, in condensed and stylized form, how ideology is actually lived.

Insofar as rituals are corporeal technologies that frame experiences, they reveal the practical substance of necroresistance as counterconduct. At the same time, rituals have a generative quality because they also shape the experience, social relations, and subjectivities of those who perform and participate in them. According to Nick Crossley, rituals are "embodied forms of practical reason" that have important effects on the constitution of (inter)subjectivity.[47] Through the analysis of these rites, we will be able to trace how these corporeal technologies function in the constitution of the militant-martyr into the subjectivity of necroresistance as well as in the making of the insurgent community as a collective subject.

Relatively new in the culture of the radical left, rituals around the weaponization of life emerged in the late 1990s and became more prevalent with the death fast struggle of 2000, even though significant variations remained in their adoption across different leftist organizations. Undoubtedly, these rituals were much more pronounced and common in the social circles of the hardliners in the death fast struggle, the militants and supporters of those organizations that initiated and continued the death fast to the end. For participants of the second group who joined the struggle after Operation Return to Life, investment in these rituals was less pronounced and dramatic and, at times, involving a critical distance. Both the variance in the attributed centrality of the self-destructive practices and sectarian considerations of political identity seem to have played a role in this diversity. The following account, therefore, aims to present a generalized sense of these rituals, without asserting that each participating organization and militant followed the same routines in exactly parallel ways.

FROM MILITANT TO MARTYR

Due to the contentious and militarized atmosphere that striated politics in the Turkey of the early 1990s, the risk of death was no stranger for a militant who was a sympathizer, supporter or member of an outlawed leftist organization. A myriad of situations, involving writing slogans on the walls, taping up posters and flyers, participating in illegal demonstrations, or attending clandestine meetings, could easily expose a militant to violence. The most traumatic and marking of these encounters with the state was torture under interrogation. Each violent encounter experienced or witnessed in the struggle tended to

confirm the militants' conviction that justice could only be attained by violence and paved the way for greater violence. As one of the participants of the
death fast struggle succinctly put it, in Turkey, "if you are going to be a revolutionary, death is always in your side pocket."[48] As a militant, you should always "carry your shroud with you," as it were, and be prepared for the worst.[49]
The very lifestyle of being a communist militant, a Marxist revolutionary, had
come to be associated with living on the edge in the culture of the radical left.

Nonetheless, there was a difference between the serious but still routine
risks that a militant would take on an everyday basis and the decision to perform self-destructive acts in which death became a more immediate, tangible,
and willed outcome of the planned action. Of course, the risk of death still
depended on the particular form of self-destruction: death might be a more
or less certain outcome (as in the offensive modalities of the weaponization
of life) or a relatively high risk that stopped short of certainty (as in long-term
hunger strikes). The fast unto death was on the border between actions of
high risk and certainty because of the indefinite duration of the hunger strike
(bounded only by the attainment of articulated demands), so it brought together the certainty that at least some participants would die (because of the
expectation that demands could only be won through the occurrence of some
deaths) and the high likelihood of long-term health consequences for many
participants (considering that the fast would eventually be terminated). Because of the serious risk of death involved in the death fast, those who volunteered to forge their lives into weapons would pass through elaborate and
sophisticated stages of selection, ideological training, and preparation.

These detailed and complex preparatory rituals, as "rites of passage," singled out the participants of the fast unto death from the rest and marked their
transition from one world to another. They constituted public acknowledgment of their new status and mission. They communicated the relation of the
militant to various interlocking collectives (the party, the community of revolutionaries, the "people") in concrete form and provided a script within which
self-destructive acts could be situated and disseminated. They transcribed the
meaning of the self-destructive act as "self-sacrifice"—a *counterconduct* against
dominant forms of conduct prescribed by the state, a selfless, ethical performance for the revolution, potent with symbolic and political significance.

These rituals acknowledged the tragically destructive nature of self-sacrifice, as the last and most significant political act of the militant, expected to
end in death, but the emphasis was on the generative nature of the same act.

Self-sacrifice was also expected to have productive force: not only would it complete the constitution of the militant into the martyr, but, through the martyr, it would create a new militancy whose power and vitality would flow back to the struggle. Through the death of the militant, the party and the nascent revolutionary community, whose symbolic representative the militant was, would gain new life. As rehearsals of funerals, in which militants participated in their own untimely parting ceremonies, preparatory rituals provided the possibility of politically and socially recognizing death before its actualization, thereby rendering its biological consummation secondary.[50] At the same time, they were occasions in which political regeneration could be celebrated. It was the firm belief in the productive aspect of self-destructive acts that injected into the preparatory rituals a strong dose of optimism, one that permeated them with *jouissance*: hope, excitement, and celebratory joy, rather than grief and mourning.

The dual quality of the weaponization of life as an end and a new beginning rendered these rituals the expression of the uninterrupted and indeed interminable continuity of the struggle. They brought the past into the present and ensured that the present would be transmitted to posterity. Through these rituals the dead reached out to the present, they structured the ethical and cultural codes of the living (codes of honor, loyalty, and commitment), illuminated the path of action to be taken, and helped shape the future of their communities. Martyrs achieved a strong and deep presence that haunted these rituals by way of the recitation of their names, invocations of their exemplary deeds, and the ornamentation of the physical spaces in which these rituals took place with their pictures. At the same time, these ceremonies were performative acts in themselves, acts that not only initiated the transformation of the militant into a martyr but also constituted the revolutionary community through, and perhaps above, history. They joined the dead and the living, the martyrs and the martyrs-to-be, while they announced the meaning of their deaths to the living and the not-yet existing.

Volunteering for Sacrifice

In the early months of 2000, well in advance of the launch of the hunger strike, militants in different prisons began to volunteer to participate, communicating their interest and enthusiasm by oral declarations, personal letters, and communiqués, addressed particularly to their comrades of higher rank.[51] In these messages they explained how they perceived the current political conjuncture, the role of the prison as an arena of struggle, the meaning of F-type prisons, the moves that the state might be expected to make, and why they thought a response in the form of a hunger strike was necessary. They expressed their expectation that the hunger strike would necessarily be a protracted battle and proclaimed their readiness to endure its consequences. They voiced their desire to take part in this "historic initiative."[52] In their messages they also recounted their reasons for volunteering, trying to convince their comrades not only of their eagerness, preparedness, and determination but also of the correctness of their motivations. Each militant who put his or her name forward for the hunger strike had to write a statement, but each statement did not automatically guarantee participation.

These statements, which the party hierarchies involved in recruitment and selection took very seriously, were important indications about the level of political consciousness the militants had attained and whether they were in fact ready to undertake self-destructive actions. Motivations of the volunteers were considered particularly important for a protracted hunger strike in which participants should not only be willing to starve themselves but also be able to sustain their starvation over a long period of time. Each organization to which individual militants pledged allegiance had to evaluate their candidacy, examining every militant's personal history and qualities, character traits, political experience, role and rank in the organization, and level of political consciousness. The leadership needed to decide, according to the specific details of each case, whether the militant was capable of carrying out a fast unto death and deserving of the lofty honor of being a martyr.

At the same time, each organization had strategic considerations beyond the merits and weaknesses of particular militants that factored into the decision making process. One of these considerations was to maintain a delicate balance between the length of the struggle and the level of participation. Organizations had to estimate the probable duration of the hunger strike as a whole, calculate the number of volunteers necessary to conduct the protest, and allocate the number of volunteers they should accept at the beginning, reserve for the future, and keep without harm. These organizations were also concerned with maintaining a proper ratio in several different ways: (1) between the size of their own prison constituency vis-à-vis that of other organizations; (2) between leadership cadres and rank-and-file militants; and (3) between females and males. Maintaining variance in the legal status of participating prisoners was also important. As the party organizations made their selections, they kept an eye on a potential amnesty (rumors about which had already began to circulate). Thus some volunteers were to be selected from those prisoners who were detained but not yet convicted, while others were to be selected from those who would most certainly remain inside, even in case an amnesty was proclaimed by the government.[53] Finally, organizations also aimed to maintain participation across different prisons over time, so the location of militants was also a criterion.

Most important, it was necessary for organizations to ensure that their volunteers wanted to participate for the right reasons. For example, a willingness to die would be prime reason for disqualification. Similarly, those who had a fatal illness were also immediately excluded because of the view that in such a situation death by starvation would be escapism, only a substitute for what was already inevitable or, even worse, an instrumental way to hasten death. The physical strength of the body was an important element, factored in to calculate how long the militant would be able to sustain the fast. If the militant's body suffered from certain ailments that rendered her weak and could potentially cause an early death, the militant would be excluded from participation, at least in the early stages of the struggle.[54] Militants who had not participated in previous hunger strikes had priority because they had not suffered any health problems due to self-starvation.

Similarly, if a militant wanted to participate primarily for self-fulfilling reasons, such as seeking personal glory, she would most surely be rejected by the party organization. "There were those volunteers," a participant of the death fast struggle explained, "who were really in this [struggle] for revolutionary heroism and they attributed themselves a chivalry. We tried not to include them in the list [of participants] as much as possible. Because we had concerns. For example, if [participation] were a personal thing, something connected to populism [i.e., being popular] and an adventurist feeling, this could lead to breaking down [before the end of the struggle]. Even if one did complete the resistance with success, one might become real trouble for the revolutionary movement and the people in its aftermath."[55] Big egos were not promoted.

Militants who volunteered themselves had to be motivated by a sound conception of the "objective" responsibility of a revolutionary, which was supposed to be altogether different from an eagerness to die. It was almost as if the decision to participate was a moral good in the Kantian sense, an autonomous and rational act of duty not only in conformity with but done for the sake of a categorical imperative to sacrifice.[56] Accordingly, the ground of the militants'

obligation to sacrifice had to be sought in pure reason (and not in the particular circumstances, expected rewards, or natural inclinations of each militant).
Sacrifice was a revolutionary *duty*. A participant explained this revolutionary
duty as follows:

> Nobody asked me if I would like to participate [in the death fast]. I
> myself volunteered and persuaded them [the leaders in the organi-
> zation]. But this is not volunteering for death. Let it not be misun-
> derstood. I have been in the struggle for thirty years. In the struggle
> people cannot make these calculations: where do I die, where do I
> survive, what if such and such happens to me there. There are things
> that must happen, things that must be done. It is like that in life. You
> think [about life] through those things that must happen. Insofar as
> you become one with things that must happen, you are no longer
> yourself, you are what you must be, you live according to what must
> be done. You evaluate yourself, too, according to what [you] must be,
> the goals, ideals you are trying to achieve, objectively. To the extent
> that you can approach yourself scientifically, seeing your place [in the
> world], seeing yourself and what you can do, you can place yourself
> within [what must be]. It is a matter of becoming one with it. Because
> I don't see revolutionary struggle only as belief; it is something
> scientific. When I looked at myself that way, I thought: I *can* do the
> death fast. I *must* do it. I volunteered. . . . And in none of my sentences
> [written to persuade my comrades] was there a wish to die. A person
> who wants to die cannot sustain this struggle. The volunteering of
> whoever wants to die would be rejected.[57]

Accordingly, the hunger strike was a task that needed to be carried out
for the revolution, so it should be undertaken only by those dedicated militants who viewed their place in the world through the lens of their role in the
struggle for revolution and considered it their duty to take on this task. For
individual militants, participation in the death fast was also an opportunity
to test the strength of one's own convictions and to renew one's commitment,
without which their lives would lack meaning. Only with a "scientific" basis to
their conviction, one that enabled them to understand what "must" be done
correctly, could they evaluate themselves accurately and make the right decision to volunteer. Their decision could not be impulsive or meant as a reaction

to circumstances; it had to be based in firm self-knowledge and political acumen, combining the scientific rationality of a materialist worldview with the
moral imperative to sacrifice for the revolutionary cause.

Once candidates were selected, they were notified ceremonially and usually in front of their peers in prison gatherings. Depending on the situation of
each individual and the overall political assessment of the party, hunger strikers were grouped into teams who would conduct their action together. With
the conversion of the hunger strike into the fast unto death, these preselected
teams would be launched consecutively. The timing in between the launching of these teams was arranged in order to spread out the expected times of
death of the participants over the duration of the struggle, relaying the flag
of struggle from one group to another, leaving a hiatus between each team,
ranging from several days in the beginning to several weeks and months in
the later stages of the struggle. Overall, the process of identification, selection,
and grouping of the candidates, and the arrangement of their concatenation
were arduous and intricately complicated tasks for these political organizations, involving a multiplicity of factors and complex calculations, in order to
strategize in advance and prepare their forces in the most effective way for the
anticipated confrontation with the state.

A Wedding with Death

Preparations commenced upon notification of the candidates. Long discussions about the meaning and implications of the hunger strike were carried out as part of ideological training. In addition to personal preparations
such as the writing of parting letters, testimonies, and wills, this period was
marked by collective ceremonies made in anticipation of the hunger strike.
One of the most noteworthy rituals almost exclusive to female militants was
the henna ceremony.

The henna night is a traditional ceremony that takes place as part of wedding rituals in Turkey. Despite local variations in how it is carried out, the
core of the ritual is the decoration of the palms of the bride-to-be with henna
in the presence of female guests. It takes place in the family home of the bride
the night before the wedding day, signifying the bride's departure from her
family home and entry into her husband's household. The bride sits in the
middle of the room dressed in red clothes, her head and face covered with a
transparent red scarf. The ritual continues as her guests walk around her in
a circle with candles, praying and singing traditional songs about separation

from loved ones to make the bride-to-be cry. Once she cries, the ritual proceeds with the mother-in-law putting a gold coin and henna in the hand of the bride-to-be, tying it with a piece of cloth that is kept there until the early hours of the morning in order to fix the ornamentation in place. After the hand of the bride is decorated, the henna cup is passed around for the guests to decorate their own hands. In some cases, the remaining henna is sent to the quarters where the groom-to-be is celebrating with male guests in order that he dye his fingers with henna as well. The night continues with singing, dancing, and celebrations.

As part of marriage celebrations, this highly gendered ritual does not only signify the passage of the bride-to-be into womanhood, but it also reproduces the relations of patriarchy.[58] It denotes a transfer of possession, the handing over of the woman from the father to the husband. This transfer is represented by the sad parting of the girl from her own parents and her reception by her future parents. The role of the mother-in-law in putting the henna in the hand of the bride-to-be signifies the new authority of the in-laws and her husband over her. The sacrificial connotations emphasize the woman's devotion to her new family. The red of the henna as well as the red of the dress of the bride-to-be connote blood, both as the end of her virginity and the sacred seal of the marriage. The ritual also involves the marking of all other women who have come of age alongside the bride-to-be, designating their readiness for the institution of marriage. The subsequent celebrations grant social approval to the marital union.

It is important to note that another use of henna is the religious ceremony that involves the marking of the sheep and rams that have been chosen for sacrifice (*kurban*) in the Islamic sacrificial fest commemorating Abraham's readiness to sacrifice his first-born son in order to obey God's command and the divine interruption of this sacrifice. This marking separates the sacrificial animal from the rest, and the henna is believed to purify the sacrifice. Occasionally, henna is also used to decorate the hands of young men who are being sent away to do their military service in order to signify their devotion to the nation and willingness to sacrifice their lives in its protection.[59]

As such, the henna ceremony has many sacrificial connotations. The appropriation of the henna ceremony by the female militants about to embark on the fast unto death underscores the role of the ritual as a rite of passage and accentuates these sacrificial connotations. Through this ritual, the ones selected for the journey toward death come of age; they move to a different stage of militancy, having reached the kind of political consciousness that enables them to devote themselves exclusively to the cause. The decoration of other women as part of the ritual, like the marking of girls eligible for marriage, signifies that others are also coming of age. And if they might not yet be among the elect few who were accepted to participate in the fast unto death, their turn too will eventually come.[60]

The militant iteration of the henna ritual also implies that the promise to conduct the act of self-sacrifice is congruent to the promise of marriage. Through this ceremony, female militants are prepared for a marriage with the revolutionary cause, a marriage that will last until death. At the same time, this is a marriage with death for the revolutionary cause.[61] Just as the traditional henna ritual celebrates the union of woman with man, while, at the same time, it laments the woman's exit from her father's house, the revolutionary iteration celebrates the union of the female militant with the political cause, while it laments her exit from the world of the living. Just as the traditional ritual signifies the woman's entry into her husband's household and subjection to her husband's and his parents' authority, the revolutionary ritual signifies the female militant's entry into the world of the dead and her submission to the authority of the political cause represented by the revolutionary party. The henna seals this sacred bond with the color of blood, which is the same as the color of the revolutionary flag. The ensuing celebrations, similar to the traditional ceremony, signify the recognition and approval of this new union by the revolutionary community.

According to the testimony of female political prisoners in Uşak Prison, where a henna night was celebrated, this ceremony was a preparation for death: "In this path, which will be taken so that oppression is tamed with death, volunteering for death comes to mean that those who are left behind will be able to live a humane life. That's why people prepare for death like they prepare for a wedding. This is the celebration for a great sacrifice."[62] The henna ceremony embellished the act of volunteering for sacrifice with the connotations of a marital union, while it also marked the passage between life and death. On the one hand, this was an experience most of these women would probably never have due to the political path they had chosen for themselves. On the other hand, having this ceremony in a militant form further propelled them on the same political path, sealing their promise to the revolutionary cause and marking a point of no return. The women imagined themselves as brides, "brides of the revolution."[63] Yet their wedding dress, as they pictured it, would not be white but scarlet—the coffin wrapped in the scarlet flag of the party, adorned with red carnations. "'We are brides, too,' one of them sa[id], 'our coffins will be all red.'"[64]

Overall, the revolutionary appropriation of the henna ceremony presents a complex image, both affirming and subverting gender roles.[65] The analogy between conducting self-destructive violence and getting married is both an affirmation of the idea and institution of marriage (as the proper thing for a woman to do, as the sacrificial act par excellence) and its subversion (in the association of marriage with death). On the one hand, it inscribes the act of self-sacrifice into the continuum of sacrifices expected from a woman as wife, mother, and daughter. It reveals that patriarchal and paternalistic values attached to the institutions of family and marriage are internalized and that the father and husband as structural positions in the gendered web of power relations continue to frame the female experience, even on the radical left. On the other hand, the same ritual is reinterpreted by these women as a means of empowerment and self-assertion. The idea of marriage with the political cause and, eventually, with death, is, at the same time, a forceful declaration of the female militant's free will and political agency. It transforms the experience of self-destruction into a joyous rite of passage and opens this form of militancy, otherwise reserved for their male comrades, to women. It constitutes a tacit critique of the patriarchal order, which expects women to get married. It enables women to refuse this path, albeit by substituting a political union in place of a familial union. The political agency of these women, therefore, denies the construction of womanhood solely according to patriarchal norms and unsettles the gendered nature of the ritual itself.[66] It is interesting to note that this unsettling was further reinforced when male militants also participated in the henna ritual alongside female militants and ornamented their palms together, particularly in settings where women and men could begin the hunger strike jointly. The revolutionary iteration of the henna ceremony also points to its profound politicization and militarization. This can be observed in the transformation of the bride's act of parting from her family house into a parting from the world of the living.[67] Similarly, the bride's entry into the new family now signifies her initiation into the world of martyrs. If the self-destructive path of action becomes the venue to attain the posthumous glory otherwise inaccessible to women, the choice of the communist star as the pattern with which to decorate their palms reinscribes traditional signs of marriage into this new, politicized sphere of meaning, marked by violence and guided by the light of the red star.

Of the 122 martyrs that the death fast movement has claimed for itself, 48 were women, making up 40 percent. Of these women, 31 died of self-starvation, 6 burned themselves to death (5 of these women were also on a fast unto death), 9 were killed by the state's security forces (5 of these women were also on a fast unto death), and, finally, 2 others died on suicide missions. Since female militants constituted such a significant part of the death fast struggle, the reappropriation of this gendered ritual and its reconfiguration in political terms were not insignificant. They symbolized in a poignant way how the cultural codes of these militants were radically reconfigured, in line with their political consciousness and orientation toward martyrdom. Ironically, however, this ritual, even in its subversion, could also be taken to signify how men and women were finally able to obtain a more equal start in the "race of death," one that was usually beyond reach in the gendered experience of female militants in the race of life.[68]

Tying the Red Headband

The principal ritual that set the stage for the self-destructive act was one that cut across gender, however. This ritual combined taking an oath in public, putting on a red headband, and making a speech, which announced the transformation of the hunger strike into a death fast. It thereby marked the initiation of a new stage in the struggle in which death would henceforth always be at arm's length, if not closer. It made the commitment of militants public and the possibility of withdrawal socially and politically more difficult. Due to its centrality, this ritual was highly anticipated, elaborately planned, and performed as a memorable event.

Carried out before an audience of militants in the prison wards (or before supporters in the shantytowns when the death fast spilled outside prisons), these rituals provide a precious window into the world of the revolutionary community. Attending to testimonies of prisoners and participants of the death fast, we can piece together the setting and procedures of this ritual in broad strokes (but it should be noted that the context, speeches, and details varied according to organization, prison, and timing of the ceremony). The focus of the ceremony was the public recognition of individuals who were chosen to pursue the fast unto death. They would be asked to come on stage and stand before their community. The stage would be adorned with flowers, mostly carnations, and the podium would be covered with party flags or red cloth. The background would also be adorned with large party flags, posters and banners that carried the slogans of the death fast struggle, pictures and paintings of martyrs, including, most notably, the figure of the leader.[69]

Before the militants took the stage, the meaning of the gathering would be announced in speeches delivered by party representatives. Solidarity messages from other prisons, from organizations outside the prison, national and international, would also be read aloud. Then each militant took the stage in turn, delivering speeches in which they promised allegiance to the cause, declared their determination to take the struggle to its victorious ending, proclaimed their commitment to their comrades, the martyrs, and the people(s) of Turkey in whose name they were struggling, and, finally, announced their desire "to conquer death" in the name of all.[70] The high point of the ceremony came at the end of the speech when the militant received the headband. The headband, which became the main symbol of the death fast, was often a dark red piece of cloth (occasionally, it would also have the symbol of the party on the red cloth).[71] It would be tied around the militant's forehead by another militant (who was either already on the death fast or a higher-ranking militant in the party), who would thereby confer upon the militant the status of being a death fast warrior.[72] The militant who tied the headband on the new warrior would usually end the procession by kissing the militant's forehead upon the headband and embracing the militant. The audience would, of course, join in by singing marches, shouting slogans, clapping, and cheering.

While each organization carried out its own ceremony, joint ceremonies were also conducted in certain large prisons with high numbers of political prisoners with different affiliations. These ceremonies are particularly important since they reflect the spirit and ideological core of the coalition that was built around the hunger strike. The speeches delivered in these ceremonies are testimonies to how the movement understood, explained, justified, and presented itself to itself as well as to the broader revolutionary community. They show how the state's high security prison project was perceived from the marginal spaces of prison wards and why it was considered to constitute a fundamental affront to the prisoners. Reflecting the formal views of these parties organizing the death fast, these speeches also set the stage for individual militants to situate themselves in the movement. They shed light on the ideational and symbolic content of ritual practices inaugurating the death fast.

The following speech, delivered by a male militant at the joint ceremony held at Sağmalcılar Prison in Bayrampaşa, Istanbul (where the Central Coor-

dination of Prisons was located), communicates to its audience the views animating the movement, as understood by the representatives of leftist political
organizations leading the death fast struggle, while it also marks the end of the
first month of the hunger strike and its conversion into a fast unto death. It
celebrates the 109 militants on hunger strike in this prison, 13 of whom would
embark on the fast unto death on this occasion. As a telling artifact of the
death fast struggle, it is worthy of a detailed analysis:

> Friends, Comrades,
> Our general resistance, which we started on October 20, [2000,]
> as TKP(ML), DHKP-C, and TKİP, has transformed into a death
> fast since November 19. As the Bayrampaşa Prison [*sic*], on No-
> vember 25, our ten comrades from DHKP-C and three comrades
> from TKP(ML) have armored themselves with scarlet bands and
> embarked on a path to write a new death fast legend. Today, we have
> gathered to congratulate them once again and to share their feelings.
> Friends, Comrades,
> We have talked and debated for months. We have concurred that
> imperialism and the fascist government have laid siege to the revolu-
> tionary movement of Turkey and that they want to liquidate the revo-
> lution. We have come to be in agreement on the fact that the center of
> this offensive is the cell policy and thus that prisons and revolution-
> ary captives are the focal point for repelling this [offensive]. We have
> come together in word; we have diverged in action.
> *This was not a clash of spaces, but a clash of wills. This was an ideological
> war.* And, in order to win this war, it was necessary to take upon our-
> selves the slogan "We will die, but we will never surrender" from our
> comrades whose blood has merged together. This was a holistic and
> comprehensive offensive, too, [one whose outcome] would deter-
> mine the future of the revolution of Turkey, the peoples of Turkey. In
> order to write the history of liberation of our peoples, it was neces-
> sary to be the continuers of the bequest of unity that our martyrs of
> the death fast of '96 have knitted with their bodies. The path of vic-
> tory, the path of knitting together the unity of the people, and, before
> all else, the path of defending revolutionary ideology [and] socialism
> pass through this point. The path to erect the peoples of Turkey,
> who carry very strong revolutionary dynamics, as an organized force

against imperialism and fascism, would pass through the addition of new rings to the [chain of] heroic legends that we have created in the '96 death fast and in Ulucanlar [Prison].

As DHKP-C, TKP(ML), and TKİP we are honored and relieved to advance in the path shown by our martyrs and our history. We are proud to have made the unity we have created in '96 the future, not past history. 1996 has shown us that where revolutionary unity comes together with correct politics, it creates magnificent victories. 2000 is also a date when revolutionary unity meets correct politics. And our victory will be magnificent with our comrades, who move toward death cell by cell, and with our martyrs, and it will increase the hope not only of the peoples of Turkey but also of the peoples of the world. It will demolish the liquidation by imperialism and fascism; the revolution will grow in the path opened by our comrades who break the siege with their bodies. We have no doubt about this; no one should have any doubts about this.

Friends, Comrades,

Our comrades with scarlet bands are the guarantees of the future of our peoples and our revolution. Those of us who lie down to death are the inheritors of the unity of the revolutionary movement of Turkey, created cell by cell in the '96 death fast. And they are carrying the flag of this valuable bequest presented to the revolution of Turkey at the cost of twelve martyrs in 1996 in their hands, [the flag] of this honor on their foreheads. Saying that *"it is as important to carry forward to the future a historic resistance, a legend of heroism, as it is to create it,"* they are keeping the promise that we have made to our martyrs of the 1996 death fast and in Ulucanlar [Prison]. The power of the revolutionary will, the greatness of revolutionary values, the invincibility of the revolution will once again become flags through their bodies. Once again will the legend of self-sacrifice for the history of the revolution of the world and of Turkey be spread cell by cell. Through such resistance, in which victory is absolute, our peoples will win; we will win.

Who is revolutionary, who is not; who wants the revolution, who does not; who is determined to create the unity of the people, who is not . . . will once again become clear; our resistance will lead to polarization. This polarization will flow into the revolution.

> *To believe is the precondition of victory.*
> We believe!
> To pay a price is the guarantee of victory.
> We are paying a price.
> Martyrs are the final point of victory.
> We will give martyrs![73]

One of the most immediate features of the speech is its military vo-cabulary; it is replete with references to warfare, offensive, assault, death, surrender, invincibility, blood, and martyrs. As its content is about war, its performance serves as a declaration of war. The text provides the political diagnosis of the present from the point of view of the prisoners, expressed as a confrontation between the prisoners and the state. The state's policy of high security prisons is interpreted both as the imposition of a new penal regime and, more important, as an assault upon the people's revolutionary impulse, an assault that is part of a new wave of oppression. Such a view results from the evaluation of the F-type prisons as part of a grand policy of "cellulariza-tion" that is not confined to the prison. "Cellularization," according to the prisoners, is not simply the doing of the "fascist" state but is also supported by (Western) imperialist centers to which the state is seen as intimately tied and dependent; politics and economics go hand in hand in the making of the F-type prisons.

At stake in this confrontation is the wholesale repression of the left in the person of the prisoners, who view themselves as the vanguard of the people and facilitator of the revolution. The prisoners see themselves in a state of "siege"; they are besieged not so much because they are imprisoned but by virtue of the state's imminent offensive on prisons. It is clear that prisoners see the prison wards as *their* spaces, islands under their control, as it were, sur-rounded by the hostile seas of the state. The speech intimates that the siege is becoming tighter and more constricting by the day and that the revolutionar-ies are in waiting for the intrusion or invasion from the outside.

According to the speech, since the assault is directed upon the prisons, placing them at the forefront of the struggle, the proper, most militant, re-sponse should emerge from the same spaces. It thus accounts for the decision on the timing of the hunger strike. We have already seen how this position, advanced by the hardliners, was criticized by other organizations who consid-ered the launch of the hunger strike early and who postponed participation until after Operation Return to Life. This speech depicts how the hardliners' position is placed within the perspective of a vanguardist orientation that provides the justification for launching the struggle from the prisons without waiting for social mobilizations to develop outside; in fact, as a means to incite them by leading the way. It also justifies the choice of self-starvation as the most militant tactic appropriate in fighting an "ideological war" based on the "clash of wills" between the state and the prisoners.

Another important feature of the speech is its performative quality, which attempts to confer unity and solidarity on the movement. Despite (or, perhaps, because of) internal disagreements within the prisoners' coalition, which we have already explored, the speech constructs and emphasizes a shared tradition of resistance inherited from the past. Given the particularly sectarian culture of the Turkish left, the significance of this declaration of unity cannot be overemphasized. The common experience of repression in prisons, the multiple acts of resistance, and security operations in which many prisoners have lost their lives (such as the one in Ulucanlar Prison), the argument goes, have created solidarity among revolutionaries and paved the ground for further unified action. Although the speech mentions that consensus has not yet been attained ("We have come together in word; we have diverged in action."), it signals the possibility of future cooperation by singling out the 1996 death fast as a defining moment in the history of the left with respect to attempts to achieve unity. Their "blood has merged together"; the left's unity has been "knitted together" via individual bodies, cell by cell, death by death, martyr by martyr. The speech thus contends that those who have died in that struggle have been the exemplary force promoting leftist solidarity across otherwise acrimoniously divided factions, rendering 1996 the legitimate precursor for the current death fast.[74] The victorious ending of the 1996 death fast is also utilized as an invitation for nonparticipating organizations to join.

The speech also reveals the logic of necroresistance: political gain can only be attained through death. Victory, the speech asserts, can only be accomplished by "paying a price"; in this case the price is "giving martyrs" for the attainment of the revolutionary cause. The political diagnosis thus offers only one prescription. The only way for the prisoners to fight is by forging their lives into weapons. It is the possibility of victory that allows the resignification of self-destructive acts into acts of self-sacrifice. However, the performance of sacrificial acts, it is expected, will accomplish more than simply to "repel" the offensive and to "break the siege": it will produce the very spark that will ignite the fire of revolution. The necessity and inevitability of victory therefore hinge on the necessity and inevitability of sacrifice. In this light, it is important to note that the retrospective construction of a singular narrative of collective resistance is achieved by focusing mainly on sacrificial acts, each instance designating a different stage in the eschatological passage from oppression to emancipation. Such a construction reveals a historical understanding in which the past is "legendary" and the future is "victorious." While the audience is invited to take part in the "heroic legends" of the past, they are also called upon to "write a new death fast legend," to "advance in the path shown by [their] martyrs and [their] history."

Martyrs do significant political, moral, and affective work in this speech as well as in other speeches. Their invocation attests to the continuing presence and influence of the dead in the world of the living. The speech thus solidly affirms the dual quality of sacrifice: what might have been an end for particular militants is, at the same time, a new beginning for the revolutionary collective, a leap forward in the establishment of strength that arises out of unified action and a common ideological stance, another step toward victory. As the present is built upon the sacrifices of the past, the future will be built upon the sacrifices of the present. The citation of martyrs affirms that true revolutionary behavior, the path to be taken, and the values to live by may all be found in their examples. The legacy of the martyrs gives meaning and endows legitimacy to new acts of self-destruction, which will be the means by which the struggle is maintained, unity established, and victory reached. The speech repeatedly assures that victory is certain: "We have no doubt," "we believe," "we will win."

It is also worth underscoring that the metaphor of the cell [hücre], both in this speech and throughout other discursive artifacts of the death fast struggle, functions as a multifaceted and evocative emblem of its politics. Most important, the idea of the cell calls to mind two forces that the death fast struggle sought to construct as polar opposites: the disciplinary penal regime built on high security prisons with cells and the corporeal technique of struggle against them whose protracted labor of dying is experienced daily by the death of somatic cells. In the first sense the cell implies a premonition. Unless something is done, the speaker intimates, the whole country is in danger of becoming a "penal colony" in the Kafkaesque sense, a large prison cell where domination will be absolute, resistance will be stifled, and the revolution will be "liquidated." Revelatory proof for this imminent danger can be found in the state's desire to confine the revolutionaries in the cells. In the second sense the cell is a bulwark. In response to the policy of "cellularization," the corporeal strategy of protest seeks to prove that absolute domination is not possible, that each cell of the body is a barricade against the attempts of government. The metaphor of the cell cogently encapsulates the contradiction between *biosovereignty* and *necroresistance*.

But that is not all. The cell also stands for the imagined relation of the militant to the collectivities in the name of which self-destruction is performed. The militants view themselves as the smallest clandestine unit—the cell—of their organizations. At the same time, each militant is a cell of the grand revolutionary organism that is the peoples of Turkey. Imagining militants as cells is an assurance that they will continue the struggle even as singular units, in case they are isolated from their comrades and put in a prison cell on their own, and that the grand revolutionary organism will be made to survive through the work of each cell. This organic metaphor reveals a reconfiguration of vanguardism from a relation of representative leadership to one of *synecdochic embodiment*. Each individual militant now stands for the masses. On the one hand, this means that what is done to them, to their bodies, is done to all. On the other hand, their struggle means the struggle of the masses, which will continue to advance through their bodies.

Finally, the cell also functions as the means for bringing into being the community-to-come that the hunger strikers proclaim themselves to be fighting for. The future community will be built "cell by cell" (*hücre hücre*); it will be called into being in and through the death of each cell, somatic and militant. The dispensability of the life of each cell in order to ensure the survival of the revolutionary organism connects the militant's mortality to the immortality of the cause. The party's longevity assures the possibility of eventual victory and therefore overrides the transience of the militant's life; each militant is only one cell among countless others who personify the party's will. The connection of the militant's life to the larger-than-life cause is forged through sacrifice: the sacrifice of each cell will ensure that the collective lives on despite the deaths of its members. Martyrdom ensures both the permanence of the struggle and the immortality of the dead. The primary slogan of the movement gains particular importance in this light: "Long Live Our Death Fast Resistance!"

Permeated as it is with the pioneering role of sacrifice, the celebratory speech announcing the inauguration of the death fast is thus symptomatic of the intimate relationship with death and immortality forged within Marxism, transforming the latter into the expression of an existential, passionate, and total commitment. In the theologization of leftist politics, martyrdom combines the secular and the sacred, the past and the present, the living and the dead. The speech that launches the militant on the path to martyrdom culminates in tying the red headband. In the speech the headband is metaphorized as the "armor" that protects the militants in war; it signifies the sheer power of will, which guides them in their resistance. But the headband is also the tangible artifact that marks the militant as a sacrifice; it signifies that the militant has assumed a sacred quality by being chosen for the honor of martyrdom and has embarked on the path that will eventuate in it. The scarlet headband is the material incarnation of the connection that binds together martyrs and militants; it is passed on from martyrs to militants, through the party, and forward to new martyrs. It is the seal of the promise of death.

THE CORPSE AS MILITANT AND MARTYR

As the material remains of the spectacle of death, the corpse constitutes the second moment of the dialectic between the living and the dead through which the weaponization of life operates. The dialectical moment signified by the corpse fuses the militant and the martyr in the same body in a contradictory unity. The social construction of the corpse and the resignification of death are therefore critical for understanding the culture of the radical left in Turkey today.[75]

We have seen how preparatory rituals functioned as rehearsals of funerals. However, these rites do not replace the actual funerals that take place when biological deaths are consummated through the performance of the sacrificial act. Each death calls forth a communal gathering, which becomes a celebration of the fact that the militant, who had already stepped into martyrdom by taking the oath and tying the headband at the inauguration of the fast, has kept the promise to die. Like preparatory rituals, funeral rites are strongly imbued with the dual quality of the sacrificial performance, both as an end and as a beginning, through the collective meanings invested in the corpse. The corpse, as already dead but not yet evicted from the world of the living, becomes an interface that allows the living to interact with the dead. It contributes to the perceived continuity between the past, the present, and ultimately, the future, by constituting the most visible and immediate yet transcendent link in this continuity, both its relay and testimony. It is possible to read the relationship of the community to sacrifice through its reverence of the corpse: the endurance of the collective is predicated on the sacrificial deaths of its members and the endurance of martyrs on the continued existence of the collective itself. The revolutionary community gains its longevity through the mortality of the militant upon which it bestows immortality.

Funeral rituals include preparing the corpse for public display, demonstrations of respect and solidarity toward the corpse, and the performance of public salutations. One of the publications issued by the participants of the death fast struggle provides a detailed description of the various rites that take place until the burial.[76] The description entails the immediate aftermath of the death of Gülsüman Dönmez, a thirty-seven-year-old woman and the single mother of a twelve-year-old boy, who passed away in April 2001, after 147 days on the death fast.[77] The publication indicates that Dönmez joined the death fast struggle as a member of the Solidarity Association for the Families and Relatives of the Arrested (TAYAD) and was part of the first team of death fasters outside the prisons in a "resistance house" in the shantytown of Küçükarmutlu, Istanbul. Her participation was intended to highlight the continuity between the inside and the outside, with the purpose of showing that the state's policy of "cellularization" was not limited to prisons and that, therefore, prison resistance against "cellularization" should be supplemented with resistance outside prisons.[78]

According to the anonymous and composite testimonial narrative, published and disseminated by the movement, the events after Dönmez's death went as follows: news of her death was announced in the neighborhood where she had been fasting, upon which people began to gather for a funeral procession. Meanwhile, Dönmez's caretakers and comrades prepared her corpse for display.[79] Her body was placed upon a catafalque not too high from the floor in one of the rooms in the house. Candles were lit around her head. Her hair was neatly combed and her red headband was left on her forehead. A white piece of cloth was tied around her chin, fastened right above her head to keep it locked. Her body was covered with a large red fabric and her face left uncovered. The catafalque was decorated with carnations.[80] The walls and floor around her corpse were ornamented with pictures and posters of other martyrs.

Once the corpse was ready, people were let into the room to say good-bye. The first ones to be allowed inside were other death fasters. Each approached the catafalque, kneeled before the corpse, and kissed the forehead of her dead body. The visitors uttered promises to continue the fight, shouted slogans, and paid their respects.[81] After the completion of this initial farewell, the corpse was carried out of the house amidst slogans. After being taken around in the streets of the neighborhood on the shoulders of her comrades, surrounded by torches and lit candles, she was brought to the yard of the public building used as a common gathering and prayer space for the Alevi community (*cemevi*), accompanied by slogans, applause, and whistles (*zılgıt*).[82] There she was placed upon another catafalque where young men took turns keeping vigil until morning, one standing before her head, the other before her feet. These men, according to the narration, stood like soldiers with their left fists in the air to pay their respects and guard the corpse as visitors came in to see the corpse throughout the night.[83] Finally, the next morning, a large cortege gathered, in the front of which walked Dönmez's son, carrying his mother's picture, with his left fist in the air, shouting slogans. After the corpse was taken through the streets of the neighborhood one last time, it was placed in the ambulance that would head to the morgue. The final stages of the procession were accompanied by slogans: "Gülsüman Dönmez Is Immortal!"[84]

As a piece of political propaganda, this account is written in a way that glorifies the dead and paints the funeral in admirable terms. In spite of its didactic and lionizing qualities, it is still helpful in pinpointing the successive steps of parting rites that have emerged around the weaponization of life, containing clues to their overall significance. First of all, the gathering around the corpse demonstrates that these funerals are as concerned with the departure of the militant as they are with the arrival of the martyr. As the dead body is resignified into the *militant-martyr*, the body is elaborately prepared into a picturesque image—simple and humble, yet powerful in its presence and unwavering in its revolutionary claim, this style encapsulates much of the political message that the death fast struggle would like to convey to the world. The pronounced visibility of the dead in the revolutionary community presents a great contrast with the broader cultural context wherein death is experienced, mourned, and remembered in private, hidden away from sight.[85]

Second, the individual salutations of the corpse (the kissing of the red headband, taking oaths, shouting slogans, making promises, paying respects with fists in the air, and scattering carnations) are occasions for the militants who are also on the hunger strike to renew their oaths and for the supporters of the struggle to affirm their commitment to the cause. These salutations, while acknowledging the death of the militant-martyr, treat the body as if it were still alive, avowing the strong impact of its sacred aura upon the living.

This aura largely emanates from the red headband, which is conspicuously left upon the corpse, thereby assuring its enduring and sacrosanct status. The militant has lived up to the honor of the red headband, carried it with grace, and fulfilled the oath she has taken. By kissing the headband, each militant partakes of its aura and reaffirms its honorable, sacrosanct quality.

Third is the way in which the corpse is not fully wrapped until burial, which defies the conventional separation between the dead and the living. Scholars have noted how in most societies the corpse is perceived as a symbol of danger, pollution, and abjection, leading to the invention of a host of funereal practices that eliminate direct contact with the dead as soon as possible.[86] Traditional practices in Turkey are no different: the corpse is washed along with prayers, wrapped completely in white shroud, and sealed away in the coffin until burial, as soon as possible. By contrast, the militant-martyr is only covered with red fabric, with the face and the headband left completely visible, which amplifies the sacred aura. The opportunity for generous contact between the community and the corpse is intended to remind everyone of what happened, that there has occurred a great sacrifice, a sacrifice undertaken in their name, on their behalf.

Fourth, the applause, whistling, hymns, revolutionary songs, and slogans uttered while the corpse is carried around in the neighborhood add to the continued public presence of the militant-martyr. The silent presence of the corpse as a relic of the sacrificial performance, like a testimony to the raison d'être of the revolutionary collective, stands in dramatic contrast to the vigor and clamor of public salutations. If the dead body can no longer speak to the world, now the *political voice* of the militant-martyr speaks to posterity. In these salutations the community takes its turn to acknowledge the militant's well-deserved status as a martyr and to fulfill the reverential obligations due her corpse. These salutations also function to allay the grief of those who are left behind and provide occasions for the collective venting of anger as a way to cope with loss. However, the awareness that the funeral is a public display, oriented toward the larger audience of the "people" and the state, makes these rites engineered occasions for the conveyance of the revolutionary community's self-understanding and political message to the world.[87] In these rites, mourning is accordingly constrained and the ways in which pain and sorrow are expressed are implicitly yet actively regulated.

Public expressions of mourning are channeled into selected slogans, hymns, revolutionary songs, and poems. Instead of wailing, there are whistles and applause.[88] The regulation of bereavement circumscribes excessive manifestations of grief and relegates them to private enclaves away from the public gaze. By circumscribing the expression of individual sorrow, the community does not seek to upend a shared conception of the "grievability" of life so much as it attempts to convert the act of mourning into a collective manifestation of solidarity, resolve, and a pledge of retribution.[89] The speeches and slogans emphasize the call for justice in the face of what is perceived to be an acute injustice perpetuated in a highly asymmetric situation between the state and the revolutionary community. It is hoped that sadness is replaced by fury, which, unlike sadness, is mobilizing and generative of further political action.

The regulation of mourning strikes a delicate balance between the contesting claims of a "right to live" and a "right to die." What is at stake here is the value attributed to the life of each militant in itself and as part of the life of the community. The latter, of course, rests on the transience of the militant's life, its expendability for the cause, and its enduring political (rather than biological) existence through the continuity of the revolutionary cause. On the one hand, it is necessary to avoid creating the impression that the revolutionaries do not value life, that they view each militant's life as merely dispensable political currency. On the other hand, life should not be overexalted by excessive mourning, which would jeopardize the whole struggle, particularly its overarchingly necropolitical strategy. So while the revolutionaries must treat the death as a loss, they must also make sure to emphasize its gains by focusing on its effects, such as its ability to convey their political message to the broader public.

Central to this message is that the power of life and death has been usurped from the state by the militant-martyr, through whom the revolutionary community expresses an alternative claim to power, a sovereignty hoped for. This alternative claim is lodged in the very bodies upon which the sovereignty of the state is built, robbing the state of its power one insurgent at a time. The gathering around the dead body of the insurgent dramatically rehearses this alternative claim to power as it enacts the emergence of a novel political community out of the "state of nature"—from the murky netherworld of Turkey's revolutionary underground, militants surface as a collective, answering the call of the sacrificial death to unite them into a new whole. They come to pay their last respects to their deceased comrade while, at the same time, they assert their own existence, which is now endowed with a new dose of legitimacy through the performance of another sacrifice in their name. In the funeral gathering, grief and mourning for the insurgent's body are therefore transformed into the assertion of power by the body politic of the insurgent community. The public interactions with the corpse disseminate its sacredness onto the living members, purifying, elevating, and consecrating them as a community for which the sacrifice has been made. As such, the dead body is treated with great reverence, as if it were a sacred canvas on which the whole history of oppression and the hope of emancipation have been painted in red.

The paradoxical conjuncture of the materialist centrality of the corpse with its transcendent and intangible aura highlights the dual status that brings together the militant and the martyr in a contradictory unity in the same body. It cogently conveys the ambivalent movement between the secular and the sacred that underlies the theologization of politics, contributing to the production of a sacrificial Marxism. The imbrication of the secular and the sacred is intensified as funeral rituals become more vital sources of endurance and reconstitution for Turkey's radical left. Insofar as the history of the left now unfolds through a "chain of sacrifice," the increasing centrality of the funeral only confirms the willingness to further the cycle of sacrificial violence, leading to further deaths and more funeral gatherings. Depressing as this prospect is, it can be interpreted to show that not only the bodies but also the hearts and minds of insurgent citizens remain devoted to an alternative order.

THE MARTYR AS MILITANT

The rituals surrounding the corpse sculpt the death of the militant into a glorious sacrifice, an honorable and sacred martyrdom, which becomes, politically and symbolically, no death at all. On the contrary; the corpse is the vehicle of rebirth: it rejuvenates and consecrates the community in whose name the self-destructive act has been performed, provides the rationale for its coming together, asserts its claim to power, and generates the continuity of the struggle.[90] In funerary rituals the revolutionary community strives to memorialize the militant-martyr through the resignification of death and the reverent reappropriation of the insurgent's body by the community. The funeral becomes the occasion of converting mourning into a unifying political stance for the community. The success of this conversion depends as much on the aftermath of the funeral, however, as it does on the funeral itself.

In the aftermath of parting rituals are processes that incorporate the militant-martyr into collective memory.[91] In what Allen Feldman has termed the "sacrificial construction of memory," the dead are integrated into collective memory by the translation of their act of sacrifice into a political narrative, the circulation of their bodies in "surrogate forms" such as images, and their integration into the everyday lives and spaces of their communities.[92] The sharing of recollections about the militant-martyr, the recitation of the events that led up to the decision to participate in the movement, and the narration of the "correct" understanding of the act of self-destruction as a sacrificial death are mechanisms by which a collective history of the revolutionary community slowly shapes into being. This history is constructed piecemeal, by iterations of a myriad of memories concerning individual interactions with the militant-martyr.[93] These memories are carefully filtered and the instances that are permitted to enter circulation are selectively reconstructed such that each of them reveals something about the militant-martyr's strength of character, virtues, commitment, determination, courage, and exemplary conduct, at times in a didactic way. Disseminated in both oral and written form, these individual memories soon acquire a communal character.

Collective memory inserts the past into the present and projects it into the future. It conveys a past that is not past, a present that is imminent eternity, and a future that is prefigured by the past and the present moment. It becomes the conduit through which the martyr's continuing presence in the world of the living fills the hovering void created by the militant's death. But this presence is not a constant one. There are periods in which the memory of the militant-martyr lies dormant. This memory is revived again and again on occasions such as the anniversary of the militant's death or the next instance of sacrificial death. Neither is the memory fixed; rather, it evolves as part of a living narrative within the trajectory of the movement. The survivors of the death fast struggle find themselves responsible for the way in which the memory of the militant-martyr is kept alive. According to a participant of the death fast,

> When a comrade is martyred, you feel as if you have been pushed out of the trench. You feel as if you have been reduced to a spectator to your comrade's fight until death, as if you have been swept aside. This is an incommensurable pain. Upon the death of your comrades, all the moments you have shared with them, all that you have gone

through together rush to your heart. You feel upon your shoulders the immense responsibility of making them live on. You become the live witness of those comrades for the people. With all your actions, your words, your gestures, you need to reflect that those comrades live on through you. The continuity of our struggle depends on us, on how we narrate our martyrs, on how we carry forward the memories, the common heritage, and the struggle our comrades have left behind. The courage they have displayed as they died, the conviction of the rightness of our cause, the attitude toward the enemy, put forth with their blood and bodies, which all aim to destroy the last vestiges of fear: this is the stance that we have to incorporate, that we have to take as our guide, that we have to pass on to future generations. *It is the responsibility of the living to make the dead live on.*[94]

These evolving practices of remembrance evoke and appropriate the militant-martyr back into the community. The quotidian expression of memory is most commonly demonstrated by the decoration of spaces with pictures of the dead. Every headquarters of a leftist journal or newspaper, every cultural center operated by leftist organizations and their legal affiliates, every office of prisoner rights organizations and associations for prisoner families displays pictures and posters of martyrs on their walls, particularly of those who stand out among others for their exemplary deeds. Pictures of martyrs, with their gaze fixed upon the living, saturate the present and attest to the willful conflation of past and present. Sometimes, accompanying the pictures, are slogans or quotes attributed to the martyrs written on large placards. Occasionally, there are particular corners devoted to the martyrs in which memorabilia from the deceased, such as letters they have written, handicrafts they have produced, and other personal belongings are exhibited. These corners share the sacrosanct aura of the martyrs. Revered and decorated with fresh carnations, these corners become reliquaries that ceaselessly inject the memory of the sacrificial act of the militant-martyr into the continuum of the struggle in its presently lived moment. The immaterial permanence of the struggle meets the materiality of enduring images and artifacts that are left behind by the dead. These marginal sites of insurgent struggle are constantly remade by the dead that haunt them. "Our sons and daughters are not dead," say the parents of death fasters who have become martyrs, "they live with us."[95]

The images of the dead function as repositories of memory that "reinforce a sense of social order [and act] as a means to instigate social disorder."[96] On the one hand, these images have made up the essential backdrop to the preparatory rituals, where they set the stage for the headband and oath-taking ceremonies; they have been placed on the walls where the hunger strikers could easily see them as they lay in bed waiting for death; they have adorned the surroundings of the catafalques of corpses.[97] The images of martyrs have thus been abundantly used throughout the hunger strike, embellishing the spaces in which performances of death were staged, constantly gazing upon militants as they lived and died. They have thus reinforced their communal bonds, their political purpose, and commitment to the cause. On the other hand, these images have also been used more subversively, as a moral-political indictment of the state, in public events, demonstrations, sit-ins, and protests. On these occasions their presence has been a silent indication of the oppression, injustice, and violence experienced at the hands of the existing order and an incitement to continue the struggle.

The names of martyrs have also made their way into the everyday world of the living, as places, offices, halls, cultural centers, and new teams of hunger strikers have been named after them, in recognition of the prominent and distinctive roles they have played. Even though no singular figure has emerged in the struggle to occupy the spotlight, some of these militant-martyrs have become, in their own right, iconic figures whose images were utilized in demonstrations outside Turkey in solidarity with the struggle. The image of one of the militant-martyrs, Sevgi Erdoğan (no relation to Turkey's current prime minister, Tayyip Erdoğan), has traveled to Northern Ireland, where it has been memorialized as a mural.[98]

With the multiple ways in which they have been employed and the varied significations they have taken on, these names and images have not simply been mnemonic devices to aid the recollections of the living. They have also been instrumental in endowing militant-martyrs with a new capacity for agency, a higher form of militancy, as it were, in which they continue to be politically active long after they have departed from the world of the living. By continuously injecting the memorable past into the flow of everyday life in the present, the militant-martyrs have actively created the foundation for a shared heritage and countertradition that will be transmitted to posterity—the tradition of *necroresistance*. A "tradition of the oppressed" perhaps, in the Benjaminian sense, but one in which the dead have the central role. Militant-martyrs are the bearers of history: they constitute reference points for the past and become part of the oral almanac of their organizations. But they also give meaning to the present and help shape the future, structuring the temporal experience of the living in a continuum. Militant-martyrs thus serve to bind their community together with a sacrificial bond, constitute an ongoing fount of legitimacy for the struggle, affirm the longevity of their community, and act as vehicles by which their revolutionary ideology is spread and passed on to new generations of militants. They thereby contribute to the reproduction of their political cause through their iconic status, which, among other things, aids in the recruiting of new members.

The collective memory created in the margins is pitted against the history written by the state and the mainstream media, where these deaths are either repressed or converted into statistics. As such, collective memory becomes a counterhegemonic tool against official historiographies, endorsed and promulgated by the state, for those who remain at the margins of the political.[99] The collective memory generated around martyrdom functions as a refutation of the hegemonic intrusion of the state's unilateral and repressive narrative, which has no space for these militants within it except as casualties in the "war against terror." In the face of the political asymmetry reproduced in the battlefield of memory, it is not simply the act of remembering these deaths, but, rather, the staunch *refusal to forget* them that becomes an act of resistance in itself. The counterhistory and sacrificial ideology that the cultural practices sprouting around the weaponization of life have engendered thus grow to be the necessary link between the performance of self-destructive acts and their desired political consequences.

The most potent symbolic expression of this counterhistory is the red headband. Because of its emblematic centrality as the primary abstraction for the militant-martyr as the new subject of revolutionary struggle, the stylized image of the headband itself serves as a commemorative symbol that stands for the death fast struggle. In the words of a participant:

> For us, martyrdom is immortality. Death is not an end. True, biologically, humans are born, they live, and they die. What is important is not that we live and die, but *how* we live and die. If you know how to live, death is never an end. We prefer to live in resistance, to live a life that carries the beauty of our fight. It is crucial that the anger and the rebellion in our heart are never silenced. Instead of living a dirty life

for sixty years, we would rather live ten years, or even an hour, but of an honorable life. *We remember and revere the headband as the expression of this honor.*[100]

The symbol of the red headband powerfully conveys the abstraction of political life from the material lives of bodies. It becomes the new material artifact of the collective will that supports each sacrificial act and attains a sacred aura that points to the theologization of politics. It is the strongest evidence for how the Marxism of the death fast struggle has been infused with a strongly sacrificial ideology, which is a new form of "political spirituality." With its abstract and capacious anonymity, the red headband also approximates the Tomb of the Unknown Marxist, a paradoxical tomb that seemed so absurd to Benedict Anderson that he thought it could never exist. The headband is no monument, but it does share a "ghostly" quality that guides the revolutionary cause through its tragic dialectic between the living and the dead.

Chapter 6
Contentions Within Necroresistance

From the uneasy coexistence, mutual penetration, and eventual merger of sovereignty and biopolitics, there emerges a new configuration of power—the biosovereign assemblage, in which the traditional power *of* life and death is imbricated by new forms of power *over* life and death. This incipient configuration is generative of novel forms of resistance. Self-destructive practices, enveloped by martyrdom and sacrifice, respond to the dominant characteristics of this power regime, which elevates *life* to sacrosanct status (by killing, when necessary) through a fundamental reversal, the *politicization of death*. Necroresistance, then, is the most immediate product of the biosovereign assemblage that functions to destabilize and disrupt its operations and processes of reproduction.

Necroresistance is an emergent repertoire of action that is based on the appropriation of the power of life and death into the hands of those who resist. The predominant characteristic of necroresistance is its negation of life through the technique of self-destruction, transforming death into a "counterconduct," with a whole range of rituals and discourses that theologize its politics. In its defensive and offensive forms, the weaponization of life as a tactic directly communicates with and responds to the sovereign core of the biosovereign assemblage. But it does so in ways enabled by biopolitics itself; it emerges on the field of possibilities opened up by the politicization of life and its attendant forms of corporeality. The insurgent's body becomes the concrete battleground of domination and resistance, subjugation and subversion, sovereignty and sacrifice.

However, just as the biosovereign assemblage is a contradictory amalgam of the differential logics of biopower and sovereign power, so is necroresistance. It would be inaccurate to claim that necroresistance is free of contradictions, inconsistencies, reversals, and internal tensions. To the contrary: necroresistance is multivalent. The very antinomy of modern political reason that Foucault identifies in the realm of power, namely, the paradoxical coexistence of the politics of life and politics over life, also occurs in the field of resistance. The staging of absolute *refusal* that characterizes the weaponization of life coexists with its inverse, with the assertion and negotiation of demands for greater rights and privileges, better conditions and standards of well-being. On the one hand, this coexistence is literal. Alongside self-destructive practices, we can still observe conventional forms of struggle that make rights demands, ask for welfare and recognition: strikes, sit-ins, boycotts, legal actions, armed struggle all continue to take place while the new repertoire of necroresistance emerges from the margins. On the other hand, there is a different kind of coexistence that can be observed *within* the domain of necroresistance itself. This is the imbrication of these differential logics within the same repertoire, a situation in which necroresistance contains elements that are both life-affirming and life-negating.

The death fast struggle presents a complex picture in which individuals staging acts of necroresistance evaluated their own actions and the movement as a whole in radically different terms, evincing the copresence of differential logics. We have already explored the structure of the death fast struggle as a coalition of organizations. However, what I mean by the copresence of opposing logics cannot be explained away by the presence of different factions in this coalition, nor even by the ideological differences and tactical disagreements among the organizations that made up these factions. True, the complexity of the movement was compounded by the fact that it was formed by a coalition of organizations with differing ideological-political viewpoints. Furthermore, the ebbs and flows of the movement, varying degrees of public support, the disagreements between the two major factions of the coalition, and their reactions to changing circumstances added further complications. Nevertheless, I would like to underscore how the shifting pieces of this picture were undergirded by the multiplicity of meanings that the individual participants attributed to their own actions all along. The performers of necroresistance had a plurality of intentions, motivations, and desires, and this diversity was reflected upon the different ways in which they interpreted the objectives of the struggle, viewed different forms of self-destructive violence, and justified resorting to them. The multivalent character of necroresistance, saliently expressed in this diversity of viewpoints, belies any simple generalization about the overall structure and alleged uniformity characterizing movements that utilize the weaponization of life, and asks us to be attentive to the contentions within the emergent repertoire of necroresistance itself.

Harvesting different perspectives from oral narrations and prisoner letters, this chapter presents an analysis of the movement that captures the complexity of necroresistance. Based on a critical reconstruction of the voices of the participants of the death fast struggle, I put forth distinct and internally coherent strands of interpretation that shed light on the differential logics of necroresistance whose coexistence and articulation shape the movement as a whole. These strands, while analytically separate, tend to exist in an intermingled and amalgamated way in reality. They do not neatly correspond to the views held by different groups or to consecutive stages of the movement. Rather, they are positions I have distilled out of the highly individual stories of the participants, the overlapping, shifting, discontinuous, and, at times, inconsistent statements that reflect the divergent experiences, differing opinions, latent conflicts, and evolving collective narratives of the movement. The content of this analysis comes from the voices of the participants of the movement, but their categorization and subsequent analysis do not.

I argue that three interpretative strands best encapsulate the multifaceted nature of the death fast struggle. These depict the movement as: (1) an act of *resistance*, a defensive struggle against torture and oppression in the name of human dignity; (2) an act of *war*, a manifestation of the struggle among classes; and (3) an act of *refusal,* an exodus that expresses a desire to break away from the existing order. Each of these distinct strands corresponds to a different political problem that the movement sought to address: (1) democracy and human rights, (2) neoliberal capitalism, and (3) the changing nature of sovereign power and domination. Among these three strands, the negation of life coexists with the affirmation of life, the politicization of death with the politicization of life, the "right to die" with the "right to live" and to live well.

As an act of resistance, the death fast was a democratic struggle for the expansion of prisoner rights. It strove to bring the arbitrary limitations of and infringements upon those rights to an end. High security prisons represented the authoritarian state tradition, its violent treatment and criminalization of dissent, and the violations of rights that came with such authoritarianism. Accordingly, the death fast struggle asserted the demand for better conditions of imprisonment, the recognition of "political" status, and the overturning of cellular isolation as an affront to human dignity. As an act of war, the death fast was part of the struggle against neoliberal capitalism by the oppressed classes. It was a confrontation between the state, as the representative of the ruling classes and therefore the "class enemy," and the political prisoners as the vanguard of the people. From this perspective, the introduction of high security prisons was conceived as part of the restructuring program of neoliberalism, which entailed the marriage of the punitive state with the deregulation of the capitalist economy. The death fast struggle sought to advance the proletarian cause against capitalism by asserting the proletarian right to live well, pushing back against the criminalization of class struggle, and politicizing the masses by vanguardist action. As an act of refusal, the death fast was the expression of the desire not to be oppressed and to exit the existing order whose increasingly fixed relations of oppression and injustice were being reinstated along with the refurbishment of the sovereign power of the state. It was the assertion of a "right to die" in response to the tightening grip of domination over life. By virtue of its refusal of life and the irrevocable exodus of its members, it also comprised an ideological offensive against biosovereign power whose legitimacy depended on the "sanctity" of human life.

The distinction between these different strands in the death fast struggle hinged on how the struggle's predominant tactic, the weaponization of life, was interpreted. The latter, in turn, was dependent upon the ways in which individuals related to their bodies, how they conceived the political nature of their lives, how they interpreted the meaning of death, and the efficacy they attributed to political self-sacrifice. These reflections of the participants of the death fast struggle also give us occasion to revisit the open question of the relationship between necroresistance and what Agamben calls "bare life." The ways in which death fasters considered their actions and interpreted their lives present us with invaluable clues regarding whether necroresistance functions as an emphatic appropriation of bare life or whether it is more akin to its rejection.

Overall, the participants' different views regarding the questions of life, death, the body, and self-destructive violence reveal to us that the weaponization of life was not free of contestation but remained at the source of political tensions, paradoxes, and ideological deflections that rendered the movement novel and problematic at once. The different strands within the movement show that, like the biosovereign assemblage, necroresistance is best understood as a complex amalgam, one that echoes the complex structure of articulation of the power regime which produces it and to which it responds. Just as the biosovereign assemblage articulates the conjunction of different modalities of power as a becoming, necroresistance, too, is marked by a process of fluidity and flux.

HUMAN DIGNITY AGAINST TORTURE

"I would rather live a day with dignity than a dishonorable life that lasts hundreds of years. I know that if I let them trample my dignity, if I sell my dignity, I know that I will no longer be human."[1] This sentiment recapitulates the choice that some prisoners felt they were forced to make: either they would concede to imprisonment in F-type prisons or they would join the protest to protect their dignity. Punishment in high security prisons was not limited to the suspension of one's liberty, but compounded by the violation of prisoners' bodily and mental integrity. In other words, cellular confinement was a *double* confinement. The cell was a "prison inside the prison" and corresponded to an insidious and invisible form of torture.[2] The disciplinary penal regime embodied in the F-type prison project meant conforming to a certain "way of life" robbed of political identity. It involved the prisoners' reduction to a biological existence. Willfully submitting to this double confinement meant trading away their dignity simply in order to survive torture. A prisoner's letter, written months before the hunger strike was launched, cogently expressed this position: "We have made our decision; we will not give up on it. We will not go into the cells. We will not accept a *torturous death* in the cells."[3]

The prisoners were not alone in equating the isolation of cellular imprisonment with torture. Solitary confinement, though not officially recognized as torture by the prevalent international human rights regime, is widely considered to be a form of "inhuman treatment."[4] Its deleterious impact particularly on mental integrity (leading, for example, to feelings of emptiness, hopelessness, fear, and the loss of time/space perception) has been an area of substantial research, which shows that sensory and social deprivation can be more damaging than the experience of naked violence.[5] In addition to studies focusing on solitary practices, ethnographies of high security prisons in the West have provided a valuable window on prisoner lives in "total institutions" that portend a troubling future for prisoners around the globe.[6]

In this light, prominent human rights organizations and advocates, in Turkey and abroad, were critical of F-type prisons, even before they were opened.[7] Representatives of various civil society organizations, who were allowed to inspect a model F-type prison in the summer of 2000 as part of a public relations event organized by the Ministry of Justice, published criticisms and concerns regarding isolation if these prisons were to be put into use.[8] Intellectuals, writers, legal professionals, physicians, and psychiatrists in Turkey have also been at the forefront of bringing isolation to the center of the public debate on F-type prisons, critiquing its potential negative impact on the prisoners' physical and especially psychological well-being.[9] Civil society organizations, such as the Istanbul Bar Association, the Turkish Medical Association (TTB), and the various branches of the Architects' and Engineers' Chambers Association of Turkey (TMMOB), were vocal critics of the F-types.[10] And once these prisons were opened, human rights organizations continued to draw attention to how the actual practices of isolation violated human rights.[11] For example, Amnesty International, Human Rights Watch, and the Helsinki Citizens' Assembly drew global attention to isolation in F-type prisons with various statements and publications.[12] Human Rights Association of Turkey (İHD) went a step further and designated isolation as a form of torture, calling it "white terror" or "psychoterror."[13]

For the prisoners, the equivalence established between cellular imprisonment and torture had several different sources. The first source was historical, arising out of the history of prison practices in Turkey. Cells played a central role in the brutal administration of prisons, particularly during the 1980 military coup. Throughout this period, cells were often utilized as a tool to punish prisoners' noncompliance or disobedience, to threaten, intimidate, and break their will, and to secure their submission to authority. The prisoners called the solitary cells of military prisons *coffins*: small, barren, damp, and dirty holes with low ceilings, making it difficult to stand up, without windows or toilets. The leadership cadres of the left and those who could initiate and lead collective action were confined in the cells for years on end and subjected to recurrent visits by handpicked wardens sent over to give them beatings, extract confessions, or "convince" prisoners either to spy on their fellows or to show remorse for their actions. As a result, cells became arenas of fierce contestation where the individual prisoner confronted state violence while striving to keep his integrity and identity as a dissident intact. Against the cells as "exceptional" spaces of violence, the wards, reconfigured by collective organization and resistance, became the spaces of normality, signifying solidarity among prisoners and noncompliance with the state. Commanding such a history, the cells of high security prisons served as a vivid reminder of the unbridled violence of the military prisons. F-type prisons were thus conceived as vestiges of the exceptional regime and spaces where the state would shed its liberal-democratic veneer and reveal, to each individual now isolated from other prisoners, that violence constituted its unchanging core.

A second way in which the cell was associated with torture depended on the prisoners' understanding of human nature. The prisoners maintained that a human being was foremost a social being and that individuality could be defined only as part of a community. Taking away the possibility of collective life in prisons and depriving the individual of social ties deeply compromised and fatally injured the individual's humanity. The solitary individualism of the cell appeared to the prisoners as a form of deindividualization imposed through a forcibly induced alienation. Strongly objecting to the state's claim that the new "rooms" in F-type prisons, by affording prisoners private spaces, would enable independent growth and autonomy, prisoners interpreted such privacy as deprivation, both sensory and human. Against the argument that F-type prisons contained spaces for common use, prisoners pointed to the prerequisite of "successful" participation in state-run "treatment and rehabilitation programs" imposed by officials. Since these programs were ideologically driven by the state's interest in molding them into compliant and docile citizens, participation in these programs would imply remorse for the prisoners' political identity as dissidents, deeply conflicting with their very self-understanding as *political* prisoners. For a political prisoner, there would be no surer sign of being "broken" than such compliance. Prisoners therefore maintained that, since they would not participate in such programs, the common areas of F-type prisons were bound to remain unused. Furthermore, they argued, in the F-type prisons, the basic human need for sociality would constantly be held against them either as a method of intimidation or as a carrot dangled by officials for extracting individual concessions. Agreeing to make concessions in order to socialize would do nothing other than bring the prisoners dishonor and shame. These prisoners considered themselves to be fighting for a penal reform in which they would not be compelled to renounce their ideological beliefs and political identities to gain access to conditions that addressed their human needs.

A third way in which the cell was equated with torture lay in the absolute vulnerability the cell created for the prisoner inside. The solitude of the cell, the prisoners expected, would place them at the mercy of the administration, exposing them to infringements of their rights and capricious tactics of violence and intimidation: the conducting of arbitrary searches; damage, destruction, or confiscation of personal belongings; limitations on family visits; subjection of prisoners and family members to degrading treatment (such as body and cavity searches); restrictions on access to legal counsel and infringements on the confidentiality of meetings with lawyers; restrictions on and obstructions of access to health care; censorship of letters; control over the circulation of newspapers and journals; and the imposition of other arbitrary disciplinary punishments. The prisoners were only too familiar with all these tactics and thus highly skeptical that such practices would now come to an end. If anything, they argued, these practices would become more widespread with the transition from wards to cells. What the F-type prisons meant, then, was the reversal of achievements in de facto prisoner rights achieved through decades of prison struggles.

The prisoners also feared for their physical safety in the absence of other prisoners with whom they could weather the intrusions of security personnel much more effectively. In the wards, not only were the prisoners stronger (since they could act as human shields for each other), they could also rely on each other as witnesses. Conditions within the prison were already risky enough when they were housed together in wards, the prisoners reasoned, so what might happen to them when they were left on their own? Citing the security operations conducted within prisons, such as those at Buca, Burdur,

Ulucanlar, and Diyarbakır Prisons, which ended with prisoner casualties, prisoners argued that they could much more easily become the victims of massacres in the high security prisons. With no one to bear witness to the actions of prison staff, going into the cell meant agreeing to endure whatever forms of inhumane treatment were inflicted on them and awarding these officials with undeserved impunity. That high security prisons were constructed away from urban centers in remote locales, difficult and expensive to reach, rendered them even more vulnerable and invisible to the public gaze. Equally important, the administrative practices within these high security prisons were shielded from outside observers by the absence of unofficial mechanisms of public scrutiny. The existing venues for expressing and inspecting prisoner grievances appeared to prisoners as far too superficial and contrived. High security prisons were the most opaque of all institutions of confinement for the general public.

After describing prisoner grievances with respect to access to lawyers, health care, visitors, letters, and physical safety, a participant of the death fast expressed prisoner sentiment this way:

> Of course, F (cell) type prisons will only deepen these problems and concerns. Because even in the current form [of prisons], even while we were together with our friends, we have experienced various attacks in which tens of our friends have died. They will not be able to fool us about this so-called treatment program. Because we have seen what treatment is at Ulucanlar, Burdur, and Bergama [Prisons]. Either [be] someone without character, without identity, someone turned into dregs or [be] dead. This is what they force upon us. Our choice is, without doubt, the second. *Because the bodily existence of someone whose soul has died is nothing.* Having lived through these examples, we have no reason to trust the state.[14]

For all these reasons, political prisoners envisioned their struggle against the high security prisons as the opposition to cellular confinement defined as a form of torture. They fought to alter the conditions of their confinement and to demand recognition of their status as *political* prisoners. In so doing, they also acted out their political identity by taking part in the venerable tradition of prisoner resistance against torture and inhumane treatment. From this perspective, theirs was a *defensive* struggle against the violence of the state. It defended the "right to resist" in the face of oppression and violation. At the same time, it aimed to advance rights and deepen the liberties available to the citizens of Turkey, both inside and outside prisons. It was motivated by human rights norms and acted in the name of a humanity that transcended prison walls. These prisoners interpreted "cellularization" as a metaphor for the growing power of the state over society.[15] If the death fast struggle could succeed in putting an end to arbitrary usurpations of rights in prisons, it would not only have secured an important feat for democracy but also constitute an example for other struggles. The participants of the death fast struggle therefore considered themselves to be part of a broader struggle for the deepening of democracy. The inclusion of more general concerns about Turkey's system of criminal justice in the initial list of demands, they argued, could be considered a reflection of this motivation.

The interpretation of the death fast struggle as an act of resistance resonates with the reading advanced by Gürcan Koçan and Ahmet Öncü in one of the very few scholarly studies on the hunger strike in Turkish prisons. These authors define the hunger strike as a nonviolent form of resistance against injustice that is carried out for the public good on behalf of all citizens. While few hunger strikers considered the distinguishing quality of the hunger strike to be non-violence (in fact, most deemed hunger striking as a form of violent protest), they certainly viewed their struggle as advancing the rights of all citizens and contributing to the democratization of Turkey as a whole. However, as we shall see, this was only *one* facet of the death fast struggle.

The prisoners who saw themselves as taking part in the democratic struggle for the advancement of human rights invariably considered the hunger strike to be dictated as a result of the circumstances in which they found themselves. The main reason why the hunger strike became the predominant tactic of struggle was the unavailability of other means of expressing their grievances in prison.[16] Whatever other means were available had already been exhausted without any effect. This is why the prisoners had to resort to the only means they had at their disposal: their bodies. The hunger strike was thus a tactic of *last resort*, a "final remedy" for being heard.[17] A participant of the death fast argued, "The death fast is something that can be done as a last solution; it is not something that can be used all the time. It is not something we exalt. One says: I would rather die than live like this. It is not something done for the greatness of the act. They kill people slowly in the cell. *This is the last solution.*"[18]

These prisoners saw their bodies as instruments for winning concessions from the state. Through the deployment of their bodies, they could use their lives as bargaining chips to attain the right to a dignified life behind bars. In the words of a participant of the hunger strike: "We had to use our bodies as means. This method was not something that we desired very much, but it was something that we had to do because we did not have any other means."[19] The use of the body amounted to self-defense against torture and oppression, which targeted the same bodies as their objects. According to the same hunger striker:

> We did not have any other means of resistance than our bodies at hand. Either our bodies would be transformed into weapons against us, through torture, or we would use those bodies as a means of resistance against the state. At the end of the day, our bodies have always been used against us as a means of torture. We only conducted a counteroffensive by transforming the same means into a means of resistance. Because in those conditions when no death fast was there, our bodies went through torture. . . . They were hanged. Torture up to even the flaying of skin. Many horrible things. At the Burdur massacre, Buca massacre, Ulucanlar massacre, all of them. We did this because we had no other choice but to use the same bodies against the state as a means of resistance. Now there are various claims, or misunderstandings, that we are sacralizing death here. We are not sacralizing any death, but we are sacralizing the kind of death that is shaped by resistance. Because it is really something sacred. Because there is something called a right of resistance. Everyone has a right of resistance against the policies directed toward us. We only used that right.[20]

From this perspective, the insurgent's body was not something that emerged ex nihilo. It was brought into being by the relations of power that have operated upon it, violated and tortured it, forced it to submit. Insurgent bodies had been used as weapons against their bearers by the state to make them break, confess, repent, accept, yield, and surrender. The state had already victimized these bodies by subjecting them to violence, pain, and deprivation when prisoners were first taken into police custody, when they were put in the cells, or when they were attacked in the prison operations that they recalled as "massacres." Using their bodies in this struggle meant, in effect, turning them against the state. This was a reversal of torture and an effective way to prevent further attempts of violation. Indeed, such a reversal or reappropriation of the body as a site of resistance from what it had previously been, namely, the site of domination and subjection, was a direct consequence of and response to the politicization of the body by the state.[21] In order to overturn the state's victimization of bodies, bodies had to be seized back from the state, even if this was to be achieved through the "enactment of modes of violence typically performed by the state."[22] What is noteworthy in this point of view, forcefully expressed by the hunger striker who described her experience of torture, is the stark separation between the body and the identity of its bearer. It is the body that goes through torture, that is hanged, whose skin is flayed, that experiences "many horrible things," while the hunger striker as the bearer of this body describes this experience by dissociating herself from her body and embracing her identity as a political prisoner who resists.[23] The body without the bearer's identity is likened to dregs; it is reduced to an existence that is not worth keeping: *"Because the bodily existence of someone whose soul has died is nothing."*[24] The dignity of the person is not reducible to her bodily integrity; instead, it is abstracted from the body and lodged in the prisoner's political identity. This abstraction becomes necessary for political prisoners to transform their bodies from being victims of the state to active instruments of resistance.

As Allen Feldman also argues for the dirty protest and the 1981 hunger strike of Irish political prisoners, the "counterinstrumentation" of the prisoner's body constitutes "the principle of [the prisoners'] dissociation from the rituals of domination" under interrogation as well as in the prison cell.[25] The state constructs the prisoner as its "other" and invests it with alterity. Ultimately, however, it is through the separation of the prisoner from her body, what Feldman calls "the *self-bifurcation* of the prisoner," that enables the radical utilization of the body.[26] The alterity is turned against the state because of the agential power of the prisoner that enables a mimetic reversal. The interiority of the prisoner, uncolonized by sovereignty precisely because of its bifurcation, provides the possibility of utilizing the body against the state in the protection of the prisoners' political identity.

With the instrumental use of the body in the hunger strike, it is transformed from the *object of violence* into the *subject of resistance*. According to these participants, the marks and scars inscribed on their bodies by torture were not thereby erased, but they were channeled into a productive, progressive, and redeeming purpose. These bodies thereby became sources of empowerment for the prisoners, restoring their agency over their own lives, even if this empowerment was dependent on taking charge of one's own starvation. Either way, these prisoners reasoned, they had no alternative: if they did not use their bodies, the state would seize them anyway. Conceptualizing the cell as torture, the prisoners thus resorted to the body—the former object of torture and thus the most obvious terrain of struggle—in their resistance against the torture of cellular confinement.

We can also consider the statements of these participants of the death fast struggle regarding their bodies as revealing a fundamental distinction between biological life and political life that has played a significant role in motivating their decisions to participate in the hunger strike. According to their view, since dignity resided only in a properly political identity, without which it was not possible to have a fully human life, and not in the body, keeping one's dignity meant refusing the equivalence between the value of biological existence and that of a political life. Cellular confinement entailed a redefinition of life as biological existence, which they equated to a prolonged and torturous death through the erosion of dignity. The cells of the high security prisons threatened to reduce prisoners to nothing more than "dregs," by subjecting their politically qualified life to sovereign violence.[27] If we were to use the concept of "bare life," we could evaluate the struggle of these prisoners as an attempt to resist the status of absolute vulnerability and dispoliticization into which sovereign power was striving to manufacture their lives, by stripping them of their political identity and situating them in a zone of "exception" where they could be violated with impunity. Hence we could surmise that, contra Agamben, the prisoners' self-understanding involved, at the same time, resistance to being reduced to bare life. The following reflections of a death faster aptly summarized this position: "Either we were going to eat, drink, and live dishonorably or we were going to venture our bodies and protect our dignity against [the state's] attack."[28]

According to Koçan and Öncü, the hunger strike was a struggle for dignity in the Kantian sense because the hunger strikers fought for the "right to determine the circumstances of one's own life."[29] From this perspective, the state's pressure on physicians to resuscitate hunger strikers meant an affront to their dignity as moral and autonomous agents who could make their own decisions. It was not that hunger strikers opposed medical intervention because they wanted to die but because they wanted to be able to make the decision to live or die themselves rather than allow the state to make it for them. However, while Koçan and Öncü emphasize that the state's treatment of the prisoners was against their dignity, because they were reduced to a "mere means," the authors also consider the death fast to be an infringement of dignity because it meant "lessening one's rational agency to gain some instrumental value."[30] Needless to say, such an interpretation deeply contradicts how death fasters interpreted their own actions.[31]

Even though these participants of the struggle viewed themselves as fighting for dignity, they were skeptical of equating the hunger strike with the "right to die." The death fast, they contended, was conducted in order to win and not, as they were often criticized, in order to die. Their actions were not opposed to the fundamental human "right to live" but were rather an assertion of that right. In the words of Koçan and Öncü, the hunger strikers "do not mean the negation of life but, on the very contrary, the affirmation of it."[32] This statement, while misleading when generalized to the whole movement, cogently summarizes the strand within it that views the struggle as an act of resistance. We can interpret the explanations of some hunger strikers regarding how they tried to prolong their process of self-starvation as much as possible, by taking vitamins, by drinking more water, and by sheer willpower from the perspective that privileges the account of the death fast as an act of resistance. Accordingly, their commitment to life was what sustained these prisoners on the hunger strike. They thought that it was important to live longer, if only by one more day, "in spite of the enemy."[33] Instead of a willingness to die, these prisoners argued, the death fast expressed a willingness to live, an extremely great and passionate desire for life. In fact, in their opinion, the hunger strike as a tactic was predicated on the strong will to live, a "life drive" rather than a "death drive." In this line, one participant of the death fast explained,

> [A person who wants to die] cannot do what must be done in a hunger strike. [She] cannot drink that water even though the body does not want it. Only a person clinging onto life can do these things. Things that one totally dislikes. You smell horrific. You smell like a corpse. People on hunger strike smell horribly bad because their cells die. Every day is a war of the will. A person who wants to die cannot do what it takes to sustain a hunger strike: drinking water, eating salt, eating sugar, maintaining oneself on these through the day, coming face to face with wardens all the time, dealing with those who come

to intervene [medically]; a person not tied to life, not wanting to live, cannot do these. A person who wants to die will kill oneself. It is very important to be in good spirits. We would always stimulate one another throughout the death fast so that we would not let ourselves go . . . Because you are very weak. We were constantly stimulated in order to be awake intellectually, to be tied to life. Without these, it is impossible to conduct a hunger strike. A person who wants to die cannot sustain a hunger strike even a single day. She would not have that power. It is very difficult for one to fight one's own body. When you are on hunger strike, you are constantly fighting your body.[34]

Starving oneself without letting go of life: this took meticulous effort, great persistence, and stoic self-discipline. These prisoners saw themselves as carrying out an intimate struggle with their own bodies: on the one hand, the body resisted dying despite the starvation imposed upon it by the will; on the other hand, the will resisted the desires of the body to nourish itself or else to give in to death. This was a "war of the will" that had to be renewed everyday, a struggle in which only the most dedicated, disciplined, and experienced militants could succeed. If it were not for the purpose of winning, the prisoners asked, how could this be done? "In the beginning, [the death fast] goes well, but later vomiting begins. Nausea . . . We could not take liquids or anything. It became a torture to drink the sugary water. Our friends quit [drinking] water in order to prevent vomiting. But you don't do this [hunger strike] to die. You have specific demands, a goal, you are doing it to win. . . . We took the sugary water insistently despite our reluctance."[35]

Chosen because there were no other means, the prisoners could only persevere in their deep physical suffering because of their conviction in the possibility of winning their demands and thus ending their hunger strike before they lost their lives to it. Death, they assured themselves, was not a certain outcome of their tactic, only a risk to bear: "You can die while you are hanging placards, you can be shot, you can die while you are being beaten up. But the death fast is on the agenda when there is no other means left to use, when all other means are exhausted and in the last stage. Otherwise, it would not mean anything other than squandering oneself."[36]

According to these participants, the death fast should not be viewed as an act of self-sacrifice. While they did consider dying in resistance sacred and glorious, they adamantly refused the criticism that they were glorifying death, which was advanced in some public discussions. The death fast struggle was not about the attainment of martyrdom but the attainment of real, concrete concessions against the F-type prisons. In the words of a participant of the death fast,

> The death fast is not an act of sacrifice. . . . You transform your body into a weapon because there is nothing else you can do. And it is an expression of ideological strength, political development, organizational talent, [and] cultural wealth because you express your commitment to life with death. You don't think of death, but you know that you might die. That's why it is not an act of sacrifice. I went on the death fast saying I will not die, I said I will be on my feet even in my last moment. Even if I am in bed, my hands will be in the air, if I can't hold my hands up, my hair will be standing. This is not an act of sacrifice. I might die, but this is not intended, it is a consequence. In an act of sacrifice, death is intended.[37]

Rather than an act of self-sacrifice, the hunger strike was a means to advance their self-interest. In fact, some of these participants refused to call their action a death fast at all; instead, they referred to it as a "hunger strike of indefinite duration." The hunger strike was not sacrificial because it was not undertaken out of devotion to others, or in the name of the "people," but for the prisoners themselves. Because the finitude of protest in the hunger strike imposed an urgency, it was the best way to inspire and mobilize the masses to act on behalf of the prisoners so that they could pressure the state to assuage the concerns of the prisoners. While they emphasized the continuity of the struggle inside and outside the prisons, they argued that social mobilization outside was central for the achievement of prisoner demands.[38] From their perspective, the mobilizations outside would be more decisive in getting results than the hunger strike itself.

The protagonists of this strand of interpretation of the death fast struggle considered the hunger strike to be qualitatively different from other modalities of self-destruction. They marked their distance from suicide attacks and disowned tactics like self-immolation and varieties of self-mutilation. Among these corporeal tactics, they singled out hunger striking as the only form of action that did not have a blind, emotive devotion to the cause and that did not involve an absolute orientation toward death. The distance these individuals took from other forms of the weaponization of life was due less to a normative problem with the use of violence per se than their view that those tactics were ineffective and therefore a waste of militant life. In contrast, the hunger strike was a rational, cognitively driven method of bargaining, much like conventional forms of protest. According to a participant of the death fast who interpreted his involvement as an act of resistance,

> It is wrong to my mind to call the death fast an act of sacrifice. The death fast is done for oneself, to protect oneself. You don't think about others. The F-type threat is coming at you and you are doing this for yourself, *to live better.* It would be an act of sacrifice if you have devoted your life, you are walking to death, [and] there is absolutely no turning back. But there is a turning back in the death fast: how? If your demands are met or if you are subject to [medical] intervention, you turn back from death. If your demands aren't met, you will die, but this is still not sacrifice. . . . The death fast is part of a long-term struggle. Suicide bombings are sacrifice because there is no turning back. One has put on the bomb. And it is wrong. Why should I kill myself with an act of sacrifice when there are better things to do? The death fast is not an act of sacrifice. Its real purpose is to trigger the masses into action.[39]

Among different interpretations of the death fast struggle, it was, without a doubt, this strand that resonated most with the public and that led to the most compassionate reception of the hunger strikers. The prisoners appeared as victims; the vulnerable citizens of an oppressive state. To the extent that the movement found support and instigated mobilizations in the domain of civil society, it was mainly due to the depiction of the movement as a democratic struggle and an act of rightful resistance to violations of human rights. The humanitarian discourse of the lawyer Behiç Aşçı, which emphasized the detrimental effects of isolation and the sanctity of human life, should be assessed as the movement's ultimate convergence with this interpretation of the death fast, an interpretation that had been there all along. Without the prioritization of this interpretation vis-à-vis others, the final mobilizations that helped end the death fast struggle would probably not have taken place.

CLASS WAR AGAINST NEOLIBERALISM

If the interpretation of the struggle as an act of resistance was the most ame-
nable to popular support, the interpretation as class struggle was the most
conducive to militant support. Many prisoners saw the high security prisons
as the embodiment of the interests of the ruling class with one fundamental
goal: "confining dissent."[40] In this conception, the state was an instrument
of capital, the cell was an instrument of the state, and therefore the cell was
an instrument of capital. The function of the cell was to tame disobedient
citizens and forge them (and, in their example, the masses) in the interests
of capital.

At stake was not a generic capitalism, but capitalism in its neoliberal version in a neocolonial setting. These prisoners saw an intimate connection
between high security prisons and the particular brand of neoliberalism put
into practice in this fringe country of Europe, dependent on foreign investment and subject to the intensive extraction and exploitation of its human
and natural resources. According to the prisoners, neoliberalism entailed the
dismantling of the welfare state and the privatization of many of the state's
vital, protective functions. Through extensive privatizations of economic enterprises owned and operated by the state, it entailed the transfer of public
wealth to private, often foreign, hands. The free reign of market forces could
not be established without the intervention of the state in order to ensure the
suppression of dissenting forces. The strengthening of the punitive arm of the
state for the market found its expression in the implementation of high security prisons. True, this was different from the privatization of penal institutions
or the utilization of prison populations as a pool of cheap and forced labor, as
in the United States, but only temporarily. Such developments might follow
in due time, but, for now, the looming threat was the state's attempt to crush
social opposition by confining its leaders in the cells.

These prisoners postulated that since the International Monetary Fund
was fully supportive of (and partly responsible for) the matchmaking between
the neoliberal economy and the authoritarian state, it must also prescribe and
support the high security prisons. As they saw it, the market-friendly policies
and harsh economic stabilization programs dictated by the IMF, involving the
destruction of the welfare state and the curbing of rights to social security,
health care, education, collective bargaining, and political expression, necessitated the high security prison cell because it promised to isolate and even-

tually destroy political opposition and to profit from this by lowering costs of supervision and control. In order to make this connection more obvious, these prisoners associated the F of the F-type prison project with the F in the International Monetary Fund. Referring to this connection as "IM(F)," they argued that the security interests of the state and the class interests of capital now formed a unified "historic bloc."[41] In this confrontation the state acted as the institutional agent of the unified bloc, whereas the political organizations of the prisoners (naturally outlawed by the ideologically motivated laws of the capitalist state) acted as the authentic representatives of the people.

As the radical political opposition in the country, the prisoners saw themselves as the only forces not afraid to object to the consolidation of the ideological hegemony of the neoliberal agenda and to fight for the proletarian cause (especially in the absence of mass movements and working class militancy). Their politics focused on opposing the state as the handmaiden of neoliberalism and the F-type prisons as the material embodiment of punitive neoliberalism. Their view of the state as the archenemy was reciprocated by the state, they believed, evinced by the fact that they were singled out for imprisonment in the high security prisons. The prisoners thus saw their struggle against the F-type prison not only as part of the class struggle against capitalism but as constituting its frontline.

Viewing themselves as the *vanguard* of the people, the prisoners believed that any submission to the state on their part would enable, if not facilitate, the submission of the rest of society. The cell attacked the community of prisoners directly, but, through them, it attacked the communal ties of the masses. Atomization in either sphere would render collective opposition impossible. "Cellularization," then, was the ideological war launched by the state to secure its hegemonic control over the hearts and minds of the masses, breaking their ties of solidarity, robbing them of their fundamental and collective rights, frightening them through the criminalization of class struggle, and securing their consent by inducing a competitive individualism. In the words of one of the participants, "this attack, the F-type prison, with the IM(F)-type life that it forces upon workers and laborers, is a very comprehensive attack. It aims to massacre the captives in prisons, to bury them alive in the grave, leaving the working and laboring people without a vanguard (*öncü*)."[42] The prisoners thus viewed themselves as human shields, barricading the state's attack on the people. If the bodies of these prisoners were to be confined in the cells of the high security prisons, they contended, the "hope of the people" would be locked up with them.⁴³ In order to prevent the state from triumphing and capturing the "people" in the person of the prisoners, the prisoners could not submit, whatever the cost: "What they desire to confine in the cell is the struggle of our people against oppression and exploitation; [they desire] to make us surrender. Calculations are being made over how much easier it would be to take over the people of a country whose revolutionary captives have been taken over in the prisons. This is why our resistance is not limited to ourselves; it is related to the liberation of our people and their future. In this frame, what is forced upon us is this: either surrender or die."⁴⁴

It is highly revealing that these prisoners called themselves "revolutionary captives" rather than prisoners or inmates. Prisoners acknowledged captivity only as a matter of fact. They rejected the legitimacy of the state's power over them and the legitimacy of its laws, from which their imprisonment had issued. Rather, they viewed themselves as having temporarily been captured by the state in the revolutionary war. While the prison held their bodies in captivity, the prisoners maintained, their minds were free. The high security cell would not only destroy the camaraderie that nourished the revolutionaries in prison wards but would also attempt to destroy their thoughts and convictions. In the words of a death faster, "Was the problem of prisons one of sovereignty? The state was always sovereign over prisons. Whenever it wanted, it could count us, for example. From this perspective, the state had no problems, ever. But the state was never sovereign over the consciousness of those inside. Neither is it sovereign over the consciousness of those now inside F-type cells."⁴⁵ From this perspective, the state appeared to be a machine that literally captured the masses, one individual at a time. The physical captivity was only a segue into ideological captivity, making individuals consent, conform, and accept the order of things—the state's ultimate goal. The reign of the state, however, would not be complete as long as communist prisoners continued to exist and fight. The challenge to the prisoners posed by the F-type prisons was to stay *in* the order, without, however, assenting to become *of* the order. "This is a psychological war. They are trying to finish us in the head rather than physically,"⁴⁶ argued a death faster. As a result, the struggle against high security prisons was not simply a war against neoliberal capitalism but also a war to preserve the very existence of revolutionary, communist politics. In response to their impending ideological annihilation, the prisoners envisioned their struggle as a war in which one of the parties would ultimately be destroyed:

"The state wants to annihilate whoever opposes its oppression, torture, and exploitation; it wants to annihilate you, us. And we don't want to be annihilated. This is the foundation of the problem."[47]

The death fast struggle, according to this conception, was much more than an act of resistance against torture and the assertion of human rights. It was an act of *class warfare* against the state and, through the state, against neoliberal capitalism. The prison was only one act in the theater of permanent class war, staged now in the cells, then on the streets, at the factories, and in the universities. "The beds in which we lie down are no longer normal beds," a participant of the death fast remarked, "they are trenches."[48] In a letter to the press, one team of death fasters wrote from prison: "A war has been going on in prisons for many years. And this war does not consist of a war between us revolutionaries and the state. It is a class war between the oppressors and the oppressed, between political government and the people."[49]

Envisioning the death fast as an episode of class war implied a different approach to why hunger striking became central to the struggle. Accordingly, the use of the body was a result of strictly instrumental calculations based on the needs of the struggle. Its deployment via the hunger strike was not a necessity but an option, not unavoidable but willfully chosen, not dictated by circumstances in which other means were not available but suggested by calculations in which other means were less preferable. The hunger strike was deemed to be the best, most efficient, and formidable instrument of protest that could potentially be used to confront the state's offensive. This was predicated on the interpretation of the hunger strike as a war tactic, a *proactive counterattack* mounted from the trenches of the prison wards against the state. The hunger strike was not a desperate act of last resort but one of *strategic choice*.

The strategic nature of this approach to the hunger strike was more a reflection of the collective agency of the political organizations and parties that coordinated and conducted the struggle than of the agency of individual prisoners themselves. These organizations represented the collective will of the prisoners. While individual prisoners participated in the construction of a revolutionary collective by fatally committing their own bodies, the organizations to which they pledged allegiance made decisions based on factors such as their overall conception of strategy, the availability of mass support, organizational strength, and competition and cooperation among similar organizations. To these outlawed political parties, which viewed themselves as vanguards in the class war against the state, individual prisoners were rank-and-file militants, no different from ordinary soldiers, who constituted their political force and enacted their strategic calculations.

There were several instrumental reasons why these parties preferred the hunger strike over other forms of struggle. First of all, self-starvation carried significant moral power over and against the state, which militated against the fasters' construction as "terrorists" by the state. Prisoners on hunger strike constituted silent yet potent indictments of the legitimacy of the capitalist state and the authoritarian tradition of political rule that manifested itself in oppressive penal practices against the revolutionaries. Each time a prisoner's corpse would publicly emerge into the world outside the prison walls, it would starkly demonstrate the state's failure in fulfilling its very basic duties, ensuring safety and security.[50] The political parties thought they could capitalize on the embarrassment of the state before its citizens and the rest of the world, caused by prisoner deaths, and use this embarrassment to strengthen their call for concessions against high security prisons.

Second, the hunger strike had symbolic and pedagogic power over the masses, which these organizations wanted to channel into their confrontation with the state. The famished bodies of prisoners pointed to the structural violence of the capitalist economy by making its effects visible on those bodies that refused to be co-opted into it. These bodies served as a metaphor for the relation of the people to capitalism in the person of the prisoners, reinforcing the latter's role as the vanguard of the people. The starvation of prisoners in the face of "IM(F)"-dictated prisons figuratively preempted and enacted the starvation of the people in the face of IMF-dictated neoliberal capitalism. In the image of the starving body, the communist parties could show the people the effects of capitalism in a visceral, everyday register. They could convince them that class war persisted, despite its concealment by the facade of the so-called liberal-democratic order. The suffering bodies, which materially evidenced the "truth" of capitalism, would function to educate the masses about the real intent of the state in imprisoning the whole country and annihilating radical dissent by installing high security prisons. Despite the state's efforts at marginalizing the prisoners as "terrorists," the parties' deployment of self-starvation sought to reinforce the self-definition of prisoners as the committed vanguards of the people whose fate was inextricably entwined with the fate of the proletarian revolution.

A third reason for choosing the hunger strike was the parties' expectation that it would generate social mobilization, based on the successful working out of the moral, symbolic, and educational implications of this tactic. Ideologically, the parties argued that social mobilization would arise insofar as the people could be convinced that the project of "cellularization" was not limited to prisons alone but related to the restructuring of social relations based on neoliberal capitalism. The parties tried to harness the people's prevailing discontent against the government's economic and social policies favoring capitalist interests with the argument for "cellularization," inciting them to struggle together with the prisoners. Practically, however, these organizations argued for the necessity of backing up their ideological stance on "cellularization" with concrete, vanguard action, which the masses expected to see in order to decide favorably on participating in the struggle. The hunger strike was thought to have the vanguard quality necessary to fulfill this expectation. And should the radicalism and commitment of the prisoners on hunger strike not suffice to motivate the masses into action, then, the parties expected, the violent reaction of the state triggered by the hunger strike would expose its true colors. The high numbers of deaths on the prisoners' ledgers, it was thought, would augment the persuasive power of their protest in exposing the "truth" of the Turkish state and the seriousness of the challenge these parties constituted against the state. In this light, resorting to other forms of self-destruction, such as suicide bombings and self-immolations, was also a strategically motivated intervention, chosen in order to escalate the situation and incite the masses further.

As a result of these considerations, the insurgent body of the prisoner was inserted in the matrix of rational and strategic political calculations of class warfare and resignified as an instrument of illegal political organizations. This instrumentalization stood in contrast to existential commitment of individuals, marking a significant difference between the approach to the hunger strike articulated at the level of the organizations and the level of individual participants. For individuals, the organizational calculus was perceived as duty. Each militant was motivated by a desire to fulfill the "revolutionary responsibility" assigned to them by their parties.[51] Their task was to complete the mission as best as possible, for this would be their contribution to the class war. In this sense, being selected to participate in the hunger strike was an emblem of prestige. The individual militant's reputation depended on the successful completion of this task, as any other. In the words of a participant of the death fast struggle, "Let's imagine we are playing chess. There, in order to win, you would give away the pawn if need be. Because you don't value each piece individually, you value winning. We can give away our life in order to win, if need be. It is not possible to understand us looking from the individualist world. Understanding is only possible if one leaves the individualist world and frees oneself of selfishness. What is important is the perpetuation of political warfare. If my death is necessary for that, I will die."[52]

Participants of the death fast struggle who shared this view insisted that the gravity of the likelihood of death involved in this mission should not be exaggerated. Death could be conceived either as a risk to be born or simply as an inevitable outcome, but it should not be viewed as something extraordinary. From the perspective of warriors, which they considered themselves to be, death was to be expected. Just as they live for the communist cause, militants must be able to die for it, especially if this might advance their cause. As a participant of the death fast put it, "Everybody will die one day. Everybody will die. One must know how to die for what one lives for."[53] If a militant could ever choose and shape his or her own death, this was the moment.

While discussing their intentions for participating in the hunger strike, these participants preferred to frame them not in terms of a willingness to live or a willingness to die, but in terms of the strength of their dedication to the communist cause. "You've got to do what you've got to do," they would repeat, highlighting the importance of attaining the consciousness of a true warrior.[54] Such a consciousness, they contended, led them to focus not on the painful experience of self-starvation but on the goal, making sure not to fail in their revolutionary mission. Giving in to pain would mean jeopardizing the struggle's potential gains. In this light, a participant of the death fast narrated the experience of fasting:

> We had come to blows with the enemy; we weren't even aware of [that we were on] the death fast. The target before us was clear. We concentrated on that. Was our arm dislocated, was our head smashed, was our bone broken? We could not really feel it. Because we were always subjected to torture. . . . We didn't really care. Because we knew in our mind that these attacks could happen, that their goal was to make us give up, to make us surrender. That's why our goal was not to surrender. And our attitude would determine

this. Therefore, we weren't even aware that we were thinning, that our bodies were melting."[55]

Instead of the desire to reclaim the body that has been subjected to torture as a site of resistance, what is more pronounced in this account is a certain nonchalance about the body and its dispensability as a function of duty. The body had already been lost to the state through torture; it had already experienced pain at the hands of the enemy. These were expected, even bound to happen, and no longer relevant. At the point of direct confrontation, the corporeal damage incurred faded in significance, leaving only a battle of wills between enemies. The individuals, narrated almost as if they had fused into a singular body with the same arm, head, and bone, were locked into not surrendering, not yielding in the struggle, and keeping their responsibility of defeating the enemy to such an extent that they even forgot they were actually dying.

This emphasis on fulfilling one's responsibility in the communist struggle was also projected on the significations attributed to sacrifice. Participation in the death fast was viewed as a modest rendition of fighting for a larger-than-life cause rather than a great act of self-sacrifice. One participant of the death fast argued: "What we are doing is not at all a great sacrifice, even a heroic deed, as some say. In fact, we are doing this merely as a revolutionary, as a communist, acting with such consciousness. It is no different from your taking the bus to go somewhere. You would get on the bus even if the bus was too crowded because you have to go there. You take it, even though it makes you uncomfortable. For us too. The death fast has death at its end, but it has to be done because this attack can only be stopped by a death fast. And I saw myself at the forefront of this."[56] Accordingly, these participants did not see any significant differences between being a guerrilla fighter and a death faster, between a death faster and a suicide bomber. They were missions all the same. A participant of the death fast contended: "Just like a guerrilla becomes immortal by giving his last breath, there is no difference for us in essence [with the death fast]. He has a weapon around his waist, whereas our bodies are weapons."[57] They compared their acts of self-destruction to the acts of the workers of the Paris Commune: "We argue that there is no difference between our actions today and those of the workers who have died fighting at the barricades of the Paris Commune, workers who have died in any kind of class conflict."[58]

Making sacrifices was part of the ordinary course of being a militant;
however, sacrificial ideology was pernicious and incompatible with communism. Distinguishing acts of self-sacrifice from the exaltation of sacrifice,
these participants argued against attributing a heroism and exceptionality to
self-destructive performances on the grounds that such heroism would drive
a wedge between the masses and the militants acting on their behalf. Communist sacrifice had to be desacralized and normalized: "It is very important
that this death becomes ordinary."[59] The following account by a participant of
the death fast provides a clear summary of this approach:

> We never saw [participation in the hunger strike] as heroism
> because this means differentiating it qualitatively [from other acts],
> abstracting it from the masses, abstracting this even from yourself
> and separating those among you who are heroic, who have special
> talents. . . . Sacrifice, when defined in terms of altruism, will need to
> point either to privileged, particularly talented types of human beings
> or to something that is based on mystical powers, supernatural be-
> liefs. . . . We have no belief in God; in the last instance, earth is where
> our bodies will go. That's why we must separate our understanding
> from that of sacrifice. What we do is similar to distributing flyers in a
> public square; it is something we do as part of class struggle. . . . We
> believe that we have made a contribution similar to that of any one of
> our friends distributing flyers. These actions are the same in essence;
> a guerrilla, a militant who distributes flyers on the street, a death
> faster . . . these are all the same. *It is necessary to routinize death.*[60]

For these avowedly atheist participants for whom a discourse on sacrifice
did not reflect their scientific Marxism, the goal of the death fast struggle was
a matter of advancing the anticapitalist struggle and politically harming their
"enemy." The real victory, of course, would be the realization of the communist cause. While they were aware that the death fast struggle would not be
sufficient to achieve such a feat, they nonetheless believed that it could have
invaluable effects, not necessarily limited to winning immediate concessions
that ameliorated prison conditions. Instead, they maintained that the death
fast struggle should be evaluated as an episode in the long-term struggle toward communism, whose actual effectiveness and success could not be con-
jectured from the present but only assessed retrospectively, once the real vic-

tory was won. Therefore, in evaluating the death fast struggle, these prisoners contended, we must think in terms of the abysmal counterfactual in which class war had been completely suppressed: what might have happened if there had been no death fast? In the words of a participant, "At the end, this is a war. Just like in a war, sometimes a bomb is more effective, whereas at other times a single bullet is more effective. The effectiveness of this action [i.e., the hunger strike] depends on current conditions. It is wrong to say these [actions] are unsuccessful. In their absence, not a single voice will be heard."[61]

Armored with such a fervent militancy, however, these participants were also aware that the war they were fighting was one that diverged from its orthodox formulations by Marx and Engels or even from its subsequent iterations by Lenin, Mao, or Che. The novelty was their extensive, repeated reliance on the weaponization of life as the primary tactic of struggle. While they wanted to distance themselves from a "politics conducted over corpses," they also admitted that the number of corpses mattered. The increasing number of casualties, produced by self-destructive acts of militants, they believed, would have an exponential impact on their audience. "We don't conduct politics over the death of people. But we also know that, after a point, class struggle can only secure its achievements through the death of individuals."[62] In their assessment of the current political conjuncture, with harsh repression by the state, asymmetric conditions of warfare, and little mass following, necroresistance constituted the correct strategy that would enable them to emerge victorious in the struggle. Despite the repeated comparisons they made between themselves and the generations of workers and militants who had lost their lives in class struggle to advance the claim that the prominence of the self-destructive form of their struggle was nothing out of the ordinary, they also argued that death had become the only viable path to victory. In other words, they were aware that necroresistance transformed class war into something new, even though its novelty and implications were far from fully worked out. In this instance practice was ahead of theory.

Overall, the interpretation of the death fast struggle as an act of revolutionary class warfare did help mobilize the constituencies of these outlawed parties and their supporters but did not do well in enhancing the image of the prisoners in the eyes of the broader public. Already suspect as "terrorists," the prisoners were rendered more marginal by a narrative that coded them as the foot soldiers of party leaders who used them for their own strategic interests. The allegedly impending revolution these parties fought for found little resonance in public opinion and expectations, which became painfully obvious with the meager working-class support the death fast struggle was able to generate. The prisoners and their supporters starved, immolated, and exploded their bodies, calling out to the masses for a revolutionary uprising, but they could not reach out to the everyday concerns of the masses from their position of marginality. The strategic calculations of these parties might have worked differently in a setting marked by the ongoing presence of radical mass mobilizations, but the disconnect between these parties and the masses led these parties to misread the world outside prisons. The militants were sincere and committed to their convictions, ready to die for the communist cause, but the urgency of their struggle and demands, their political views and tactics had come to be so removed from the people that it rendered their deaths more tragic and moot. From the perspective of its participants, the struggle for communism had grown inseparable from the struggle for prison wards, but the idea that the prison was the main trench in the war between classes met only meager support among the toiling masses in whose name these militants died self-inflicted deaths. To put it another way, the stronger the disconnect between the militants and the masses, the more fervent, violent, and marginal the prisoners' struggle became.

REFUSAL AGAINST BIOSOVEREIGNTY

A third strand of interpretation that emerges from participant narratives involves the construction of the death fast struggle as an act of *refusal*. This view comes out most vividly from the accounts of prisoners who considered the cell to be the vehicle of totalitarian domination, due not simply to the coercion or intimidation directed at the body but to the subtle mechanisms for the generation and cultivation of consent. Accordingly, the F-type prison cell was the instrument of containing and invading each person, in body and mind, in order to ensure total subjugation. At stake was more than obedience; the cell, more perniciously, required consent to the legitimacy of the state and turned each individual into a vehicle for reproducing its ideological hegemony. From this perspective, the cell was an embodiment of the state, which, in turn, was the institutional agent of sovereignty. Sovereignty became more biopolitical; it expanded its control over different facets of life, while, at the same time, it built its legitimacy on its ability to protect life and enhance its well-being. It enveloped individuals as it dominated them, it turned them into vehicles of their own domination. The opposition to the cell, or to the state that acted through the cell, could not therefore proceed by making demands and extracting concessions from the state. It had to target the core of its capacity to dominate, its sovereignty. The ideological delegitimization of sovereignty could only be carried out, according to these participants, through a withdrawal of consent. Withdrawal from the domain of sovereign power meant withdrawal from the life defined and promoted by the state, from life produced by biosovereign power.

To this group of participants, it was appropriate neither to demand the "right to live" in prison with human dignity nor to wage war against the neoliberal project forced upon society by their existential class enemy. While these were important and shared concerns, demanding better conditions in prisons and asking for the protection and betterment of their lives, rights, and welfare were ultimately bound to end up strengthening the legitimacy of the state, even as these demands might be won. While resistance advancing demands for rights could be effective in obtaining concrete results, nonetheless, it remained within the parameters of politics established and maintained by sovereign power itself. In other words, such resistance was reformist and compromising, even instrumental. It was therefore inadequate, if not misleading altogether.

By contrast, these prisoners argued, dramatic and incisive action was necessary in order to begin to think outside the system of power that wrapped itself around individuals like an invisible web and threatened to smother them. In light of the threat of the complete colonization of life and the stifling of opposition by the totality of power that was bound to envelop prisoners in the cells, it was necessary to fight not only the superficial manifestations of this colonization, but the core of power orchestrating this colonization. As a counterpoint to forms of resistance based on demands for better life conditions, which these prisoners interpreted as furthering their subjection to power, it was necessary to turn life itself back upon power. As such, the struggle must involve the willful usurpation of the power of life and death into their own hands. It was therefore crucial to *assert* (and not demand) a "right to die" as a sign of the withdrawal of consent to power. This was deemed to be the only way in which these individuals thought they could enter a frontal collision with the state, as the embodiment of sovereignty, and to refuse its grasp first on the prisoners and, through them, on the people. Against the totality of domination, "We have come to the point where death will speak, where our dead will speak," wrote a prisoner in a letter from prison.[63]

Unlike the interpretations of the movement as an act of resistance or class war, the *form* of struggle was not incidental or instrumental but central to this third conception. The corporeality of the death fast was extremely important as the spatial medium through which the power of life and death was exercised. At the same time, corporeality was extremely insignificant in light of the ultimate meaning of the same struggle. On the one hand, the body was exalted as it was transformed from a site of subjection into the venue of a decisive, radical, and noncompromising political intervention, the medium of asserting a voice from the margins of the political sphere. On the other hand, the body was denounced as simply a vessel of life and death, one that was worthy only by way of its destruction, only insofar as its destruction was made to convey a political voice that would otherwise remain mute. Since the self-destruction of the body was the conduit of political voice, and death was fully intended, expected, and, to a certain extent, even desired in the struggle, the centrality of the body was displaced onto the centrality of death. According to this conception, the political meaning of self-destructive acts was intimately tied to the metaphysical meaning of life and death, increasingly abstracted from the body.

The meaning of life and death that nourished the self-destructive actions of these individuals resulted from the ideology of "sacrifice" that endowed them with a theological conception of militancy and an attendant investment in martyrdom. The conviction of the need to sacrifice one's life for the political cause and that sacrifice was the (only) path to the success of the cause, equipped these participants with the determination and stamina necessary to carry out self-destructive acts. According to one death faster, "In attacks like these, what is more important than physical power is psychological power. That is, what really matters is your head ... your ideology. And the resistance made us stronger. *Our ideology is that we can venture death.*"[64] Because the destruction of the body was conducted within a matrix of meaning that valued sacrifice above all else, self-induced death was clearly demarcated from suicide. The choice involved in the weaponization of life was not between life and death but between biological death and ideological death. Real suicide was to concede to ideological death by compromising to stay alive.

In this light, the decision to participate in the death fast for these prisoners was a decision between biology and ideology. In the life that sovereignty
defined, produced, and permitted in the cells, the preservation of the body
meant the annihilation of the communist cause. "The state wants to strip us of
our identity, to make us naked," one participant said, encapsulating the repeated sentiment of many others.[65] By contrast, for these prisoners, ideological
self-preservation, at the detriment of biological survival, was the precondition
for the survival and endurance of the cause. According to a participant, "I sacrifice my life so as not to sacrifice my thoughts. That's why I don't think that I
am sacrificing anything. To the contrary, I am doing this to protect myself, for
my beliefs, my thoughts. Only if I had forgone my thoughts, would I have sacrificed; I would have squandered [myself]."[66] The sacrifice of one's convictions
would compromise the prisoner as a communist militant because it meant
conceding to the sovereignty of the state. A communist could only concede to
requisites of the political cause. As one of the death fasters put it, "Our bodies are not unsacrificeable. Society is being contaminated through our bodies.
When our thoughts and our bodies contend with one another, we relinquish
our bodies, not our thoughts. Because our thoughts express the free future of
society. Our thoughts are important, the body is sacrificeable. We could damage our bodies, not our thoughts."[67]

Since only ideological death was truly synonymous with ceasing to exist,
incurring corporeal damage or losing one's life lost their significance. Living a
life without one's political identity was like being the *living dead*: "They want
to turn us into the living dead. . . . We said, we will die if necessary but will not
be turned into the living dead."[68] On the hunger strike, a participant explained,
"the body is finished, but you don't feel it's coming to an end. Because you
are feeding your brain—that's what's important; it's your imagination, what
sustains you is your imagination."[69] The imagination she referred to was that
of an alternative order based on communism. Her bodily existence could be
sacrificed for the advent of the order she envisaged; that imagination nourished her while she starved her body. As another participant put it, "To give
up on one's thoughts is the real sacrifice. The body becomes worn out within
the flow of life anyway. This is a choice, too. But the wearing out of the body
becomes less of a problem in the death fast. *We understand that death is not
connected to self-preservation.*"[70]

In this account the paradoxical severing of death from self-preservation
implied a latent but prevalent logic, based on an exchange between life and

death, that defined an economy of sacrifice. One's relation to death was established neither through the idea of risk nor responsibility, but rather through the mediation of a different category: price or toll (*bedel*). The price of biological self-preservation was political death while the continuation of political existence could be gained at the expense of bodily existence. "I am twenty-two years old," wrote a female prisoner in her letter to the public, "and on the death fast for over a hundred days. Death does not intimidate me. Because if I cannot live a human life when I live, death is more than welcome."[71]

The sacrificial economy established a quid pro quo between different forms of life: "There are many living beings in life. Human beings have values; this distinguishes them from other living beings. Breathing, eating, drinking is *not* living. What we cannot give up is the fight that human beings put up for their values. In a way, we are paying for this fight."[72] At the same time, each death in the struggle called for due measure: "We have paid our price," the common slogan of the death fast went, "and we will make them pay!" ("*Bedel ödedik, bedel ödeteceğiz!*"). In the economy of sacrifice, retribution meant getting back each death's due in the form of political survival.

In this economy, corporeal violence was transformed into an exchange value abstracted from the real suffering of the concrete body. The neutralization of the violence of self-destruction in the conception of a "price to be paid" enabled the reinscription of the performance of death as the equivalent of commanding political voice. A death faster wryly summarized the dilemma of self-inflicted violence as the price of voice: "A death faster is not harming himself. This is an illusion. He is shouting with his body. Day by day, hour by hour, minute by minute, he is *shouting*."[73] The more the body approached death, the louder politics spoke through it.

"They are trying to annihilate us," a veteran of the movement asserted, "I understand this better [now]. 'Revolutionism will come to an end on the soil of this country,' this is the calculation of the sovereign. We are *dying to exist* as revolutionaries."[74] Being a revolutionary meant living a politically defined life, a life with values and convictions, defined not by but in opposition to sovereign power. This conception was juxtaposed against the biologically defined life that was deemed as the highest value in the state's discourse. Biological life was not commensurate with human life, and to defend their equivalence was already a concession to an individualist, self-serving, and conformist way of life, which stood at the basis of the ideological legitimation of sovereignty. "In our country, to live a human life has a very heavy toll, unfortunately. If I avoid

paying this toll just because my life will be shorter, or if I do not live as I should
... this would be egoism."[75]

The state upheld the "sanctity of life," but what it sought to protect was
the mere act of living. The medical interventions sanctioned by the state to
resuscitate hunger strikers clearly demonstrated that it was the biological life
of prisoners the state was concerned with. Moreover, this biological life was
dispoliticized, one that would be stripped of its political qualities precisely
because its permission to live would be granted on the basis of its letting go
of the "right to die." If we put this in Agamben's terms, what was at stake in
the attempts to feed the hunger strikers through nonconsensual medical intervention was precisely the production of "bare life" by sovereign power, which
turned medicine into its instrument. The prisoners refused this reduction,
both by conducting a fast unto death and by insisting on the "right to die,"
fighting to continue their fast by pulling out the IV in their arms each time
they became conscious and found themselves being fed against their will.[76]
A participant of the death fast remarked, "The doctor, the prison guard, the
psychologist, they are all representatives of the state, they are part of the same
grinder that tries to break the resistance. They were even trying to turn our
families against us."[77] "Today, we are only a handful, our numbers are meager,"
another former death faster remarked, "but we are doing what no one else was
able to do."[78]

Like those participants who viewed the struggle as an act of resistance,
those who viewed it as an act of refusal shared the distinction between biological life and political life. They concurred that biological survival was only
a travesty of a fully human life that must involve living according to one's
ideology. They similarly viewed the cell as the threat of being reduced to a
life in which they were asked to trade their survival for their convictions. In
this light we can observe that both groups converged in how they understood
their struggle vis-à-vis the meaning of life; namely, as the opposition to the
reduction of their existence to bare life or what they called the "living dead."
However, those who represented the overall movement as an act of refusal opposed bare life not simply because it indicated a life vulnerable to exceptional
violence, or because it constituted an assault on their dignity as persons with
a "political" identity, but, what is more important, because their opposition
entailed a *withdrawal* from sovereignty. They viewed themselves as paying a
price for securing the possibility of a political existence beyond the Turkish
state and its ideological hegemony for all those left behind.

As Marx has persuasively argued, equivalent exchange in the "free" market does not prevent the creation of surplus value. Similarly, in the death fast struggle, equivalent exchange in the political market between different forms of life did not prevent the creation of a surplus spectrality—martyrdom. The growing centrality of martyrdom, especially among the proponents of the interpretation of the struggle as an act of refusal, not only celebrated death as the "price" for political existence, but elevated it into the very vehicle for bringing forth an alternative political order, beyond sovereignty. This order would be built by *militant-martyrs*, and, once established, it would stand upon their haunting presence. Death was the form of refusal of sovereign power, martyrdom was the form of acceding to a reconfigured sovereignty to come. Relinquishing their biological existence, militant-martyrs did not merely add to the political existence of their cause; they also asserted the possibility of a form of dissident political existence that transcended the dichotomy of biological and political life. Instead, they advanced a new form of "sacrificial" existence that would thrive on the *absence* of its agent. "What is forced upon us is this: 'to die as we live.' Our alternative is this: 'To become immortal as we die.'"[79]

The sacrificial interpretation of Marxism provided the alternative matrix of meaning that sustained this economy of exchange between different forms of death. Sacrificial ideology became a prism that established the highest value as the survival of the cause and the revolutionary collective at the expense of the survival of each individual. Class consciousness in this ideology was supplanted by a "sacrificial consciousness," that is, the moral-political awareness that the communist vanguard must conduct "acts of sacrifice" to incite the masses into struggle. "One who does not have the consciousness to sacrifice has no chance of victory," a participant of the death fast struggle explained.[80] The spectacular acts of death had the potential to be effective on the masses because they reached out to the sacrificial consciousness that already existed in nascent form in popular morality. Acts of sacrifice spoke to the altruism of ordinary people, the participants claimed, which should be sufficient to inspire, if not compel, any individual to participate in the death fast struggle or at least to support it. This was because, they argued, in the simplicity of the act of giving one's life for the sake of the masses, the masses could recognize and heed the righteousness of the death fasters' cause and their selfless identification with the will of the people. The masses could also relate to the individuals giving up their lives, even without a highly sophisticated political consciousness. The noble simplicity of the act of sacrifice communicated, in abbreviated and ordinary form, the ideology of Marxism as a whole and the meaning of the communist project. Neither did the revolutionaries need an elaborate ideological formation in Marxism. It was sufficient that they had an ethical-political stance against injustice and the knowledge that they could oppose injustice through acts of sacrifice. A participant explained this position as follows: "For a socialist, a revolutionary to sacrifice oneself, it is not necessary that one has a Marxist-Leninist formation of the highest level. It is sufficient to see the fact that one's country, one's neighbor, one's relatives are under repression and oppression. It is sufficient to be a democrat. In the last instance, it is sufficient to be human."[81]

Popular morality, in this view, was already well disposed to sacrifice. The prevalence of Islamic values in the context of Turkey, and particularly as they were understood by Alevis, further supported an ethical consciousness in which sacrifice was one of the highest values. Because Alevi identity was built on a foundational act of sacrifice within Islam and because being an Alevi in Turkey involved the historical experience of subjugation by the Sunni majority, Alevi culture was considered to contain a subterranean sacrificial tradition, a tradition that would be more receptive to political acts of self-sacrifice. However, as these participants noted, theirs was not a struggle around Alevism, nor were they all from an Alevi background. Rather, Alevism, they argued, constituted one of the many indigenous traditions that nourished a sacrificial understanding within Turkish culture, rendering their orientation toward sacrifice more accessible to the masses on an everyday level. One of the former death fasters explained: "A sacrificial consciousness is present in the culture of our people, in the culture of the Anatolian people; it is ingrained. But the ornamentation of this consciousness with revolutionary values comes with being a revolutionary. Otherwise there are many mothers, fathers, siblings who sacrifice themselves for their children. This is common experience."[82] While sacrifice was the cement of popular morality, it needed to be revitalized, reworked with the values of communism, and transformed into a revolutionary morality, which would channel the ordinary impulse to fight against injustice into support for an insurgent politics advocated by the participants of the death fast struggle.

From this perspective, no great differences existed between various types of the weaponization of life. Suicide attack and self-immolation differed from hunger striking only with respect to form, not content. The substance of each act was much the same: sacrifice. Defending this view, a participant explained: "The death fast is sacrifice. You are sacrificing your life, you give it. There are only differences of form with other acts of sacrifice. Self-immolation is a higher form of the death fast. It is the ultimate point of sacrifice. There are also those friends who explode themselves with bombs. There is no difference [among these forms] in terms of political consequences; they are all the loftiest forms of action."[83]

According to these participants, all forms of action in which life was forged into a weapon were effective, but in different ways. In the case of suicide attack, the physical damage done to the enemy was of primary importance, whereas with the hunger strike and self-immolation the damage was more ideological. In the hierarchy of sacrificial acts, the most valuable was the one that had the greatest certainty of death. However, all self-destructive acts, regardless of their specific modality, functioned to expose the "truth." A participant of the death fast struggle stated, "Acts of sacrifice explain political realities to the people, they arouse emotions, they affect and organize the people. [The hunger strike] is a method of explaining the political realities in prisons, but the political realities in prisons are a consequence, they mirror those of the country. The political realities of the country are experienced there; this is what is explained."[84]

The most important target of the death fast struggle, the "truth" it sought to expose, was that the ideological hegemony of the state was built on its role as the protector of life. By provoking the state to violence, self-destructive acts could help reveal what was actually behind this role: "The political-ideological stance of the death fast is that it reveals to the masses the mask worn by this attack [of the state]."[85] Unmasking the state means showing the illegitimacy of the state's sovereignty, which, these participants argued, could only be done by taking the power of life and death away from the state. Taking their lives into their own hands, these participants believed that they could create damage of a different caliber: "You don't only cause actual damage against the power you are warring. . . . This is what you say there [in the act of sacrifice]: this life is mine, I will end it if I want, in the way that I want, it will go on if I don't want [to end it], you [the state] cannot decide upon that, I will decide how this life must be lived."[86]

The radical aspect of self-destructive violence, according to this interpretation of the movement embedded within a sacrificial ideology, lay in its capacity to delegitimize biosovereignty ideologically. Through the appropriation of the power of life and death from the state into the hands of the individuals, it rendered individuals sovereign over their own lives, if only by authoring their own deaths. But the participants were clear about not juxtaposing the individual against the state. Rather, the individual, as the representative of the revolutionary collective, facilitated the emergence of the latter as an alternative locus of sovereign power through this usurpation of the power of life and death from the state. Individual claims to sovereignty by way of sacrifice slowly brought into being the revolutionary collective as a recipient of political sacrifice alternative to the state, challenging what I have called the state's *monopsony* of sacrifice.

If the death fast movement was therefore able to present itself as the harbinger of a new political order, at the basis of this order were the ward communes, which represented the future in embryonic form in the prison. The lived communism of the wards rendered these sites into the *constituent spaces* of an alternative order. According to one of the participants, "Unless the enemy intervenes in and silences the life in prisons in line with its own will, it knows that the people will think as follows: how can a state that cannot keep a leash on those imprisoned within its four walls keep a leash on those who are outside? Both the state and the left know that this is how the people will think and that the people will soon slide into those organizations against the state. But the state has already lost hold of its leash."[87]

The proponents of this interpretation argued that their position was not simply allegiance to a different sovereign (which it was), but, more significantly, to a different kind of sovereignty. Accordingly, the "sovereignty" of the revolutionary collective was different from state sovereignty because it articulated the power of a community in which both the antagonism between social classes and the opposition between the individual and the collective had already been surpassed. Furthermore, "revolutionary sovereignty" subverted the hierarchy in the vitalism of state sovereignty, which was obsessed with self-preservation, survival, sanctity of life, and well-being at any cost. Against the exaltation of life as the supreme and sacred value of modern societies, "revolutionary sovereignty" asserted the survival of the revolutionary cause at the expense of individual and even collective survival. In other words, ideological survival (not the preservation and sanctity of biological life) was the new source of legitimation for this alternative sovereignty. It was on the basis of "revolutionary sovereignty" that the death fast struggle could gain a counter-hegemonic character.

Self-destruction enabled the withdrawal of consent from the ideological hegemony of state sovereignty by way of the withdrawal of bodies. It sought to lift the ideological veil of sovereignty—the preservation and the sanctity of life—and expose that its "truth" was grounded in violence. It asserted a "right to die," while expressing a defiant stance against injustice, a fundamental desire not to be oppressed, and a yearning for an alternative order to come. This radical departure from the existing order necessitated death as a way of severing the bonds that kept individuals in captivity to the existing order. Death rendered the movement an *exodus*. Writing on the Irish hunger strike, Feldman contends, "the highly revealing proposal of the mass hunger strike, that undifferentiated rush of the collective body to the 'edge' and beyond, indicates the extent to which the Hunger Strike as a medium of political action was considered analogous to the prison escape."[88] This is largely true, yet incomplete in case of the death fast struggle. This "escape," enacted by the collective staging of self-destruction, was as much out of the clasp of the state's sovereign power as it was out of the prison. By authoring their deaths, these prisoners believed they were subtracting themselves from power and exiting the order in which their lives were being administered in a totalizing way. Moreover, this exit, when collectively performed, was expected to create the rupture that would awaken the oppressed; as a refusal, it would therefore also pave the way out of the order for the masses, by bringing into view the way to withdraw consent and by bringing into being an alternative order.

According to the participants who viewed their actions as a form of refusal, they were taking part in an ideological war without end, which was already won simply by virtue of their perspicacity in waging the war in this self-destructive form: "To make the decision for the death fast is to get ahead 1–0 against the state. This is an ideological war. [The state] wants to annihilate you; you claim that you will exist with the deaths. We are now carrying out a war upon deaths; upon deaths, disabilities, veterans. To make the decision for the death fast *is* our victory."[89] The victory of the death fast struggle was already won and yet always deferred because it lay in waiting for the masses to follow the prisoners in their final exodus.

Interpreted as an act of resistance, class war, and refusal, the death fast struggle was in fact the unstable and multifaceted amalgam of these different conceptions of struggle. In its advocacy of the rights of political prisoners, it sought to resist cellular confinement as torture and ward off arbitrary intrusions and usurpations of fundamental rights that had no place in an ostensibly liberal-democratic regime. As part of an anticapitalist struggle, it fought cellular penal policy as an instance of the neoliberal program and sought to advance proletarian interests against the state by acting as the vanguard of the oppressed. Finally, as an act of refusal, it waged an ideological battle against state sovereignty, especially its consensual foundations of legitimacy in the value of self-preservation and sanctity of life. By staging an exodus based on the appropriation of the power of life and death and adopting a sacrificial ideology as the legitimating source of a "revolutionary sovereignty," it sought to rupture the existing order and expose the possibility of an alternative order worthy of loyal and existential commitment. Overall, the contested significations enveloping the weaponization of life as a tactic characterized the multifaceted nature of the movement and caused its oscillation between different logics of struggle, including the affirmation of life and the advancing of demands, on the one hand, and the negation of life and advocacy of fatal exodus, on the other. Necroresistance worked as a complex amalgam, containing within itself different interpretations of the same struggle, and internal tensions, contradictions, and even oppositions among these interpretations. As a result, necroresistance was simultaneously within, against, and beyond the biosovereign assemblage, rehearsing its subversion in multiple ways, albeit without success.

Table 6.1 MARTYRS OF THE DEATH FAST STRUGGLE, 2000–2007

	NAME	LAST NAME	AFFILIA-TION	DATE OF DEATH	PLACE OF DEATH	CAUSE OF DEATH	G	AGE	HUNGER STRIKE START DATE
1	Cafer	Dereli	DHKP-C	09-Dec-00	Rotterdam, Netherlands	stabbed to death while on hunger strike	M	22	N/A
2	Nilüfer	Alcan	DHKP-C	19-Dec-00	Bayrampaşa Prison	died in prison operation while on death fast	F	36	14-Dec-00
3	Ali	Ateş	DHKP-C	19-Dec-00	Bayrampaşa Prison	died in prison operation while on death fast	M	30	19-Nov-00
4	Cengiz	Çalıkoparan	DHKP-C	19-Dec-00	Bayrampaşa Prison	died in prison operation while on death fast	M	32	29-Nov-00
5	Seyhan	Doğan	DHKP-C	19-Dec-00	Bayrampaşa Prison	died in prison operation	F	27	
6	Özlem	Ercan	DHKP-C	19-Dec-00	Bayrampaşa Prison	died in prison operation while on death fast	F	23	14-Dec-00

7	Aşur	Korkmaz	DHKP-C	19-Dec-00	Bayrampaşa Prison	attempted self-immolation and died in prison operation while on death fast	M	28	19-Nov-00
8	Murat	Ördekçi	TKEP/L	19-Dec-00	Bayrampaşa Prison	died in prison operation	M	28	
9	Gülseren Yazgülü Güder	Öztürk	DHKP-C	19-Dec-00	Bayrampaşa Prison	died in prison operation while on death fast	F	28	19-Nov-00
10	Fırat	Tavuk	DHKP-C	19-Dec-00	Bayrampaşa Prison	attempted self-immolation and died in prison operation while on death fast	M	29	19-Nov-00
11	Şefinur	Tezgel	DHKP-C	19-Dec-00	Bayrampaşa Prison	died in prison operation	F	29	
12	Gülser	Tuzcu	DHKP-C	19-Dec-00	Bayrampaşa Prison	died in prison operation while on death fast	F	34	14-Dec-00
13	Mustafa	Yılmaz	DHKP-C	19-Dec-00	Bayrampaşa Prison	died in prison operation	M	32	

14	Murat	Özdemir	DHKP-C	19-Dec-oo	Bursa Prison	attempted self-immolation and died in prison operation while on death fast	M	39	19-Nov-oo
15	Ali İhsan	Özkan	TKP(ML)	19-Dec-oo	Bursa Prison	attempted self-immolation and died in prison operation while on death fast	M	26	19-Nov-oo
16	İlker	Babacan	DHKP-C	19-Dec-oo	Çanakkale Prison	died in prison operation while on death fast	M	22	14-Dec-oo
17	Fidan	Kalşen	DHKP-C	19-Dec-oo	Çanakkale Prison	attempted self-immolation and died in prison operation while on death fast	F	36	19-Nov-oo
18	Fahri	Sarı	PKK-DÇS	19-Dec-oo	Çanakkale Prison	died in prison operation	M		
19	Sultan	Sarı	PKK-DÇS	19-Dec-oo	Çanakkale Prison	died in prison operation	F		
20	Hasan	Güngörmez	DHKP-C	19-Dec-oo	Çankırı	attempted self-immola-	M	36	19-Nov-oo

#					Prison				
						tion and died in prison operation while on death fast			
21	İrfan	Ortakçı	DHKP-C	19-Dec-00	Çankırı Prison	died in prison operation while on death fast	M	29	19-Nov-00
22	Halil	Önder	DHKP-C	19-Dec-00	Ceyhan Prison	attempted self-immolation and died in prison operation while on death fast	M	30	19-Nov-00
23	Alp Ata	Akçayöz	DHKP-C	19-Dec-00	Ümraniye Prison	died in prison operation	M	29	
24	Umut	Gedik	DHKP-C	19-Dec-00	Ümraniye Prison	died in prison operation	M	23	
25	Ahmet	İbili	DHKP-C	19-Dec-00	Ümraniye Prison	attempted self-immolation and died in prison operation while on death fast	M	32	19-Nov-00
26	Ercan	Polat	DHKP-C	19-Dec-00	Ümraniye Prison	died in prison operation	M	26	

#	First Name	Surname	Organization	Date	Prison	Description	Sex	Age	Date
27	Rıza	Poyraz	DHKP-C	19-Dec-00	Ümraniye Prison	died in prison operation	M	29	
28	Berrin	Bıçaklar	DHKP-C	19-Dec-00	Uşak Prison	attempted self-immolation and died in prison operation while on death fast	F	22	19-Nov-00
29	Yasemin	Cancı	DHKP-C	19-Dec-00	Uşak Prison	attempted self-immolation and died in prison operation	F	33	
30	Gültekin	Koç	DHKP-C	03-Jan-01	Istanbul	suicide attack	M	24	19-Nov-00
31	Cengiz	Soydaş	DHKP-C	21-Mar-01	Sincan F-Type Prison	death fast	M	29	19-Nov-00
32	Adil	Kaplan	TKP(ML)	07-Apr-01	Edirne F-Type Prison	death fast	M	37	19-Nov-00
33	Bülent	Çoban	DHKP-C	07-Apr-01	Kandıra F-Type Prison	death fast	M	27	29-Nov-00
34	Gülsüman	Dönmez	TAYAD	09-Apr-01	Istanbul	death fast	F	37	14-Nov-00
35	Nergiz	Gülmez	TKP/ML	11-Apr-01	Kartal Special Type Prison	death fast	F	31	19-Dec-00

36	Fatma	Ersoy	DHKP-C	11-Apr-01	Kütahya E-Type Prison	death fast	F	27	19-Nov-00
37	Celal	Alpay	TKP(ML)	12-Apr-01	Buca Prison	death fast	M	28	19-Nov-00
38	Abdullah	Bozdağ	DHKP-C	12-Apr-01	Buca Prison	death fast	M	26	19-Nov-00
39	Tuncay	Günel	TİKB	12-Apr-01	Edirne F-Type Prison	death fast	M	26	19-Dec-00
40	Erol	Evcil	DHKP-C	13-Apr-01	Sincan F-Type Prison	death fast	M	35	15-Dec-00
41	Murat	Çoban	DHKP-C	14-Apr-01	Sincan F-Type Prison	death fast	M	28	29-Nov-00
42	Canan	Kulaksız	TAYAD	15-Apr-01	Istanbul	death fast	F	20	29-Nov-00
43	Gürsel	Akmaz	DHKP-C	16-Apr-01	Buca Prison	death fast	M	41	15-Dec-00
44	Endercan	Yıldız	TKP(ML)	18-Apr-01	Sincan F-Type Prison	death fast	M	41	29-Nov-00
45	Şenay	Hanoğlu	TAYAD	22-Apr-01	Istanbul	death fast	F	35	14-Nov-00
46	Sibel	Sürücü	TKEP/L	22-Apr-01	Kartal Special Type Prison	death fast	F	33	19-Dec-00

47	Kazım	Gülbağ	DHKP-C	23-Apr-01	Regensburg, Germany	self-immolation	M	36	
48	Hatice	Yürekli	TKİP	24-Apr-01	Ankara Ulucanlar Prison	death fast	F	33	19-Nov-00
49	Sedat	Karakurt	DHKP-C	25-Apr-01	Edirne F-Type Prison	death fast	M	24	29-Nov-00
50	Erdoğan	Güler	DHKP-C	25-Apr-01	Izmir	death fast	M	29	29-Nov-00
51	Fatma Hülya	Tumgan	DHKP-C	28-Apr-01	Ankara Ulucanlar Prison	death fast	F	33	19-Nov-00
52	Hüseyin	Kayacı	MLKP	06-May-01	Buca Prison	death fast	M	32	3-Jan-01
53	Cafer Tayyar	Bektaş	TKP(ML)	07-May-01	Sincan F-Type Prison	death fast	M	25	19-Nov-00
54	Uğur	Türkmen	DHKP-C	27-May-01	Mersin (upon release from Sincan F-Type Prison)	death fast	M	29	29-Nov-00
55	Veli	Güneş	DHKP-C	16-Jun-01	Kandıra F-Type Prison	death fast	M	45	19-Nov-00

56	Aysun	Bozdoğan	TKEP/L	26-Jun-01	Kartal Special Type Prison	death fast	F	25	19-Dec-00
57	Zehra	Kulaksız	TAYAD	29-Jun-01	Istanbul	death fast	F	23	21-Nov-00
58	Gökhan	Özocak	DHKP-C	05-Jul-01	İzmir (upon release from Buca Prison)	death fast	M	41	15-Dec-00
59	İsmail	Karaman	DHKP-C	06-Jul-01	Istanbul	killed	M	24	
60	Ali	Koç	DHKP-C	12-Jul-01	Sincan F-Type Prison	death fast	M	30	29-Nov-00
61	Sevgi	Erdoğan	DHKP-C	14-Jul-01	Istanbul (upon release from Uşak Prison)	death fast	F	45	19-Nov-00
62	Muharrem	Horoz	TKP/ML	03-Aug-01	Kandıra F-Type Prison	death fast	M	34	19-Dec-00

63	Osman	Osmanağaoğlu	DHKP-C	14-Aug-01	Istanbul (upon release from Kandıra F-Type Prison)	death fast	M	44	19-Nov-00
64	Hülya	Şimşek	TAYAD	31-Aug-01	Istanbul	death fast	F	38	19-Dec-00
65	Gülay	Kavak	DHKP-C	07-Sep-01	Istanbul (upon release from Kartal Special Type Prison)	death fast	F	29	19-Nov-00
66	Uğur	Bülbül	DHKP-C	10-Sep-01	Istanbul	suicide attack	M	25	
67	Ümüş	Şahingöz	DHKP-C	14-Sep-01	Istanbul (upon release from Ümraniye Prison)	death fast	F		19-Nov-00
68	İbrahim	Erler	DHKP-C	17-Sep-01	Tekirdağ F-Type Prison	self-immolation while on death fast	M	29	11-May-01
69	Abdülbari	Yusufoğlu	TAYAD	20-Sep-01	Istanbul	death fast	M	21	6-May-01

70	Ali Rıza	Demir	DHKP-C	27-Sep-01	Istanbul (upon release from Kandıra F-Type Prison)	death fast	M	30	19-Nov-00
71	Zeynep Arıkan	Gülbağ	DHKP-C	27-Sep-01	Istanbul (upon release from Ümraniye Prison)	death fast	F	33	19-Nov-00
72	Özlem	Durakcan	TAYAD	28-Sep-01	Istanbul	death fast	F	19	4-Jun-01
73	Ayşe	Baştimur	DHKP-C	28-Sep-01	Istanbul (upon release from Çanakkale Prison)	death fast	F	34	19-Nov-00
74	Ali Ekber	Barış	KPİÖ	18-Oct-01	Kandıra F-Type Prison	death fast	M	39	1-May-01
75	Bülent	Durgaç	TAYAD	05-Nov-01	Istanbul	died during police raid in Armutlu	M	27	

76	Arzu	Güler	TAYAD	05-Nov-01	Istanbul	died during police raid in Armutlu while on death fast	F	23	4-Jun-01
77	Barış	Kaş	TAYAD	05-Nov-01	Istanbul	died during police raid in Armutlu	M	20	
78	Sultan	Yıldız	TAYAD	05-Nov-01	Istanbul	died during police raid in Armutlu	F	28	
79	Eyüp	Samur	DHKP-C	07-Nov-01	Kandıra F-Type Prison	self-immolation while on death fast	M	23	11-May-01
80	Muharrem	Çetinkaya	DHKP-C	07-Nov-01	Sincan F-Type Prison	self-immolation while on death fast	M	29	3-Jun-01
81	Nail	Çavuş	DHKP-C	07-Nov-01	Tekirdağ F-Type Prison	self-immolation while on death fast	M	37	11-May-01
82	Tülay	Korkmaz	DHKP-C	19-Nov-01	Kartal Special Type Prison	death fast	F	25	11-May-01
83	Ali	Çamyar	TİKB	02-Jan-02	Kırklar F-Type Prison	death fast	M	32	11-May-01
84	Zeynel	Karataş	TKP(ML)	05-Jan-02	Tekirdağ F-Type Prison	death fast	M	25	3-Jun-01

85	Lale	Çolak	TİKB	08-Jan-02	Istanbul (upon release from Kartal Special Type Prison)	death fast	F	27	11-May-01
86	Yusuf	Kutlu	DHKP-C	08-Mar-02	Sincan F-Type Prison	death fast	M	29	3-Jun-01
87	Yeter	Güzel	TKP(ML)	10-Mar-02	Bayrampaşa Prison	death fast	F	38	26-Sep-01
88	Doğan	Tokmak	DHKP-C	16-Mar-02	Kandıra F-Type Prison	death fast	M	30	3-Jun-01
89	Tuncay	Yıldırım	MLKP	21-Mar-02	Izmir (upon release from Kırıklar F-Type Prison)	death fast	M	31	28-Jul-01
90	Meryem	Altun	DHKP-C	01-Apr-02	Kartal Special Type Prison	death fast	F	26	3-Jun-01
91	Okan	Külekçi	TİKB	23-May-02	Tekirdağ F-Type Prison	death fast	M	26	26-Sep-01

92	Semra	Başyiğit	DHKP-C	30-Jul-02	Kartal Special Type Prison	death fast	F	24	28-Jul-01
93	Fatma	Bilgin	DHKP-C	10-Aug-02	Malatya Prison	death fast	F	30	3-Jun-01
94	Melek Birsen	Hoşver	DHKP-C	21-Aug-02	Malatya Prison	death fast	F	32	26-Sep-01
95	Gülnihal	Yılmaz	DHKP-C	26-Aug-02	Kütahya Prison	death fast	F	34	3-Jun-01
96	Fatma Tokay	Köse	DHKP-C	31-Aug-02	Kütahya Prison	death fast	F	35	28-Jul-01
97	Hamide	Öztürk	DHKP-C	10-Sep-02	Bakırköy Prison	death fast	F	32	3-Jun-01
98	Serdar	Karabulut	DHKP-C	08-Nov-02	Sincan F-Type Prison	death fast	M	32	28-Jul-01
99	İmdat	Bulut	DHKP-C	19-Nov-02	Kandıra F-Type Prison	death fast	M	36	3-Jun-01
100	Zeliha	Ertürk	DHKP-C	30-Nov-02	Kartal Special Type Prison	death fast	F	24	3-Jun-01

101	Feridun Yücel	Batu	DHKP-C	01-Dec-02	Kırklar F-Type Prison	death fast	M	33	1-May-02
102	Feride	Harman	DHKP-C	15-Dec-02	Istanbul (upon release from Malatya Prison)	death fast	F	29	28-Jul-01
103	Berkan	Abatay	DHKP-C	20-Dec-02	Tekirdağ F-Type Prison	death fast	M	27	11-May-01
104	Özlem	Türk	DHKP-C	11-Jan-03	Sincan F-Type Prison	death fast	F	27	26-Sep-01
105	Orhan	Oğur	DHKP-C	26-Feb-03	Tekirdağ F-Type Prison	self-immolation	M	22	
106	Yusuf	Aracı	DHKP-C	26-Mar-03	Sincan F-Type Prison	death fast	M	31	1-May-02
107	Şengül	Akkurt	DHKP-C	20-May-03	Ankara	suicide attack	F	26	
108	Muharrem	Karademir	DHKP-C	27-Feb-04	Kandıra F-Type Prison	self-immolation while on death fast	M	31	20-Oct-03
109	Günay	Öğrener	DHKP-C	04-Mar-04	Uşak Prison	self-immolation while on death fast	F	31	20-Oct-03

110	Ümit	Günger	DHKP-C	31-Mar-04	Tekirdağ F-Type Prison	self-immolation while on death fast	M	32	30-Nov-02
111	Selma	Kubat	DHKP-C	01-May-04	Gebze M-type Prison	self-immolation while on death fast	F	26	20-Oct-03
112	Ali	Şahin	DHKP-C	22-May-04	Edirne F-Type Prison	leukemia/medical neglect after death fast	M	24	1-May-02
113	Hüseyin	Çukurluöz	DHKP-C	22-Jun-04	Sincan F-Type Prison	self-immolation while on death fast	M	42	20-Oct-03
114	Bekir	Baturu	DHKP-C	23-Jun-04	Sincan F-Type Prison	self-immolation while on death fast	M	34	20-Oct-03
115	Semiran	Polat	DHKP-C	24-Jun-04	Istanbul	suicide attack	F	29	
116	Salih	Sevinel	DHKP-C	21-Jul-04	Tekirdağ F-Type Prison	heart attack/medical neglect	M	38	
117	Selami	Kurnaz	DHKP-C	12-Aug-04	Tekirdağ F-Type Prison	death fast	M	40	20-Oct-03
118	Sergül Hatice	Albayrak	DHKP-C	28-Dec-04	Istanbul (upon release from Uşak	self-immolation while on death fast	F	26	25-Jul-04

					Prison)				
119	Faruk	Kadıoğlu	DHKP-C	26-May-05	Tekirdağ F-Type Prison	self-immolation while on death fast	M	28	9-May-05
120	Eyüp	Beyaz	DHKP-C	01-Jul-05	Ankara	suicide attack	M	25	
121	Serdar	Demirel	DHKP-C	07-Jan-06	Sincan F-Type Prison	death fast	M	42	9-May-05
122	Fatma	Koyupınar	DHKP-C	27-Apr-06	Istanbul (upon release from Gebze M-Type Prison)	death fast	F	34	9-May-05

Conclusion
From Chains to Bodies

I n the juxtaposition of the two death-events, of Mehmet the hunger striker and Damiens the regicide, that opened chapter 1, we have seen the vivid contrast between two kinds of violence inflicted upon the insurgent's body. The bloody and dismembering violence performed upon Damiens's body by Samson, the king's executioner, marks a poignant and telling distance from the silent and decomposing violence performed upon Mehmet's body by no one other than himself. One was directed against the insurgent by the state, the other by the insurgent against the state. One was alone on the scaffold, the other, though alone in bed, not on his own—he was acting as part of a movement that involved hundreds of others. Sovereign power, or the *power of life and death*, is the common core that inheres in the violence in both these death-events and establishes an equivalence between them. However, these death-events are also symptomatic scenes of different power regimes and their corresponding forms of resistance.

The transformation of Damiens's refusal to utter a confession into Mehmet's corporeal and self-directed, though no less fatal and unyielding, refusal to give obedience to domination provides clues to the ways in which both power relations and resistance have changed. The juxtaposition between the two death-events permits us to see the movement from an absolute and monarchical sovereignty to a biopolitical and democratic sovereignty as well as the emergence of a new form of resistance based on self-destruction. The novelty of necroresistance, accordingly, is twofold: on the one hand, it usurps the power of life and death from the state, thereby constituting an active challenge to sovereign power; on the other hand, it operates on a discursive and practical terrain that is enabled by the biopoliticization of sovereignty, one that mimics its delineation of life as the object of power but responds by its inversion.

The distance between Damiens and Mehmet becomes all the more obvious by the statement that can be found in a pamphlet issued by the movement of which Mehmet was a part. The statement reads as follows: "We have nothing to lose but our bodies. But we have a great world to win!"[1] This is a reiteration of the famous statement penned by Marx and Engels in "The Manifesto of the Communist Party": "The proletarians have nothing to lose but their chains. They have a world to win."[2] Damiens hails to us from a time before the full development of capitalism and its attendant social and political antagonisms, a time before Marxism, whereas Mehmet's movement partakes in, and, indeed, cannot but be thought against the background of a rich tradition of revolutionary struggle that finds its inspiration, guidance, and voice through Marxism.

In the "Manifesto," Marx and Engels present a critique of the existing order from the perspective of social relations of production brought about by capitalism whose deep inequalities and differences in power and status are masked by the legal and political order that ostensibly provides freedom and equality to citizens. They call upon workers to unite in struggle and to unshackle themselves from the chains that keep them tied to the capitalist system. At the same time, Marx and Engels make a political intervention in the domain of theory by performatively staging this struggle, announcing that a "specter is haunting Europe" while becoming the very "specter" that they thereby announce.

The shift enacted by the reiteration of this statement by proponents of the death fast struggle in Turkey is important because it constitutes a direct response to the "Manifesto" while, at the same time, it reveals what is novel about this struggle. The most visible shift in this rewriting is that the statement no longer addresses proletarians as a third, external party but uses the "we" in assuming the identity of the proletariat. This identification accentuates its performative quality, enacting the proletarian perspective not only by issuing an answer to Marx and Engels's call to action, but also by responding to that call from within action. The statement performs the coming into being of the proletariat as an active subject in struggle who has now appropriated its own voice. It equates political prisoners with the proletariat not simply as their representative but as their vanguard embodiment. Each Mehmet stands for the proletariat singly, the death fast struggle stands for it collectively.

More important, however, is that the rewriting of this famous statement, subtle and yet radical, signifies a conceptual and political transformation that can be discerned from the substitution of chains with bodies. This substitution implies that, in the current political and social order, proletarians' own bodies have replaced the invisible chains that hold individuals in bondage. In this new call the standpoint of material production and reproduction as a point of critique of the existing order recedes into the background while a new material standpoint takes over. This standpoint is that of the individual body, from whose perspective there is a dual shift.

The first aspect of this shift is the biopolitical register. It reveals the understanding that proletarians are tied to the existing social and political order not simply by the enchainment imposed by those in power but by their own entailment in its reproduction through their biological, ideational, affective, and libidinal investment. By entrusting their material existence to the state's biopolitical protection, by accepting the life granted to them by the existing order, they have participated in rendering their bodies the invisible chains that keep them tied to their subjection. The existing order, wherein life conceived as survival has been rendered devoid of political meaning, has given them corporeal security in exchange for their obedience.

The second element is a shift in the way the struggle to overcome proletarian subjugation to that order is now conceived. If subjugation is now lodged in the corporeal register, so is liberation. The rewritten statement announces that propelling the proletarians further on the path toward that "great world to win" will be achieved by the negation of the corporeal existence through the

government of which obedience to the existing order is secured and reproduced. Implicit here is the idea that by negating bodily existence as the basis
of the particular form of life that is allowed, securitized, and sanctified by the
state's political rule, a truly political life, one whose relation to justice has not
been severed, can be made possible.

However, unlike the "specter haunting Europe" whose advent is so men-
acingly announced in the "Manifesto," it is the withdrawal of the death fast
struggle from the scene of politics that continues to haunt us today. This is
because the local reiteration of Marx and Engels's statement by Mehmet's
movement does not simply offer a new interpretation of radical politics, but it
calls into being a new form of agency that permeates and indeed enables that
radical politics by way of its self-destruction. *Human weapons*, the actors who
resort to weaponizing their lives to stage their political intervention, continue
to menace politics not merely by their appearance but also by their disappearance, especially after they have authored their own deaths. How, then, may we
come to terms with their troubling legacy?

PRACTICAL-POLITICAL EFFECTS

Before gesturing toward an evaluation of the success and failure of human
weapons in more general terms, I want to begin the assessment, once again,
from the concrete case of the death fast struggle. The caveat in drawing up
a balance sheet in order to evaluate a movement is that its success or failure
is never completely reducible to immediate, tangible changes that it is able
to effect. The equivocal status of the results is particularly pronounced for
movements that resort to the weaponization of life, which is itself polyvalent.[3] This is because, while there is an *instrumental* aspect to the battle such
movements wage, which can be related to their expressed objectives (whether these are about prison conditions, rights' violations, demands for welfare
and recognition), there is also an *expressive* aspect, irreducible to the specific
demands they make. The latter dimension, related to the independent effects
of the weaponization of life as a *form* of political action, is much more intangible, long-term, and invisible in its political, ideological, and cultural effects.
These reverberations can be rippling, difficult to assess in the immediate aftermath of the political intervention of human weapons, and highly ambiguous in their measurability.

In both practical-political and theoretical terms, it must be acknowledged that the death fast struggle presents us with a mixed record. In keeping with the practical-political goals of the death fast struggle, it would not be inaccurate to say that the movement has largely failed in securing its immediate objectives. The death fast struggle was able neither to halt the opening of F-type prisons nor to prevent the larger project of the "cellularization" of Turkey's carceral landscape where high security prisons have now become permanent fixtures. In these prisons the disciplinary penal regime is currently enforced with utmost diligence. In addition to the F-type prisons in various provinces, now numbering fourteen, there are two other high security prisons: Diyarbakır D-type and Erzurum H-type. In total these prisons can house about six thousand people, a figure that already falls short of the number of political prisoners, whose current numbers (in 2011) are around eighty-five hundred, including both convicts and detainees.[4]

The total prison population itself has risen to an all-time high, reaching approximately 130,000 people. With the construction of new prisons and the renovations and adjustments made to existing ones, over 70 percent of the existing carceral capacity has been modified according to the new penal regime. Decked with different letters of the alphabet (D, E, H, L, M, and T-types), these prisons have been made or remade according to a spatial layout of small cells and modular units, in each of which a maximum of eight to ten people are allowed.[5] In other words, *in all the prisons across the country, collective confinement in wards is gradually being replaced by solitary or small-group confinement in cells.*

Now, there is some truth to the official claim that these new prisons are much cleaner, better lit and heated, and more comfortable than the traditional ward-based prisons, whose overcrowding and poor physical conditions (involving lighting, heating, cleaning, bedding, among others) presented enormous difficulties for everyday life. Despite the improvements in material conditions brought along with the F-type prisons, however, hailed in the name of "civilization" and "modernity" by state officials, it is far from certain that the social and political conditions of prisons have become better.[6] In addition to the obvious problem of social and sensory deprivation associated with cellular confinement in the new prisons, human rights defenders and legal professionals continue to report that degrading body searches on visitors, incursions on rights to health care, personal letters, journals, and books, and, more important, allegations of beatings, torture, and other human rights abuses continue, even though at a lesser intensity and frequency than before.[7] The disciplinary penal regime, which initially only selectively targeted political prisoners, is now slowly expanding to take the rest of the prison population within its fold.

At the same time, access to socialization remains precarious. On this score, despite its overall failure to stop the enforcement of the disciplinary penal regime, the struggle's success in managing to secure the right to socialization must be recognized: up to ten hours per week of social time for ten prisoners at a time, which is not conditional upon participation in prison-administered "rehabilitation programs" in the high security prisons. Even though this is hardly a great victory, particularly given the ambitious list of demands of the struggle at its inception, the impact on the everyday lives of prisoners of the relaxation of absolute isolation in conditions of cellular imprisonment cannot be underestimated. Unfortunately, however, prisoner letters to the parliament's Human Rights Commission attest that, despite the decree of the Ministry of Justice authorizing access to socialization, its application continues to be arbitrary, fluctuating, and ridden with tensions between the prison administrations and the prisoners.[8] As a result, the threat of social and sensory deprivation in the cells and the possibility of arbitrary practices and usurpations of hard-earned rights continue to be salient problems for Turkey's prisoners.

Paradoxically, however, it is those ambitious demands initially voiced by the death fast struggle, such as the abolition of the state security courts, reforms in the criminal justice system, even changes in the constitution, i.e., demands that appeared the most unattainable, that have come true today. In the last decade the beginning of Turkey's accession negotiations with the European Union and the changing political dynamics under the three successive Justice and Development Party (AKP) governments have greatly accelerated Turkey's democratization process.[9] The changes that have been wrought in the legal, jurisprudential, and political spheres, in line with the Copenhagen criteria of the EU and AKP's own liberalizing mission, have curbed the entrenched role of the military in politics, led to important constitutional amendments through the referendum of September 12, 2010, and brought welcome enlargements in terms of rights and liberties (at least de jure).[10] However, while the construction of a new constitution is under way, Turkey continues to be in a process of transition in which it is unclear whether a *real* democratization that tackles Turkey's thorny issues (such as the Kurdish question, secularism, social justice, and reconciliation with the past) will effectively take place.

Serious questions abound regarding the fairness and impartiality of the proceedings of the trials of military officials (for having conspired in planning a coup) and those of other prominent journalists, bureaucrats, and intelligence and police officers (for colluding with criminal intent).[11] Prisons now host prisoners, such as former members of the High Command, whose trial, let alone indictment, was previously simply unthinkable. At the same time, the usual suspects, namely, journalists, lawyers, human rights defenders, and activists, continue to fill up the prisons, at an unprecedented rate. On the one hand, high-profile trials of individuals and groups considered to have been related to the "deep state," i.e., the forces that often escaped the control of democratically elected governments and acted beyond the laws with impunity in the name of the security interests of the state, signal that the "untouchables" of the authoritarian past are fast eroding. On the other hand, ongoing restrictions on the freedom of expression and assembly cast grave doubts on the commitment of the new ruling elite to democracy.[12] When, for example, as recently as June 2013, the mass protests that developed in opposition to the cutting of trees in Istanbul's Gezi Park to make way for a shopping mall styled after an Ottoman military barracks spread like wildfire across the country and brought into the open the accumulated grievances and worries concerning the authoritarian tendencies of the AKP government, they were forcefully repressed by the riot police who showed little restraint in its use of batons and plastic bullets and deployed inordinate amounts of pressured water and pepper spray on mostly nonviolent protestors. Such events serve as a mirror that reflects the dark face of the Turkish state, a face with which political prisoners, dissenters, and forces of opposition in this country have been only too familiar for many decades.

Therefore, while the Kemalist elite, with its top-down approach to society, authoritarian secularism, ethnicist construction of citizenship, and hostility toward class struggle, have suffered a big blow from the conservative, populist political Islamists brought to power by almost 50 percent of the popular vote, it would be overly optimistic to conclude that the strong state tradition has thereby entered a process of silently withering away. Overall, the question of democratization has become further complicated by the burden of "dominant-party politics," under the hegemonic and majoritarian leadership of AKP (now celebrating its third term in government), whose increasingly authoritarian attitude toward dissent raises serious doubts about future prospects.[13]

While it is unclear how and to what extent the death fast struggle has contributed to the process of democratization (if at all), it still remains the case that the death fast struggle did a lot of work to raise the popular level of consciousness about the general conditions of the country's prisons as the underside of its democracy. As an act of resistance, it pushed back against the state to secure the rights of prisoners and called public attention to the intimate connection between the isolation in prison cells and torture. Even if it was not able to expand prisoners' rights significantly, it managed to expose the weak enforcement of the human rights regime in these marginal spaces and the Turkish state's highly checkered history of treating dissent. The death fast struggle also performed a great service in demonstrating how the mainstream social-democratic left in Turkey has lost some of its fundamental reflexes about human rights, democracy, and justice by bringing to light the very irony that, in the face of prison unrest, the Turkish state's responses of conducting a highly militarized security operation in the prisons, endorsing censorship and repression, the deflection of real human rights concerns to a discourse on security, and the sanctioning of medical intervention through artificial feeding were all orchestrated under a coalition government led by Ecevit's Democratic Left Party (DSP). DSP, as the rising star of the center-left in the 1990s and the party with the highest votes in the 1999 elections (22 percent of the total), experienced a bitter defeat in the elections of 2002, receiving just above 1 percent. While its abrupt decline in popularity cannot simply be attributed to its handling of the death fast struggle (a decline that was precipitated by its failures in handling the economic recession as well as the leadership struggles within the party), its stance toward the "prisons problem" was surely another symptom of its eroding credibility. The death fast struggle was able to bring this erosion into public view, even if its ability to provide a real alternative was frustrated by its own politics and inability to stimulate the masses into large-scale collective action on its behalf.

On the other hand, when viewed as part of an ongoing class war, the movement failed to make significant strides. Most obviously, it was unable either to defend or to gain popular support for the lived experience of communism in the wards that had become the prisoners' sanctuaries. Further, the movement's contention that the prison was a trench of class struggle, on equivalent footing with other arenas like the factory, workshop, office, university, and the street, and even the foremost trench in the battle with the state, due to the specific political circumstances of the present, did not seem to resonate much with the masses on whose behalf the prisoners claimed to be fighting. In fact, the prominence accorded to the prison may have added to the prisoners' alienation from popular support. While the connection between neoliberal capitalism and F-type prisons, pointing out the dual processes of the erosion of the welfare state and the refurbishing of the penal apparatus, was an important political thesis, which emphasized how the state was actively creating individualized, dispoliticized subjectivities for the smooth functioning of the market, the diffusion of this thesis as the dominant claim of the struggle remained limited. Overall, the aspirations of the movement in advancing class struggle stayed largely within the framework of vanguardist politics, whose radical and spectacular interventions into politics from marginal spaces were expected to lead to mass mobilizations and uprisings. Despite some public support generated at the beginning and ending of the movement (though less on the basis of discourse that centered on class struggle than one based on democracy and human rights), the level of mass mobilization remained far below expectations. And whatever popular support did materialize was either censored or forcefully repressed by the security forces, thus confining the death fast struggle to the margins out of which it emerged. In turn, the death fast struggle was unable to develop its counterhegemonic discourse and impose its political agenda upon a broad coalition of oppositional forces that might have been able to carry at least some of its aspirations forward.

Finally, interpreted as an act of refusal, the death fast struggle had a dramatic effect that is difficult to capture by the yardstick of success or failure precisely because of the way in which the weaponization of life defies instrumentality through its disruption of the means-ends relation. Here it is helpful to point to the fact that the repeated acts of self-destruction performed by prisoners and their supporters presented a complex challenge to the Turkish state that it could not ignore. The resort to multiple forms of violence, including conventional urban guerrilla tactics along with defensive and offensive forms of self-destruction, did not only undermine the state's legitimate monopoly of the use of force. By usurping the power of life and death from the state through violent acts of self-destruction, which were resignified and justified as acts of political self-sacrifice necessary for bringing into being an alternative order, the movement also challenged what I have called the state's *monopsony* of sacrifice, i.e., its status as the only legitimate recipient of political sacrifice.

If the weaponization of life thereby threatened the sovereign power of the state, it also challenged the ideological hegemony of the state based on the sanctification and the protection of the "right to live." By asserting the controversial "right to die," the participants of the death fast struggle negated the life that was permitted to them, a life they saw as profoundly unjust. Their ideological attack was to bring into view how the form of life sanctified by the increasingly biopolitical nature of the sovereignty of the state was a biological life that was stripped of politics and to deny the desirability of this form of life as the basis of obedience. Instead, they upheld the primacy of their political over their biological existence and advocated the withdrawal of consent from the existing order by way of self-destruction.

On the other hand, the dramatic impact of the weaponization of life was continuously submerged, repressed, and co-opted by the strategic choices and practices of the state (whose force and capacity the participants of the struggle significantly underestimated). The state *did* consider the radical left to be a real threat to its own sovereignty and, as a result, proceeded to mobilize and employ the traditional instruments of sovereign power to eliminate it, rather than ignoring this threat or addressing it only with superficial measures. However, in so doing, it consistently fused these instruments with biopolitical tools, such as the selective management of populations and interventions that target life and well-being within a rubric of humanitarian government. In order to solve the "prisons problem," which had become a public embarrassment, the state introduced a new penal regime that became the emblem of its drive toward biopoliticization so as to strengthen and renew its sovereignty. In order to reinvent itself as a *biosovereign assemblage* and implement a new modality of rule, which it considered more efficient, technological, modern, cost-effective, and "humane," it made law, waged war, and dictated its own terms for peace.

The Turkish state first expediently reduced the unruly prison "crowd" by *making law*, providing the conditions of possibility of implementing a disciplinary penal regime. It then put the high security prisons into immediate use, despite a public lack of confidence in and consent to them (as well as the government's quickly reneged promise to cultivate a public consensus), by *making war* against the prisoners on hunger strike in existing prisons and, through the mediatized images of this war, against the public at large. The state resorted not only to ordinary forms of violence, with its military might, but also to more nuanced, symbolic, and personalized forms of violence, such as torture, inhumane treatment, and the strategic negligence of the prisoners' needs and concerns. Extremely important among these forms of violence was nonconsensual artificial feeding, which not only enlisted medicine as a biopolitical tool of government but also, because of its improper administration, left hundreds of prisoners with disabilities. And, finally, the state secured the future of the penal regime and eliminated the recalcitrant insurgency in the cells of the new prisons by *making peace,* issuing reprieves and pardons, thereby ejecting prisoners out of the prisons into the care of their own families and reestablishing itself as the benevolent protector even of its unruly citizen-subjects.

These stratagems involved the instrumentalization of law, the deployment of collective and individualized violence, and the exercise of legal, medical, psychological, and other specialized knowledges upon carefully singled out populations in order to implement a biopoliticized modality of sovereignty. Not only did the prisoners incorrectly estimate the agility of the Turkish state in attending to its own wounded sovereignty, but they also failed to appreciate the cynicism with which the state was able to churn out whatever shame it was supposed to suffer as a result of the deaths of prisoners from self-starvation and self-immolation in the form of a self-righteous display of pride and strength in its struggle against "terrorism." In the meantime, the discursive field of "terror" continued to expand exponentially, not only in Turkey but around the globe after 9/11, subsuming the already questionable tactics of the prisoners within the repertoires of "terrorist" action and the state strategies of coping with them within processes of securitization.

THEORETICAL IMPLICATIONS

This book cast the death fast struggle as a concrete instance, a revealing example, that crystallizes the tensions and contradictions of a global political conjuncture in which the process of the *biopoliticization of sovereignty* meets the *necropoliticization of resistance.* Using a framework of analysis that builds on Foucault's analysis of power relations was prompted by my effort to consider the specificity of the new form of resistance performed through self-destructive techniques. As a counterpoint to arguments in the literature addressing self-destructive practices, which focus on explanations based on religious convictions, individual motivations, psychological orientations, and histories of trauma, on the one hand, or strategic organizational choices in conditions of asymmetric warfare, on the other, I have maintained the necessity of pursuing a critical approach that also problematizes the conditions that produce these practices and attends to the power relations in response to which these self-destructive practices come into being and take on their specific *form*. Because of the corporeal register in which these struggles unfold, I have contended that a biopolitical approach, which accounts for how life becomes an object and objective of power relations, should be deployed in order to understand why and how death becomes constituted into a distinct vehicle of resistance.

The biopolitical framing of the narrative of the death fast struggle has several advantages over competing approaches. Most important is that it affords us the possibility of analyzing the nature of power relations in which the agents who resort to the weaponization of life are situated and through which their subjectivities and political practices are shaped as well as challenged. It allows us to venture beyond a narrow model of rational choice, because it gives us a perspective on political subjectivities as the complex products of power relations and their contestation, subjectivities whose active political choices may be based on expressive and noninstrumental as well as instrumental rationality. It offers a different view of the agency of individuals, enabling us to trace the way choices and decisions are shaped by the spaces in which individuals are situated and the experience of these spaces that they transform through their own social relations. It casts light on the ways in which individuals live through and perceive power relations as well as how they comprehend the range of possibilities available to them for their contestation. It thus helps delineate the individual in its profound political and ethical complexity: with motivations, beliefs, and commitments, with choices that are a function not simply of prior experiences of trauma, loss, or psychopathology, but also of a complex constellation of negative and positive experiences that are conditioned by a politics of space and devotion to a cause: in the Turkish example the marginality and asymmetry of the space of the prison as well as its social appropriation into *ward communes* where communism was put into practice.

Foucault's analysis of the panoptic spatiality of the prison is of utmost importance for understanding how asymmetry shapes both power and resistance in such modern institutions. As such, it allows us to question the boundaries of the political by paying attention to the body not merely as the object of power and site of subjection but also, and what is more important, as a site of resistance. The body now becomes the vehicle of a desubjectivization through which a counterpolitics finds material basis. The biopolitical approach concretizes the body as the material space of contestation where opposing forces, sovereignty and resistance, intersect in a battle that takes place on a micro as well as a social scale. Finally, Foucault's theoretical apparatus encourages us to pay attention to the particularities of each situation and struggle, the web of relations in which these struggles are situated and through which agents make their own interventions, thereby enabling us to call into question grand narratives that run from the early martyrs of the various religious traditions to contemporary human weapons as if they would seamlessly constitute a singular, trans-historical lineage that explains our world today.

While utilizing a Foucauldian perspective on power relations in order to analyze the novelty and significance of the death fast struggle, I have taken as my point of departure two theses that characterize the biopolitical argument: first, that in modern regimes of power, life itself has become the object of political rule and regulation and, second, that, with this transformation, death is pushed outside the boundaries of the political. As a result, many theorists of biopolitics have tended to argue that the transformation from sovereignty into biopolitics entails the replacement of sovereignty by biopolitical techniques of government. At the same time, the totalizing narrative of governmentality, penetrating and molding ever more spheres of life, has tended to construe a bleak potential for resistance, if any, and to theorize resistance as a residual, fragmentary, localized, and restricted response to power relations. At best, resistance has been tied to an affirmation of life as the object of biopolitics, which functions by making claims for greater rights, welfare, and recognition, mimicking the nature of power relations in their contestation.

The book provides a response to both of these arguments, both theoretically and through the in-depth study of the death fast struggle. First, through a close reading of Foucault, I have argued that, while some of the contradictions in Foucault's own writings, and especially the ambiguities in his theorization of the problem of the articulation of sovereignty with new modalities of power, have authorized or at least lent credence to the reading that posits the disappearance of sovereignty, it is also possible to identify another strand of theorization in Foucault, which presents important clues regarding the complicated and imbricated interrelationship between sovereignty and biopolitics. The signpost of this strand in Foucault's thought is the argument regarding the reversal of the politics of life into its opposite, the politics of death, a reversal he identifies as the paradox that profoundly shapes the Nazi and Soviet experiences in the Second World War but that also conditions the rule of every modern state more generically, if less pronouncedly and more insidiously. For Foucault, this paradox arises from the coexistence of sovereignty, discipline, and security, sharpened into a contradictory conjunction of the machinery of death and the management of life.

Extrapolating from and building on Foucault's observations on the modulations enacted by the emergence and confluence of these different modalities of power, I have put forth the theorization of the contemporary power regime as an incipient configuration, characterized not only by this confluence but a changing structure of articulation. *Biosovereignty* denotes an emergent regime of power, an assemblage of discourses and practices, signs and actions, one that surfaces at the intersection of the power to kill and the power to regulate life. Its dominant characteristics, tactics, and the specific forms of violence it deploys are defined by the structure of articulation among different modalities of power in highly contextualized, historically situated forms. The theory of biosovereignty sharpens and provides the groundwork to explore the latent strand in Foucault's writings, a strand that otherwise remains embryonic, ambiguous, and at times, incongruous.

Second, I have maintained that the same paradox of the reversal of the politics of life into the politics of death can be observed in the field of resistance. Alongside movements that demand greater rights and well-being, resources and recognition, we now find struggles that make a political intervention by staging a total rejection of domination and disrupting the political rationality of biosovereignty. In my attempt to theorize these forms of political action, especially in the absence of a sophisticated biopolitical theorization of resistance, I have found it necessary to carry out a critical reconstruction of Foucault's writings in order to identify distinct forms of resistance as they correspond to different modalities of power relations. Providing a multifaceted portrait of resistance in Foucault, from Damiens's refusal to confess on the scaffold to the uprisings in Iran, I have delineated different threads of theorization that can shed light on the struggles of the present based on the weaponization of life. In this inquiry I have isolated Foucault's controversial writings on the Iranian revolution to be particularly resourceful in the conceptualization of sacrifice as a form of *counterconduct* that stages a complete *refusal* of obedience, albeit when these reflections are reconsidered in conjunction with his analysis of governmentality in light of present developments. My main contention in working through the possibilities and limitations of different instances of resistance in Foucault's work has been the necessity to pressure the biopolitical approach to shed light on paradoxical copresence of struggles that politicize life both in affirming and negating forms as well as in their inter-relationships. The latter form of struggles, which I have called *necroresistance*, constitutes the blind spot of Foucauldian biopolitics and the main contribution of this book.

In developing the theorization of necroresistance, I have also found it necessary to engage in detail with Agamben, one of the most influential critics of Foucault, whose thesis on "bare life" has provocatively and forcefully reconfigured the biopolitical approach. Examining Agamben's critique of Foucault and his arguments, especially from the perspective of its implications for resistance, I have critiqued his reconfiguration of biopolitics in a metaphysical and transhistorical direction based, on the one hand, on the conceptualization of sovereignty as always already biopolitical and, on the other hand, on rendering life the abstract and disempowered function of sovereignty without any real potential for resistance. Nonetheless, exploring scholarship that utilizes both Foucault's and Agamben's work to analyze contemporary struggles that resort to self-destructive practices, I have contended that the questions raised by the Agambenian inflection of the biopolitical approach concerning the relationship between necroresistance and bare life cannot be satisfactorily answered without developing a concurrent grasp of how these struggles take place on the ground and how the agents that resort to the weaponization of life understand their own relation to life and death, power and resistance.

Having scrutinized the ethnographic material that constitutes the in-depth study of the death fast struggle, we are now at a point to reconsider the theorization of biosovereignty and necroresistance advanced in the beginning of this book. The analysis of the death fast struggle allows us to push back against the theoretical apparatus that was deployed to frame and present it and to evaluate the extent to which the analysis demonstrates the arguments elaborated theoretically, complicates the concepts developed, and suggests directions for further development.

One of the claims of the book, and the underlying logic of its architecture, is to cast power and resistance both in a binary opposition and as complementary parts of the same story by exposing how the center appears from the point of view of those in revolt in the margins and how the margins of power appear from the point of view of the state. Each point of view, captured in situ through the narrations of a multiplicity of actors, functions to unveil a certain "truth" of the other, allowing us a glimpse into the other's hidden reality.

From the perspective of the margins, the study of the death fast struggle lends important empirical illustration and support to the theoretical argument advanced earlier regarding the recalcitrance and ongoing vitality of sovereignty within the biopolitical problematic. This demonstration is not the simple verification of the rather obvious, continued existence of the modern state and its role in contemporary politics. Rather, it strives to make visible the continuous presence, indeed refurbishment, of the sovereign core of power, wrapped as it increasingly is, within layers of disciplinary, regulatory, and ostensibly more "humane," benevolent, tolerant, and respectful mechanisms of domination. The permeation and modification of the supreme power of life and death by disciplinary and biopolitical tactics make it stronger and, insofar as it is able to take these tactics into the fold of its traditional prerogatives, they enable the revamping of sovereignty. However, the new, biopolitical tools of government that sovereignty deploys in order to augment itself also require reinforcement by conventional tactics of power, thereby referencing a mutual instrumentalization and interpenetration. If we revisit the contradiction between the sovereign power of life and death and the vitalist idiom of biopower (with the attendant humanitarian discourse on the sacredness of life and the supremacy of survival, with which sovereignty, and especially its extraction of corporeal loyalty, is now paradoxically justified), from the point of view of the mutual imbrication of sovereignty and biopower, we can see that the analysis of biosovereignty fundamentally problematizes the narrative of sovereignty as a progressive tale of the accumulation of freedoms, deepening self-government, and enlightened domination.

On a more specific register, the analysis evinces the process by which the biosovereign assemblage is constituted in the Turkish context as well as its specific structure of articulation. If sovereignty takes the lead in doing the work of amalgamating, incorporating, implementing, and instrumentalizing biopolitical goals and tactics, the latter also transform sovereignty from within. In light of the authoritarian impulses of the Kemalist tradition of statecraft in Turkey, that sovereign power should take the primary initiative is perhaps unsurprising. However, the result, the emergent assemblage as analyzed here, presents a contradictory ensemble of power relations that is no longer simply reducible either to sovereignty as it is classically conceived or to biopolitics in its pure form. Rather, it is a complex and evolving formation, reinventing and reconstituting itself anew in each exceptional "crisis."

When human weapons take into their own hands the power of life and death, they challenge the core of sovereign power, latent and subdued through biopoliticization, with which they find themselves in confrontation. In the moment of their self-induced death, they wrench the power of life and death away from the apparatuses of the modern state in which sovereignty is conventionally vested. But, the analysis of the death fast struggle reminds us, this is only part of the picture. That is because their protest is in turn occasioned by the increasing biopoliticization in government, which attempted to render their lives and well-being into the practical and discursive object of power in the first place. As a result, the exercise of political agency in opposition to biosovereignty takes specific forms whose corporeality and relation to death are occasioned not only as a response to sovereignty but also as directly enabled and conditioned by biopolitics and its valorization of life. Indeed, the *politicization of death* appears radical and disruptive precisely because of the evolving nature of power relations and the expansion of the limits of their field of intervention, increasingly based on the *politicization of life*. This is what marks the distinction of the death fast struggle from a movement that simply contests the sovereignty of the state. Rather, what the analysis shows is that the movement is directed at disrupting the biopoliticization of sovereign power through death insofar as that biopoliticization renders death into a possible site of resistance at the margins of power. Consequently, biosovereignty relegates death to its margins, but it also enables the deployment of death as a challenge emerging from those margins.

In contrast, from the perspective of the center, the analysis of the death fast struggle complicates the limited and pessimistic account of resistance provided by theorists of biopolitics, according to whom the increasing penetration of power into every facet of life shapes subjectivities in ways that preclude or greatly limit the potential of resistance. Such a view should best be considered as the ultimate desire of power, though a desire that is constantly thwarted by the new forms of resistance that biosovereignty produces and encounters. For the center, acts of resistance are frustrating first because they exist at all, showing the points of weakness in the web of relations woven into the growing network of the biosovereign assemblage. However, the acts of resistance based on self-destruction appear particularly trying in comparison to more conventional forms of struggle that demand better conditions of life and greater well-being because, while struggle and negotiation with the latter are always possible, necroresistance's negation of life and thereby the power over life makes it difficult to subsume it within the biosovereign assemblage. This is a radical challenge not only because it disrupts the functioning and reproduction of power relations but also because it puts into question the sacredness of life, that survival reigns supreme over any other value, which lies at the foundation of biosovereignty. Necroresistance thereby presents a constant line of flight that destabilizes and prevents the consolidation of the biosovereign assemblage into a stable, self-reproducing, smoothly functioning *apparatus*.

From this point of view, necroresistance appears to continuously frustrate the attempt of the biosovereign assemblage to produce its subjects not only as docile and obedient but also as the sources of consent to the prioritization of biological survival and the sacralization of being alive, i.e., to the values that lie at the basis of biosovereign legitimation. Translating into the terms used by Agamben, who claims that the constitutive feature of "bio-sovereignty" (which I have distinguished from what I call biosovereignty) is the biopolitical production of life as "bare," we may say that necroresistance interrupts the forcible baring of life as such, i.e., its *dispoliticization*. Alternatively, we may take the study of the death fast struggle as providing a powerful counterpoint to Agamben's claim that the production of bare life is a constitutive facet of "bio-sovereignty." This study shows that the production of life as bare is only the utmost fantasy of power. This is because even in conditions under the most totalizing and penetrating control, such as those of the prison, power cannot prevent resistance. Furthermore, since the attempt to elude the grasp of power by death, by appropriating the power of life and death from the biosovereign assemblage, is also the assertion of a *politicized* understanding of life as superior to the alternative of simply being alive to which individuals are increasingly threatened to be reduced, it would be more accurate to construe this resistance not as the resistance *of* bare life but as resistance *to* bare life. Because the resistance of bare life already assumes the reduction of individual lives to the defining feature of vulnerability through the inclusive exclusion, it overlooks the very political meaning that these individuals attribute to their lives and the radical interventions they attempt to make at the cost of their lives. The assertion of a politicized life over and against survival and the prioritization of political causes and ideological convictions over biological existence do not only challenge the foundations of the existing order but also force us to reconsider the turn taken in the biopolitical approach that uses the category of bare life rather indiscriminately and uncritically and, worse, that assumes it to be a matter of fact rather than a biosovereign fantasy. It is important here to recall Foucault's remark about revolt, whether it is carried out by one person or the masses: "no power is capable of making it absolutely impossible."[14]

At the same time, the analysis of the death fast struggle complicates the unitary and internally consistent appearance of necroresistance from the point of view of the central apparatuses of power. Even though, as a movement, the death fast struggle attempted to present itself as a coherent whole, this study allows us to see the multiple and, at times, conflictual and contradictory strands within it, which make up a complex and polyvalent reality that is not reducible to one facet alone. Most significantly, the difference between the *offensive* and *defensive* forms of the weaponization of life and the varying degrees of support these modalities find among individuals who actively participate in the struggle itself present a nuanced picture of necroresistance as an emergent repertoire of political action whose internal configuration, justifications, tactical distinctions, and rituals of conduct are far from unitary or complete. The divergent self-narrations and varying interpretations of the participants depict the sphere of struggle as a differentiated amalgam, both as the dynamic intersection of different viewpoints, discourses, and practices, and as the evolving assemblage of forces that changes with the vicissitudes of the struggle itself. Such an account cautions us against reductionist interpretations of necroresistance, conveying its multifaceted reality and calling attention to its internal struggles and transformations.

On the particular register of the Turkish case, the analysis depicts the process by which different oppositional forces assemble and disassemble, as particular strands within the movement take precedence over the others, both discursively and practically. While the current that privileges the weaponization of life as the primary strategy of struggle is in ascendance, we see the assertion of the "right to die" as a radical and uncompromising stance that privileges the site of the prison as the frontline of social and political struggle, resorts to recurrent acts of self-destruction by way of escalation, and assumes a vanguardist idiom in which spectacular acts are expected to take the lead in mobilizing the masses. Given the predominantly vanguardist heritage of the extraparliamentary leftist groups in Turkey, the ascendance of this current within the struggle is not unexpected, even though this still involves a substantive reconfiguration of what vanguardism entails. On the other hand, when the more moderate current assumes dominance, we witness the transformation of the discourse of the struggle to one of human rights and opposition to isolation as torture, presenting the weaponization of life as a tactic of last resort of those whose field of political action is limited by the marginality of prison conditions. Such an approach is marshaled to seek broad alliances with the public, through mass mobilization or the deployment of figures of public stature to motivate mass mobilization, with the use of moral arguments in order to exert pressure on the government as the main means of political intervention. Both the internally fraught coalition structure of the movement and the ebbs and flows in the trajectory of the struggle as a whole have provided space for this moderate current to carve an important role for itself, alongside the hardliners' vanguardist current. Because these currents do not necessarily replace one another chronologically but coexist in an unstable whole, they give complexity to the movement and point to the ongoing presence of multiple contentions that are never fully resolved.

At the same time, the polyvalent nature of the death fast struggle in particular and of necroresistance in general provides different opportunities for its co-optation by the biosovereign assemblage with varying degrees of efficacy. On the one hand, the repetitive authoring by individuals of their own self-destruction refuses the framework of instrumental action, functioning in effect as a conduit to convey the frustration of the oppressed under conditions of asymmetry and injustice produced through biosovereign government. When the expression of political voice takes the form of putting into question the very sanctity of life and the value of survival, and thereby the legitimacy of domination, necroresistance amounts to a defiant refusal in the face of which no government can remain untarnished. The withdrawal of consent by the irreversible act of death is, at the same time, the withdrawal of the bodies that are the vehicles and conduits of power. Such a withdrawal, through the severing of the body from subjection, also unsettles the very structure that defines what the center and margin are through their relationality. On the other hand, the simultaneous assertion of demands, ranging from the abolition of high security prisons to broader prisoner rights, from the cessation of arbitrary violations to the transformation of antidemocratic laws and the penal system, presents a framework in which negotiation and compromise are possible and indeed invited by the movement. This allows an opening for the biosovereign assemblage to take the resistance back within its fold, an opening that was initially foreclosed by the hawkish faction within the state but eventually utilized successfully to bring the movement to an end. Concurrently, what is more interesting is that the very coexistence of these different facets in the opposition has enabled the pitting of one against the other by the state. Because the discursive regime of the biosovereign assemblage prioritizes the sanctity of life but also jealously reserves to itself the power of death, it is also able to subsume the claim for a "right to die" and to use it against its own proponents, even against those who participated in the struggle with the overarching purpose of securing basic rights and deepening democracy, by using the construction of the struggle as "inhumane" and its performers as "terrorists." It therefore becomes possible to justify the exercise of biosovereignty by virtue of the necessity of rescuing lives, against actual lives, in the name of Life itself. In the Turkish context, such justification was utilized for the large-scale violence of security operations, individualized medical resuscitation, as well as the issuing of selective pardons. However, even if the biosovereign assemblage is thereby capable of containing the lines of flight, it nonetheless suffers from the necessity to secure popular consent for its operations by making certain concessions, even if in the long run, for it must assure its further self-reproduction. The final concession of the state, relaxing isolation in high security prisons, becomes more intelligible in this light.

Consequently, the study of the death fast struggle not only illustrates the dual tendency of the biopoliticization of sovereignty and the necropoliticization of resistance but also significantly complicates the way in which these tendencies operate, how they react to one another and transform each other, how the struggle of these tendencies conceived at a metatheoretical level occasions novel consequences regarding the dynamics of resistance. Of these consequences, two are particularly relevant to conceptualizing the full import of the emergence of human weapons as a new mode of agency on the scene of politics, with the weaponization of life as a new repertoire of action for radical political resistance in the present.

First is the theologization of politics that follows from the independent effects of the self-destructive *form* of resistance. The study of the death fast struggle draws attention to how the weaponization of life, even when adopted by Marxist groups that are openly secular (if not atheist) paves the way for the emergence of a political spirituality in which martyrdom assumes a place of prominence and becomes the new vehicle of a sacrificial vanguardist militancy, generating a whole set of practices that can be conceptualized as counter-conduct. It is necessary to underscore the difference of this theologized politics, however, from a religious politics. It is precisely the absence of any openly held religious belief, and, further, the espousal of a materialist worldview, by the performers of the weaponization of life, at least in the Turkish context, that render the emergence of a new "secular" theology around martyrdom and sacrifice paradoxical and interesting. The *militant-martyr*, whose role in the

history of the oppressed now reimagined as an endless chain of sacrifice is always already reserved, replaces the communist militant as the epitome of the
political subjectivity emergent in and through necroresistance. Given that the
political theology of human weapons exhibits itself in concrete and elaborate
rituals that revolve around the marking, politicization, resignification, and remembrance of death, this emergence also suggests that such a political theology might indeed be a necessary supplement for the weaponization of life as
an existentially committing form of struggle in order to ensure its reception by
a community, its sustenance and further reproduction.

Second is the ambiguous nature of the form of community that is upheld
as an alternative political horizon by human weapons. Even while politicizing
death against the biosovereign assemblage, thus pursuing a tactic that constitutes a refusal precisely in its negation of life as the object of power relations,
individuals who resort to the weaponization of life also sustain a positive political project. The ward commune is an example of this project brought to life
on a small, limited scale under very difficult conditions. Although this project
is never fully articulated on a theoretical register by participants of the death
fast struggle, it involves an assumed commitment to the reorganization of the
existing social and political order along communist lines, while also upending
the asymmetry in which they find themselves and redressing the injustices
that they have experienced in person and that the proletariat continues to experience as a result of authoritarian neoliberal capitalism. However, whereas
the disruptive, subversive aspect of this struggle is clear, the constructive,
positive aspect is more abstract and ambiguous, if not aporetic, especially in
relation to how power relations would operate within the future order. While
these individuals oppose the biosovereign assemblage and express a desire for
nondomination and nonoppression, do they call into being another form of
community founded on premises and power relations that are substantially
different than those that characterize the present? Or do they tend to conform
to and reproduce biosovereignty, in their own political structures and communities, discourses and practices, even as they attempt to go beyond it? Do the
relationships fostered between the individuals in this movement, the political
parties and organizations with which they are affiliated, and the communities
that support their practices constitute the embryonic forms of an alternative
form of communal power that is not based on either the sovereign power to
kill or the biopolitical power to make live, but is rather inherently connected
with justice? Or is it that the expressive form and apocalyptic terms in which

the struggle is increasingly lodged foreclose the possibility of thinking about the future, deferring the definition and specification of the positive political project into an ever receding horizon? These questions remain open—unanswered, perhaps unanswerable in a satisfactory way, in light of the political theology that imbues the weaponization of life and the affective and corporeal nature of the spectacles of death that, on the one hand, enable a radical politics while, on the other hand, becoming the impediments of a critical contemplation about the future.

Nonetheless, the death fast struggle of Turkey leaves an important legacy, not simply for Turkish politics, nor only for the region, but also for the globe. As the long and troubling decade in which the political prisoners of Turkey hailed from their prisons to the rest of the world by staging spectacles of death comes to an end, a decade whose chronologically inaccurate but politically relevant global beginning can be traced to the suicide attacks on the World Trade Center and the Pentagon on September 11, 2001, the world witnessed the self-immolation of a Tunisian man, Muhammad al-Bu'azizi, whose self-destructive act then became the trigger for the revolutionary upheavals in North Africa and the Middle East. Forging his life into a weapon of struggle as he set himself on fire, Muhammad al-Bu'azizi was in close kinship not only with the prisoners in Turkey but also the detainees in Guantánamo, Nafha and Beer Sheva Prisons in Israel, the migrants across detention centers and refugee camps in the United States, Australia, Greece, France, Japan, Malaysia, Iraq, Afghanistan, Bahrain, and many other places, too numerous to name, where individuals, either singly or collectively, continue to resort to this emergent repertoire of political struggle. Whether by starving, immolating, exploding, or mutilating their bodies, these individuals perform violent spectacles. They exercise their moral and political agency by way of violence, either defensively, by directing violence toward their own bodies, or more offensively, by targeting others. Either way, they make their entry on the stage of politics by authoring their exit. The conduit of this exit is the destruction of the body, the real tie that connects agents to power, the "chains" of the late modern age.

This book has attempted to restore the agency of these actors by taking them seriously as interlocutors and to present an account of how and why self-destruction becomes a way to negate biosovereignty. For unlike the spectacle of Damiens's death in the hands of the executioner on the scaffold, which is intended for the people to watch and remain in awe of the magnific, terrifying, and overwhelming power of sovereignty, the spectacle of Mehmet's death, or of al-Bu'azizi death, or of the nonconsensually prevented deaths of Guantánamo detainees calls upon the people in a different way. These counterspectacles ask us to become cognizant of the nature of power relations in which we live and die, the asymmetries and injustices they entail, and our own investment and complicity in them. As acts of violence they attempt to make visible the violence that is normalized and routinized and therefore rendered invisible by the existing order. By resisting power, perhaps they even seek to dispel our fear of transgression and the inertia of habituation that is easily confused with consent, thereby imploring us to build bridges of solidarity, to act collectively, to mobilize against what is unjust in our own way. This book is my response to that call. Not to excuse or justify human weapons, nor to condemn or vilify them, but to reckon with them; to engage, earnestly and critically, with their intervention into politics. For their voices are part of our common history. Or, rather, as Foucault poignantly remarked, "it is precisely because there are such voices that human time does not take the form of evolution, but that of 'history.'"[15]

Notes

Introduction

1. The "repertoire" of action, as relatively routine and coherent scripts of claims-making practices performed as part of contentious politics, comes from Tilly, *Contentious Performances*, 14–17.

2. Global Detention Project is a repository that documents some of these protests. See www.globaldetentionproject.org. Last accessed November 12 2013.

3. On recent hunger strikes in immigration and refugee detention centers, see, among others, McGregor, "Contestations and Consequences of Deportability"; Bailey, "Up Against the Wall"; Edkins and Pin-Fat, "Through the Wire"; Ticktin, *Casualties of Care*; Siméant, "La Violence d'un Repertoire."

4. See, for example, Buntman, *Robben Island*; Carlton, *Imprisoning Resistance*; Silver, "Palestinian Threats as Jail Hunger Strike Starts."
5. Amnesty International, *United States of America*.
6. Olshansky and Gutierrez, *The Guantánamo Prisoner Hunger Strikes*.
7. Ibid., 7.
8. For the struggle in the H-Blocks, see Campbell, McKeown, and O'Hagan, *Nor Meekly Serve My Time*; O'Malley, *Biting at the Grave*; Beresford, *Ten Men Dead*; and Feldman, *Formations of Violence*. For background, see Sweeney, "Irish Hunger Strikes and the Cult of Self-Sacrifice," 422, and "Self-Immolation in Ireland."
9. Associated Press, "Some Guantánamo Prisoners Have Gone on Hunger Strike." Also see Olshansky and Gutierrez, *The Guantánamo Prisoner Hunger Strikes*, 10.
10. Lewis, "Guantánamo Prisoners Go on Hunger Strike."
11. Nicholl et al., "Forcefeeding and Restraint of Guantánamo Bay Hunger Strikers"; Annas, "Hunger Strikes at Guantánamo"; Rubenstein and Annas, "Medical Ethics at Guantánamo Bay Detention Centre"; Dyer, "Force Feeding at Guantánamo Breaches Ethics."
12. Rhem, "Guantánamo Tube Feedings Humane."
13. U.S. Department of Defense, "News Briefing with Secretary of Defense Donald Rumsfeld."
14. U.S. Department of Defense, "Medical Program Support for Detainee Operations." Article 4.7.1 reads as follows: "In the case of a hunger strike, attempted suicide, or other attempted serious self-harm, medical treatment or intervention may be directed without the consent of the detainee to prevent death or serious harm."
15. Olshansky and Gutierrez, *The Guantánamo Prisoner Hunger Strikes*, 8.
16. Dodds, "Terror Suspects at Guantánamo Attempted Mass Hanging."
17. Ibid.
18. U.S. Department of Defense, "News Briefing with Secretary of Defense Donald Rumsfeld."
19. Wood, "Three Guantánamo Bay Detainees Die of Apparent Suicide."
20. Ibid.
21. Ahmad, "Resisting Guantánamo."
22. Welch, "Guantánamo Bay as a Foucauldian Phenomenon"; Scraton and McCulloch, *The Violence of Incarceration*.
23. For a historical overview, see Scanlan, Stoll, and Lumm, "Starving for Change."

24. However, unlike what James Scott calls "weapons of the weak," I interpret the *weaponization of life* as encompassing actions that are overt and frontal confrontations, indeed collisions, with power. The suggestive term, coined by Scott, refers to everyday forms of peasant resistance, a wide range of spontaneous, unplanned, more or less anonymous, self-helping, petty, and yet stubborn and persistent acts that fall short of openly challenging and directly confronting authorities and dominant relations of power. Examples are foot dragging, evasion, dissimulation, false compliance, pilfering, feigned ignorance, slander, arson, and sabotage. By contrast, the *weaponization of life* involves open, visible, and spectacular challenges to dominant symbols, with clearly articulated political goals, a collective agency, and organized will. Cf. Scott, *Weapons of the Weak*, see especially 28–47.

25. Grojean, "Violence Against the Self," 110.

26. Biggs, "Dying Without Killing." In this light, Biggs maintains: "The suicidal attack is an extraordinary weapon of war whereas self-immolation is an extreme form of protest" (173).

27. Dingley and Mollica, "The Human Body as a Terrorist Weapon"; Hopgood, "Tamil Tigers, 1987–2002," 68–69; Bornstein, "Ethnography and the Politics of Prisoners" and "Palestinian Prison Ontologies"; Nashif, *Palestinian Political Prisoners*; Rosenfeld, *Confronting the Occupation*; Ergil, "Suicide Terrorism in Turkey"; Bozarslan, *Violence in the Middle East*; Grojean, "Violence Against the Self," 107; Criss, "The Nature of PKK Terrorism in Turkey"; Cline, "From Ocalan to Al Qaida."

28. On the simultaneous use of different modalities of self-destruction, Biggs, for example, recognizes that there is a range or continuum of actions that can be classified as self-immolation, such as self-destruction by cyanide, jumping off buildings, fasts unto death, and other self-mutilations ("Dying Without Killing," 192–95). However, he continues to construe hunger striking as a categorically different form of action. He also makes the claim that self immolators "do not incline towards suicidal terrorism, or indeed any actions intended to kill their opponents" (ibid., 183). For him, the PKK and DHKP-C constitute "two marginal exceptions, both from Turkey" (ibid., 183–84).

29. On this point, also see Grojean, "Violence Against the Self," 106.

30. According to Bell, the existential element is rather located in the aesthetic effects evoked by self-destructive acts. The sensory dislocation these violent acts produce, particularly horror, leads us to search

for answers to existential questions raised by that dislocation. Bell's
reflections pertain to suicide attacks, but they can also be extended to
other forms of self-destructive violence. See Bell, "The Scenography of
Suicide."

31. Fanon, *The Wretched of the Earth*, 84, 86, 93–94.
32. For this argument, see Khosrokhavar, *Suicide Bombers*, 45–52; and
    Bozarslan, *Violence in the Middle East*, 10–13, 132–36.
33. Fanon, *The Wretched of the Earth*, 38, 41.
34. Benjamin, "Critique of Violence," 248.
35. While I argue for the specificity and irreducibility of *form*, however, I
    do not think its effects abolish the possibility of politically motivated
    human agency altogether. This is what Faisal Devji appears to suggest
    when he argues that

> the attacks of 9/11, immaculately planned and executed though they
> were, lacked intentionality because Al-Qaeda could neither control
> nor even predict their global repercussions. Hence the actions of this
> jihad, while they are indeed meant to accomplish certain ends, have
> become more ethical than political in nature, since they have resigned
> control over their own effects, thus becoming gestures of duty or risk
> rather than acts of instrumentality properly speaking. This might be
> why a network such as Al-Qaeda, unlike terrorist or fundamentalist
> groups of the past, has no coherent vision or plan for the future.

Even if their intentions are instrumental, the argument goes, the un-
controllable effects of their actions at the global level, transform their
actions into ethics rather than politics. Devji, *Landscapes of the Jihad*,
3–4.
36. Durkheim, *Suicide*, 217–40, 283–90.
37. McGray, "Bobby Sands, Suicide, and Self-Sacrifice"; Stern-Gillet, "The
    Rhetoric of Suicide"; and O'Keeffe, "Suicide and Self-Starvation."
38. Sluka, *Death Squad*; George, *Western State Terrorism*; and Wright, *State
    Terrorism in Latin America*.
39. For an emphasis on fanaticism that is versatile and open to religious,
    sectarian, or nationalist valences, see Laqueur, *The New Terrorism*.
    For the particularly religious modality of fanaticism, see, for example,
    Juergensmeyer, *Terror in the Mind of God*; and Stern, *Terror in the Name*

of God. For interpretations of terrorism as predominantly based on religious motivation, see Hoffman, *Inside Terrorism,* especially 81–130; and Israeli, "Islamikaze and Their Significance."

40. Khosrokhavar, *Suicide Bombers.* But Khosrokhavar also identifies different strands of martyrdom within Islam, based on the writings of thinkers such as Ali Shariati, distinguishing between *mujahids* (the conductors of jihad), who risked death on the battlefield, and *shahids* who faced death and persecution without the possibility of immediate success in order to demonstrate the righteousness of the sacred cause (ibid., 41–48).

41. King, "They Who Burned Themselves for Peace," 139–40; Khosrokhavar, *Suicide Bombers,* 5.

42. Juergensmeyer, *Terror in the Mind of God,* 10–15, 61–84.

43. Oliver and Steinberg, *The Road to Martyr's Square,* xxiii; Reuter, *My Life Is a Weapon,* 14.

44. Grojean, "Violence Against the Self," 109–14; Bozarslan, *Violence in the Middle East,* 132–36.

45. Hafez, "Dying to Be Martyrs," 55, 61–75.

46. Andriolo, "Murder by Suicide." Also see Stern, *Terror in the Name of God,* xxi–xxii; and Reuter, *My Life Is a Weapon,* 19–39. Reuter draws a line of succession between the assassins and al-Qaeda, through Khomeini. On the story of Hassan Sabbah, see Lewis, *The Assassins.*

47. Boyarin, *Dying for God;* and Bowersock, *Martyrdom and Rome.*

48. Cohn, *The Pursuit of the Millenium,* especially 127–47. Sacrificial practices, such as fasting, self-flagellation, self-abnegation and suffering, as well as the *imitatio Christi,* as the ritual repetition of the sacrificial act in order to prevent the imminent apocalyptic catastrophe of the world, were common during the Middle Ages. For fasting in particular, see Bynum, *Holy Feast and Holy Fast.*

49. King, "They Who Burned Themselves for Peace," 127–50.

50. Asad, *On Suicide Bombing.*

51. For a discussion of the complex and multilayered account of motives, see Gambetta, *Making Sense of Suicide Missions.*

52. Elster, "Motivations and Beliefs in Suicide Missions," 243.

53. Pape, *Dying to Win,* 21, 45–47, 83–94.

54. Gambetta, "Can We Make Sense of Suicide Missions?" 261.

55. Victor, *Army of Roses.*

56. For a discussion on the rationality of suicide bombers, see Hafez, "Dying to Be Martyrs"; Caplan, "Terrorism"; Sprinzak, "Rational Fanatics."

57. Gambetta, *Making Sense of Suicide Missions*, 24–26, 71, 111–14, 142–46, 239–42.

58. Ibid., 89, 94, 99, 102, 159–63.

59. Reuter, *My Life Is a Weapon*, 18; Pape, *Dying to Win*, 29–33.

60. On the changing nature of warfare, see Kaldor, *New and Old Wars*; Münkler, *The New Wars*; and Jabri, *War and the Transformation of Global Politics*.

61. Kalyvas and Sánchez-Cuenca, "Killing Without Dying," 210–25; Pape, *Dying to Win*, 30.

62. Reuter, *My Life Is a Weapon*, 87.

63. Crenshaw, "The Logic of Terrorism"; Bloom, *Dying to Kill*, 120–41. On the contagion effect, see Reuter, *My Life Is a Weapon*, 13; Moghadam, *The Globalization of Martyrdom*; Nacos, "Revisiting the Contagion Hypothesis."

64. Bloom, *Dying to Kill*, 91–97.

65. Hill, "Kamikaze, 1943–45," 1–42; Kalyvas and Sánchez-Cuenca, "Killing Without Dying," 209–32; Laqueur, *The New Terrorism*, 16–46; Reuter, *My Life Is a Weapon*, 33–51; Andriolo, "Murder by Suicide," 738.

66. Foucault, *The History of Sexuality*, 1:136–41.

67. Foucault, *Discipline and Punish*.

68. Foucault, *Security, Territory, Population*.

69. Extensive studies of various institutions and practices show the relevance of Foucault's insights regarding their role in social control and the constitution of subjectivities. See, for example, Garland, *Punishment and Welfare* and his *The Culture of Control*; Garland and Young, *The Power to Punish*; Cohen, *Visions of Social Control*; Donzelot, *The Policing of Families*; Turner, *Regulating Bodies*; Petersen and Bunton, *Foucault*; Rose, *Governing the Soul*; Dean, *Governmentality*, among others.

70. Agamben, *Homo Sacer*.

71. Işık and Pınarcıoğlu, *Nöbetleşe Yoksulluk*; Erman, "The Politics of Squatter (Gecekondu) Studies in Turkey."

72. Mignolo, *Local Histories/Global Designs*.

73. Taussig, "Culture of Terror—Space of Death."

74. See, for example, Sharma and Gupta, *The Anthropology of the State*; Ferguson and Gupta, "Spatializing States"; Hansen and Steppput, *States of Imagination*; and Das and Poole, *Anthropology in the Margins of the State*.
75. Das and Poole, "State and Its Margins," 4.
76. Feldman, *Formations of Violence*, especially 147–217.
77. Foucault, *"Society Must Be Defended,"* 7.
78. Althusser, *Machiavelli and Us*, 42, 63, 80.

1. Biosovereignty and Necroresistance

1. Mehmet is the name I have chosen to call this hunger striker to conceal his identity.
2. There is no in-depth study of Küçükarmutlu's history. However, studies of other shantytowns provide comparable findings regarding the development of these neighborhoods, their grassroot organization often based on familial and ethnic ties, the struggles around access to infrastructural and municipal services, and the involvement of their inhabitants in radical politics. See, for example, Aslan, *1 Mayıs Mahallesi*; and Erder, *İstanbul'a Bir Kent Kondu*.
3. According to Holston, such urban spaces are "heterogeneous and outside the state" and sites where the boundaries of membership are contested. Holston, "Spaces of Insurgent Citizenship."
4. Loïc Wacquant persuasively captures a trend within the United States between the ghetto and the prison create a "single institutional mesh." He argues that these sites are brought together through a functional equivalency, structural homology, and cultural fusion in which the penal management of poverty redefines citizenship through the criminalization of race. In the Turkish context, it is difficult to make a similar observation at a general level. While there is a certain connection between the wards of political prisoners and the shantytowns in which their supporters live, exacerbated through radical politics, it is not accurate to characterize these spaces as homologous sites of governmental intervention combining the problem of poverty with racial criminalization. Cf. Wacquant, "Deadly Symbiosis."
5. Interview with a participant of the death fast, May 18, 2005.

6. Interview with family members of a participant of the death fast, February 15, 2005.

7. Interview with a participant of the death fast, January 24, 2005.

8. Interviews with participants of the death fast, May 19–20, 2005.

9. Interview with a participant of the death fast, May 23, 2005.

10. Quoted in Foucault, *Discipline and Punish*, 3.

11. Ibid., 5.

12. Ibid., 3, 5.

13. See Weber, "Politics as a Vocation," 33.

14. Foucault, *"Society Must Be Defended,"* 247.

15. Foucault, *The History of Sexuality*, 136, *"Society Must Be Defended,"* 240–41.

16. It is also possible to deduce alternative traditions of sovereignty from the history of political thought. One such tradition is sovereignty as constituent power. For the elaboration of this tradition and its distinction from sovereignty as command, see Andreas Kalyvas, "Popular Sovereignty, Democracy, and the Constituent Power." Foucault does not consider this tradition, but rather takes the theory of sovereignty in its repressive, unitary, and juridical modality as his point of reference for sovereignty in Western societies.

17. Foucault, *"Society Must Be Defended,"* 37, *The History of Sexuality*, 144, *Discipline and Punish*, 141, 215.

18. Foucault, *"Society Must Be Defended,"* 34–39.

19. Foucault, *Security, Territory, Population*, 11, 65, 96.

20. Foucault, *Abnormal*, 82–83, *Discipline and Punish*, 3–6, 33–35, 47, *The History of Sexuality*, 135–36.

21. Bodin, *On Sovereignty*, bk. 1, ch. 8, 1.

22. Foucault, *Psychiatric Power*, 73–79.

23. Foucault, *Discipline and Punish*, 26–27, 138, 170, 203.

24. Ibid., 26.

25. Foucault, *"Society Must Be Defended,"* 35–36.

26. Foucault, *Psychiatric Power*, 27, 46; *"Society Must Be Defended,"* 36; *Discipline and Punish*, 208.

27. Foucault, *Psychiatric Power*, 39–62, *The History of Sexuality*, 31–33, 49, 82–83, *Discipline and Punish*, 170, 183, 208, *"Society Must Be Defended,"* 37.

28. Foucault, *Discipline and Punish*, 222, *"Society Must Be Defended,"* 37, 56, *Psychiatric Power*, 64.

29. Foucault, *Security, Territory, Population*, 79.

30. Foucault, *"Society Must Be Defended,"* 241.

31. Foucault, *Security, Territory, Population*, 11, 20, 45, 96.

32. Foucault, *"Society Must Be Defended,"* 241.

33. Foucault, *The History of Sexuality*, 138.

34. Ibid., 139.

35. Foucault, *Security, Territory, Population*, 237, 246.

36. Foucault, *"Society Must Be Defended,"* 248.

37. Foucault, *The History of Sexuality*, 138, 140, *Psychiatric Power*, 66.

38. Foucault, *The History of Sexuality*, 136, 144, *Discipline and Punish*, 208.

39. Foucault, *Discipline and Punish*, 221.

40. Foucault, *The History of Sexuality*, 138–39.

41. Foucault, *Security, Territory, Population*, 8.

42. Ibid., 9–10.

43. Foucault, *Discipline and Punish*, 194, 222, *The History of Sexuality*, 144.

44. Foucault, *"Society Must Be Defended,"* 37, *Psychiatric Power*, 110; *Power/ Knowledge*, 73.

45. Foucault, *The History of Sexuality*, 139.

46. Foucault, *"Society Must Be Defended,"* 241–42, 248–60, *Security, Territory, Population*, 8, 107.

47. Foucault, *Psychiatric Power*, 64–66.

48. Ibid., 81–87.

49. Foucault, *Discipline and Punish*, 170, 232.

50. Ibid., 16.

51. Foucault, *Security, Territory, Population*, 36–37, 44–45, especially 66.

52. Foucault, *Discipline and Punish*, 217.

53. Foucault, *Security, Territory, Population*, 312, 322–27.

54. Ibid., 109.

55. Foucault, *"Society Must Be Defended,"* 254.

56. Ibid., 254, 260.

57. Foucault, *"'Omnes et Singulatim,'"* 311.

58. Foucault, *"The Political Technology of Individuals,"* 405.

59. Foucault, *Security, Territory, Population*, 106.

60. Ibid., 107.

61. Deleuze and Guattari, *A Thousand Plateaus*, 585.

62. Ibid., 87–88.

63. Phillips, *"Agencement/Assemblage,"* 109.

64. Rabinow situates the concept of assemblage between problematization and apparatus in terms of scale and endurance. He argues:

> Assemblages are secondary matrices from within which apparatuses emerge and become stabilized or transformed. Assemblages stand in a dependent but contingent and unpredictable relationship to the grander problematizations. In terms of scale they fall between problematizations and apparatuses and function differently from either one. They are a distinctive type of experimental matrix of heterogeneous elements, techniques, and concepts. They are not yet an experimental system in which controlled variation can be produced, measured, and observed. They are comparatively effervescent, disappearing in years or decades rather than centuries. Consequently, the temporality of assemblages is qualitatively different from that of either problematizations or apparatuses.

> Rabinow, *Anthropos Today*, 56

65. Deleuze and Guattari, *A Thousand Plateaus*, 24.
66. Tampio, "Assemblages and the Multitude," 394.
67. Venn, "A Note on Assemblage," 107.
68. For a discussion of Foucault's apparatus and Deleuze's assemblage and the occasional slippage in Foucault's lectures between the two concepts, see Legg, "Assemblage/Apparatus."
69. The concept of assemblage has recently been productively deployed to theorize a wide range of phenomena, ranging from the combination of new technologies and politics to the composition of cities and the conjunction between nationalism and homonormativity. See, for example, Ong and Collier, *Global Assemblages*; and Farias and Bender, *Urban Assemblages*; Puar, *Terrorist Assemblages*.
70. Ong, "Scales of Exception," 120–21.
71. Despite the wealth of studies that Foucault has inspired, the literature on resistance informed by Foucault's ideas is relatively (and surprisingly) thin. An important example of scholarship that addresses resistance from a perspective informed by Foucault is Scott, *Domination and the Arts of Resistance*. Also see Sawicki, *Disciplining Foucault*; Diamond and

Quinby, *Foucault and Feminism*; Pile and Keith, *Geographies of Resistance*; Butler, *Bodies That Matter*; and Selmeczi, "' . . . we are being left to burn because we do not count.'"

72. Foucault, "The Subject and Power," 342.
73. Foucault, *The History of Sexuality*, 95–96.
74. Foucault, "The Subject and Power," 346.
75. Simons, *Foucault and the Political*, 6.
76. On Foucault and resistance, see Poulantzas, *State, Power, Socialism*, 146–53; Pickett, *On the Use and Abuse of Foucault for Politics*, especially 35–54; Giddens, *A Contemporary Critique of Historical Materialism*, 158–81.
77. McCarthy, "The Critique of Impure Reason," 258.
78. Habermas, "Some Questions Concerning the Theory of Power"; Fraser, *Unruly Practices*, 283.
79. Bernstein, "Foucault," 229.
80. Foucault worked for prison reform through the "Groupe d'information sur les prisons" [Prison Information Group (GIP)] with Jean-Marie Domenach and Pierre Vidal-Naquet. See Patton, "Of Power and Prisons"; "Michel Foucault on Attica"; and Foucault, *Remarks on Marx*, 41, 138. On the prison struggles in France in the 1970s, see Soulié, "Années 70."
81. Thompson, "Forms of Resistance."
82. Kantorowicz, *The King's Two Bodies*, 1–23.
83. Foucault, *Discipline and Punish*, 3.
84. Ibid.
85. Ibid., 4.
86. Ibid., 38.
87. Ibid., 67.
88. Ibid., 73.
89. Ibid., 29, 170.
90. Ibid., 197.
91. Ibid., 237.
92. Foucault, *Abnormal*, 87.
93. Ibid., 96–102.
94. Foucault, *Discipline and Punish*, 285.
95. Garland, *Punishment and Modern Society*, 154, 167–173.

96. "Michel Foucault on Attica," 154–61; Patton, "Of Power and Prisons," 109–10.

97. McNay, *Foucault and Feminism*; Foucault, *Power/Knowledge*, 163–64.

98. Foucault, *Power/Knowledge*, 161.

99. Feldman, *Formations of Violence*, 144.

100. Ibid., 178.

101. Ibid., 177. Feldman relies on a Nietzschean framework in order to conceptualize the body as the product of "unequal and differential effects of intersecting antagonistic forces" (ibid., 176).

102. Ibid., 178.

103. Siméant, *La Cause des Sans-Papiers*, 302–10.

104. Foucault, "Alternatives to the Prison," 12–24.

105. Foucault, *Discipline and Punish*, 268, 270.

106. Foucault, *The History of Sexuality*, 95–96.

107. Ibid., 145.

108. Ibid.

109. For the relatively recent turn to recognition in political and social struggles, see Taylor, *Multiculturalism and "the Politics of Recognition"*; and Honneth, *The Struggle for Recognition*. However, for a critical theory of recognition that fruitfully combines with redistributive struggles, see Fraser, "From Redistribution to Recognition?"

110. According to Prozorov, who insists on keeping sovereignty and biopower apart: "If resistance to sovereignty . . . consists in *disobedience* and *revolt* either for the purposes of establishing a new form of sovereignty or refusing sovereignty as such in a variably conceived ideal of anarchism, resistance to biopower must entail the *refusal of care*, an attitude of indifference no longer to the threat of power, but to its loving embrace." Prozorov, "The Unrequited Love of Power," 62.

111. Foucault, *Security, Territory, Population*, 125–29.

112. Ibid., 154.

113. Ibid., 195.

114. Ibid., 193–216.

115. Ibid., 200–1.

116. Ibid., 196.

117. Ibid., 228.

118. Ibid., 198–99.

119. Ibid., 204.

120. Ibid., 204–15.

121. Ibid., 355.

122. Ibid., 356.

123. Foucault, *The History of Sexuality, Vol. 3: The Care of the Self,* and *The Hermeneutics of the Subject.*

124. Afary and Anderson provocatively suggest that Foucault's turn to the "aesthetics of existence" was directly influenced by his experience with the Iranian revolution. Afary and Anderson, *Foucault and the Iranian Revolution,* 4–5.

125. Foucault, *Remarks on Marx,* 134.

126. Ibid., 135.

127. Ibid., 136 (my emphasis).

128. Ibid., 139.

129. For a collection of Foucault's writings on Iran, see Foucault, "Appendix: Foucault and His Critics."

130. Foucault, "Tehran," 201–2.

131. Foucault, "The Revolt in Iran Spreads on Cassette Tapes," 216.

132. Foucault, "What Are the Iranians Dreaming [Rêvent] About?" and "Is it Useless to Revolt?" 209 and 265, respectively.

133. "Dialogue Between Michel Foucault and Baqir Parham," 186–87. Also Foucault, "What Are the Iranians Dreaming [Rêvent] About?" 208.

134. Foucault, "Tehran," and "Iran," 201 and 255 respectively.

135. Foucault, "Is It Useless to Revolt?" 264.

136. "Iran," 255.

137. Foucault, "Tehran," 202–3.

138. Foucault, "Is It Useless to Revolt?" 265.

139. Foucault, "What Are the Iranians Dreaming [Rêvent] About?" 204, 207, 209.

140. Foucault, "A Revolt with Bare Hands" 211.

141. "Iran," 254.

142. Ibid., 257.

143. Foucault, "Is it Useless to Revolt?" 264.

144. Miller, *The Passion of Michel Foucault,* 308, 314, 324.

145. Afary and Anderson, *Foucault and the Iranian Revolution,* 106–62. The authors critique Foucault's assessment of the Iranian revolution as seduced by an orientalist appreciation of the non-West that leads him to an erroneous assessment of what eventually became a theocracy in

Iran. Of central importance to their critique is Foucault's enthusiasm for antimodernism and his blindness to gender, especially as it plays out in the Iranian context. I think Afary and Anderson are largely correct in their feminist critique of Foucault. However, their framing of Foucault's reaction to the Iranian revolt as a function, on the one hand, of his personal fascination with death and non-Western homosexuality, and, on the other hand, of his hostility to Western modernism and rationality, does not do justice, in my opinion, to Foucault's complexity as a thinker, and especially to his attention to alternative forms of rationality and his nuanced critique of modernity, which remains well attuned to appreciating different forms of "political spirituality" rather than writing them off as antimodern.

146. "Iran," 253.

147. Foucault, "The Mythical Leader of the Iranian Revolt," 222.

148. "Iran," 253.

149. For the different articulations of the relationship between sovereignty and biopower, with an increasing emphasis on their conjunction and mutual operation, see Butler, "Indefinite Detention"; Connolly, "The Complexities of Sovereignty"; Dillon, "Correlating Sovereign and Biopower"; Reid, *The Biopolitics of the War on Terror*; De Larrinaga and Doucet, "Sovereign Power and the Biopolitics of Human Security."

150. Agamben, *Homo Sacer*.

151. Ibid., 7, 111.

152. Schmitt, *Political Theology*.

153. Agamben, *Homo Sacer*, 7. Also, Agamben, "Form-of-Life." For a critique of Agamben's philological generalizations and how they color his conclusions, see Dubreuil, "Leaving Politics."

154. Agamben, *Homo Sacer*, 7.

155. The sovereign in Hobbes's *Leviathan* best exemplifies this case. In this political formation the sovereign has absolute power over each and every individual in order to assure his self-preservation as well as the preservation of the whole. The sovereign preserves the "state of nature," the violence, and the "exception" within the political state, even though he is the source of law. The dissenters to this new juridical order are considered to have stayed in (or reverted back to) the "state of nature" and are stripped of their right to the civil order; they become *homo sacer*. Agamben, *Homo Sacer*, 107.

156. "Bare" or sacred life is not the equivalent of natural life. For an elaboration of four different conceptions of life in Agamben, see Mills, *The Philosophy of Agamben*, especially 59–80.

157. For a critique of Agamben's genealogy of homo sacer, see Fitzpatrick, "Bare Sovereignty."

158. Agamben, *Homo Sacer*, 85.

159. Ibid., 83.

160. Ibid., 6.

161. Agamben indicates this structural relationship as follows: "The sovereign is the one with respect to whom all men are potentially *homines sacri*, and *homo sacer* is the one with respect to whom all men act as sovereigns." Agamben, *Homo Sacer*, 84.

162. Ibid., 89.

163. Ibid., 101.

164. In fact, all of the occurrences of the term "bio-sovereignty" in the existing scholarly literature are tied to Agamben's arguments. According to Caldwell, "bio-sovereignty" is "a form of sovereignty operating according to the logic of the exception rather than law, applied to material life rather than juridical life, and moving within a global terrain now almost exclusively biopolitical" (par. 7). She coins the term as an amalgamation of the Schmittian "exception" and the Agambenian articulation of life and power, but expands its applicability to the sphere of international politics. She asserts that "bio-sovereignty" is what replaces nation-state sovereignty on a global scale (par. 35) and acts directly on a universalized construct of "humanity" (par. 40). See Caldwell, "Bio-Sovereignty and the Emergence of Humanity." On the other hand, Kalyvas uses the concept to denote a specifically Agambenian inflection of sovereignty. Kalyvas, "The Sovereign Weaver." Finally, according to Ong, "bio-sovereignty" is the exercise of state control over biological resources by claiming the realm of "sheer life" as a domain for ethical intervention. Discussing the example of Indonesian authorities' refusal to share samples of the bird flu and its reception by the world health community and drug companies, Ong argues that the exertion of sovereign rights over virus samples is a way in which the realm of biological life is claimed from the domination of global capital through the mechanism of the "exception." For Ong, then, "bio-sovereignty" is less about the form or nature of power that is exercised than about

the domain in which it is exercised and claimed. "Bio-sovereignty," in this conception, remains juridical and tied to the Schmittian definition of the right to decide on the "exception." Thus Ong's use of the term, while important in the way in which it pinpoints the exercise of state control over the realm of life, reveals little about the changing nature of sovereignty in tandem with its exercise in the biopolitical domain. Ong, "Scales of Exception," 124.

165. Agamben, *Homo Sacer*, 9.

166. Agamben, *Remnants of Auschwitz* and *Homo Sacer*, 185.

167. Agamben, *Means Without Ends*, 41.

168. Agamben, *Homo Sacer*, 20, 119, 123 and *State of Exception*.

169. Agamben, *Homo Sacer*, 166.

170. Ibid., 124–25, 139–40.

171. Ibid., 9–10.

172. Ibid., 142.

173. Agamben, *Remnants of Auschwitz*, 155.

174. Fitzpatrick, "These Mad Abandon'd Times."

175. Laclau, "Bare Life or Social Indeterminacy?" 11.

176. Lemke, "A Zone of Indistinction," 10.

177. For a comparative discussion of Agamben and Foucault's method in which the camp as paradigm ostensibly replaces the panopticon as paradigm, see de la Durantaye, *Giorgio Agamben*, 219–26.

178. Agamben, *Homo Sacer*, 142.

179. Ibid., 187.

180. Bigo, "Detention of Foreigners," 12.

181. Mitchell, "Geographies of Identity"; Masters, "Femina Sacra"; Ziarek, "Bare Life on Strike"; Sanchez, "The Global E-rotic Subject."

182. Reinert, "The Persistence of Sacrifice," par. 28.

183. Lemke, "A Zone of Indistinction," 8.

184. Ibid.

185. DeCaroli, "Boundary Stones," 46.

186. Fitzpatrick, "Bare Sovereignty," note 24.

187. Huysmans, "The Jargon of Exception," 175.

188. Agamben, *Homo Sacer*, 59. For a further elaboration of this rather elusive, nonetheless provocative alternative, see Agamben, *The Coming Community*, and his *Means Without Ends*. A helpful review is by Mills,

"Agamben's Messianic Politics."
189. Agamben, "Form-of-Life," 154.
190. Agamben, *Homo Sacer*, 188.
191. Agamben, "Form-of-Life," 154.
192. Agamben, *Homo Sacer*, 48.
193. Ibid., 62. For Agamben's interpretation of Bartleby, see his "Bartleby, or On Contingency."
194. Agamben, "Bartleby, or On Contingency," 254.
195. For a comparative evaluation of Deleuze's and Agamben's interpretations of Bartleby, see Cooke, "Resistance, Potentiality and the Law."
196. For a critique of Agamben's messianism, see Sinnerbrink, "From *Machenschaft* to Biopolitics."
197. Passavant argues that Agamben's theory is ridden with a fundamental contradiction in that his subjects can only move beyond sovereignty if they violate his theory of sovereignty. Accordingly, the potentialities of refusal and exodus embedded within the figure of Bartleby, anomic carnivals, and messianism do not constitute meaningful political action. Passavant, "The Contradictory State of Giorgio Agamben."
198. Rajaram and Grundy-Warr, "The Irregular Migrant as *Homo Sacer*"; Ahmetbeyzade, "Gendering Necropolitics"; Biehl, "Vita"; Enns, "Bare Life and the Occupied Body"; Jenkins, "Bare Life"; Parfitt, "Are the Third World Poor Homines Sacri?"; Žižek, "Biopolitics"; Cadman, "Life and Death Decisions in Our Posthuman(ist) Times."
199. Mbembe, "Necropolitics."
200. Ibid., 40.
201. Ibid., 27.
202. Ibid., 39.
203. Instead of necropolitics, Murray calls this form thanatopolitics because, he argues, the politics of the suicide bomber is not reducible to a politics of the corpse but should rather "invoke the inassimilable mythic and rhetorical dimensions of Thanatos, with its long tradition from the Greeks through to Freud." Murray, "Thanatopolitics."
204. Mbembe, "Necropolitics," 36.
205. Edkins and Pin-Fat, "Through the Wire," 3.
206. Ibid., 20.
207. Ziarek, "Bare Life on Strike."

208. Following Maurice Blanchot, Guenther argues that the human relation to alterity, which persists despite the destruction of the subject,
remains the source of resistance. In other words, even in the greatest
abjection there exists an intersubjective dimension whose presence
provides the possibility of resistance. Guenther purports "*life is never
bare*—not because *bios* cannot be separated from *zoē*, but because the
relation to the Other cannot be destroyed. Even when reduced to a
'naked relation to naked existence,' even when exposed to an unimagi-
nable extremity of need and affliction, even when forced to steal from
others in order to secure one's own survival, the subject retains a relation to alterity which provides a starting point, however minimal, for
resistance." Guenther, "Resisting Agamben," 75.
209. Feldman, *Formations of Violence*, 144, 178.
210. Enns, "Bare Life and the Occupied Body," par. 33.
211. Ibid., par. 28.
212. Ibid., par. 31.
213. Ibid., par. 38.
214. Owens, "Reclaiming 'Bare Life'?" 578.
215. Weigel, "The Critique of Violence."
216. Bailey, "Up Against the Wall."
217. Ibid., 121.
218. Ibid., 118–19.
219. Murray, "Thanatopolitics," 195.

2. Crisis of Sovereignty

1. Heper, *The State Tradition in Turkey*.
2. Heper, "The Ottoman Legacy and Turkish Politics."
3. *CHF Programı*.
4. Parla, *Türkiye'de Siyasal Kültürün Resmi Kaynakları* 3:40, 325.
5. An important exception is the brief period of the first National Assembly in Ankara (1920–23) before the proclamation of the republic. Mete
Tunçay, *Türkiye Cumhuriyeti'nde Tek Parti Yönetiminin Kurulması*.
6. Parla, *Türkiye'de Siyasal Kültürün Resmi Kaynakları*.
7. For the origins of the Father State image and its role in constructing
national identity, see Delaney, "Father State, Motherland, and the Birth

of Modern Turkey."

8. Zürcher, *Political Opposition in the Early Turkish Republic*; and Weiker, *Political Tutelage and Democracy in Turkey*. The "tutelary" character of the Kemalist regime refers to the role of the governing elite in deciding when the masses become mature enough for democracy and to the justification of their authoritarian rule through the unrealized conditions of socioeconomic development that necessitate their intervention. In contrast, scholars from the modernization school have interpreted "tutelage" as a transitory phase of authoritarianism between traditional and modern government where the regime creates the conditions conducive to democracy and prepares the nation through the inculcation of democratic values to ensure the success of the transformation. In the meantime, the very success of a tutelary regime in this transitional/preparatory role is expected to undermine the grounds for its own legitimate existence. However, this view is inflicted with a linear schema of development and the problem of attributing a predetermined democratic essence to the tutelary regime. Cf. Özbudun, "The Nature of the Kemalist Political Regime"; and Köker, *Modernleşme, Kemalizm ve Demokrasi*, 210–21, 235.

9. Parla, *Türkiye'de Siyasal Kültürün Resmi Kaynakları* 3:40, 326.

10. Yerasimos, "The Monoparty Period," 69ff. Similarly, despite the incorporation of secularism into Kemalist ideology, definitions of national identity involved monosectarian religious interpretations based on Sunni Islam as a supplementary aspect of the homogeneous and indivisible nation.

11. Parla, *Türkiye'de Siyasal Kültürün Resmi Kaynakları* 3:41–44, 326.

12. Some scholars hold populism to be the "source of democratic rights" of the Kemalist regime because of its dimension of legal equality, dis missing the implications of the latter corporatist part. See Karal, "The Principles of Kemalism." Others argue that the initial formulation of the principle entailed an anticapitalist content. See Özbudun, "The Nature of the Kemalist Political Regime." Yet evidence for an anticapitalist substance depends on a few commentaries by Mustafa Kemal Atatürk that might also be evaluated as tactical maneuvers to accommodate leftist opposition or to maintain a left-leaning image. An ex post facto evaluation of Kemalist practices would validate the maneuver view.

13. Boratav, *Türkiye'de Devletçilik.*
14. Hershlag, "Ataturk's Étatism."
15. Boratav, "Kemalist Economic Policies and Etatism"; Tezel, *Cumhuriyet Dönemi'nin İktisadi Tarihi.*
16. Köker, *Modernleşme, Kemalizm ve Demokrasi,* 180.
17. Ibid., 209. Mehmet, "Turkey in Crisis"; Tachau, "The Political Culture of Kemalist Turkey."
18. The substitution of science in place of religion, as a modernizing step in societal evolution, reflected the influence of the Comtean project of positivism over the Kemalist secularizers. According to Kadıoğlu, it "gave secularism a teleological as well as a theological character." Kadıoğlu, "Republican Epistemology and Islamic Discourses," 5–7.
19. According Sakallıoğlu, Islamic elements were incorporated into national discourse in the early years of the republic to establish legitimacy. This incorporation led to the formation of the "double discourse" of the state, i.e., the repeatedly used strategy of combining the control and exclusion of Islam with its accommodation and inclusion. Sakallıoğlu, "Parameters and Strategies of Islam-State Interaction in Republican Turkey."
20. Parla, *Türkiye'de Siyasal Kültürün Resmi Kaynakları* 3: 45, 328; İnsel, "Laiklik, Cumhuriyet ve Sosyalist Hareket."
21. Especially after 1980, the inclusion of Islamic elements into Kemalist ideology became more overt and systematic, both as a "bulwark against communism and a substitute for class-based ideologies" as well as a means of legitimizing policies of economic liberalization. Sakallıoğlu, "Kemalism, Hyper-Nationalism and Islam in Turkey," 262. For the latter point, see Birtek and Toprak, "The Conflictual Agendas of Neo-Liberal Reconstruction"; Öniş, "The Political Economy of Islamic Resurgence in Turkey"; and Yavuz, "Turkey's Fault Lines and the Crisis of Kemalism."
22. Dumont, "The Origins of Kemalist Ideology," 38.
23. With language reform, the Ottoman Turkish word for "reform" or "transformation" (*inkılâp*) was replaced with the new Turkish word for "revolution" (*devrim*) in 1935, but it was later changed back to its original. The dual usage still continues to date, signifying different ideological interpretations of the Kemalist past.

24. Parla, *Türkiye'de Siyasal Kültürün Resmi Kaynakları* 3: 47, 328.
25. Adak, "National Myths and Self-Na(rra)tions."
26. Gramsci, *Selections from the Prison Notebooks.*
27. Özbek, "Osmanlı'dan Günümüze Sosyal Devlet."
28. Akın, "*Gürbüz ve Yavuz Evlatlar*"; Alemdaroğlu, "Politics of the Body and Eugenic Discourse"; Buzgan, "History of Vaccination Policies, in Turkey"; Evered and Evered, "State, Peasant, Mosquito," "Governing Population, Public Health, and Malaria," and "Syphilis and Prostitution."
29. Ergin, "'Is the Turk a White Man?'" and "Biometrics and Anthropometrics."
30. Aybers, "Eugenics in Turkey During the 1930s"; Salgirli, "Eugenics for the Doctors."
31. Köker, *Modernleşme, Kemalizm ve Demokrasi,* 236.
32. Özbek, "Osmanlı'dan Günümüze Sosyal Devlet," 20–26.
33. Sunar, "Populism and Patronage."
34. According to Carl Schmitt, "sovereign is he who decides on the exception." Schmitt, *Political Theology,* 5.
35. As Schmitt teaches us, the right of naming the enemy is one of the most important qualities of a political entity's claim to sovereignty and a constitutive quality of its own identity. See Schmitt, *The Concept of the Political,* 38–39.
36. According to Paker, the continuous expectation of danger from internal and external threats, always aiming to weaken, divide and destroy the country, acts as a "paranoid fantasy" that has become a consistent feature of the security discourse of the state. Paker, "Paranoyanın Zaferi," 33.
37. Mardın, "Opposition and Control in Turkey."
38. Tunçay, *Türkiye'de Sol Akımlar 1908–1925*; Tunçay and Zürcher, *Socialism and Nationalism in the Ottoman Empire*; Harris, *Origins of Communism in Turkey*; Quataert and Zürcher, *Workers and the Working Class in the Ottoman Empire*; Sayılgan, *Türkiye'de Sol Hareketler*; and Şişmanov, *Türkiye İşçi ve Sosyalist Hareketi Kısa Tarihi* are important resources for this turbulent period in Turkish history. For a study of the way in which the founders of the Communist Party were collectively eliminated, see Gökay, "The Turkish Communist Party."

39. An instance of this precarious position of the Communist Party of Turkey toward the Kemalist regime was the ethnic revolt of 1925, in relation to which the socialists supported the Kemalist "bourgeois" government against the "feudal" dissenters (in line with the view of the Communist International). However, the Law for Maintenance of Order (Takrir-i Sükûn) promulgated as a preventive measure by the government was soon to ban all opposition, outlawing, first and foremost, all socialist and communist organizations. See Akdere and Karadeniz, *Türkiye Solu'nun Eleştirel Tarihi* 1:158–59.

40. One of the predecessors of the turn of the socialists toward the promotion of a "Third Way," that is, a strategy of development that was not capitalist and that constructed the unity and interests of the "nation" as superior to those of the working class, was the Kadro movement, which materialized around a journal published by a group of leftist intellectuals affiliated with the socialist movement. Interestingly, the members of this movement also partook of the initial attempts of the ideological formulation of Kemalism. For more information, see Türkeş, "The Ideology of the Kadro [Cadre] Movement."

41. Landau, *Radical Politics in Modern Turkey*, 96–103.

42. For information related to the socioeconomic transformations of the early Republican and Democrat Party periods, see Hershlag, *Turkey*; Keyder, "The Political Economy of Turkish Democracy" and *State and Class in Turkey*; Owen and Pamuk, *A History of the Middle East Economies*.

43. Samim, "The Tragedy of the Turkish Left," 66.

44. For a history of the party, see Aybar, *Türkiye İşçi Partisi Tarihi*; and Aren, *TİP Olayı*.

45. The term comes from Yerasimos, "The Monoparty Period." For the politics of transition to democracy, see Eroğul, "The Establishment of Multiparty Rule."

46. For the evolution of the Turkish left after the 1950s, see *Sosyalizm ve Toplumsal Mücadeleler Ansiklopedisi*, vol. 7.

47. Samim, "The Tragedy of the Turkish Left," 61.

48. Alevis constitute the Shia community in Turkey. A heterodox and tolerant sect, the Alevis have usually supported the Republican People's Party and secular politics. They have also been a major source of sup-

port for the social-democratic and radical left. For a history of Alevi politics in Turkey, see, in particular, Çamuroğlu, "Alevi Revivalism in Turkey"; Korkmaz, *Alevilere Saldırılar*; van Bruinessen, "Kurds, Turks and the Alevi Revival in Turkey"; Erman and Göker, "Alevi Politics in Contemporary Turkey"; and Poyraz, "The Turkish State and Alevis."

49. DİSK was allowed to reopen only in 1991.

50. These figures come from TİHV, *İşkence Dosyası*, 19. Also available in *Cumhuriyet*, "Darbenin Bilançosu"; and *Radikal*, "12 Eylül'le 20 Yıl."

51. In 1980 individuals between the ages fifteen and sixty-four made up 25 million of Turkey's total population, which was about 45 million.

52. Among those who were eventually executed by the military regime, eighteen were leftists, eight were rightists, twenty-three were convicted of "ordinary" crimes, and one was a militant of ASALA (the Armenian organization responsible for the assassination of Turkish diplomats abroad). These figures come from TİHV, *İşkence Dosyası*, 19. According to Tanör, the number of approved executions was fifty-five, out of which thirty-five were convicted of political crimes. Two of these executions were approved in 1984 by the first civilian parliament constituted after the elections of 1983. Tanör, *Türkiye'nin İnsan Hakları Sorunu*, 28–29.

53. Öniş, *State and Market*; and Aricanli and Rodrik, *The Political Economy of Turkey*.

54. As Article 68 of the new constitution stipulated, "The statutes and programmes, as well as the activities of political parties shall not be in conflict with the independence of the state, its indivisible integrity with its territory and nation, human rights, the principles of equality and rule of law, sovereignty of the nation, the principles of the democratic and secular republic; they shall not aim to protect or establish class or group dictatorship or dictatorship of any kind, nor shall they incite citizens to crime" (http://www.anayasa.gov.tr/Mevzuat/Anayasa1982/). Last accessed November 15, 2013.

55. Campaigning against the new constitution before the referendum was illegal. However, the constitution was approved with the support of an overwhelming majority of voters (91.4 percent). Turnout for the referendum was also quite high (91.3 percent of the registered electorate), partially due to the stipulation in the new constitution forbidding

electoral participation for those who failed to cast their votes for the next five years (Provisional Article 16).

56. For example, according to Article 13 of the constitution, "Fundamental rights and freedoms may be restricted by law, in conformity with the letter and spirit of the Constitution, with the aim of safeguarding the indivisible integrity of the state with its territory and nation, national sovereignty, the Republic, national security, public order, general peace, the public interest, public morals and public health." Similarly, Article 14 stipulated:

None of the rights and freedoms embodied in the Constitution may be exercised with the aim of violating the indivisible integrity of the State with its territory and nation, of endangering the existence of the Turkish State and Republic, of destroying fundamental rights and freedoms, of placing the government of the State under the control of an individual or a group of people, or establishing the hegemony of one social class over others, or creating discrimination on the basis of language, race, religion or sect, or of establishing by any other means a system of government based on these concepts and ideas.

Constitution of the Republic of Turkey (http://www.anayasa.gov.tr/ Mevzuat/Anayasa1982/). Last accessed November 15, 2013.

For the legal critique of the 1982 Constitution, see Tanör's *Türkiye'nin İnsan Hakları Sorunu*, 249–61, and his *İki Anayasa*, 97–114. For a comparative political analysis of Turkey's constitutions, see Parla, *Türkiye'de Anayasalar*.

57. Schmitt, *Political Theology*, 5.

58. The so-called Provisional Article 15 of the 1982 Constitution guaranteeing the impunity of military commanders from any allegation of criminal, financial, or legal responsibility for their use of sovereign authority in this interim period has only recently been rescinded with the referendum of September 12, 2010.

59. Batman, Bingöl, Bitlis, Diyarbakır, Hakkari, Mardin, Siirt, Şırnak, Tunceli and Van were the ten provinces kept longest under this "state of emergency." Hakkari and Tunceli were taken out on July 30, 2002,

Diyarbakır and Şırnak were the last ones to return to normalcy on
November 30, 2002.

60. The definition of "internal threat" comes from the Secretariat General
of the National Security Council, www.mgk.gov.tr/Turkce/sss.html
(last accessed June 7, 2010).

61. United Nations, *Report of the Committee Against Torture*, 9. On allegations of widespread and systematic torture in Turkey in the 1980s and
1990s, see, for example, Amnesty International, *Torture in the Eighties*, 217–20 and *Turkey: Still Waiting for Change*; TİHV, *Türkiye İnsan
Hakları Raporu '91* and *İşkence Dosyası*.

62. On Islamist politics in the shantytowns, see White, *Islamist Mobilization in Turkey*. However, the same phenomenon has been interpreted as
a manifestation of growing poverty and the increased marginalization
of the shantytowns. Cf. Işık and Pınarcıoğlu, *Nöbetleşe Yoksulluk*.

63. See Terörle Mücadele Kanunu. This law was promulgated in lieu of
Articles 140, 141, 142, and 163 (with the exception of 142/3) of the Penal
Code. All of these articles contained significant restrictions on freedom
of expression and organization. Hence, despite the problems regarding the stipulations of this law (see further on in this chapter), it also
intended to lift some of the previously imposed restrictions. For a legal
critique of the antiterror law and the evaluation of the legal system
from the perspective of human rights, see Tanör, *Türkiye'nin İnsan
Hakları Sorunu*.

64. The prevalence of torture in the 1990s has been well documented by
international and national sources alike. See, for example, Amnesty
International, *Turkey: Torture, Extrajudicial Executions, Turkey: Recom-
mendations for Action*, and *Turkey: No Security Without Human Rights*;
Helsinki Watch, *Nothing Unusual* and *Twenty-One Deaths in Deten-
tion in 1993*; Human Rights Watch, *Turkey: Torture and Mistreatment*;
İnsan Hakları Derneği İstanbul Şubesi, *Cezaevleri Komisyonu Raporu*;
İstanbul Barosu Cezaevleri Komisyonu, *Cezaevleri Durum Raporu*;
Yıldız and McDermott, *Torture in Turkey*; Pişkinsüt, *Filistin Askısından
Fezlekeye*; and Sevimay, *TBMM İnsan Hakları Komisyonu Raporlarında
Resmen İşkence*. For a scholarly collection on different aspects of the
human rights regime in Turkey, see Arat, *Human Rights in Turkey*.

65. The term was coined by Candar, "Redefining Turkey's Center."

66. For the rise of political Islam, see Yavuz, *Secularism and Muslim Democracy in Turkey*.

67. Rumford, "Human Rights and Democratization in Turkey"; Keyman and İçduygu, "Globalization, Civil Society and Citizenship in Turkey"; and Özbudun, "Democratization Reforms in Turkey."

68. I use the concept of the "crowd" both as a counterpoint to the official discourse on "overcrowding" (see further on in this chapter) and in order to capture the political character of the prisoners as a "face-to-face" "living and many-sided," riotous ensemble. My understanding of the crowd is indebted to E. P. Thompson and George Rudé whose historical work on the preindustrial and protoindustrial crowds have rescued the concept from its pejorative connotations (criminal, irrational, and racist) in previous works (such as Le Bon, *The Crowd*) and given it a social and political character in contrast to psychologist and behaviorist explanations. See Thompson, *The Making of the English Working Class* and his "The Moral Economy of the English Crowd"; and Rudé, *The Crowd in History*.

69. Law for the Struggle Against Terror (Terörle Mücadele Kanunu) went into effect at the date of its publication in the Official Gazette on April 12, 1991.

70. This article was amended in 1995, obliging the state to show criminal intent and reducing prison sentences for offenses that fell under this article as "thought crimes."

71. For example, the right to remain silent and the right to inform family members were only allowed with legal amendments in 1998 and 2002.

72. Law No. 2845 on State Security Courts and Law No. 3842 on the Criminal Procedural Code were amended in 1997. This amendment limited detention periods for "terror" suspects in collectively committed crimes to four days, which could be extended to seven by the public prosecutor. In regions under the "state of emergency," this period could be extended up to ten days. The amendment also permitted detainees to meet with their lawyers, though not immediately with detention, but after the extension of detention (after two days for individual crimes, four days after collective crimes).

73. Interview with state official, July 5, 2005.

74. *Hürriyet*, "Devletin İtirafı"; *Radikal*, "Devletin Cezaevi İtirafı."

75. *Sabah*, "Cezaevleri Suç Fabrikası Gibi."

76. See, for example, İstanbul Barosu İnsan Hakları Merkezi Cezaevi Çalışma Grubu, "Cezaevleri Sorunları ve Çözüm Yolları" and *1999–2000 Yılları Çalışma Raporu*.

77. TBMM, *Genel Kurul Tutanakları*, November 21, 2000, 49.

78. According to the statistics released at the time, the political prisoner population was 9,642 out of 73,748 individuals. According to updated statistical information currently published by the Ministry of Justice, the political prisoner population was made up of 10,348 out of 68,764 individuals at the end of 1999. The overall percentage ranges between 13–15 percent of the whole population (depending on the figures). See Adalet Bakanlığı Ceza ve Tevkifevleri Genel Müdürlüğü (hereafter ABCTGM), "Statistics," www.cte.adalet.gov.tr/. Last accessed December 1, 2012.

79. A list of prisoners as of May 2002 according to political affiliation is available in Taşkın, *Cezaevi İstatistikleri*, 294–5.

80. This security operation took place after political prisoners in the fourth and fifth wards invaded the seventh ward allotted to "ordinary" prisoners. This internal invasion was conducted because of the excessive crowding in the political prisoners' wards. On September 2, 1999, the prisoners tore down the wall separating these wards and claimed the enlarged space for themselves until the security operation on September 26. TBMM İnsan Haklarını İnceleme Komisyonu, *26 Eylül Ulucanlar Cezaevi Raporu*, 112 ff.

81. ABCTGM, "Açlık Grevi ve Ölüm Orucu Eylemlerinin Gerçek Nedenleri." This document has now been removed from the official Web site. Last accessed August 19, 2003.

82. While the share of the Ministry of Justice in the government's budget was 3 percent until 1960s, it decreased steadily in the following years. Since 1996 this share had decreased to less than 1 percent of the general budget. In 2000 its share was 0.77 percent. In contrast, for example, the share of the Ministry of Defense was 8.1 percent.

83. On the problem of governing prisons by executive decrees, Erdal, "Devletin Cezaevi Politikası."

84. TBMM, *Genel Kurul Tutanakları*, November 21, 2000, 50.

85. Ibid.

86. Ibid.

87. Agha is a term used for powerful local landlords who dominate and exploit peasants connected to them through semi-feudal ties. TBMM, *Genel Kurul Tutanakları*, November 21, 2000, 63 (my emphases).
88. Ibid.
89. Ibid., 54–55 (my emphasis).
90. Weber, "Politics as a Vocation," 33.
91. The term was introduced into modern economics by Robinson, *The Economics of Imperfect Competition*.

3. The Biosovereign Assemblage and Its Tactics

1. Churchill and Vander Wall, *Cages of Steel*; Immarigeon, "The Marionization of American Prisons"; King, "The Rise and Rise of Supermax"; Kurki and Morris, "The Purposes, Practices, and Problems of Supermax Prisons"; Mears, and Reisig, "The Theory and Practice of Supermax Prisons"; Pizarro and Stenius, "Supermax Prisons"; Sparks, Bottoms, and Hay, *Prison and the Problem of Order*; and Ward and Werlich, "Alcatraz and Marion."
2. ABCTGM, "Ülkemizde Ceza İnfaz Kurumları."
3. Kaptanoğlu, "Panopticon'dan F Tipine Tecrit," 33.
4. TBMM, *Genel Kurul Tutanakları*, November 21, 2000, 51.
5. ABCTGM, "Açlık Grevi ve Ölüm Orucu Eylemlerinin Gerçek Nedenleri."
6. Interviews with state officials, July 5–8, 2005.
7. Council of Europe, *Report to the Turkish Government on the Visit to Turkey Carried Out by the European CPT from 16 to 24 July 2000*, especially 11–12. While endorsing the new prisons, the CPT did caution, however, that the "moves towards smaller living units for prisoners in Turkey must be accompanied by measures to ensure that prisoners spend a reasonable part of the day engaged in purposeful activities outside their living unit" (12). This recommendation, repeated in the 2001 report, in fact dated from an earlier visit. See Council of Europe, *Report to the Turkish Government on the Visit to Turkey Carried Out by the European CPT from 19 to 23 August 1996*.
8. Green, "Turkish Jails, Hunger Strikes."
9. Interviews with state officials, July 5–6, 2005.

10. Interview with state official, July 6, 2005 (my emphasis).

11. DSP Genel Merkezi, *Ne İstedi, Nasıl Çıktı?* 33–34 (my emphases).

12. Ibid. (my emphases).

13. Ibid.

14. In fact, a similar committee had been utilized for the talks that ended the 1996 death fast.

15. The members of this committee were Orhan Pamuk, Yaşar Kemal, Oral Çalışlar, Can Dündar, Zülfü Livaneli, Enver Nalbant, and Mehmet Bekaroğlu. The prisoners were represented by Şadi Özbolat, Ercan Kartal, and Aydın Hanbayat.

16. Ecevit declared: "I wish them success in the *mission of humanity* they have undertaken. We will properly evaluate the information and suggestions they will bring us as a result of their observations." DSP Genel Merkezi, *Ne İstedi, Nasıl Çıktı,* 34 (my emphasis).

17. The members of this committee were Kamer Genç, Mehmet Bekaroğlu, Tunay Dikmen, and the commission secretary. The member of the ultranationalist MHP who chaired this committee was asked by the prisoners not to participate in the talks.

18. DSP Genel Merkezi, *Ne İstedi, Nasıl Çıktı,* 40–1.

19. Ibid.

20. The militant who conducted this attack was Ahmet Metin Koyuncu, allegedly a member of the illegal MLKP. *Sabah,* "Kimliği Parmak İzinden Bulundu."

21. The group of hunger strikers claimed that twenty-two-year-old Cafer Dereli was attacked by supporters of a fascist group from Turkey. *Hürriyet,* "Destek Orucu Kana Bulandı."

22. In this incident, Özkan Tekin was killed and two militants were wounded. *Yaşamda Atılım,* "Özkan, Cafer, Ahmet Hucrelere Barıkat."

23. All those organizations that issued the October 21 declaration about the premature launching of the hunger strike (with the exception of TKEP/L) now participated in the struggle by going on hunger strike.

24. TKP(ML) later admitted that the timing for the attack was wrong and would have been correct only if it had been conducted after the Operation Return to Life. In their critical assessment of the death fast struggle, the party conceded that their mistake gave ammunition to state propaganda against the death fast. See *Sınıf Teorisi,* "20 Ekim 2000," 43.

25. *Sabah*, "Polis de Yürüdü" and "Müdürlerini Çiğnediler."
26. The riot police make up a separate branch of the police force since 1983. They are responsible for establishing security and order at events such as political demonstrations, meetings, labor strikes, press conferences, protests, house demolitions, funeral processions, symposia, concerts, festivals, contests, and natural disasters.
27. *Hürriyet*, "Ecevit: Devlete Dayatma Kabul Edilemez."
28. Ibid.
29. Ibid.
30. At this point, the composition of this committee was slightly different than the one before. In addition to the prisoner representatives, the committee now comprised of Mehmet Bekaroğlu (member of parliament and the Human Rights Commission), Yücel Sayman (head of the Istanbul Bar Association), Metin Bakkalcı (associate president of the Turkish Medical Association), Kaya Güvenç (president of the Architects' and Engineers' Chambers Association of Turkey), Oral Çalışlar (columnist of the newspaper *Cumhuriyet*), Behiç Aşçı (lawyer representing many hunger strikers), and Tekin Tangün (president of the Solidarity Association for Families and Relatives of the Arrested [TAYAD]).
31. See Dündar, "Ölüm Koridoru." For excerpts from the transcriptions of the meetings, see *Kurtuluş Yolu*, "Ölüm Orucu Direnişinin Talepleri Üzerine Görüşme Tutanakları," 129–60.
32. *Hürriyet*, "Bekaroğlu: Ölüm Orucu Bugün Biter."
33. Ibid.
34. *Hürriyet*, "Ölüm Orucunda İpler Koptu."
35. DSP Genel Merkezi, *Ne İstedi, Nasıl Çıktı*, 51.
36. *Hürriyet*, "Ölüm Orucuna DGM Yasağı."
37. Although the issuing of parliamentary amnesties is not a new practice in Turkey, it is highly controversial. In the history of the Turkish republic, forty-three amnesties have been issued prior to this one, ranging from general and unconditional to partial and specialized amnesties and conditional releases. The 1982 Constitution foreclosed the issuing of a "general amnesty" (by Articles 14, 87, and 169). Prisoners convicted of crimes committed with the purpose of disrupting the "indivisible unity of the State with its country and nation," destroying basic rights

and liberties, harming the "democratic and secular republic" as well as burning, annihilating or contracting forests were deemed ineligible for amnesty (Constitution, http://www.anayasa.gov.tr/Mevzuat/Anayasa1982/). Last accessed November 15, 2013.

38. See TBMM, *Genel Kurul Tutanakları*, December 8, 2000, 443.

39. Ibid., 462.

40. Ibid., 482.

41. In fact, if the constitutional court decided that the bill contradicted the equality clause in the constitution, the effect would be to expand the scope of the law. In which case, prisoners convicted with "terror crimes," including prisoners associated with PKK, for example, might also benefit from conditional release.

42. TBMM, *Genel Kurul Tutanakları*, December 8, 2000, 447.

43. This firm stance was taken by the coalition government despite the ambivalence of Nationalist Action Party (MHP). Member of Parliament Mehmet Şandır, speaking on behalf of MHP, argued: "In this law's text . . . there are elements that we are not satisfied with, either. Forgive me, we are not the ones that made the promise to society, as MHP, we are not responsible for these mistakes, for this issue coming to this point." When a member of the opposition cut him off and said, "Don't give your vote, propose a motion, then," Şandır responded, "Of course, we are evaluating the issue from where we stand. We say, this problem, which demands urgency before society, which cannot be postponed, which becomes a problem for society, which leads to the polarization of society, its separation into fronts, which has the tendency to block the agenda of Turkey, has to be solved in some way and at once. Therefore, because of this necessity, we will support this bill, despite all our worries and objections" (ibid., 453–54).

44. Ibid., 465.

45. For example, capital punishment for crimes against the state could not be commuted even while capital punishment for murder in the first degree could.

46. Ibid., 467.

47. Ibid., 444 (my emphasis).

48. The expression "organization camp" is commonly used in Turkish political discourse to refer to the headquarters of "terrorist" parties. Ibid., 459.

382 3. The Biosovereign Assemblage and Its Tactics

49. In addition to the antiterror law, which stipulated that high security prisons would be allotted for prisoners held for terror crimes, Article 13 of the Law for the Struggle Against Interest Based Criminal Organizations promulgated in 1999 (Law No. 4422) added that those imprisoned for crimes according to this law should also be subject to Article 16 of the antiterror law. In other words, those imprisoned for crimes relating to the mafia and criminal gangs were also to be kept in high security institutions designated for terrorist offenders. Further, according to the Bylaw for the Execution of Sentences (Article 78/B), among those held for "ordinary" crimes, prisoners who created unrest, instigated uprisings, and were not responsive to "rehabilitation programs" in medium security prisons would also be transferred to these high security institutions.

50. DSP Genel Merkezi, *Ne İstedi, Nasıl Çıktı*, 33–34 (my emphases).

51. Sezer, "Türkiye Cumhurbaşkanlığı Belgesi," 32–33.

52. *Hürriyet*, "Her An Ölebilirler."

53. Devletoğlu, "Demir Leydi 20 Yıl Önce Söylemişti."

54. *Hürriyet*, "İşte Avrupa'nın F Tipi Raporu," and "Türkiye Haklı."

55. These prisons were Adana Kürkçüler, Ankara Ulucanlar, Aydın, Bartın, Sağmalcılar (Bayrampaşa), Buca, Bursa, Ceyhan, Çanakkale, Çankırı, Elbistan, Ermenek, Gebze, Kırşehir, Malatya, Nevşehir, Nazilli, Niğde, Uşak, and Ümraniye Prisons.

56. Interview with state official, July 5, 2005.

57. *Hürriyet*, "Düğmeye Böyle Basıldı."

58. *Sabah*, "Operasyonu Bir Yılda Hazırladık."

59. *Hürriyet*, "Türk: Şefkat Operasyonu."

60. Interview with state official, July 5, 2005.

61. Interviews with state officials, July 6–7, 2005.

62. Interview with state official, July 5, 2005.

63. Interview with state official, July 6, 2005.

64. Ibid.

65. Interview with state official, July 8, 2005.

66. DSP Genel Merkezi, *Ne İstedi, Nasıl Çıktı*, 58.

67. *Hürriyet*, "Operasyonun Bilançosu."

68. The prisons where the greatest resistance was put up against the operation were the Sağmalcılar and Ümraniye Prisons in Istanbul and the Çanakkale Prison.

69. 942 prisoners were taken to three F-type prisons put into immediate use: 308 prisoners were taken to Sincan F-type Prison in Ankara, 317 prisoners were taken to Edirne F-type Prison, and 317 prisoners were taken to Kocaeli F-type Prison. 95 female prisoners were taken to Bakırköy Women and Children's Prison and Kartal Special Type Prison. 237 prisoners were taken to hospitals. *Hürriyet*, "Hayata Dönüşün Bilançosu."

70. Interview with state official, July 5, 2005.

71. Upon visiting Sincan F-type Prison on December 22, 2000, in the immediate aftermath of the December 19 operation, ten lawyers issued a joint statement drawing attention to the severity of the prisoners' situation. Lawyers Kazım Bayraktar et al., "Basına ve Kamuya Açıklama." A direct testimony of Bilal Ertürk, who was imprisoned for alleged participation in street protests against the F-type prisons before the operation and discharged soon after being transferred to Sincan F-type Prison, confirmed the violent procedures of entry into the high security prison, procedures including severe beatings and degrading body searches. See Göktaş, "F Tipinde Üç Gün Yetti."

72. The report prepared by the Contemporary Lawyers' Association (ÇHD), based on the initial observations of lawyers and families, documented the prisoners' injuries due to exposure to violence during the operation. Çağdaş Hukukçular Derneği İstanbul Şubesi, *Cezaevleri Çalışma Komisyonu Raporu.*

73. İHD İstanbul Şubesi, *F Tipi Cezaevleri Raporu*, 3–5.

74. Bekaroğlu, *TBMM İnsan Hakları İnceleme Komisyonu Başkanlığı'na Sunulan Rapor.*

75. DSP, *Ne İstedi, Nasıl Çıktı*, 60 (my emphases).

76. In order to emphasize that only the unruly prisoners were transferred, the minister noted that the prisoners affiliated with PKK had been left in their wards. These prisoners were not participating in the death fast.

77. *Hürriyet*, "Cezaevlerindeki Terör Karargahları Temizlendi." However, according to Judge Taşkın at the Ministry of Justice, "it would be very wrong to reduce the reason for carrying out the Operation Return to Life to hunger strikes. Even if there had not been any hunger strike, a prison operation would have been carried out under a different name. The operation does not concern an event but the system; it is not destruction, but a transition; it is not the end to the hunger strike or a

similar event, but the beginning and end of a system." Taşkın, *Basında Cezaevleri ve Gerçekler*, 193.

78. The two soldiers who died in the operation were Nurettin Kurt and Mustafa Mutlu. It has been alleged that their deaths were caused by friendly fire.

79. Foucault, *Discipline and Punish*, 50, 58.

80. Bora, "'Hayata Dönüş' ve Medya," 45–47; Görmüş, "'Hayata Dönüş'te Medya"; Fatih Polat, "Bir Savaş ve Operasyon Gücü Olarak Medya"; Demirer and Özgür, "'Andıç'lı F-Tipi Medya."

81. *Milliyet*, "Sahte Oruç, Kanlı İftar."

82. *Hürriyet*, "Devlet Girdi."

83. Mengi, " Devlet Uyandı!"; Altaylı, "Halkı Anlasalardı Böyle Olmazdı!"; Ülsever, "Cezaevi Operasyonlarında Hükümeti Destekliyorum"; Çölaşan, "İnsan Hakları!"; Korkmaz, "Nihayet . . . ".

84. *Sabah*, "Sol Örgütlerin Cinnet Eylemi"; *Hürriyet*, "Yakılanlar Kurban" and "Kadın Militanı Yaktılar."

85. Kaliber, "F Tipi Gelişmeleri ve Cezaevleri Operasyonu," 97.

86. The alleged conversations over cell phones smuggled into prisons were considered suspect by various human rights groups because they contained expressions used primarily by the police. Cell phone companies also announced that they had shut off communications in the area of the Sağmalcılar Prison, Bayrampaşa, Istanbul, when the operation began. TİHV, "Ölüm Orucuna Müdahale Devam Ediyor."

87. DSP Genel Merkezi, *Ne İstedi, Nasıl Çıktı*, 58.

88. Right before the operation, there were 287 prisoners on the death fast and 1,269 prisoners on hunger strike, making a total of 1,556 prisoners. Taşkın, *Basında Cezaevleri ve Gerçekler*, 386. On December 26 the number of prisoners on hunger strike was reported as 1,596, of whom those on the death fast numbered 432. Türk, "Press Conference."

89. *Yaşadığımız Vatan*, "Şişli Emniyet Müdürlüğüne Yönelik Feda Eylemi," 8–9.

90. Until the 1970s, artificial feeding has been a major tool used by governments around the world for the termination of hunger strikes. This practice goes back to the early 1900s, when British suffragettes on hunger strike were resuscitated with this method. A major turning point in this policy occurred when two prisoners (the Price sisters)

sued the Ministry of Interior Affairs in Britain for nonconsensual feeding. Government policy changed after the British Medical Association adopted the position that no doctor could be pressured to perform nonconsensual medical intervention and that the final decision on intervention should be left to individual doctors. As a result of this shift, the Provisional IRA militants on hunger strike in 1976 and 1981 were not subjected to artificial feeding, resulting in casualties. Elsewhere, artificial feeding is still being used. For example, GRAPO militants were artificially fed in the 1989 hunger strike in Spain, Moroccan militants were artificially fed in their 1990 hunger strike, and prisoners on hunger strike at Guantánamo Bay were artificially fed in 2002 and 2005.

91. DSP, *Ne İstedi, Nasıl Çıktı*, 60 (my emphasis).

92. Artificial feeding in Turkey was first sanctioned by an executive decree (No: 25–167) issued by the Ministry of Justice on December 31, 1997, as a response to the 1996 death fast that ended with a death toll of twelve prisoners. Accordingly, those prisoners on hunger strike whom the doctors find to be at risk of death or to have lost consciousness can be artificially fed.

93. For the ethics of treating hunger strikers, see Johannes Weir Foundation for Health and Human Rights, *Assistance in Hunger Strikes*; Annas, "Hunger Strikes"; Keeton, "Hunger Strikers"; Fessler, "The Implications of Starvation Induced Psychological Changes."

94. World Medical Association, *Declaration of Tokyo.*

95. World Medical Association, *Declaration of Malta on Hunger Strikers.*

96. *Hürriyet,* "Müdahale Etmeyen Hekime Soruşturma Açılacak"; World Medical Association, "WMA Warned About Mounting Campaign Against Turkish Doctors."

97. Lewey, "Force-Feeding"; Thorborn, "Croaker's Dilemma"; "The Law and Force-Feeding"; Gregory, "Personal Views."

98. Dr. Metin Bakkalcı, interview by Beraç Günçıkan.

99. Türk Tabipleri Birliği Merkez Konseyi, "Cezaevleri" and "Cezaevlerindeki Açlık Grevleri İçin Acil Çağrı Metni"; Soyer, "Açlık Grevleri/Ölüm Oruçları."

100. Hatun, "Ölüm Oruçları ve Hekimlik."

101. Oguz and Miles, "The Physician and Prison Hunger Strikes," 171 (my emphasis).

102. İnsan Hakları Derneği, *Ölüm Oruçları*. Of these individuals subject to interventions, eleven individuals suffered memory loss, six were diagnosed with Korsakoff syndrome and another with Korsakoff psychosis.

103. The amendment to the Turkish Penal Code and the Law for the Administration of Prisons (Law No. 4806), passed on February 5, 2003, upheld medical intervention on those whose life is endangered or whose consciousness is lost in a hunger strike or death fast, regardless of the consent of the prisoner concerned. The same law stipulated that those preventing the nourishment of prisoners (including those who encourage or convince prisoners to conduct hunger strike) would be punished with two to four years of imprisonment. In case death followed such action, the sentence would be increased to ten to twenty years (Article 307/b in Penal Code). The same stipulations were adopted in the new Turkish Penal Code (Law No. 5237) passed on September 26, 2004 (Türk Ceza Kanunu, www.tbmm.gov.tr/kanunlar/k5237.html). Last accessed November 2012.

104. See *Yaşadığımız Vatan*, "Polis Otosuna Silahlı Saldırı," 39.

105. The prisoners survived for much longer durations on this hunger strike in comparison to previous fasting experiences (where the horizon of survival was restricted to forty to seventy days) mainly because they supplemented their otherwise restricted diet with vitamin B1.

106. For a list of the names of the dead, see table 6.1.

107. Foucault, *Discipline and Punish*, 256, 269.

108. The antiterror law was amended on May 1, 2001, and this amendment went in effect on May 5, 2001, when it was published in the Official Gazette No. 24393.

109. The law for these specialized courts (Law No. 4675) was passed in the parliament on May 16, 2001, and was put in effect with its publication in the Official Gazette No. 24410 on May 23, 2001. With this law, 140 new courts were established. The law for monitoring boards (Law No. 4681) was passed on June 14, 2001, and went into effect on June 21, 2001 with its publication in the Official Gazette No. 24439; 130 monitoring boards have been established since then. For a complete list of changes introduced by the Ministry of Justice as part of the "penal reform" in the fields of legislation, prison construction, and educational services to personnel, see ABCTGM, "Cezaevi Reformu Çalışmaları ve İnsan Hakları."

110. One of the vocal critics of this proposal was Mehmet Bekaroğlu, a member of the parliament's Human Rights Commission and part of the committee conducting the talks with the prisoners before December 19, 2000. While he welcomed the establishment of monitoring boards, he argued that these should be comprised of members not appointed by the state but chosen out of a list proposed by civil society institutions in the province of the relevant prison. He argued that the selection procedure of who would serve on these boards, as outlined in the current proposal, was based on the Justice Commission (upon recommendations by the governor of that province), which meant, in effect, that they would be appointed by the state. As such, he argued, the members would be like civil servants and greatly limited in their actions. See TBMM, *Genel Kurul Tutanakları,* June 12, 2001, 53.

111. İnsan Hakları ve Mazlumlar için Dayanışma Derneği Cezaevleri Komisyonu, *Cezaevi...*

112. Türk, "Press Conference," and Taşkın, *Basında Cezaevleri ve Gerçekler,* 32.

4. Prisoners in Revolt

1. *Devrimci Demokrasi,* "Devrimci Tutsaklar Teslim Alınamaz!"
2. Interview with a participant of the death fast, May 23, 2005.
3. Marx and Engels, "The German Ideology," 47.
4. Interviews with participants of the death fast, February 15, May 18, and May 23, 2005.
5. Interview with a participant of the death fast, May 23, 2005.
6. Interview with a participant of the death fast, February 15, 2005.
7. Interview with a participant of the death fast, January 24, 2005.
8. Interview with a participant of the death fast, February 15, 2005.
9. De Certeau, *The Practice of Everyday Life.*
10. Interview with a participant of the death fast, May 22, 2005.
11. Yılmaz, *İçimizdeki Hapishane.* On the problem of the widespread use of violence in factional conflict within the radical left, see Boyoğlu, *Ölümden Öte.*
12. Interviews with participants of the death fast, February 15, May 18, and May 23, 2005.

13. Lefebvre, *The Production of Space.*

14. According to Wacquant, we can find the phenomenon of "advanced marginality" produced through the uneven development and forms of exclusion that operate in urban centers of post-Fordist economies. This marginality, as a structural position, is not unlike the marginality of these prisons vis-à-vis the public sphere, even though economic factors are not the main determinants of the exclusion of prisoners. However, Wacquant associates advanced marginality with a loss of a positive identification with space as a source of identity. By contrast, in the case of prison wards, the radicalization of identity through a positive and intense identification with space becomes the driving force of violent forms of self-expression. See Wacquant, "The Rise of Advanced Marginality."

15. Gould, *Insurgent Identities.*

16. On the concept of constituent power, see Negri, *Insurgencies.* However, the spatial dimension of constituent power has not been fully explored. A notable exception is Schmitt, *The Nomos of the Earth.*

17. On the spatialities of resistance, see Pile and Keith, *Geographies of Resistance.*

18. Öztürk, *Türkiye Solunun Hapishane Tarihi,* 123–24.

19. Coşkun, "Nâzım Hikmet'in Açlık Grevi," 16.

20. Öztürk, *Türkiye Solunun Hapishane Tarihi,* 224.

21. Fişekçi, "Nâzım Hikmet'i Açlık Grevine Götüren Yol," 9.

22. Coşkun, "Nâzım Hikmet'in Açlık Grevi," 31; Öztürk, *Türkiye Solunun Hapishane Tarihi,* 226–27.

23. Behram, *Darağacında Üç Fidan,* 94–95.

24. Ibid., 96–97.

25. For testimonies of former political prisoners from various prisons since the 1980s, see Mavioğlu, *Asılmayıp da Beslenenler.* For testimonies of female political prisoners of three generations, see Çelik, *Demir Parmaklıklar Ortak Düşler.*

26. Bozyel, *Diyarbakır 5 Nolu;* Zana, *Prison No. 5;* Zeydanlıoğlu, "The Period of Barbarity"; Çürükkaya, *12 Eylül Karanlığında Diyarbakır Şafağı;* Welat, *Auschwitz'den Diyarbakır'a 5 No'lu Cezaevi;* Kısacık, *İşkence ve Ölümün Adresi;* Miroğlu, *Dijwar.*

27. Kukul, *Bir Direniş Odağı Metris.*

28. Bora, "Hapishane Rejimi," 17, 20.

29. "Political" wards stood in stark contrast with the wards of the "independents," where militants who had broken down under interrogation in police custody (usually involving torture) or those who would like to break away from their organizational affiliations were placed during the military coup. See Mavioğlu, *Asılmayıp da Beslenenler*, 60.

30. Interview with families of participants of the death fast, January 20 and May 18, 2005.

31. İnsan Hakları Derneği, *1981–1995 Cezaevlerinde Yaşamını Yitirenler*.

32. Yetkin and Tanboğa, *Dörtlerin Gecesi*; and Yüce, *12 Eylül Sömürgeci-Faşist Rejimine Karşı Diyarbakır Zindan Direnişi*.

33. Mavioğlu, *Asılmayıp da Beslenenler*, 109–10. On Mamak, also see Dönmez, *Mamak . . . Ey Mamak*.

34. Interview with a participant of the death fast, May 31, 2005.

35. See Kukul, *Bir Direniş Odağı Metris*, and Karataş et al., *12 Eylül'de Direniş Ölüm ve Yaşam*.

36. ABCTGM, *1 Ağustos Genelgesi*, July 7, 1988. On this also see Mavioğlu, *Asılmayıp da Beslenenler*, 309–10.

37. Şeşen, *Tutsak Aileleri*.

38. İHD İstanbul Şubesi, *Sessiz Çığlık*, 102.

39. Kanar, "Azaphane ya da Cezaevleri," 70.

40. Mavioğlu, *Asılmayıp da Beslenenler*, 311; TİHV, *İşkence Dosyası*.

41. See TİHV, *Türkiye İnsan Hakları Raporu '91*, 109–16.

42. For the various decrees, see ABCTGM, *Genelgeler*, May 6, 1996, May 9, 1996, and September 29, 1997.

43. Council of Europe, *Report to the Turkish Government on the Visit to Turkey Carried Out by the European CPT from 19 to 23 August 1996*.

44. Several accounts of 1996's resistance are available. See, for example, *Direniş Ölüm ve Yaşam-II*; Okuyucu, *'96 Ölüm Orucu*; Uğur, *Zafere Mahkum Edilenler Ölümü Küçülterek Yenerler*; and Yılmaz, *Ölümü Yenenleri Kimse Yenemez*. As the 2000 death fast began, the family organization of the prisoners published a brief pamphlet to remind the public of what had happened in 1996. TAYAD, "12 İnsan."

45. Interview with a participant of the death fast, May 29, 2005.

46. In 1999, when Kemal Ertürk and Bülent Ertürk, two prisoners under arrest as the suspects of the assassination upon the Governor of Çankırı, were transferred to Eskişehir Special Type Prison from Ankara Central Closed Prison, they went on hunger strike. The CCP coordinated

prisoners around the country to create greater pressure on the Ministry of Justice by acts such as resisting counts, invading different sections of their prisons, and taking wardens hostage. Forty-three wardens were taken hostage overall. These actions came to an end when the demands of the CCP were met. Interviews with participants of the death fast, April 22, May 22, and May 29, 2005.

47. For a narrative of the prisoner resistance at Ulucanlar Prison, see Bektaş, *Zafere Halay*; and TAYAD, "Yalanları Parçalayan Ulucanlar Katliamı." For a collection of accounts of the operation by lawyers, see Bayraktar et al., *Ulucanlar*. For a list of allegations of other infractions on prisoner rights during this period, see Özgür TAYAD, "Hapishaneler Gerçeği."

48. TBMM İnsan Haklarını İnceleme Komisyonu, *26 Eylül Ulucanlar Cezaevi Raporu*, especially 112–20.

49. Interview with a participant of the death fast, May 29, 2005. In order not to hasten the looming security operation on all prisons, the CCP did not coordinate prison riots across the country when the security operation in Burdur Prison took place. Other tactics, such as boycotting court appearances, were pursued.

50. TKP(ML) was later renamed as MKP.

51. *Devrimci Demokrasi*, "Devrimci Tarihi(ni) Unutma . . .!" 3.

52. *Devrimci Demokrasi*, "Devrimci Tutsaklar Teslim Alınamaz!" 8.

53. These three organizations made up over two-thirds of the prison population on the Turkish left, corresponding to over one thousand individuals.

54. *Kızılbayrak*, "Hücre Saldırısını Püskürtmenin Sorunları ve Sorumlulukları."

55. *Kızılbayrak*, "Hücre Saldırısı ve Yeni Zindan Direnişi."

56. Interview with a participant of the death fast, May 10, 2005.

57. *Devrimci Demokrasi*, "Devrimci Tarihi(ni) Unutma! . . . " 3; *Kızılbayrak*, "Hücre Saldırısı ve Yeni Zindan Direnişi."

58. *Alınterimiz*, "Faşizm Hücre Tipi Cezaevi Hükmünü Yürütüyor," 1.

59. *Yaşamda Atılım*, "Ölüm Hücrelerini Yıkacağız," 1, 9.

60. *Ufuk Çizgisi*, "Ölüm Orucu Değerlendirmesi (II)."

61. Ibid.

62. Interview with a participant of the death fast, January 24, 2005.

63. Interview with a participant of the death fast, July 1, 2005.

64. Interview with a participant of the death fast, February 15, 2005.

65. Saçılık, "Burdur Saldırısı Planın Bir Parçasıydı"; *Devrimci Demokrasi*, "Saldırı F Tipi Projesinin Provasıdır," 16 and "F Tipine Geçişin Provası ve Burdur Direnişi," 12; *Yaşamda Atılım*, "Buca'da Burdur Provası," 5; *Ufuk Çizgisi*, "Ölüm Orucu Değerlendirmesi (II)."

66. *Devrimci Demokrasi*, "Devrimciliğin Yeniden Sınandığı Keskin Bir Dönemeçten Geçiyoruz," 3.

67. *Ufuk Çizgisi*, "Ölüm Orucu Değerlendirmesi (II)."

68. *Yaşadığımız Vatan*, "Hapishanelere Yönelik Provokasyonlara Tutsaklardan Tepki," 21.

69. Anderson, "'To Lie Down to Death for Days,'" 820.

70. *Devrimci Demokrasi*, "Süresiz Açlık Grevi Direnişi Başladı," 1; TAYAD Komite Nederland, *Documentation on the* Death Fast *in Turkey*; TİHV, *2001 Türkiye İnsan Hakları Raporu*.

71. *Bağımsız Vatan*, "Direniş Tarihimize Onurla Yazılan Yeni Sayfalar Eklemeye Devam Ediyoruz," 5, 12–13; *Devrimci Demokrasi*, "Direniş Tarihimize Onurla Yazılan Yeni Sayfalar Eklemeye Devam Ediyoruz," 13. The participation of prisoners associated with TKİP was announced separately. *Kızılbayrak*, "Öleceğiz ama hücrelere girmeyeceğiz! . . ." 1; *Yaşadığımız Vatan*, October 30, 2000, 5, 16.

72. *Bağımsız Vatan*, "Direniş Tarihimize Onurla Yazılan Yeni Sayfalar Eklemeye Devam Ediyoruz," 5, 12–13; *Devrimci Demokrasi*, "Direniş Tarihimize Onurla Yazılan Yeni Sayfalar Eklemeye Devam Ediyoruz," 13.

73. Ibid.

74. Ibid.

75. Ibid.

76. State security courts were established according to Article 143 of the 1982 Constitution, which assigned them the responsibility of dealing with "offences against the indivisible integrity of the State with its territory and nation, the free democratic order, or against the Republic whose characteristics are defined in the Constitution, and offences directly involving the internal and external security of the State." Constitution of the Republic of Turkey, www.anayasa.gov.tr/Mevzuat/Anayasa1982/. Last accessed November 15, 2013.

77. ABCTGM, *Protokol*, January 14, 2000. Available in İHD İstanbul Şubesi, *Sessiz Çığlık*, 30–50.

78. Established in 1992, All Judicial and Penal Institutions Employees' Union has ten thousand members working in the justice system, ranging from prisons to the Ministry of Justice and the Constitutional Court. The trade union is organized as part of the Confederation of Public Laborers' Trade Unions (KESK).

79. While the Kurdish prisoners lent support to the death fast of 1996, this did not happen in 2000. Instead, the Kurds distanced themselves from the death fast struggle. Their position on the 2000 death fast was summarized by their leader, writing with the pseudonym Ali Yılmaz in "F Tipleri, Devlet, Sol ve PKK Açısından Cezaevleri."

80. *Yaşadığımız Vatan*, October 30, 2000, 4.

81. Interviews with participants of the death fast, February 15, April 17, and May 23, 2005.

82. Yücel, "Galatasaray."

83. The Intelligentsia and Artist Initiative Against the F-type Prison (F-Tipi Cezaevine Karşı Aydın ve Sanatçı Girişimi) was comprised of intellectuals such as İlhan Selçuk, Adalet Ağaoğlu, Oral Çalışlar, Halil Ergün, Gencay Gürsoy, Ercan Karakaş, Yaşar Kemal, Zülfü Livaneli, Orhan Pamuk, and Eşber Yağmurdereli.

84. The proceedings of this conference are available: TAYAD, "Hapishaneler Gerçeği, Yaşanan Sorunlar ve Çözüm Önerileri Kurultayı."

85. See *Yaşadığımız Vatan*, December 11, 2000, 34.

86. For the full text of this declaration, see *Yaşadığımız Vatan*, November 20, 2000, 6.

87. *Yaşamda Atılım*, "Uyarı Hepimize!" 1.

88. *Ufuk Çizgisi*, "Ölüm Orucu Değerlendirmesi (V)."

89. *Yaşadığımız Vatan*, December 11, 2000, 6.

90. *Yaşadığımız Vatan*, December 4, 2000, 49; *Devrimci Demokrasi*, "Avrupa'da Tutsaklarla Dayanışma Eylemleri Sürüyor," December 1–16, 2000, 19.

91. *Evrensel*, "Cezaevlerinde Ölüm Engellensin."

92. For a self-critique issued by TKP(ML) on this attack, see *Sınıf Teorisi*, "20 Ekim 2000," 43.

93. İHD İstanbul Şubesi, "Ölum Oruçlarına İlişkin Ön Rapor"; Çağdaş Hukukçular Derneği İstanbul Şubesi, "19.12.2000 Tarihinde Başlatılan Cezaevleri Operasyonu."

94. *Hürriyet,* "Hayata Dönüşün Bilançosu." It is also noteworthy that although thirty prisoners died in these operations, the Death Fast Struggle only claims twenty-eight of these deaths as its "martyrs" (see table 6.1). The two other prisoners who died, Haydar Akbaba and Muharrem Buldukoğlu, have allegedly been killed by other prisoners while Operation Return to Life was taking place at Ümraniye Prison in Istanbul. These prisoners, who were allegedly executed as "enemies of the people," were affiliated with MLKP, which later issued a self-critique about these executions in 2004, retracting the "false" accusations about them and restoring their names by the affirmation that these two prisoners were still in the revolutionary ranks when they died. See Özcan, "Akbaba ve Buldukoğlu'yu Hapiste Kim Öldürdü?"

95. For an overview of the report concerning Sağmalcılar (Bayrampaşa) Prison, where twelve prisoners were killed, see the newspaper article by Şık, "Gerçeğe Dönüş." For a detailed list of the causes of death for each prisoner, see Şık, "İşte Böyle Öldüler." According to the autopsy reports, only seven prisoners have died directly because they set themselves on fire while the remaining twenty-three were fatally shot, burned, or suffocated. These reports also proved that the prison scenes were not kept "as is" for legal inspection after the operation. Instead, some spots with large pools of blood were covered with cement or piles of books and other furniture, suggesting tampering with evidence to conceal the disproportionate use of violence. After the operation, Minister of Justice Türk claimed that prisoners had fired upon security forces with Kalashnikov guns and burned themselves to death. Minister of Interior Affairs Sadettin Tantan argued that no weapons were used by security forces, whereas prisoners utilized Kalashnikov guns, hunting guns, and hand grenades. See *Radikal,* "'Mahkumlar Ateş Etti' Demişlerdi." Tantan also revealed that the operation had been planned weeks before it actually took place and that the gendarmes were well-trained (using model prisons), putting into doubt the sincerity and value of negotiations with the prisoners. Keskin, "Resmi Yalanlar."

96. *Yaşadığımız Vatan,* "Şişli Emniyet Müdürlüğüne Yönelik Feda Eylemi," 8–9.

97. İHD İstanbul Şubesi, "Press Release on January 20, 2001" and "Press Release on February 8, 2001," in *F Tipi Cezaevleri Raporu 2.*

98. See Tüm Yargı-Sen Genel Merkez Yönetim Kurulu, "Sendikamıza Yönelik Baskılar." Courtesy of Oral Çalışlar.

99. "Partiler, Dergiler, Yazarlar Ne Dediler?"; *Yaşadığımız Vatan*, "Sol Ne Tarafta?" "ÖDP, Kaçınılmaz Tartışmayı Yaşıyor," and "ÖDP: Ölüm Orucu Gündemimiz Değil." Also available in Kartal, *Büyük Direniş ve Sol*, 84–93, 118–21, 203–5.

100. Güler, "Sola Dair," 3.

101. Özgür, "Terörize Et ve Yönet."

102. Laçiner, "'Hayata Dönüş!'" 14.

103. Ibid., 15.

104. Devecioğlu, "'Biz'den Uzaklaşan Hapishaneler," 41.

105. Ibid. For a critical exchange on these essays, see Uygun, "Hapishaneler Üzerine"; Poyraz, "Ömer Laçiner'e Mektup"; Laçiner, "Cevap Yerine."

106. *Devrimci Demokrasi*, "F Tipi Ölüm Hücrelerinde Direniş Büyüyor," 1.

107. *Yaşamda Atılım*, "Ölürüz ama Teslim Olmayız," 2.

108. *Yaşadığımız Vatan*, "F Tiplerinde İşkence," 4.

109. Türk, "Press Conference."

110. Even though prisoners associated with Kurdish nationalism, generally imprisoned for cases related to the outlawed PKK, did *not* participate in the death fast struggle (except for marginal support), there was one faction on the Kurdish left actively supporting the death fast struggle. This was a splinter group called Revolutionary Line Warriors (Devrimci Çizgi Savaşçıları) that had broken off from PKK after the capture and imprisonment of Abdullah Öcalan, the party leader. Prisoners of the PKK-DÇS group began a hunger strike of indefinite duration on December 3, 2000. *Yaşadığımız Vatan*, December 11, 2000, 37. Among prisoners associated with the Kurdish struggle, only members of this group were transferred to F-type prisons, along with others from the Turkish left.

111. Cf. Anderson, "'To Lie Down to Death for Days,'" 820.

112. *Yaşadığımız Vatan*, March 25, 2001, 14.

113. Interviews with participants of the death fast, January 20, February 15, April 17, and May 31, 2005.

114. The latter situation arises when the termination of the hunger strike lacks the appropriate vitamin B1 support. When sugary liquids are fed into the body through the veins, without additional thiamin, the already critical levels of thiamin in the body are depleted in the process-

ing of sugar, giving rise to the Wernicke-Korsakoff disorder. For an important study on the issue, see Gökmen,"Mayıs 1996 Açlık Grevi-Ölüm Orucu Katılımcılarının Klinik Değerlendirilmesi." Other relevant medical studies on former hunger strikers and death fasters from Turkey reveal the full range of damage due to Wernicke-Korsakoff, despite the use of B1. Gürvit et al., "Hunger-Strike Related Wernicke-Korsakoff Disease"; Başoğlu et al., "Neurological Complications of Prolonged Hunger Strike"; Kınay et al.,"Early and Late Stage EEG Findings in Wernicke-Korsakoff Syndrome."

115. The most common symptoms of the Wernicke-Korsakoff syndrome are confusion, attention deficit, disorientation, vision impairment, hypothermia, hypotension, ataxia, and amnesia. Wernicke and Korsakoff can be diagnosed separately as two different disorders, but they are generally considered to be different stages of the same disorder, Wernicke being the acute phase while Korsakoff is the chronic. Korsakoff syndrome tends to develop as Wernicke's symptoms diminish. Wernicke's encephalopathy is mainly associated with damage to the central nervous system whereas Korsakoff psychosis is mainly associated with the impairment of memory. Mayda, "Wernicke-Korsakoff Hastalığı ve Rehabilitasyonu."

116. Ufuk Çizgisi, "Ölüm Orucu Değerlendirmesi (VI)."

117. Ufuk Çizgisi, "Ölüm Orucu Değerlendirmesi (VII)."

118. Ibid.

119. Ufuk Çizgisi, "Ölüm Orucu Değerlendirmesi (VII)."

120. When the declaration was first published at the end of May 2001, it was signed, rather vaguely, by "All Detainees and Convicts in Resistance." A week later, however, it was republished, with the signatures of ten organizations now part of the movement. The list of signatories comprised DHKP-C, TKP(ML), TKİP, TKP/ML, TİKB, DH, TDP, MLKP, DY, and THKP-C/MLSPB. For the former version, Yaşadığımız Vatan, May 28, 2001, 12. For the latter, see Yaşadığımız Vatan, June 4, 2001, 6.

121. The publication of the diary of a hunger striker who suffered from memory loss due to medical intervention is a poignant testimony to this problem. See Sadiç, Puslu Aydınlık.

122. The antiterror law was amended on May 1, 2001, and this amendment went in effect on May 5, 2001, when it was published in the Official Gazette No. 24393.

123. The law for the specialized courts (Law No. 4675) was passed in the parliament on May 16, 2001, and was put in effect with its publication in the Official Gazette No. 24410 on May 23, 2001. The law for monitoring boards (Law No. 4681) was passed on June 14, 2001, and went into effect on June 21, 2006, with its publication in the Official Gazette No. 24439. However, political prisoners considered these changes to be superficial gestures that did not address the real problem. Instead, they argued, these "reforms" further entrenched the F-type prisons and provided no basis for addressing their concerns. For a critique of these special courts prepared by the Izmir Bar Association with actual examples of their stipulations, see İzmir Barosu, "İnfaz Hakimlikleri."

124. Hundreds of prisoners were eligible due to the effects of self-starvation. See Taşkın, *Basında Cezaevleri ve Gerçekler,* 32.

125. Interview with a participant of the death fast, May 29, 2005.

126. The headline of the newspaper *Sabah* on the day of the raid announced the impending operation: "This Is Istanbul, Not Palestine." Hopalı, "Burası Filistin Değil Istanbul."

127. Erdoğan, Sayman, and Özkan, "Open Letter"; Erdoğan (president of the Ankara Bar Association), Acar (president of the Antalya Bar Association), Sayman (president of the Istanbul Bar Association), and Özkan (president of the Izmir Bar Association), "Üç Kapı, Üç Kilit"; and İstanbul Barosu Merkez Kurulu ve Meslek Odaları Merkez Kurulları, "Statement on the Death Fasts in Prisons." Courtesy of Yücel Sayman.

128. Of these individuals, 8 were on hunger strike of indefinite duration and   142 were on the death fast. By the end of 2001, 182 convicted prisoners had received reprieve on their sentences and were discharged from prison according to Criminal Procedural Code Article 399 and 71 prisoners under arrest were discharged from prison by court decisions at their ongoing trials. Türk, "Press Conference." In addition, the president had pardoned another 25 prisoners based on Article 104 of the Constitution. In the following months this policy would be continued. By October 2004 the number of prisoners discharged went up to 660 (out of which 189 were permanently pardoned by the president, 391 received postponements of their sentences, renewable every six months, and 80 were released by court decisions). See Taşkın, *Basında Cezaevleri ve Gerçekler,* 32.

129. A list of signatory organizations and individuals to the proposal appeared in print: *Cumhuriyet,* "Ölümleri Durdurmak İçin Bir Çözüm."

Different branches of the trade unions, as well as union confederations such as DİSK and Türk-İş also issued a press release announcing their support on January 11, 2002. For news articles about the approach of the prisoners versus the Minister of Justice, see *Evrensel*, "Üç Kapı Üç Kilit Tartışması"; and *Cumhuriyet*, "'Üç Kapı Üç Kilit'e Ret."

130. Adalet Bakanlığı, "İstanbul, Ankara, İzmir ve Antalya Barolarının Birlikte Hazırladıkları 'Üç Kapı Üç Kilit Projesi.'"

131. Kansu, "'3 Kapı 3 Anahtar' Teşvikçi Önerisi."

132. TKP(ML)-affiliated ex-prisoners withdrew from the death fast outside in January 2002; MLKP affiliated ex-prisoners followed suit in May 2002. DHKP-C affiliated ex-prisoners and TAYAD members continued. *Devrimci Demokrasi*, "Alibeyköy Direniş Evi," 8; *Evrensel*, "Bir Grup Tutuklu Ölüm Orucunu Bitirdi," 15.

133. Kama et al., "Halkımıza!" 9.

134. *Ekmek ve Adalet*, no. 11 (3 June 2002), 5.

135. With the 2002 general elections, the parliament's composition had greatly changed. The coalition government of Democratic Left Party (DSP), Motherland Party (ANAP), and Nationalist Action Party (MHP) was now replaced by the majority government of Justice and Development Party (AKP) under the leadership of Recep Tayyip Erdoğan, with 354 out of the 550 seats in the parliament. The major party in opposition was Republican People's Party (CHP) led by Deniz Baykal. Of the previous coalition, neither the Democratic Left Party nor the Nationalist Action Party could enter parliament, having received less than 10 percent of the votes of the general electorate. Motherland Party, from the previous government, obtained only twenty seats in this parliament.

136. Aşçı had his "last supper" as part of the ceremony initiating him into revolutionary martyrdom with a large circle of militants, colleagues, friends, and members of TAYAD on April 4, 2006. His red headband was tied by Ahmet Kulaksız, the father of two militant-martyr Canan and Zehra, both of whom had fasted outside prison walls. See the news article in *Istanbul Indymedia*, "Devrimci Avukat Behiç Aşçı Ölüm Orucunda."

137. Behiç Aşçı, "Letter to the Public," quoted in Temelkuran, *Ne Anlatayım Ben Sana!* 155–59.

138. Behiç Aşçı, interviewed by Ahmet Tulgar, in Aşçı, "'Bu 10 Dakikada Çözülecek Sorun.'"

139. *Istanbul Indymedia*, "Devrimci Avukat Behiç Aşçı Ölüm Orucunda."

140. Ibid.

141. Aşçı is a respected member of the Istanbul Bar Association, he serves on the general board of the progressive Contemporary Lawyers' Association (ÇHD) and he has worked in the activist bureau called the People's Law Bureau (Halkın Hukuk Bürosu) since 1994.

142. Interviews with human rights defenders, June 11, June 17, June 20, 2005.

143. Laçiner, "Hayata Dönüş!" 15; *Ufuk Çizgisi*, "Ölüm Orucu Değerlendirmesi (VII)."

144. Interviews with human rights defenders, June 21, June 25, July 1, 2005.

145. There is a substantial body of research that confirms the negative health implications of solitary confinement. See, among others, Andersen et al., "A Longitudinal Study of Prisoners on Remand"; Glancy and Murray, "Psychiatric Aspects of Solitary Confinement"; Haney, "Mental Health Issues"; Hrassian, "Psychopathological Effects of Solitary Confinement"; Miller and Young, "Prison Segregations"; Rhodes, "Pathological Effects of the Supermaximum Prison."

146. Aşçı, "'Bu 10 Dakikada Çözülecek Sorun."

147. düzkan, *behiç aşçı kitabı*, 63–64.

148. Kalyvas, "Hegemonic Sovereignty."

149. Aşçı, "Behiç Aşçı Kimdir?"

150. Similarly, in the speech he gave at his red headband ceremony, Aşçı explained: "Why did I volunteer for the death fast? There are many things to be said. Imperialism, attacks against the peoples of the world, the oppression, terror, isolation, and censorship in Turkey. But one of the reasons of utmost determining significance from my perspective arises because I take up this problem as a problem of conscience. One hundred and twenty-one people have fallen martyr. I know a great many of them. I participated in their funerals. All of this accumulated. In a place where all this was lived, it would have been a lack of conscience to be cut off from this process." See *Istanbul Indymedia*, "Devrimci Avukat Behiç Aşçı Ölüm Orucunda."

151. In the interview by Tulgar, Aşçı distinguished the death fast from an act of suicide as follows: "If I had thought that the death fast was an act of suicide, I would throw myself down from here and at least I would not have to endure the pains induced by hunger. It is not like that, we have a demand at stake. I don't have an intention to die, neither did the 122 people who have died until today. I want to live, too. But the

problem is how and in what way we shall live. If what is demanded from lawyers like myself is to turn [our] back against the living conditions of our clients, we can never accept such a life." See Aşçı, "Bu 10 Dakikada Çözülecek Sorun." Also see ayşe düzkan, *behiç aşçı kitabı,* 42.

152. Temelkuran, *Ne Anlatayım Ben Sana!* 161.

153. This irony finds expression in the hunger striker's desire to be the final sacrifice in the death fast, the "sacrifice to end all sacrifice," the last death that wins a victory for the movement. Fatma Koyupınar was the last death faster to die in the struggle. She passed away on April 27, 2006, three weeks after Behiç Aşçı began fasting. On May 1, 2006, Sevgi Saymaz began her fast unto death. In Sevgi Saymaz's words: "Fatma had said, 'Let me be the last.' Now I am saying the same thing. But the only condition for this is the abolition of isolation." Saymaz, "Tecridin Sona Erdirilmesi Talebiyle."

154. The declaration stated, "Aşçı has started his "death fast" action in his home in Istanbul with the demand of abolishing isolation. Both inside prisons and outside, the death fast action against isolation continues. The health and life of all of them is in danger. . . . The voice of lawyer Behiç Aşçı, who has put his life on the line in order to defend his clients' right to live, must be attended to." For the full declaration, see "Tecrit İşkencedir!"

155. Temelkuran, *Ne Anlatayım Ben Sana!* 152.

156. ABCTGM, *Genelge 45/1,* January 22, 2007.

5. Marxism, Martyrdom, Memory

1. "Iran: The Spirit of a World Without Spirit," 255.
2. *Sosyalizm ve Toplumsal Mücadeleler Ansiklopedisi,* vol. 7.
3. Aydınoğlu, *Türk Solu.*
4. Cinemre and Çakır, *Sol Kemalizme Bakıyor.*
5. Samim, "The Tragedy of the Turkish Left," 63–64.
6. Stephenson, "Kemalizmden Sonra Sol Nereye?"
7. Samim, "The Tragedy of the Turkish Left," 67.
8. Atılgan, *Yön-Devrim Hareketi,* 52–60; Şener, *Türkiye Solunda Üç Tarz-ı Siyaset,* 77–171; Kahraman, "Türk Solunun Çıkmaz Sokağı," 48–53.
9. Landau, *Radical Politics in Modern Turkey,* 122–70; Lipovsky, *The Socialist Movement in Turkey,* 21–48; Şener, *Türkiye Solunda üç Tarz-ı Siyaset,* 301–24.

10. Boran, *İki Açıdan Türkiye İşçi partisi Davası*, 8off. Also see Karpat, "Socialism and the Labor Party of Turkey."

11. Aren, *TİP Olayı (1961–1971)*.

12. Lipovsky, *The Socialist Movement in Turkey*, 125–30, and "The Legal Socialist Parties of Turkey."

13. Şener, *Türkiye Solunda üç Tarz-ı Siyaset*, 231–47.

14. Ibid., 175–207.

15. Belli, *Milli Demokratik Devrim*.

16. According to Aydın, what was inherent in this thesis was the supposition that the initial "good" state had been replaced by the ruling class of the comprador bourgeoisie and collaborationist classes. If these dominant strata could be overthrown with the help of the national classes, the "good" state could be reestablished. See Aydın, "Türkiye'de 'Devlet Geleneği' Söylemi Üzerine," 75.

17. Doğan, "Türk Solunun Kısa Tarihi," 136–40.

18. Ulus, *The Army and the Radical Left in Turkey*.

19. Akdere and Karadeniz, *Türkiye Solu'nun Eleştirel Tarihi*, 250–53.

20. Perinçek, *Sosyal-Emperyalizm ve Revizyonizme Karşı 1970'te Açılan Mücadele*. Also see Şener, *Türkiye Solunda üç Tarz-ı Siyaset*, 210–14.

21. Perinçek, *Kemalist Devrim-1*; Kahraman, "Türk Solunun Çıkmaz Sokağı," 69–72.

22. Şener, *Türkiye Solunda Üç Tarz-ı Siyaset*, 225–30.

23. Kaypakkaya, "Şafak Revizyonizminin Kemalist Hareket, Kemalist İktidar Dönemi, İkinci Dünya Savaşı Yılları, Savaş Sonrası ve 27 Mayıs Hakkındaki Tezleri," in *Seçme Yazılar*, 127–97.

24. Kaypakkaya, "TİİKP Program Taslağı Eleştirisi," in *Seçme Yazılar*, 97, "Türkiye'de Ulusal Sorun," in *Seçme Yazılar*, 211–16.

25. Kaypakkaya, "Türkiye'de Ulusal Sorun," 252–53.

26. Kaypakkaya, "Şafak Revizyonizmi ile Aramızdaki Ayrılıkların Kökeni ve Gelişmesi," in *Seçme Yazılar*, 356–64.

27. *THKO Davası*; Akdere and Karadeniz, *Türkiye Solu'nun Eleştirel Tarihi*, 313.

28. Töre, "THKO'nun Doğuşu-Gelişimi ve Sonu," 2170–1.

29. Çayan, "Kesintisiz Devrim I," in *Bütün Yazılar*, 234, 287; Şener, *Türkiye Solunda Üç Tarz-ı Siyaset*, 214–23.

30. Çayan, "Kesintisiz Devrim II-III," in *Bütün Yazılar*, 292.

31. Ibid., 303.

32. Ibid., 311.

33. Ibid., 318–20.

34. Anderson, *Imagined Communities*, 9.

35. Ibid., 7.

36. Ibid., 10.

37. Bloch, "Karl Marx, Death and the Apocalypse."

38. Ibid., 39.

39. Ibid, 41.

40. The Alevi sect, as the local Shia community in Turkey, has been historically subjugated and oppressed by the Sunni majority. Alevis have been long-standing supporters of leftist politics.

41. Faith here should be understood as an unqualified certitude in the theoretical premises of one's position such that they are taken for granted as the truth and the legitimate basis of actions. Faith can thus arise in the absence of an overt fusion of Marxist theory with religious thought.

42. Freud uses the term *displacement* to indicate the process of dream work in which the various components of latent, preconscious thought-material is shifted upon a different object or impressionistic residue of the dream-day, distorting the dream-thoughts such that they become difficult to recognize in the dream-content. Althusser also adopts the term, but applies it to the social formation in which the overdetermined contradictions are diverted, serving the preservation of the status quo. My use of the term is informed by the work of both of them, but is restricted to the conceptual articulation and alignment of the theoretical elements of ideology, i.e., how these elements are deflected, dislocated, and reconfigured as a result of the introduction of elements largely foreign to that ideology. For Freudian displacement, see Freud, "On Dreams." For Althusser's version, see Althusser and Balibar, *Reading Capital*, 99-101, 243-50.

43. Unlike the religious forms of martyrdom, secular forms of martyrdom have not been thoroughly studied. For the religious roots of martyrdom, see Boyarin, *Dying for God*; Gregory, *Salvation at Stake*; and Shepkaru, *Jewish Martyrs in the Pagan and Christian Worlds*.

44. The word *shahadat* in Arabic also implies bearing witness or testimony (like its Christian counterpart). However, this is not an active conna-

tion in contemporary Turkish usages. On the social aspect of bearing witness, see Euben, "Killing (For) Politics."

45. According to Becker, this might not be a paradox at all since the quest for heroism is a defense mechanism against the universal fear of death. However, such an approach is based on generalizations about human nature, whether psychological or philosophical, which I find problematic. Cf. Becker, *The Denial of Death*.

46. The movement from the hunger strike into the death fast can be fruitfully compared to the movement from the economic (and/or political) strike to the proletarian general strike in the thought of Georges Sorel. The first is limited and extortionist, while the latter aspires for a total break. The proletarian general strike, like the death fast, has its theological connotations, which Sorel associates with "myth." For the contrast between the political general strike and the proletarian general strike, see Sorel, *Reflections on Violence*.

47. Crossley, "Ritual, Body Technique, and (Inter)Subjectivity."

48. Interview with a participant of the death fast, February 15, 2005.

49. Interview with a participant of the death fast, April 8, 2005.

50. Parry, "Sacrificial Death and the Necrophagus Ascetic."

51. *Yaşadığımız Vatan*, December 11, 2000, 43–46.

52. Interview with a participant of the death fast, January 17, 2005.

53. Interview with a participant of the death fast, March 18, 2005.

54. In spite of this decision to exclude those who had formerly participated in a death fast from the current one, some organizations later reversed their decision and allowed some of their 1996 death fast veterans to participate in 2000. This change was dictated mainly by the length of the struggle and the need for more participants. However, in the aftermath of the death fast, such relaxation of the participation criteria was considered to be a mistake and became a source of self-criticism. The decision was considered to be a mistake because the burden of sustaining a lengthy death fast on a body already suffering from the aftereffects of the former death fast turned out to be particularly heavy, leading to earlier and more difficult deaths or permanent disabilities. Such participation also turned out to be one of the accentuating factors behind the decision of many militants to leave the ranks of the struggle and, at times, to break with their organizations completely.

55. Interview with a participant of the death fast, March 18, 2005.

56. As Kant argues: "For in the case of what is to be morally good, that it conforms to the moral law is not enough; it must also be done for the sake of the moral law." Kant, *Grounding for the Metaphysics of Morals,* 3.

57. Interview with a participant of the death fast, January 24, 2005.

58. Ustuner, Ger, and Holt, "Consuming Ritual."

59. Kaplan, "Din-u Devlet All Over Again?"

60. Interview with a participant of the death fast, May 31, 2005.

61. According to Reuter, the association of death with the wedding celebration goes back to the events that led to the formation of the Shia tradition. In Karbala, Hussayn's nephew Qasim died before his wedding. See Reuter, *My Life Is a Weapon,* 48.

62. Berrin, *Başeğmeyen Kadınlar,* 43.

63. Interviews with participants of the death fast, April 7, May 18, and May 22, 2005.

64. Berrin, *Başeğmeyen Kadınlar,* 76.

65. Hasso, "Discursive and Political Deployments," 35.

66. de Mel, "Body Politics."

67. Acara, "The Militarization of Henna."

68. Interview with a participant of the death fast, May 31, 2005.

69. The leader of each organization is different, though, perhaps not surprisingly, all leaders are exclusively male.

70. Interviews with participants of the death fast, January 17, January 20, May 29, May 30, and May 31, 2005.

71. In public discussions the similar use of the red headband in the religious ceremonies of the Alevi community has been singled out as evidence that the ideology of the death fast struggle is a form of Alevi leftism. While one could perhaps argue that this is an appropriation of Alevi cultural symbolism by the death fasters, the identification of the death fast with Alevism is an interpretation that, in my opinion, should be rejected because of the absence of declared Islamic beliefs by the participants of the movement.

72. In some organizations the comrade tying the headband is not chosen from among those who rank higher in the party. This is intended as a measure to challenge the fixity of hierarchies among militants. Interview with participants of the death fast, January 17 and March 11,

2005.

73. Speech delivered in the headband ceremony of TKP(ML) and DHKP-
C militants in Sağmalcılar Prison, Bayrampaşa, Istanbul on November
26, 2000, *Devrimci Demokrasi*, "Kızıl Bantlı Direnişçilerin Kararlılığı,
Zaferin Finalini Muştuluyor," December 16–31, 2000, 8.

74. An example of this leftist solidarity is the rare occasion of a joint publication on the 1996 death fast by different organizations that participated in it, giving an account of the demands, process, martyrs, and
achievements of the struggle. See Okuyucu, ed. *'96 Ölüm Orucu.*

75. Seale, *Constructing Death,* 50–72.

76. Dönmez, *Yaşatmak icin Öldüler,* 131–40.

77. Gülsüman's brother was imprisoned in 1995, an experience that connected her with other prisoners' families. Gülsüman herself had been
detained multiple times and once imprisoned in 1997 for four and a half
months because of her activism in prisoner rights organizations set up
by families and relatives of prisoners. Ibid., 485–86.

78. Gülsüman began the death fast on the same team with her best friend
and neighbor, Şenay Hanoğlu, also a prisoner's relative and the mother
of two children. Fasting together with Gülsüman for many months,
Şenay died less than two weeks after Gülsüman did. For the details of
their comraderie and consecutive deaths, see ibid., 67–182.

79. In her analysis of undertakers, Howarth calls this process "humanizing
the body." Howarth, *Last Rites,* 147.

80. See picture in Dönmez, *Yaşatmak icin Öldüler,* 486.

81. Ibid., 138.

82. *Cemevi* is a house of worship and communal gathering place for
practices including the eating of common meals, the conduct of
celebrations and funerals, and the performance of cultural activities. It
is mainly associated with urban Alevi communities as a social site for
a variety of communal occasions. The overall significance of the Alevi
house of worship is overdetermined, as its social-religious quality has
been supplemented with a political one as a result of the repression
of Alevi identity in Turkey. The funeral ceremonies of death fasters
of Alevi background were conducted in these spaces located in the
shantytown neighborhoods.

83. Dönmez, *Yaşatmak icin Öldüler,* 138.

84. There was another funeral ceremony for Gülsüman in another shantytown—the Gaziosmanpaşa neighborhood. She was buried, as she had

stated in her will, in the Cebeci Cemetery along with the martyrs of the Operation Return to Life.

85. Townsend, *Vile Bodies*.
86. Kristeva, *Powers of Horror*.
87. Seale, *Constructing Death*, 193–210.
88. On the similar ways in which mourning is regulated in Plato's *Laws*, see Naas, "History's Remains."
89. On the relation between the precariousness of life, its grievability, and the "right to life," see Butler, *Frames of War*.
90. On symbols of fertility in funeral rituals, see Bloch and Parry, "Introduction: Death and the Regeneration of Life."
91. Nora, "Between Memory and History."
92. Feldman, "Political Terror and the Technologies of Memory," 65–66.
93. Interviews with family members of participants of the death fast, May 18 and June 11, 2005.
94. Interview with a participant of the death fast, January 17, 2005 (my emphasis).
95. Interviews with family members of participants of the death fast, May 18 and June 11, 2005.
96. Hallam, Hockey, and Howarth, *Beyond the Body*, 42.
97. See Berrin, *Başeğmeyen Kadınlar*, 151. According to the excerpts from the diary of Sevgi Erdoğan, published in this book, she would begin every day of the death fast by saluting the pictures of the dead hung on the wall across from her bed.
98. "Support the Turkish Hunger Strike," republican mural, Divis Street, Falls, West Belfast, 2001. Photographed by Tony Crowley.
99. The use of memory as a counterhegemonic device approximates Foucault's term *counter-memory*. See Foucault, "Nietzsche, Genealogy, History."
100. Interview with a participant of the death fast, January 17, 2005 (my emphasis).

6. Contentions Within Necroresistance

1. Interview with a participant of the death fast, January 17, 2005.
2. Kamel and Kerness, "The Prison Inside the Prison."
3. Kesici, "Letter to Oral Çalışlar from Sağmalcılar Prison" (my emphasis). Courtesy of Oral Çalışlar.

4. Evans and Morgan, *Preventing Torture*.

5. Many analyses produced by human rights organizations have drawn attention to the human rights violations of supermax security prisons. See, for example, Human Rights Watch, *Cold Storage; Red Onion State Prison*; and *Out of Sight*.

6. See, for example, Sykes, *The Society of Captives*; Jacobs, *Stateville*; Rhodes, *Total Confinement*; Drake, *Prisons, Punishment and the Pursuit of Security*.

7. Human Rights Watch, "Small Group Isolation in Turkish Prisons."

8. See, for example, Ankara Barosu, *Sincan F Tipi Cezaevi Gözlem Raporu ve "Cezaevleri Sorunu" Üzerine Görüşler*; İstanbul Barosu İnsan Hakları Merkezi Cezaevi Çalışma Grubu, *"Kocaeli F Tipi Cezaevi" Gözlem Raporu*; İnsan Hakları Derneği, *F Tipi Cezaevi Modeli*; Türk Tabipleri Birliği, *F Tipi Cezaevlerine İlişkin Türk Tabipleri Birliği Raporu*.

9. Ankara Barosu İnsan Hakları Komisyonu, *Türk İnfaz Sisteminin Sorunları*; Çağdaş Hukukçular Derneği, "F Tipinden Yeni İnfaz-İzolasyon Yasasına"; Özgür Hukuk Bürosu, "F Tipine İlişkin Bazı Tespitler" and "F Tipleri"; Koşan, "Emperyalizmin Ölüm Anıtları"; Çalışlar, "Eza-Tipi ya da F-Tipi"; Günçıkan, "Hücre"; Kanar, "'İktidar Aklı' Cezaevleri"; Kaptanoğlu, "Panopticon'dan F Tipine Tecrit," 34–36; İşlegen, "F Tipi Cezaevleri, İnsan Hakları, Sağlık"; Cinmen, "Tecrit Politikası."

10. Ankara Tabip Odası, *Açlık Grevleri/Ölüm Oruçları ve Cezaevlerindeki Son Süreçle İlgili İzlem Raporu*; TMMOB Mimarlar Odası İzmir Şubesi, "F Tipi Cezaevi Raporu."

11. İnsan Hakları Derneği İstanbul Şubesi, *Tecrit ya da F Tipi İnfaz Sistemi*; Le Pennec and Eberhardt, *The F-Type Prison Crisis*.

12. Amnesty International, *Turkey: "F Type" Prisons*; Human Rights Watch, *Turkey: Small Group Isolation in F-type Prisons*; Helsinki Citizens' Assembly, *F Type Prisons' Report*.

13. İnsan Hakları Derneği İstanbul Şubesi, *Sessiz Çığlık*.

14. Aydoğmuş "Letter to Oral Çalışlar from Ümraniye Prison." Courtesy of Oral Çalışlar.

15. Anderson, "'To Lie Down to Death for Days,'" 820.

16. Siméant also finds that the hunger strike, or more generally the body, is a common resort as a medium of protest for those who have limited access to other forms of protest, particularly illegal migrants and others

who demand status or contest the status assigned to them by the state. See Siméant, *La Cause des Sans-Papiers*, 302–10.

17. Bora, "Hapishane Rejimi," 17.

18. Interview with a participant of the death fast, January 24, 2005 (my emphasis).

19. Interview with a participant of the death fast, June 17, 2005.

20. Ibid.

21. Scarry, *The Body in Pain.*

22. Feldman, *Formations of Violence*, 178; Anderson, "'To Lie Down to Death for Days,'" 830.

23. Interview with a participant of the death fast, June 17, 2005.

24. Aydoğmuş, "Letter to Oral Çalışlar from Ümraniye Prison."

25. Feldman, *Formations of Violence*, 138.

26. Ibid., 178.

27. Koçan and Öncü, "From the Morality of Living to the Morality of Dying," 359.

28. Interview with a participant of the death fast, January 17, 2005.

29. Koçan and Öncü, "From the Morality of Living to the Morality of Dying," 357.

30. Ibid., 358.

31. At the same time as Koçan and Öncü interpret the hunger strike as a struggle for Kantian autonomy, they also assert that the hunger strike was a struggle for recognition in the Hegelian sense. The F-type prisons, in their argument, were "aiming to subordinate them [the prisoners] to a particular self-consciousness without granting them any recognition. The prisoners' self-consciousness is denied by taking away their freedom and rights" (ibid., 362). Accordingly, the prisoners' denial of servitude led to a life-and-death struggle with the state as the "master." Their ability to face death was their attainment of a new morality along with a new subjectivity. The authors claim that this new morality was an expression of *ressentiment* in the Nietzschean sense, a reactive experience of frustration and the "desire to put an end to domination and oppression and a will to power denied to them" (ibid., 361). While interesting and provocative, the interpretation of Koçan and Öncü superimposes multiple philosophical frameworks on the death fast (for example, Kantian, Hegelian, and finally Nietzschean) that tackle different aspects of the struggle without adjudicating the relative merits of

each perspective, the tensions among them when taken together, and how they refract the actual voices and views of the participants in the struggle.

32. Ibid., 360.
33. Interviews with participants of the death fast, January 17, January 20, May 29, May 31, July 1, 2005.
34. Interview with a participant of the death fast, January 24, 2005.
35. Interview with a participant of the death fast, January 24, 2005.
36. Interview with a participant of the death fast, January 26, 2005.
37. Interview with a participant of the death fast, July 1, 2005.
38. Anderson, "'To Lie Down to Death for Days,'" 820.
39. Interview with a participant of the death fast, January 26, 2005 (my emphasis).
40. Neier, "Confining Dissent."
41. Gramsci, *Selections from the Prison Notebooks*, 60–61, 137.
42. Gürbüz, "Letter to Oral Çalışlar." Courtesy of Oral Çalışlar.
43. Interviews with participants of the death fast, January 17, May 22, May 29, July 1, 2005.
44. Karabulut, Gardaş, and Eren, "Open Letter to the Press and Public from Aydın Prison." Courtesy of Oral Çalışlar.
45. Interview with a participant of the death fast, June 17, 2005.
46. Interview with a participant of the death fast, January 17, 2005.
47. Captives of DHKP-C, TKP(ML), TKİP Cases Who Continue Their Hunger Strike in All the Prisons, "Letter to Çalışlar." Courtesy of Oral Çalışlar.
48. Interview with a participant of the death fast, January 17, 2005.
49. Demirel, Kaya, and Çoban, "Letter to the Press and to the Public from Aydın Prison." Courtesy of Oral Çalışlar.
50. Feldman, *Formations of Violence*, 232.
51. Interview with a participant of the death fast, June 10, 2005.
52. Interview with a participant of the death fast, July 15, 2005.
53. Interview with a participant of the death fast, June 17, 2005.
54. Interview with a participant of the death fast, January 24, 2005.
55. Interview with a participant of the death fast, January 20, 2005.
56. Interview with a participant of the death fast, July 15, 2005.
57. Interview with a participant of the death fast, January 17, 2005.

58. Interview with a participant of the death fast, April 7, 2005.

59. Interview with a participant of the death fast, January 20, 2005.

60. Interview with a participant of the death fast, April 7, 2005
(my emphasis).

61. Ibid.

62. Ibid.

63. Nazik, "Letter to Oral Çalışlar from Sincan F Type Prison." Courtesy of Oral Çalışlar.

64. Interview with a participant of the death fast, July 15, 2005
(my emphasis).

65. Interview with a participant of the death fast, May 22, 2005.

66. Interview with a participant of the death fast, January 24, 2005.

67. Interview with a participant of the death fast, January 20, 2005.

68. Interview with a participant of the death fast, January 17, 2005.

69. Interview with a participant of the death fast, February 15, 2005.

70. Interview with a participant of the death fast, January 24, 2005
(my emphasis).

71. Türkmen, "Letter from Niğde Prison." Courtesy of Oral Çalışlar.

72. Interview with a participant of the death fast, June 17, 2005.

73. Interview with a participant of the death fast, January 17, 2005.

74. Interview with a participant of the death fast, May 30, 2005
(my emphasis).

75. Interview with a participant of the death fast, May 22, 2005.

76. Interviews with participants of the death fast, April 20, May 18, 22, 25, and 29, 2005.

77. Interview with participants of the death fast, January 20 and May 23, 2005.

78. Interview with a participant of the death fast, May 31, 2005.

79. Interview with a participant of the death fast, April 7, 2005.

80. Interview with a participant of the death fast, June 17, 2005.

81. Interview with a participant of the death fast, May 31, 2005.

82. Interview with a participant of the death fast, June 17, 2005.

83. Interview with a participant of the death fast, May 30, 2005.

84. Interview with a participant of the death fast, May 31, 2005.

85. Interview with a participant of the death fast, January 17, 2005.

86. Interview with a participant of the death fast, May 22, 2005.

87. Interview with a participant of the death fast, May 22, 2005.
88. Feldman, *Formations of Violence*, 249.
89. Interview with a participant of the death fast, May 30, 2005.

Conclusion

1. Joint statement issued by political prisoners of different affiliations condemning the preparations for a military intervention in prisons and calling for public support, dated October 10, 2000, printed in *Yaşadığımız Vatan*, October 16, 2000, 21.
2. Marx and Engels, "The Manifesto of the Communist Party," 500.
3. Anderson, "'To Lie Down to Death for Days,'" 840.
4. ABCTGM, "Statistics." Since 2011, the Ministry of Justice has stopped publishing statistics that list "terror" crimes separately from "ordinary" crimes on its Web site.
5. ABCTGM, "Ülkemizde Ceza İnfaz Kurumları."
6. Mavioğlu, "'Eski Günlere' Dönüşün Emareleri."
7. Some of these problems have also been reported by the parliament's own Human Rights Investigation Commission. See TBMM İnsan Haklarını İnceleme Komisyonu Başkanlığı, *Bolu F-Tipi Cezaevi Raporu.*
8. Başaran, "Cezaevleri İsyanlara Gebe"; Çağdaş Hukukçular Derneği, "F Tipi Cezaevinde Tecrit Ölüm Getirdi."
9. Amnesty International, "Turkey: Briefing on Present State of Human Rights."
10. Human rights organizations point to the continuation of serious human rights violations despite ongoing reforms. See, for example, Amnesty International, *Turkey: Memorandum on AI's Recommendations.*
11. See, for example, Balbay, *Silivri Toplama Kampı.*
12. For a passionate indictment of the new ruling elite, see Şık, *Pusu.*
13. Muftuler-Bac and Keyman, "The Era of Dominant Party Politics."
14. Foucault, "Is It Useless to Revolt?" 263.
15. Ibid., 266.

Bibliography

Acara, Eda. "The Militarization of Henna." *Fe Dergi: Feminist Eleştiri* 2, no. 2 (2010): 91–94.

Adak, Hülya. "National Myths and Self-Na(rra)tions: Mustafa Kemal's *Nutuk* and Halide Edib's *Memoirs* and *The Turkish Ordeal*." *South Atlantic Quarterly* 102, nos. 2/3 (Spring/Summer 2003): 509–27.

Adalet Bakanlığı [Ministry of Justice]. "İstanbul, Ankara, İzmir ve Antalya Barolarının Birlikte Hazırladıkları 'Üç Kapı Üç Kilit Projesi' ile İlgili Açıklama" [Declaration on the 'Three Doors, Three Locks Project' Jointly Prepared by the Istanbul, Ankara, Izmir, and Antalya Bar Association]. Press release, January 14, 2002.

Adalet Bakanlığı Ceza ve Tevkifevleri Genel Müdürlüğü [Ministry of Justice General Directorate of Prisons and Detention Houses]. *1 Ağustos Genelgesi* [August 1 Decree]. No. Ks. 4/V: R/4-E-234–87, July 7, 1988.

——. "Açlık Grevi ve Ölüm Orucu Eylemlerinin Gerçek Nedenleri ve Hayata Dönüş Operasyonu" [The Real Reasons of Hunger Strike and Death Fast Actions and Operation Return to Life]. Public Statement, [January 2001]. http://www.adalet.gov.tr/cte/olaylar/hayatadonus.htm. (Last accessed August 19, 2003.)

——. "Cezaevi Reformu Çalışmaları ve İnsan Hakları" [Progress on Prison Reform and Human Rights]. Press release. http://www.cte.adalet.gov.tr/ inshak/insan_hak.htm. (Last accessed March 9, 2007.)

——. *Genelge 45/1* [Decree 45/1.] No. B:03.0.CTE.0.00.00.04 / Ankara, January 22, 2007.

——. *Genelgeler* [Decrees]. No. Ks/11 V: R Ankara 96018784, May 6, 1996; No. Ks/11 V: R Ankara 96019603, May 9, 1996; No. Ks/11 V: R Ankara 96019605, May 9, 1996; and No. 4-E-2/19–218 Ankara, September 29, 1997.

——. *Protokol* [Protocol]. No. KS: 4V. R 1-E-2 3/18, January 14, 2000.

——. "Statistics." http://www.cte.adalet.gov.tr/. (Last accessed December 1, 2012.)

——. "Ülkemizde Ceza İnfaz Kurumları" [Prisons in Our Country]. http:// www.cte.adalet.gov.tr/. (Last accessed December 1, 2012.)

Afary, Janet, and Kevin B. Anderson. *Foucault and the Iranian Revolution: Gender and the Seductions of Islamism.* Chicago: University of Chicago Press, 2005.

Agamben, Giorgio. "Bartleby, or On Contingency." In *Potentialities.* Trans. Daniel Heller-Roazen, 243-71. Stanford: Stanford University Press, 1999.

——. "Form-of-Life." In *Radical Thought in Italy: A Potential Politics,* ed. Paolo Virno and Michael Hardt, 151–56. Minneapolis: University of Minnesota Press, 1996.

——. *Homo Sacer: Sovereign Power and Bare Life.* Trans. Daniel Heller-Roazen. Stanford: Stanford University Press, 1998.

——. *Means Without Ends: Notes on Politics.* Trans. Vincenzo Binetti and Cesare Casarino. Minneapolis: University of Minnesota Press, 2000.

——. *Remnants of Auschwitz: The Witness and the Archive.* Trans. Daniel Heller-Roazen. New York: Zone, 1999.

——. *State of Exception.* Trans. Kevin Attell. Chicago: University of Chicago Press, 2005.

——. *The Coming Community.* Trans. Michael Hardt. Minneapolis: University of Minnesota Press, 1993.

Ahmad, Muneer I. "Resisting Guantánamo: Rights at the Brink of Dehumanization." *Northwestern University Law Review* 103, no. 4 (2009): 1683–758.

Ahmetbeyzade, Cihan. "Gendering Necropolitics: The Juridical-Political Sociality of Honor Killings in Turkey." *Journal of Human Rights* 7, no. 3 (2008): 187–206.

Akdere, İlhan, and Zeynep Karadeniz, *Türkiye Solu'nun Eleştirel Tarihi 1908–1980* [A Critical History of the Left of Turkey 1908-1980]. Vol. 1. 2d ed. Istanbul: Evrensel Basım Yayın, 1996.

Akın, Yiğit. "*Gürbüz ve Yavuz Evlatlar*": Erken Cumhuriyet'te Beden Terbiyesi ve Spor ["Sturdy and Tough Children": Physical Education and Sports in the Early Republic]. Istanbul: İletişim Yayınları, 2004.

Alemdaroğlu, Ayça. "Politics of the Body and Eugenic Discourse in Early Republican Turkey." *Body and Society* 11, no. 3 (September 2005): 61–76.

Alınterimiz. "Faşizm Hücre Tipi Cezaevi Hükmünü Yürütüyor" [Fascism Is Executing Its Cell Type Prison Sentence]. January 18, 1999, 1.

Altaylı, Fatih. "Halkı Anlasalardı Böyle Olmazdı!" [It Would Not Have Been Like This Had They Understood the People!]. *Hürriyet*, December 20, 2000.

Althusser, Louis. *Machiavelli and Us.* Ed. François Matheron. Trans. Gregory Elliott. London: Verso, 1999.

————, and Etienne Balibar, *Reading Capital.* Trans. Ben Brewster. London: Verso, 1997.

Amnesty International. *Torture in the Eighties.* London: Amnesty International, 1984.

————. "Turkey: Briefing on Present State of Human Rights Development During the Pre-accession Process." *Briefing Paper,* no: EUR 44/041/2002, September 2002.

————. *Turkey: "F Type" Prisons: Isolation and Allegations of Torture or Ill-Treatment.* Report, no. EUR 44/025/2001, April 2001.

————. *Turkey: Memorandum on AI's Recommendations to the Government to Address Human Rights Violations.* Report, no: EUR 44/027/2005, August 2005.

————. *Turkey: No Security Without Human Rights.* Report, no. EUR 44/084/1996. September 30, 1996.

————. *Turkey: Recommendations for Action to Combat Systematic Violations of Human Rights.* Report, no. EUR 44/006/1995. January 1, 1995.

————. *Turkey: Still Waiting for Change—Information on Continuing Human Rights Abuses.* Report, no. EUR 44/26/1991. February 1, 1991.

————. *Turkey: Torture, Extrajudicial Executions, "Disappearances."* Report, no. EUR 44/039/1992. April 30, 1992.

——. *United States of America: Cruel and Inhuman. Conditions of Isolation for Detainees at Guantánamo Bay*. Special Report, no. AMR 51/051/2007, April 5, 2007. London: Amnesty International, 2007.

Andersen, H. S., D. Sestoft, T. Lillebaek, G. Gabrielsen, R. Hemmingsen, and P. Kramp. "A Longitudinal Study of Prisoners on Remand: Psychiatric Prevalence, Incidence and Psychopathology in Solitary vs. Non-Solitary Confinement." *Acta Psychiatrica Scandinavica* 102, no. 1 (2000): 19–25.

Anderson, Benedict. *Imagined Communities: Reflections on the Origin and Spread of Nationalism*. Rev. ed. London: Verso, 1991.

Anderson, Patrick. "'To Lie Down to Death for Days': The Turkish Hunger Strike, 2000–2003." *Cultural Studies* 18, no. 6 (November 2004): 816–46.

Andriolo, Karin. "Murder by Suicide: Episodes from Muslim History." *American Anthropologist* 104, no. 3 (2002): 736–42.

Ankara Barosu [Ankara Bar Association]. *Sincan F Tipi Cezaevi Gözlem Raporu ve "Cezaevleri Sorunu" Üzerine Görüşler* [Sincan F Type Prison Observation Report and Views on the "Prisons Problem"]. Report, July 22, 2000.

Ankara Barosu İnsan Hakları Komisyonu [Ankara Bar Association Human Rights Commission]. *Türk İnfaz Sisteminin Sorunları* [Problems of the Turkish Execution System]. İnsan Hakları Dizisi [Series on Human Rights], no. 5, Ankara, January 2000.

Ankara Tabip Odası [Ankara Physicians' Chamber]. *Açlık Grevleri/Ölüm Oruçları ve Cezaevlerindeki Son Süreçle İlgili İzlem Raporu* [Observation Report Concerning Hunger Strikes/Death Fasts and the Recent Process in the Prisons]. Report, January 25, 2001.

Annas, George J. "Hunger Strikes." *British Medical Journal*, no. 311 (1995): 1114–15.

——. "Hunger Strikes at Guantánamo—Medical Ethics and Human Rights in a 'Legal Black Hole.'" *New England Journal of Medicine* 355, no. 13 (September 28, 2006): 1377–82.

Arat, Zehra F. Kabasakal, ed. *Human Rights in Turkey*. Philadephia: University of Pennsylvania Press, 2007.

Aren, Sadun. *TİP Olayı (1961–1971)* [The Event of the Workers' Party of Turkey (1961–1971)]. Istanbul: Cem Yayınevi, 1993.

Aricanli, Tosun, and Dani Rodrik, eds. *The Political Economy of Turkey: Debt, Adjustment, and Sustainability*. New York: St. Martin's, 1990.

Asad, Talal. *On Suicide Bombing*. New York: Columbia University Press, 2007.

Aslan, Şükrü. *1 Mayıs Mahallesi: 1980 Öncesi Toplumsal Mücadeleler ve Kent*

[The May 1 Neighborhood: Social Struggles and the City Prior to 1980].
Istanbul: İletişim Yayınları, 2004.

Associated Press. "Some Guantánamo Prisoners Have Gone on Hunger Strike." *New York Times*. July 22, 2005. http://www.nytimes.
com/2005/07/22/politics/22gitmo.html?_r=1. (Last accessed November
12, 2013.)

Aşçı, Behiç. "Behiç Aşçı Kimdir?" [Who Is Behiç Aşçı?] Press release,
Istanbul Indymedia, January 11, 2007. http://istanbul.indymedia.org/
news/2007/01/165307php. (Last accessed January 12, 2007.)

——. "'Bu 10 Dakikada Çözülecek Sorun'" ["This Is a Problem That Can
Be Solved in 10 Minutes"]. Interview by Ahmet Tulgar. *Birgün*, June 21,
2006. http://www.tecritekarsi.com/basinden/ahmet_tulgar.html. (Last
accessed January 10, 2007.)

Atılgan, Gökhan. *Yön-Devrim Hareketi: Kemalizm ile Marksizm Arasında Geleneksel Aydınlar* [The Direction-Revolution Movement: Traditional Intellectuals Between Kemalism and Marxism]. Istanbul: Yordam Kitap, 2008.

Aybar, Mehmet Ali. *Türkiye İşçi Partisi Tarihi* [History of the Workers' Party
of Turkey]. 3 vols. Istanbul: BDS Yayınları, 1988.

Aybers, Orhan. "Eugenics in Turkey During the 1930s." PhD diss., Middle
East Technical University, 2003.

Aydın, Suavi. "Türkiye'de 'Devlet Geleneği' Söylemi Üzerine" [On the "State
Tradition" Discourse in Turkey] *Birikim*, nos. 105/106 (January/February 1998): 63–82.

Aydınoğlu, Ergun. *Türk Solu: Eleştirel Bir Tarih Denemesi (1960–1971)* [The
Turkish Left: An Attempt at a Critical History (1960–1971)]. Istanbul:
Belge Yayınları, 1992.

Aydoğmuş, Nahit. "Letter to Oral Çalışlar from Ümraniye Prison." [In Turkish.] N.d., private collection.

Bağımsız Vatan. "Direniş Tarihimize Onurla Yazılan Yeni Sayfalar Eklemeye
Devam Ediyoruz" [We Continue to Add New Pages to Our History of
Resistance Written with Honor]. October 23, 2000, 5, 13.

Bailey, Richard. "Up Against the Wall: Bare Life and Resistance in Australian Immigration Detention." *Law and Critique* 20, no. 2 (August 2009):
113–32.

Bakkalcı, Metin. Interview by Berat Günçıkan. *Cumhuriyet Dergi*, December
31, 2000. http://www.ttb.org.tr/aclik_grevleri/mbakkalci_sy.html. (Last
accessed December 1, 2012.)

Balbay, Mustafa. *Silivri Toplama Kampı: Zulümhane* [The Silivri Camp: House of Oppression]. Istanbul: Cumhuriyet Kitapları, 2010.

Başaran, Rıfat. "Cezaevleri İsyanlara Gebe" [Prisons Are Prone to Riots]. *Radikal*, May 30, 2010.

Başoğlu, M., Y. Yetimalar, N. Gürgör, S. Büyükçatalbaş, T. Kurt, Y. Seçil, and A. Yeniocak. "Neurological Complications of Prolonged Hunger Strike." *European Journal of Neurology* 13, no. 10 (October 2006): 1089–97.

Bayraktar, Kazım et al., eds. *Ulucanlar* (Istanbul: Şubat Basım Yayım, 2000).

Bayraktar, Kazım, Dilek Mıdık, Elif Uysal, Betül Vangölü, Selçuk Kozağaçlı, Özgür Sarıyıldız, Filiz Kalayci, Özlem Şen, Sait Kıran, and Serkan Arıkanoğlu. "Basına ve Kamuya Açıklama" [Statement to the Press and Public]. Press release, December 22, 2000.

Becker, Ernst. *The Denial of Death*. New York: Free Press, 1973.

Behram, Nihat. *Darağacında Üç Fidan* [Three Saplings on the Gallows]. Istanbul: Everest Yayınları, 2008.

Bekaroğlu, Mehmet. *TBMM İnsan Haklarını İnceleme Komisyonu Başkanlığı'na Sunulan Rapor* [Report Submitted to Chair of the Grand National Assembly of Turkey Human Rights Investigation Commission]. Report, January 3, 2001.

Bektaş, Cafer Tayyar, ed. *Zafere Halay: Belgeleri ve Tanıklarıyla Ulucanlar Direnişi* [Dance to Victory: The Ulucanlar Resistance with Documents and Witnesses]. Istanbul: Kardelen Yayımcılık, 2002.

Bell, Vikki. "The Scenography of Suicide: Terror, Politics, and the Humiliated Witness." *Economy and Society* 34, no. 2 (May 2005): 241–60.

Belli, Mihri. *Milli Demokratik Devrim* [National Democratic Revolution]. Ankara: Aydınlık Yayınları, 1970.

Benjamin, Walter. "Critique of Violence." *Selected Writings*, vol. 1: *1913–1926*, ed. Marcus Bullock and Michael W. Jennings, 236–52. Cambridge: Belknap Press of Harvard University Press, 1996.

Beresford, David. *Ten Men Dead: The Story of the 1981 Irish Hunger Strike*. London: Grafton, 1987.

Bernstein, Richard. "Foucault: Critique as a Philosophical Ethos," *Critique and Power: Recasting the Foucault/Habermas Debate*, ed. Michael Kelly, 211–42. Cambridge: MIT Press, 1994.

Berrin, Yasemin, ed. *Başeğmeyen Kadınlar: Büyük Direnişin Uşak Cephesi* [Unruly Women: The Uşak Front of the Great Resistance]. Istanbul: Boran Yayınevi, 2004.

Biehl, Joao. "Vita: Life in a Zone of Social Abandonment." *Social Text* 19, no. 3 (2001): 131–49.

Biggs, Michael. "Dying Without Killing: Self-Immolations, 1963–2002." In *Making Sense of Suicide Missions*, ed. Diego Gambetta, 173–208. Oxford: Oxford University Press, 2005.

Bigo, Didier. "Detention of Foreigners, States of Exception, and the Social Practices of the Control of the Banopticon." In *Borderscapes: Hidden Geographies and Politics at Territory's Edge*, ed. Prem Kumar Rajaram and Carl Grundy-Warr, 3–33. Minneapolis: University of Minnesota Press, 2007.

Birtek, Faruk, and Binnaz Toprak. "The Conflictual Agendas of Neo-Liberal Reconstruction and the Rise of Islamic Politics in Turkey: The Hazards of Rewriting Modernity." *Praxis International*. 13, no. 2 (1993): 192–212.

Bloch, Ernst. "Karl Marx, Death and the Apocalypse." In *Man on His Own: Essays in the Philosophy of Religion*, trans. E. B. Ashton, 31–72. New York: Herder and Herder, 1970.

Bloch, Maurice, and Jonathan Parry. "Introduction: Death and the Regeneration of Life." In *Death and the Regeneration of Life,* ed. Maurice Bloch and Jonathan Parry, 1–44. Cambridge: Cambridge University Press, 1982.

Bloom, Mia. *Dying to Kill: The Allure of Suicide Terror.* New York: Columbia University Press, 2005.

Bodin, Jean. *On Sovereignty.* Ed. Julian H. Franklin. Cambridge: Cambridge University Press, 1992.

Bora, Tanıl. "Hapishane Rejimi: Bir 'Seri Katil' Zihniyeti" [The Prisons Regime: A "Serial Killer" Mentality]. *Birikim*, no. 136 (August 2000): 17–21.

——. "'Hayata Dönüş' ve Medya" ["Return to Life" and the Media]. *Birikim*, nos. 142–143 (February-March 2001): 45–47.

Boran, Behice. *İki Açıdan Türkiye İşçi Partisi Davası: İfade ve Savunma* [The Workers' Party of Turkey Case from Two Perspectives: Testimony and Defense]. Istanbul: Bilim Yayınları, 1975.

Boratav, Korkut. "Kemalist Economic Policies and Étatism." In *Ataturk, Founder of a Modern State*, ed. Ergun Özbudun and Ali Kazancıgil, 165–90. Hamden, CT: Archon, 1981.

——. *Türkiye'de Devletçilik* [Étatism in Turkey]. 2d ed. Ankara: Savaş Yayınları, 1982.

Bornstein, Avram. "Ethnography and the Politics of Prisoners in Palestine-Israel." *Journal of Contemporary Ethnography* 30, no. 5 (2001): 546–75.

——. "Palestinian Prison Ontologies." *Dialectical Anthropology* 34, no. 4 (2010): 459–72.

Bowersock, G. W. *Martyrdom and Rome.* Cambridge: Cambridge University Press, 2002.

Boyarin, Daniel. *Dying for God: Martyrdom and the Making of Christianity and Judaism.* Stanford: Stanford University Press, 1999.

Boyoğlu, Erdal, ed. *Ölümden Öte: Sol İçi Şiddeti Sorgulamak ve Aşmak* [Beyond Death: Questioning and Overcoming Violence Within the Left]. Istanbul: Belge Yayınları, 2010.

Bozarslan, Hamit. *Violence in the Middle East: From Political Struggle to Self-Sacrifice.* Princeton: Weiner, 2004.

Bozyel, Bayram. *Diyarbakır 5 Nolu* [Diyarbakır Number 5]. 5th ed. Diyarbakır: Deng Yayınları, 2008.

Buntman, Fran Lisa. *Robben Island and Prisoner Resistance to Apartheid.* Cambridge: Cambridge University Press, 2003.

Butler, Judith. *Bodies That Matter: On the Discursive Limits of Sex.* New York: Routledge, 1993.

——. *Frames of War: When Is Life Grievable?* London: Verso, 2009.

——. "Indefinite Detention." In *Precarious Life: The Powers of Mourning and Violence,* 50–100. London: Verso, 2004.

Buzgan, Turan. "History of Vaccination Policies, in Turkey" (Türkiye'de Dünden Bugüne Aşılama Politikaları)." *Journal of Pediatric Infection (Çocuk Enfeksiyon Dergisi)* 5, Supplement 1 (April 2011): 235–38.

Bynum, Caroline Walker. *Holy Feast and Holy Fast: The Religious Significance of Food to Medieval Women.* Berkeley: University of California Press, 1987.

Cadman, Lisa. "Life and Death Decisions in Our Posthuman(ist) Times." *Antipode* 41, no. 1 (2009): 133–58.

Caldwell, Anne. "Bio-Sovereignty and the Emergence of Humanity." *theory and event* 7, no. 2 (2004). https://muse.jhu.edu/login?auth=0&type=summary&url=/journals/theory_and_event/v007/7.2caldwell.html. (Last accessed November 13, 2013.)

Campbell, Brian, Laurence McKeown, and Felim O'Hagan, eds. *Nor Meekly Serve My Time: The H-Block Struggle 1976–1981.* Belfast: Beyond the Pale, 1994.

Candar, Cengiz. "Redefining Turkey's Center." *Journal of Democracy* 10, no. 4 (October 1999): 129–41.

Caplan, Bryan. "Terrorism: The Relevance of the Rational Choice Model." *Public Choice* 128, no. 1–2 (July 2006): 91–107.

Captives of DHKP-C, TKP(ML), TKİP Cases Who Continue Their Hunger Strike in All the Prisons. "Letter to Çalışlar." [In Turkish.] October 31, 2000, private collection.

Carlton, Bree. *Imprisoning Resistance: Life and Death in an Australian Supermax.* Sydney: Institute of Criminality Press, 2007.

CHF Programı [The Republican People's Party Program]. Ankara: TBMM Matbaası, 1931.

Churchill, Ward, and J. J. Vander Wall, eds. *Cages of Steel: The Politics of Imprisonment in the United States.* Washington, DC: Maisonneuve, 1992.

Cinemre, Levent, and Ruşen Çakır, eds. *Sol Kemalizme Bakıyor* [The Left Is Looking at Kemalism]. Istanbul: Metis Yayınları, 1991.

Cinmen, Ergin. "Tecrit Politikası, F Tipi Ceza ve Tutukevleri" [Policy of Isolation, F Type Prisons and Detention Houses]. *Birikim,* no. 136 (August 2000): 63–65.

Cline, Lawrence E. "From Ocalan to Al Qaida: The Continuing Terrorist Threat in Turkey." *Studies in Conflict and Terrorism* 27, no. 4 (July 2004): 321–35.

Cohen, Stanley. *Visions of Social Control: Crime, Punishment, and Classification.* Cambridge: Polity, 1985.

Cohn, Norman. *The Pursuit of the Millenium: Revolutionary Millenarians and Mystical Anarchists of the Middle Ages.* Rev. ed. Oxford: Oxford University Press, 1970.

Connolly, William. "The Complexities of Sovereignty." In *Sovereign Lives: Power in Global Politics,* ed. Jenny Edkins, Véronique Pin-Fat, and Michael Shapiro, 23–40. New York: Routledge, 2004.

Constitution of the Republic of Turkey. http://www.anayasa.gov.tr/Mevzuat/Anayasa1982/. (Last accessed November 15, 2013.)

Cooke, Alexander. "Resistance, Potentiality and the Law." *Angelaki: Journal of the Theoretical Humanities* 10, no. 3 (2005): 79–89.

Coşkun, Kıymet. "Nâzım Hikmet'in Açlık Grevi" [The Hunger Strike of Nâzım Hikmet]. In *Nâzım Hikmet'in Açlık Grevi* [The Hunger Strike of Nâzım Hikmet], ed. Yeşim Bilge Bengü, 15–33. Istanbul: Istanbul Bilgi Üniversitesi Yayınları, 2011.

Council of Europe. *Report to the Turkish Government on the Visit to Turkey Carried Out by the European Committee for the Prevention of Torture and*

Inhuman or Degrading Treatment or Punishment (CPT) from 19 to 23 August 1996. Report, no. CPT/Inf (2001) 1, Strasbourg, March 1, 2001. http://www.cpt.coe.int/documents/tur/2001-01-inf-eng.htm#Report. (Last accessed November 22, 2013.)

——. *Report to the Turkish Government on the Visit to Turkey Carried Out by the European Committee for the Prevention of Torture and Inhuman or Degrading Treatment or Punishment (CPT) from 16 to 24 July 2000.* Report, no. CPT/Inf (2001) 25, Strasbourg, November 8, 2001. http:// www.cpt. coe.int/documents/tur/2001-25-inf-eng.htm. (Last accessed November 22, 2013.)

Crenshaw, Martha. "The Logic of Terrorism: Terrorist Behaviour as a Product of Strategic Choice." In *Origins of Terrorism: Psychologies, Ideologies, Theologies, States of Mind,* ed. Walter Reich, 7–24. New York: Cambridge University Press, 1990.

Criss, Nur Bilge. "The Nature of PKK Terrorism in Turkey." *Studies in Conflict and Terrorism* 18, no. 1 (1995): 17–37.

Crossley, Nick. "Ritual, Body Technique, and (Inter)Subjectivity." In *Thinking Through Rituals: Philosophical Perspectives,* ed. Kevin Schilbrack, 31–51. New York: Routledge, 2004.

Cumhuriyet. "Darbenin Bilançosu" [The Balance Sheet of the Coup]. September 12, 2000.

——. "Ölümleri Durdurmak İçin Bir Çözüm; Üç Kapı Üç Kilit" [A Solution to Stop the Deaths; Three Doors Three Locks]. January 16, 2002.

——. "'Üç Kapı Üç Kilit'e Ret" [Rejection of 'Three Doors Three Locks']. January 10, 2002.

Çağdaş Hukukçular Derneği [Contemporary Lawyers' Association]. "F Tipi Cezaevinde Tecrit Ölüm Getirdi" [Isolation Brought Death in the F Type Prison]. Press release, April 13, 2010.

——. "F Tipinden Yeni İnfaz-İzolasyon Yasasına: Mahpusluktan Kürek Mahkumluğuna" [From the F Type to the New Execution-Isolation Law: From Imprisonment to Galley Slavery]. Special Issue. *Çağdaş Hukuk,* July 2004.

Çağdaş Hukukçular Derneği İstanbul Şubesi [Contemporary Lawyers' Association Istanbul Branch]. *Cezaevleri Çalışma Komisyonu Raporu (10.04.1999–31.03.2001)* [Report of the Working Commission on Prisons (April 10, 1999-March 31, 2001)]. Report, Istanbul, 2001.

——. "19.12.2000 Tarihinde Başlatılan Cezaevleri Operasyonu ile İlgili

Açıklama" [Briefing Concerning the Prisons Operation of December 19, 2000]. Press release, December 25, 2000.

Çalışlar, Oral. "Eza-Tipi ya da F-Tipi." [Torment-type or F-type]. *Cumhuriyet Dergi*, no. 748, July 23, 2000, 2–3.

Çamuroğlu, Reha. "Alevi Revivalism in Turkey." In *Alevi Identity: Cultural, Religious and Social Perspectives*, ed. Tord Olsson, Elisabeth Özdalga and Catharina Raudvere, 79–84. Istanbul: Swedish Research Institute, 1998.

Çayan, Mahir. *Bütün Yazılar* [Complete Works]. Istanbul: Atılım Yayınları, 1992.

Çelik, Mukaddes Erdoğdu. *Demir Parmaklıklar Ortak Düşler: Üç Dönem Üç Kuşak Kadınlar* [Iron Bars, Common Dreams: Three Eras, Three Generations of Women]. Istanbul: Ceylan Yayınları, 2005.

Çölaşan, Emin. "İnsan Hakları!" [Human Rights!]. *Hürriyet*, December 21, 2000.

Çürükkaya, Selim. *12 Eylül Karanlığında Diyarbakır Şafağı* [Diyarbakır Dawn in the Darkness of September 12]. Cologne: Ağrı Yayınları, 1990.

Das, Veena, and Deborah Poole, "State and Its Margins: Comparative Ethnographies." In *Anthropology in the Margins of the State*, ed. Veena Das and Deborah Poole, 3–34. Santa Fe: School of American Research Press, 2004.

——, eds. *Anthropology in the Margins of the State*. Santa Fe: School of American Research Press, 2004.

Dean, Mitchell. *Governmentality: Power and Rule in Modern Society*. London: Sage, 1999.

DeCaroli, Steven. "Boundary Stones: Giorgio Agamben and the Field of Sovereignty." In *Giorgio Agamben: Sovereignty and Life*, ed. Matthew Calarco and Steven DeCaroli, 43–69. Stanford: Stanford University Press, 2007.

De Certeau, Michel. *The Practice of Everyday Life*. Trans. Steven Rendall. Berkeley: University of California Press, 1984.

de la Durantaye, Leland. *Giorgio Agamben: A Critical Introduction*. Stanford: Stanford University Press, 2009.

De Larrinaga, Miguel, and Marc G. Doucet. "Sovereign Power and the Biopolitics of Human Security." *Security Dialogue* 39, no. 5 (2008): 517–37.

Delaney, Carol. "Father State, Motherland, and the Birth of Modern Turkey." In *Naturalizing Power: Essays in Feminist Cultural Analysis*, ed. Sylvia Junko Yanagisako and Carol Delaney, 177–99. New York: Routledge, 1995.

Deleuze, Gilles and Felix Guattari. *A Thousand Plateaus: Capitalism and Schizophrenia*. Trans. Brian Massumi. Minneapolis: University of Minnesota Press, 1987.

de Mel, Neloufer. "Body Politics: (Re)Cognising the Female Suicide Bomber in Sri Lanka." *Indian Journal of Gender Studies* 11, no. 1 (February 2004): 75–93.

Demirci, Arzu, and Hülya Üçpınar, *İzmir Barosu İnsan Hakları Hukuku ve Hukuk Araştırmaları Merkezi: F Tipi Cezaevlerinin Ceza İnfaz Hukuku Açısından Değerlendirilmesi* [İzmir Bar Association Human Rights Law and Legal Studies Center: The Evaluation of F Type Prisons from the Perspective of Penal Execution Law]. İzmir: Egetan, January 2001.

Demirel, İlhan, Barış Kaya, and Murat Çoban. "Letter to the Press and to the Public from Aydın Prison." [In Turkish.] November 29, 2000, private collection.

Demirer, Temel, and Gökçer Özgür. "'Andıç'lı F-Tipi Medya" [F-type Media with a Military Intelligence Memorandum]. *Özgür Üniversite Forumu*, no. 12 (October-December 2000): 27–55.

Devecioğlu, Ayşegül. "'Biz'den Uzaklaşan Hapishaneler" [Prisons That Drift Away from "Us"]. *Birikim*, nos. 142–43 (February-March 2001): 37–44.

Devji, Faisal. *Landscapes of the Jihad: Militancy, Morality, Modernity*. Ithaca, NY: Cornell University Press, 2005.

Devletoğlu, Jan. "Demir Leydi 20 Yıl Önce Söylemişti" [The Iron Lady Had Said So Twenty Years Ago]. *Sabah*, December 15, 2000.

Devrimci Demokrasi. "Alibeyköy Direniş Evi" [Alibeyköy Resistance House]. January 16–31, 2002, 8.

———. "Avrupa'da Tutsaklarla Dayanışma Eylemleri Sürüyor" [Solidarity Actions with Prisoners Continue in Europe]. December 1–16, 2000, 19.

———. "Devrimci Tarihi(ni) Unutma! ... " [Don't Forget (Your) Revolutionary History! ...]. July 1–16, 2000, 3.

———. "Devrimci Tutsaklar Teslim Alınamaz!" [Revolutionary Captives Cannot Be Taken Over!]. March 1–16, 2000, 8.

———. "Devrimciliğin Yeniden Sınandığı Keskin Bir Dönemeçten Geçiyoruz" [We Are Passing Through a Sharp Turning Point in Which Revolutionism Is Being Tested Again]. October 1–16, 2000, 3.

———. "Direniş Tarihimize Onurla Yazılan Yeni Sayfalar Eklemeye Devam Ediyoruz" [We Continue to Add New Pages to Our History of Resistance Written with Honor]. October 16–31, 2000, 13.

——. "F Tipine Geçişin Provası ve Burdur Direnişi" [The Rehearsal for the Transition to the F Type and the Burdur Resistance]. August 1–16, 2000, 12.

——. "F Tipi Ölüm Hücrelerinde Direniş Büyüyor" [Resistance Grows in F Type Death Cells]. January 16–31, 2001, 1.

——. "Kızıl Bantlı Direnişçilerin Kararlılığı, Zaferin Finalini Muştuluyor" [The Determination of The Resistors With Red Headbands Bespeaks the Finale of Victory]. December 16–31, 2000, 8.

——. "Saldırı F Tipi Projesinin Provasıdır" [The Attack Is the Rehearsal for the F Type Project]. July 16–31, 2000, 16.

——. "Süresiz Açlık Grevi Direnişi Başladı" [The Hunger Strike Resistance of Indefinite Duration Has Begun]. October 16–31, 2000, 1.

"Dialogue Between Michel Foucault and Baqir Parham." In *Foucault and the Iranian Revolution: Gender and the Seductions of Islamism.* Trans. Janet Afary. Annotated by Janet Afary and Kevin B. Anderson, 183–89. Chicago: University of Chicago Press, 2005.

Diamond, Irene, and Lee Quinby, eds. *Foucault and Feminism: Reflections on Resistance.* Boston: Northeastern University Press, 1988.

Dillon, Michael. "Correlating Sovereign and Biopower." In *Sovereign Lives: Power in Global Politics,* ed. Jenny Edkins, Véronique Pin-Fat, and Michael Shapiro, 41–60. New York: Routledge, 2004.

Dingley, James, and Marcello Mollica. "The Human Body as a Terrorist Weapon: Hunger Strikes and Suicide Bombers." *Studies in Conflict and Terrorism* 30, no. 6 (2007): 459–92.

Direniş Ölüm ve Yaşam-II: Devrim Kuşağının Kahramanları [Resistance Death and Life-II: Heroes of the Revolution Generation]. Istanbul: Haziran Yayıncılık, 1997.

"Diyarbakır Zindanı." http://www.diyarbakirzindani.com. (Last accessed January 19, 2013.)

Dodds, Paisley. "Terror Suspects at Guantanamo Attempted Mass Hanging and Strangling Protest in 2003, U.S. Military Reports." *Associated Press Worldstream.* January 25, 2005. Available at http://www.highbeam.com/doc/1P1–104672517.html. (Last accessed November 5, 2012.)

Doğan, Erkan. "Türk Solunun Kısa Tarihi: Sosyalizmi Milliyetçilikle Eklemlemek" [The Short History of the Turkish Left: To Articulate Socialism with Nationalism]. *Doğu Batı* 15, no. 59 (2011): 135–55.

Donzelot, Jacques. *The Policing of Families.* Trans. Robert Hurley. Baltimore:

Johns Hopkins University Press, 1997.

Dönmez, Hasan. *Mamak . . . Ey Mamak* [Mamak . . . Oh, Mamak]. Istanbul: Su Yayınları, 2007.

Dönmez, Şenay. *Yaşatmak için Öldüler* [They Died to Make Live]. Istanbul: Boran Yayınevi, 2003.

Drake, Deborah. *Prisons, Punishment and the Pursuit of Security*. Hampshire: Palgrave Macmillan, 2012.

DSP Genel Merkezi (Democratic Left Party Central Office). *Ne İstedi, Nasıl Çıktı? Af ve Rahşan Ecevit: Cezaevleri ve F Tipi* [What Did She Want, How Did it Come Out? Amnesty and Rahşan Ecevit: Prisons and the F Type]. Ankara: Ajans-Türk Basım ve Basın, October, 2001.

Dubreuil, Laurent. "Leaving Politics: Bios, Zōē, Life." *diacritics* 36, no. 2 (Summer 2006): 83–98.

Dumont, Paul. "The Origins of Kemalist Ideology." In *Ataturk and the Modernization of Turkey*, ed. Jacob M. Landau, 25–44. Boulder: Westview, 1984.

Durkheim, Émile. *Suicide: A Study in Sociology*. Trans. John A. Spaulding and George Simpson. New York: Free Press, 1951.

Dündar, Can. "Ölüm Koridoru" [Death Corridor]. *Sabah*, December 20, 2000. Available at http://www.candundar.com.tr. (Last accessed October 28, 2010.)

düzkan, ayşe. *behiç aşçı kitabı* [The Behiç Aşçı Book]. Istanbul: Versus Kitap, December 2006.

Dyer, Owen. "Force Feeding at Guantanamo Breaches Ethics, Doctors Say." *British Medical Journal* 332, no. 7541 (March 11, 2006): 569.

Edkins, Jenny, and Véronique Pin-Fat. "Through the Wire: Relations of Power and Relations of Violence." *Millennium: Journal of International Studies* 34, no. 1 (August 2005): 1–24.

Elster, Jon. "Motivations and Beliefs in Suicide Missions." In *Making Sense of Suicide Missions*, ed. Diego Gambetta, 233–58. Oxford: Oxford University Press, 2005.

Enns, Diane. "Bare Life and the Occupied Body." *theory and event* 7, no. 3 (2004). http://muse.jhu.edu/login?auth=0&type=summary&url=/journals/theory_and_event/v007/7.3enns.html. (Last accessed November 13, 2013.)

Erdal, Meryem. "Devletin Cezaevi Politikası" [The State's Prison Policy]. *Birikim*, no. 136 (August 2000): 57–62.

Erder, Sema. *İstanbul'a Bir Kent Kondu: Ümraniye* [A City Squatted to Istanbul: Ümraniye]. Istanbul: İletişim Yayınları, 1996.

Erdoğan, Sadık, Gürkut Acar, Yücel Sayman, and Noyan Özkan. "Üç Kapı Üç Kilit" [Three Doors, Three Locks]. Press release, November 28, 2001, private collection.

Erdoğan, Sadık, Yücel Sayman, Noyan Özkan. "Open Letter." [In Turkish.] Press release, April 5, 2001.

Ergil, Doğu. "Suicide Terrorism in Turkey." *Civil Wars* 3, no. 1 (Spring 2000): 37–54.

Ergin, Murat. "Biometrics and Anthropometrics: The Twins of Turkish Modernity." *Patterns of Prejudice* 42, no. 3 (2008): 281–304.

———. "'Is the Turk a White Man?' Towards a Theoretical Framework for Race in the Making of Turkishness." *Middle Eastern Studies* 44, no. 6 (2008): 827–50.

Erman, Tahire. "The Politics of Squatter (Gecekondu) Studies in Turkey: The Changing Representations of Rural Migrants in Academic Discourse." *Urban Studies* 38, no. 7 (2001): 983–1002.

———. and Emrah Göker. "Alevi Politics in Contemporary Turkey." *Middle Eastern Studies* 36, no. 4 (2000): 99–118.

Eroğul, Cem. "The Establishment of Multiparty Rule: 1945–71." In *Turkey in Transition: New Perspectives*, ed. Irvin C. Schick and Ertuğrul Ahmet Tonak, 101–43. New York: Oxford University Press, 1987.

Euben, Roxanne. "Killing (for) Politics: Jihad, Martyrdom, and Political Action." *Political Theory* 30, no. 1 (February 2002): 4–35.

Evans, Malcolm D., and Rod Morgan. *Preventing Torture: A Study of the European Convention for the Prevention of Torture and Inhuman or Degrading Treatment or Punishment.* Oxford: Clarendon, 1998.

Evered, Kyle T., and Emine Ö. Evered. "Governing Population, Public Health, and Malaria in the Early Turkish Republic." *Journal of Historical Geography* 37, no. 4 (October 2011): 470–82.

———. "State, Peasant, Mosquito: The Biopolitics of Public Health Education and Malaria in Early Republican Turkey." *Political Geography* 31, no. 5 (June 2012): 311–23.

———. "Syphilis and Prostitution in the Socio-Medical Geographies of Turkey's Early Republican Provinces." *Health and Place* 18, no. 3 (May 2012): 528–35.

Evrensel. "Bir Grup Tutuklu Ölüm Orucunu Bitirdi" [A Group of Prisoners Ended the Death Fast]. May 14, 2002, 15.

———. "Cezaevlerinde Ölüm Engellensin" [Death Should Be Prevented in Prisons]. December 19, 2000.

———. "Üç Kapı Üç Kilit Tartışması" [The Three Doors Three Locks Debate]. January 10, 2000.

Fanon, Frantz. *The Wretched of the Earth.* Trans. Constance Farrington. Intro. Jean-Paul Sartre. New York: Grove, 1963.

Farias, Ignacio, and Thomas Bender, eds. *Urban Assemblages: How Actor-Network Theory Changes Urban Studies.* Oxon: Routledge, 2010.

Feldman, Allen. *Formations of Violence: The Narrative of the Body and Political Terror in Northern Ireland.* Chicago: University of Chicago Press, 1991.

———. "Political Terror and the Technologies of Memory: Excuse, Sacrifice, Commodification, and Actuarial Moralities." *Radical History Review,* no. 85 (Winter 2003): 58–73.

Ferguson, James, and Akhil Gupta. "Spatializing States: Toward and Ethnography of Neoliberal Governmentality." *American Ethnologist* 29, no. 4 (2002): 981–1002.

Fessler, D. M. T. "The Implications of Starvation Induced Psychological Changes for the Ethical Treatment of Hunger Strikers." *Journal of Medical Ethics* 29, no. 4 (2003): 243–47.

Fişekçi, Turgay. "Nâzım Hikmet'i Açlık Grevine Götüren Yol" [The Road That Led Nâzım Hikmet to Hunger Strike]. In *Nâzım Hikmet'in Açlık Grevi* [The Hunger Strike of Nâzım Hikmet], ed. Yeşim Bilge Bengü, 7–14. Istanbul: Istanbul Bilgi Üniversitesi Yayınları, 2011.

Fitzpatrick, Peter. "Bare Sovereignty: Homo Sacer and the Insistence of Law." *theory and event* 5, no. 2 (2001). http://muse.jhu.edu/login?auth=0&type=summary&url-/journals/theory_and_event/v005/5.2fitzpatrick.html. (Last accessed November 12, 2013.)

———. "These Mad Abandon'd Times." *Economy and Society* 30, no. 2 (2001): 255–70.

Foucault, Michel. *Abnormal: Lectures at the Collège de France, 1974–1975.* Ed. Valerio Marchetti and Antonella Salomoni. Trans. Graham Burchell. New York: Picador, 2003.

———. "Alternatives to the Prison: Dissemination or Decline of Social Control?" *Theory, Culture, and Society* 26, no. 6 (2009): 12–24.

———. "Appendix: Foucault and His Critics, an Annotated Translation." In

Foucault and the Iranian Revolution: Gender and the Seductions of Islamism.
Trans. Karen de Bruin et al. Annotated by Janet Afary and Kevin B. Anderson, 180–277. Chicago: University of Chicago Press, 2005.

——. "A Revolt with Bare Hands." In *Foucault and the Iranian Revolution:
Gender and the Seductions of Islamism.* Trans. Karen de Bruin and Kevin
B. Anderson. Annotated by Janet Afary and Kevin B. Anderson, 210–13.
Chicago: University of Chicago Press, 2005.

——. *Discipline and Punish: The Birth of the Prison.* Trans. Alan Sheridan.
New York: Vintage, 1977.

——. "Intellectuals and Power: A Conversation Between Michel Foucault
and Gilles Deleuze." In *Language, Counter-Memory, Practice: Selected Essays and Interviews by Michel Foucault,* ed. Donald F. Bouchard, 205–217.
Ithaca: Cornell University Press, 1977.

——. "Is It Useless to Revolt?" In *Foucault and the Iranian Revolution: Gender
and the Seductions of Islamism.* Trans. Karen de Bruin and Kevin B. Anderson. Annotated by Janet Afary and Kevin B. Anderson, 263–67. Chicago:
University of Chicago Press, 2005.

——. "Nietzsche, Geneaology, History." In *Language, Counter-Memory,
Practice: Selected Essays and Interviews by Michel Foucault,* ed. Donald F.
Bouchard, 139–64. Ithaca: Cornell University Press, 1977.

——. "*Omnes et Singulatim*': Toward a Critique of Political Reason." In *Essential Works of Foucault* (1954–1984), vol. 3: *Power,* ed. James D. Faubion,
trans. Robert Hurley et al., 298–325. New York: New Press, 2001.

——. *Power/Knowledge: Selected Interviews and Other Writings 1972–1977.* Ed.
Colin Gordon. New York: Pantheon, 1980.

——. *Psychiatric Power: Lectures at the Collège de France, 1973–1974.* Ed.
Jacques Lagrange. Trans. Graham Burchell. Hampshire: Palgrave Macmillan, 2006.

——. *Remarks on Marx: Conversations with Duccio Trombadori.* Trans. R.
James Goldstein and James Cascaito. New York: Semiotext(e), 1991.

——. *Security, Territory, Population: Lectures at the Collège de France, 1977–
1978.* Ed. Michel Senellart. Trans. Graham Burchell. Hampshire: Palgrave
Macmillan, 2007.

——. "*Society Must Be Defended*": Lectures at the Collège de France, 1975–1976.*
Ed. Mauro Bertani and Alessandro Fontana. Trans. David Macey. New
York: Picador, 2003.

——. "Tehran: Faith Against the Shah." In *Foucault and the Iranian Revolu-

tion: Gender and the Seductions of Islamism. Trans. Karen de Bruin and Kevin B. Anderson. Annotated by Janet Afary and Kevin B. Anderson, 198–203. Chicago: University of Chicago Press, 2005.

———. *The Hermeneutics of The Subject: Lectures at the Collège de France 1974–1975.* Ed. Arnold I. Davidson. Trans. Graham Burchell. Hampshire: Palgrave Macmillan, 2005.

———. *The History of Sexuality,* vol. 1: *An Introduction.* Trans. Robert Hurley. New York: Vintage, 1990.

———. *The History of Sexuality,* vol. 3: *The Care of the Self.* Trans. Robert Hurley. New York: Vintage, 1988.

———. "The Mythical Leader of the Iranian Revolt." In *Foucault and the Iranian Revolution: Gender and the Seductions of Islamism.* Trans. Karen de Bruin and Kevin B. Anderson. Annotated by Janet Afary and Kevin B. Anderson, 220–23. Chicago: University of Chicago Press, 2005.

———. "The Political Technology of Individuals." In *Essential Works of Foucault* (1954–1984), vol. 3: *Power,* ed. James D. Faubion, trans. Robert Hurley et al., 403–17. New York: New Press, 2001.

———. "The Revolt in Iran Spreads on Cassette Tapes." In *Foucault and the Iranian Revolution: Gender and the Seductions of Islamism.* Trans. Karen de Bruin and Kevin B. Anderson. Annotated by Janet Afary and Kevin B. Anderson, 216–20. Chicago: University of Chicago Press, 2005.

———. "The Subject and Power." In *Essential Works of Foucault* (1954–1984), vol. 3: *Power,* ed. James D. Faubion, trans. Robert Hurley et al., 326–48. New York: New Press, 2001.

———. "What Are the Iranians Dreaming [Rêvent] About?" In *Foucault and the Iranian Revolution: Gender and the Seductions of Islamism.* Trans. Karen de Bruin and Kevin B. Anderson. Annotated by Janet Afary and Kevin B. Anderson, 203–9. Chicago: University of Chicago Press, 2005.

Fraser, Nancy. "From Redistribution to Recognition? Dilemmas of Justice in a 'Post-Socialist' Age." *New Left Review,* no. 212 (July–August 1995): 68–93.

———. *Unruly Practices: Power, Discourse, and Gender in Contemporary Social Theory.* Cambridge: Polity, 1989.

Freud, Sigmund. "On Dreams." In *The Freud Reader,* ed. Peter Gay, 142–72. New York: Norton, 1989.

Gambetta, Diego. "Can We Make Sense of Suicide Missions?" In *Making Sense of Suicide Missions,* ed. Diego Gambetta, 259–99. Oxford: Oxford University Press, 2005.

———. ed. *Making Sense of Suicide Missions.* Oxford: Oxford University Press, 2005.

Garland, David. *Punishment and Modern Society: A Study in Social Theory.* Chicago: University of Chicago Press, 1990.

———. *Punishment and Welfare: A History of Penal Strategies.* Aldershot: Gower, 1985.

———. *The Culture of Control: Crime and Social Order in Contemporary Society.* Chicago: University of Chicago Press, 2001.

Garland, David, and Peter Young, eds. *The Power to Punish.* London: Heinemann, 1983.

George, Alexander, ed. *Western State Terrorism.* New York: Routledge, 1991.

Giddens, Anthony. *A Contemporary Critique of Historical Materialism.* London: Macmillan, 1981.

Glancy, Graham D. and Erin L. Murray. "Psychiatric Aspects of Solitary Confinement." *Victims and Offenders* 1, no. 4 (2006): 361–68.

Global Detention Project. http://www.globaldetentionproject.org. (Last accessed November 12, 2013.)

Gould, Roger V. *Insurgent Identities: Class Community, and Protest in Paris from 1848 to the Commune.* Chicago: University of Chicago Press, 1995.

Gökay, Bülent. "The Turkish Communist Party: The Fate of the Founders." *Middle Eastern Studies* 29, no. 2 (1993): 220–35.

Gökmen, Emel, Hakan Gürvit, Demet Kınay, Nermin Demirci, Hüseyin Şahin, Rezzan Tuncay, Emre Öge, and Gençay Gürsoy. "Mayıs 1996 Açlık Grevi-Ölüm Orucu Katılımcılarının Klinik Değerlendirmesi" [The Clinical Evaluation of Participants of the May 1996 Hunger Strike-Death Fast]. http://www.ttb.org.tr/aclik_grevleri/turkce4.html. (Last accessed December 1, 2012.)

Göktaş, Kemal. "F Tipinde Üç Gün Yetti" [Three Days Were Enough at the F Type]. *Radikal,* December 28, 2000.

Görmüş, Alper. "'Hayata Dönüş'te Medya" [The Media in "Return to Life"]. *Taraf,* November 30, 2010.

Gramsci, Antonio. *Selections from the Prison Notebooks.* Ed. Quintin Hoare and Geoffrey Nowell Smith. New York: International, 1971.

Green, Penny. "Turkish Jails, Hunger Strikes and the European Drive for Prison Reform." *Punishment and Society* 4, no. 1 (2002): 97–101.

Gregory, Bernadette. "Personal Views: Hunger Striking Prisoners: The Doctors' Dilemma." *British Medical Journal* 331, no. 7521 (October 15, 2005): 913.

Gregory, Brad S. *Salvation at Stake: Christian Martyrdom in Early Modern Europe.* Cambridge: Harvard University Press, 1999.

Grojean, Olivier. "Violence Against the Self: The Case of a Kurdish Non-Islamist Group." In *The Enigma of Islamist Violence,* ed. Amélie Blom, Laetitia Bucaille and Luis Martinez, trans. John Atherton, Ros Schwartz and William Snow, 105–20. New York: Columbia University Press, 2007.

Guenther, Lisa. "Resisting Agamben: The Biopolitics of Shame and Humiliation." *Philosophy and Social Criticism* 38, no. 1 (2012): 59–79.

Güler, Aydemir. "Sola Dair" [On the Left]. *Sosyalist İktidar,* no. 203, December 22, 2000.

Günçıkan, Berat. "Hücre: Ruh da Üşür Beden de" [The Cell: The Soul Feels Cold and So Does The Body]. *Cumhuriyet Dergi,* no. 749, July 30, 2000, 1, 6–9.

"'Güneşimizi Karartamazsınız!' Şiarıyla Kahramanlık ve Bağlılık Eylemi Gerçekleştiren Yoldaşlar" [Comrades Who Commit Acts of Heroism and Commitment With The Slogan 'You Cannot Darken Our Sun']. Fedai Şehitler Albümü [Album of Sacrificial Martyrs]. *Serxwebun,* no. 26 (2001): 78. Available at http://www.serxwebun.org/sehitler/fedaisehit-leralbumu/. (Last accessed December 1, 2012.)

Gürbüz, Cafer. "Letter to Oral Çalışlar." [In Turkish.] N.d., private collection.

Gürvit, H., E. Gökmen, D. Kınay, H. Şahin, N. Demirci, R. Tuncay, A. Boyaciyan, E. Öge, and G. Gürsoy. "Hunger-Strike Related Wernicke-Korsakoff Disease." *Journal of the Neurological Sciences* 150, Supplement 1: S39. Available at http://www.ttb.org.tr/aclik_grevleri/ingmetin7.html. (Last accessed December 1, 2012.)

Habermas, Jürgen. "Some Questions Concerning the Theory of Power: Foucault Again." In *The Philosophical Discourse of Modernity,* trans. Frederick G. Lawrence, 266–93. Cambridge: MIT Press, 1987.

Hafez, Mohammed M. "Dying to Be Martyrs: The Symbolic Dimension of Suicide Terrorism." In *Root Causes of Suicide Terrorism: The Globalization of Martyrdom,* ed. Ami Pedahzur, 54–80. London: Routledge, 2006.

Hallam, Elizabeth, Jenny Hockey, and Glennys Howarth. *Beyond the Body: Death and Social Identity.* London: Routledge, 1999.

Haney, Craig. "Mental Health Issues in Long-Term Solitary and 'Supermax' Confinement." *Crime and Delinquency* 49, no. 1 (2003): 124–56.

Hansen, Thomas, and Finn Stepputat, eds. *States of Imagination: Ethnographic Explorations of the Postcolonial State.* Durham, NC: Duke University Press, 2001.

Harris, George S. *Origins of Communism in Turkey.* Stanford: Stanford University Press, 1967.

Hasso, Frances S. "Discursive and Political Deployments by/of the 2002 Palestinian Women Suicide Bombers/Martyrs." *Feminist Review,* no. 81 (2005): 23–51.

Hatun, Şükrü. "Ölüm Oruçları ve Hekimlik" [Death Fasts and Medicine]. *Radikal 2,* December 31, 2000. Available at http://www.ttb.org.tr/aclik_grevleri/shatun_sy.html. (Last accessed December 1, 2012.)

Helsinki Citizens' Assembly. *F Type Prisons' Report: Solitary Confinement in F-Type Prisons Must Be Ended!* Report, July 10, 2001.

Helsinki Watch. *Nothing Unusual: Torture of Children in Turkey.* Special Report, January 1, 1992.

———. *Twenty-One Deaths in Detention in 1993.* Report 6, no. 2, January 1994.

Heper, Metin. "The Ottoman Legacy and Turkish Politics." *Journal of International Affairs* 54, no. 1 (Fall 2000): 63–82.

———. *The State Tradition in Turkey.* North Humberside: Eothen, 1985.

Hershlag, Z. Y. "Ataturk's Étatism." In *Ataturk and the Modernization of Turkey,* ed. Jacob M. Landau, 171–180. Boulder: Westview, 1984.

———. *Turkey: The Challenge of Growth.* Leiden: Brill, 1968.

Hill, Peter, "Kamikaze, 1943–5." In *Making Sense of Suicide Missions,* ed. Diego Gambetta, 1–42. Oxford: Oxford University Press, 2005.

Hoffman, Bruce. *Inside Terrorism.* Rev. ed. New York: Columbia University Press, 2006.

Holston, James. "Spaces of Insurgent Citizenship." In *Cities and Citizenship,* ed. James Holston, 155–76. Durham: Duke University Press, 1999.

Honneth, Axel. *The Struggle for Recognition: The Moral Grammar of Social Conflicts.* Cambridge: MIT Press, 1996.

Hopalı, Tayfun. "Burası Filistin Değil İstanbul" [This Is Istanbul, Not Palestine]. *Sabah,* November 5, 2001.

Hopgood, Stephen. "Tamil Tigers, 1987–2002." In *Making Sense of Suicide Missions,* ed. Diego Gambetta, 43–76. Oxford: Oxford University Press, 2005.

Howarth, Glennys. *Last Rites: The Work of the Modern Funeral Director.* New York: Baywood, 1996.

Hrassian, Stuart. "Psychopathological Effects of Solitary Confinement." *American Journal of Psychiatry* 140, no. 11 (1983): 1450–54.

Human Rights Watch. *Cold Storage: Super-Maximum Security Confinement in Indiana.* New York: Human Rights Watch, 1997. http://www.hrw.org/reports/1997/usind/. (Last accessed December 1, 2012.)

———. *Out of Sight: Super-Maximum Security Confinement in the United States.* Special report 12, no. 1 (G), 2000. http://www.hrw.org/reports/2000/supermax/. (Last accessed December 1, 2012.)

———. *Red Onion State Prison: Super-Maximum Security Confinement in Virginia.* New York: Human Rights Watch, 1999.

———. *Turkey: Small Group Isolation in F-type Prisons and the Violent Transfers of Prisoners to Sincan, Kandıra, and Edirne Prisons on December 19, 2000.* Report 13, no. 2 (D), 2001. http://www.hrw.org/reports/2001/turkey/index.htm. (Last accessed December 1, 2012.)

———. "Small Group Isolation in Turkish Prisons: An Avoidable Disaster." *Briefing Paper,* May 24, 2000.

———. *Turkey: Torture and Mistreatment in Pre-Trial Detention by Anti-Terror Police.* Special report, March 1, 1997. http://www.hrw.org/legacy/reports/1997/turkey/. (Last accessed November 12, 2013.)

Huysmans, Jef. "The Jargon of Exception—On Schmitt, Agamben, and the Absence of Political Society." *International Political Sociology* 2 (2008): 165–83.

Hürriyet. "Bekaroğlu: Ölüm Orucu Bugün Biter" [Bekaroğlu: The Death Fast Ends Today]. December 13, 2000.

———. "Cezaevlerindeki Terör Karargahları Temizlendi" [The Terror Headquarters in the Prisons Were Cleaned Out]. December 21, 2000.

———. "Destek Orucu Kana Bulandı" [Solidarity Strike Got Bloody]. December 11, 2000.

———. "Devlet Girdi" [The State Went In]. December 20, 2000.

———. "Devletin İtirafı: Cezaevlerini Teröristler Yönetiyor" [The Confession of the State: Terrorists Rule the Prisons]. October 15, 1999.

———. "Düğmeye Böyle Basıldı" [How the Green Light Was Given]. December 20, 2000.

———. "Ecevit: Devlete Dayatma Kabul Edilemez" [Ecevit: Impositions Upon the State Cannot Be Accepted]. December 11, 2000.

———. "Hayata Dönüşün Bilançosu" [The Balance Sheet of Return to Life]. December 24, 2000.

———. "Her An Ölebilirler" [They Can Die Any Moment]. December 16, 2000.

———. "İşte Avrupa'nın F Tipi Raporu" [So This is Europe's F Type Report]. December 14, 2000.

———. "Kadın Militanı Yaktılar" [They Burned a Female Militant]. December 22, 2000.

———. "Müdahale Etmeyen Hekime Soruşturma Açılacak" [Physicians Who

Do Not Intervene Will Face Prosecution]. December 22, 2000.

——. "Operasyonun Bilançosu: 2 Asker Şehit Oldu, 15 Mahkum Öldü" [The Balance Sheet of the Operation: 2 Soldiers Martyred, 15 Convicts Dead]. December 19, 2000.

——. "Ölüm Orucuna DGM Yasağı" [The DGM (State Security Court) Ban on the Death Fast]. December 15, 2000.

——. "Ölüm Orucunda İpler Koptu" [Bridges Burned in the Death Fast]. December 15, 2000.

——. "Türk: Şefkat Operasyonu" [Türk: Compassion Operation]. December 19, 2000.

——. "Türkiye Haklı" [Turkey Is Right]. December 15, 2000.

——. "Yakılanlar Kurban" [Those Who Were Burned Are Victims]. December 22, 2000.

Immarigeon, Russ. "The Marionization of American Prisons." *National Prison Project Journal* 7, no. 4 (1992): 1–5.

"Iran: The Spirit of a World Without Spirit: Foucault's Conversation with Claire Brière and Pierre Blanchet." In *Foucault and the Iranian Revolution: Gender and the Seductions of Islamism.* Trans. Alan Sheridan. Annotated by Janet Afary and Kevin B. Anderson, 250–60. Chicago: University of Chicago Press, 2005.

Israeli, Raphael. "Islamikaze and Their Significance." *Terrorism and Political Violence* 9 (1997): 96–121.

Istanbul Indymedia. "Devrimci Avukat Behiç Aşçı Ölüm Orucunda" [Revolutionary Lawyer Behiç Aşçı Is On The Death Fast]. April 12, 2006. http://istanbul.indymedia.org/news/2006/04/114692.php. (Last accessed January 12, 2007.)

Işık, Oğuz, and M. Melih Pınarcıoğlu, *Nöbetleşe Yoksulluk: Sultanbeyli Örneği* [Taking Turns in Poverty: The Example of Sultanbeyli]. Istanbul: İletişim Yayınları, 2001.

İnsan Hakları Derneği [Human Rights Association]. *F Tipi Cezaevi Modeli, Sorunlar ve Öneriler: CPT'ye (Avrupa Konseyi İşkencenin Önlenmesi Komitesi) Sunulan Rapor* [F Type Prison Model, Problems and Suggestions: The Report Presented to CPT (Council of Europe Committee for the Prevention of Torture)]. Report, July 16, 2000.

——. *1981–1995 Cezaevlerinde Yaşamını Yitirenler* [1981-1995 Those Who Lost Their Lives in The Prisons]. Report, n.d.

——. *Ölüm Oruçları: 200. Gün Raporu* [Death Fasts: Report On the 200th Day]. Report, July 2001.

İnsan Hakları Derneği İstanbul Şubesi [Human Rights Association Istanbul Branch]. *Cezaevleri Komisyonu Raporu: 93 Ocak Şubat Mart Nisan* [The Report of the Prisons Commission: 93 January February March April]. Report, May 1993.

——. *F Tipi Cezaevleri Raporu 2* [F Type Prisons Report 2]. Special Report, 2002.

——. "Ölum Oruçlarına İlişkin Ön Rapor" [The Preliminary Report Concerning The Death Fasts]. *Bulletin*, no. 1. December 19, 2000.

——. *Sessiz Çığlık: Hücreler* [Silent Scream: The Cells]. Special Report, 2001.

——. *Tecrit ya da F Tipi İnfaz Sistemi* [Isolation or The F Type Execution System]. Report, 2003.

İnsan Hakları ve Mazlumlar İçin Dayanışma Derneği Cezaevleri Komisyonu [Solidarity Association for Human Rights and the Oppressed Prisons Commission]. *Cezaevi ... Cezaevi ... : Yeni Yasal Düzenlemeler Üzerine Değerlendirme* [Prison... Prison...: An Evaluation Concerning New Legislation]. Report, May 2001.

İnsel, Ahmet. "Laiklik, Cumhuriyet ve Sosyalist Hareket." *Birikim*, no. 2 (June 1989): 25–34.

İstanbul Barosu Cezaevleri Komisyonu [Istanbul Bar Association Prisons Commission]. *Cezaevleri Durum Raporu 1995/1997* [Report on the Prisons Situation, 1995–97]. Report, October–December 1997.

İstanbul Barosu İnsan Hakları Merkezi Cezaevleri Çalışma Grubu [Istanbul Bar Association Human Rights Center Working Committee on Prisons]. *Cezaevlerinde Son Gelişmeler: Koğuşlardan Hücrelere 19 Aralık Cezaevleri Operasyonları* [The Most Recent Developments in Prisons: The Prisons Operations of December 19 From Wards To Cells]. Special Report, February 2001.

——. "Cezaevleri Sorunları ve Çözüm Yolları" [Problems of Prisons and Solution Routes]. Roundtable Meeting, December 11, 1999. Private collection.

——. *"Kocaeli F Tipi Cezaevi" Gözlem Raporu* ["Kocaeli F Type Prison" Observation Report]. Report, June 16, 2000.

——. *1999–2000 Yılları Çalışma Raporu* [Working Report on Years 1999–2000], Report, 2000.

İstanbul Barosu Merkez Kurulu ve Meslek Odaları Merkez Kurulları [Istanbul Bar Association Central Board and Central Boards of Occupational Chambers]. "Statement on the Death Fasts in Prisons" [In Turkish.] Press release, December 5, 2000, private collection.

İşlegen, Yeşim. "F Tipi Cezaevleri, İnsan Hakları, Sağlık" [F Type Prisons, Human Rights, Health]. *Birikim*, no. 136 (August 2000): 40–43.

İzmir Barosu [Izmir Bar Association]. "İnfaz Hakimlikleri: Cezaevlerinin DGM'si" [Courts for the Penal Execution of Sentences: The State Security Courts of Prisons]. Special issue, *Çağdaş Hukuk* (July 2004): 59–124.

Jabri, Vivienne. *War and the Transformation of Global Politics.* 2d ed. London: Palgrave Macmillan, 2010.

Jacobs, James B. *Stateville: The Penitentiary in Mass Society.* Chicago: University of Chicago Press, 1978.

Jenkins, Fiona. "Bare Life: Asylum-Seekers, Australian Politics and Agamben's Critique of Violence." *Australian Journal of Human Rights* 10, no. 1 (2004): 79–95.

Johannes Weir Foundation for Health and Human Rights. *Assistance in Hunger Strikes: A Manual for Physicians and Other Health Personnel Dealing with Hunger Strikes.* Amersfoort: Johannes Weir Foundation for Health and Human Rights, 1995.

Juergensmeyer, Mark. *Terror in the Mind of God: The Global Rise of Religious Violence.* 3d ed. Berkeley: University of California Press, 2003.

Kadıoğlu, Ayşe. "Republican Epistemology and Islamic Discourses in Turkey in the 1990s." *Muslim World.* 88, no. 1 (1998): 1–21.

Kahraman, Hasan Bülent. "Türk Solunun Çıkmaz Sokağı: Kemalizm (Ordu) İlişkisi" [The One Way Street of the Turkish Left: The Kemalism (Army) Relationship]. *Doğu Batı* 15, no. 59 (2011): 35–76.

Kaldor, Mary. *New and Old Wars: Organized Violence in a Global Era.* Cambridge: Polity, 1999.

Kaliber, Alper. "F Tipi Gelişmeleri ve Cezaevleri Operasyonu Vesilesiyle Türkiye'de Yöneten-Yönetilen İlişkisine Bir Bakış" [A Look at the Relationship Between the Rulers and the Ruled in Turkey on Occasion of F Type Developments and the Prisons Operation]. *Birikim*, no. 145 (May 2001): 92–98.

Kalyvas, Andreas. "Hegemonic Sovereignty: Carl Schmitt, Antonio Gramsci, and the Constituent Prince." *Journal of Political Ideologies* 5, no. 3 (2000): 343–76.

———. "Popular Sovereignty, Democracy, and the Constituent Power." *Constellations* 12, no. 2 (June 2005): 223–44.

———. "The Sovereign Weaver: Beyond the Camp." In *Politics, Metaphysics, and Death: Essays on Giorgio Agamben's* Homo Sacer, ed. Andrew Norris, 107–34. Durham: Duke University Press, 2005.

Kalyvas, Stathis N., and Ignacio Sánchez-Cuenca. "Killing Without Dying: The Absence of Suicide Missions." In *Making Sense of Suicide Missions*, ed. Diego Gambetta, 209–32. Oxford: Oxford University Press, 2005.

Kama, Bayram, Yunus Aydemir, Cemal Çakmak, Kenan Güngör, Aytunç Altay, Ramazan Sadıkoğulları, Hasan Yüksel, and Özgür Aslan. "Halkımıza!" [To Our People!] Public Statement. *Devrimci Demokrasi*, June 1–16, 2002.

Kamel, Rachael, and Bonnie Kerness. "The Prison Inside the Prison: Control Units, Supermax Prisons, and Devices of Torture." *Justice Visions Briefing Paper*. Philadelphia: Community Relations Unit, American Friends Service Committee, 2003. http://www.afsc.org/justicevisions.htm. (Last accessed April 17, 2005.)

Kanar, Ercan. "Azaphane ya da Cezaevleri" [Torment Houses or Prisons]. *Birikim*, no. 82 (February 1996): 63–70.

———. "'İktidar Aklı' Cezaevleri" [Prisons of Raison D'état]. *Demokratik Dönüşüm*, no. 2 (July 2001): 13–18.

Kansu, Işık. "'3 Kapı 3 Anahtar' Teşvikçi Önerisi." ["Three Doors, Three Locks": The Proposal of Promoters]. *Cumhuriyet*, January 12, 2002.

Kant, Immanuel. *Grounding for the Metaphysics of Morals*. 3d ed. Trans. James W. Ellington. Indianapolis: Hackett, 1993.

Kantarowicz, Ernst H. *The King's Two Bodies: A Study in Mediaeval Political Theology*. Princeton: Princeton University Press, 1957.

Kaplan, Sam. "Din-u Devlet All Over Again? The Politics of Military Secularism and Religious Militarism in Turkey Following the 1980 Coup." *International Journal of Middle East Studies* 34, no. 1 (February 2002): 113–27.

Kaptanoğlu, Cem. "Panopticon'dan F Tipine Tecrit" [Isolation from the Panopticon to the F Type]. *Birikim*, no. 136 (August 2000): 31–39.

Karabulut, Suat, Burhan Gardaş, and Sinan Eren. "Open Letter to the Press and Public from Aydın Prison." [In Turkish.] November 29, 2000, private collection.

Karal, Enver Ziya. "The Principles of Kemalism." In *Ataturk, Founder of a Modern State*, ed. Ergun Özbudun and Ali Kazancıgil, 11–35. Hamden, CT: Archon, 1981.

Karataş, D., İ. Erdoğan, T. Özkök, A. Turan, Ş. Şen, Z. Polat, and M. Göleli, *12 Eylül'de Direniş Ölüm ve Yaşam* [Resistance Death and Life Under September 12]. 3d ed. Istanbul: Boran Yayınevi, 2000.

Karpat, Kemal H. "Socialism and the Labor Party of Turkey." *Middle Eastern Journal* 21, no. 2 (1967): 157–72.

Kartal, Ercan, ed. *Büyük Direniş ve Sol* [The Great Resistance and the Left]. Istanbul: Boran Yayınevi, 2011.

Kaypakkaya, İbrahim. *Seçme Yazılar* [Selected Writings]. Istanbul: Umut Yayımcılık, 1992.

Keeton, G. R. "Hunger Strikers: Ethical and Management Problems." *South African Medical Journal*, no. 83 (1993): 380–81.

Kesici, Gülizar. "Letter to Oral Çalışlar from Sağmalcılar Prison." [In Turkish.] June 24, 2000, private collection.

Keskin, Adnan. "Resmi Yalanlar" [Official Lies]. *Radikal*, July 4, 2001.

Keyder, Çağlar. *State and Class in Turkey: A Study in Capitalist Development.* London: Verso, 1987.

———. "The Political Economy of Turkish Democracy." *New Left Review*, no. 115 (May–June 1979): 3–21.

Keyman, E. Fuat, and Ahmet Içduygu, "Globalization, Civil Society and Citizenship in Turkey: Actors, Boundaries and Discourses." *Citizenship Studies* 7, no. 2 (July 2003): 219–34.

Khosrokhavar, Farhad. *Suicide Bombers: Allah's New Martyrs.* Trans. David Macey. London: Pluto, 2005.

Kınay, Demet, Betül Baykan, Ayşen Gökyiğit, Emel Gökmen, Hüseyin Şahin, Candan Gürses, Rezzan Tuncay, Gencay Gürsoy, and Hakan Gürvit. "Early and Late Stage EEG Findings in Wernicke-Korsakoff Syndrome Due to Long-Standing Starvation: Correlation with the Clinical and MRI Findings." Poster presentation in the European Neurological Society Meeting, June 5–9, 1991, Milan, Italy. Available at http://www.ttb.org.tr/aclik_grevleri/ingmetin3.html. (Last accessed December 1, 2012.)

Kısacık, Raşit. *İşkence ve Ölümün Adresi: Diyarbakır Cezaevi* [The Address of Torture and Death: Diyarbakır Prison]. Istanbul: Ozan Yayıncılık, 2011.

Kızılbayrak. "Hücre Saldırısını Püskürtmenin Sorunları ve Sorumlulukları" [The Problems and Responsibilities of Repelling the Cell Attack]. August 12, 2000.

———. "Hücre Saldırısı ve Yeni Zindan Direnişi" [The Cell Attack and the New Dungeon Resistance]. November 21, 2000.

———. "Öleceğiz ama hücrelere girmeyeceğiz! . . . " [We Will Die But We Will Not Enter the Cells! . . .]. October 21, 2000, 1.

King, Roy D. "The Rise and Rise of Supermax: An American Solution in Search of a Problem?" *Punishment and Society* 1, no. 2 (1999): 163–86.

King, Sallie B. "They Who Burned Themselves for Peace: Quaker and Buddhist Self-Immolators During the Vietnam War," *Buddhist-Christian Studies* 20 (2000): 127–50.

Koçan, Gürcan, and Ahmet Öncü. "From the Morality of Living to the Morality of Dying: Hunger Strikes in Turkish Prisons." *Citizenship Studies* 10, no. 3 (July 2006): 349–72.

Korkmaz, Esat. *Alevilere Saldırılar* [Attacks on Alevis]. Istanbul: Pencere Yayınları, 1997.

Korkmaz, Tamer. "Nihayet . . . " [Finally . . .]. *Zaman*, December 21, 2000.

Koşan, Ümit. "Emperyalizmin Ölüm Anıtları: Yüksek Güvenlik Cezaevleri (Hücreler)" [The Death Monuments of Imperialism: High Security Prisons (Cells)]. *Evrensel Kültür*, August 2000, 16–19.

Köker, Levent. *Modernleşme, Kemalizm ve Demokrasi* [Modernization, Kemalism and Democracy]. Istanbul: İletişim Yayınları, 1990.

Kristeva, Julia. *Powers of Horror: An Essay on Abjection*. New York: Columbia University Press, 1982.

Kukul, Sinan. *Bir Direniş Odağı Metris: Metris Tarihi* [Metris, a Focus of Resistance: History of Metris]. Istanbul: Haziran Yayınevi, 1984.

Kurki, Leena, and Norval Morris. "The Purposes, Practices, and Problems of Supermax Prisons." *Crime and Justice* 28 (2001): 385–424.

Kurtuluş Yolu. "Ölüm Orucu Direnişinin Talepleri Üzerine Görüşme Tutanakları: Kim Ne Dedi?" [Records for Meetings on the Demands of the Death Fast Resistance: Who Said What?], February 2005, 129–60.

Laclau, Ernesto. "Bare Life or Social Indeterminacy?" In *Giorgio Agamben: Sovereignty and Life*, ed. Matthew Calarco and Steven DeCaroli, 11–22. Stanford: Stanford University Press, 2007.

Laçiner, Ömer. "Cevap Yerine: Bir Eleştiri Mantığı ve Üslubuna Dair" [In Lieu of a Response: On a Logic and Tone of Criticism]. *Birikim*, no. 145 (May 2001): 105–8.

——. "'Hayata Dönüş!'" ["Return to Life!"]. *Birikim*, nos. 142–43 (February–March 2001): 10–6.

Landau, Jacob M. *Radical Politics in Modern Turkey*. Leiden: Brill, 1974.

Laqueur, Walter. *The New Terrorism: Fanaticism and the Arms of Mass Destruction*. Oxford: Oxford University Press, 1999.

Le Bon, Gustave. *The Crowd: A Study of the Popular Mind*. London: Fisher Unwin, 1896.

Lefebvre, Henri. *The Production of Space.* Trans. Donald Nicholson-Smith. Oxford: Blackwell, 1991.

Legg, Stephen. "Assemblage/Apparatus: Using Deleuze and Foucault." *Area* 43, no. 2 (2011): 128–33.

Lemke, Thomas. "A Zone of Indistinction: A Critique of Giorgio Agamben's Concept of Biopolitics." *Outlines: Critical Social Studies* 7, no. 1 (2005): 3–13.

Le Pennec, Elsa, and Sally Eberhardt. *The F-Type Prison Crisis and the Repression of Human Rights Defenders in Turkey: Report from a Fact-Finding Mission to Istanbul and Ankara.* Observer Mission Report. Copenhagen: Euro-Mediterranean Human Rights Network, the Kurdish Human Rights Project, and the World Organizations Against Torture, October 2001.

Lewey, Lila. "Force-Feeding: A Clinical or Administrative Decision?" *Canadian Medical Association Journal* 116, no. 4 (February 19, 1977): 416–19.

Lewis, Bernard. *The Assassins: A Radical Sect in Islam.* New York: Basic Books, 2003.

Lewis, Neil A. "Guantánamo Prisoners Go on Hunger Strike." *New York Times.* September 18, 2005.

Lipovsky, Igor. "The Legal Socialist Parties of Turkey, 1960–80." *Middle Eastern Studies* 27, no. 1 (1991): 94–111.

——. *The Socialist Movement in Turkey, 1960–1980.* Leiden: Brill, 1992.

Mardin, Şerif. "Opposition and Control in Turkey." *Government and Opposition* 1, no. 3 (1966): 375–88.

Marx, Karl, and Friedrich Engels. "The German Ideology." In *Collected Works,* vol. 5. New York: International Publishers, 1976.

——. "The Manifesto of the Communist Party." In *The Marx-Engels Reader,* ed. Robert C. Tucker, 469-500, 2d ed. New York: Norton, 1978.

Masters, Cristina. "Femina Sacra: The 'War on/of Terror,' Women and the Feminine." *Security Dialogue* 40, no. 1 (February 2009): 29–49.

Mavioğlu, Ertuğrul. *Asılmayıp da Beslenenler: Bir 12 Eylül Hesaplaşması* [Those Who Were Not Hanged but Fed: Settling Accounts with September 12]. Istanbul: Babil Yayınları, 2004.

——. "'Eski Günlere' Dönüşün Emareleri" [Signs of Return to the "Old Days"]. *Radikal,* November 16, 2007.

Mayda, İbrahim. "Wernicke-Korsakoff Hastalığı ve Rehabilitasyonu" [Wernicke-Korsakoff Disorder and Its Rehabilitation] *Toplum ve Hukuk* 2, no. 5 (Winter 2003): 95–99.

Mazlumder [Solidarity Association for Human Rights and the Oppressed]. *1998 Yılı Cezaevleri Raporu* [1998 Prisons Report]. Report. http://mazlumder.org/yayinlar/detay/yurt-ici-raporlar/3/mazlumder-1998-yili-cezaevleri-raporu-1998/1003. (Last accessed November 13, 2013.)

Mbembe, Achille. "Necropolitics." *Public Culture* 15, no. 1 (2003): 11–40.

McCarthy, Thomas. "The Critique of Impure Reason: Foucault and the Frankfurt School." *Critique and Power: Recasting the Foucault/Habermas Debate*, ed. Michael Kelly, 243–82. Cambridge: MIT Press, 1994.

McGray, James W. "Bobby Sands, Suicide, and Self-Sacrifice." *Journal of Value Inquiry* 17 (1983): 65–75.

McGregor, JoAnn. "Contestations and Consequences of Deportability: Hunger Strikes and the Political Agency of Non-Citizens." *Citizenship Studies* 15, no. 5 (2011): 597–611.

McNay, Lois. *Foucault and Feminism: Power, Gender and the Self*. Boston: Northeastern University Press, 1993.

Mears, Daniel P., and Michael D. Reisig. "The Theory and Practice of Supermax Prisons." *Punishment and Society* 8, no. 1 (2006): 33–57.

Mehmet, Özay. "Turkey in Crisis: Some Contradictions in the Kemalist Development Strategy." *International Journal of Middle East Studies* 15, no. 1 (1983): 47–66.

Mengi, Güngör. "Devlet Uyandı!" [The State Woke Up!]. *Sabah*, December 20, 2000.

"Michel Foucault on Attica: An Interview." *Telos* 19 (1974): 154–61.

Mignolo, Walter. *Local Histories/Global Designs: Coloniality, Subaltern Knowledges, and Border Thinking*. Princeton: Princeton University Press, 2000.

Miller, Holly A., and Glenn R. Young. "Prison Segregations: Administrative Detention Remedy or Mental Health Problem?" *Criminal Behavior and Mental Health* 7, no. 1 (1997): 85–94.

Miller, James. *The Passion of Michel Foucault*. New York: Simon and Schuster, 1993.

Milliyet. "Sahte Oruç, Kanlı İftar" [Fake Fast, Bloody Meal]. December 20, 2000.

Mills, Catherine. "Agamben's Messianic Politics: Biopolitics, Abandonment and Happy Life." *Contretemps* 5 (December 2004): 42–62.

———. *The Philosophy of Agamben*. Montreal: McGill-Queen's University Press, 2008.

Miroğlu, Orhan. *Dijwar: Faili Meçhul Cinayetler ve Diyarbakır Cezaevi'ne Dair Her Şey* [Tough: Everything About Extrajudicial Executions and the

Diyarbakır Prison] 3d ed. Istanbul: Everest Yayınları, 2009.

Mitchell, Katharyne. "Geographies of Identity: The New Exceptionalism." *Progress in Human Geography* 30, no. 1 (2006): 95–106.

Moghadam, Assaf. *The Globalization of Martyrdom: Al Qaeda, Salafi Jihad, and the Diffusion of Suicide Attacks.* Baltimore: Johns Hopkins University Press, 2008.

Muftuler-Bac, Meltem, and E. Fuat Keyman, "The Era of Dominant Party Politics." *Journal of Democracy* 23, no. 1 (January 2012): 85–99.

Murray, Stuart J. "Thanatopolitics: On the Use of Death for Mobilizing Political Life." *Polygraph* 18 (2006): 191–215.

Münkler, Herfried. *The New Wars.* Trans. Patrick Camiller. Cambridge: Polity, 2005.

Naas, Michael. "History's Remains: Of Memory, Mourning, and the Event." *Research in Phenomenology*, no. 33 (2003): 75–96.

Nacos, Brigitte L. "Revisiting the Contagion Hypothesis: Terrorism, News Coverage, and Copycat Attacks." *Perspectives on Terrorism* 3, no. 3 (September 2009): 3–13.

Nashif, Esmail. *Palestinian Political Prisoners: Identity and Community.* New York: Routledge, 2008.

Nazik, Ali. "Letter to Oral Çalışlar from Sincan F Type Prison." [In Turkish.] February 15, 2001, private collection.

Negri, Antonio. *Insurgencies: Constituent Power and the Modern State.* Trans. Maurizia Boscagli. Minneapolis: University of Minnesota Press, 1999.

Neier, Aryeh. "Confining Dissent: The Political Prison." In *The Oxford History of the Prison: The Practice of Punishment in Western Society,* ed. Norval Morris and David J. Rothman, 350–80. New York: Oxford University Press, 1995.

Nicholl, David J., Holly G. Atkinson, John Kalk, William Hopkins, Elwyn Elias, Adnan Siddiqui, Ronald E. Cranford, Oliver Sacks, on behalf of 255 other doctors. "Forcefeeding and Restraint of Guantanamo Bay Hunger Strikers." *Lancet* 367, no. 9513 (March 11, 2006): 811.

Nora, Pierre. "Between Memory and History: Les Lieux de Memoire." *Representations,* no. 26 (Spring 1989): 7–24.

Oguz, N. Y., and S. H. Miles. "The Physician and Prison Hunger Strikes: Reflecting on the Experience in Turkey." *Journal of Medical Ethics* 31, no. 3 (2005): 169–72.

O'Keeffe, Terence. "Suicide and Self-Starvation." *Philosophy* 56 (1981): 349–63.

Okuyucu, Yasemin, ed. *'96 Ölüm Orucu: Ölümün Ufkundaki Zafer* ['96 Death Fast: The Victory at the Horizon of Death]. Istanbul: Yar Yayınları, 1998.

Oliver, Anne Marie, and Paul Steinberg. *The Road to Martyr's Square: A Journey Into the World of the Suicide Bomber.* Oxford: Oxford University Press, 2005.

Olshansky, Barbara, and Gitanjali Gutierrez. *The Guantánamo Prisoner Hunger Strikes and Protests: February 2002–August 2005.* Special Report by the Center for Constitutional Rights. New York: Center for Constitutional Rights, 2005. Available at http://www.ccr-ny.org. (Last accessed January 3, 2013.)

O'Malley, Padraig. *Biting at the Grave: The Irish Hunger Strikes and the Politics of Despair.* Belfast: Blackstaff, 1990.

Ong, Aihwa. "Scales of Exception: Experiments with Knowledge and Sheer Life in Tropical Southeast Asia." *Singapore Journal of Tropical Geography* 29 (2008): 117–29.

——, and Stephen J. Collier, eds. *Global Assemblages: Technology, Politics, and Ethics as Anthropological Problems.* Malden: Blackwell, 2005.

Owen, Roger, and Şevket Pamuk. *A History of the Middle East Economies in the Twentieth Century.* Cambridge: Harvard University Press, 1998.

Owens, Patricia. "Reclaiming 'Bare Life'? Against Agamben on Refugees." *International Relations* 23, no. 4 (2009): 567–82.

Öniş, Ziya. *State and Market: The Political Economy of Turkey in Comparative Perspective.* Istanbul: Boğaziçi University Press, 1998.

——. "The Political Economy of Islamic Resurgence in Turkey: The Rise of the Welfare Party in Perspective." *Third World Quarterly.* 18, no. 4 (1997): 743–66.

Özbek, Nadir. "Osmanlı'dan Günümüze Sosyal Devlet" [The Welfare State from the Ottomans to Our Day]. *Toplum ve Bilim,* no. 92 (Spring 2002): 7–33.

Özbudun, Ergun. "Democratization Reforms in Turkey, 1993–2004." *Turkish Studies* 8, no. 2 (June 2007): 179–96.

——. "The Nature of the Kemalist Political Regime." In *Ataturk, Founder of a Modern State,* ed. Ergun Özbudun and Ali Kazancıgil, 79–102. Hamden, CT: Archon, 1981.

Özcan, Emine. "Akbaba ve Buldukoğlu'yu Hapiste Kim Öldürdü?" [Who Killed Akbaba and Buldukoğlu in Prison?] *Bia Haber Merkezi.* http://www.bianet.org/2006/04/10/77429.htm. (Last accessed March 11, 2007.)

Özgür, Ayhan. "Terörize Et ve Yönet" [Terrorize and Manage]. *Evrensel,*
December 25, 2000.

Özgür Hukuk Bürosu. "F Tipine İlişkin Bazı Tespitler" [Some Observations
on the F Type]. *Savunma,* no. 4 (January–February 2001): 3–5.

——. "F Tipleri: Siyasi Mahkumları Günahlarından Arındırma Projesi" [F
Types: A Project to Purify Political Prisoners of Their Sins]. *Savunma,*
no. 3 (October–November 2000): 15–18.

Özgür TAYAD. "Hapishaneler Gerçeği" [The Reality of Prisons]. *Tutuklu
Aileleri Bülteni,* no. 3, April 2000.

Öztürk, Şaban. *Türkiye Solunun Hapishane Tarihi* [The Prison History of the
Left of Turkey]. Istanbul: Yar Yayınları, 2004.

Paker, Murat. "Paranoyanın Zaferi" [The Victory of Paranoia]. *Birikim,* no.
142–43 (February–March 2001): 27–36.

Pape, Robert A. *Dying to Win: The Strategic Logic of Suicide Terrorism.* New
York: Random House, 2005.

Parfitt, Trevor. "Are the Third World Poor Homines Sacri? Biopolitics, Sovereignty, and Development." *Alternatives: Global, Local, Political* 34 (2009):
41–58.

Parla, Taha. *Türkiye'de Anayasalar* [Constitutions in Turkey]. Istanbul:
İletişim Yayıncılık, 1993.

——. *Türkiye'de Siyasal Kültürün Resmi Kaynakları: Kemalist Tek Parti
İdeolojisi ve CHP'nin 6 Oku* [The Official Sources of Political Culture in
Turkey]. Vol. 3. Istanbul: İletişim Yayıncılık, 1992.

Parry, Jonathan. "Sacrificial Death and the Necrophagus Ascetic." In *Death
and the Regeneration of Life,* ed. Maurice Bloch and Jonathan Parry,
74–110. Cambridge: Cambridge University Press, 1982.

"Partiler, Dergiler, Yazarlar Ne Dediler?" [Parties, Journals, Writers, What
Did They Say?]. *Teori ve Politika,* no. 21 (Winter 2001). http//www.teor-
ivepolitika.net. (Last accessed January 12, 2012.)

Passavant, Paul A. "The Contradictory State of Giorgio Agamben." *Political
Theory* 35, no. 2 (April 2007): 147–74.

Patton, Paul. "Of Power and Prisons: Working Paper on *Discipline and Punish.*" In *Michel Foucault: Power, Truth, Strategy,* ed. Meaghan Morris and
Paul Patton, 109–47. Sydney: Feral Publications, 1979.

Perinçek, Doğu. *Kemalist Devrim-1: Teorik Çerçeve* [The Kemalist Revolu-
tion-1: Theoretical Framework] 5th ed. Istanbul: Kaynak Yayınları, 1995.

——. *Sosyal-Emperyalizm ve Revizyonizme Karşı 1970'te Açılan Mücadele.*

[The Struggle Against Social-Imperialism and Remission Since 1970].
Istanbul: Aydınlık Yayınları, 1976.

Petersen, Alan, and Robin Bunton, eds. *Foucault: Health and Medicine*. London: Routledge, 1997.

Phillips, John. "Agencement/Assemblage." *Theory, Culture and Society* 23, no. 2–3 (2006): 108–9.

Pickett, Brent. *On the Use and Abuse of Foucault for Politics*. Lanham, MD: Lexington, 2005.

Pile, Steve, and Michael Keith, eds. *Geographies of Resistance*. London: Routledge, 1997.

Pişkinsüt, Sema. *Filistin Askısından Fezlekeye: İşkencenin Kitabı* [From the Palestinian Hanger to the Graft Investigation: The Book of Torture]. Ankara: Bilgi Yayınevi, 2001.

Pizarro, Jesenia, and Vanja M. K. Stenius. "Supermax Prisons: Their Rise, Current Practices, and Effect on Inmates." *Prison Journal* 84, no. 2 (2004): 248–64.

Polat, Fatih. "Bir Savaş ve Operasyon Gücü Olarak Medya" [Media as a War and Operation Power]. *Özgür Üniversite Forumu*, no. 12 (October–December 2000): 7–26.

Poulantzas, Nicos. *State, Power, Socialism*. Intro. Stuart Hall. Trans. Patrick Camiller. London: Verso, 2000.

Poyraz, Bedriye. "The Turkish State and Alevis: Changing Parameters of an Uneasy Relationship." *Middle Eastern Studies* 41, no. 4 (2005): 503–16.

Poyraz, Cemal. "Ömer Laçiner'e Mektup" [Letter to Ömer Laçiner]. *Birikim*, no. 145 (May 2001): 102–4.

Prozorov, Sergei. "The Unrequited Love of Power: Biopolitical Investment and the Refusal of Care." *Foucault Studies*, no. 4 (February 2007): 53–77.

Puar, Jaspir. *Terrorist Assemblages: Homonationalism in Queer Times*. Durham, NC: Duke University Press, 2007.

Quataert, Donald, and Eric Jan Zürcher, eds. *Workers and the Working Class in the Ottoman Empire and the Turkish Republic 1839–1950*. London: I.B.Tauris, 1995.

Rabinow, Paul. *Anthropos Today: Reflections on Modern Equipment*. Princeton: Princeton University Press, 2003.

Radikal. "Devletin Cezaevi İtirafı" [The Prison Confession of the State]. October 8, 1999.

———. "'Mahkumlar Ateş Etti' Demişlerdi" [They Had Claimed 'The Prisoners Fired']. July 2, 2001.

———. "12 Eylül'le 20 Yıl" [20 Years with September 12]. September 12, 2000.

Rajaram, Prem Kumar, and Carl Grundy-Warr. "The Irregular Migrant as *Homo Sacer*: Migration and Detention in Australia, Malaysia, and Thailand." *International Migration* 42, no. 1 (2004): 33–64.

Reid, Julian. *The Biopolitics of the War on Terror: Life Struggles, Liberal Modernity, and the Defence of Logistical Societies*. Manchester: Manchester University Press, 2006.

Reinert, Hugo. "The Persistence of Sacrifice: Some Notes on Larry the Luckiest Lamb." *borderlands* 6, no. 3 (2007). Available at http://www.borderlands.net.au/vol6no3_2007/reinert_larry.htm. (Last accessed November 5, 2012.)

Reuter, Christopher. *My Life Is a Weapon: The Modern History of Suicide Bombing*. Princeton: Princeton University Press, 2004.

Rhem, Kathleen T. "Guantanamo Tube Feedings Humane, Within Medical Care Standards." *American Forces Press Service*. December 1, 2005. Available at http://www.defense.gov/news/newsarticle.aspx?id=18672. (Last accessed December 1, 2012.)

Rhodes, Lorna A. "Pathological Effects of the Supermaximum Prison." *American Journal of Public Health* 95, no. 10 (2005): 1692–95.

———. *Total Confinement: Madness and Reason in the Maximum Security Prison*. Berkeley: University of California Press, 2004.

Robinson, Joan. *The Economics of Imperfect Competition*. London: Macmillan, 1933.

Rose, Nikolas. *Governing the Soul: The Shaping of the Private Self*. 2d ed. London: Free Association Books, 1989.

Rosenfeld, Maya. *Confronting the Occupation*. Stanford: Stanford University Press, 2004.

Rubenstein, Leonard S., and George J. Annas. "Medical Ethics at Guantanamo Bay Detention Centre and in the US Military: A Time for Reform." *Lancet* 374, no. 9686 (July 25, 2009): 353–55.

Rudé, George. *The Crowd in History: A Study of Popular Disturbances in France and England 1730–1848*. New York: Wiley, 1964.

Rumford, Chris. "Human Rights and Democratization in Turkey in the Context of EU Candidature." *Journal of Contemporary European Studies* 9, no. 1 (May 2001): 93–105.

Sabah. "Cezaevleri Suç Fabrikası Gibi" [Prisons Are Like Crime Factories].

September 26, 1999.

———. "Kimliği Parmak İzinden Bulundu" [His Identity Was Found From His Finger Print]. November 24, 2000.

———. "Müdürlerini Çiğnediler" [They Walked Over Their Superiors]. December 14, 2000.

———. "Operasyonu Bir Yılda Hazırladık, Bir Haftada Bitirdik" [We Prepared the Operation in One Year, We Finished it in One Week]. December 20, 2000.

———. "Polis de Yürüdü" [The Police Walked as Well]. December 13, 2000.

———. "Sol Örgütlerin Cinnet Eylemi" [The Insanity Action of Left Organizations]. December 23, 2000.

Saçılık, Veli. "Burdur Saldırısı Planın Bir Parçasıydı" [The Burdur Attack Was Part of the Plan]. Interview by Tacim Coşgun. *Evrensel*, August 20, 2000.

Sadiç, İsmail H. *Puslu Aydınlık: Belleğini Yitiren Bir Direnişçinin Güncesi* [Misty Light: The Diary of a Resistor Who Lost His Memory]. Istanbul: Şubat, 2001.

Sakallıoğlu, Ümit Cizre. "Kemalism, Hyper-Nationalism and Islam in Turkey." *History of European Ideas* 18, no. 2 (1994): 255–70.

———. "Parameters and Strategies of Islam-State Interaction in Republican Turkey." *International Journal of Middle East Studies* 28, no. 2 (1996): 231–51.

Salgirli, Sanem Güvenç. "Eugenics for the Doctors: Medicine and Social Control in 1930s Turkey." *Journal of the History of Medicine and Allied Sciences* 66, no. 3 (2011): 281–312.

Samim, Ahmet. "The Tragedy of the Turkish Left." *New Left Review*, no. 126 (March-April 1981): 60–85.

Sanchez, Lisa E. "The Global E-rotic Subject, the Ban, and the Prostitute-Free Zone: Sex Work and the Theory of Differential Exclusion." *Environment and Planning D: Society and Space* 22 (2004): 861–83.

Sawicki, Jana. *Disciplining Foucault: Feminism, Power, and the Body*. New York: Routledge, 1991.

Sayılgan, Aclan. *Türkiye'de Sol Hareketler 1871–1972* [Leftist Movements in Turkey 1871–1972]. Istanbul: Hareket Yayınları, 1972.

Saymaz, Sevgi. "Tecridin Sona Erdirilmesi Talebiyle Uşak Cezaevi'nde Ölüm Orucu Sürdüren Sevgi Saymaz Hayatını ve Eyleminin Nedenlerini Anlatiyor" [Sevgi Saymaz on the Death Fast in Uşak Prison with the

Demand of Ending Isolation Narrates Her Life and the Reasons for Her Act]. Interview by Halkın Sesi TV, December 21, 2006. http://www. tecrit.worldpress.com. (Last accessed January 12, 2007.)

Scanlan, Stephen J., Laurie Cooper Stoll, and Kimberly Lumm. "Starving for Change: The Hunger Strike and Nonviolent Action, 1906–2004." In *Research in Social Movements, Conflicts and Change,* ed. Patrick G. Coy, 28: 275–323. Bingley: Emerald, 2008.

Scarry, Elaine. *The Body in Pain: The Making and Unmaking of the World.* New York: Oxford University Press, 1985.

Schmitt, Carl. *Political Theology: Four Concepts of the Concept of Sovereignty.* Trans. George Schwab. Intro. Tracy B. Strong. Chicago: University of Chicago Press, 2005.

——. *The Concept of the Political.* Trans. George Schwab. Chicago: University of Chicago Press, 1996.

——. *The Nomos of the Earth in the International Law of the Jus Publicum Europaeum.* Trans. G. L. Ulmen. New York: Telos, 2003.

Scott, James C. *Domination and the Arts of Resistance: Hidden Transcripts.* New Haven: Yale University Press, 1990.

——. *Weapons of the Weak: Everyday Forms of Peasant Resistance.* New Haven: Yale University Press, 1985.

Scraton, Phil, and Jude McCulloch, eds. *The Violence of Incarceration.* New York: Routledge, 2009.

Seale, Clive. *Constructing Death: The Sociology of Dying and Bereavement.* Cambridge: Cambridge University Press, 1998.

Selmeczi, Anna. "' . . . we are being left to burn because we do not count': Biopolitics, Abandonment, and Resistance." *Global Society* 23, no. 4 (2009): 519–38.

Sevimay, Devrim. *TBMM İnsan Hakları Komisyonu Raporlarında Resmen İşkence* [Official Torture in Grand National Assembly of Turkey Human Rights Commission Reports]. Istanbul: Metis, 2001.

Sezer, Ahmet Necdet. "Türkiye Cumhurbaşkanlığı Belgesi" [Document of the Presidency of Turkey]. No. B.01.0.KKB.01 KAN. KAR. : 39–18/A-1–2000–984, December 5, 2000. In *23 Nisan 1999 Tarihine Kadar İşlenen Suçlardan Dolayı Şartla Salıverilmeye, Dava ve Cezaların Ertelenmesine Dair Kanunun Değerlendirilmesi* [The Evaluation of The Law for Conditional Release and Postponement of Court Cases and Punishments for

Crimes Committed until April 23, 1999], ed. Erdener Yurtcan, Hamide
Zafer, and Sibel İnceoğlu, 32–33. Istanbul: Doga Basım Yayın, n.d.

Sharma, Aradhana, and Akhil Gupta, eds. *The Anthropology of the State: A
Reader.* Malden, MA: Blackwell, 2006.

Shepkaru, Shmuel. *Jewish Martyrs in the Pagan and Christian Worlds.* Cambridge: Cambridge University Press, 2006.

Sınıf Teorisi. "20 Ekim 2000 Ölüm Orucu ve Sonuçları Üzerine Genel Bir
Yorum" [A General Evaluation on the Death Fast of October 20, 2000
and Its Consequences], no. 2 (June–July 2003): 42–46.

Silver, Eric. "Palestinian Threats as Jail Hunger Strike Starts." *Independent,*
August 16, 2004. http://www.independent.co.uk/news/world/middle-
east/palestinian-threats-as-jail-hunger-strike-starts-556750.html. (Last
accessed June 7, 2010.)

Siméant, Johanna. *La Cause des Sans-Papiers.* Paris: Presses de Sciences Po,
1998.

———. "La Violence d'un Répertoire: Les Sans-Papiers en Grève de la Faim."
In *La Violence Politique dans Les Démocraties Européennes Occidentales,* ed.
Phillippe Braud, 315–38. Paris: L'Harmattan, 1993.

Simons, Jon. *Foucault and the Political.* London: Routledge, 1995.

Sinnerbrink, Robert. "From *Machenschaft* to Biopolitics: A Genealogical
Critique of Biopower." *Critical Horizons* 6, no. 1 (2005): 239–65.

Sluka, Jeffrey A., ed. *Death Squad: The Anthropology of State Terror.* Philadelphia: University of Pennsylvania Press, 2000.

Sorel, Georges. *Reflections on Violence.* Ed. Jeremy Jennings. Cambridge:
Cambridge University Press, 1999.

Sosyalizm ve Toplumsal Mücadeleler Ansiklopedisi [Encyclopedia of Socialism
and Social Struggles]. Vol. 7. Istanbul: İletişim Yayıncılık, 1988.

Soulié, Christophe. "Années 70—Contestation de la Prison. L'information
est une Arme." *Raison Présente,* no. 130 (1999): 21–38.

Soyer, Ata. "Açlık Grevleri/Ölüm Oruçları, TTB ve Son Tartışmalar"
[Hunger Strikes/Death Fasts, TMA (Turkish Medical Association) and
Recent Debates]. *Evrensel,* January 6–10, 2001. Available at http://www.
ttb.org.tr/aclik_grevleri/a_soyer.html. (Last accessed December 1, 2012.)

Sparks, Richard, Anthony Bottoms, and Will Hay. *Prison and the Problem of
Order.* Oxford: Clarendon, 1996.

Sprinzak, Ehud. "Rational Fanatics." *Foreign Policy,* no. 120 (September/October 2000): 66–74.

Stephenson, Chris. "Kemalizmden Sonra Sol Nereye?" [Whither the Left After Kemalism?]. *Marx-21*, no. 1 (Winter 2011): 6–79.

Stern, Jessica. *Terror in the Name of God: Why Religious Militants Kill*. New York: HarperCollins, 2003.

Stern-Gillet, Suzanne. "The Rhetoric of Suicide." *Philosophy and Rhetoric* 20, no. 3 (1987): 160–70.

Sunar, Ilkay. "Populism and Patronage: The Demokrat Party and its Legacy in Turkey." *Il Politico* 60, no. 4 (1990): 745–57.

"Support the Turkish Hunger Strike." Republican mural, Divis Street, Falls, West Belfast, 2001. Photographed by Tony Crowley. Murals of Northern Ireland Collection. Claremont Colleges Digital Library. http://ccdl. libraries.claremont.edu/col/mni. (Last accessed November 1, 2012.)

Sweeney, George. "Irish Hunger Strikes and the Cult of Self-Sacrifice." *Journal of Contemporary History* 28, no. 3 (July 1993): 421–37.

———. "Self-Immolation in Ireland: Hungerstrikes and Political Confrontation." *Anthropology Today* 9, no. 5 (October 1993): 10–14.

Sykes, Gresham M. *The Society of Captives: A Study of a Maximum Security Prison*. Intro. Bruce Western. Princeton: Princeton University Press, 2007.

Şener, Mustafa. *Türkiye Solunda Üç Tarz-ı Siyaset: YÖN, MDD ve TİP* [Three Styles of Politics on the Left of Turkey: Direction, National Democratic Revolution and Workers' Party of Turkey]. Istanbul: Yordam Kitap, 2010.

Şeşen, Gülten, ed. *Tutsak Aileleri, 12 Eylül ve TAYAD* [Families of Captives, September 12 and TAYAD]. Istanbul: Haziran Yayınları, 1991.

Şık, Ahmet. "Gerçeğe Dönüş" [Return to Reality]. *Radikal*, July 2, 2001.

———. "İşte Böyle Öldüler" [This Is How They Died]. *Radikal*, July 3, 2001.

———. *Pusu: Devletin Yeni Sahipleri* [Trap: The New Owners of the State]. Istanbul: Postacı Yayınevi, 2012.

Şişmanov, Dimitr. *Türkiye İşçi ve Sosyalist Hareketi Kısa Tarihi 1908–1965* [Short History of Workers' and Socialist Movement in Turkey 1908–1965]. Istanbul: Belge Yayınları, 1978.

Tachau, Frank. "The Political Culture of Kemalist Turkey." In *Ataturk and the Modernization of Turkey*, ed. Jacob M. Landau, 57–76. Boulder: Westview, 1984.

Tampio, Nicholas. "Assemblages and the Multitude: Deleuze, Hardt, Negri, and the Postmodern Left." *European Journal of Political Theory* 8, no. 3

(2009): 383–400.

Tanör, Bülent. *İki Anayasa* [Two Constitutions]. Istanbul: Beta Yayınları, 1986.

———. *Türkiye'nin İnsan Hakları Sorunu* [Turkey's Human Rights Problem]. 2d ed. Istanbul: BDS Yayınları, 1991.

Taşkın, Ahmet. *Basında Cezaevleri ve Gerçekler* [Prisons in the Media and Realities]. Ankara: Eda Matbaası, 2005.

———. *Cezaevi İstatistikleri (1997–2002)* [Prison Statistics (1997–2002)]. Istanbul: Zirve Basım, 2002.

Taussig, Michael. "Culture of Terror—Space of Death. Roger Casement's Putumayo Report and the Explanation of Torture." *Comparative Studies in Society and History* 26, no. 3 (July 1984): 467–97.

TAYAD [Solidarity Association for the Families of the Arrested], ed. "Hapishaneler Gerçeği, Yaşanan Sorunlar ve Çözüm Önerileri Kurultayı" [Congress on the Reality of Prisons, Problems Experienced and Proposed Solutions]. *Tutuklu Aileleri Bülteni*, no. 11, March 2001.

———, ed. "12 İnsan: Ne İstiyorlardı?" [12 People: What Did They Want?] *Tutuklu Aileleri Bülteni*, no. 7, September–October 2000.

———, ed. "Yalanları Parçalayan Ulucanlar Katliamı: Belgeler ve Anlatımlar" [Ulucanlar Massacre Smashing the Lies: Documents and Narratives]. *Tutuklu Aileleri Bülteni*, no. 2 (n.d.).

TAYAD Komite Nederland. *Documentation on the Death Fast in Turkey*, 2002. Available at http://prisonsenturquie.free.fr/hungerstrike.pdf. (Last accessed June 7, 2010.)

Taylor, Charles. *Multiculturalism and "the Politics of Recognition."* Princeton: Princeton University Press, 1992.

"Tecrit İşkencedir!" [Isolation Is Torture!] Public Declaration, December, 2006. http://www.tecritekarsi.com/ilan_metni.html. (Last accessed January 12, 2007.)

Temelkuran, Ece. *Ne Anlatayım Ben Sana!* [What Can I Tell You!] Istanbul: Everest, 2006.

Terörle Mücadele Kanunu [Law for the Struggle Against Terror]. No. 3713, April 12, 1991. http://www.mevzuat.adalet.gov.tr/html/809.html and http://www.icj.org/IMG/Turkey1991law.pdf. (Last accessed December 1, 2012.)

Tezel, Yahya S. *Cumhuriyet Dönemi'nin İktisadi Tarihi (1923–1950).* [The

Economic History of the Republican Era (1923-1950)]. Ankara: Yurt
Yayınları, 1983.

"The Law and Force-Feeding." *British Medical Journal* 2, no. 5921 (June 29, 1974): 737–38.

THKO Davası [The THKO Case]. 2d ed. Istanbul: Akyüz Yayınları, 1991.

Thompson, E. P. *The Making of the English Working Class*. New York: Random House, 1964.

———. "The Moral Economy of the English Crowd in the Eighteenth Century." *Past and Present*, no. 50 (1971): 76–136.

Thompson, Kevin. "Forms of Resistance: Foucault on Tactical Reversal and Self-Formation." *Continental Philosophy Review* 36, no. 2 (June 2003): 11–38.

Thorborn, Kim Marie. "Croaker's Dilemma: Should Prison Physicians Serve Prisons or Prisoners?" *Western Journal of Medicine* 134, no. 5 (May 1981): 457–61.

Ticktin, Miriam. *Casualties of Care: Immigration and the Politics of Humanitarianism in France*. Berkeley: University of California Press, 2011.

Tilly, Charles. *Contentious Performances*. Cambridge: Cambridge University Press, 2008.

TMMOB Mimarlar Odası İzmir Şubesi [TMMOB Architects' Chamber Izmir Branch]. "F Tipi Cezaevi Raporu" [F-type Prison Report]. In *F Tipi Cezaevleri Değerlendirme Raporları* [F-type Prisons Assessment Reports], ed. İzmir Meslek Odaları Platformu, 71–77. Izmir: Egetan, August 2001.

Townsend, Chris. *Vile Bodies: Photography and the Crisis of Looking*. Munich: Prestel, 1998.

Töre, Teslim. "THKO'nun Doğuşu-Gelişimi ve Sonu" [THKO's Birth, Development and End], *Sosyalizm ve Toplumsal Mücadeleler Ansiklopedisi*, 7:2170–71. Istanbul: İletişim Yayıncılık, 1988.

Tunçay, Mete. *Türkiye Cumhuriyeti'nde Tek Parti Yönetiminin Kurulması (1923–1931)* [The Establishment of Single Party Rule in the Republic of Turkey (1923–1931)]. Ankara: Yurt Yayınları, 1981.

———. *Türkiye'de Sol Akımlar 1908–1925* [Leftist Currents in Turkey 1908–1925]. Ankara: Bilgi Yayınevi, 1978.

———, and Erik Jan Zürcher, eds. *Socialism and Nationalism in the Ottoman Empire, 1876–1923*. London and New York: British Academic Press and I.

B.Tauris, 1994.

Turner, Brian S. *Regulating Bodies: Essays in Medical Sociology*. London: Routledge, 1992.

Tüm Yargı-Sen Genel Merkez Yönetim Kurulu [Central Board of Tüm Yargı-Sen]. "Sendikamıza Yönelik Baskılar" [Repression Against Our Trade Union]. Press release, March 2, 2001.

Türk, Hikmet Sami. "Press Conference." Television Broadcast, *TRT2* [Turkish Radio Television Channel 2], January 9, 2002.

Türk Ceza Kanunu [Turkish Penal Code]. No. 5237, September 26, 2004. http://www.tbmm.gov.tr/kanunlar/k5237.html. (Last accessed November 1, 2012.)

Türk Tabipleri Birliği [Turkish Medical Association]. *F Tipi Cezaevlerine İlişkin Türk Tabipleri Birliği Raporu* [The Turkish Medical Association's Report on F Type Prisons]. September 20, 2000. http://www.ttb.org.tr/rapor/f_tipi.html. (Last accessed December 1, 2012.)

Türk Tabipleri Birliği Merkez Konseyi [Turkish Medical Association Central Council]. "Cezaevleri" [Prisons]. Press release, December 22, 2000.

———. "Cezaevlerindeki Açlık Grevleri İçin Acil Çağrı Metni" [Urgent Call for the Hunger Strikes in Prisons]. Press release. February 7, 2001.

Türkeş, Mustafa. "The Ideology of the Kadro [Cadre] Movement: A Patriotic Leftist Movement in Turkey." *Middle Eastern Studies*. 34, no. 4 (1998): 92–119.

Türkiye Büyük Millet Meclisi [Grand National Assembly of Turkey]. *Genel Kurul Tutanakları* [Proceedings of the General Convention]. 21st Period, 3d Legislative Year, 18th Convention, 2d Session, November 21, 2000. Ankara: TBMM Basımevi, 2001.

———. *Genel Kurul Tutanakları*. 21st Period, 3d Legislative Year, 27th Convention, 1st Session, December 8, 2000. Ankara: TBMM Basımevi, 2001.

———. *Genel Kurul Tutanakları*. 21st Period, 3d Legislative Year, 115th Convention, 5th Session, June 12, 2001. Ankara: TBMM Basımevi, 2001.

Türkiye Büyük Millet Meclisi İnsan Haklarını İnceleme Komisyonu [Grand National Assembly of Turkey Human Rights Investigation Commission]. *Bolu F-Tipi Cezaevi Raporu* [Bolu F-Type Prison Report]. Special Report, October 2003.

———. *26 Eylül Ulucanlar Cezaevi Raporu* [September 26 Ulucanlar Prison Report]. Ankara: TBMM Basımevi, June 2000.

Türkiye İnsan Hakları Vakfı [Human Rights Foundation of Turkey]. *İşkence*

Dosyası: Gözaltında ya da Cezaevinde Ölenler (12 Eylül 1980–12 Eylül 1995)
[The Torture File: Those Who Have Died in Custody or in Prison (September 12, 1980–September 12, 1995)]. Ankara: TİHV Yayınları, March
1996.

———. "Ölüm Orucuna Müdahale Devam Ediyor" [Intervention in the Death
Fast Continues]. *Urgent Information Brief*, December 21, 2000.

———. *Türkiye İnsan Hakları Raporu '91* [Turkey Human Rights Report '91].
Ankara: TİHV Yayınları, January 1992.

———. *2001 Türkiye İnsan Hakları Raporu* (Ankara: TİHV Yayınları, 2001).
Available at http://www.tihv.org.tr/2001-insan-haklari-raporu/. (Last
accessed November 15, 2013.)

Türkmen, Yeliz. "Letter from Niğde Prison." [In Turkish.] March 8, 2001,
private collection.

Ufuk Çizgisi. "Ölüm Orucu Değerlendirmesi (II)" [Evaluation of the Death
Fast (II)]. No. 16, June 15, 2005. Republished at http://www.alinteri.org/.
(Last accessed November 15, 2012.)

———. "Ölüm Orucu Değerlendirmesi (V)" [Evaluation of the Death Fast
(V)]. No. 19, July 27, 2005. Republished at http://www.alinteri.org/.
(Last accessed November 15, 2012.)

———. "Ölüm Orucu Değerlendirmesi (IV)" [Evaluation of the Death Fast
(IV)]. No. 20, August 10, 2005. Republished at http://www.alinteri.org/.
(Last accessed November 15, 2012.)

———. "Ölüm Orucu Değerlendirmesi (VII)" [Evaluation of the Death Fast
(VII)]. No. 21, August 24, 2005. Republished at http://www.alinteri.org/.
(Last accessed November 15, 2012.)

Uğur, Can Ali, ed. *Zafere Mahkum Edilenler Ölümü Küçülterek Yenerler* [Those
Who Are Doomed for Victory Defeat Death by Belittling It]. Istanbul:
Altınçağ Yayımcılık, 1997.

Ulus, Özgür Mutlu. *The Army and the Radical Left in Turkey: Military Coups,
Socialist Revolution and Kemalism.* New York: I. B. Tauris, 2011.

United Nations. *Report of the Committee Against Torture: Addendum.* Special
Report, no. A/48/44/Add.1. Official Records of the General Assembly,
Forty-eighth Session, Supplement 44, November 15, 1993.

U.S. Department of Defense. "Medical Program Support for Detainee Operations." Instruction. No. 2310.08E. June 6, 2006. Available at http://www.dtic.
mil/whs/directives/corres/pdf/231008p.pdf. (Last accessed November 23,
2012.)

——. "News Briefing with Secretary of Defense Donald Rumsfeld and Gen. Peter Pace." *News Transcript.* November 01, 2005. Available at http://www.defense.gov/transcripts/transcript.aspx?transcriptid=1440. (Last accessed November 22, 2012.)

Ustuner, Tuba, Guliz Ger, and Douglas B. Holt. "Consuming Ritual: Reframing the Turkish Henna-Night Ceremony." *Advances in Consumer Research* 27 (2000): 209–14.

Uygun, Ayşe. "Hapishaneler Üzerine" [On Prisons]. *Birikim*, no. 145 (May 2001): 99–101.

Ülsever, Cüneyt. "Cezaevi Operasyonlarında Hükümeti Destekliyorum" [I Support the Government in Prison Operations]. *Hürriyet*, December 21, 2000.

van Bruinessen, Martin. "Kurds, Turks and the Alevi Revival in Turkey." *Middle East Report*, no. 200 (July-September 1996): 7–10.

Venn, Couze. "A Note on Assemblage." *Theory, Culture and Society* 23, no. 2–3 (2006): 107–8.

Victor, Barbara. *Army of Roses: Inside the World of Palestinian Women Suicide Bombers.* n.p.: Rodale, 2003.

Wacquant, Loïc. "Deadly Symbiosis: When Ghetto and Prison Meet and Mesh." *Punishment and Society* 3, no. 1 (2001): 95–134.

——. "The Rise of Advanced Marginality: Notes on Its Nature and Implications." *Acta Sociologica* 39, no. 2 (1996): 121–39.

Ward, David A., and Thomas G. Werlich. "Alcatraz and Marion: Evaluating Super-Maximum Custody." *Punishment and Society* 5, no. 1 (2003): 53–75.

Weber, Max. "Politics as a Vocation." *The Vocation Lectures*, ed. David S. Owen and Tracy B. Strong. Trans. Rodney Livingstone. Indianapolis: Hackett, 2004.

Weigel, Sigrid. "The Critique of Violence: Or, the Challenge to Political Theology of Just Wars and Terrorism with a Religious Face." *Telos*, no. 135 (Summer 2006): 61–76.

Weiker, Walter F. *Political Tutelage and Democracy in Turkey: The Free Party and Its Aftermath.* Leiden: Brill, 1973.

Welat, İrfan. *Auschwitz'den Diyarbakır'a 5 No'lu Cezaevi* [From Auschwitz to Diyarbakır Prison Number 5]. Istanbul: Aram Yayınları, 2010.

Welch, Michael. "Guantanamo Bay as a Foucauldian Phenomenon: An Analysis of Penal Discourse, Technologies, and Resistance." *Prison Journal* 89, no. 1 (March 2009): 3–20.

White, Jenny B. *Islamist Mobilization in Turkey: A Study of Vernacular Politics.* Seattle: University of Washington Press, 2002.

Wood, Sara. "Three Guantanamo Bay Detainees Die of Apparent Suicide." *American Forces Press Service.* June 10, 2006. Available at http://www. defense.gov/news/newsarticle.aspx?id=16080. (Last accessed November 15, 2012.)

World Medical Association. *Declaration of Malta on Hunger Strikers.* November 1991. http://www.wma.net/en/30publications/10policies/h31/index. html. (Last accessed November 15, 2012.)

——. *Declaration of Tokyo: Guidelines for Physicians Concerning Torture and Other Cruel, Inhuman or Degrading Treatment or Punishment in Relation to Detention and Imprisonment,* adopted by the 29th World Medical Assembly, Tokyo, Japan, October 1975, and revised by the 170th and 173d WMA Council Sessions in France in May 2005 and May 2006. http://www. wma.net/en/30publications/10policies/c18/index.html. (Last accessed November 15, 2012.)

——. "WMA Warned About Mounting Campaign Against Turkish Doctors." Press release, January 2, 2001. Available at http://www.wma.net/en/40n ews/20archives/2001/2001_19/index.html. (Last accessed December 1, 2012.)

Wright, Thomas C. *State Terrorism in Latin America: Chile, Argentina, and International Human Rights.* Lanham: Rowman and Littlefield, 2007.

Yaşadığımız Vatan. "F Tiplerinde İşkence ve Direniş Sürüyor" [Torture and Resistance Continues in the F Types]. January 9, 2001.

——. "Hapishanelere Yönelik Provokasyonlara Tutsaklardan Tepki" [Reaction from Captives Against Provocations Upon Prisons]. October 16, 2000, 21.

——. October 16, 2000, October 30, 2000, November 20, 2000, December 4, 2000, December 11, 2000, March 25, 2001, May 28, 2001, and June 4, 2001.

——. "ÖDP, Kaçınılmaz Tartışmayı Yaşıyor" [ÖDP (Liberty and Solidarity Party) Goes Through the Inevitable Debate]. January 29, 2001.

——. "ÖDP: Ölüm Orucu Gündemimiz Değil: Devrimciler Ölür, Akıllı Solcular Yaşasın" [ÖDP (Liberty and Solidarity Party): Death Fast Is Not Our Agenda: Revolutionaries Die, Let the Smart Leftists Live]. April 2, 2001.

——. "Polis Otosuna Silahlı Saldırı" [Armed Attack Upon Police Car]. April 9, 2001.

———. "Sol Ne Tarafta? Devrimcilik Ne?" [On Which Side Is the Left? What Is Revolutionism?]. January 9, 2001.

———. "Şişli Emniyet Müdürlüğüne Yönelik Feda Eylemi" [Sacrificial Action Against the Şişli Police Headquarters]. January 9, 2001.

Yaşamda Atılım. "Buca'da Burdur Provası" [The Burdur Rehearsal in Buca]. September 16, 2000, 5.

———. "Ölüm Hücrelerini Yıkacağız, Politik Tutsaklara Özgürlük" [We Will Demolish the Death Cells, Freedom to Political Captives]. September 16, 2000.

———. "Ölürüz ama Teslim Olmayız" [We Will Die But Not Surrender]. December 27, 2000.

———. "Özkan, Cafer, Ahmet Hücrelere Barikat" [Özkan, Cafer, Ahmet Are Baricades Against the Cells]. December 16, 2000.

———. "Uyarı Hepimize!" [The Warning Is to All of Us!]. November 18, 2000.

Yavuz, M. Hakan. "Turkey's Fault Lines and the Crisis of Kemalism." *Current History* 99, no. 633 (2000): 33–38.

———. *Secularism and Muslim Democracy in Turkey.* Cambridge: Cambridge University Press, 2009.

Yerasimos, Stéphane. "The Monoparty Period." In *Turkey in Transition: New Perspectives,* ed. Irvin C. Schick and Ertuğrul Ahmet Tonak, 66–100. New York: Oxford University Press, 1987.

Yetkin, Fevzi, and Mehmet Tanboğa, *Dörtlerin Gecesi* [The Night of the Four]. Ankara: Yurt Kitap-Yayın, 1990.

Yıldız, Kerim, and Juliet McDermott. *Torture in Turkey: The Ongoing Practice of Torture and Ill-Treatment.* Great Britain: Kurdish Human Rights Project, January 2004.

Yılmaz, Ali. "F Tipleri, Devlet, Sol ve PKK Açısından Cezaevleri" [F Types and Prisons from the Perspective of the State, the Left and the PKK]. *Özgür Halk Dergisi,* January 15, 2001.

Yılmaz, Aytekin. *İçimizdeki Hapishane: Labirentin Sonu* [The Prison Inside: The End of the Labyrinth]. Istanbul: İletişim Yayınları, 2003.

Yılmaz, Ulaş Osman. *Ölümü Yenenleri Kimse Yenemez: Süresiz Açlık Grevi ve Ölüm Orucu Direniş Güncesi* [Nobody Can Defeat Those Who Defeat Death: Hunger Strike of Indefinite Duration and Death Fast Resistance Diary]. Istanbul: Öz Basım-Yayım, 1997.

Yüce, Mehmet Can. *12 Eylül Sömürgeci-Faşist Rejimine Karşı Diyarbakır Zindan Direnişi: Direniş Eylemleri, Anlamı ve Sonuçları* [The Diyarbakır

Dungeon Resistance Against the Imperialist-Fascist Regime of September 12: Acts of Resistance, Their Meaning and Consequences]. Köln: Weşanen Serxwebün, 1991.

Yücel, Hacer. "Galatasaray; Ana Yüreği" [Galatasaray: Mother's Heart]. *Evrensel*, September 10, 2000.

Zana, Mehdi. *Prison No. 5: Eleven Years in Turkish Jails*. Watertown, MA: Blue Crane, 1997.

Zeydanlıoğlu, Welat. "The Period of Barbarity: Turkification, State Violence and Torture in Modern Turkey." In *State Power and the Legal Regulation of Evil*, ed. Francesca Dominello, 67–78. Oxford: Inter-Disciplinary, 2010.

Ziarek, Ewa Płonowska. "Bare Life on Strike: Notes on the Biopolitics of Race and Gender." *South Atlantic Quarterly* 107, no. 1 (Winter 2008): 89–105.

Žižek, Slavoj. "Biopolitics: Between Terri Schiavo and Guantanamo." *Artforum*, December 2005. Available at http://www.lacan.com/zizartforum1205.htm. (Last accessed November 22, 2013.)

Zürcher, Erik Jan. *Political Opposition in the Early Turkish Republic: The Progressive Republican Party*. Leiden: Brill, 1991.

Index

martyrdom and, 68; of militant-
martyrs, 245–47; organizational, 23;
personal, 23; of prisoner demands,
195; of prison revolts, 59; for self-
destruction, 19, 22
Muselmann, 72, 79, 80
Mysticism, 237

National democratic revolution (NDR),
229–34, 238, 400*n*16
Nationalism (Six Arrows), 90–91, 98
Nationalism, cultural roots of, 236
Nationalist Action Party (MHP), 100,
113, 381*n*43
Nationalist Front (Milliyetçi Cephe),
100
National Salvation Party (Milli Selamet
Partisi), 100
National security, political prisoners
and, 133
National Security Council, 103
Nazism, 50, 94, 339
NDR, *see* National democratic revolu-
tion
Necroavailability, 75
Necropoliticization, of resistance, 27–28,
31–32, 337
Necropolitics, definition of, 78
Necropower, 77–78
Necroresistance, 27, 32–34, 63, 68, 165,
341, 346; bare life and, 77–82, 85–86,
341; biosovereign assemblage and,
309, 344; biosovereignty and, 30, 32,
63, 83, 85, 259, 341, 344; centrality
of, 224; circle of violence and, 220;
class war and, 297; complexity of,
273, 275; death fasts and, 272–73;

definition, 27, 271–72; forms of, 85;
legitimacy and, 241; logic of, 257;
Marxism and, 235–36; performances
of, 273; self-destruction and, 272–73;
theorization of, 68, 70, 341; *see also*
Self-destruction; Weaponization
of life
Neoliberal capitalism, 164, 225, 274, 288,
348; cellularization and, 293; F-type
prisons and, 335; IMF, 288–89, 292;
revolutionary warfare against, 291
Neoliberalism, class war against, 288–98
9/11 (September 11th), 212, 349, 354*n*35
Non-violence, 15, 280
Northern Ireland, 30, 59, 128, 268

Obedience, 45, 65–66, 68, 69, 133, 298,
329, 330, 336
Oktay, Seyfi, 184
Ong, Aihwa, 53
Operation Return to Life, 2–4, 149,
379*n*24; aftermath of, 201–2, 205–6,
383*n*71; amnesty legislation and,
8–9; asymmetric warfare of, 150–51;
casualties in, 160, 201–2, 393*n*94,
393*n*95; death fasts and, 154, 384*n*88;
Ecevit on, 150; female political
prisoners in, 151, 383*n*69; justification of, 153–54; in media, 153, 201,
203; prisoner demands and, 202;
prisoner injuries in, 383*n*72; prison
resistance and, 382*n*68; public
criticism of, 153; rationale for, 150;
self-immolation, 200–201; social opposition to, 203–4; sovereignty and,
201; symbolism of, 154; violence of,
150–51, 153–54, 200–201, 383*n*72